The Hebrew Humanism of MARTIN BUBER

The Hebrew Humanism of MARTÍN BUBER

by Grete Schaeder
Translated by Noah J. Jacobs

Wayne State University Press, Detroit, 1973

Published simultaneously in Canada by the Copp Clark Publishing
Company, 517 Wellington Street, West Toronto 2b, Canada.

Library of Congress Cataloging in Publication Data

Schaeder, Grete.
The Hebrew humanism of Martin Buber.

Translation of Martin Buber; Hebräischer Humanismus.
1. Buber, Martin, 1878–1965. I. Title.
B3213.B84S2713   1973   296'.092'4 [B]   70–39691
ISBN 0–8143–1483–X

Grateful acknowledgment is made to the Morris and Emma Schaver
Publication Fund for Jewish Studies for financial assistance in the publication
of this book.

Originally published as *Martin Buber: Hebräischer Humanismus*, copyright
© 1966, Vandenhoeck & Ruprecht, Göttingen.

This translation from the German has been made by permission of the
German publisher, Vandenhoeck & Ruprecht, Göttingen © Vandenhoeck &
Ruprecht in Göttingen.

FOR ERNST SIMON
WHO ACCOMPANIED MARTIN BUBER ON THE ROAD TOWARD
INTERNATIONAL RECONCILIATION

CONTENTS

PREFACE

THIS BOOK is the outcome of a personal meeting I had with Martin Buber and our friendship during the years 1961–1965.

The two works to which I am most indebted are Hans Kohn's *Martin Buber* and Maurice Friedman's *Martin Buber: The Life of Dialogue.*

Martin Buber donated a large part of the Erasmus Prize awarded to him in 1963 to the Leo Baeck Institute, which was founded in 1955 for the scientific study of the Holocaust. For a German to contribute to this study is not inconsistent with Buber's interpretation of the Institute's purpose.

INTRODUCTION

BUBER'S "HEBREW HUMANISM" is not an ideology; it is a conception of man. Nor is it meant to be used as a formula to help us derive a doctrine from Buber's work. It is rather that "narrow ridge" between systems which he regarded as his proper place. Even in the last years of his life he declared, "I have no doctrine," and described himself as "atypical" and not confined to any particular intellectual system. Buber was neither a theologian nor a philosopher in the usual sense. He interpreted the Bible for his contemporaries, but he also took a definite stand with respect to the political events of his day. He was familiar with the ecstatic experiences of mystics, but his universal spirit was aware of the problems of the world. He was a popular educator and he could admonish like a prophet, but he was also a scholar who constantly applied himself to speculative problems. His style never degenerated into academic jargon, and was never permitted to obscure his unforgettable human comment. No one culture can claim him as its own. The path of Hebrew humanism that he followed unites the West with the East, the Western freedom of the spirit with the wisdom of the Orient for the sake of "the one thing that is needful" (Luke 10:42).

The phrase *Hebrew humanism* comes from Buber himself and appears as the title of an essay he published in 1941, but the subject it treats was of interest to him as early as 1903 when he spoke of Zionism as a "Jewish Renaissance" and supplemented Herzl's conception of a Jewish state with his call for a regeneration of the Jewish people. For he regarded the Zionist movement as part of a deep historical process that was destined to renew the nation and give birth to a new man. He

11

had stated in 1918 in one of his *Addresses on Judaism (Reden über das Judentum)*: "Not Hebraism, but Hebrew humanism, must be the core of a movement of Jewish regeneration." The renewal of Judaism appeared to him a phenomenon similar to that of the Italian Renaissance —a national movement, to be sure, but also one that was of deep significance for mankind for it proceeded from the chosen people, the exemplary people of the Bible.

Buber's Hebrew humanism until World War I was the product of the tension between his German and his Jewish legacy. European humanism, to which his idea of a Jewish revival was oriented, appeared to him on three historical planes: the Italian Renaissance, which he, a student of Dilthey, saw as the springtime of national life and a transition to a new, life-affirming humanity; German classicism, which came to him chiefly through Hölderlin; and the tragic-heroic philosophy of Nietzsche, whose magic melodies by the time he was seventeen had turned his head.

In his youth Buber was subject to periods of overpowering emotional exaltation although he was not a mystic in the traditional Jewish sense. His precocious passion for direct mythical experience reminds us of Chagall. The exuberant imagination of this great East European Jewish painter in depicting the animate and inanimate world found a corresponding note in Buber's naive pan-sacramentalism—for both had retained and preserved some deep creative impulse which is concealed in the lives of the common people. It was this impulse that later led Buber to give special prominence to a specific Jewish type which in his opinion still survived in the religion of the common people and which he recognized in the ecstasies of the Hasidim "on whom the spirit descends from above," as it once did on the prophets and bearers of biblical charisma. Something of this quality was preserved in Buber's Jewish heritage, a quality that was in conflict with his Western trained intellect and its urge for an enlightened, rational ordering of the intellectual world and for "universal understanding," as defined by Dilthey. This conflict led to severe inner tensions and explains the many contradictory elements in Buber's early life—on the one hand, the pantheistic cast of his youthful mind and, on the other hand, the rationalism of his psychological interpretation of the origin of the gods, in the manner of Simmel.

Nietzsche's pseudoprophetic voice haunted Buber for many years. The quality of charisma, which in the Bible is bound to Israel's election, becomes in Nietzsche's late phase of European humanism a natural phenomenon and the prerogative of human genius. Nietzsche's doctrine of the "evolving God" and self-redemption, his interpretation of creative genius which transformed ancient biblical traditions, and especially the literary cult of prophecy developed by his followers, constituted a real danger for Buber in his formative years. In his youth, moreover, Buber was dominated by the idea of an overpowering creative will, and in his thoughts about the Jewish Renaissance we find a prominent place given to "the creators" as the bearers of a new folk culture.

A subtle, disintegrating Nietzschean influence around the turn of the century succeeded in changing the meaning of the concepts *life, mysticism, myth,* and effaced the boundaries between the various intellectual disciplines. *Mysticism* became a synonym for rapturous intoxication with life; the art myths of the poets allowed furtive glimpses of man as God incarnate, apotheosized; a vague, romantic pantheism became the religion of the educated classes. Buber did not remain immune to the shifting intellectual currents of his day, but he was saved from their aberrations by his deep religious fervor and by his prolonged study of mysticism and myths. Even in those early days his method of studying religion was not historical but comparative, intent on discovering the earliest forms of religious experience common to both East and West. In the founders of the great religions he perceived the truth of a teaching that is lived and practiced, which was later to become the secret of his own influence and is often derived from his "existentialism." In Buddha, Lao-tzu, or Jesus he found the "fulfilling" man who is himself the "teaching," the truth that is handed down from generation to generation as a way of life and not as knowledge about the nature of being.

In his study of the many religions, Buber first examined the primordial myth of man's realization of the divine. Myth was for him "an eternal function of the soul," man's creative answer to the Unconditioned which he is always called upon to fashion anew. This development reached its culmination in 1913 with the completion of his own philosophic-religious myth, a work composed in the form of a Platonic dialogue and bearing the biblical title *Daniel*, wherein the author expounded a life view that is in the main ethical and not strictly religious, because it is chiefly concerned with the attempt to understand the basic facts of human life "mythically" as man's participation in the cosmic process of realizing God. The work was designed to be a synthesis between East and West, to present the triumphant progress of the "realizing" man, of the "I of the world"—but Western thought predominates. Here Buber may be regarded as a forerunner of modern existentialism, whereas in his later work his European and Jewish heritages are equally balanced.

During World War I Buber experienced a religious breakthrough in his thinking. This was accompanied by a series of signs and revelations which culminated in one intense religious experience: God, the God of the fathers, God as Person and Presentness—the eternal Thou —not the God of the philosophers, nor the godly that is in all beings and things, but "the Lord of the Voice, the One!" Man and God meet, the finite and the infinite interlock and, behold, man is transformed. He no longer stands "realizing" in the center of being; he is now a Person who lives in the sight of a personal God. As a result of Buber's changed conception, biblical man now became the criterion of his Hebrew humanism and the Bible the source of his religious experience, the arena of his confrontation with God, the distinctive ground of man's life and his human condition. It was here that God first came forth to converse with man and spoke his first Thou, to be repeated after him by man in addressing his fellowman—so that the personal pronoun Thou became the symbol connecting the correlative biblical commandments that enjoined man to love God *and* his fellowman. It is only when man relinquished his futile faith in himself as a self-sufficient entity and entered into fellowship with others that he became an "open" person, a member of the community. The community of Israel also must remain "open" to humanity, to community as a messianic category.

The "openness" of the person of which Buber spoke stemmed from the fact that the world is "creation," and as such all things within it are interrelated to form one whole as if informed by "a vital dialogue in the heart of the world." Buber's conception of man was now determined by the trinity: creation, revelation, redemption. The essential thing in this conception is that each term of the trinity was conceived not as a unique event relegated to remote antiquity or to the far-distant future at the end of time, but as a continuous process. That revelation takes place here and now Buber himself experienced—how God speaks to man with his ceaseless creation and how man answers by establishing a "being" relationship to this realm of creation and thus contributes to the fulfillment of the meaning of creation. To live thus is to add "a drop of messianic perfection" every moment and to sanctify God. The vexing problem of time in the perishable world of things, so acute in Buber's generation, was thus overcome. The very certainty of a timeless creation, revelation, and redemption sanctified time. In an age of demythologizing, Buber was able as a result of his biblical studies to recover the "mythical" element of faith in which the mystery became sensuous and concrete as the "Thou" between man and God, as the ever-present intuition of creation, revelation, and redemption. Not mysticism but myth was the fateful word that defined Buber's relationship to God. In his early *Addresses on Judaism*, he rediscovered the mythical element in the Jewish religion as the bearer of the "being-tradition" in the people, as the language of deep personal emotion, and as the embodiment of the holy, which is the very breath of religion.

"Ye shall be holy, for I the Lord am holy" was the commandment that Buber recognized unconditionally and which he took as a corollary of man's being created in the image of God. The sole purpose of Jewish law with its network of commandments and prescriptions was to direct all human activity to the service of God. Buber strove to achieve this same end from within by having man hallow God in his own personal life and by making his every act a sacrament that bound him to God. This was the worship of the sanctification of everyday life which Buber found exemplified in Hasidism and which he proclaimed as its "message," a worship in which the priestly people of the Bible could unite with the pious of the whole world. Its foundation was envisaged by Buber to be a new "metapolitical" community—the Jewish settlement in Palestine was to serve the world as a living example of a model community based on peace and justice. A necessary requisite for this must be the "return to the normative, elemental forces of the people" as revealed in the Bible. Hebrew humanism was an endless road that stretched from the myth of a primeval beginning to a messianic humanity.

The Word was put into the mouth of the prophets who were charged with transmitting God's message to the people. Buber knew that he had to bear witness to God but also that what he had to say must be expressed in human speech. We need only compare the intimations he gave us of his being addressed by "signs" in the middle of an ordinary day with Jeremiah's visit to the potter's house to recognize that something of the prophetic spirit had survived in him. In connection with the ecstatic confessions of the mystics he once spoke of their "impossible message"; his own life bore witness to the tragedy of being unable to convey to his contemporaries a message he felt to be urgent. One of his biblical verses most often quoted is the complaint of him who is called but not chosen: "In the shadow of his hand hath he hidden me, and made me a polished shaft; in his quiver hath he hid me" (Isa. 49). Buber's humanism was not without its tragic aspects.

After he had settled in Palestine, Buber made three attempts to convey a "message" to his people by way of historical examples. He wrote the book *Moses* to describe the character of the founder of Israel's unique position as a people and as a religious community among the nations of the world. In a second book, *Israel and Palestine*, he pointed out the close connection between land and people felt by every Jew in Palestine, and he showed how this mutual relationship had been strengthened throughout the centuries by the belief in Israel's religious mission. *The Hasidic Message (Die chassidische Botschaft)*, his third book, proclaimed the sacramental sanctification of daily life, an attitude that made Hasidism for Buber the model for both a social and a religious renewal of mankind in his day. But his words remained unheard.

Another way to proclaim a "message" in our time is through great poetry. Buber wrote a mystery play called *Elijah*, and his deepest insights into Hasidism are to be found in the chronicle *For the Sake of Heaven (Gog und Magog)*. He wrote poems until the last year of his life, although they fell short of great poetry and were not acknowledged by his contemporaries. He used his poetic talents to serve God in his prodigious labor of translating the Bible and of interpreting the "message" of the Hasidic legends, whose publication eventually became a classic of world literature.

Buber was also a humanist in the European tradition as is shown by his steadfast allegiance to language, thought, and science, never despairing in his attempt to convey his religious experiences in the rational modes of expression developed by the modern spirit and translating them into the language of philosophy, whose subject-object category of conceptualization hardly did justice to their inner life. His determination to investigate man's condition and to follow truth wherever it might lead was the result of his Western training, as was also the precision and vitality of his language. His passion to salvage for the European spirit its lost legacy never deserted him; he had hoped to make visible "a neglected, obscured, ancient reality."

Buber had no doctrine; he himself *was* a doctrine, when we consider the influence of his personality despite the loneliness of his life—a trait common to all great religious spirits. The listening post to which his faith summoned him was the precarious "narrow ridge" of his Hebrew humanity: "facing God and being at the same time united with his fellow men." A poem he composed on February 9, 1964, expresses his final legacy:

Eine fremde (laute) Stimme spricht:

Ein Seil ist über die Tiefe gestreckt,
Setz deinen Fuss nun darauf
Und, eh dein Schritt den Widerspruch weckt,
Lauf!

Ein Seil ist über die Tiefe gespannt,
Versag dich unterwegs allem Hier!
Schon winkt von drüben dir eine Hand:
"Zu mir!"

Die vertraute (leise) Stimme spricht:

Folge nicht dem heischenden Ruf!
Der dich schuf
Meinte dir zu: "Sei bereit
Für jede irdische Zeit!"
Immer schon hält dich seine Hand—
Bleib liebend der Welt zugewandt!

                                                [Ungedruckt]

A strange (loud) voice speaks:

A rope is stretched across the deep,
Place your foot upon it
And, before your step arouses contradiction,
Run!

A rope is stretched across the deep,
Renounce along the way all that is here!
A hand on the other side is already beckoning:
"Come to me!"

The familiar (gentle) voice speaks:

Follow not the imperious voice!
He who created
You meant: "Be prepared
For every earthly season!"
His hand has ever held thee—
Remain lovingly facing the world!

                                                [Unpublished]

1
The Beginnings

MARTIN BUBER was born in Vienna on February 2, 1878. The old Austria where he spent his childhood and youth has been described in glowing colors by his countryman, Stefan Zweig, in *World of Yesterday*, a nostalgic book of memoirs about his life in exile as he looked back on a lost age of innocence, the golden era of a supranational culture which had preserved the spiritual, humane atmosphere of the old Europe.

The peaceful coexistence of so many different nations within a single state made the Danube monarchy at the turn of the century a natural haven for writers from all countries of Europe who still dreamed of a united Europe. This was a potent factor in the historical development of the country and accounts for the peculiar character of the Austrian people among the South German races. In Vienna "all the streams of European culture converged; at court, among the nobility, and among the people the German was related in blood to the Slavs, the Hungarians, the Spanish, the Italian, the French, the Flemish: and it was the peculiar genius of this musical capital that dissolved all these contrasts harmoniously into something new and unique, the Austrian, the Viennese. . . . It was delightful to live here, in this atmosphere of spiritual conciliation, and subconsciously every citizen became supranational, cosmopolitan, a citizen of the world." [1] Centuries of living together had produced an Austrian way of life that was characterized by a "passion for the inconsequential," [2] akin to the English "understatement"; this was enhanced by Adalbert Stifter's "law of gentleness" as an enduring principle in support of quiet nobility and humble virtues.

19

The Austrian way of life, radiating from the capital and making itself felt throughout the Empire, combined urbanity with natural confidence, accepting as a matter of course the concomitant risks of frivolity, sentimentality, and indolence.

The imperial city of Vienna, with its prudent, easygoing attitude of "live and let live," was an unrivaled center of assimilation[3] whose diversities and contradictions were reconciled by its innate musicality and strong sense of continuity. The ability of the city to attract and assimilate foreign elements was evident not only in its attitude to its Slavic and Hungarian subjects but also in its treatment of the Jews who had migrated from the East. At the turn of the century the assimilated Jewish population of Vienna had attained a position of eminence equal only to that of the Jews in Spain in the fifteenth century. The Jews were prominent in the artistic world and had made significant contributions in all the intellectual disciplines, contributions which were not "specifically Jewish but which, on the contrary, through the miracle of empathy . . . were successful in giving to that which was specifically Austrian and Viennese its most intensive expression." [4] The European reputation enjoyed by Austrian poetry and music, and by the Vienna School in many of the sciences, owes much to the achievements of prominent Jews.[5] The simple magic of the Austrian character is nowhere more perfectly expressed than in the work of the partly Jewish Viennese poet, Hugo von Hofmannsthal. No one has better preserved the patriarchal atmosphere and the deep sense of fellowship that unified the Austrian family of nations than Richard Beer-Hofmann in his reminiscences of Vinzek and of the dog Querschtl in his *Paula—ein Fragment* [Paula, a fragment]—the same poet who dreamed the great dream of Jacob's election and who composed *Lullaby for Miriam [Schlaflied für Mirjam]* for his people. The novel of the fading Austrian Empire, the *Radetzkymarsch*, was written by the Jewish poet, Joseph Roth.

The old Austria, which had given hopeful signs of a united Europe of the future, revealed at an early stage the dangers that threatened her. The same Vienna that loved music and theater above all else, that esteemed its actors and singers more than its statesmen, and that was more interested in festive processions and flower-bedecked carriages than in the solution of political problems, was at the same time the hotbed of a nationalistic pan-German and petty bourgeois anti-Semitism, the city of von Schönerer and Karl Lueger, where Hitler first conceived his political ambitions. And, to complete its contradictions, it was the city where Jews had lived most peacefully as an integral part of the population and where they had become, by dint of their creative achievements, more completely naturalized than in any other country in Europe; it was this city that gave birth not only to Hitler's fanatical nationalism but also to Theodor Herzl's fervent and at the time seemingly utopian Zionism.

Just as barely a century earlier, even before the diplomats at the Congress of Vienna had concluded their celebrations, new revolutionary impulses proceeding from France were beginning to shake the foundations of reactionary Europe, so now beneath the surface of an opulent and gay bourgeois culture new political realities were being felt in Austria. Austrian prose and poetry at the end of the last century seem to us to have had a dreamlike, magical quality. Poetry, music, and pure thought had become the sole arbiters of culture, although Austria was still far from comprehending the full import of Hofmannsthal's later insight that "spirit is reality that has been penetrated and mastered."

The Jews of Vienna had contributed in a large measure not only to the gaiety and musicality of Austrian life but also to the ethereal, unworldly aspect of its culture. It was with good reason that the young Hofmannsthal was called Ariel by his friends and described by Arthur Schnitzler's widow in her book of memoirs, *Spiegelbild der Freundschaft* [Mirror of friendship], as "a being strangely compounded of color, flight, dreamy pensiveness, and aloofness." Olga Schnitzler also preserved for us one of Beer-Hofmann's characteristic remarks during his last years in Vienna: "Why, then, do I need roots; I have wings." [6]

In a discerning introduction to Beer-Hofmann's collected works (1963), Buber spoke of the prominence of the death motif in the writings of the Viennese Jewish poets and its significance: "It is as if this circle of Viennese poets, bound together by strong ties of friendship, had been granted another peculiar common element [the death-motif]." [7] In this connection Buber alluded to a prophetic remark of Schnitzler's: "They will have a premonition that their world is coming to an end . . . for the end of their world is drawing nigh."

Arthur Schnitzler was not only the poet of "the sweet Viennese girl" and of the brooding aesthetes imprisoned in their lonely egos but he also looked at the world around him with the penetrating eye of a physician and diagnosed the symptoms of its decadence. His *Hands Around [Reigen]* does not celebrate the joy of living; it is characterized by deep despair and the hopelessness of a *danse macabre*.[8] Schnitzler basically is closely allied to the great nonconformist founder of psychoanalysis, Sigmund Freud, the unmasker of all the traditional certainties of our culture. In a letter that Freud sent him on his sixtieth birthday, the scientist called the poet his "doppelgänger," and described him as one who possessed intuitively what he [Freud] had acquired by painstaking research.[9] Just as the polarity of love and death constitutes the central theme in Schnitzler's work, so is the interplay between Eros and the death-impulse in Freud's *Beyond the Pleasure Principle* the primary force that governs life. In recent years the historian Friedrich Heer studied the attempts of Austrian Jewry to overcome its premonition of the end as it was expressed in the creative arts, and in this connection has pointed to the significant role played by psychoanalysis: "Modern depth psychology and psychoanalysis arose in Vienna from a deep Jewish anxiety and uneasy apprehension of the neglected, dark areas of man's inner being as it came into contact with the lower elements of the Austrian Empire, the 'lower masses of society' infected with anti-Semitism." [10] He also spoke with candor of the great loss suffered by Austrian culture as a result of the Jewish catastrophe: "The intellectual provincialism of present-day Austrian culture—its lack of standards, its loss of international recognition, its failure to concern itself with world-wide questions—is a direct consequence of the annihilation of the Jews and their expulsion from Austria." [11] Heer's judgment, although one-sided, is in the main accurate.

Stefan Zweig's observation that "what one has breathed from the air around him in his childhood enters the blood and cannot be taken from him" [12] had not the same meaning for Buber as for the author of the *World of Yesterday* who as a child grew up in the liberal cosmopolitan atmosphere of Viennese Jewry. At the age of three Buber was taken from his parents and brought up in the home of his grandparents in Galicia. Viennese culture, it is true, had penetrated to the furthermost corners of the empire, and Buber was able to receive a humanistic education in the Austrian *gymnasium* in Lemberg. But for one who experienced the vast expanse of the Danube monarchy from his home in Galicia and had become involved in the daily problems of its diverse population, a purely humanistic understanding of the world must have been in the long run superficial and inadequate.

We learn something of Buber's childhood and youth from "Autobiographical Fragments" which were collected several years ago and published in a slender volume entitled *Begegnung* [Meeting].[13] Buber's purpose in this autobiographical work was not simply to relate isolated personal incidents but to include only those experiences that had had a profound influence on the course of his life. Nor was it his purpose to present a coherent account of his philosophical development but rather, as he was fond of saying, to let his memory "act like a sieve," relying more on the unknown but vital principle derived from life itself than on consciously selected episodes. We thus find less attention given to books and to intellectual disputes and more to personalities who made a strong impression on him and to those chance incidents that influenced his early development. Like the Hasidic anecdotes which he collected and recounted for more than half a century, the experiences he recalled of his past life all have some deep exemplary significance, experiences in which some incident coincided with a revealing phrase or in which some mute occurrence spoke to him with subtle assurance "even as a vital process speaks." [14]

One of Buber's deepest experiences, derived from "the atmosphere of the time," is related to the diversity of languages spoken by the heterogeneous population of Lemberg: "In the home of my grandparents, as in the home of my parents, German speech prevailed, but the language of the street and the school was Polish; only the Jewish quarter hummed with uncouth and tender Yiddish; and in the synagogue resounded, vibrant as ever, the robust tones of Hebrew antiquity." [15] This vital contact with the pulsating life of East European

Jewry, in which the voice of antiquity resounded in his ear "as vibrant as ever," was of decisive importance to Buber for the remainder of his life. In his account in *My Way to Hasidism* he recalls the lasting impression made upon him by the life of the Hasidic communities in the small town of Sadagora, an impression remembered by him as "image and feeling" despite the magic and superstition that had long since tarnished the purity of this great mystical movement.

The distinction between German and Jewish cultural interests was not totally disregarded in the home of Buber's grandparents, as it was in most of the Jewish homes in Vienna, but both were cultivated side by side in a peculiar manner. As the editor of Hebrew books of biblical interpretation *(midrashim)*, Buber's grandfather was a highly respected scholar and had introduced his grandson to the language and tradition of his forefathers. He himself was a living example of talmudic learning combined with scientific methods of modern Western philology. In the festschrift in honor of Martin Buber's fiftieth birthday, *Aus unbekannten Schriften* [From unknown writings], Friedrich Thieberger gives an admirable description of Salomon Buber's way of thinking, his scholarly as well as his personal attitude to language—how he proceeded from concrete facts to trace a word through its ramified meanings back to its ultimate origin, to its uncorrupted pristine root still preserved in the sacred books of the Bible. Thieberger's observations not only cast a light on the grandson's Bible translation but also raised the general question as to whether the impartial objectivity of modern philology might not have something to learn from the personal involvement of the Jewish scholar. The love of tradition and of what Buber called the "elemental Jewishness" of his grandfather were in a peculiar way compatible with the spirit of Enlightenment that prevailed in the house of his grandparents and which was, in the case of his grandmother Adele Buber, characterized by a deep attachment to the German classics.

The grandmother, who conducted her husband's extensive business affairs, a common practice among the Jews of East Europe, so that he could devote his leisure to the study of the Talmud, was a woman in whom naiveté and deep feeling were peculiarly mixed. Her grandson was impressed not so much by her efficiency as by her "pithy and splendid command of German which she guarded like a treasure." Her wide familiarity with classical German poetry was reflected in her daily speech.

In his father's house, where Buber spent his vacations and to which he returned at the age of fourteen, the spirit of the Enlightenment was evident in the practical conduct of daily life. His father was a landowner with advanced ideas, who made use of the latest achievements of science and technology to increase the yield of his estates, and whose personal relationship to his subordinates might be described as paternalistic. His attitude to nature was unromantic and born of a deep sense of responsibility. He had, moreover, an original gift for story-telling.

In short, the atmosphere in which Buber grew up was characterized by a deep respect for tradition and for the dignity of labor, by an appreciation of poetry and a candid acknowledgment of responsibility, by an atmosphere of enlightened sincere piety.

Buber recalled the people he met in those early years chiefly by the way in which they spoke "their word" to him—for speech was to him the very air he breathed, and his primary concern always remained the reality of language, its truth and purity. His later talent for "meeting" had been prepared in childhood. The unsaid word also belonged to the basic experiences of his early days. The superficial tolerance and lack of mutual understanding between the Christian and Jewish students at the Polish *gymnasium* were brought home to him on one occasion when, hard-pressed in a dialogic confrontation with the headmaster, he failed to find the right word.

Language studies constituted the most important aspect of Buber's education. Daily life in the Galician capital demanded a knowledge of several languages but Buber, aside from this practical consideration, early displayed a talent for languages which was fostered by the humanistic ideals of his grandmother. Thoughts about the nature of language occupied him at an early age: "The multiplicity of human languages, their wonderful variety in which the white light of human speech is at the same time fragmented and preserved, presented a problem for me even while I was still in my boyhood. . . ." [16] The problem of the One and the Many—the need of a dialogic relationship—

was beginning to disturb him. Early in life he realized that in every
language, indeed in every word, something lived that was unique, and
that something was always lost in the process of translation: "The
world of the Logos and of the Logoi opened up to me, grew dim,
brightened, and grew dim again." [17] Just as Goethe once conceived a
novel in which the various members of a family, dispersed in different
parts of the world, exchanged impressions in the different languages of
their respective countries, so Buber conceived of bilingual conversations between a German and a Frenchman, a Hebrew and a Roman.
The preoccupations of the future translator are already evident. From
the time when he made his earliest translations together with his grandfather until his famous translation of the Bible, he followed a long and
arduous road along which he was guided by a deep fidelity to the precise inner truth that dwells in the living word. The word was for him
always the *spoken* word, the living voice that is heard, summoned up
from the distant past and destined to influence the present.

> Sleepest thou, Miriam?—Miriam, my child
> We are the shore, and deep within us runs
> The blood of what has once been—rolling towards
> That which is to come; blood of our fathers,
> Filled with restlessness and pride.
> *In* us are *all*. Who feels himself to be alone?
> *Thou* art their life—their life is thine—
> Sleep, Miriam, my life, my child—sleep! [18]

Thus sang the poet Richard Beer-Hofmann in 1897, the same year in
which the First Zionist Congress met in Basel. The manner in which
Buber described the familiar figures of his childhood reveals an appreciation for his heritage. That science could be "the organic possession
of the entire person" had been demonstrated by his grandfather. His
familiarity with poetry, a legacy from his grandmother, reminds us of
Goethe's well-known description of his mother's talent for storytelling.
Throughout his life Buber was an occasional poet in the Goethean
sense; poetical language, in addition to scientific, was for him an indispensable form of expression. His father, on the other hand, exhibited a
sense of responsibility and earnestness in his conduct of the household.

What do these recollections teach us about the character of the child? In this respect his very first composition, which has the title "Die Mutter" [The mother], is revealing. He was separated from his mother in the third year of his life, and only a year later the cruel truth was revealed to him by an older playmate who told him: "No, she will never come back." This shattering revelation could not of course be fully grasped by the child's conceptual powers, but "it remained fixed in me, and it clung to my heart with greater force with the passing years; but only after some ten years did I begin to feel it as something that concerned not only me but all men. . . . I suspect that all I have learned of genuine meeting in the course of my life had its origin in that hour on the wooden porch." [19] Considering Buber's reticence in relating personal matters, this must be considered an important confession.

The age in which a child loses the love of his mother is considered by psychologists to be of decisive importance for his future development. Such a loss leaves a deep wound in the child's tender soul—not a trauma in the psychoanalytical sense—and a lasting sense of insecurity which, in a sensitive child, could not fail to have serious effects. It expressed itself with terrifying vehemence when the child felt the force of powers that were beyond his understanding. Thus, Buber recounted how he was overwhelmed by intense emotion when the principal of the school asked him to describe the rude behavior of some of his classmates and how, a few years later at the age of fourteen, he was almost driven to the verge of madness brooding over philosophical antinomies, and again the death of one close to him when he was seventeen affected him as an almost self-destructive experience.

Highly instructive in this connection is his early composition "Das Pferd" [The horse]. Since his grandfather and his father owned estates, from his early childhood he was accustomed to associate with animals. In the fragment "Der Vater" [The father], he tells us that his father knew intimately each of his horses and that he used to greet them in a personal manner. This habit was also adopted by his son who often stroked the neck of his favorite horse, which always acknowledged this friendly gesture with a faint snort. For the sensitive lad this was not just a passing pleasure but "a deeply emotional event": he felt as if "the element of vitality itself" had touched his skin.[20] He experienced his playmate as a Thou who trusted him implicitly without thereby losing "the immense otherness of the Other." One day, however, the animal failed to respond to his tender gesture, and the boy experienced this interruption of unreserved contact between them as man's first fall—for it was precisely on this day that he had failed to give himself unreservedly to the animal and felt self-conscious of his experience on touching it.

As a sensitive child Buber had developed an unusual aptitude for deep experiences, something in the nature of an additional sense, an antennalike organ of the soul; "meeting" could also take place outside the human sphere. The creature that "faced him in an elemental way on a Thou to Thou basis" was in a single, undivided act felt as both a sensuous *and* a spiritual experience, and this conjunction of sensuous and spiritual spontaneity as an inseparable unity in the depths of the soul was characteristic of Buber's personality and is the key to the understanding of his philosophy. Even as late as 1958, in his epilogue to a new edition of *I and Thou*, he insisted that a "meeting" in the full sense of the word was also possible with inanimate nature, a point which other philosophers frequently treated with misgiving. Poets will readily understand this, although it would be an error to underestimate Buber as a philosopher simply because of his undeniable poetical gifts. We are dealing here with a dimension of existence that not only goes back to the common root of poetical and religious-philosophical experience but also transcends the purely poetical.

Even as a child Buber experienced abstract, intellectual phenomena with a sense of physical participation. When he reflected on the misunderstandings that arise among people attempting to communicate with one another in different languages, his heart began to pound within him.[21] He felt as if he were probing the secret of the meeting of the two languages at the point of their intersection. And does not something of that same tension remain, he was to ask later, when people of different temperament and character speak the same language? Has a word ever precisely the same meaning for any two people? The basic problem here is whether serious dialogue is at all possible without grave misunderstandings. Is it the philosopher or the poet who raises this question? The problem is beyond the competency of both. These questions, which concern man as a whole but find no place in any philosophical system, are precisely the questions that are characteristic of Buber's thinking.

The loneliness of his early years as well as the affinity of his genius for sensuous impressions aggravated the child's sensitivity and elemental insecurity. His intensive experiences, which affected his whole being, and his deep insecurity in facing the world contradicted and complemented each other. This feeling of elemental insecurity was most conspicuous in his speculations on time and space which engaged his mind at the age of fourteen. Time and space, mysteriously held together by the adhesive power of man's mind, now became for him problematical, and his inability to fathom their nature, to imagine them concretely as finite or infinite, drove him to the verge of despair: "I always had to try again and again to imagine the edge of space or its infiniteness, a time with a beginning and end, and both were equally impossible and hopeless—and yet there seemed to be only the choice between one or the other absurdity. Led by an irresistible compulsion I reeled from one to the other, at times threatened by a fit of insanity, so that I seriously considered the possibility of escaping by a timely act of suicide." [22]

Again he is relentlessly driven to express an abstract, intellectual phenomenon in concrete terms in order to find a resting place for his spirit. The lecture he gave in 1938, "Das Problem des Menschen" [The problem of man], in which he speaks of this perilous quest of the spirit, shows us how the question of What is man? became the crucial problem of a philosophical anthropology. In this connection Buber made a characteristic distinction in the history of the human spirit between epochs of *Behausing* (in which man feels at home in the universe) and epochs of *Hauslosigkeit* (in which man feels homeless, marooned in the universe, and inclined to regard himself as problematical). In Pascal's question "qu'est-ce qu'un homme dans l'infini?" we hear for the first time the anxious voice of modern man and his feeling of insecurity in the Copernican universe. In the seventeenth century it was space that was the demonic power that threatened to demolish the defenses of man's ego; now the elusive, fugitive concept of time was even more alarming: "the reality of the world was at stake; the world in which we live and move had taken on an absurd and uncanny aspect." [23]

From these melancholy reflections Buber was liberated by reading Kant's *Prolegomena to Any Future Metaphysics [Prolegomena zu einer jeden künftigen Metaphysik]*; from that he learned that space and time are nothing more than the forms of our intuition and are not "real qualities that adhere to the things-in-themselves," that man can comprehend the world only through time and space, and that being itself is removed from the alternatives finite or infinite. Kant's conception of time left open the question of eternality and the existence of God, and held out the hope "that there is an Eternal which is something wholly different from the Infinite, just as it is wholly different from the finite, and that there can still be ties between me (man) and the Eternal." [24] The fragment "Philosophers" shows us that even in that early period a way was still open to him to find genuine security in a world that no longer need be dreaded "since there is Eternity." This would mean finding a way that led from Kant's question, "What is man?" to the question of the Psalmist, "What is man, that thou art mindful of him?" without, however, abandoning the world that Kant had made safe for science and logic.

The "Autobiographical Fragments" tells us nothing of Buber's early religious life. Ernst Simon informs us in his study "Martin Buber and German Jewry" [25] that for his bar mitzvah speech Buber chose not the customary pentateuchal weekly text but Schiller's "The Words of Faith." Soon thereafter he apparently underwent a severe religious crisis. When he was fourteen, he ceased his hitherto scrupulous observation of religious customs and no longer put on phylacteries during morning prayers. [26] In his grandfather's house his close relationships were "firmly fixed," despite many doubts. But not long after his return to his father's house he became alienated from Judaism and was driven in a state of "effervescent spirituality" into the turmoil of the times: "Until my twentieth year, and to some extent even later, my spirit was in constant movement, undergoing various kinds of tensions and susceptible to solutions that constantly assumed new forms but without a unifying core or growing substance . . . remaining in an agitated fullness of spirit but without Judaism, without humanity, and without the presence of the godlike." [27]

The reassurance and comfort that the boy of fourteen received from the reading of Kant's *Prolegomena* was not of long duration; two years later this hard-won philosophic freedom was again shattered when he read Nietzsche's *Thus Spake Zarathustra*.

In the fragment "Philosophers" Buber describes his Zarathustra experience as catastrophic. The strong words he uses in this connection, like "sudden assault" and "deprivation of freedom," indicate what he must have meant by catastrophic: the negative equivalent of "turning" or *tshuva*, the biblical concept which is so central to Buber's religious thought, denoting a critical "turning" that comes about not as a result of man's decision but by the intervention of a higher power.

Buber also acquired a new conception of time from his reading of *Zarathustra*, that is, the doctrine of the "eternal recurrence of the same" or the conception of time "as an unending sequence of finite processes, which are similar to one another in all respects, so that the terminal phase of the process passes over into its initial phase." [28] Here also, as in the case of Kant and the Psalmist, an appropriate biblical verse can be cited [from the book of Ecclesiastes]: "The thing that hath been, it is that which shall be; and that which is done is that which shall be done: and there is no new thing under the sun." The ancient Jew of the Old Testament, nevertheless, recognized his dependence on God and observed His commandments. The new prophetic voice, however, began with the proclamation: God is dead! and counseled man to abandon his belief in God and morality and turn to the fullness of life which is the inexhaustible, eternal source of ever-developing forms.

Although Buber could not accept Nietzsche's interpretation of time even when he was only seventeen, he later speaks of the "seduction" and "fascination" of *Zarathustra* in those early days. The very choice of these words shows that he was enchanted by a personality and not by a doctrine. At that time books were for Buber propitious or ominous powers. The reading of Kant's difficult *Prolegomena* had been for him an intimate personal experience; he now read Nietzsche and embraced that solitary, homeless thinker as a demonic brother-in-spirit and learned to love him "as a close and distant friend." In Nietzsche he recovered his own passion for questioning, and found in him a thinker who could convert the most abstract knowledge into powerful feelings and who struggled with a thought "as one struggles with one's destiny which seizes the whole man and takes him captive. . . ." [29] It is idle to ask whether Nietzsche is a philosopher or a poet, for his philosophizing is a vital act of man as a whole, the complete man who is also capable of poetic expression which he feels is indispensable to his thought.

When he was twenty-two, Buber published his reflections on this theme under the title "Nietzsche und die Lebenswerte" [Nietzsche and life values] in which he pointed out that this lonely thinker escapes every attempt at classification and cannot be definitely characterized as a poet, a psychologist, or the founder of a new society: "Many arise in his name, but each out of a wholly personal impulse since he finds in him that which is peculiarly his own, the release of his own powers which through him are transformed into active energy." [30] Thus, his final characterization of Nietzsche was that of a "thought-poet" who was also an "emissary of life."

"Life" for Nietzsche was first of all a concept of struggle. [31] "Concept" is perhaps too comprehensive a term, since, in the last analysis, "life" remains for him undetermined and is, as Jaspers says, "one of the *signa* of Nietzschean philosophizing" that has not become a concept like "creativity," "eternal recurrence," "will to power"; it is an ultimate incomprehensibility which he took for granted, one which can be "transfixed but not conquered by a word." [32] In his second *Thoughts Out of Season* Nietzsche's conception of life is synonymous with the struggle for genuine culture against historical positivism and the philistine belief in progress, against "an Alexandrian scientific culture that is anemic, pedantic, alienated from myth and from life, a culture in which optimism and faith in rationalism have been triumphant. . . ." [33] Genuine culture is, in Nietzsche's view, unity of artistic style in every outward expression of the people's life: "The people that can be called cultured must be in a real sense a living unity, and cannot be miserably cleft asunder into form and substance." [34] "Antiquarian" history, the history of the life of thought and the preservation of tradition, maims the "plastic power" of a people, and it must be overcome by an unhistorical attitude, that is, the courage to forget and learn to live by superhistorical powers, by art and science. "Monumental" history, which Nietzsche sets up in opposition to the "antiquarian," is not concerned with the continuity of the world-process but with the great men of all times who are in communication with one another in a kind of ghost-like conversation. The language of the past is an oracle which is deciphered only by those who know how to build for the future: "You can only explain the past by what is highest in the present." [35] It is thus youth above all to whom Nietzsche addresses his *memento vivere.*

Buber's essay "Nietzsche und die Lebenswerte" testifies to the enthusiasm with which he answered Nietzsche's challenge. The heroic life to which he is here summoned, the glorification of the lonely great man, the vaguely radiant formulation of his basic concepts—"riddle-intoxicated" and "twilight-rejoicing," Zarathustra calls his disciples—must have had an overpowering fascination for Buber's sensitive nature. It was precisely the idealistically minded of his generation who regarded Nietzsche as the great ethical teacher, who against his will lived on the rich moral heritage of German integrity and piety, and whose ardent philosophizing proceeded from a deep sorrow for mankind.

It was above all the ambiguous concept "creation" that caused Buber the greatest difficulty. To the degree that "life" is not interpreted as struggle in Nietzsche's work it is understood primarily as "creation." The creative act of the great man and the creative development of the cosmos respond to the same rhythm. Buber, like Nietzsche, developed the concept of "creation" along several lines. In the narrowest sense he understood it as self-creation: Nietzsche's confident assertion that man has the freedom to determine his self-being was in those early years a stirring thought for Buber. Self-creation, becoming a unified whole, meant not only the frank acknowledgment of the imperious claims of the body and its senses but also the submission of man as a whole to the spiritual. One must not only *have* the truth, one must *be* truth; or, as Buber put it in an early lecture, "The Old and New Community": "We do not want revolution; we are revolution." [36] In Buber's struggle to achieve unity amid the conflicting and contradictory forces within him, Nietzsche's influence was strong and was still apparent in *Daniel* and in his early *Addresses on Judaism*; even in his conception of "self-creation as self-improvement," when he began the study of Hasidism, the spell of Nietzsche's intense vision did not desert him.

"Creation" also means creative participation in the culture of one's people and of humanity. Nietzsche's attitude to the Germans has to some extent a parallel in Buber's relation to Judaism. Both struggled against the petrified cultural values of the time and against an alienated tradition; both wished to penetrate to the sources, to the hidden energies in the depths of the nation's life.[37] They meet one another as they both confront Hölderlin's question: "When do you appear whole, soul of the fatherland?" Just as Hellas was a highly idealized Germany for Hölderlin and Nietzsche, so did the ancient history of his own people serve Buber as a beacon and guide. In his characterization of the Jew, Buber was also influenced by Nietzsche's heroic-tragic conception of man. The belief expressed in the *Birth of Tragedy*, that the moribund myth of a people can be revived and become the symbol of a national renaissance, was developed in Buber's Jewish thought far beyond its mythical aspects. Zionism was to him from the very outset more than a movement with political and social goals; it was a movement directed to the renewal of nationhood. In the first years of his Zionist activities his advocacy of Judaism as "reality" was influenced no less by Nietzsche's concept of culture than by the glorious past of his own people. Among Buber's early Zionist writings is an essay written in 1902 with the characteristic title: "Die Schaffenden, das Volk und die Bewegung" [The creators, the people and the movement]. Here the "creators," who are not to be confused with the intellectuals, are the bearers of the "culture-producing forces"; they are "the secret kings of the people." [38] A "creation" is demanded which is both life and a life-enhancing force.

The concept "creation" has still a third dimension, creation that rises above itself: to create a being higher than ourselves . . . to create above and beyond ourselves.[39] Nietzsche sees man as a bridge and as a transition to a higher godlike form of being, in the realizing of which life as "becoming" and as "the will to power" gains its real meaning. It is characteristic that the later essays which appeared under this title were to bear the superscription "The Innocence of Becoming." [40] Since God for Nietzsche is dead, man must redeem himself by becoming a superman. The form he is to take is a creation of faith, and thus Nietzsche also called him "the redeeming man": "Sometime or other he must come, the redeeming man . . . he who gives the earth its due . . . this conqueror of God and of Nothing." [41] This superbeing, in whom all that is corporeal and earthy is transfigured, is anticipated by the creator-philosopher Zarathustra, whose mission it is to prepare the way for him, to help him emerge from the realm of thought to reality. He himself remains a challenge and a boundary figure.

The thought of creating something that surpasses man also finds an echo in Buber's article on Nietzsche: "Over against the God of the world's beginning he set up a formidable adversary, the becoming God to whose development we can contribute, the envisaged product of future evolutions." And again we find in "Die Schaffenden, das Volk und die Bewegung": "The creative man will, of course, always receive the watchword not from yesterday but from tomorrow, and the Law not from the God who has reigned from time immemorial but from the becoming God."

When Buber became interested in the study of German and Jewish mysticism around the turn of the century, Nietzsche's "becoming God" found a place in his thought not as a dogma or evolutionary doctrine but as "image and feeling." The concept thereby underwent a significant change; instead of the becoming God we now have a God that is realized by man: "Man appeared to me to be the being through whose existence the Absolute resting in its truth can acquire the character of reality." [42] Buber's thoughts about the "fulfilling" or "central" man in his prewar essays and in *Daniel* are dangerously close to Nietzsche's "superman" as the "redeeming" man, that is, the bearer of human self-redemption, although he could have arrived at this notion independently along other intellectual paths. Hans Kohn has pointed out [43] that Buber in 1903 was writing a philosophical work which was never published: "Das Schaffen als Erlösung oder Evolution und Revolution" [Creation as redemption or evolution and revolution]. The juxtaposition of "creation" and "redemption" in the title, which again goes back to Nietzsche, is instructive in that it shows how Buber and his contemporaries regarded the mystics of former generations and what they themselves understood by mysticism in their own day. The medieval mystics, especially Meister Eckhart, were looked upon as great creative figures and bearers of the Christian myth. Nietzsche's life ecstasy and the pantheistic inclinations of his followers tended to ignore the ecclesiastical attachments of the Christian mystics and to emphasize the newly discovered affinity between mysticism and myth.

Nietzsche, who was a philosopher, poet, and "prophet" all in one, endowed man with unprecedented significance as a creator and as his own redeemer. The concept "revelation" also appeared in the new light of creative inspiration: "Has anyone at the end of the nineteenth century any distinct notion of what poets in a stronger age understood by the word inspiration? The idea of revelation, in the sense that something which profoundly convulses and upsets one becomes visible and audible with indescribable certainty and accuracy, describes the simple fact. One hears and one does not seek; one takes and does not ask who gives; a thought suddenly flashes up like lightning; it comes with necessity, without faltering—I have never had a choice in the matter. There is an ecstasy so great that the immense strain is sometimes relaxed by a flood of tears, during which one's steps involuntarily rush and anon involuntarily lag. There is a feeling that one is utterly out of hand, with the very distinct consciousness of an endless number of fine thrills and titillations descending to one's toes; there is a depth of happiness in which the most painful and gloomy parts do not act as antitheses to the rest but . . . as necessary shades of color in such an overflow of light. . . . Everything happens quite involuntarily, as if in a tempestuous outburst of freedom, of absoluteness, of power and divinity." [44] This life-shattering revelation, experienced by a prophet without God, is characterized by him as a deep and basic phenomenon in the life of the creative man. Forms of experience which for centuries had been the exclusive domain of religious revelation and mystical ecstasy were now usurped by an intensified aesthetic experience that defied classification. Among Nietzsche's followers this resulted in a dangerous confusion of boundaries and concepts, and raised audacious man to an unprecedented height. Buber, whose deep religious disposition made him susceptible to ecstatic experiences, also succumbed to this pseudo-religious feeling of the time; and this lasted until the era of World War I when he developed a maturer appreciation for genuine religion.

Nietzsche created within Western Christian culture a type of ecstatic personality that is basically different from the mystic, one that receives his "revelations" in a state of Dionysian frenzy: "then the intellect is just as much at ease or at home in the senses as the senses are at ease or at home in it. . . ." The most sensuous things are "transfigured by a simile-intoxication of the highest spirituality." [45] In this condition of effulgent radiance and transfiguring frenzy, things reflect their own ecstasy. It is this feeling that Buber had in mind when he later spoke of the "kingdom of sublime intoxication" into which he was seduced by *Zarathustra*.

At one of the critical points of his Dionysian experience, time became for Nietzsche "the eternal recurrence of the same": the very use of the word *eternal* instead of *endless* reveals the faith symbol that is hidden in his doctrine.[46] In his detailed interpretation of Nietzsche's doctrine of the "great noonday," O. F. Bollnow has shown[47] that the conception of time as *eternal recurrence* signifies "a conceptual interpretation of eternity experienced in the highest joy of noonday." Man's subjective conception of time is here proclaimed as a form of objective occurrences in time. By failing to recognize the subjective character of the inner sense of time, which operates on several planes, this theory conceived time as a recurrent cycle.

The time problem that perplexed Buber was part of the atmosphere of that period, and it was only through Nietzsche that it assumed for him the dimensions of a personal crisis. Just as the representation of space in the Copernican world view produced the "anthropological unrest" of Pascal's generation, so did the problem of the nature of time become a burning problem in the last decade of the nineteenth century, and continued long thereafter to affect Buber's intellectual development. Bergson's distinction between time as duration, experienced in terms of life, and time as divisible or measurable revealed that time is differently conceived and experienced where "life" is the highest metaphysical concept. It was only gradually recognized that this profound revolution in our conception of time was symptomatic of an existential imbalance or giddiness and that this was basically the result of a religious crisis. Buber confessed that he also suffered from this vertiginous imbalance that was characteristic of the time, and that he wrestled with this problem for years "without the presence of the godly."

At the end of 1896 Buber left Galicia to begin his studies at the University of Vienna where eight years later he received his doctor's degree. He did not regard the city of his birth and early childhood as his native city, and he spoke of it as the "home where he was a stranger," where he first experienced "the world" somewhat in the sense in which one spoke of "Dame World" in the Middle Ages. This enchanting, poetry-intoxicated city on the Danube, which breathed an intellectual atmosphere that was so congenial to the assimilated Jews of Vienna, must have been a pleasant relief for Buber, whose roots were deeper in the East and who bore within him the tensions of the Slavic soul. The lectures he attended in his first year at the university do not seem to have made a deep impression on him. Only in the seminars, where teacher and students interpreted a text in common, did he discover that "spirit" was something that exists *between* people.

In the theater as well it was the human confrontation, the spoken word in contradistinction to the written word, that fascinated him. The poet of his youth was Hugo von Hofmannsthal. He rediscovered Goethe's euphoric verse, "I am prodigality; I am poetry," in Hofmannsthal's poem "Lebenslied": "This easy extravagance of the 'prodigal' inheritors of the ancient treasure enchanted my heart; it penetrated my speech and writings. Two decades passed until, in the storm of the World War which revealed the innermost dangers that beset man, I disciplined myself to the service of the Word and through bitter struggle acquired the heritage in a way I had never expected." [48] But the thoughts of the young Austrian poet were to occupy Buber for a long time; as late as 1958, on the occasion of his eightieth birthday, Albrecht Goes spoke of the "austere Hofmannsthal grace" of Buber's language.

Austria never succeeded in establishing a proper relationship to Martin Buber any more than she had with many other of her famous sons. He who wrote a truly classical German and whose language until the end betrayed his Viennese origin wrote in 1957: "I am a Polish Jew. . . ." [49] This relationship could perhaps best be described by a word coined by Buber himself, *Vergegnung*, "mis-meeting", to indicate the failure of true *Begegnung*, "meeting".

Austria is greater than Vienna and must be grasped in its totality if we would properly assess Buber's participation in Austrian life. Nor must we forget the cultural significance of Prague, the Slavic gate of the Danubian monarchy. Here we must step out of the "World of Yesterday" and listen to Buber's younger contemporary, Friedrich Heer, who described the period at the beginning of the century not as a golden era but as an already decadent age soon destined to pass away.[50]

Even while the old Austria was crumbling it showed signs of greatness, for it was conscious of its high mission and of the difficult task it had set for itself, namely, to preserve the traditional order of Europe, to reconcile the old patriarchal culture with the revolutionary impulses of the rising masses and the large admixture of foreign elements in the population. The solicitude for the "neglected substratum" of the folk-soul had produced not only psychoanalysis and depth psychology but also another Jewish achievement of historical significance, namely, "Austrian poetry between Kafka and Broch," which attempted to reflect the doubts and misgivings of the old Empire and give them permanent expression in the "high form" of poetry. A further attempt to rescue the traditional values of Europe is seen by Heer in the new religious existential thinking that culminated in Martin Buber. It is no accident that Ferdinand Ebner and Martin Buber, who independently of one another rediscovered the Thou of human fellowship, were both Austrians. In the Danubian monarchy the art of living together was in the very air. Buber's achievement in integrating the despised, nameless mass of East European Jews into the "upper" world of culture was, according to Heer, not only a Jewish but also an Austrian achievement and represented the harmonious integration of Jewish genius with Austrian *humanitas*.

Heer described his country's intellectual and social relations as an Austrian historian and hence tended to see Buber from a distance and somewhat impersonally, for he was still unacquainted with Buber's "Autobiographical Fragments." Buber's Austrian characteristics, nevertheless, stand out clearly as we look back over the years of his development, even though the circle of Viennese writers and poets of his day regarded him as an outsider. The problem of Austrian nationalities was familiar to him because of the various languages he heard around him as a child; he also inherited a restlessness from his Slavic background as well as the intellectual tensions of his Jewish heritage. Tolerance, as a form of social convenience and an enlightened human attitude, was a basic element of the Austrian character. In Buber it was combined with the ancient Jewish striving for the supranational and the universally human, and constituted a counterpoise or antidote to his passionate Zionism. His rediscovery of Hasidism as a popular religious movement was also facilitated by the social relations that existed naturally in Austria between the upper classes and the common people; the attitude of his father to his subordinates exemplified this for Buber.

The convictions that there is a divine spark in all human beings that can be redeemed and that man's native goodness can find expression in an atmosphere of tolerance were among Buber's basic beliefs. The hardships of his early years awakened in his deeply religious nature a restlessness which, according to St. Augustine, "finds its rest only in God." To the outside world his restlessness was expressed as an "out-going soul element," as a vital spiritual force which imparted to every "meeting" a specific color and illumination. In the "Autobiographical Fragments" this vital interest in human fellowship speaks to us in clear tones and illuminates Buber's early years as he considered them in retrospect. Again and again the merely conceptual and the sensuously opaque are transformed in the pure flame of this life into the same soul-element of a warmer and yet not too intimate humanity. In the "Fragments" the personalities and events of his youth pass before us as the spoken and heard elemental words of his existence, bound to the fleeting moment and preserved by memory and imagination in an ultimate harmony as lived and irrevocable decision.

TEACHERS

The typical figure of the respected teacher does not appear in the "Autobiographical Fragments." The young student did not find such a teacher either in his first year at the University of Vienna or during his two semesters at Leipzig (1897–98 and 1898–99), where he attended lectures in psychiatry and psychology in addition to his main studies in philosophy, the history of art and Germanics. The teacher he found most congenial was the famous Wilhelm Dilthey who had succeeded Lotze at the University of Berlin in 1882 and remained there until his death in 1911. Buber studied at the University of Berlin in the summer of 1898 and in the autumn of 1899; after receiving his degree he lived in the vicinity of Berlin from 1906 to 1916 as a free-lance writer. In addition to Dilthey's lectures at the university, he also attended those of Georg Simmel whose friend he later became.

Buber's fragment "A Lecture" [50a] ["Ein Vortrag"] is particularly revealing for it deals with his first year at Leipzig and with the transitional period before he became a teacher. In the introduction, apparently without any connection to the events he described subsequently, Buber spoke of the impression that Bach's music made upon him; it was not the "sorcery" of glorious sounds that enchanted him but the hidden meaning of life, conjured up by the music, that liberated his soul.

Buber was invited by a Socialist society to give a lecture on Ferdinand Lasalle, in whose life and work he had been interested for some time. As an admirer of Nietzsche and Carlyle he was ill-prepared to treat the problematical figure of Lasalle, and he presented him as an impetuous, heroic figure, consumed by boundless passion that ended in tragedy. Even as he spoke, Buber realized that he had not fully understood the problem of historical understanding and that he was guilty of gross simplification in turning historical figures into idols or caricatures, and in making historical facts conform to preconceived ideas of greatness.

"Bach helped me," Buber noted. Bach's music was played in Leipzig with consummate artistic craftsmanship, and its penetrating power transported Buber into an absolute world of its own, divorced from all finite historical context, into a realm of inexpressible religious responsibility.

The problem of historical understanding was formulated by Wilhelm Dilthey. History for Nietzsche had no meaning except as the servant of life and action; he never really grasped it in its totality, and considered the historical sense "a malady from which men suffer." The great figures of the past became for him more and more the tragic symbols of his own existence. His preoccupation with history did not lead him to any objective area of reality; historical self-determination had for him, rather, an "unbounded power";[51] he used history to confirm his "hybrid self." To feel the history of mankind, with all its hopes and defeats, as one's own history "requires a piece of good fortune that mankind has not yet known—a godlike fortune, full of power and love, full of tears and laughter," as it is written in *Die Fröhliche Wissenschaft* [The gay science], Aph. 337.

Dilthey reproached Nietzsche[52] for having formed his conception of man from introspection: "Man recognizes himself only in history, never through introspection" (7:279). The general conception "man," apart from his historical objective manifestations, was nonexistent for Dilthey. Man does not have a history, he *is* history: "I am an historical being down to the deepest unattainable depths of my Self" (7:278). We do not know what possibilities of realization the future holds for man. The "totality" of human nature is to be found only in history and will emerge only from the totality of all objective manifestations.[53] Life cannot be divorced from history. "What is philosophy . . . ? History must be consulted to find out what philosophy is" (8:208). All our basic questions find their answers in history.

Early in his career Dilthey began to seek the meaning of the creative principle of "life" in the manifold forms of its historical manifestation. The ultimate riddle of life is not thereby solved: "In life's secret, unfathomable countenance, with its laughing mouth and melancholy eyes, all the generations of thinkers and poets have sought to find an answer, and this also is endless" (6:287). The philosophical question concerning the meaning of life is immensely complicated, even when it is limited to the human, historical world, and becomes a true adventure of the spirit. For all basic research in the social sciences must proceed from the initial assumption that here life must be grasped in terms of life; there is no absolute point of departure (cf. 1:419; 5:110). It is as if one were to be asked to draw lines and construct solid figures in a flowing stream (cf. 7:280). Dilthey undertook this seemingly impossible task with incredible intellectual passion and perseverance. The interpretation of the social and intellectual history of Europe in this undertaking went hand in hand with reflections on the basic problems of philosophical and historical research. Starting from his famous trinity, experience—expression—understanding, Dilthey attempted to investigate the prerequisites of a hermeneutics of life, to set up categories of life, and to study the nature and components of a world view; and thus, proceeding from the simple to the complicated, he constructed his method of research in the social sciences.

Dilthey proceeds from the view that the world is an articulated whole wherein each individual finds his place through the interrelationships of a common life that binds all men together by means of institutions in which "life" develops and in which the manifold life relations of the individual converge. Even before a child begins to speak he is part and parcel of a common system of relations (7:208 f.), and, to a limited extent, "understands" the world in which he finds himself: every life relation also entails a life understanding.[54] The experience of one's self always includes an experience of the world. On a preconceptual level the I and the world are one; the separation of subject and object is effected only by thought. The original "interiority" in which reality exists for us is displaced by the activity of the understanding—a thought that comes close to Buber's distinction between the I-Thou and the I-It relation. Every individual opens up into a world of his own. Life is transfixed and made comprehensible by means of expression; living together implies a natural mutual understanding. Proceeding from these simple, basic ideas Dilthey attempts to find a path to the great historical relations: "We leave the stream of life, and the unending sea takes us up" (7:252). The categories that apply to the life of the individual are now transferred to the historical world and its effective relations. Every historical epoch, by reason of its specific "horizon," has a distinctive spiritual form that distinguishes it from all others.

"The basic thought that underlies my philosophy is that until now experience as a whole, entire and unfragmented, has never served as the ground of philosophizing, and certainly not entire reality as a whole" (7:171; cf. 1:123). In the preface to his *"Einleitung in die Geisteswissenschaften"* [Introduction to the social sciences], written as early as 1883, Dilthey pointed out that the empiricists and Kant were concerned only with the "knowing subject" and not with the man of flesh and blood. His purpose, however, was to relate every component of present-day abstract scientific thinking to the whole of human nature as it is given in experience and in the study of language and history (1:xviii). For the age in which he lived was characterized by "an insatiable longing for reality" (1:123). A basic science of reality comprising "human nature" and history is the philosophical anthropology he envisaged. Dilthey considered himself to be in the tradition of Kant's transcendental philosophy (cf. 8:14 and 174 f.), although he did not take for his starting point man's creative cognitive faculty.[55] The history of ideas, as he understood it, is not concerned with changing concepts and their relations but with modifications of the entire man in his total reality.[56] History is concerned with the contact of life with life: the task of *Geistesgeschichte* is to retranslate the immeasurable historico-social reality back into the "spiritual vitality" from which it sprang (5:265).

Philosophy is an engagement of the entire man, a striving to capture "full, unmutilated experience," to feel the force of the "spiritual vitality" in historical understanding whose secret is to be found not in reason but in the affective and conative aspects of human nature. On all these points Buber was from the very outset an enthusiastic disciple of Dilthey; in his I and Thou, for example, he also constructed the human world on the basis of the simplest facts of life.

It was to a large extent Dilthey's vacillating attitude to Nietzsche, which was sometimes intimate and sometimes distant, that predestined him to be Buber's teacher. Both Dilthey and Nietzsche were "philosophers of life"—except that the road chosen by the former led to science. He thus served as a counterpoise to Nietzsche's revolutionary pathos and, from a historical point of view, as a transitional figure uniting two epochs.

The poet of Dilthey's youth was Hölderlin, and he was thus faced with the task of reconciling the basic poetical and philosophical attitude of German classicism toward reality and the exact sciences with the tendencies of his own age. Dilthey may be characterized as a scientist with a poet's vision. Nietzsche was also an admirer of Goethe, but his understanding was unhistorical and in time he abandoned it in favor of his polemics against the culture of his age; Goethe remained the ideal of his inner vision, perhaps the only one he never betrayed.

"Never did the atmosphere of a living being bear a closer affinity to the atmosphere of a poem," said Hugo von Hofmannsthal of Dilthey *in memoriam.*[57] Poets were for him the "seers of mankind" and the authentic interpreters of life. Nietzsche's thought also strove toward poetic utterance—Thomas Mann spoke of his *Erkenntnislyrik* (poetry in search of knowledge)—but he felt more at home in the twilight zone between philosophy and poetry. Dilthey was able, however, because of his deep appreciation of the German classics, to achieve a fine balance between thought and feeling in his prose style. In this respect Buber was also like his teacher: the poetical element as a basic component of his language was meant to engage the reader's emotions and thus expressed his conviction that philosophy must concern itself with the entire man. It was such intellectual attitudes that teacher and student had in common, more than the knowledge transmitted in the classroom, that made their relationship fruitful.

One of the most moving testimonies of Dilthey's humanity is the talk he gave to students and friends on the occasion of his seventieth birthday in 1903 [58] in which he tells how Raphael's *The School of Athens* appeared to him in a dream. His chief aim, he declared, had always been to transmit to his students methods of research, the "art of dissecting reality," which is the hallmark of a philosopher and of historical thinking—not a ready-made solution of life's riddle but the vital sense of inner freedom that springs from a historical consciousness. He related how he was startled in his dream by the consciousness of the disunity of philosophical schools whose representatives were depicted in Raphael's picture. Modern man realizes that he cannot expect philosophy to give him valid knowledge concerning ultimate questions: "The pure light of truth can only be perceived by us in its differently refracted rays." Philosophy is left with the task of arranging and organizing the experimental sciences. The philosophical spirit is present wherever the basic principles of a science are studied and a connection with the other sciences sought, wherever a method and its cognitive value are tested and their relation to the idea of knowledge ascertained. Real freedom, however, is given to us through history; for history teaches us to respect the portion of truth that is to be found in every world view.

This philosophical insight accompanied Buber throughout his life. There are teacher-student relations that are realized not so much by concrete results as by the direction a teacher gives to the energies of the student. Buber learned from Dilthey how to formulate historically the question concerning man, and this desire to understand man soon led him to the study of myth and mysticism. One can readily detect Dilthey's influence in Buber's thoughts concerning the rebirth of Judaism or concerning mysticism and myth. Dilthey's studies of the late Middle Ages and the beginnings of the Renaissance, in which the development of European national cultures appeared to give rise to a new spiritual world, confirmed Buber's conviction that the renewal of the Jewish nation through the development of the total energies of the individual Jew as a whole, both of body and soul, need not be an idle dream. No less important was his teacher's gospel of work which made a deep impression on him, but which he could realize only gradually as he pursued his own tasks. From Dilthey he also learned how to approach complex intellectual questions from different points of view and patiently to await their clarification. Although the affinity of his genius for his teacher's life philosophy grew weaker with the years because of his own religious experience, Buber still held fast to Dilthey's "philosophical spirit." He did not adopt any particular theological mode of thought, but devoted himself as a mature and independent thinker to the study of the boundary areas between religion and science.

On the centenary of Georg Simmel's birth in 1958 a *Buch des Dankes* was issued in which more than fifty friends and former students contributed words of appreciation. Buber in his essay, the shortest in the volume, relates how Simmel once anxiously asked him what in his opinion had been his influence on his students, and that he had answered: "You have taught them to think"—an answer that did not seem to displease Simmel,[59] for it hit the mark and was confirmed by almost all the contributors to the volume. Simmel's peculiar manner of thinking accounts for his success among the students and for the failure of his academic career. His thinking was not that of a "knowing subject" but of a man with a body and soul, and his students took part in his lectures as in a living experience. He was a master of precise formulation: "his intense manner of speaking reflected the tension of his thought; he presented only the abstract, but he did so as part of a common endeavor and as lived participation, so that the listener's interest also became part of life, and comprehension followed of itself." [60]

Thinking was for Simmel a passion, an inner compulsion to see all things *sub specie philosophiae*. The first essay, in his collection of posthumous essays with the title *Brücke und Tür* [Bridge and door],[61] is a good example of Simmel's method of probing into the daily things around him and extracting their deep philosophical significance. He inquired into the meaning of destiny, love, and death; he philosophized about nature as landscape and about the art of acting. He was a philosopher with a soul, with what Margarete Susman calls a "pre-analytical" soul [62]—which today is no longer in fashion. And the "salvation of the soul"—which he distinguished from sanctity and immortality—the soul's premonition of ultimate bliss and perfection, became the subject of those short, artistically constructed philosophical essays, a style created by him. But even a comprehensive work such as his *Philosophy of Money* was called by an enthusiastic reader an "intellectual poem" and a "universal work of art." [63]

Simmel's inspired philosophizing soared into the realm of thought from its roots in life itself, and yet it remained locked up in the heart of the thinker and unable to grasp reality. An incident related by Friedrich Meinecke[64] illustrates this type of thinking. He recalled how Simmel visited him before he left for Strasbourg and how he refused the chair his host offered him but remained standing while he delivered an impromptu discourse on the philosophy of chairs and on the custom of offering one to a guest—which must surely have struck his host, who was a realistic historian, as highly inappropriate. One of Simmel's most significant works, *Goethe*, was described by Troeltsch as a "grand panorama of being," and yet it fails to capture the essential message of the great poet. In the case of Dilthey and Buber we can speak of a universal, human relationship to poetry; Simmel, however, experienced poetry through a filter of philosophic speculation.

Whereas Dilthey's influence is still felt, Simmel's name is hardly mentioned today. The motto he chose as a superscription to his posthumous diary indicates that he realized he would leave no spiritual heirs behind him. He is, like Dilthey, a transitional phenomenon. In an age that celebrated the triumphs of materialism and positivism, he looked back to Kant and Goethe. He died in 1918 and did not live to see the great social and political upheavals that marked the aftermath of World War I in Germany.

The first sentence of an unfinished autobiographical sketch which Simmel wrote as an introduction to the *Buch des Dankes* reads: "My starting point was epistemological and scientific Kantian studies with which historical and social studies went hand in hand." To Kant's question, How is nature possible? he added, How is history possible? How does an event become history? Following Kant's solution Simmel separated the content of a historical event from its form. The realm of ideal existence, which we call history, is formed for Simmel, as "nature" was for Kant, by the a priori categories of the human spirit.

The problem of historical understanding was treated by both Simmel and Dilthey as a special instance of understanding. But whereas Dilthey, as a historian, seeks this understanding by viewing man as part of his historical milieu, Simmel is concerned with the theory of historical understanding and the nature of historical time, and tries, as Margarete Susman expresses it, "to understand understanding." [65] This leads him to question how it is at all possible for one man to "understand" another. The common nature shared by all men is not the indispensable condition for our understanding one another; nor do we understand only that which we ourselves have experienced. We understand one another as a whole, as a unity. The category of Thou is for Simmel "a primary phenomenon of the human spirit, like seeing and hearing, thought and feeling or like objectivity in general, like time and space, like the I; it is the transcendental basis of man's existence as a "political animal." [66] These thoughts, which were published in 1918 but which are already apparent in the opening chapter of his *Sociology*, foreshadow an area in which Buber was later to break through to his philosophy of the dialogic principle, set forth with an astonishing simplicity that would have been beyond the powers of his teacher.

We also find Buber struggling to express this basic principle in another area of thought. In 1905 he began to publish *Die Gesellschaft*, of which forty volumes appeared in the seven years of its existence. In

Buber's introduction to the first volume we first meet the concept "between man and man" although not in the sense he used later[67] to mean a "distinct dimension" of the personal relationship between individuals, but synonymous with "social," and referring to group relations. He thus defines the problem with which the collection *Die Gesellschaft* is concerned: "The living together of people in all its forms, patterns and activities, as seen from the new social-psychological point of view." [68] A wide field is here staked out for the new collection: "Sociology is a science of the forms of human relations between man and man, whose patterns are dealt with by ethics, political economy, political science, jurisprudence, etc., and whose activities constitute the subject matter of historical science: the history of economics, society, and culture." The social-psychological point of view presented here points to Simmel, but the elaboration of the concept *zwischenmenschlich* is Buber's interpretation of what Simmel understood by *Vergesellschaftung,* "socialization." Furthermore, the highly abstract language of Buber's introduction and the precise formulations that touch on so many areas of thought also show strong traces of Simmel's thought.

As the founder of a formal sociology Simmel did not attract many followers. The methodological principle he employed came from a critical examination of the question: How is society possible? Simmel arrives at his new concept of sociology "by separating the forms of *Vergesellschaftung* from the contents, that is, the impulses, aims, and subject matter which become social only after having been subjected to the reciprocal influences between individuals." The investigation of these reciprocal influences is in his view the task of "pure sociology." [69]

In his fragmentary recollections Simmel pointed out that this concept of reciprocal influences, from the standpoint of its sociological significance, had become for him "a purely comprehensive metaphysical principle." He also learned to look upon the concepts truth, value, and objectivity as "reciprocal effects." In an age of skeptical distrust of the Absolute and Eternal, an age which regarded cognition as an independent, detached process "whose elements mutually determine their respective positions, as is also the case in masses of matter where it is effected by means of gravity," [70] a world structure of pure relationship in which all things bear and sustain one another seemed to be the only possibility of making this disintegrating world of phenomena visible as a whole.[71]

Simmel's thinking was pluralistic, marked by a vivid sense of life's unending and varied relations—a characteristic that must have had a strong influence on Buber. To Simmel the great philosophers signified basic anthropological approaches in comprehending the wholeness of life; every philosophy is an objectification of a definite human type and gives us only one aspect of the totality of life; "The apple of the Tree of Knowledge was not ripe" is as characteristic for his thinking in this matter as his dictum concerning the Absolute: "I did not see it, but it was there." [72]

Simmel contributed a slender volume for *Gesellschaft*, called *Die Religion* (1906), in which God is present but not visible: the question of God's existence is treated purely sociologically, and the origin of the belief in God is given a socio-psychological explanation. God is the transcendent meeting-place of the group's forces. The relations between man and man are elevated to the transcendental by the impulse of the religious life process and find their expression in the idea of the godly. The dynamics of religious life naturally tend toward objectification in the form of the Absolute.[73] The chief concern here is with the origin of religion; the question of God's existence is not discussed. In this work Simmel distinguished between religion as the objective world of belief and religiosity as a category of feeling, an innermost quality of being that colors one's entire experience, a force that creates religion out of itself.

Simmel's profoundest thoughts on religion are reserved for his later book *Lebensanschauung* [Conception of life] with the subtitle "Vier Metaphysische Kapitel." Here his thoughts about life are given a metaphysical basis, and in the process he presses forward to an absolute life concept. A philosophical system did not emerge from this attempt, but rather something that Simmel called "attitudes to life," a view of the relation of life to itself. The deep contradiction between life as creative movement, on the one hand, and form as a world-formative principle, on the other, is here resolved by the notion of "transcendence of life." Simmel seeks to interpret the struggle that goes on in all areas of the spirit between dynamic life and the forms it produces by finding a more comprehensive principle of life's most primary movement; "transcendence of life" means that life in one and the same act creates more-life and more-than-life. Life has the power to produce not only itself but at the same time objective forms as well. The cultural forms it creates are at first receptacles in which life finds a temporary habitation until it outgrows them. In this way life creates religions and then in time abandons them.

Simmel found the empirical basis for his theory in self-consciousness: "The subject that turns itself into its own object is the symbol or the real expression of life." That spirit can confront itself and still retain its unity and know its own being is a primary phenomenon of life: self-consciousness is the timeless basic form of life.[74] The venturesome leap that is made here from the life of the individual to the life of society is instructive for the understanding of Simmel's "attitudes," that is, the determining factors which he claimed to discern behind the surface states and processes. We can detect a strain of mysticism, a mysticism which was understood at that time as a kind of complementary concept to skepticism and constantly threatened by it; this becomes apparent, for example, in the title of Gustav Landauer's *Skepsis und Mystik* and in Fritz Mauthner's philosophy of language.

Buber's pantheism at that time was of another kind. He was carried away by the unadulterated experience of the moment and failed to appreciate the precise effects of its intellectual aspects. Under Simmel's influence his mystical feeling was subjected to a kind of secular-scholastic discipline. Here Buber found a teacher with a comprehensive view of all areas of life, and a thinker who could capture the most elusive experience in his conceptual net. As one of his students said of him: "He gave us concepts in bodily form." [75] Buber was exposed to the danger of this mode of thinking until he wrote *Daniel*, namely, the illusion that such universal thinking, however deeply experienced, can in itself pierce reality and attain "realization."

Of great significance for Buber was above all Simmel's distinction between religion and religiosity, which not only provided a basis for his early essays on Judaism but also was still evident in his later confrontation with Christianity in *Zwei Glaubensweisen* [Two ways of faith].

Simmel's distinction between belief as "taking something to be true" and belief as an innermost attitude of the whole man could only be made by a thinker who might indeed be devout and given to mysticism but who did not feel bound by any particular religion—a not infrequent phenomenon of that day. Simmel's religiosity, divorced from religion, was an abstraction that owes more to a creative impulse than to religious feelings, and in the end remained as alien to human reality as is his talented portrayal of Goethe. The danger that beset Simmel here as elsewhere was his tendency to isolate the phenomenon he was investigating, cleanse it of all impurities, and then imbue it with a spurious vitality that was not in harmony with actual life.

An example of this peculiar lack of a sense of life's reality was the debate that took place at the meeting of sociologists in October 1910 after Troeltsch's lecture on "Stoic-Christian Natural Law and Modern Secular Natural Law" when Simmel raised the question whether any social or sociological significance was to be attached to Christianity and whether its only problem was that of "God and soul." Buber, who followed him, expressed his doubts about mysticism as a sociological category, for he saw in mysticism "the most absolute realization of religiosity as that peculiar mode of self-apprehension and that intensity of self-exaltation which makes possible an 'apperception of God,' a personal relationship to a soul-content that is felt to be God," and then contrasted this religiosity of mysticism with a religion which is "a sociological entity constructed on the basis of religiosity." Utilizing Simmel's categories, Buber came to the conclusion that mysticism might be designated as "religious solipsism."

In his rejoinder Troeltsch pointed out that Simmel placed too much emphasis on mysticism in his interpretation of religion; and in his answer to Buber he argued that we cannot speak of mysticism itself but only of its historical manifestations. Buber's view is similar to Maeterlinck's, namely, that in the life of the early Christian mystics community played an important part.[76]

Simmel's conception of religion was supplemented and deepened by an extremely individualistic ethic which he discussed in the last chapter of *Lebensanschauung*. Buber also found Simmel's concept "individual law" congenial to his mode of thought, a concept that was similar to Nietzsche's proclamation of the ancient doctrine: Become the one thou art.

In the realm of ethics as well Simmel took Kant for his starting point. In the Ought, which was for him as for Kant an absolutely valid category, Simmel saw once more the operation of that astounding reversal whereby the form that is created and nourished by life turns against life. But Simmel was careful not to make Kant's universal reason the criterion of the ethical, applying it only to human acts. He conceived the Ought as something individual, springing from the innermost lives of unique human beings: "The individual law is the objective Ought of an individual, the challenge that comes from *his* life and is addressed to *his* life." [77] That such an individual law cannot be derived from life alone was demonstrated two years later by Peter Wust in his *Auferstehung der Metaphysik* [The resurrection of metaphysics].[78] But the creative character that the Ought assumes in an "individual law" greatly appealed to Buber in both Nietzsche and Simmel. That his own ethics remained largely formal and individualistic has been held against Buber to this day by his friends and critics. He had indeed learned from his profound religious experience that individual law has its roots in transcendence, that it completes that which the Creator had intended for man, and signifies the realization of the life form that resides in him.

2
Mysticism and Myth

SIMMEL IN his treatment of philosophical questions always returned to Kant as his starting point; Dilthey was also of the opinion that "the basic problem of philosophy had been formulated by Kant for all time . . . (5:12). In his *Hauptproblemen der Philosophie* [Main problems of philosophy], however, Simmel recognized in Eckhart's type of mysticism another possible mode besides Kant's of comprehending being as a whole: the soul spark that comes from the divine ground leaps from life to life and illumines the world that flows from God.[1] Dilthey's interest was also directed to a transcendental theology which goes beyond dogmas and religious forms "to an ever-present and constantly active human godliness in the soul that produces all these forms of the religious life (2:109; cf. 2:77); and in another passage we learn that "only from the standpoint of pantheism is it possible to have an interpretation of the world that fully exhausts its meaning" (4:260). For both thinkers it is man's creative faculty that leads from mysticism to Kant. But they were too conscious of the demands of their own age to adopt an uncritical romantic attitude to mysticism. Buber's generation, on the other hand, had been deeply influenced by Nietzsche's conception of the creative man, and had embraced mysticism unreservedly with no misgivings about its historical irrelevance: it found in mysticism its own life feeling.

Buber's doctoral dissertation at the University of Vienna in 1904 dealt with an aspect of German mysticism and was entitled: "Zur Geschichte des Individuationsproblems (Nikolaus von Cues und Jakob Böhme)" [The history of the problem of individuation—Nicholas of

Cusa and Jacob Boehme]. It was intended as part of a larger work which would comprehend the problem of individuation from Aristotle to Leibniz. This larger work was never completed, but it is apparent from the dissertation, which is unpublished,[2] that the author's knowledge went far beyond the assigned theme; that he had a comprehensive view of the history of the problem of individuation in Western philosophy.

That Buber chose Nicholas of Cusa as his starting point shows the influence of his teacher Dilthey, whose interest in humanistic studies of early modern times is stressed in the introduction to the dissertation. The Renaissance as Dilthey saw it was not a return to the values of the ancient world, but a movement of supranational significance that proclaimed the rebirth of man and the dawn of a new spiritual world. At the same time, however, Dilthey showed in his treatment of the life of Petrarch the great inner tensions that existed in the life feeling and creative will of the early Renaissance and its deep-seated conflict with traditional Christian values.

In the case of Nicholas of Cusa, who was a cardinal of the Church, there was no conflict between belief in revelation and philosophical knowledge. Buber ignored the Christian component of Cusa's thought and spoke of his "relative monistic system" which he took to be a "more relative pantheism" compared to Bruno, a pantheism "that sees God in everything and outside of everything, and that looks upon nature as the realm in which we experience God who is not limited, however, to the natural world but points to a transcendental realm beyond experience; that sees every single being as divine and as only an emanation from an indivisible origin whose unity and wholeness are not impaired by this radiation or unfolding." Aside from this reservation he treated the imagery and similes of Cusa as concepts of a philosophical system that resembles Neoplatonism. Dilthey also saw in Cusa the highest expression of an "objective mysticism . . . in which the relation of the whole and the part determined the relation of the individual to the invisible whole and its visible manifestation." [3] Buber spoke of an "objective individualism" and, starting from Cusa's basic concepts, "unfolding" and "participation," he showed how the manifold emanates from the one divine world ground. All beings participate with God, although in varying degrees, and the gradations of participation are not indicated. Buber was able to demonstrate that these assigned degrees of participation are at first only inchoate in the individual and only gradually develop from potentiality to actuality. The greater this development the more complete is the degree of participation, i.e., of the primary image at its source, and the attainment of God: "It is not the depersonalizing but rather the personalizing process that leads things to God."

It was characteristic of the philosophers and writers around the turn of the century to underestimate the Christian element in German mysticism. Karl Jaspers,[4] in a recent study of the philosophical and theological questions treated by Cusa, concludes that the belief in revelation is evident in almost all his writings, that this belief is the source of his speculative thought and its general tenor, and that it signifies the development of belief by the methods of philosophy. He cautions us not to attribute to Cusa a false modern notion of spiritual freedom because of the bold way in which he anticipates the use of reason: "We may regard Cusa as the last peak of the Christian-ecclesiastical Catholic belief that constitutes the unity of the West, with its clear philosophical concepts, before the final inroads of 'modernity.' He seems to be completely at home in eternity." [5]

Jaspers sees Cusa's limitation precisely in the fact that his peculiar view of knowledge as conjecture or learned ignorance, his bold search for paradoxes, suddenly find refuge in the doctrine of revelation when his transcendental thinking is most intense. The notion of creation penetrates his metaphorical language of the unfolding God. Whereas Buber believes that "Cusa thinks of the world-process as an unfolding of God," Jaspers thinks that for Cusa the world as world is not a divine process: "God is not the seed from which the world grows; God himself is not a becoming God." [6] All the greatness of creation is a reflection of the Deity. As a being who is made in the image of God, man is confident of his own powers of creation, but "as the image of Otherness, he is humble because, being separated by an abyss, he is always inadequate." [7] All human perfection is perfection in the realm of symbols. As an example of his own view in contradistinction to that of Nicholas of Cusa, Jaspers cites Mirandola's conception of man's absolute freedom as described in his "On the Dignity of Man." The philosophy of Nicholas of Cusa is not a coherent system; it is "a meditative movement of thought led by objective guides." [8] Man, according to him, in order to develop and complete the primary image of his individuality needs faith in Christ; indeed, he needs to be transformed into him: the path from individuality to self-being leads through Christ; he alone is "mankind in its highest degree and in all its fullness."

No less important is the fact that Buber fails to consider Nicholas of Cusa's trinitarian thinking which he, as a non-Christian, could not always take seriously. It is precisely man's highest faculty of reason, involved in all thinking and constituting man's prerogative, dignity, and freedom, that is presented to us as trinitarian. In reason God created an image of his own three-fold nature. Even as the world came into being through God's trinitarian thinking, so does our conceptual world come into being through the ideas of reason—unity, uniformity, association of ideas. "All creatures are the unfoldings of God; but only reason is the image of in-folding." [9]

The second part of the dissertation deals with Jacob Boehme whom Buber called the individualist of German mysticism. He saw Boehme poised even more precariously than Nicholas of Cusa on the boundary between theism and pantheism, a position that in his case led to deep human conflicts. Also for Boehme the problem of individuation is at the same time the problem of creation. For him the ultimate transcendent unity of God is removed from the category of human thought and conceived in changing symbols as an unfathomable eternal will without being, or, in Buber's words, as "the unity of an irrational dynamic potentiality and not that of a substance however absolutely thought." This potential infinity is represented as a striving toward "realization" in a twofold sense: through motion and through knowledge. God wants to find himself, that is, to know and to reveal himself, to actualize himself; and he attains both through the actualization of the individuation that is latent within him.

In Buber's further interpretation of Boehme, God enters into creation so completely that we may identify it with his actualized powers. All things in God are One Body containing many members bound to one another by subtle mutual influences on which its being rests. Buber cited Boehme's image of the organ where each pipe emits a characteristic tone, and yet there is but *one* stream of air in all the pipes. For Boehme, as for Nicholas of Cusa, God is wholly in every thing, and hence each thing must bear all things latent within itself. Creation is not a process that has ended, a closed circle. God remains the dynamic principle of individuation in nature, the "eternally productive power," so that here as well "everything is in the process of creation." In the wake of divine self-revelation every being strives to realize the form implicit in its creation, and all the contradictions in the world only serve to quicken and enhance the peculiar individuality of each thing. But besides this movement of repulsion of things "against one another," there is contrary to it a basic movement of attraction of things "for one another," whereby all things long to return "with one another" to the unity in God.

From Boehme's obscure language Buber was able to extract and clearly explain the myth by which the "philosophus teutonicus," as Boehme was called, had influenced the Romantic movement and German idealism, and helped determine the "German line" in philosophy from Eckhart to Hegel, a modification of the ancient Neoplatonic-gnostic-Jewish myth of the "becoming" God. Buber recognized that ever since the age of the Renaissance the question of the nature of God was at the same time the problem of individuation, and he traced its ramified connections from Nicholas of Cusa through Paracelsus and Valentin Weigel down to Jakob Boehme.

The God who realizes himself in the world has been found by modern man to be the conception that was most congenial to his new mode of thinking. Even though we may find some thinkers of this period who believe that man has the ability to extract nature's secrets from the depths of a divine Being, this conviction did not militate against their belief in creation. Just as Boehme's *Ungrund*, "nonground," can only be comprehended as a triune God, so is the seal of the trinity stamped on nature and on man. The belief in creation and in creatureliness is still vital and deeply felt. When Boehme says: "Heaven, earth, stars and the elements are all in man, and in addition the triune of the Godhead . . ." [10] then this is the being-one and the being-all of man as image and likeness, which does not exclude man's

Otherness over against God, just as the stamped wax is not the seal. Boehme never loses sight of the fact that the world is fallen creation and that man must be born again in Christ. This is attested to not only by the deep piety that pervades his shorter religious writings but also by his explanation of the "Charts of the Three Principles" in his *Mikrokosmos* [Microcosm]. "In this chart man is presented as an image of all three worlds, corresponding to soul, spirit, and body, as he was at the beginning after his creation, what he became after the Fall as the result of temptation and error, and what he is to be in his rebirth through the spirit of Christ, this being a true, essential image of the three principles of divine revelation as emanating from the Word of the divine Will." Man's ethical task remains untouched by nature-philosophical speculations, namely, his task to renew the face of the earth by being born again in Christ and to restore the divine body of creation.

In his essay on Nietzsche Buber stressed the fact that this philosopher had raised up a formidable adversary against the God of the world's beginning: "The becoming God in whose development we can participate, the product of future evolutions of which we have a presentiment." The God of creation is for him inseparable from the becoming God. Buber also found in Boehme a spirit of prophetic power which has its place between philosophy, mysticism, and poetry. With all its obscurity Boehme's language is intensely vivid and picturesque, and it must have attracted Buber by its power to render the most abstract thought in words of sensuous intuition. Boehme, like Nietzsche, not only required myth but also helped to transmit it. At that early date Buber had not yet realized, as he later acknowledged,[11] how close Boehme's mystical speculations were to the cabbala. From the standpoint of their inner relationship to Jewish tradition Boehme's thoughts must have appealed to him more than Nietzsche's "dogma of evolution." Boehme was a visionary, creative spirit who thought in symbols and whose rational powers were not as highly developed as his plastic style and prophetic consciousness. He did not succeed in reconciling his Christian belief with the many nature-philosophical and theosophical ideas which had influenced him, and in fusing the two into a single unified conception, a unity which he no doubt beheld in his inner vision. Buber, on the other hand, achieved a coherent unity in the representation of his myth which he developed as a philosophical doctrine of the pantheist Boehme. He was able to do this successfully because he refrained from taking issue with the Christian aspect of Boehme's philosophizing. A not unimportant factor which contributed to his success was no doubt his personal interest and participation in the problems with which he struggled.

These views naturally do not emerge as clearly in the dissertation as in the essay "Über Jakob Böhme" [On Jacob Boehme] which appeared in *Wiener Rundschau* as early as 1901.[12] The very first sentence betrays Buber's own interest rather than a desire to do justice to the seventeenth-century mystic: "The basic problem around which all of Boehme's thoughts revolve is the relation of the individual to the world." And soon thereafter this impression grows stronger when the world is described as a "riddle" and man as "hopelessly alone."

Buber correctly perceived that Boehme was primarily concerned not with an abstract notion of God but with the actual form of the godlike in reality, with a "theologia ex idea vitae deducta," as already noted by Oetinger.[13] In the seventeenth century, a century torn by dissension and discord, Boehme was primarily concerned with the question of "the hidden God." The problem was how the indissoluble contradictions and irrational disunities in a world of good and evil, light and darkness, could emanate from the original activity of the divine Being, and how they could be understood as the manifestations of God. The Jewish cabbalists had likewise turned to the inner secrets of the divine life in order to escape from the oppressive life of the Diaspora; and in both instances the depth and poignancy of personal questioning helped to extend the framework of orthodox doctrine.

In the simplified and personal form in which Boehme's world myth is reproduced in Buber's essay, less emphasis is placed on the contrast between God's anger and God's love than on the harmony of creative forces, the play of love that gives rise to the unfolding world and impels its creatures to participate in its development. Buber emphasized above all that the world is not a creation that was completed in a single act but, rather, a constant unfolding of God, a self-revelation in which man, consciously or unconsciously, participates. All struggle and discord serve this end; the inner longing of all things for one another leads to God because, as Buber says, "in it all beings are united to God . . . and it is the way to the new God whom we create, to the new unity of forces."

In the essay on Nietzsche, which is concerned with "the evolving God in whose development we can participate," Buber speaks of "the new God whom we create," and he clarifies his conception by quoting Feuerbach's dictum: "Man by himself is man (in the ordinary sense); man with man—the unity of I and Thou—is God." In a later epilogue to his *Schriften über das dialogische Prinzip*[14] [Writings on the dialogic principle], Buber called this sentence "a pseudo-mystical construction" through which "an anthropological God-substitute" is created. He was at that time, however, obviously not aware how far Feuerbach's anthropocentric formulation was removed from Boehme's vivid imagery and from the ancient myth of the reversion of all things to God. Buber significantly welcomed this restriction to an I-Thou relationship that could be grasped by the senses; he only objected to Feuerbach's attributing the new unity to the difference between one man and another: "We are today closer to Boehme than to the teachings of Feuerbach, closer to the feeling of St. Francis of Assisi who called the birds and stars his brothers and sisters, and still closer to the Vedanta."

Tat twam asi is the symbol created by the Occident to express the doctrine that man is not only united to the world but also that the world *is;* it is the symbol of the microcosm which, according to Buber, was felt more deeply and expressed more beautifully by Boehme than by any other German mystic: "Heaven and earth with all beings, and even God himself, reside in man." And to this Buber added a confession that goes far beyond his theme: "This marvellous world-feeling has become peculiarly our own. We have woven it into our innermost experience. When I take a piece of fruit to my mouth I feel: this is my body; and when I take wine to my lips, I feel: this is my blood. And we are sometimes overcome with a desire to put our arms around a young tree and feel the same life-rhythm that pulsates in us or to read in the eyes of a dumb animal our very own secret. We experience the rise and disappearance of the most distant star as something happening to us. And there are moments in which our organism is an altogether different piece of nature."

On reading these lines many will recall the verses of Hugo von Hofmannsthal:

> The weariness of wholly forgotten nations,
> I cannot cast from my eyelids,
> Nor keep from my frightened soul
> The silent falling of distant stars.[15]

We must be careful, however, not to dismiss Buber's words as the mere poetical sentiment of an adolescent. Again we must refer to the epilogue of the 1958 edition of *I and Thou* in which Buber, then in his eighties, still maintained that a meeting with dumb, inanimate nature was possible, and that the wide sphere wherein this could take place "extends from stones to stars"; that a tree can answer a man who addresses it in its wholeness and unity as a being.[16] In his youth this meeting was experienced as the being-one and the being-all of mysticism.

It was a mysticism that expressed itself through the medium of a myth, that is, as a life-feeling that was conscious of having found its way back to an original revelation which rises now and then like a star in the history of mankind, then fades away and loses itself in what Buber in his old age, in connection with the I-Thou meeting, called a "neglected, obscured, primordial reality." The youthful candor of the pantheistic confession in this essay on Boehme, reminding us of the words with which Christ ordained the sacraments required for salvation, could be regarded by hostile critics as a form of literary blasphemy. In reality, however, it expresses a naive pan-sacramentalism characteristic of poets and of those who are religiously inclined. It was a conspicuous trait in Goethe's youth and is still evident in the seventh book of his autobiography, *Poetry and Truth*, where he speaks of "the symbolic or sacramental meaning" of man and its significance for the development of a culture. Buber later described the pan-sacramentalism of primitive people as a preliminary stage for the "sacramental existence" of the Hasidim, an indication that he was also aware of the emergence of a primordial reality. Buber's remark, that "there are moments in which our organism is an altogether different piece of nature," suggests an ecstatic experience; Buber's idea, under the influence of Nietzsche, to create "the new, becoming God" would then be—although he was not aware of it—the present-day form for directing the divine will as was done by the magician of prehistoric times.

In 1930 Buber wrote an introduction to his *Dialogue* which he called "Original Remembrance." [17] There he tells us of a recurrent dream that came to him at certain intervals, a life dream such as many people have experienced, in which the deepest desires and disappointments of the soul become an "open secret." It is highly significant that in this dream Buber should invariably find himself in a world that is reminiscent of primitive, prehistoric conditions, and that the dream should so often begin with an animal tearing his arm to pieces. The actual content of the dream is practically devoid of all action. It consists of a long, drawn-out call by the dreamer, a wordless, melodious call that is answered by another counter-call coming from the distance—not an echo but a counter-melody, the answer to a question that is not uttered but on which the soul's salvation depends. On one occasion the dreamer fails to hear the expected counter-cry and, still dreaming, becomes aware of a personal experience—such as that of his meeting with the horse in his early youth. But now he felt as if his life depended on his receiving an answer; he waits for it with his whole being, all his senses becoming one single organ of hearing—and behold, a mute answer comes to him on a silent breeze, as if it had always been in the air around him.

The world that is conjured up in this dream is closely related to the myth that sees God in all things. The terrifying world of struggle and combat—the animal that attacks him—vanishes, and the dreamer enters the realm of real being where the voices in the cosmos, as in Boehme's image of the world as an organ, answer one another, because God is the air that contains and sustains them all. The dreamer goes astray in attempting to direct the experience when he adopts an attitude which Buber elsewhere calls "reflexion" *(Rückbiegung)*, an attitude that reminds us of the gestures of a magician toward God. It is also significant that the dream does not terminate in a nightmare like the life-dreams heard by psychoanalysts. The answer is borne to the dreamer by a gentle breeze and he succumbs to it as to the voice of the "vanishing silence" in which the prophet Elijah once heard the words of the Lord; and this answer that he hears is all the more beatific since it had always been there and since without it the cry would not have been possible.

Once we recognize the deeper significance of this dream of a primeval age, we understand how Buber in *I and Thou* assumed that the natural, original form of the basic I-Thou relationship resides in the life of the primitive races and of the child.[18] In both cases the I-Thou relationship functions effectively even before an I-consciousness comes into being, for it is primarily a relationship that is experienced as an impulse that passes through the entire body like a flash of lightning. The sentence "I see the tree" destroys the primary relationship in which the tree lives and has its being over against him. This must be kept in mind when Buber insisted that a "meeting" with inanimate nature is possible in the realm of real human events. "In the beginning was relation": the fragmentary glimpses into prehistoric humanity afforded us by the study of primitive races are supplemented and confirmed by our observation of the early development of children wherein we can trace the development of the human race and recognize "the a priori of relation," "the inborn Thou."

The character of a genius, especially of an artist, displays a "childlike" quality in his understanding of the world which enables him to retain a sense of novelty and naive wonder long after adolescence, and it is only when an abnormal one-sided development retards the natural processes of growth that we can speak of "infantilism." In this connection Goethe speaks of a "repeated puberty" and observes that, although unusual, it is by no means an abnormal life-process. In sacramental experience this natural faculty is raised to a religious union and imbued with a sacred character.

We now return to the pantheistic confession that we find in the essay on Boehme. The digression indicates that Buber's attitude to nature as "a flowing omnipresence" is to be taken seriously and in its full sensuous concreteness. We see how a knowledge of prehistoric times was present in Buber as a kind of anamnesis, which is to be understood not in the sense of cynical resignation as recently described by Gott-fried Benn in his study of poetic creation among primitive people, but rather as a devout simplicity of heart, a genuine relation to the natural-spiritual which in recent times can be compared to the nature expe-riences of Hölderlin. For Hölderlin wine and bread are the divine traces that Christ, the brother of Dionysus and Heracles, left behind him in the universe. He also was no stranger to mythic suffering that comes from the feeling of being forsaken and isolated, for he was al-ways exposed to the flash of lightning hidden in every being, to the ele-mental ray of its violent passions. He was overwhelmed by the prime-val recollection of God's ubiquity through which nature becomes a "holy, living, intimate Universe" governed by an "ontic Eros" which flows like a boundless current between the Inner and the Outer. Höl-derlin's "abysmal world-interiority" is the fate of the poet who is a seer.[19]

The life that the poet lived in sacramental union with a mythical world was shattered; his exhausted spirit, weighted down by a super-abundance of signs, reverted to the secure refuge of the great Mother. Buber, however, passed through this charmed circle unscathed: "I have called thee by thy name; thou art mine. When thou passest through the waters, I will be with thee; and through the rivers, they shall not ov-erflow thee: when thou walkest through the fire, thou shalt not be burned; neither shall the flame kindle upon thee" (Isa. 43: 1).

To be sure, he was not spared grave ordeals. The "Autobiographi-cal Fragments" reveal how Buber's exuberant imagination from his earliest childhood exposed him to lurking terrors and painful confu-sions. The loss of his mother at an early age was a cruel blow to the sensitive child. While still an adolescent, he was driven to the brink of madness by thoughts of suicide because of his philosophical speculations on the nature of time and space which had become for him bleak fictions in a capricious, unregenerate world. Thus, at the age of seven-teen the death of a man he had known made him feel as if death had thrown a lasso around his neck: "That there was death in the world be-came for me a sin for which I had to do penance. My feeling of isola-tion prevented me from sleeping, and a loathing of life kept me from taking nourishment. . . ." He was sent to a secluded place in the mountains; surrounded there by nature and the elements as by an "active divine power," he one day envisaged chaos and cruel destruction as the deadly struggle of the primordial powers in a mythical world. He described the landscape: ". . . I saw everything as cloudy forms in which all distinctions were dissolved. Light and darkness mingled together; all form had passed beyond its limits and burst into an iridescent serpent coil of colors which enclosed the spectral horizon." He described Man: "Instead of the flowing simplicity of the animated human form I found myself to be double: half life and half death, and in both I experienced not states but powers—in the one, the imperious urge of sprouting nature; in the other, the compulsion of all perishable things. And while the movement of pulsating life surged through the first, the latter was being convulsed by decay and disintegration, both being intensified to such a degree, however, that I felt I lay beneath them like an anvil and suffered the double hammer blows." [20] Rebirth came to him as a final union of life and death.

The realization that his experiences had carried him to the precarious edge between health and sickness may have terrified him at times. We know that he studied psychiatry for three semesters. His restless spirit felt more secure after he had become acquainted with Paula Winkler during his summer semester in Zurich. His marriage when he was twenty-one helped him find the inner unity he was seeking. This inner unity, which remained elemental and bound to a mythical being-relation, first looked to Boehme for adequate expression, but soon found its own independent interest in the realm of "I and world" rather than in the abstruse theosophical speculations of his predecessor. The God of Boehme, who realizes himself far removed from the fallen world of sin, becomes "the new God whom we create, a new unity of forces"; he becomes the focal point of a creative all-encompassing unity which Buber, seeking a concrete sensuous expression, related to Feuerbach's dictum, "Man with man—the unity of I and Thou—is God"— which he placed on the same level as the vital life feeling of the Vedanta and St. Francis of Assisi.

From his *Dialogue* we learn that Buber in his youth experienced ecstatic states which transported him beyond the framework of time and space and liberated him from the world's tortured embrace. In later years he described these ecstatic experiences as "godlike joyous hours," a hybrid attempt to experience eternity as "life" and to confine it within the limits of his own soul. Buber described these religious experiences, which approach those of the mystics, as an "experience of an Otherness that is not part of the structure of life" and which abandons the "I" to the manifold. Time divides and separates; "rapture, illumination and ecstasy reign in a timeless realm that knows no causal nexus." [21] The union he experienced penetrates his body and soul like a flash of lightning. Since Buber's religious experience in those years was marked by a strong creative consciousness of self, the question arises as to what extent he was influenced by Nietzsche's description of creative inspiration which is expressed in the language of mysticism: a hearing and seeing of indescribable assurance, a lightning-like illumination, a rapture that transports him "in a tempest of feeling and freedom, of absoluteness, of power, of godliness." [22] The pantheists of the twentieth century, who experience the godlike in the unending movement of self-creative life, identify man's having been created in God's image with man's creative faculty.

When Buber's youthful productions are contemplated, it is frequently asked whether the life feeling of a poet is what is revealed in his mysticism. The same question also arises when we read the early works of Hugo von Hofmannsthal because he also started from an all-embracing unity of life only in the end to find himself a mystic without mysticism, one who traces the "world-secret" in the myths of the various races—"the I as universe" as he called it in one of his autobiographical sketches. In his diary Hofmannsthal observed: "The tragic primary myth: the world, fragmented in individuals, yearns for unity; Dionysus Zagreus longs to be born again." And in one of his early drafts we find: "Doctrine of mysteries: we are of *one* flesh with all that ever was, with Alexander, with Tamerlane, with the vanished gigantic lizards and gigantic birds, with all the gods and the prodigies of the human race." Hofmannsthal also was fascinated by the way in which the individual forms of life strive to attain their lost life-unity. The real life, the life of the gods, is lived only by the poet who in a retrogressive movement binds the living individual to a common destiny that bears all souls within itself. "The poet: Pambios" is a notation written by Hofmannsthal in January 1895 [23]—the poet whom he regards as the magician who "as in a dream" sympathizes with the lot of all men on earth. Hofmannsthal went further and became engrossed in the mystery of sacrifices whose meaning he discovered in the circumstance that he who offers up a sacrifice identifies himself with the animal being sacrificed and for a moment feels that he is being slaughtered with it, experiencing his own body as the "symbol" through which he gains access to universal unity. This reminds us of Buber's words concerning the moments "in which our organism is an altogether different piece of nature."

We thus see that Hofmannsthal was familiar with a mystical world experience without a mystical doctrine. This was the dream of the poet as a world-moving magician, already anticipated by Novalis's magical idealism whereby the boundless ego of the poet can reduplicate itself into manifold roles of self-dramatization of alien lives. But Hofmannsthal also experienced, as his Greek dramas testify, a strong Nietzschean phase (in addition to Schopenhauer's influence) after which he turned to Christian-Neoplatonic mysticism. The motto he took to illustrate his path through life came from the *Vita Mosis* of Gregory of Nyssa: "He, the lover of the highest beauty, regarded what he saw only as the symbol of that which he had not yet seen and he longed to take delight in this itself, in the primary image." [24]

The experience of immanency, consisting of an intermixture of religious and poetic experiences, belonged at the beginning of the century to the "secret of contemporaneity," to those who were in their twenties. Rainer Maria Rilke's *The Book of Hours* was inspired by a mystic world experience which finds God in "things," by a religious feeling of being at home in the universe that came to the poet from communion with God and from the companion of his Russian journey, Lou Andreas-Salomé, a remarkable woman older than himself to whom he was passionately attracted and for whom he composed many strophes included in this volume. Poetry was endowed with sacred significance in Stefan George's demand for cultural renewal through art. Hofmannsthal's address "Der Dichter und diese Zeit" [The poet and the times] in 1907 boldly proclaimed that the man with a book in his hand has supplanted the kneeling worshiper of the past. He goes on to say that the modern reader looks to the poet for salvation, and the poet answers this religious supplication in his tormented struggle to create a "world of relations," a world formerly sanctioned and made safe by its relation to transcendence. Despite its confident tone, Hofmannsthal's address is accompanied by a presentiment of the unending perils that await the poet in his heroic attempt to bring transcendence down to earth and to impart to the world a new dimension which until now "it possessed only in God." In an age when traditional spiritual values no longer afforded man ultimate security, the poet regained the title of seer conferred upon him in ancient days. Buber's teacher Dilthey was also convinced that poetry was destined to become more significant than ever before for the consciousness of modern man. When we recognize that "there is no formula that contains the truth, that every religious dogma and every scientific explanation of the world's structure are symbols for something whose real nature no myth, no dogma, and no concept can fathom or express . . . it is the artist, speaking only in images and symbols, who seems to possess the most truthful language." [25]

Buber published poems and dramatic fragments in periodicals in the early part of the century; in his reproduction of Hasidic tales he first chose the form of a free rendering or paraphrase. At that time he probably attributed to his poetic talent more significance than it later appeared to merit. Again we must recall Buber's closeness to Hölderlin, the poet who was at the same time a seer, conscious of his religious vocation in the interests of his people and bearing a message of salvation, and whose creative genius shone like a beacon to guide the talented dreamers who came after him. In his monograph Hans Kohn recalls an evening devoted to a reading by Buber of his story "Der Sommerheld" [The summer hero] and an act from his drama *Elijah*; he also mentions a letter written in December 1906 in which Buber spoke of being engaged in writing a trilogy of stories—Elohim, Adonai, Jahve—which showed him to be in a state of intense religious excitement: "I have a new answer to give to everything . . . I have grown into my heaven—my life begins. I experience nameless woe and nameless mercy." [26] The poem he wrote in 1904, "Das Wort an Elijahu"

[The word addressed to Elijah], reflects his consciousness of a religious vocation:

> Mourning they sank into the grave
> —Hear in the air the wail—
> Speak, son of man:
> *Ye linger long* in coming.
>
> Suffering thirst they sank into the grave
> —Feel how all thirst is unquenched—
> Speak, son of man:
> *The time is fulfilled.*
>
> Blessing they sank into the grave
> —Behold the frozen gesture—
> Speak, son of man:
> *Let it become!* [27]

This religious message of creation obviously refers to the renaissance of the Jewish people through Zionism, a movement that Buber supported from the very outset. The Zionist movement gave him a sense of reality by presenting him with concrete tasks which demanded action and at the same time saved him from too great a passion for abstract truth and disembodied ideals that characterized the impersonal and generalizing mode of thought of many of the German poets and writers of his time.

Even his early talks and essays on Judaism, such as "Die Schaffenden, das Volk und die Bewegung" in 1902, show that Buber's conception of "creation" referred not only to literature and the intellectual disciplines but also to the whole of life. The *creators* are the "strong and complex personalities in whom human events conjoin in order to attain new developments in spirit and in deed." The artists, on the other hand, are always more intent on "making" than in seeing that anything should come into being. "There are creators who fashion their material out of human souls, races, and cultures; others fashion their material out of their own being; and still others out of unattached values and revelations. The creator can also produce things which belong to the inner life, are beyond all speech, but are nevertheless able to move other human beings." [28] All "becoming" manifests itself only to the extent that it takes on form, so that creation is always related to fashioning and constructing. In "Das Gestaltende" [The formative], an address given in 1912, which betrays richer experience and a maturer grasp of the problem, Buber spoke of a constant force of inertia inherent in life that resists being shaped, so that man's labors often remain incomplete and in danger of being like the famous torsos of Michelangelo that we see in Florence. It is at bottom the desire for a genuine work of perfect form that leads Buber from reality to poetry. His novel *For the Sake of Heaven* and his mystery play *Elijah*, which he had begun at the beginning of the century, were published when he was advanced in age. The deep thoughts he had developed after studying Hasidism for forty years, thoughts that no scientific analysis can express, found their proper mode of expression in the novel: it is only in poetry that we can have pure realization and attain the form which, as Hofmannsthal expressed it, "disposes of the problem." Buber's poetical word, however, was not arbitrary and detached but pressed into the service of life, representing only one of the many expressive forms of his vocation; for Hofmannsthal there had never existed any other form.

Buber's creativity in the years of his apprenticeship was based on what he called *Urhebertrieb,* the urge to be the author of a work and to take an active part in the formation of things.[29] In his essay on Alfred Mombert (1922), Buber, speaking of the creative personality, characterized *Urhebertrieb* as the knowledge a man has that he is "of God's lineage and his apprentice in the work of creation." The myth of the creation of the world is the language of this basic relationship; it always refers to the never-ending process of creation and not to the dogma according to which creation was a unique act that occurred at a particular time and place; and its basic thought is: "The world does not become; the world is made." [30] The idea of "man made in the image of God, conceived as deed, as becoming, as task" made a lasting impression on Buber when he discovered it in the Baal-Shem with which he began his long years of Hasidic studies: "Let man develop the quality of zeal with his whole heart. May he arise from his sleep with zeal, for he has become holy and another man and is worthy to testify, having taken on the quality of the Holy One, praised be He, when He created worlds." [31]

The concrete idea expressed by *Urhebertrieb,* namely, that man and God are partners in the work of creation, is the basic notion of the poem "Das Wort an Elijahu," in which the "son of man" is man summoned to become God's coworker. Here is an allusion to Christ similar to that found in the essay on Boehme in the words, "This is my body." Just as Christ, in the one case, appears as a "demigod" and as the brother of man, in the spirit of Hölderlin, so does he appear in the other as the newly risen Christ as depicted in Buber's essay on the Isenheim Altar of Mathias Grünewald: "the man of every age and every place, of the here and now, in the process of perfecting himself to become the I of the world" [32]—one who is reconciled unto himself and who, because of his comprehension of the cosmos, is able to consummate the creative, redeeming act.

Grünewald, the creator of "the Altar of the spirit in the West," is described at the beginning of Buber's essay as the kindred spirit of one who had flourished in the same vicinity two centuries before: Meister Eckhart. He who wishes to understand Buber's "son of man," the figure of both the creative and the redemptive man, cannot ignore the deep influence Eckhart exerted on him in his early days.

Buber has given us no comprehensive characterization of Eckhart. In his dissertation, however, Eckhart's sermons are often quoted, and an important passage in his "What Is Man?" *(Das Problem des Menschen)* states: "Since 1900 I was first influenced by German mysticism from Meister Eckhart to Angelus Silesius, both of whom believed that the ultimate ground of being, the nameless impersonal Godhead, first comes to "birth" in the human soul; and then I came under the influence of the later Cabbala which teaches that man has the power to unite the God who reigns above the world with his shekinah which dwells within the world. Thus there developed in me the thought of the realization of God through man; man appeared to me as the being through whose existence the Absolute, resting in its truth, can acquire the character of reality." [33] The connection between Meister Eckhart and the Cabbala which Buber made prior to 1914 in this short account of his world view is clarified by a reference in his work *Der grosse Maggid* (1922) in which East European Jewish mysticism, which seeks to unite the transcendental God with the God indwelling in beings and things, is correlated with Meister Eckhart's "maxim of brotherly love": "The noble man is that only begotten son of God whom the Father eternally begets"—one of the propositions rejected in 1329 by Pope John XXII.[34]

In Meister Eckhart we have the beginning of the conception of the myth of God's path through creation which Buber had traced from Cusa to Boehme. Eckhart was also a man who belonged wholly to the Middle Ages, for whom the problem of individuation had not yet arisen and for whom creatures in themselves were "simply nothing." Buber associated Eckhart, more than any other mystic, with the basic experiences expressed in his image of the "son of man": the unshakeable certainty of man's essential equality with God and his partnership with Him in the work of creation—the doctrine that man is "of divine race and of God's kin," as is written in the *Book of Divine Consolation*.

Religious pantheism in the early part of the century regarded Eckhart as a kindred spirit and a Christian heretic. Modern research has been more skeptical of this judgment.[35] A careful comparison of Eckhart's German sermons with his Latin writings and a close examination of his thought reveal that in many points his alleged pantheistic teachings could be interpreted as Catholic panentheism. The various methods used in medieval biblical exegesis, with their subjective judgments and venturesome speculations, have grown unfamiliar to us and we no longer have the intermediate logical steps necessary for their proper understanding. As for the scholastic Eckhart, who profited enough from the intellectual discipline and education of his order to rise to the highest responsible positions, Catholic research will surely regain much ground by his method—but the ultimate and deepest experience of the great mystic will continue to be elusive.

It was far from Eckhart's intent to transform the created into the Creator: "I can err, but I cannot be a heretic; for the first refers to the mind, the second to the will," he declared in his "Rechtfertigungsschrift" [Letter of justification]. The difficulties of his doctrine for his contemporaries arose from the passionate fervor with which he presented Christian beliefs and animated the most abstract notions as, for example, the vividness with which the dogma of God-man became real for him, impelling him to regard the Church as the mystic body of Christ, as the mysterious spirit-life with Christ and in Christ. He took St. Paul's words, "Not I live, but Christ lives in me," in deep earnest, as he did the words in the prologue to the Gospel of John which speaks of men "who are born of God." His chief concern was to break open the husks, extract the kernel, and not "to be left with unattached symbols"; he could not content himself with an "abstract" God who is only the object of thought, but longed for a "God of the present" who is closer to man than his own body.

With the same boldness that Eckhart made abstract thoughts concrete by restoring their original vesture in the world of sense, he also bore witness to the artless way in which God reveals himself to the human soul, in a sudden illumination which is the divine light itself. He always found new names for the soul ground in which all spiritual forces become one and "being," and in which the union with the one and only God is consummated. Since this innermost process escapes the categories of thought and can be rendered only in symbols, he expressed this tremendous experience in a double image—the eternal begetting of the son in man through God and the birth of God in the soul ground here and now.

This language of sincere deep emotion which borders on the ineffable, where personal feelings vanish and melt into a nameless unity, is called by Buber "brotherly speech." In the frank confessions of his early essays and poems in which the creation phrase *Let there be* is attributed to the *son of man,* he had in mind Eckhart's graphic imagery, and his experience of an all-embracing unity breaks forth in the words: "This is my body; this is my blood."

Eckhart also taught that man must be in harmony with himself in order to find God, as is written in the sermon "Of the Noble Man": "The one with the One, one of the One, one in the One, and in one the One eternally!" The way that leads to God, according to Eckhart, is that of separation, renunciation, un-becoming; man must leave himself and all creatures if he would receive the sonship of God: only in complete poverty of spirit can God's work be accomplished in the world.

Buber could not follow Eckhart along this path. The notion of immanence and the modern consciousness of personality had by the beginning of the century been too far removed from the spirituality of the man of the Middle Ages. Here we note the significant role that Hasidism, the East European mysticism of the eighteenth century, subsequently played in Buber's thinking. Not through "un-becoming" or by turning one's back on the world does man prove himself worthy of being God's coworker, but rather through sanctification of the world by actively participating in its work and by assuming responsibility for the fate of creation.

THE RENEWAL OF HASIDISM

Hasidism, or East European Jewish mysticism, was one of the two great movements by which East European Jewry overcame the dominance of medieval religious legalism. The other movement, through which the adjustment to the growth of Western culture was made, was the Enlightenment *(Haskalah)*. Both movements were concerned with the renewal of Jewish life, and from the very beginning they were recognized by Buber as spiritually indispensable for the national renaissance of Judaism through Zionism.

We thus find in one of Buber's early Zionist essays, "Renaissance und Bewegung" [Renaissance and movement] (1903), a brief sketch of Hasidism in which its basic features are clearly set forth. He calls Hasidism "a mysticism which is as strong as it is soulful . . . the doctrine of active feeling as the bond between man and God," a doctrine which, far from denying the Law, helped to revive it. All activity that flows from a pure heart is divine worship: "Creative activity endures forever; creation is continuous and unending, and man takes part in it through power and love." [36]

A year later Buber withdrew from political activity and devoted himself to an intensive study of Hasidic writings in which he found the "original Jewish" expression of the ancient mystical treasures of mankind: "the creation of man in the image of God, conceived as deed, as becoming, as task." Hasidism did not demand asceticism and "un-becoming" as did medieval mysticism. In the spiritual leaders of the Hasidic communities, the *zaddikim*, Buber recognized the ideal of the "perfect man" and his kinship with Eckhart's "noble man"—and in the revelation of that moment he assumed the task "of proclaiming it to the world." [37]

The difficulties that this task imposed upon him were enormous. Since the basic theoretical principle of Hasidism flowed from the theosophical speculations of the later Cabbala, this study involved a difficult and still unexplored branch of mystical philosophizing. In the transmission of popular books, the lives of the great Hasidim and their oral traditions have come down to us garbled and distorted. The legends were jotted down in a formless and careless manner, so that often the original meaning could hardly be recognized. Buber described how his first attempts to produce a free translation of the stories of Rabbi Nachman proved a failure, and how only an independent paraphrase could do justice to the spirit behind the stories, especially when he came to the legends of the Baal-Shem. Although the result of his labors must be described as "an arbitrary paraphrase of traditional themes," his fidelity to the subject matter increased as he became less dependent on the texts before him. This method did not violate Hasidic tradition: Rabbi Nachman himself hit upon the idea of storytelling when he became aware that his teachings had "no clothes": thus a mystical idea or a life maxim which he wished to transmit to his students was imperceptibly turned into a meaningful tale.[38]

The same circumstances which marked Buber's relation to German mysticism now appears on another plane: his studies had kindled in him the consciousness of a vocation which he felt to be both religious and poetical. His work gains greater coherence and reflects a deeper sense of reality by being placed in the service of Zionist culture, the idea that only by a confident appropriation of its past in the interests of the living present could Judaism regain its lost creativity and greatness. As early as 1901 Buber had suggested that a new Jewish art which would find its material in the life of the people would constitute the most effective Jewish education.

For a short period after he had joined the Zionist movement in 1898, Buber, in his criticism of culture and in his insistence on creative activity in its national aspirations, was a disciple of Nietzsche. His primary concern was to instill into the atrophied life of the ghetto a new sense of nationhood, to infuse it with a new vital spirit and restore its "creative cultural force" that had been moribund for centuries. When Buber speaks of the "self-redemption, resurrection and salvation" of the nation in his first Zionist essays, we hear echoes of the pseudoreligious prophetic voice of Nietzsche.[39] His own passion for creation, *Urhebertrieb,* which impelled him to take part in the creation of things, was first directed almost exclusively to the renewal of national life, to poetry and culture. He states in a short review, "Drei Stationen" [Three stations] (1929): "When we first began our service for Israel, our slogan was culture. We yearned, actively, to see the Jewish people give valid expression to its 'reborn' nature in a world of its own making." [40]

The study of German mysticism and his own ecstatic experiences had imparted greater religious depth to Buber's cultural nationalism and a new significance to his "becoming God." Numerous points of contact can be found between the speculations of Jewish mysticism on how the world with all its abundance and diversity emanates from one Godhead and the ideas developed by Buber in his study of German philosophy from Cusa to Boehme. The Cabbala also taught that God in creating the world "restricted himself"; "becoming" issued forth from an absolute Being; God is at the same time transcendent and present in his glory, the shekinah. Sparks of light burst forth at the creation, overflowed into the spheres, and became imprisoned in matter. Man has the task of releasing these sparks from their bondage and reuniting God and his shekinah.

It was not the theosophical speculations of Hasidism but its teachings of the relation of man to God and the world which made a lasting impression on Buber and which he came to regard as his "message" to the world. Not theories about the origin of the world but rather the doctrine of man's participation in its redemption became the object of his passionate interest. Through this partnership with God in the work of redeeming the world, man's *Urhebertrieb* became a vocation and his creative energy was imbued with religious consecration. "Man's admittance into power," which Buber took from the legacy of the Baal-Shem, appealed to his nature and enlisted his deepest allegiance.

Not "God and the soul" but "God and the world" is the insistent theme which informed all Hasidic thought and action. The problem was how to bridge the gap between the holy and the profane, how to render visible the divine sparks scattered throughout the world, and how to make all that is earthly and corporeal a part of holy living by treating it as holy and consecrated to God: the mystery of man is that he has been appointed to act as the cosmic intermediary.[41]

The magic that flows from Buber's paraphrased legends and tales resides in man's cosmic union with all creatures and with inanimate creation. God is in all things and constitutes their essential being—in Him all are one.[42] All creatures present themselves to man and are by him raised to God. Piety and mercy create an atmosphere in which man feels at home in creation: lost children are watched over by beggars whose infirmities prove to be the true gifts of life. The question here is not one of cultivating sympathy for our fellowmen but of learning how to live with them, and out of deep love to bear their woes in our heart "as one bears the life of a tree with all its absorption of water and shooting forth of buds and its dream of roots and the craving of the trunk and the thousand tracks of its branches, or as one bears the life of an animal with all its gliding and stretching and grasping, and all the joy of its sinews and joints, and the dull tension of its brain. . . ." So to live with one's fellowman means to realize the truth "that all souls are one, but each is a spark from the primordial soul, and the whole of the primordial soul is in each." [43] Almost forty years ago Wilhelm Michel wrote that Buber's Hasidic legends move in a region where the concept piety is irrelevant since it does not preclude the possibility of not-being-pious: "with these Hasidim, however, existence and being-pious coincide." [44]

In the introduction to the *Legend of the Baal-Shem* Buber tells us that in recreating the legends he was concerned neither with "real" life nor with what is customarily called local color: "My narration stands on the ground of Jewish myth, and the heaven of Jewish myth is above it." [45] He gives us a vivid account of this myth in the section, "The Life of the Hasidim," which, as G. Sholem points out, has justly become famous. Buber himself called the introduction "An Account" but he gives us much more than a general account of the relation of the

Hasidim to God and the world, and the teachings that constitute the basis of this relation. Buber was primarily concerned with the forces that shape the lives and activities of this pious community: *hitlahavut*, "fervor," ecstasy; *avoda* "service"; *kavvana* "intention"; *shiflut* "humility"—to each of which the introduction devotes a section.

Ecstasy and service are "the poles between which the life of the holy man oscillates." *Hitlahavut* is the flight of the soul to a region beyond time and space and, above all, thought. In its "unrefracted light" all things are simple and in their proper place; the things of the world are one. A man who has experienced ecstasy thenceforth shares the destiny of the shekinah, "the indwelling presence of God" which is to be found in the world in exile; for him the world reverts into nothingness, and he strives to attain the unity which existed before anything was created.

For such a man who lives with God, service in time and space is directed to a divine Being who is beyond our comprehension. Here the infinitude of life accompanies the most insignificant act, and the soul also seeks its unity within its innermost sphere. Service is not only an affair of the individual but also the concern of the community. Through common service, through the unity of the manifold, the world reverts to its divine origin, and a "becoming" is consummated which one day will unite the original oneness, "God's being which has departed from his creatures," with the indwelling presence of God. Only prayer that aspires to this unity truly lives. Every service that is consecrated to God by an undivided soul is acceptable; but he serves best who has himself become Nothing and is prepared for every kind of service.

By *kavvana*, "intention," Buber understands "the mystery of the soul directed to a goal." Intention does not mean will power; it is not directed to an individual goal but to the one common goal to which all roads lead: redemption. When a man feels his power increasing as a result of consciously directing his prayers and actions, it is because *kavvana* is "a ray of God's glory," of the shekinah which emanates from it and which aspires to redemption. Hence, redemption does not mean the salvation of the individual, but the salvation of the world. All men are the abodes of wandering souls, and all things contain divine sparks which can be redeemed by every man, each in his allotted sphere, if he would deal with his fellowman and with all things in holiness. But here also there is a highest form and perfection: the *kavvana* of the creator who is empowered with the Word which binds heaven and earth to one another.

Ecstasy and intention exhibit man in his "being introduced into power"—*shiflut,* "humility," like *avoda,* is directed toward the world and signifies the knowledge that the individual is only a part of the cosmos, a wave in the unending sea of universal generation. Only a soul at rest in Nothing is unconstrained by limits and is able to live with all beings and find God in them. Such a "living together" is love: it is not something that is desired or consciously known, but something that just happens between creatures; it is in the world and in God.

Buber's introduction can be described neither as a simple account of the life of the Hasidim nor as poetical variations on the theme of Hasidic mysticism. The beliefs, explained and illustrated by numerous quotations, represent to him both everyday life and mystery; they are the powers with whose help man fulfills his function as "cosmic mediator." For "above and below is one Unity," "God is in each thing as its original essence," [46] and man is given the task of making the hidden divine element visible: to bind things "to their upper root" and to bring together the separated spheres by fashioning his own life in the active service of prayer. That which appears as "fervor of the heart's service" from his personal point of view is, looked at objectively, the power of God that has been sent forth with the world and into the world, and whose impulse to revert to the unity of God is set in motion by man. It is the godly element in him that prepares itself for God's work. Every man is a link in the shekinah; his suffering comes from its suffering and can only be assuaged through its redemption. He who combines fervor with service has overcome all things in the world that make for division and separation: "He is the brother of created things and feels their glance as if it were his own, their footsteps as if made by his own feet, their blood as if it were flowing in his own body. He is the son of God and places his soul in his immense Hand, anxiously and confidently aspiring to all the heavens and earths and unknown worlds." [47]

The language of this last passage leads us back to the essay on

Boehme where Buber recognized man's mystical unity with the world body in its circular spheres and life waves; and the "son of God" is the "son of man" in the poem, "Das Wort an Elijahu," and the brother of Meister Eckhart's "noble man." [48] In Buber's conception of German and Jewish mysticism a recurrent unity of image and thought is discernible. This is to be attributed to the fact that Boehme had been influenced by cabbalistic speculations. Two years after the completion of the *Baal-Shem* we learn from the introduction to *Ekstatische Konfessionen* [Ecstatic confessions] the nature of the real problem, namely, the great myth that "runs through the ages of mankind: the myth of unity that becomes multiplicity, because it wishes to look and be looked at, recognize and be recognized, love and be loved and, while remaining a unity itself, comprehends itself as multiplicity; the myth of I that begets a Thou; of the primordial self which transforms itself to world, and of the Godhead which transforms itself to God." [49]

The poetical language which helps to harmonize the life forces of Hasidic piety with the sayings of its Masters, combining both into a coherent image of high poetical beauty, introduces us at the same time into the heart of the legends. Just as the commonplace intermingles with the miraculous in Hasidic life, so also does its poetry cast a sense of mystery on all earthly things; it is the husk around the kernel of the divine element that shines mysteriously within us and in the world around us in the reflection of the primal light. The poetical word illumines the depths of the mystical life: it proclaims ecstasy as the symbol of the divine primal unity, the tension of the soul between the universe and nothingness, and makes its way through nothingness to unity; at the same time it signifies the being of the soul in God and its human otherness.

Buber pointed out in 1949, in the introduction to the *Tales of the Hasidim*, that the Baal-Shem cannot be described as a spiritual man in the ordinary sense of the word but rather as one who "draws his strength from an extraordinary union between spiritual and tellurian powers, between heavenly and earthly fire; it is the sublime which determines the earth-sustained frame. The life of such a man is a constant receiving of fire which is transformed into light." [50] It was this characterization of the Baal-Shem as a combination of fire and light that

Buber had in mind forty years earlier when he wrote the legend "Die Offenbarung" [Revelation].

This legend relates how the Baal-Shem, while still unknown, was the host of an inn at the edge of the Carpathian mountains and when the time came for his calling to be revealed, he was visited by a rabbi. The guest expressed his desire to travel further after a short rest, but as he continued his travels he soon felt his carriage was entering a chaos and that a fearful abyss had opened up under him, eager to swallow him. A gigantic figure in sheepskin, resembling his host, came to his aid and directed the carriage safely back to the inn. A similar experience occurred on the following day and on the day thereafter. Each time the customary order of the world was reduced to chaos and turmoil; an endless abyss separated the beings that are enclosed within themselves as in a prison, until the gigantic man appeared among the creatures in the firmament and with his overarching presence restored the brotherly fellowship of creation.

The actual revelation occurred on the following night. The rabbi was impelled to enter the room of the mysterious host. When he arrived the room was filled with flames as high as a man, but they gave off no smoke, and amid the flames he beheld his Master:

> And further the Rabbi saw: there was a division in the fire, and it gave birth to a light, and the light was as a roof over the flames. The light was double. Below it was bluish and was part of the fire, but the upper light was white and motionless, and it spread around the head of the Master as far as the walls. The bluish light was the throne of the white one; the white light rested on it as on a throne. The colors of the bluish light kept changing incessantly, at times to black and at times to a wave of crimson. But the white light above never changed, and remained always white. Now the bluish light was all embedded in the fire, and what the fire consumed it consumed. But the white light that rested on it was not consumed and had nothing in common with the flame.
>
> The Rabbi looked, and behold the Master's head was standing wholly in the white light, and the flames rose up round the body of the Master. But the flames that rose turned to light, and thus from time to time there was more and more light.
>
> The Rabbi saw how the entire fire had become light. And

the blue light began to force its way into the white, but each wave that pressed through became white and changeless.

The Rabbi saw that the Master was standing wholly in a white light. But above his head rested a hidden light, colorless and invisible, revealed only to the gaze of the earthly onlooker as a secret mystery.[51]

The mysterious light above the head of the Master is the shekinah. This we learn from a word of the Baal-Shem with which Buber concluded the section *avoda* of the introduction, in which the thrones, appearing as visions of colored light, are mentioned: "He makes his body a throne of life, and of life a throne of the spirit and of the spirit a throne of the soul and the soul the throne of the light of God's glory, and the light streams all around him, and he sits in the midst of the light and trembles and rejoices."

"*Die Offenbarung*" displays Buber's poetical gift at its best and is, above all, characteristic of his method. The vision of fire and light originated in a meditation on the mystical character of the Baal-Shem's life. The reader who has not yet been persuaded by the aptness and force of the imagery that the visions are actually beheld and are not an arbitrary invention will be convinced by the reference to the words of the Baal-Shem and his characterization in the *Tales of the Hasidim*. But the motif of the struggle between light and fire has wider implications. It is very likely that Buber, while thinking about the spiritual and tellurian elements in the Baal-Shem, had in mind the speculations of Jacob Boehme, found at the end of his dissertation, concerning the amalgam of light and fire in man's nature and in God's essence. "Light" is here synonymous with the eternal striving to realize God; "fire," however, represents the will for self-destruction inherent in nature and the return to a primordial condition, for it is its nature, according to Boehme, "to soar above the light and yet is unable to do so." It longs to consume and destroy everything, and yet it remains a minion of the light's will which is directed to the existence and preservation of the world. That Boehme could interpret this duality as a "twofold will in God" was a remarkable thought that engrossed Buber in the early years of the century. We thus find in the first edition of the *Legend of the Baal-Shem* (1908) a passage (later deleted): "Everything is God; and everything serves God." In the first edition of the *Legends of Rabbi Nachman* there are also sentences whose pantheistic wording was changed in later editions.[52]

The experiences of the rabbi in the legend also led him into a mythical world and show us creation in the conflict of the elements. The mystic Nothing is presented as the abyss between beings and things and as the condition of the soul transported back to chaos to be used by God in a new work of creation. The meaning that is attributed to "Nothing" in every section of the introduction as an indispensable transitional stage on the way to perfection is proof that Buber's thoughts had their roots in the world of mysticism.

At that time Buber regarded the free paraphrasing of the legends as a necessary medium to render the piety of the Hasidim intelligible to his contemporaries. In this attempt his overestimation of the poet as seer, which was the prevailing notion of that day, was not a negligible factor. There is, however, another explanation that derives from the very nature of the situation: the mystical life that Buber attempted to present was bound up with the renewal of a myth. The line from Goethe, "In all elements God's presence"—later used by Buber as a superscription to the first edition of *I and Thou*—reveals the true nature of the problem. The God-wrought creation evolves in the cosmic struggle of natural forces; fire, which loses its igneous force, is confirmed as an element of godliness. Only a poetic representation could evoke the sensuous-supersensuous atmosphere that is the life ground of his legends.

Another important factor which influenced Buber's poetical aspirations, hitherto neglected, was his wife who was also a poet and in 1912 published her first work, a volume of mythical stories called *Die unechten Kinder Adams* [The illegitimate children of Adam] under the pseudonym Georg Munk. In the preface to *Dialogue* Buber indicated the importance he attached to this life partnership with his wife:

> The abyss and the light of worlds,
> The need of the times and the longing for eternity,
> Vision, event and poem:
> Dialogue it was and is with thee.

Three years after his wife's death Buber published *Geister und Menschen* [Spirits and people] (1961), a selection of stories taken from three of her books. In the preface he related how his wife, who had the gift of endowing natural phenomena with poetical form, possessed rare insight into the uncanny forces of elemental nature. In addition to her poetical gifts and her remarkable affinity for natural mysteries, Paula Buber also possessed a masculine strength and independence. In contrast to the godlike inwardness of Buber's legends, in which the elements are sanctified and elevated to a higher order, her mythical thinking shows the influence of the heathen world of antiquity, being an unrestrained natural force that expressed itself in opposition to—and often in revolt against—Christianity. The circumstance that gave rise to this attitude is soberly described in clear, austere language: "In the very heart of this reality figures arise and accost men. Out of the air and ground, water and mountain, from the very inclinations and acts of man and from the relations with which they animate the space between them, powers arise that take on human form, look, and voice, which otherwise pass us by without uttering a sound or casting a glance." [53]

It would be interesting to compare Buber's all-embracing mythical imagery with his wife's literary style. We shall content ourselves with pointing out the poetic element common to both. A single example will suffice to show how she experienced man's encounter with nature, an example taken from one of her stories that is closest to Buber's legend style, "Sankt Gertrauden Minne" [St. Gertraude's love]: "The things that surrounded her were to her eye no longer an image, to her hand no longer an object; all things were in her and she was in all things. She grew amid grass and plants; she was the foot that trod and also the trodden plant, the hand that plucked and the fading flower; she blossomed in the tree, ripened in the fruit, fell as the withered leaf, floated in the wind, and the wind was like the breath of her mouth. In autumn days she descended from the clouds, hardened in the frozen earth, was a buried grain of seed and the resurrected stalk. She was the sparrow hawk that circled, cried, and swooped down, and bled in the dismembered bird; she was poured out in the moonlight and rose to heaven on the foam of a wave. The dreadful beast of the forest did not flee when she passed among the tree trunks, but grazed as her shadow fell upon it. When she washed at the stream, the thirsty stag did not raise its head." [54] Paula Buber's tales describe not only man's encounter with inanimate nature but also speak of beings which are at the same time both man and tree and which, being born of the elements, return to them. The ghostlike *doppelgänger* that drives man to self-destruction, described by Buber in "Demon in the Dream," [55] turns out to be, in "Sankt Gertrauden Minne," a figure that walks about in the light of day.

In the preface to *Chinesische Geister-und Liebesgeschichten* [Chinese ghost and love stories],[56] which grew directly out of that magic circle of common poetical activity, Buber confessed that in this "song of kindred and enamoured elements" more than anything else it was the intimacy between demons and men that appealed to him: "The demons are beings of our world, only that they are born in a deeper, darker level. . . . The orderly processes of nature, however, are here not discontinued but only extended; at no point is life's ceaseless profusion interrupted, and all things that live bear the seed of the spirit. It is not only in animals, plants, and rocks that the demonic flourishes and seeks to ripen, like a fruit, into human form: that which your hand has shaped longs to breathe and to be wedded to a breathing being; that which your mind has devised, stirs and reaches out to become visible like a real thing; any act whatever can engender a demon who enters your home as your friend, as your wife, as your son, and requites you. But all this is not strange; it is as familiar as home; it is life." The spiritual qualities that one must possess to be able to walk this common road together are less familiar to us today; at that time, however, this gifted couple earnestly hoped that through the medium of poetry they would be capable of expressing something more than fiction. They were seriously concerned in the work of renewing the oldest language of mankind, the myth.

In his posthumous work *Nachlese* [Gleanings], whose contents Buber had selected shortly before he died, we find a poem which he had written in his wife's copy of *Tales of the Hasidim* in which he recalls the early years they had spent together:

> Do you still know how we in our young years
> Sailed together on this sea?

Visions came, great and marvellous,
We beheld them together, you and I.
How image joined itself to image in our hearts!
How a mutually moving portrayal
Arose from it, and lived between you and me!
We were there, and still wholly here
And wholly together, roaming and grounded.
Thus the voice awoke, and since then proclaims
And attests the ancient glory, as new,
True to itself and you and our being together.
Take then also this witness in your hands,
It is an end and yet has no end,
For eternity hears it and hears us,
As we resound from it, I and you.[56a]

Buber's poetical activity in cooperation with his wife testifies to his interest in myth, insofar as it is directed to folk tales and to the life of the common people, and not treated as religion or philosophy— although these latter studies were not altogether neglected or dismissed. The development of myths is a unified, coherent process; this is true whether the "central figure" is a hero or a prophet, for heroes were originally the sons of gods also. In the mythical view they are comprehended intuitively as a whole, in their irrational, underivative unity as products of the divine will seeking to realize itself in the world. In *Die vier Zweige des Mabinogi*, [The four branches of Mabinogi] published by Buber, the gods live with men on intimate terms, as they do in the Chinese demon myths, and around the deeds of the heroes there still lingers an atmosphere of uncanny power and magic which testifies to their former divine nature.

The Finnish epic *Halewala*, however, republished by Buber in 1914, is concerned with the power of man and not of the gods: it is the epic of the magical power of the enchanted word.[57] This epic is at the same time the creation of an entire people and the work of an individual collector, Elias Lönnrot, who accomplished for the Finnish myth what Buber had in mind for the preservation and revival of Hasidism. He introduced unity and coherence into the Finnish folk songs and incantations, as Buber had done into the formless and unorganized traditional legends of the Hasidim. Here and there the collector turns out to be an epigone; he is not a poet for he does not work independently, nor is he a scholar for he is not motivated by scientific interest. Both can be classified as storytellers or narrators, and any new creation that emerges from their work happens because the subject matter already existed: "Born of the ancient dreams of the folk and matured in the spacious life of folk history, it was given coherent structure by one who had come out of the blood and destiny of those folk-circles which represented and preserved the folk spirit," Buber wrote in his introdcction to *Halewalah.*[58] And in the preface to his *Legend of the Baal-Shem*, he said of his own work in the Hasidic folk books: "I have retold the legends as one who was born later. I bear in me the blood and the spirit of those who created them, and they became new out of my blood and spirit."[59]

EKSTATISCHE KONFESSIONEN

In those early years Buber studied not only popular books and collections of legends but he also selected and edited the sayings of the mystics of all ages and nations, insofar as they were linguistically accessible to him, and published them as *Ekstatische Konfessionen* (1909). Except for his work in Hasidism, his study of mysticism to which he had devoted so many years was completed.

These collections remind us of that earlier period in German history when Herder began to collect folk songs in *Stimmen der Völker in Liedern* (1778). Buber's interest stems in part from the Enlightenment, for his primary concern in these mystical revelations and confessions is "man" in the sense of a philosophical anthropology or, more exactly, the human voice in its attempt to utter the inexpressible. Buber's spiritual interests became widespread when he was studying the myths and religious texts of all ages and cultures in order to understand—in the sense of Dilthey's *Verstehen*—the basic problems concerning man and his relation to God. But the mystical texts of *Ekstatische Konfessionen* revolve around one focal point which at the time was Buber's most vexing problem: the word of man who must return from his ecstatic experience to everyday life and who, after having experienced boundless unity, must again face the motley world. This is the tragedy of the soul which envisages the One that is beyond all communication and can only express the Other in images, dreams, and visions, but not Unity.

The theme of *Ekstatische Konfessionen* is not the mystery of *unio mystica* but man's inability to transmit "the impossible message," the voice "in which the word burns," the word in its original, pristine state. The function of speech in the life of the community is to express that which is common to all, to attain understanding; but at the same time it secretly longs to leave the hustle and bustle of daily life and become something wholly different, something perfect: "truth, purity, poetry." For Buber *speech* is the primary act of the spirit. In a letter to Henri Borel in 1917 he wrote: "The creation of the word is for me one of the most mysterious processes of the life of the spirit; yes, I confess that in my view there is no essential difference between what I here call the production of the word and what has been called the emergence of the Logos. The becoming of a word is a mystery that takes place in the enkindled, open soul of the world-poetizing, world-discovering man." [60] This statement helps us bridge the gap to the somewhat abrupt conclusion in the introduction to *Ekstatische Konfessionen* where mankind's primordial myth of unity that becomes multiplicity is taken by Buber as the symbol of the mystic's experiences. The masters who always recreated this myth also experienced unity, and then progressed from this unity to multiplicity. But out of their experience came not the language of confession but the allegorical language of myth.

Buber concluded with questions which are tantamount to a pantheistic confession: "But is myth a chimera? Is it not a revelation of the ultimate reality of being? Is not the experience of one who has ecstasies a symbol of the original experience of the world-spirit? Are not both a living experience? We hearken to our inmost selves, and we know not which sea's murmur we hear."

After this confession, which Buber modified in *I and Thou*, it is instructive to recall his remarks about the experience of ecstasy in his introduction: "What is experienced in ecstasy (if indeed we can speak of a *what* in this case) is the unity of the I." [61] Do not the last two words express too much, especially from the standpoint of one who is skeptical of the mystical union with God? Can we vouch for anything more than "unity," and is not "unity of the I" a generally accepted interpretation around 1900, just as *unio mystica* was formerly accepted by believers when religion was still a living force? The introduction to *Ekstatische Konfessionen* contains a similar synthesis of pantheism, understanding, and enlightenment, which was also characteristic of Dilthey. The basic attitude behind this synthesis reminds us of Buber's contribution to the debate that took place at the Congress of Sociologists in 1910 where he spoke of mysticism and solipsism. Where the world spirit is the unending sea of life, ecstasy cannot remain *unio mystica* in the old sense. In the ecstasies of modern pantheism, I and the universe are complementary experiences, as instant and eternity. Eternity intrudes upon the I in an instantaneous flash—and, devoid of being, it is delivered over to "profusion of the manifold." "Rapture, illumination, and trance" reign in these "deified, joyous hours" when we feel one with the mighty stream of life; but a God that is experienced in this manner is always a "momentary God." Mysticism around 1900 was not bound to any doctrine that rested on a cognitive basis, and it was therefore constantly threatened by radical changes. It was the product of skepticism and longing, according to Nietzsche, an ecstasy that was not rooted in faith: "je suis mystique et je ne crois à rien"—as expressed by Flaubert in an oft-quoted dictum.

Although Buber's ecstatic experiences and his affinity with the mystics of the past, based on long and intense study of their works, are not to be confused with those of the aesthetic writers of his time for whom the word *mystic* had degenerated to *mysterious,* a closer look at the older mystical texts shows how atypical were his thoughts and feelings. Buber's mystical experiences did not revolve around the theme of God and soul, for this was precluded by his belief in God as world spirit, which he called the Absolute or the Unconditioned, but around the mysterious concept of the "realization" of man and God—the realization of God with respect to and through the world which, if pursued far enough, leads ultimately to the deification of man.

In this connection Buber's much too theoretical distinction between religion and religiosity, which he took from Simmel,[62] played a significant role. He regarded the mystic as the embodiment of religiosity, although a year later Troeltsch reminded him that historical dis-

tinctions are also applicable to this area, and that what is true of Maeterlinck need not be true for the medieval mystics. In this radical rejection of all religious systems with rigid dogmas and prescribed duties,
Buber tended to underestimate the significance of the humble daily
worship of a lived religion for the experience of ecstasy or the significance of the "we" of a religious community of service and prayer
whose members are dedicated wholly to God. *Unio mystica* is here su-
perseded by a life form of voluntary service that rests on the firm foundation of dogma. In Buber's life, however, the "religious" was at that
time tangential to the problems of daily life—so that the soul, cast out
from the Universe into empty Nothingness, can complain only of the
lost unity of the I. Buber failed to see that for most of his predecessors
mysticism was not only a living experience but also a road that must be
traversed, and that this constituted the reciprocal influence between ecstasy and lived religion.

Thoughts of this kind found little understanding around the beginning of the century. Although a man of genius is a child of his time
and its *Zeitgeist*, his insurgent energies will reach out beyond his age
and seek a way back to origins and sources. Buber was not content
with a mysticism that remained nothing more than an ephemeral mood.
From the ecstasy of the mystic that can never be expressed in
"speech," he turned to another being form of the unified man: to the
"teaching" that is not knowledge but a Way and a lived revelation.
The original meaning and habitat of the word he had in mind is at the
same time the *fons et origo* of religion itself, and it is to be found in
those men who are glorified by myth: in Buddha, in Jesus, in Lao-tzu.

MYTH

The deep seriousness with which Buber and his contemporaries
devoted themselves to mysticism and myth proceeded from an insight
contained in one of Dilthey's observations already quoted, namely,
"that there is no formula that contains the truth, that every religious
dogma and every scientific formula concerning the structure of the
world is a symbol for something that no myth, no dogma, and no con-

cept can exhaust or express as it really is *an sich. . . .*" [63] This school
of thought was characterized by a skepticism of the absolute validity of
thought and an overestimation of man's irrational creative powers, and
this went hand in hand with the longing of all youth to comprehend
the complete and whole reality of life. The decline of modern Western
culture, in which knowledge, experience, and action no longer flow
from a common source, was related by Nietzsche to the gradual disappearance of the myth: "Without myth . . . every culture loses its
healthy creative natural power; it is only a horizon encompassed with
myths." [64] Buber's friend, Gustav Landauer, also wrote in 1907:
". . . only where myth is found does a new people arise." [65]

In a scholarly essay on "Myth and Culture" [66] (1922), Arthur
Liebert pointed out that Nietzsche's idea of culture as the unity of artistic style as expressed in all the vital aspirations of a people is itself a
myth and shows Nietzsche to be a disciple of Goethe and the classical
Greek ideal. Liebert goes on to prove that every absolute evaluation of
a particular province of culture involves man's myth-forming talent.
Myth is not confined to the realm of religion; even positivism, when it
claims absolute validity, is a myth.

In Buber's view the creation of myths is not confined to the past:
"Myth is an eternal function of the soul," he wrote in 1914.[67] There is
no unambiguous definition as to what is to be understood by "myth."
In ancient times it was an expression of a collective life feeling; in our
day it has become the label for the ideology of a political party. Buber's
own interpretation, given at the beginning of his address "Myth in Judaism," goes back to Plato. It takes myth to be "an account of a divine
occurrence as a sensuous reality." In other words, a myth must not
only recount the deeds and sufferings of a god but a sensuous-concrete
event must also be conceived by man as absolute, that is, as occurring
outside the realm of causal nexus and otherwise inexplicable. Myth testifies to a sense of the intuitive apprehension of the Absolute.

Buber takes this conception of myth to refer to an original receptive and reactive faculty in man which is not wholly moribund even in
rational cultures. For the most part this faculty becomes active in
boundary situations or at the critical stages of a deep personal experience when man recognizes "occurrences in the world as being of

supra-causal significance and as the expression of a central meaning which, however, is to be comprehended not by thinking but by the power of the vigilant senses and with the passionate impulses of the entire person, as an intuitive reality given in all its multiplicity." This sense for the irrational aspects of an experience, for that which flares up in a thing only here and now, beyond thought and beyond speech, is predominant among primitive people and is understood by them with all the soul's "fervor" and "tension."

Buber's interest in primitive people and his use of the word *fervor* as a central concept in the *Legend of the Baal-Shem* indicate that we are once more in the same sphere of pan-sacramental experience which was the basis of his mystical confession in the essay on Boehme. "In the beginning is relation"[68]—and relation is at first a swift, lightning-like experience felt with body and soul. It can be experienced either as magical unification and expressed in the language of mystical identification or it can be regarded from the standpoint of man's creative spontaneity and as his answer to "the world's productive energies," in which case we find ourselves in the realm of myth with its relational *force* and *spiritual* unification. Regarded as an "eternal" function and viewed as part of Buber's own situation, myth signifies the creative answer of one who is by nature sacramentally disposed to apprehend the godlike in sensuous phenomena.

Mysticism and myth have for Buber a common root in life. This explains his attitude to the mystics in *Ekstatische Konfessionen*, which was a rare mixture of sublime empathy and aloofness. The ecstasy he was most familiar with did not come from meditation and absorption in God, but was the result of an intensified elementary relation-phenomenon. This connection between mysticism and myth was significant in 1900, far beyond Buber's individual case in its effect on Neopantheism; it characterized the attitude of Buber's close friend, Gustav Landauer, to Eckhart. We have already referred to Friedrich Hölderlin, the poetic genius who had anticipated this world experience with a radiant purity that was no longer attainable a century later. Even Hölderlin, who regarded himself as a seer, in his day was acknowledged only as a poet. Around 1900 only the poets seemed to experience the life unity of mysticism and myth and give it artistic form. Since language seeks to utter the ineffable mystical experience in the form of symbols and images, it stands to reason that the creative answer of myth is unthinkable without poetical language.

Buber's life feeling was closer to that of Rainer Maria Rilke than to any other contemporary, the poet for whom all "things" were impregnated with God's presence, and in whose saying "song is existence" we hear a clear echo of the voice of Hölderlin. In 1914 he wrote: [69] "When I would taste a piece of fruit now and then, and felt it dissolve on my tongue, it was already like a word of the spirit." Rilke had also known Buber's mystical experience in which inanimate nature responds to man. Once on leaning against a tree he felt "as if from the inside of the tree almost imperceptible vibrations were being transmitted to him . . . he thought he had never been caressed by gentler movements; his body, as it were, was being treated like a soul. . . ." [70] In this all-embracing universal relation, the boundaries between the inner and the outer may sometimes disappear. Rilke recalls an hour "when a bird-call without coincided with one within him for it did not break, as it were, at the limits of the body, but both converged in an unbroken space in which, mysteriously protected, only a single spot of purest, deepest consciousness remained. At this moment of rapture, he closed his eyes so as not to be disconcerted by the contour of his body, and the infinite passed into him so subtly from all sides that he thought he felt the light presence in his breast of the stars which in the meantime had risen." [71] Rilke's friend, Lou Andreas-Salomé, who approached all artistic experience and creativity with the categories of her teacher, Sigmund Freud, characterized these two experiences as the expression of infantile eroticism, as frustrated and abortive attempts to achieve a work of art, and as a retrogression to purely bodily functions. At that time myths could also be formed from submerged secondary phenomena. [72]

Rilke's creative responses to his mystic experience are universally known: the mythical angel of his *Duino Elegies*, the symbols of the "world's inner space," the myth of the singer Orpheus whose "endless traces" live in all things that bloom and sing in nature. "Dance the orange . . . it has been deliciously converted into you" (*Sonnets to Orpheus* I.15), that is, do not be content only to smell, taste, and see the orange but dance it also to reveal all its possible relations to the world—thus proclaiming the same poignant body-soul experiences considered by Buber as indispensable for the origin of the myth. Rilke was a lonely poet who trod the steep path between the glory and the dark, described by the English poet, Wystan Hugh Auden: [73]

> And Rilke, whom "die Dinge" bless,
> The Santa Claus of loneliness . . .

That the poet offers rich gifts to the solitary soul and writes only for a limited circle without attempting to express a collective life feeling constitute the weakness and tragedy of this modern myth. Rilke at any rate attained world fame as a poet, whereas other myth-making poets, such as Alfred Mombert, failed to achieve this high distinction. The mythical figures of Mombert's poetry, created with so much pathos, are today forgotten, and their prophetic pretensions make them appear somewhat ludicrous.

In the first decades of the century *myth* was not only an affair of the poet and limited to mystical experience but was also pervaded by an air of religious consecration; authors frankly appealed to the religious and philosophical sentiments of the reader. It is thus that myth arose around a historical figure whose portrayal is not concerned with the historical but with the "eternal" form, adopting a style between scientific language and poetical language. Gundolf's famous book on Goethe belongs to this category and, above all, Ernst Bertram's *Nietzsche* with the subtitle *Essay on Mythology*. The introduction to this latter book is called "Legend" and contains an excellent theoretical discussion of what in this literary category is understood by *myth*. As Buber did in his preface to the *Legend of the Baal-Shem*, Bertram finds the boundaries between myth and legend fluid: [74] "All occurrences tend to become image, all that lives legend, all reality myth." Bertram's initial assumption is that historical writing can never reconstruct past reality, since it transposes its object to another category of being and, consciously or unconsciously, involves making evaluations; its end result is therefore never life itself but its legend. The process of legend making, however, is only in part an affair of posterity; great men of the spirit radiate a myth-making power from beyond the grave, and summon us to recreate and complete their image: "No single individual can possibly compose the last word of their legend, the complete myth of their being." [75] A kind of *mana* thus emanates from the great personality, an effective power that creates a coherent relational structure to which the myth is an answer.

But living men can also radiate a will for immortality. The secret of the Stefan George Circle resided precisely in the concept myth. Here we have a poet who, assured of his role as the seer of a new era, advanced the claim to be "bearer of the holy fire and guardian of the temple." [76] Beauty was proclaimed as the highest value to consecrate everyday life, and the perfect man as the sole revelation of the divine. We here encounter, even more plainly than in Nietzsche, the dangers typical in the German veneration of the ancient Greeks. George, like his predecessor Hölderlin, is concerned with the renewal of German culture; his chief desire is to rescue it from barbarism and materialism by enlisting the spiritual forces of the Circle and its system of values in order to create a new type of German man. But the result was the undisguised deification of man of the "Maximin" myth [named after Maximilian Kronberger, a beautiful and gifted youth who died in 1904 at the age of sixteen and whom George glorified in his poetry]. In 1933, the Circle fell apart and the dream of the new age vanished with it.

All these manifestations of the new myth had many points in common with Buber's ideas, but when the two are compared we see that these ideas are as atypical here as they were when compared with the mystics of *Ekstatische Konfessionen.* His affinity to Hölderlin and Hofmannsthal has already been touched upon.[77] For him Hölderlin embodies in the noblest and most natural manner man's "answer" to divine omnipresence, "the sense for the intuition of the Absolute." Buber and Hofmannsthal walk the same path through the spiritual world, through the myths and cultures of the different races, but Hofmannsthal was a poet, and his deep mystical experience is concerned with problems of form and "the magic of configuration." Rilke's solution, despite the intensity with which he experienced the unity of Inner and Outer, remained purely poetical and removed from the turbulent stream of human development. Buber, like George, wanted to live life deeply and triumphantly, but not through an esoteric "Circle" with its aesthetic doctrine of salvation. Like Gundolf and Bertram he fixed his gaze on the "eternal" form, but he did not conceive it as isolated from life—and his *Moses* was one day to show us this form in conjunction with the history of religion.

The myths that were prevalent in Buber's day represented only partial solutions—valuable perhaps as personal insights but, like islands in a sea, without rule or compass. Buber envisaged man as a whole and the answer to his problems as a whole. He gave *ratio* its due, and did not shun any problem that could be solved by knowledge. This occupied him for years and, like Dilthey, he took the broad road of history in attempting to solve the problem of man. In the question of man's relation to God he had in mind not the individual of a given time and place but man in general. Mystical experiences were not foreign to him, but Simmel's severe philosophizing made itself felt within the inner sphere of religion when he attempted to give a sociopsychological explanation of man's worship of the divine and the phenomenon of ecstasy. The language of poetry is an indispensable part of his style, but he did not permit its magic to involve him in spurious profundity or to betray the stern test of truth and propriety. He did not confuse religious consecration with aesthetic incense; his mind remained open for the whole answer.

To find his own language Buber attempted to go back to the original speech of mankind. He listened to the religious voices of the different races across vast spaces stretching from the Occident to Buddha and Lao-tzu, and in Jewish history from Abraham to the prophets. The glad tidings of God's realization went forth from the Orient.

The Orient was for Buber, as it was for German classicism and romanticism, a spiritual unity. Despite the complex composition of its diverse population, it was governed, as an organism, by a uniform vital structure which is as recognizable today as those described in the documents of Asia's antiquity. The Oriental type is clearly distinguished from the Occidental. In Buber's terminology this type is inclined to be "motor," whereas the European type is inclined to be "sensory." In the former the impressions made on the soul tend to find release in action, whereas in the latter they seek release in image and form. The Oriental lives in the chain of generations, in the "becoming" of things and in their interrelations; the man of the Occident strives to attain to being and to establish order in space, and hence vision is his most highly developed sense. Plato called the essence of the things beheld *eidos*, that is, image, form; the Chinese philosopher speaks of *Tao* or *Path*.

From Buber's description of the "motor" type it seems that he, as a Jew, regarded his original home to be the Orient. That which was natural for the Oriental was exceptional for the Occidental: "The senses of this (Oriental) type are closely connected with one another and with the dark life of the organism; an impression that strikes one of his senses has a powerful impact on all of them, and the specific sense-qualities pale before the force of the total impact." [78] From this we learn what *relation,* whose initial spark can culminate in ecstasy, meant for Buber. Thus, in the introduction to *Ekstatische Konfessionen,* Buber states that ecstasy is more common—more "normal"—in the Orient than in the Occident. The Oriental experiences the world as something that happens to him, something that takes hold of him; unending relation runs through him like a stream. But deep within him is a quiet passive core which feels itself to be at one with the hidden sense of the world, and this sense of unification leads him to recognize his essential task: to make manifest the truth of the world. He was aware of its preestablished inner unity which in the world of phenomena appears in the form of polar opposites or antitheses: good and evil in Persian thought, world and illusion in Hindu philosophy, yes and no in the Chinese conception. In the Orient, however, there is a common desire to lead the true life, to find the right road that leads man to his proper vocation: to create a unified being of duality. Discursive thought is for the Oriental nothing more than an adumbration, a projection; only when it is lived does it become a reality. No matter by what name the message is called that leads to "the Way," the Way itself is one—"the Way of God in the world." He who takes this Way walks in the "footsteps of God," well aware that the "fate of the world depends on the acts of the human agent to a degree that no man can fathom."

None of the great religious doctrines had its origin in the West. What is missing in Europe now, as in the past, is the teaching of "the one thing that is needful," the teaching of the Way: "The true life as the basic metaphysical principle that is underived and irreducible."

These thoughts are outlined in Buber's address "The Spirit of the Orient and Judaism" and are elaborated in the essay "The Teaching of Tao" 1909), later included in the final edition of his *Works*, for it represents an important stage in his development.

Buber proceeded from the point of view that in the Orient there is, besides science and law, a third basic power of the spirit: teaching. Science is based on the duality of postulate and deed. Teaching develops independently of these: it is directed to "the one thing that is needed." It is lived truth that demands nothing; it only proclaims itself and is fulfilled in the "central man." This fulfillment is the genuine, the unified life.

The language of the central, the fulfilling man is the parable, which is not based on the duality of content and form but on the inseparable unity of spirit and life, the Absolute in the world of things. After his death the life of central man is raised to the Unconditioned: it becomes myth. Myth in turn leads to religion, which is already mixed with the elements of law and knowledge: this is "the Path" of the teaching in the world.

The Way of the teaching in the Orient can be followed in its three manifestations: the Jewish teaching of the Kingdom of God, the Indian teaching of redemption, the Chinese teaching of Tao. All three attain their perfection in a man: in Jesus, in Buddha, in Lao-tzu. When the unity of the teaching is translated from lived life to content and form, it disintegrates into the message of the Kingdom of Heaven and of men as the children of God, the message of redemption through suffering and the holy path, and that of Tao and non-activity *[wu-wei]*.

The "central man" realizes the unity of the world that is inherent in every human life and of which every Oriental has innate knowledge. The fulfillment of the teaching is always an act in the sense of a decision, whereby the Way that is found becomes the one and Unconditioned. In his address "The Renewal of Judaism," Buber cited as an example the saying of Jesus that he came not to destroy but to fulfill the Law and the prophets. Jesus' assurance in the next verse that not a single letter of the Law will pass away until all things have been accomplished means: "until the teaching of the Unconditioned will be fulfilled in all purity and sincerity of soul, until the world is hallowed and deified by the absolute deed." [79] The message of Jesus is the postulate of unconditioned decision which raises man into the Kingdom of God: all Wholeness is God's image and likeness; and when man chooses with his whole soul, a mystery takes place: "unified man partakes of God's essence." [80] To decide with one's whole soul always means to decide for God who illumines every Wholeness. In every decision where duality is overcome, "the primal meaning of the world is fulfilled eternally as if for the first time." Buddha's renunciation of the world is also a deed and a decision, born together instantaneously and of eternity; his knowledge is the fulfilling being that has no need to return in a future life. [81]

What is Tao? It is the Unknowable and the Ineffable. In the becoming of the world it appears as primal existence, as "the mother of all beings." In the being of the world it appears as the world's order; it is unity within change; it is the unity of all opposites, for example, masculine and feminine which do not exist separately in the world but are always found together. Everything reveals Tao by its way, by its life. There is not a thing in which Tao is not wholly present as the thing's self. The self of things has its essence in the manner in which things answer one another. Tao is in things only potentially; it takes effect only when it comes into contact with other things.

In man Tao appears as the element that unifies, completes, and reconciles, and that redeems things of all duality. In the perfect man Tao not only appears, it *is*. Tao presses toward realization; it realizes itself in the authentic life of the fulfilling man. Just as the Tao of things becomes alive and manifest only through contact with other things, so also does the Tao of the world become alive and manifest only through its contact with unified man. It is he who rediscovers his unity in the world and in all things, who conjures up the Tao of the world, revives its passive unity and makes it manifest, and is, according to Tao teaching, a creator: "The perfect man is self-contained, supremely secure, united by Tao, unifying the world, a creator, God's comrade: the comrade of all-creating eternity. The perfect man has eternity. Only the perfect man has eternity. The spirit wanders through all things until it blossoms forth in the perfect man to all eternity. . . . In the perfect man Tao returns to itself from its world-wide wanderings through phenomena. It becomes fulfillment." [82]

In this path traversed by Tao through the world of phenomena back to itself, Buber recognized the basic form of myth that he had already encountered in German and Jewish mysticism: the myth of God's way in the world and its realization. Just as Tao is in every thing "as the Self of the thing," so is God wholly in every thing as that thing, according to Nicholas of Cusa and Jacob Boehme, being in both instances a potentiality to be realized. The teaching of being-at-one with the world that Buber had found in Boehme, he later discovered as an Oriental doctrine by which man's deepest core, radically removed from all contradiction, is identical with the hidden sense and essence of the world.

German and Jewish mysticism were bound to a theistic religious system, and the path of man's realization was more or less determined by this religion. However, this mysticism had not yet attained the religiosity that Buber had in mind: the pure religiosity of being and not of knowledge, of the free deed and not of the prescribed service. To find such religiosity he had to go back to the early beginnings of the world's great religions and to the myth that proclaimed their founders. In Buddha, Jesus, and Lao-tzu he met with truth that is lived and transmitted, the fulfilling man who is himself teaching. Through the profound teachings of the Orient "the mystery is lifted out of the abyss." [83] Here Buber learned an ethical principle he could unreservedly acknowledge, the unconditionality of the deed: "a great religiosity is basically not concerned with *what* is done, but only whether it is done within human limitations or divine unconditionality." [84]

Meister Eckhart's conviction that man is "of godlike race and God's kin" is confirmed by Tao teaching which regards man as the partner of creative Being, and the "unified one" as united with the universe, comprehending the polarity of the world, the Tao of things. This all-embracing intimacy by means of an unknown and formless principle appealed to Buber's pantheism; an inner-worldly ethical principle imbued creative force with religious consecration. In Tao teaching, as in Hasidism, man has a task to fulfill with respect to things, a task that does not proceed from knowledge but from man's self-composed united being. What is generally called knowledge involves taking a stand over against something and is bound to a dialectic of subject and object. Only the unity of being, however, is true knowledge; it embraces all things in its being, that is, in its love.[85] This knowledge is the true act, an act of the entire being that proceeds from collected unity and self-composure and is, as Lao-tzu called it, "the doing of not-doing." The love of the perfect man "comprehends"—an important, recurrent concept for Buber—and is the unconditioned love which is liberated in things by Tao.

It is Tao's "message" which was elaborated by Buber: that aspect which was turned to humanity. The Chinese features are as inconspicuous in his presentation as is the trinity in his presentation of German mysticism. The enthusiastic interpretation of the creative function of inactivity, of non-doing, was tacitly corrected in *Daniel.*

From the great founders of religion Buber learned the teaching of the "lived truth," and made it part of his own character and influence. It compelled him to acknowledge the imperious claims of the spirit, and it gave him the basic components of what has been called his "existentialism"—an atypical and world-rejoicing existentialism that could not possibly have come from Kierkegaard.

In the teachings of Lao-tzu, with which he became acquainted through the poet-philosopher Chuang-tzu, Buber found the elements for a religious existentialism that is beyond all religion. The basis for this conception was provided by the worldwide dispersion of the primordial myth. Buber thus discovered features of Tao teaching in the Greek philosopher Heraclitus: "The thoughts of Heraclitus—the unknowable but universally operative *logos,* unity which is at the same time both nameless and named, the proclamation of an eternal world-order, the eternal transformation of the manifold to unity and of unity to the manifold, the harmony of opposites, the relation between the waking state and dreaming in the life of an individual, and that between life and death in the world's existence—all these are more closely related to Tao teaching than to any other." [86] Wherever myth prevails, truth is experienced in the sensuous image, in the living content of meaning which is at once body and soul, inseparable and indivisible. The godlike dwells in beings and in things—Tao, *logos*, sheki-nah—indeed, every word, as an indivisible unity of spirit and body, is attached to the *logos* as "symbol of the primordial being," to the "Word that is in the beginning." In a letter Buber wrote to Henri Borel [87] we find: "The creation of the word is a mystery that takes place in the kindled, open soul of world-poetizing, world-discovering man." And in this same letter he adds that for him there is no essential difference between word creation and that which has been called the emergence of the *logos*. Few modern non-Christian Europeans have displayed such a deep insight into the meaning of "incarnation."

"The parable is the introduction of the Absolute in the world of things; myth is the introduction of things in the world of the Abso-lute." [88] Teaching, parable, myth—in this trinity the living truth makes its way through all times and spaces by constantly giving rise to new life. Myth is an eternal function of the soul.

"Sensuous reality is godlike, but it must be realized in its godli-ness," Buber writes of Hasidism in his address "Myth in Judaism." The shekinah resides within the depths of every being and can be re-deemed by man: "Every man is thus summoned to determine God's fate with his own life; every living being is thus deeply rooted in the living myth." [89]

How Buber extracted a coherent language of religiosity from Oriental teachings, enabling him to "comprehend" the different reli-gions, is revealed in his description of the risen Christ on the closed wings of the Isenheim Altar. In this painting the manner in which Christ unites in himself the various hues of earthly existence and bears them heavenward is for Buber the mystery of how multiplicity be-comes unity: "This is not the Jew Yeshua trodding the soil of Galilee and teaching in his day; it is also Yeshua; this is not the incarnate *Logos* that descends from its timeless pre-existence into time; it is also the *Logos*. This is the man of all times and places, of the here and now, who is perfecting himself to become the I of the world. This is the man who embraces the world. . . . He loves the world to the end of uncon-ditionality; he bears the world upward to its very self. He, the unified one, fashions the world into a unity." [90]

The "living unity" cannot be found; it can only be achieved. The essay "With a Monist" shows how a world attitude of religiosity is possible at all times and places. The monist, as a faithful believer in an absolute causal explanation of the world, enters into a dialogue with the apostle of the myth and of "the one thing that is needful." Although Buber is considered a mystic, he rejected every form of mysticism that believes it can find God by turning its back on the world. He granted *ratio* the right to comprehend and explain as much of the world as it can, for it is precisely in this manner that the incomprehensibility and spontaneity of the spirit are made manifest. But it can explain only common reality and, in the end, it remains incomprehensible, for the glorious paradox of our existence is that "the comprehensibility of the world is only a footstool of its incomprehensibility." Reality is not a fixed, unchanging condition; it is capable of being heightened and intensified if approached not with the categories of the understanding but with "the active senses of one who loves." Reality arises through the "contact between the ineffable movement of things and the animating energies of my senses . . . which are spiritual powers anchored in the body." [91] The "effective" reality of things—their "activity," their formative and yielding qualities—is revealed to the loving man who takes them absolutely and for whom they are incomparable: "In the features of the loved one, whose self he realizes, he discerns the enigmatic face of the universe." [92] This knowledge, which is a loving comprehension, is called by Buber "the great reality," and he found it in the primary relations of the spiritual life. "Genuine art is the art of one who loves"—and this is also true in science and philosophy. The secret form and inherent potentiality of life, and the mysterious sense of things reveal themselves in this way—as the Tao of the world.

"Every genuine deed is the deed of one who loves. Every genuine deed is the result of contact with a loved thing and flows into the universe. Every genuine deed establishes unity in the world out of a lived unity. Unity is not a quality of the world, but its task. To create unity out of the world is our never-ending work." [93]

Here Buber sought to introduce elements of Oriental teaching into Western thought. He who creates unity within himself and concentrates on a thing with the "magic of direction" until it "springs up to meet him" in its formative unity and uniqueness, actualizes that which is present in him as possibility, lifts it to a higher level of reality, and realizes God while he is realizing the world. Hugo Bergmann, who compared Buber's "great reality" with the "great experience" of Zen Buddhism, pointed out that here the unifying act of man has cosmic significance: [94] it accomplishes God's way in the world.

The world's godliness is found in all beings and things as cosmic love-unity, and this is to be realized by man. This teaching, however, should not be spread "zealously," but "in one's being"—so that each one may discover it in himself. St. Paul, whom Buber called "a violent man," transformed the living truth of Jesus into a dialectic; Chuang-tzu, the poet, was the apostle of Tao teaching to the things of the world. Poets are the guardians of the mythical view; their work introduces the parable of the teaching into the world. Rationalists regarded Chuang-tzu as useless because he lived obscurely and without a profession, "gathering in himself many folk parables." Here Buber, like Elias Lönnrot, had in mind specific ideas of his own. Just as Plato was the poet of the Idea, Chuang-tzu was the poet who in poetical form proclaimed Tao, the Way, "as the ground and the meaning of the unified life, its universal ground and universal meaning." [95]

The radical affinity between religious and poetical experience appeared to Buber not only as tension and opposition; he saw it as an interdependence rooted in the creativity of the bearers and guardians of the primordial process of "Incarnation," of the penetration of world matter by spirit: teaching and parable in their descent from the godlike to the world of senses and myth in raising things to the Absolute. Thus the poet in his own inviolate piety appeared as the brother of the "fulfilling man." In this sense Buber continued his work of transmitting the Hasidic legends. His existentialism is confident of the innocence and ultimate significance of man's creative answer to religious mystery, and is far removed from Kierkegaard's conflict between the aesthetic and the religious life form.

In 1913 all of Buber's studies and experiences in mysticism and myth culminated in his first large work *Daniel*, whose subtitle *Dialogues on Realization* indicates its resemblance to the style form of a Platonic dialogue. *Realization* here means God wants to be realized—not through "religion" but through every individual who in his own sphere does what is right, unifying, and formative, and who "loves the world to the end of unconditionality." *Daniel* is a life teaching without fixed religious obligation, an existentialism which at the same time signifies a West-East synthesis. To be, as poet-philosopher, an apostle of Eastern teaching to the West is the task Buber had set before himself in writing *Daniel.* The spirit that this work breathes can be summed up in the concluding words of the dialogue with the monist: "Let us believe in man!"

Realization

TO EACH of the five *Dialogues on Realization* in *Daniel*, Buber prefixed an introduction together with a place name. The geographical locality of each of the dialogues expresses more than the local setting; it signifies a symbolical landscape or scene, since meaning for Buber was not something that is injected into the world of things from without or superimposed from above, but something that constitutes their life's innermost secret.

"Of Direction," the title of the first dialogue, takes place on the mountain slopes amid crags that rise up as if animated by a spirit of challenge. The second dialogue, concerning "of reality," takes place in "Above the City," which is filled with the feverish haste and barren activity of urban life. The garden, with its varied but organic growth, is the delightful scene of the dialogue that deals with "Meaning." "After the Theater"—the setting for the mystery of the spirit on earth—treats polarity. The dialogue "By the Sea" contains all contrasts within its secret depths and reveals the meaning of all realization: unity.

Buber's introduction to *Legend of the Baal-Shem* was based on the primary words of mystical experience. In an essay on Buddha[1] (1908), he spoke of the fortress of ancient basic words where we could take shelter from the hustle and bustle of daily life. In *Daniel* he was also concerned with primary conceptions, such as Goethe had contemplated in his *Urworten Orphisch* in which, as in these dialogues, an East-West synthesis was attempted, that is, the revival of a vanished mythology for present-day life in the Occident. Like Goethe's primary words—demon; *tyche,* "the accidental"; Eros; *ananke,* "compulsion"; and *elpis,* "hope"—Buber's guiding symbols are not abstract concepts but forces with which we have to deal in life and which involve grave decisions. For Goethe, man's metamorphosis was predetermined by these primary words, the way in which human existence conforms to the growth and modification of all life. But Buber was also concerned with bringing the "path" within us into harmony with the basic factors of the external world.

The form of the dialogues recalls the philosopher of the dialogic principle; it also reveals that a critical stage had still to be overcome before he could attain the mature spiritual form of his later works. The dialogues are deliberately based on common incidents of daily life and, as in the Platonic dialogue, these are meant to lead us to the basic factors of human existence. Later, when Buber became more aware of the perils involved in every genuine dialogue, he would not have adopted this form of presentation. In fact, the character of the dialogues is not always of the same quality throughout. The figure that is drawn with the greatest consistency and in sharpest outline is the Woman in the first dialogue. The decision to introduce her again into the dialogue demonstrates the intellectual interests he and his wife had in common. The highly emotional participants in the third and fifth dialogues must be conceived as Daniel's younger friends; in reality, however, they represent earlier stages in Buber's own development and pose questions which perplexed him at the time and to which he could find no answer. In the second and fourth dialogues the participants have no deep significance, and merely repeat key words that reflect a hardheaded, skeptical attitude to life. The third and fifth dialogues actually consist of a single speech and a refutation—Daniel's long explanations here are somewhat in the nature of a monologue.

The Occident, as Buber tells us, has science, art, and religion; it also possesses freedom of thought and comprehensive philosophical systems. But it lacks "the one thing that is needful." Buber did not underestimate the greatness of Europe and its significance for the human spirit, and he surely did not ask the European to become an Oriental. But he was eager to bring to the West something of the greatness of the Orient: the authentic life, the "teaching" that is one with life:

Why should I labor thus the path to find,
If not to show it unto all mankind?

[Goethe, Dedication]

Religious truth is not a doctrine but a way, a way that is not found but lived. In this sense teaching and myth are never completed, but are, rather, man's imperfect creative answer to the Unconditioned. The word *creative* here does not refer to the prerogatives of talent, but is synonymous with spontaneous, original; it is an enduring quality of the human heart which accepts every occurrence as absolute and recognizes in it the sign of the Eternal. The dialogues in *Daniel* attempt to show us the Way that is bound to no religion but follows the path taken by myth in the history of mankind, the form in which living teaching expresses itself.

The dialogue in the mountains discloses a mythical landscape with two people, representing the basic polarity of man and woman. Daniel is the masculine speaker, but his partner has no name and is simply called the "Woman"—woman as mother and as companion. She represents the maternal forces of being: the alternations of day and night, of sleep and waking; the blessing of the earth's rhythm, the "again" as the recurrent jubilant cry of human life. For her the earth is the formless element, the maternal womb, and the origin of all being. Daniel, however, strives to free himself from the maternal force that keeps pulling him down to earth. His path leads upward; spaceless unity that knows no multiplicity is his home. Over against the powers of the earth he opposes the magic of the soul, its innate "direction." A man's directional tension is like a torch to which the lightning from above is wedded. The earth seeks to draw the soul into the chaotic turmoil of events; the infinitude of possibilities, tensions, and feelings press in upon it and threaten to destroy it. Only gods and demons can cope with this infinitude without direction; over against it, however, the soul must rely upon its own peculiar, indigenous powers: "Direction is that primary tension of the human soul which impels it from time to time to choose this and no other from the infinitude of possibilities and to realize it in action." [2] The soul that knows its direction is stronger than the whirlwind. It is not only united in itself; in everything it approaches with a perfect sense of direction the portals of the One open before it. To illustrate this experience Buber again took the example of a tree, a stone pine: "With all your directed strength receive the tree, surrender yourself to it until you feel its bark as you feel your skin, and the springing forth of a branch from the trunk like the pull in your muscles; until your feet cling and grope like roots and the skull of your head arches like a resplendent crown; until you recognize your children in the blue fir-cones; yes, until you have been transformed. But also in the transformation you do not relinquish your direction, and through it you experience the tree so that you attain unity within it. For it pulls you back into yourself; the transformation vanishes like a fog, and around your direction a being arises, the tree, so that you experience its unity, unity itself. It is no sooner transplanted from the earth of space into the earth of the soul but it tells its secrets to your heart, and you become aware of the mystery of reality. Was it not one tree among others? But now it has become the tree of eternal life" (p. 54).

This experience is highly instructive for the understanding of Buber's mystical speculations and for the manner in which he appropriated the teaching of Tao. Our initial assumption must again be that the ecstasy he experienced was an intensified relation-phenomenon: One who in his innermost being feels at one with all the unending life cycles of nature, who feels the roots of his being deeply intertwined within him, who immerses himself in a thing or a being with a concentrated and directed unity until the instantaneous force of the relation strikes him and consummates the mystical identification. But the experience as such, without the magic of self-direction, would be "only a dream of unification," for "it pulls you back into yourself; the transformation vanishes like a fog." He who surrenders himself to an ecstasy without direction falls from the life of the universe into nothing, and the powers of chaos threaten to tear him limb from limb. This is Daniel's answer to the Woman's question: whether by losing oneself in the Universe, in ecstasy, will one find the solution for the suffering that comes from the sense of isolation. He who maintains his direction, however, experiences the miracle of becoming creative in the task to which he has devoted himself, and he feels that "our life's force is confirmed with immortal seals" (p. 51). He who enters into an ecstatic state with the self-possessed music of his inner self, as Orpheus descended into the realm of Hades with a lyre to die and rise from the dead with Dionysus, experiences unity in a formative sense as "the mystery of reality": the form of the tree reveals itself, and the isolated tree has become the "tree of eternal life." Only by preserving his own direction is man able to experience the rhythm of the earth as "sacrament," as death and renewal of the soul.

The attitude that Buber had in mind here is the *wu-wei* of Tao teaching, the non-activity that comes from self-possessed unity, which signifies the perfection of all activity, non-activity as an effect of the entire being that refrains from participating in the world's work but which experiences the unity of all things in its own unity: "He who is in complete harmony with himself is surrounded by the receiving love of the world." [3] In this harmony with one's self and with things, man makes the passive Tao in the world "active and manifest," lifts it up into being. Tao, "the mother of all being," is realized through man. As in *Daniel*, the earth's rhythm becomes a "sacrament," and its vital life becomes eternal form through the directed and unified man. Now Daniel's union with the Woman also reveals itself as an alliance with the powers of the earth, as a freely chosen community.

The theme of this community of interests, with whose symbolical figure the dialogue ends, is taken up again in the second dialogue, "Above the City." The unified, directed man had been able to realize in himself the being-form of a tree, but what was to be done with the innumerable anonymous voices of a large city? For a brief moment Daniel accepted the challenge and took it upon himself to gather the conflicting forces and diverse needs of the nameless crowd into his unified soul, so that it encompassed him as a gigantic body encompasses the throbbing human heart. But his attempt failed, for there can be no community of interests with those who know no reality: "He who does not realize, remains unreal" (p. 64).

What is meant by reality here emerges from the subsequent elaborations of the theme of the realizing and oriented attitude of man to his experiences, whereby *Daniel* became the preliminary stage of Buber's most famous work *I and Thou*. Reality here is not, as is commonly supposed, the objective world as the coherent structure of experience on which science is based, but rather the result of the orientating function which enables man to catalogue a new experience and find a place for it among his past experiences. Reality is not the primary material of our living experience, for this is never given us. The way in which one approaches an experience and becomes aware of it is in itself a formative ingredient of that experience. Pure relations, active interrelationships, are as incomprehensible as a flash of lightning; they become "reality" when a lightning-like unification is "realized" or "fulfilled." To "realize" means to relate an experience to nothing other than itself, to bring to light that within it which is unique, relation-less, and which constitutes its very essence. This is brought about and is illustrated by the example of the tree in the first dialogue, by an act of devotion, which is at the same time a steadfast resolve, an answer given by one's own creative power. To realize, then, is what Buber elsewhere called "a myth-creating attitude."

"Spirit is realization: unity of the soul, exclusiveness of life-experience, unification" (p. 77). All creative acts of the spirit have arisen from a realizing attitude: "The hero and the sage, the poet and the prophet, are unifying men; its mystery is called communion . . ." (p. 72). For Buber "communion" is the consciously fulfilled relation process dedicated to the Unconditioned. Every man is endowed with a capacity for unification, and no man can live *only* realizing—orientating periods must alternate with realizing periods. Realizing power is to be found predominantly in primitive people, in children, and in creative individuals who create in an organized and artistic form that which is present in others in an embryonic, rudimentary stage; the creative man sets "reality" before the eyes of all. Buber has here defined the significance of relation for the creative individual.[4]

Orientated behavior means finding a place in time and space for that which is experienced and ordering it with respect to cause and effect. This makes for universal comprehensibility. But by sundering in two the original unity of relation in subject and object, it falsifies it at its very core. Orientated behavior has legitimate claims: it makes possible science and vast communal projects. But it tends to identify itself too easily with utilitarian goals. An exclusive preoccupation with orientated behavior and the astounding success of its practical achievements to the detriment of creative realization are characteristic of our modern age. Those who have not experienced genuine realization, however, have been defrauded of their human prerogative. Only a rude awakening can convince them of the ghostlike character of their lives and the false security of their intellectual pretensions. To bring to them a vision of true realization and a sense of common endeavor were the tasks Buber set for himself with these *Dialogues on Realization*.

In "On Meaning. Dialogue in the Garden" direction points out the chosen way, and the process of realization creates its "reality"; but they do not yet constitute "meaning," as is revealed to us by the natural order of the world. In the previous dialogue, the great creative spirits endowed with a comprehensive faculty of realization were called by Daniel "unifiers," and their capacity for experience was characterized by him as that of a child. Thus, "meaning" is first of all the natural unification of children and young people, the central unity of their lives that comes to them as a gift in a world of miracles: "everything was responsive to me, all things were in accord with themselves and unified in themselves," as Daniel's younger friend described his lost security—all things flow into the heart of the world, into meaning (p. 82).

Reinold's naive security is unexpectedly shattered. One night the youth rowed out on the starlit sea in a blessed state of cosmic unification: "Boundlessness was the bed of my soul; heaven, night and sea its pillow" (p. 85). But as he returned to the shore, the silent infinity became for him a haunting nightmare; instead of the universe, his soul experienced nothingness: "led astray, betrayed, rejected, my soul hung in the dread of the night between sea and sky" (p. 85). Where previously he had found total unification there was now only a gaping abyss between the things of the world. The soul, as if dazed, yearns "for its sacrament, for meaning"—only to find the abyss in itself, its unity and security irretrievably lost.

Dispassionate understanding, theology, philosophy, and mysticism have built bridges for man that lead him across the abyss of being. But Reinold knows that only "thought" can set foot on these bridges, not the elemental soul: "this thing made of stone and storm and flood and flame, this Whole, this weighty, vibrating thing" refuses to reconcile itself to these thought constructions (p. 88).

Daniel interprets Reinold's experience to mean that he had reached a crossroad where he had to choose between certainty and meaning. Orientating behavior holds out a promise of certainty; it leads to truths that we can possess, to the windowless ark called *Weltanschauung*, which is sealed up with pitch to keep out the living waters. He who chooses the other Way, however, is exposed to unknown perils and perpetual risks. He knows he must realize the primordial depths that have opened up before him, and that he must withstand the abyss with the magic of his "direction," as one who would realize himself after having thrown in his lot with being. Such a life means starting each day anew at the precarious edge of being. The deed is to realizing man what magic is to primitive man; it is not something that can be found in the chain of cause and effect, but a new beginning and an act of world creation. The theologian who places God within the causal chain is far removed from this type of man who seeks to lift the submerged underived truth out of the depths, who knows that "God can be realized by man only as the innermost presence of a lived experience . . ." (p. 91). Again we find that here the absolute, the unconditioned, the world spirit of the West are mysteriously close to Eastern Tao: he who chooses direction and meaning "does not possess the world, yet he stands in its love; for he realizes all being in its reality" (p. 92). And in the light of meaning, with which the soul is innately endowed from the very beginning to enable it to preserve its experiences and to develop, the experienced world becomes for him "a sacred mirror in which the signs of primal being appear" (p. 94). Just as the realizing man is related to primitive man by the magic of his activities, so also is he related to him in his myth-creating knowledge: to him who stands in the love of the world all things become the image and seal of the eternal World Spirit. He interprets whatever befalls him as a message, and that which needs to be done as his task. Meaning is mythical truth.

The realizing man is convinced that the Unknowable comes to life through him: "For like primitive man, who finds in magic his essential deed and in myth his essential knowledge and experiences the mystery in the union and celebration of both by overcoming their separateness and uniting himself with God, so also does he who has direction and meaning feel an eternally new mystery by realizing God in all things. For God seeks to be realized, and all realization is God's realization; and none takes place except through man who realizes himself and all being" (p. 95).

The "kingdom of holy insecurity" is God and danger, which at that time appeared to Buber as the kingdom of God; danger is the portal to reality and "reality is the highest price of life and God's eternal birth" (p. 98).

The abyss also must be realized, that thousand named yet nameless polarity of all being, which is also an inner abyss. Within it can be seen the "signs of primal nature" summoning us to the task of creating unity out of all duality, establishing unity in the world "so that God's realized countenance will shine forth out of tension and current" (p. 98).

The first three dialogues in *Daniel* are more closely connected than are the last two. They form a coherent body of life teaching for the individual based on common human experience. The fourth and fifth dialogues extend the theme to include the whole of the spiritual world, although here as well a highly personal experience is now and then referred to. The two concluding parts of the work remind us that Buber had originally planned not five but twelve dialogues, seven basic ones and five of a historical nature, so that the final version suffered from extensive abridgment and condensation.[5]

The fourth dialogue resumes on a different plane the discussion of the problem of "meaning" and "polarity," the subject of the third dialogue. The introduction of the theater proved to be a fortunate artistic device which enabled Buber to continue the theme of personal realization treated in the previous dialogues and at the same time to present the phenomenon of polarity in a generalized form without having to rely on particular instances. The theater provided the proper background for mythical behavior. The players, redeemed from the tyranny of time, seem to have come from the periphery of being; they act out being and anti-being, the purest polarity which spells inevitable doom. The action on the stage takes place *sub specie aeternitatis*, reminding us of the Christian world theater with its heaven and hell. The two tragic actors, Creon and Antigone, reveal the primordial duality of the spirit that is beyond guilt and innocence, and as Daniel witnesses the first act, he feels as if he were the I of this spirit in which the polar currents between the players flow together and unite.

In the interval that follows Daniel becomes aware of another polarity. He suddenly feels that he is one of the spectators and that he constitutes, together with them, a mythical reality over against the actors. Even though the "dynamic wholeness of active participation" may be absent in many of the spectators—for in the last analysis the spectacle is still removed from daily life and cannot wholly obliterate the distinction of audience and tragedy, being and anti-being—yet, while the two actors on the stage are locked in struggle and valiantly coming to terms with their polarity, they are one with the spectators who affirm and comprehend the fate of both.

In the third act Daniel becomes aware of still another polarity, that between the hero and the actor who is playing that role. What is actually involved in this realization of the hero by the actor? Does it not involve "the secret of magic possessed by all virginal people? He who transforms himself into God lives the life, performs the deed and carries out the work of God. Did he not realize God in and with his soul as in and with his body?" (p. 114). Such a transformation succeeds by virtue of that "high excitement" felt by him who dares surrender himself to a polarity and realize his counter-pole; and this excitement, according to Buber, is "more precious and sacred to the soul than desire and pain" (p. 118).

There are three ways of fulfilling polarity: through struggle openly engaged in, through a love that embraces others, and through knowledge that transforms itself into the world, as once the youth, Dionysus, in the Bacchus play, transformed himself into God and realized him. Genuine knowledge is possible only when the one who is transformed takes part in the movement of the world in harmony with the movement of his own being, performs the world's deed and accomplishes its work: "For the secret of the world is the *kinesis* of the infinite, the union of meaning and being, and no one attains it who reflects upon it, but only he who does it; and he is the knower. He carries out the polarity in which he stands by realizing his counter-pole . . . the simulacrum that becomes creative in him is the imitation of the unknown God—is realization" (p. 119).

In the world of the theater, however, the real imitator of the unknown God, the one who realizes in himself all tensions and fulfills in himself the pole and counter-pole of all forms, is the poet. Plato called him the messenger of God, but he is also the messenger of the earth. In him the double current that flows in all animate beings is condensed and spiritualized; all tensions, which in others remain unexpressed, are cultivated and developed by him: "Of the poet it can be said that his heart is the hub in which the spokes of polarities converge" (p. 123). He loves the world and embraces its contradictions; and he is the guardian of the word which unites all opposites: "To speak the world: this means to span the world with a rainbow bridge from pole to pole" (p. 124).

The hymn to the poet and to his "fire-force" that binds God and world is not Daniel's last word. The poet is today as always the guarantee that the unity of word and life, which we call myth, is not lost. He is always the one who applies the criterion of the Unconditioned. His work struggles with contraries and embraces them. By transforming himself he consummates the work of the unknown God. Poetry leads to life, but it is not life itself. The last word in *Daniel* is spoken by man, who is the bearer of the teaching.

The fifth and last dialogue treats "of unity." Its setting is the sea in its infinity of being and becoming—"this womb giving birth to and devouring all multiplicity and all contrast" [6]—and the primary symbol of the ultimate unity to which Elias freely submits, returning to the "mother" as Empedocles did by throwing himself into the crater of Mt. Etna to be consumed by its divine flames.

The unnerving reflection on his eventual death leads Luke to Daniel. The polarity of life and death dawned on him and became the question of the world. What kind of a sea is it on which man sails forth morning after morning, accompanied by life and death? He knows the power that impels him to death, and he calls its mysterious effect "time"—but does not an unknown wind waft to him the tidings of a new becoming? "I know that somehow I am myself this unknown sea, but I cannot reach the place where I am that wind . . . I long to know the holy sea . . . I have an urge to behold what I am" (p. 132).

Daniel answers him by relating a personal experience: how as a lad of seventeen he had experienced the death of a relative,[7] and how that same gap between life and death that appeared within his friend revealed to him with tragic force the loss of elemental unification. A fierce struggle between life and death within him threatened to annihilate him; external nature appeared to him a chaos and a ghostly nightmare. Finally it was not the soul but the body that found the redeeming gesture: "My two arms raised themselves, my hands bent to each other, my fingers entwined, and over all the horror arched the God-powerful bridge. Then my body became united, the world became one for me . . . I had torn down the eternal wall, the wall within me. From life to death, from the living to the dead, flowed this deep union . . ." (p. 135).

In that hour, without knowing it, Daniel learned the deep meaning of the teaching, "the one thing that is needful." The unity behind the polarity of life and death, the I that is at the same time "the holy sea," cannot be recognized; it can only be lived—and to live means to act. The "simple act" of the body, that symbolic gesture in which the polar currents of being are united to a point of tension, had bound together life and death to the "I."

He who truly experiences the world experiences it as polarity; all the wisdom of the ages has for its subject the duality of the world. No matter how this basic duality is described by the philosophers—spirit and matter, form and material, being and becoming, reason and will—their constant endeavor is to overcome this tension and abolish it. And the unity they reach is always a resting point which is free of all turbulent tensions and the violent impact of experience. These roads had to be rejected by Daniel. The Hindu teaching that the duality of the world is only an illusion and deception was one such false road; another was Western philosophy in which duality was thought to be inseparable from unity and conjoined with it in an ultimate identity. He also found the Chinese teaching that neutralizes the opposite within itself and reduces it to a kind of non-entity to be inadequate.

Daniel tried each of these ways and then abandoned them, after having extracted from them whatever he found of value as "teaching" —until one day the entire meaning of the teaching flashed upon him: unification. As he wandered along the way, he picked up a piece of mica and examined it for some time and, behold, the duality of subject and object disappeared. While gazing at the object he was struck with a presentiment of unity: inseparability. But it was only after he had united himself with the object in complete concentration that he experienced the "I of union."

True unity cannot be found; it can only be achieved. The living soul also experiences itself as a duality, as tension, and as task: "There is in reality no 'I' that is worthy of the name except the 'I' of my tension . . . no pole, no force, no thing—only stream, only unification can become an I." What we commonly call I is a makeshift or expedient, a grammatical fact . . . "but the I of tension is something done, a reality. . . . To live world tension is the highest test of our being" (pp. 142, 143). He who attempts this is the "I of the world," the Unconditioned —planted in the midst of human life in all its inescapable conditionality.

The unity of life and death is learned only by him who takes upon himself their tension and who experiences life and death of the world within himself: "Then the I of this tension will awaken in you—the unconditioned, the unity of life and death" (p. 144).

Daniel is a transitional work not only from an autobiographical point of view. We do not do justice to this small work if we see it only as a preliminary stage of *I and Thou*. Historically, it anticipates the transition from life philosophy to existentialism in a way that was unique in its day. The pantheistic mysticism and vitalism of the life philosophies are retained as well as their basic world-rejoicing mood. It becomes "existential" because of its concentration on the subjective human pole of the relation I and the universe, which in this transitional situation actually has to bear world tension—until Buber's next work, *I and Thou*, with its compression of the universe in the Thou, restored the natural equilibrium. "Let us believe in man" describes Daniel's basic attitude to life, and this belief was shattered only after the experiences of World War I.

This existentialism is also atypical compared with later existentialist philosophies in that it did not disavow its origin in mystical religiosity. This was already evident from the saying of Scotus Erigena which Buber chose as a motto and later omitted:[8] "Deus in creatura mirabili et ineffabili modo creatur"—God is created in his creation in a marvelous and ineffable way—which expresses the idea, even before the time of Meister Eckhart, that the primordial ground of being, the nameless impersonal Godhead, is born in the soul.[9] Even in Eckhart we find that the birth of God in the human soul, together with the idea of the noble man as the only begotten son whom the Father begets eternally, constitute a single structure of thought and experience. This firm belief in the paradox of the mystical sonship is at the basis of Daniel's conception. The language of parable in the older mysticism is transferred to the mysterious concept "realization": God begets the son, that is, he realizes himself in man and through man even as man realizes God in the world.

Directly given sensory existence is godlike, but it must be "realized" in godliness. The godliness of the world is hidden in beings and things, and it can be brought to light only by man: "In the features of the beloved, whose self he realizes, man discerns the enigmatic countenance of the universe." [10] The verb *to know* always had for Buber something of its Hebrew connotation of *to embrace lovingly*; it is not something that is consummated by thought alone. To know is to touch: "the contact between the ineffable whirl of things and the vivifying powers of the senses, which are more than and different from vibrations of the ether, the nervous system, the perception and association of impressions—which are bodily spirit." [11] Thus, the realizing man feels the secret form of things with his limbs and in his heart; he acknowledges the majesty of things, "so that he may speak and celebrate it and reveal its form to men." [12] The experience of embracing a tree, described by Buber as early as 1901 in his essay on Boehme, reappeared in *Daniel* in more explicit form; but basically it is the same relation phenomenon which now becomes unification and transformation, both steadfastness and embrace, and whose meaning is fulfilled in revealing the being-form of existence. "Realization" is directed to the mystery of the real in its unimpaired sensory reality, to formative reality as it is given to us.

The unified man attains his own unity in a mysterious way. In the preface to *Daniel* this manner of knowing is proclaimed in the simple concreteness of an everyday experience: "After a downward climb, which I had to make immediately because of the approaching dusk of a dying day, I stood at the edge of a meadow, certain of the right road, and let the dusk descend upon me. Not needing a support and yet willing to accord my tarrying a fixed point, I pressed the tip of my walking-stick against the trunk of an ash tree. I then felt in twofold fashion my contact with its being: there where I held the stick, and there where the stick touched the bark. Appearing to be only where I was, I found myself nonetheless there too where I found the tree." Daniel, who realizes the being-form and through it attains his own unity, is again the "son of man" of the poem "Das Wort an Elijahu" in which the father would realize himself here and now. To repeat the creation word "Let there be" means to kindle the divine spark within things and to make manifest the hidden meaningful form within them, their Tao. In *Daniel* we see that "being made in the image of God" is creative power, and *to realize* means to make use of this formative power.

Daniel is still the brother of the mythical folk heroes, of the "sons" of God in the early days of mankind; and he is the apostle of the "teaching" of the East that never grows old and always begins anew, the messenger who brings to the Occident the knowledge of "the one thing above all that is needful." In *Daniel* we have the adumbration of an East-West synthesis and the unexpressed implication of the mediating role of Judaism between the Orient and the Occident. Daniel's message is of the here and now, and is bound to no religion or philosophy. It stands for all knowledge that is lived truth, way, unification, realization, for the "unending ethos of the moment." From the standpoint of man only "the one thing that is needful" can serve as an answer to the primal One.

Buber fully agreed with Dilthey's thesis that the question concerning the nature of man must find its answer in history. He therefore proceeded to investigate the philosophical and religious systems of the past and to trace the folk myths and sagas of the East and West. In these investigations he frequently came across the myth of the realization of the godlike on earth, of the unity that becomes multiplicity and seeks to return to unity. Buber was concerned not with the historical situation and the knowledge it affords us concerning the structure of the world, but with the way that is to be taken and the message that is to be transmitted. Precisely because the way is one and open to all men he was constrained to simplify its essence and to ignore the adventitious growth of magic, gnosticism, and dogma. The specifically historical features are the ephemeral ones; that which remains is man as the unity of the way, the truth, and life.

Buber was never content to go only part of the way; he was constantly impelled to go back to origins. In his teaching in *Daniel* he always had in mind the founders of the great religions and judged them in accordance with the highest possible standard: a being-form in which the Ought is fused into a self-proclaimed life and into a message that leaps like an electric spark from man to man. All genuine knowledge proceeds from a life form, from the unity of life and word, and is transmitted as the unity of life and word into myth, whose guardians and preservers are the poets.

Buber's concern was never with poetry as such, with the arbitrary power of the word, or with the calculated passion of "making." Here again he was impelled to seek origins, to find a form to give shape to things which are life and yet poetry. In the word, which is at the same time gesture, and expression, which is still form, he hoped to find the primordial speech of mankind. The world takes place in the word, and there is no world that does not become word. The preface to the first edition of *Daniel* thus concluded with a symbolism of unification: "At that time the dialogue appeared to me." Word here is not only concept; it is also a sign, and it is the invocation of things as signs of divine Omnipresence.

With this work Buber had hoped to renew the primal myth for his own time. The form he chose, that of the philosophical dialogue, not only does justice to the inquisitive understanding but also goes beyond it. Here Buber found the poetical element, the language of parable, to be indispensable—but it was subordinated to the service of the "teaching."

In the end Daniel, who bears the "world tension" and who embraces religions as God embraces his creation, goes beyond the founders of the teaching. He is like all human originators, even Adam, the first-born of creation. The great creative spirit always retains something of man's nearness to God before the Fall, an unmediated relationship which still knows nothing of the fear of the Lord. Again and again the cardinal sin of pride arises in him, and "the grace which makes him who is borne the bearer" becomes at the same time the temptation of human creativity. "To write poetry is presumptuous," Goethe said in his *Westöstlicher Divan*; and to the verses, "Allah need no longer create/ We create his world," he added the complementary verse, "What are you doing in the world? It is already made,/ The Lord of Creation has foreseen everything." As bold and comprehensive as the conception of this life teaching is, Daniel's "I of the world" remains powerless; the "world tension" which it bears does not go beyond the realm of literature and the subjective. Buber's demands were too exacting for ordinary mortals who, unlike him, had not given themselves to mystical speculations nor been imbued with their emotional values. His ideas, for all their conceptual beauty and depth, remained in the precarious state in which the German spirit found itself before World War I, immersed in a naive Romanticism with its excessive claims for the purely spiritual and poetical aspects of life. Not until the appearance of his *I and Thou* did Buber break through to the primal reality that is the common possession of all men.

"Eritis sicut Deus" is today, as always, the temptation of creative man. Daniel's existentialism has titanic features, and the fire he would fain bring from heaven is—and this is as true of Goethe as it is for the other proponents of "life" in the past—the eternity of the moment. It is no accident that the mysterious stranger, whose voluntary death provided the occasion for the last dialogue with Daniel, bears the name of the prophet Elijah who was granted immortality and of whom it is said: "He who dies in the completed unity of his life utters the I that is not suspended: which is the naked eternity." [13]

The titanic features we find in *Daniel* are compensated for by Buber's remarkable naiveté. His mystical experience is meant to realize God, but it fails to see that this is the path that leads to the deification of man, which was the prevalent view of his day. Man's task, which he called "realizing," is not yet the reality that is given us; and the Thou which confronts man cannot be created by him in a lightning flash of unification, but must be accepted in its otherness. The "high excitement," which is "more precious and sacred than desire and pain" and to which Daniel surrenders to achieve transformation and unification, is not yet free of "refraction" which has an independent existence of its own. It is the preform of the creative gesture with which the magicians of antiquity conjured up the "eternal" form of the Other.

The *Dialogues of Realization* thus represent the final stage of a development, pointing to that new beginning of "self-determination" with which Buber later began the "Way of Man according to Hasidic Teaching": that moment when God asked Adam: "Where art thou? Where art thou in your world?"

ADDRESSES ON JUDAISM

The basic theme that connects the life teaching of *Daniel* with *Addresses on Judaism* is that of "the renewal of the entire man." As early as 1900 Buber had defined the nature and goal of the Jewish Renaissance, which he viewed as part of the movement of a growing "self-determination of the national soul," as the form that proclaimed a new humanitarian culture for the Jewish people.[14] Buber was convinced that a true renaissance can never emerge from purely national tendencies but must be based on "humanism" and be nourished by a new conception of human nature: "Europe's national speech-cultures thus came into being because a new intellectual world was urgently seeking free expression." [15]

This world feeling came to Buber first as a vague intimation on a gentle morning breeze: "I mean that new attitude to the world that is beginning to germinate in us, the men of today who are in the vanguard, and then pass on and sprout in the men of some future generation. This human world feeling is still unexpressed today. The forming of this world feeling and the renewal of Judaism are two aspects of the same process. 'For salvation comes from the Jews': the basic tendencies of Judaism are the elements out of which a new conception of the world word is again and again created. Thus, the most deep-seated humanity of our soul and the deepest Judaism of our soul mean and desire the same thing." [16] It is the task of spiritual Zionism to free Judaism to perform "its deed in humanity" and to enable it to speak a new world word to our time.

To anticipate the content of this new world word seemed to Buber in 1911 to be premature, but he clearly saw the direction it would take: it would arise now as always from the concern "to have spirit enter into life." [17] This primal force in Judaism that resists all attempts to sever religion from ethics, the national from the social principle, and seeks to merge them into "a world of the unity of all life on earth," struck a responsive chord in the religious aspirations of that day. Men were no longer content to accept the incongruous situation wherein the soul is saved while the unredeemed world is left to go its own way. They now sought to realize the unity of spirit and world, to find true freedom, freedom in God—and here the aspiration of mankind coincided with the primal forces of Judaism.

We thus find the main theme of *Addresses* to be the same as that of *Daniel*: realization. They differ, however, in that realization is treated on another level. In place of the fictitious dialogues of realization we have actual addresses delivered to a group of young people and open to discussion and refutation. This meant that at the very outset the realm of inwardness was left behind and the ground of reality reached. "The true place of realization is the community." [18]

The message that Buber proclaimed in *Daniel* and *Addresses on Judaism* before World War I was essentially the same: the "renewal of the whole man" through the "realization" of the godlike in the world. The message in *Daniel*, which is addressed to all mankind, was not delivered in the polemical, pseudo-prophetic tone of Nietzsche. Its teaching, which was the renewal of the primal myth, was to proclaim itself; it was to restore people to a mythical relationship and encourage them to cultivate an unconditional attitude to the Absolute. Buber's message was addressed to a definite period in world history as was the message of the ancient prophets, but it had a different purpose. It looked to the world as one would look into a mirror in which the "signs of the primal being" could be deciphered by one who understands the language of mythical truth and takes every event of the past and present as a "seal of the world spirit of which he has a presentiment": "He accepts whatever befalls him as a message; he does what is necessary for him to do as a commission and a demonstration." [19]

The explanation of the world through "signs" that we find in *Daniel* proceeded, like Goethe's later mysticism of the world's "primal relations," from symbol concepts which constitute an "alphabet of the world-spirit." But the belief in a symbolic structure cannot be communicated. Even Goethe's nature symbolism was accepted by his time only when it was concealed in the garb of great poetry. It could not be conveyed simply by knowledge, for it presupposed in the reader a common basic experience, namely, that a definite concept becomes a "sign" and that a fundamental fact of being is revealed in it. The myth in Buber's *Daniel* was just as little understood as Goethe's humanistic science of nature.

Addresses on Judaism were directed to a well-defined community that could be appealed to on the basis of common memories and experiences of the Jewish past. More than any other people the Jews are a community held together by common memories,[20] preserving the Jewish legacy through the centuries because of a "passion for tradition" which came down from father to son through the peculiar "potency of the Jewish collective memory." In such a community based on common memories it was not a Romantic notion for Buber to assert that the "teaching" was not something completed, but "a mighty process of spiritual creation, a creative answer to the unconditioned which has not yet been concluded." [21] The myth of *Addresses* has not the world-wide range of *Daniel* since it is limited to the Jewish past, and so understood. The message of the renewal of man could here be contained in a familiar word which belongs to the basic concepts of the Jewish religion: *return*. Renewal, as a recovery of "buried ancient treasures," referred to well-known events and memories. Buber declared in his address "On

Youth and Religion" (1919): "Without intimate connection with his people man remains wayward and scattered when God calls him."

Addresses on Judaism owe their origin to an invitation extended to Buber by an association of Jewish students at the University of Prague which was called Bar Kochba, after a Jewish military commander who led the last revolt against the Roman domination of Judea in the second century. The young Zionist students of this association wished to learn from Buber the real meaning of Herzl's thesis that the Jews were a *people*. This was the beginning of that enduring influence that Buber had on young people and which was later to make him the great teacher of an entire generation.[22] Among those who organized and attended the addresses were some who in later years became part of Buber's intimate circle of friends and supporters. In 1930 when Buber was fifty, Hans Kohn published a comprehensive biography of him. Kohn, in his autobiography *Living in a World Revolution* (1964),[23] described the intellectual life of prewar Prague, including the activities of the Bar Kochba society and a characterization of its most prominent members, pointing out once more how much Buber's book, which marked the end of his youth, had meant to him at the time.[24]

Another outstanding member who attended the addresses was Robert Weltsch whose attachment to Buber was based primarily on their common conception of spiritual and political Zionism. For many years, until his emigration in 1938, Weltsch was the publisher of the *Jüdische Rundschau* in Berlin. For the second edition of Kohn's book in 1961, Weltsch wrote a lengthy epilogue on Buber's activities and writings since 1930 with the same reflective clarity that distinguished his smaller works on Buber.

In his introduction to Buber's *Der Jude und sein Judentum*,[25] Weltsch referred to Hugo Bergmann, an older member of the society, who is also mentioned in Kohn's *Memoirs* and who was responsible for introducing Buber to the Bar Kochba group. While still a young man Bergmann had joined the Hebrew Renaissance movement of Eastern Jewry and had become well versed in Hebrew; after World War I he emigrated to Palestine where he became professor of philosophy at the Hebrew University in Jerusalem and its first rector.

Daniel was an attempt to achieve a synthesis between the Orient and the Occident, but it failed to have any permanent influence. *Addresses on Judaism* were destined to become to a lesser extent a spiritual bridge between East and West, drawing more closely together the eastern Jews and the assimilated Jews of central and western Europe. Prague's geographical position as the gateway to the West for the Slavic world made it an ideal meeting place between East and West. It was in Prague that Kafka found his way back to Judaism after attending a performance by East European Jewish actors. Buber's personality combined elements of both East and West because of his childhood experiences among East European Jews, his dedication to the renewal of Hasidism, and his espousal of Achad Haam's cultural program in the early days of Zionism. That a man like Buber, who was so deeply imbued with the best German culture of his age, recalled the assimilated Western Jews to the original sources of their religious past which had been preserved by the East European Jews, and that he pointed to a new life of the future in which these two different segments of the nation could again be united in spirit, was under the circumstances of that day and age an achievement of considerable significance.

The first three addresses—"Judaism and the Jews," "Judaism and Humanity," and "The Renewal of Judaism"—were given in Prague between 1909 and 1911, and appeared in 1911 in book form under the title: *Drei Reden über das Judentum* [Three addresses on Judaism]. The second three addresses—"The Spirit of the Orient and Judaism," "Jewish Religiosity," and "Myth in Judaism"—were given in the years 1912 to 1914 and published in 1915 in a book with the title, *Vom Geist des Judentums* [The spirit of Judaism]. The seventh address, "The Holy War," was given in 1918 and published a year later. In the 1923 edition of the collected *Addresses*, "Herut: On Youth and Religion" was added—ten years being spent, all in all, in their preparation. For the 1923 edition, Buber wrote a preface in which he explained how the addresses formed a unit and how in preparing them many problems were clarified without, however, appreciably affecting his original basic views. To prevent this "clarification" from being misinterpreted as "conversion" he undertook to define more precisely some of the basic concepts and to rephrase formulations that might lead to misunder-standing—all of which was done, however, in order to elucidate his views and not to correct them.

Buber seemed to fear that his *Addresses* would give rise to misun-derstandings or, it may be, he had already encountered them. Even in his intimate circle there had been some criticism that they lacked a unified theme. Franz Rosenzweig, in "Die Bauleute. Ueber das Ge-setz" [The Builders. On the law], regarded them as a conversion from the conceptual construction of the "Absolute" and the "World Spirit" to the living God.[26] Hugo Bergmann, in "Martin Buber and Mysti-cism" (1963),[27] took the view that the address "Herut" represented a significant turning point which was later explicitly expressed in the 1923 preface.

It is true that the first address seems to have little in common with the religious reality that emerges so clearly and convincingly in "He-rut." It may very well be, however, that in this matter Buber's critics are the victims of a false perspective which leads them to exaggerate the differences in the basic intellectual factors in his interpretation of Juda-ism. Buber stated in his preface to "Judaism and the Jews" [27a] that the common theme of *Addresses* dealt with Judaism as a phenomenon of re-ligious reality; and by this he meant that Judaism is to be understood not as a system of abstract concepts but as lived life, and that "religious reality" refers to what takes place between man and God and not only to what takes place within man.

Thus, the first question that Buber asked in seeking to define the nature of Judaism was whether it is still possible in our day to under-stand Judaism as religion, whether Jews are still capable of a belief that is something more than "a humanity embellished with monotheism," a belief that not only recognizes God as Truth but as a Reality that one attests to with one's very life. Such a religiosity was now seen by Buber as only a memory of the past.

Another answer to the question concerning the nature of Judaism has it that the Jews constitute a nation. It was on this point especially that the Zionist society addressed by Buber sought clarification. If this answer intended nothing more than to indicate the unique character of the Jews among the nations, then another question arises: What is it that makes a people an autonomous reality in the life of an individual, so that he feels its force not only in the world around him but also within himself?

Just as a child learns only gradually to distinguish his body and his "I" from the environment, so also does the adult become aware of his environment—with its constant factors: home, language, mores—earlier than he becomes aware of the permanent substance within him which is the bearer of his impressions and experiences. But once he is touched by the feeling of immortality, he senses within him another bond that ties him to his people, one that reaches out far beyond his own life into the past and the future. He learns that "the deepest layers of our being are determined by blood, that our thinking and will are colored by it to their very core." Thus he finds his place in the chain of the generations, recognizes the past of his people as his own destiny and its future as his own task: "On the first level his people represented the world to him; now they represent his soul."

In general the community of home, language, and customs is the same as the community of blood. This, however, is not true in the case of the Jew. His essential nature cannot develop in the world around him; until he has learned that blood is the formative element of his life and the deepest force of his soul, he feels the tragic duality of his existence. In acknowledging his origin, however, he must accept not only the greatness but the tragedy and shame of the Jewish past as well, and place his hopes in the Jewish future: "My people is my soul." As he looked into the future, Buber was convinced that the powerful forces active in this most tragic and incomprehensible people have not yet been felt and that Judaism has not yet spoken its distinctive word in history.

As early as 1930 Hans Kohn stated in his book that "Judaism and the Jews" was not so much a contribution to the Jewish national consciousness as it was to the new, ethical-religious nationalism prevalent in Europe in the days before World War I.[28] In his *Memoirs* he points out the significance of Fichte's *Addresses to the German Nation* with its folk myth and its influence at that time not only in Germany but also among the Zionists of the Prague Circle who regarded their situation to be similar to that of the Germans before their War of Liberation.[29]

Furthermore, the views of Gustav Landauer could be cited in support of this comparison as we find, for example, in his letter to Hedwig Lachmann (21.6.1900): "The further we descend into the depths of our individual lives and the more we withdraw from conceptual thinking and the sensuous gazing into our most secret and ineffable self, the more do we become part of this real community with its forces of race, humanity, animality. For this world lives in us. . . ." [30] And three years later we find in his "Skepsis und Mystik": "That which man is by his very nature, that which is his innermost and most indefeasible possession, is the great community of the living within him, his lineage and his blood-community." [31]

During the period in which Landauer expressed these thoughts (1900–1903), Buber's own vague, mystical experiences of cosmic unification were similar to those of his friend. About 1910 Buber's deep interest in Hasidism became evident, and around the core of his ecstatic experience and his extensive studies in mysticism there developed a comprehensive symbolic and conceptual structure. At that time Judaism meant to him more than he expressed in his first Prague address. He was more concerned with the road that must still be traversed before genuine religious reality can be reached. This preparatory work he regarded as absolutely necessary, and in this connection his recollections of 1900 are not without significance. In Prague Buber addressed people who were about ten years younger than himself, and he may have had in mind the road that he himself had taken. His task, as he then saw it, was to help these young people, who were driven about by the *Zeitgeist* and cut off from the sources of their national culture, to achieve that unification in being on which his own living faith rested. Thus, the idea of a community of blood and destiny that he developed in his address was not the same as that of the other rising nationalisms or of the mystique of blood and origin that was in vogue at the time. To the young people who had trustingly put to him the question concerning their national consciousness, he earnestly sought to give an answer that would touch the reality of their individual lives. He thus described to them the tension between the world around them and that deep power within them for which they had no name, and he pointed out to them the way that would lead them to their common destiny where they would feel more secure. In Buber's view religious reality cannot be experienced without the mythical, primordial shudder that comes from contact with elemental powers: the road to the original powers of the spirit leads through the elemental soul, and the highest creative deed is adumbrated in the originating impulse of the body itself, in its *Urhebertrieb*. Buber experienced the elemental soul of creation as cosmic unification that was constantly reaffirmed with the intense and unclouded vision of a flash of lightning. His listeners felt as if they had been cast adrift on a dark stream that transported them back into the past history of their own people—an experience that was familiar to Buber from the days of his own youth.

The first address dealt with the duality between Outer and Inner; the second, "Judaism and Mankind," [32] dealt with the tensions within the individual. In the realm of elemental life, polarity prevails; and he who identifies himself unreservedly with the total life of the people, with its greatness and with its humiliation, finds an abyss opening up within his own soul. The Jewish people experienced the mystery of this original deep-seated duality as no other people; but they also preserved, as no other people, a striving for unity. Wherever the Jew became creative, he did so in conjunction with his search for unity— within himself, in his people, in mankind, and between God and man.

Judaism had once created the great symbol of inner duality: the separation between good and evil or sin. But in the course of its history, it had learned how to overcome this division; its creative deed was rooted in the attempt to make the soul one. Everyone who made this his personal task participated in this great process, and thus staked his life on the conviction that the powers of ancient Judaism have not been exhausted in the centuries of exile: "Judaism cannot give new materials, new meaning-contents to mankind, as other nations do, for the Jew's relation to material existence, to things, is not strong enough; it can only offer, ever anew, a unification of mankind's diverse contents, and ever new possibilities of synthesis. At the time of the prophets and of early Christianity it offered a religious synthesis; at the time of Spinoza an intellectual synthesis, at the time of socialism a social synthesis. And for what synthesis is the spirit of Judaism preparing itself today?

Perhaps for a synthesis of those syntheses." Buber here had in mind a renewal of mankind, which would be at once religious and social and which would proclaim "a world of God which needs to be realized in both the life of individual man and the life of the community: the world of unity."

In the third address, "The Renewal of Judaism," [33] Buber set forth the meaning of that rebirth and renewal of the whole man which, ever since his early days, he had envisaged as the goal of his Zionist work. He was well aware that he was dealing with concepts which must necessarily give offense in an age that believed in the dogma of evolution. Renewal means the total change to an unconditional and heroic life, to a mode of action which in ancient times was expected to change the face of the earth.

Such a mode of action must combine the three interrelated ideas that, since time immemorial, have been decisive for Judaism: the idea of unity, the idea of the deed, and the idea of the future. The Jew's striving for unity gave birth to the idea of the one living God, which was the object of the mightiest passion in human history, the passion of the prophets. The yearning for unity between God and the world was fulfilled by the shekinah, by the idea of the "indwelling" of God in the world; a Jew [Spinoza] created the idea of "God-Nature," of the world-being God. The idea of the deed has always been a focal point of Jewish religiosity, just as it has been the deed and not the belief that constitutes for the Oriental the decisive bond between man and God. Even after Jewish religiosity had petrified into law during the centuries of the Diaspora, the deed, as the unconditioned decision for God, remained the root of "absolute" life in Judaism, preserving its underground existence in the religion of the common people—the movements of the Essenes, early Christianity, and, in modern times, Hasidism bear witness to this phenomenon. Not the content of the deed but the manner in which it is performed is its decisive element. The great Hasidim taught that man himself is a Thora, an "instruction," which is both life and teaching. The original idea of Judaism, however, is messianism, the idea of the absolute future. On the outermost horizon of being, in a realm otherwise inhabited by evanescent dreams, the Jew undertook "to build a house for mankind, the house of true life." Here for the first time the Absolute was proclaimed the goal to be realized in and by humanity.

Only over against this true life of Judaism can the full extent of the degeneration and rootlessness of its present existence be measured. No reform can save us here, but only a total about-face, a "renewal from the root to all the ramifications of being." Only when every individual realizes in his own life the mighty forces of the Jewish past is there hope that the spirit will be rekindled into life: "To be prepared means to prepare."

In the two important addresses, "The Spirit of the Orient and Judaism" and "Myth in Judaism," [34] the "teaching" of the Orient is contrasted with the culture of the West, and myth, as a primary form of our creative life, is given a new basis and made more acceptable to modern man. This attempt reflects Buber's conception of the significance of myth in the years prior to World War I, [35] when his deepest concern for the fate of his people was inseparable from his own life teaching as set forth in his *Dialogues on Realization.*

That salvation will come from the Jews even in our day is a hope that Buber derived from the circumstance that the Jew has remained an Oriental. The heavens and hells experienced by the Jew in the centuries of his sojourn in the Occident have caused deep injury to his soul. The Emancipation tempted him with the glory of the world, and he succumbed to its allurements. But deep within him the primordial strength of his soul, "the immortal Jewish urge for unity," remained unimpaired. The Jews are the latecomers of the Orient, destined by history to be a mediating people and messengers of Asia's life truths to the West: "In those Jews the great idea of Asia became exemplary for the Occident—the Asia of boundlessness and of holy unity, the Asia of Lao-tzu and Buddha, which is the Asia of Moses and Isaiah, of Jesus and Paul." [36] The Jew who returned to Palestine and attempted anew the ancient task of building a model community in the ancient home of his people could thereby lay the foundation for a teaching of the future in which the spirit of the Orient and the Occident is fused into one unity: "It is up to us to seek the salvation of Jerusalem, which is the salvation of the nations."

In the comprehensive picture of the religious and historical life of the Orient presented in the fourth address, Buber reduced the whole idea of the renewal of Judaism to the central concept of the Jewish religion, the concept of *teshuvah*—return, reversal, turning-point, decision to turn to God—which he again discussed in the fifth address, "Jewish Religiosity," [37] and elaborated along historical lines.

"Renewal of Judaism means in reality renewal of Jewish religiosity": henceforth the total phenomenon of Judaism as "religious reality" was placed first in discussion. In this connection Buber distinguished sharply between religion and religiosity. Religiosity is the unmediated personal relationship to the Unconditioned, the desire for a living participation with it, the will to realize it in the world through action. Religion adopts the religiosity of a definite period with its precepts and dogmas, and gives it final form not in accordance with a creative but with an organizational principle. Religiosity begins anew with every young person; it means being shaken to the core of one's being when confronted with the mystery of life. Religion is primarily concerned with preserving and transmitting precepts, dogmas, and customs necessary for its survival and well-being.

This renewal can take place only by ever new acts of decision for God as the realization of divine freedom and unconditionality on earth. The "conversion" to the unconditioned life, which each man must make directly out of the depths of his inner duality, establishes a life communion with God which the author of the second Psalm had already captured in a mighty symbol, and which Buber again encountered in Meister Eckhart: "Thou art my son; this day have I begotten thee."

Jewish religiosity is based on "the one thing that is needful"; it knows that the truth must be done. In the unconditionality of his deed, man experiences communion with God. "God's countenance reposes invisibly in an earthen block; it must be wrought, carved out of it." We can do this by participating in the building of the true human community, in that each of us "in his own place, and in the natural context of a life shared with others will perform what is just, unifying, and formative: for God does not wish to be believed, discussed, or defended by us, but simply to be realized through us."

The true human community is the theme of the seventh address, "The Holy Way." [38] It was written in 1918, published a year later, and dedicated to Buber's friend, Gustav Landauer, who had died as a martyr for the true human community and whom he had in mind when he stated in his address: "Nothing new can be established by taking an autocratic constitution from one country and superimposing it on a communist one while life between man and man and also the methods of government remain unchanged. To bring about a true transformation of society, a true renaissance, human relations must undergo a change." True realization of God takes place *between* men; it is the "in-between," the seemingly empty space, where God is present in the immediacy of lived life.

What should Israel do to free itself from the ghostlike unreality of its present situation? Should it take the road of nationalism and be like all the other nations? Should it deny its origin and become the champion of a new humanity? Should it return to the observance of the letter of the law and the obsolete Jewish tradition? The way pointed out by Buber, the "holy way," is the way of the lived truth, and it passes through Zion. "In the true life between men will the new word be revealed. . . . True community is the Sinai of the future."

Buber placed his hope on the youth to create the new community, that "revolutionary colonization" in Palestine which he also called "lived religion." This was the younger generation, which he regarded as standing at a critical turning point in human history, to whom in a final address[38a] he once more pointed the way back to Judaism's original powers and to whom he imparted his deepest thoughts on religiosity: "There is only *one* way out of our misfortunes: that which leads us to freedom in God." *Herut*, "freedom," meant God's writing on the first tablets which had been intended for the people; law and instruction were engraved on the second. But again and again the primordial forces of the people strove to restore the mutilated traces of God's freedom. They broke through narrow dogmas and precepts to find freedom in God, for they were not content to see the godlike relegated to the world beyond, but sought to achieve unity with God through the "free act of the perfect man."

Youth is the time of "openness" in which every man is in touch with the Unconditioned, and then we see whether he withstands, evades, or passes it by; whether he degrades the touch of the Infinite to mere "experience" or whether he responds to it with his whole being: "with his spirit by apprehending the godlike in symbols, with his soul by loving the universe, with his will by meeting the test in active life."

In this trial youth can rely on a great source of strength that will come to its aid: the living community of the people, the religious creative forces of his nationhood. The soul speech of the folk religion was a treasure from which even the founders of new religions drew their inspiration. The Jews, unlike those who adopted the Christian faith, did not graft a foreign spiritual principle on heathen myths. In Judaism religious development had its origin in the soul of the people, and its creative power was not severed from its vital impulses. Thus, the task of Judaism is to hallow the world in its fullness and in its sensuous reality, and not to rest before the whole answer of man to God has been given. Hasidism represented an earnest attempt to synthesize the secular and the spiritual, to fuse deep religious feeling with the simplicity and fullness of natural life; it was in the direction of such a synthesis that Buber saw the future of Judaism: "In the growing striving for this synthesis is youth's guarantee that when it descends into the depths of Jewish religion in search of help for its soul, it will not find decomposing rocks but the waters of genuine life."

In this last address as well, Buber made a sharp distinction between religiosity and religion, and admonished youth not to flee the Unconditioned in search of rigid religious forms. We desecrate law and instruction when we accept them without saying Yea to the whole of the human soul. True Judaism that insists on the realization of God by man was for him the folk religion which leads an underground life and, "although secret and suppressed, is the authentic, productive religion in contradistinction to an official, sham Judaism whose power and whose public representation are without authority or legitimacy." [39] What passes for Judaism today is its "relative life," the succession of generations, and a barren, dialectical spirituality. Only the absolute life of a people is of permanent significance for the human spirit, only those tendencies of the folk character which can be translated into spiritual values and deeds, and which have been expressed in the history of Judaism with uncommon vigor and depth.

In this subterranean absolute life of Judaism, religious originality was at work creating myths. The presence of a myth in Jewish monotheism was for a long time unjustly denied. The ancient Jew had no other way of expressing himself except mythically, and whatever he found of interest and worth relating dealt with Yahwe's deeds over against his people and rested on an all-pervading "metaphysical causality." Buber distinguished between two basic forms of Jewish myth that had developed throughout the centuries: the saga of the deeds of Yahwe, and the legends of the life of the "central" or the "perfect realizing man"—the myth of world preservation and the myth of world redemption.

The "central" or the "perfect realizing man" is familiar to us from Buber's study of myths and from his dialogues in *Daniel*. Buber also called him the "fulfilling" man because, as a living teaching, he brought to fulfillment the religious tendencies of his people by his very existence. Religiosity for Buber was always an unmediated myth-creating life in which the experience of the godly expressed itself in symbols. The very juxtaposition of *Daniel* and *Addresses* is highly instructive in defining the nature of religiosity and its limits. The teaching of Daniel was an unanchored, free-floating creative religiosity, a bold synthesis of the myths of all peoples and cultures. Man here bears "world tension" without the support of a definite religion; he "comprehends" the world and consecrates it to God in the full presence of his total human existence. Buber in *Daniel* was not successful in conveying to his age the teaching of "the one thing that is needful."

In *Addresses*, however, religiosity is seen in the "soul-circle" of the ancestral religion. Here Buber's otherwise clear distinction between these two concepts lost some of its force and, no doubt unintentionally, their common features became more prominent. Here also Buber spoke only of the significance attached to religiosity as the bearer of Judaism's spiritual life-ground and development, but he failed to appreciate the importance of fixed forms for the preservation of religious life among the non-creative masses of believers. In *Addresses* Judaism is taken to be absolute, unconditional life, that is, myth. But this myth of Judaism reached the Jews because it was intimately connected with the religious reality of the people.

Hugo Bergmann explains the "great turning" that he seems to detect in "Herut" as the sharp distinction which Buber made in this address between God and God's proclamation to man: "In the earlier writings the godlike threatened to coalesce with the human, so that we find formulations there which remind us of Feuerbach's anthropocentrism." [40] Thenceforth, however, the Unconditioned became the great Opposite, and God's deeds over against man were the primary reality.

This affinity to Feuerbach was evident in the early work on Boehme in 1901[41] in which, as in the essay on Nietzsche written a year later, Buber spoke of a "becoming God" in a sense that obscures or even opposes a "being God." But soon thereafter, under the influence of German mysticism, he underwent a change that caused him to adopt the idea of the "realization of God by man" which dominated his early work: "Man appeared to me as that being through whose existence the Absolute resting in its truth can acquire the character of reality." [42] In Meister Eckhart this realization was represented by a symbol of the birth of God in the soul of man, a symbol that made a deep impression on Buber. But only in Hasidism did his studies of mysticism find a suitable vehicle for his personal religious experiences. The central symbol of his passionate urge for realization of the godlike became the concept with which Hasidism designated the union of God with his shekinah: yichud. This Hasidic concept is not only an acknowledgment of God's unity but also a being-act of the whole man and a meeting between God and man: "Man brings about the unity of God, that is, through him the unity of becoming, the divine unity of creation, is accomplished . . . in which the primordial unity of unseparated being finds its cosmic counter-image: unity without multiplicity in the union of multiplicity." [43] German mysticism as well as Jewish mysticism assumed that outside of God's becoming and activities in the world, there is a God who is an unattainable transcendental Being; and this signified for Buber an irrefragable certainty, a basic assumption of his thinking which is evident not only in *Der Grosse Maggid* (1922) but also in the *Legend of the Baal-Shem* and *Legends of Rabbi Nachman*. During all the years in which the addresses were given, "to realize" meant for Buber "to unify reality" and, as he stated in the preface, "to prepare the world as a place for God's reality."

He could thus with perfect justice refrain from identifying himself, as Scheler did, with the idea of a "becoming God": ". . . not as if I were uncertain of a godlike becoming in immanence, but because it is only from the deep certainty of the divine Being that we can apprehend the mysterious sense of God's becoming, his participation in Creation and his sympathy with the fate of its freedom; but without this deep assurance, God's name is but a pale pretence for the true God."

This thought was expressed in the address "Herut": "Primary reality is constituted by the effect of the unconditional upon the human mind." [44] The designation "the unconditional" is also characteristic: Buber would continue for a long time to describe the unattainable mystery of the being God with abstract concepts. We can safely say that Buber always meant "God" and not a metaphysical idea or an ethical ideal, and that God was to him not something created by man or something that has evolved in man. Buber in the preface did not succumb to the tendency of his contemporaries who saw in religion a form of human productivity which belonged to the realm of culture and in which God became more or less a fiction.

Such a fiction, however, must be carefully distinguished from myth, which man does not imagine *(einbildet)* but which is formed within him *(ein-bildet)*. Here God is the great Opposite, the "Thou *an sich.*" Man "withstands the Almighty by the strength of his vision . . . he grasps that which is in itself incomprehensible by the creation of the symbol." This is comparable to gathering up the waters of the universal streams in cups or capturing the flash of primeval light in a mirror—but it is man's most appropriate way of testifying to his meeting with the Divine. These symbols of the human spirit are also capable of growth and interiorization: "It is not God who changes but only theophany, the manifestation of the Divine in man's symbol-creating mind—until no symbol is adequate any longer, and none is needed; and life itself, in the miracle of man's being with man, becomes a symbol; until God is truly present when one man clasps the hand of another." [45]

"The theophany changes" means here that the history of the

human spirit is also true, in a figurative sense, of the individual—God can reveal himself in the life of man in different ways. To Buber this revelation first came as an elemental cosmic unification, as the flash in the divine sparks hidden in things—to use the symbolism of Jewish mysticism—as the touch of Tao in things in order to make them "alive and manifest" or in Goethe's language: "In all the elements there is God's presence." Buber's experiences are not to be dismissed as semi-aesthetic or secondary. Revelation always involves an act of surrender to the divine ray of meaning in beings and things which, through loving and steadfast devotion, becomes creative when the individual "comprehends" the Opposite with his whole human presence—whereby, of course, the unification is at first not consciously felt as an Opposite. In this process, which Buber in *Daniel* called "realizing," the confrontation of I and Thou is in this sense anticipated.

We must accept Buber's unusual pan-sacramentalism and assume the genuineness of his elemental feeling for God, if we are to understand the language of his preface of 1923. That he had overestimated man's creative possibilities in his emphasis on God realization and thus succumbed to the prevailing fashion of the *Zeitgeist* need not be denied. But his primary concern was always God and not the personal I; "to bear world-tension" meant to him the passionate task of consecrating the whole world to God. The sentence from the fifth address, cited by Bergmann, "God's countenance reposes invisibly in an earthen block; it must be wrought, carved out of it," is not to be interpreted as man's vain delusion that he could create God. The image was inspired by Michelangelo's famous torsi in Florence,[46] and reflected Buber's enthusiasm for the task of realizing God, for the being-God was at that time far removed from him and beyond any revelation.

In the matter of the origin of representations and images, Buber placed too great an emphasis on man's share in creation—for example, when he spoke at the Sociological Conference in 1910, using Simmel's social-psychological language. In the preface he clearly stated that the idea and representation of God never arise from the human spirit alone, but only from "mutual contact of the divine and the human, from meeting." *Daniel* had shown that even the noblest and purest will cannot produce religious "teaching," and that God's will and participation are also indispensable. An Esperanto religion is just as impossible as an Esperanto language. The *Addresses*, on the other hand, places Buber on the path of *re-ligio* (a binding back) and leads him back to the creative depths of his ancestral religion. This path is the stream that flows from the past into the future and bears the blood, through the elemental soul of the folk, back to its original spiritual source.

In his later years Buber spoke of "the theophany changes" as the circumstance that all his being-experiences between 1912 and 1919 had become present to him "in a growing measure as one great experience of faith. By this an experience is meant which transports a person in all his component parts, including his capacity for thought, so that, all the doors springing open, the storm blows through all the chambers." [47]

The storm is the accompanying symbol of a new revelation just as it is in another place the night, when Buber spoke of that decisive hour of personal existence "in which we must forget all that we erroneously thought we knew of God, retaining nothing traditional, nothing acquired by learning, no scraps of knowledge, but immersed in the night." [48] But storm and night are only the harbingers of an ineffable and mysterious present: "Revelation does not flash from the cloud but from the lowly things themselves; it whispers to us in the course of every ordinary day, and it is alive quite near us, quite close; the shekina dwells about us. . . . This is the history of Israel, as it is the history of the human person. . . ." [49]

The new revelation spoke the language of "vanishing silence." The "being" God, until now hidden by the abstractions, the Absolute, the Unconditioned, revealed himself as an experience in which the eternal present becomes a Voice—not Elohim, the creative power of God in nature, but "the unconfined God, the bearer of the boundless light, the Godhead, pure Being; and precisely this absolute Godhead acts as a person. . . ." [50] The absolute Being is at the same time the absolute person, and it is this person that speaks the "I" of revelation. Buber's thoughts presented here are the mystical thoughts and experiences of Hasidism, but they are at the same time declarations of his own great faith experiences of the years 1912 to 1919.

In the poem "Elijahu," which Buber wrote in 1903, we find an intimation of this Way:[51]

You wanted to descend like a storm wind
And to be mighty in deed like the tempest,
You wanted to blow being into being
And bless human souls while scourging them,
To admonish weary hearts in the hot whirlpool
And to stir the rigid to agitated light,
—You sought me on your stormy paths
And did not find me.

You wanted to soar upward like a fire
And wipe out that which did not stand your test,
Sin-powerful, you wanted to scorch worlds
And to refine worlds in sacrificial flame,
With sudden force to kindle a young nothingness
To new becoming of blessed poem,
—You sought me in your flaming abysses
And did not find me.

Then my messenger came to you
And placed your ear next to the still life of my earth,
Then you felt how seed after seed began to stir,
And all the movements of growing things encircled you,
Blood hammered against blood, and the silence overcame you,
The eternally complete, soft and motherly
—Then you had to incline upon yourself,
Then you found me.

There is in the life of a man of genius a formative anticipation which finds expression only later in life experiences and conceptual structures. The secret of these anticipations is man's "being-on-the-way," which also expresses itself in his speech, images, and symbols, reflecting the deep impulses of his heart. In this sense the legend "Die Offenbarung" [Revelation] with its image of fire that becomes light turns out to be a self-revelation: the cleansing and self-purification of the flame reproduce the process which Buber in his preface called, with reference to his own development, "clarification." These images remain faithful even in dreams: our original remembrance follows the voice of "vanishing silence," which is heard by all the senses. Whatever more is meant by such symbols one need not inquire into or discover. In the words of St. Augustine: *Secretum meum mihi,* the ultimate secret is shared by the soul with God alone.

4
The Life of Dialogue

IN THE intellectual life of Germany during the years after World War I, the ethicists separated from the aesthetes. For Buber this signified the final emergence from the misty atmosphere of creative subjectivity and a breakthrough from speculations on "realization" to reality between individuals, to the confrontation of I and Thou. That one's "I" can only be found in the tension of unification was an insight that had already been achieved by Daniel when he looked at the fragment of mica, although at that time he had still not left the realm of inwardness: "O fragment of mica," we find later in *I and Thou*,[1] "looking on which I once learned, for the first time, that I is not something 'in me' —with you I was nevertheless bound up in myself; at that time the event took place only in me, not between me and you."

This radical change in Buber is also evident in a short rhapsodic essay that he had written in the autumn of 1914, the prose hymn "To the Contemporary."[2] Here the two kinds of reality considered above were dealt with in the light of the new mood that prevailed in Buber's generation. "Power, invading power of the contemporary!" Contemporaneousness: this once meant the extension of a lived moment down to the deepest recesses of being, until "time" escaped to where it could no longer be grasped and where the present became the omnipresent: ". . . and I breathed the dreams of far distant beings; the stirrings of unknown creatures gathered in my throat, and in my blood the elements of souls mingled." Bound to one another by unending music, the great figures of all times were close to him. But this unification existed only in soul space; its contemporaneousness was subjective and nothing more than the *fata morgana* of a heightened moment.

In the autumn of 1914, however, "contemporaneousness" had become a fateful omen of blood and terror that seared the soul like a fire-brand. How could that moment which had brought to us this world-wide contemporaneousness be withstood? "Time" had become the common possession of all; the moment was the concrete today in its responsibility for the building of tomorrow. The music of reconciliation, however, remained the secret of the eternal God, the Lord of all times. The bliss of the tolling bell "All Time" may be unforgettable, but Buber will never again dismiss the Here and Now of the moment that comes but once: "Out of your fire the light is born, and nowhere is this light born except in your fire. I am consumed in you, but I am consumed into light"—again we find the image of fire that turns into light to make visible the purifying process of the soul.[3]

From these two contrasting modes of time arose the aesthetic components of Buber's ecstatic experience. The hubristic notion that in such moments man grasps the secret of world harmony is slightly intimated. Another episode of those critical years which illustrates even more convincingly the questionable intimacy between religious and aesthetic experience was recalled by Buber in the section "A Conversion" in his *Dialogue*,[4] in which he looked back on experiences that took place outside of time and space amid "rapture, flashes of illumination, transport, timeless, causeless." Here "religious" means surrendering oneself to the plenitude of life, which reminds us of the experiences of the mystics. It was after one of these "beatific hours" in which life, streaming toward death and eternity, was interrupted by a disconcerting, intruding present that an unknown young man came to see Buber. Buber received him in a friendly spirit but his soul was not present, and he failed to note that the young man was in despair and had come to him in a fateful hour of his life. By the time he had learned of this from a friend not long thereafter, the young man had already departed from this life.

Buber took this incident to heart and looked upon it as a "judgment"; from then on he regarded all timelessness that is acquired by sacrificing the moment too dearly bought. He renounced all ecstasy which removes man from daily life, and turned away from all religions which disclaim the responsibilities of every single hour. He pondered "the unending ethos of the moment" and the grave responsibilities that accrue to man every hour of his life. Time now appeared to him as a strong "spiritual bond," composed of an infinite number of moments that bind man to God and eternity.

The depth of Buber's suffering during the war can be appreciated only when we take seriously the mystical idea of world unification of his prewar days. One who was capable of feeling within himself the life of a tree with all its sap and shoots will surely be sensitive to the untold misery caused by war, and will experience its myriad sacrifices as his own annihilation. Buber was never to forget that a human being had come to him to learn the meaning of his life and had departed without receiving an answer: responsibility also included the undesired and unknown sorrow that one person unconsciously inflicts on another.

Cosmic unification once meant the proud feeling of bearing world tension. It was the language of creative love which in *Daniel* formed the "rainbow bridge from pole to pole," so that all contradictions in the soul are made fruitful and the primal polarity of life becomes one: through creative, realizing love, man demonstrates that he was made in the image of God. To a freely chosen inner world tension the war added a real world tension that brought home to Buber the impotence of creatures and the fear of God's judgment. The recreative cosmic unification is deepened into sympathy with the suffering of one's fellow creatures, and the courage to create becomes the collective strength to resist and endure. "The religious" is no longer defined as a condition nor, as Simmel defined it, "a special quality of feeling itself, a concentration or a leap, a consecration or being crushed, which in itself is religious";[5] religious experience became the confrontation of man and God, the relation to a suprahuman sphere.

During the war Buber was not a German patriot as were other Jewish philosophers of his time, among them Simmel and Hermann Cohen, nor was he politically active or a revolutionary like his friend Gustav Landauer. Like his teacher Simmel, he regarded the war as the "absolute situation" in which man is faced with a decision;[6] and, like

Landauer, he was convinced of the necessity of a spiritual renewal of mankind. But deep within his heart he was, like Hugo von Hofmannsthal, a follower of the "conservative revolution." This meant, as far as Zionism was concerned, a Jewish program of settlement in Palestine which would revolutionize the traditional forms of community life and make them more responsive to human needs; and, as far as Germany was concerned, it meant primarily educational programs and institutions: man had to change himself before he could change the forms of government. The "revolution" that Buber had in mind was the return to the inner sphere of human values, which we see from the change that took place in his own life as recorded in his fragment "A Conversion."

In 1923, ten years after the *Dialogues on Realization*, Buber's most famous work *I and Thou* appeared, a work which bore witness to a critical stage in his life and which described those being-experiences of which he became "increasingly aware as a great faith experience." [7] The earliest preliminary sketch was made in 1916, when it was conceived as the first part of an intended work of five volumes, followed three years later by what the author called "a rough copy." Two more years of "spiritual asceticism" were necessary, however, before the book appeared in its final form, for Buber was at that time still occupied with his Hasidic studies and was also preparing a course of lectures on "Religion as Presentness," to be given during 1922 in the *Freies Jüdisches Lehrhaus,* the famous institute founded by Franz Rosenzweig for the study of Judaism. This edition of *I and Thou* underwent no further changes, for it had been composed with "irresistible enthusiasm" in a language that Buber wished to preserve.

The language of *I and Thou* is unique in the history of philosophy, and its classification has to this day caused difficulties for both Buber's friends and critics. In *The Library of Living Philosophers*, volume 12, which is devoted to Buber's philosophy, it is variously described as "great poetry" and as "a philosophical-religious poem." [8] Maurice Friedman in a popular article characterized it as "a little poetic masterpiece." Among the older critics, Simon Maringer spoke of it as "dialogic theology," whereas Hermann L. Goldschmidt questioned its dialogic character and considered it the "monologue of a mystic or of a poet," for to speak of having conversations with inanimate things and invisible forces is to misunderstand the unique quality of human dialogue.[9]

In discussing the different opinions concerning this work we shall first turn to the rather lengthy concluding section called "Answer" in volume 12 of *The Library of Living Philosophers* in which Buber answered the questions and misgivings of his critics with great skill and candor. He began by describing himself as an "atypical man" who is neither a philosopher nor a theologian. He left no doubt that the basis of his philosophizing is religious: the faith experience which extended from 1912 to 1919, precisely the years in which *I and Thou* was in the making. His chief concern thenceforth was to bear witness to this faith experience: "where I may draw out of primal depths . . . I must acknowledge it." [10] Buber emphasized again and again that this experience was a purely personal one, and that it was not his task to transmit a message like the prophets or to admonish and censure in God's name, but rather to demonstrate that the experience he had and the path he took were accessible to others. He therefore had to find a conceptual language to convey the subtle texture of his nonconceptual experience to make it comprehensible to others: the language of his message had to be a philosophical one.

Buber answered the objection that such faith experiences belong to the realm of theology by asserting that he had no teaching to impart and was not authorized to make any statements on the nature of God. Although he was inclined to agree with Walter Kaufmann's characterization of him as a religious thinker rather than a philosopher, he insisted that his style of thinking differed from that of Pascal or Kierkegaard who took religion for their starting point and then attempted to harmonize their personal faith experience with it. For Buber, however, "the religious" lays claim to the entire man in the total reality of his life, without the assurance and consolation that the rigid forms of a religion afford to its believers. It is considerably more convenient to "deal with religion than with a God who banishes one from his native home and his father's house to restless wandering." [11] Buber, who rejected the idea that he has a message, still spoke with great earnestness of the "command of the task" (p. 702) and, with reference to *I and Thou*, of "the theme which has here been dictated to the experiencing thinker" (p. 692). His thinking became more responsible as a result of the "meeting" he experienced, and in his philosophizing he would never again fail to consider man as one who lives his life over against God. However, it was not a theological but a philosophical anthropology that he was attempting to formulate.

The need to make religious experience part of our common culture is a characteristic thought that is found through all of Buber's work from the end of World War I, but none of his writings testifies to it with such immediacy and such poignant language as *I and Thou*. The "irresistible enthusiasm" with which the work was written is evident in its clear, expressive formulations and its restrained yet confident tone, peculiar to the great religious documents of world literature.

Buber was spurred on by the consciousness of blazing a new path, of making a new beginning, and by a trait which Gustav Landauer had already noted in his character as early as the appearance of *Daniel*, namely, his ability to bring to the surface "being, that which lies buried, the subterranean." [12] "A neglected, obscure, primordial reality was to be made visible," as he put it in his "Answer" (p. 693). The real question was concerned with "the basic attitude in the life of every man toward all existing being" (p. 692), of the presuppositions of all philosophizing that could not be explained systematically but which could only be indicated: "I must say it once again: I have no teaching. I only point to something. I point to something in reality; I point to something in reality that has not been seen or too little seen. I take him who listens to me by the hand and lead him to the window. I throw open the window and point to what is outside." [13] In this sense Fritz Kaufmann aptly characterized Buber's philosophizing as a *Welt-Weisen*[14]—being at once world wisdom and instruction (Torah).

In reality we find the teaching which is "mighty in significance and in rescuing strength." "Being" as such reveals "the one thing that is needful," the way that could serve as a basis for "human beings to be able to live together." [15] Polarity, the world riddle of the constant disintegration of all living things, still remains part of human existence that

is beyond our understanding; but within it is to be found enduring
strength if one has the proper approach. *Daniel* has key concepts like
direction, meaning, and *unity* which open doors into life and point out a
new way, the narrow ridge above the abyss. But it was only in *I and
Thou* that Buber found the proper "primary words"—the human expressions which appear in all areas of life corresponding to the primordial movement of being, and which open up for us a new world view
from the "open window."

In the language of *I and Thou* we hear the elevated accents of
prophecy. The suggestive power of its rhythmic speech reflects the
inner participation of one who has confronted the reality of his life:

> To man the world is twofold, in accordance with his twofold atti-
> tude.
> The attitude of man is twofold, in accordance with the twofold
> nature of the primary words which he speaks.
> The primary words are not isolated words, but combined words.
> The one primary word is the combination I-Thou.
> The other primary word is the combination I-It; wherein, without
> a change in the primary word, one of the words He or She can re-
> place *It.*
> Hence the I of man is also twofold.
> For the I of the primary word I-Thou is a different I from that of
> the primary word I-It.[16]

What is expressed by the two primary words in the first section of
I and Thou? The confrontation of I and world is not something that is
fixed or permanent; it is dependent on primary words spoken by man,
that is, on two basic attitudes he can adopt with respect to the world.
"Primary words do not express something that might exist independently of them, but being spoken they bring about existence" (p. 3).
"Speaking" is understood symbolically, beyond its everyday meaning,
and denotes "the primary act of the spirit" itself; and "primary word"
contains a hidden kernel which touches on the mystery of Creation and
whose secondary meaning and connotation are only gradually developed in Buber's writings.

To speak primary words is to consummate a being-act. It involves
a decision as to which of two possibilities to be an "I" man seizes and

actualizes with his existence: I-speaking and I-existence are one for Buber, and he who speaks a primary word enters into the word and stands in it (p. 4). It is ultimately a matter of whether one faces the world and greets it with the powers of the mind or with one's unmediated being. The two primary words are not always actually "spoken," but I-Thou is always lived as elemental unification; and I-It is always a consciousness of something and involves the separation of subject and object. The one creates relation, the other knowledge, out of which the world of time and space is structured, the world view of science about which men can communicate with one another. In this world there are contents and objects; the I-Thou relation, however, is nothing but pure Presentness, limitless and incomparable: everything else lives in its light.

All transitive verbs that have something as object belong to the I-It world. Not only do "I recognize something" or "I do something" but also "I experience something," that is, inner feelings alone do not establish a relation to the world: for it is only in me and not between me and the world which does not participate in it. Here we clearly see how Buber rose above his own past. The world as experience takes place through the primary word I-It.

The relation established by the primary word I-Thou arises in three spheres: in our life with nature, with men, and with intelligible forms. In the fullest sense, the Thou can be given and accepted only in our life with men. In our life with nature, our relation is below the threshold of speech and takes place in the dark; and in our life with intelligible forms, we feel we are being addressed and we answer with our being: constructing, thinking, and acting. Buber raised the question whether it is permissible to include the extralingual sphere that lies outside of speech in the world of the primary word, and the answer he gave anticipates the third part of the work, the relation to God: "In every sphere in its own way, through each process of becoming that is present in us we look out toward the fringe of the eternal Thou; in each we are aware of a breath from the eternal Thou; in each Thou we address the eternal Thou" (p. 6).

That the world is God's creation and that all creatures are created interrelated to one another explain the fact that a tree also could become a Thou for me: here also the relation is unmediated and pure mutuality; the wholeness and unity of the tree are disclosed to me: "it is bodied over against me and has to do with me, as I with it—only in a different way" (p. 8). A light that comes from Being flares up as answer.

In the realm of art the extralinguistic relation meets with fewer obstacles to understanding than in our life with nature: "This is the eternal source of art, that a man is faced by a form which desires to be made through him into a work of art" (p. 8). This form that he beholds without its being "there" cannot be described by the artist—he can only realize it. Once it is created, it is a thing among other things—until one day it flashes upon another as Thou.

Over against the human Thou, "language" is the exchange of speech and counter-speech. The being-act which creates immediacy is often represented as feeling and hence misunderstood. One has feelings—there is love between I and Thou, and man dwells in his love: "Feelings accompany the metaphysical and metapsychical fact of love, but they do not constitute it" (p. 14). In this same sense Buber pointed out in "The Holy Way" that the realization of the godlike on earth takes place not *in* man but between men.[17] Every genuine meeting does something to man; he emerges from it different from what he was. But the I-Thou relation is fraught with tragedy: pure presentness cannot be sustained; every Thou inevitably becomes It, at least for a time. In this connection Buber spoke of the "exalted melancholy" of our fate.

"Through the Thou a man becomes I" (p. 28) means that man's I-consciousness developed only gradually from relational events. In the history of mankind and in the life of the individual the abstracted I, which is the prerequisite for the primary word I-It, is inextricably embedded in the "web of relation," in the relation to the Thou. The most important section in the first part of *I and Thou* points out that the natural preform of the I-Thou primary word is evident to us even today in the life of primitive people and in the life of children, so that it is actually a "submerged" primal form of our being to which Buber calls our attention. Where we use a concept, primitive man uses a whole sentence in which the lived relation is still preserved. I and Thou are first of all a single elemental relation—and the confrontation is conceived primarily as a reciprocal process, not as that of two people, and is felt as an exciting experience that passes through the body like a flash of lightning. Buber's assertion that the I-Thou relation produces an immediate effect in both partners is also confirmed by the life form of primitive people.

The natural preform on which the spiritual reality of the primary words rests is observed even more readily in the first years of a child's life. The child's prenatal life represents a natural unification, and it leaves in the child an impulse for universal relations, a wordless prefiguration of saying Thou which makes its appearance in the earliest stage of life. In the child we have before us a living model of human development, and we recognize in it "the a priori of relation," the "inborn Thou" (p. 27). Only after an I-consciousness has gradually separated itself from the I-Thou unification does the primary word I-It become possible.

"To man the world is twofold, in accordance with his twofold attitude" (p. 31) means that the It-world has secured for itself a coherent, ordered world in time and space—but the real world order is glimpsed by man only in the immortal moments of meeting with his Thou: every meeting is a sign of world order. The world of the "uncanny primary word" is insecure and unreliable; it is pure presentness and timeless, and cannot be communicated to others, but its melancholy departures lead to the "eternal Thou," enter into creation as an active power, and give man a glimpse of eternity (p. 33).

The first part of *I and Thou* describes the nature and function of the primary words and determines their prehistoric phenomenal form; the second part deals with the world of spirit. Where is the place of the spirit in relation to the primary words? Is it not a late product in the history of mankind, and does it not presuppose the secure I-It world as a foundation? Buber believes otherwise: "Man speaks with many tongues, tongues of language, of art, of action; but the spirit is one, the response to the Thou which appears and addresses us out of the mystery. Spirit is the word . . . spirit is not in the I, but between I and Thou. It is not like blood which circulates in you, but like the air in which you breathe" (p. 39). Spirit does not come from thought, but from the power of relation. Man can grasp the whole world with his thought and still remain enclosed within himself; every I-Thou relation, however, leads him outside himself toward life, and flows into God.

Spirit is word but also in the world of the spirit the tragedy that adheres to the I-Thou relation in life returns; every response of man to his Thou "binds up the Thou in the world of It" (p. 39). This is the price paid for the advance of knowledge, the creation of works of art, and the activity of those whose teaching is their life lived before God, circumscribed by religion.

With the formation of the I-It world, which tended more and more to dominate the history of a culture to the detriment of the relational force, the human Thou runs the danger of losing its own pulsating life, its constantly renewed life unification. Life is split into an inner and an outer. This is precisely the crisis of our time. Contemporary man has divided his life with his fellowman into two separate spheres: institutions and feelings. Institutions are the "outside," where man works and conducts his daily affairs; feelings are the "inside," where man recuperates from his institutional life (p. 43). But institutions provide no public life, and feelings alone do not constitute a Person: "True public and true personal life are two forms of unification" (p. 46). Both require a living center to which they can be related. In marriage, for example, it is not feelings that are decisive, but that two people reveal the Thou to one another so that love might reign *between* them. But the spheres of economics and politics, which embody the will to profit and the will to power, preserve their innermost life only as long as they participate in spirit and do not abjure its power. Nor can they dispense with the relational power, the living center of the spirit, although they can never realize spirit in its full purity.

Every great culture is based on a primary meeting with the divine mystery, creating a conception of the cosmos that is peculiar to itself. As long as the members of this culture help consummate the essential act of the spirit that informs it and participate in the relation to the living center, the culture will remain creative. When this ceases, the culture petrifies, until the appearance of some strong personality whose life the people can emulate and who can inspire them to return to their ancient sources. The relationship of the community and the individual

is made plain: men with authentic personal lives value their inner freedom, recognize the saving power as well as the perils in this return to
sources; they do not accept the idea of an inescapable fate.

Only the I of the primary word I-Thou is person; the I of the
other primary word is "self-willed person." Person comes into being
when the I enters into relation with other persons and makes contact
with the Thou—in every Thou we are touched with the breath of eternal life. Persons are united through their common participation in reality, through their "being together" which confirms their being. The
self-willed person, however, enjoys his separate existence, and experiences others when he needs them for his own purposes. No man is
only person, and no one is only self-willed person; every man lives in
the twofold I and oscillates between the two poles of human existence.
We need only think of Socrates, Goethe, and Jesus, and we see before
us the I of unending dialogue, the I of pure communion with nature,
and the I of unconditioned relation.

The third part of the work deals with the eternal Thou. God has
many names among men and yet is only One; all those who address the
Thou of their life mean Him. In every genuine meeting the eternal
Thou is present: "Through this mediation of the Thou of all beings
fulfillment and non-fulfillment of relations come to them: the inborn
Thou is realized in each relation and consummated in none" (p. 75).
Again and again we are disappointed to find that our Thou has become
an It. And so man has no rest until he finds the unending, eternal Thou
that by its very nature cannot be converted into an It.

This reminds us of St. Augustine's famous Inquietum: "My heart
is restless until it finds its repose in Thee, O Lord." But whereas St.
Augustine renounced the world and removed himself from it in order
to find God, Buber's relational power, although carrying us beyond the
earthly Thou, always brings us back again to the world. Only when
we fulfill each moment in its entire presentness, do we arrive at the
point which is the eternal Present. Not by annihilating the world but
by hallowing it can we find Him whom we cannot seek, the living
God. To have nothing besides God and yet to place everything within
Him—this is perfect relation. To enter the relation I must renounce

not my I but every false arbitrary desire and every impulse for self-assertion.

"He who truly goes out to the world goes out to God" (p. 79). But does not such an assertion contradict the experiences of religious history? Were not those who found God in the past for the most part the lonely souls, the great mystics who were removed from the world? To meet these objections, and to present the I-Thou relation between man and God as the "primary reality of dialogue" as he experienced it, Buber devoted a lengthy section of the third part to a discussion of the problem of mysticism.

In this connection Buber referred to the explanations he gave in his introduction to *Ekstatische Konfessionen* (1910), at the same time clarifying them in some points and modifying them in others. Even at that early date he perceived the basic phenomenon of ecstasy as that of the I becoming one, which is experienced as union with God and as unity with the world.[18] But here he was interested in distinguishing more sharply the two phenomena which he had previously been unable to separate clearly. The soul's becoming one, the concentration of all powers in the core of being, was now recognized by Buber as the most decisive prerequisite for a genuine experience of God: loneliness as innermost concentration is necessary and justified. But this becoming one is something that occurs *in* man and not between man and God. Ecstasy as union with the Deity is taken by Buber to be an illusion, as "the ecstatic dynamic of relation," and as "the marginal intensification of the relational act": "The relation itself in its vital unity is felt so forcibly that its parts seem to fade before it, and in the force of *its* life the I and the Thou, between which it is established, are forgotten" (p. 87). Buber was passing judgment on the ecstatic experiences of his own youth which were intensified relational phenomena.

Indian mysticism, in which universal being and self-being are identical and which seeks to attain this identity by entering into the pure subject, moves in the realm of the unreal since its point of departure is boundary concepts, and its comatose condition of immersion is unrelated to life as it is actually lived. God is identical neither with the Universe nor with one's Self for He embraces both, and our confrontation with Him is not exhausted by conceptual statements: when this confrontation is thought, it moves in insoluble antinomies, and yet we must live with this contradiction as if it were resolved. Thus, to the religious reality of our life, statements such as, "I am at someone's mercy" and "It is within my power" belong together: "where the *complexio oppositorum* rules, there the law of contradiction is silent." [19]

The introduction to *Ekstatische Konfessionen* concludes with a reference to the ancient myth of unity that became multiplicity, and sees in the experience of the visionary who returns to the world a "symbol of the primal experiences of the world-spirit." In *I and Thou*, however, Buber detected in the twofold nature of the primary words the distinct human expression of a metacosmic primal polarity, of a twofold movement of the world in relation to the Godhead: "A turning away from the primal Source, in virtue of which the universe is sustained in the process of Becoming, and a turning toward the primal Source, in virtue of which the universe is released in Being. . . . Our knowledge of the twofold nature is silent before the paradox of the primal mystery" (p. 101).

Loneliness and concentration are necessary—but only as unifiers do we press forward to God's reality. For this reason Buber, after his discussion of mysticism, repeated word for word the section concerning the three spheres which constitute the world of relation.[20] Only as long as the three spheres are transparent with respect to God and illumined by his Presence can Cosmos, Eros, and Logos retain their revelatory meaning.

If then the I-thou relation to God is not mysticism, according to Buber, how is life unification with the invisible mystery to be understood? How does a dialogue between man and God take place? The reader who asks this question perhaps recalls another question that may have occurred to him while reading the first part of the work and that Buber's repetition of the three spheres of relation now brings back to his mind, namely, the question as to how a mutual relation in life is possible with the speechless figures of nature and spirit. Both questions belong in fact together, and readers who feel this have a deeper understanding of Buber's real concern than do those who regard his experiences with trees as a fanciful digression that is not to be taken seriously.

The question as to how God communicates with man can be answered today as always with the single word: revelation. The nature of revelation—as personal experience and as a fact of religious history—is dealt with in the concluding portion of *I and Thou,* where the concept is comprehensively and yet concretely formulated. Revelation is to be found in prehistoric times and at critical points in the early history of mankind: "The mighty revelations to which religions appeal are essentially like the silent revelations that go on everywhere and at all times" (p. 116). The primary phenomenon common to all revelations for Buber is that man undergoes a change after meeting with God. It is not a question of an experience but of an effect: something happens to man; he receives something he did not have before, something whose origin he cannot explain.

But what he receives has no content, and it knows only of a Present that imbues one with unification, meaning, and mission, and with a feeling of certainty and confirmation that has nothing to do with knowledge. The mystery remains what it was, and life has not become easier but more difficult; at the same time, however, it has become what Buber called "heavy with meaning." Meaning as such cannot be communicated; it cannot be formulated as knowledge or as an imperative: "We can only go forth and affirm its truth" (p. 111). The I and Thou as such is the message, and the elemental penetration of meaning and mission the revelation: "That is the eternal revelation that is present here and now. I know of no revelation and believe in none whose original phenomenon would not be the same. I do not believe in a self-determination of God, in a self-determination of God before man. The word of revelation is: I am that I am; that which reveals is that which reveals. That which is *is* and nothing more. The eternal source of strength streams forth, the eternal contact persists, the eternal voice sounds forth, and nothing more" (p. 111).

It is apparent here that Buber's direct and personal experience of God, the revelation of the eternal Thou, resulted in a similar personal view of religious history. Revelation is "religion as presentness," and the responsibility of him who stands "before the Face" and is summoned in the unconditioned reality of his being is more binding than the precepts of the Jewish tradition, whose complete validity Buber never again entirely accepted for himself. He was nevertheless conscious of being closer to biblical belief than many of his Jewish contemporaries who followed the letter of the law, the belief which is faithfulness, unification of life to life, boundless trust. He knew that he had again entered into the biblical dialogue between God and man, and that he was being addressed in a kind of loving embrace which he felt was directed to the center of being.

In the later epilogue to *I and Thou*,[21] Buber sought to comprehend the Presence of God through the paradox of the "absolute person." Absolute being confronts man as absolute person and speaks the "I" of revelation. Since God brings his absoluteness with him into the relation, he never ceases by his nature to be Thou for us: "it is we only who are not always there" (p. 99). And because of this absoluteness of the eternal Thou, we need not abandon any other relation when we come to him. The relation to God is the universal relation into which every other I-Thou flows: "There we find only one stream that flows from I to Thou, always more and more unending, the one boundless stream of real life" (p. 107). Through the eternal and unconfined presence of God the other moments of the I-Thou relation, which constantly tend to degenerate into the I-It world, acquire a kind of continuity, a "world-life of unification"; and with respect to their common center they acquire a coherent structure in the life of the individual as well as in world history. Buber speaks of a "deep world involvement in the face of God," of a "love responsibility" that arises in us for the sum total of world events: "To him who steps before the Face, the world becomes fully present for the first time, illumined by eternity, and he can in One response say Thou to the beingness of all being. There is no more any tension here between world and God, but only the One reality" (p. 108).

Buber was well aware that the reciprocal relation between man and God is as undemonstrable as the existence of God himself. And nothing can better illustrate his characterization of himself as an "atypical man" than the revelation of *I and Thou*, which can be classified as neither philosophy nor theology. Emil L. Fackenheim in his study

"Martin Buber's Concept of Revelation" [22] has set forth the difficulties that confront a philosopher when he meets someone who asserts that today there are not only revelation faiths but that revelation can also exist here and now in which the critically trained mind of modern man can believe. Since Buber recognized only the directly lived I-Thou relation to God as revelation and yet saw in theology the "passage of the God-thing through religion" and the "continuity of keeping God in time and space," which proceeds from man's need to believe in a secure It, theologians find it difficult to acknowledge his "religion as presentness." But Buber's answer to both would be that it is not a question of concepts and their distinctions but a matter of concrete life in which the I-Thou relation, from the early days of primitive man to the inspiration of the creative spirit and religious revelations, is a pervasive reality.

But how far is this reality accessible to every man? With which organs do we apprehend the "secret and yet revelatory act of being touched" [23] by God's presence? It may be instructive to cite a number of instances in which Buber speaks of meeting with God and to compare them with his experiences of confrontation with nature and the visible and invisible forms of the spirit.

In *I and Thou* the revelatory presence of God is designated as "light breath"; it may also involve a struggle, something like a wrestling bout (p. 109). Both are primary experiences of the bibilical dialogue with God, similar to Buber's remark that God comes forth out of the darkness to reveal himself and that man must pass through fear and trembling to attain the love of God. To fear God means "trembling to become aware of His incomprehensibility"; it means consciousness of one's own creatureliness. [24] In *Der Grosse Maggid* the fear of God is described as a "central feeling of God's presence." [25] Buber also recognized a revelation that is a "hiding of the Countenance"; and "God's darkness must be seen with the eyes; it wants to be seen." [26] Again Buber described "meeting" as "a wind that comes to one from beyond, nearness, touch, the mystery of light out of darkness." [27] He called it a "speechless intimate grace" [28] or a "light for the seeing eye, strength for the active hand." [29] Hence, the question raised throughout concerns experiences and modes of expression, known and proclaimed by prophets and mystics as they seek their way to God. Religious experience presupposes a sensuous-supersensuous openness, an inner awareness of being in touch with transcendence, which in all religions belongs to the nature of sacrament.

But whereas this feeling for the sacramental in the case of most mystics is sensitive only to things divine, Buber's sensuous-spiritual, relational force is from the very outset directed with unusual intensity to the life of nature. In *I and Thou* Buber spoke of that secret longing for the "natural unification" of prenatal life which never wholly leaves man (p. 25). Since early youth he possessed something like a "transmitting soul element" with which he received and answered the mysterious life streams that flow from being to being and which transcend bodily limitations. In this connection we are reminded of Buber's early essay on Boehme where in a living communion with nature he experienced the mystery of transsubstantiation, and testified to an experience in which he was transported until he felt that he had been transformed: "And there are moments in which our organism is an altogether different piece of nature." [30] At that time elemental unification seemed to him to be based on the mystical teaching of the microcosm according to which the entire universe is present in man. Like Hölderlin, he experienced divine omnipresence in the life of nature.[31]

This rapture in which the life of a tree with all its sap and shoots merges with one's own organism was a consuming momentary flame which, leaping like a flash of lightning from being to being, finally exhausted itself. Buber's earlier mysticism actually preserved something of the elemental relational force found in the life of primitive man. In experiencing a complete "natural unification" that burst the bounds of individuation, it was possible that the consciousness of the other, of twoness, could disappear. But the mutual embrace and the merging into oneness that Daniel experienced in the first dialogue in his unification with the fir cone as "mystery of the real" is a subjective experience. Human creative power cannot transform the tree into a "tree of eternal life," and in the end it remains what it is, as does man. Buber's later interpretation of mysticism as "ecstatic dynamic of relation" and "marginal intensification of the relational act" accurately describes his own ecstatic experiences: the unifying "realization" of God that man experienced took place beyond the life of nature—and here the mystical merging into one proved to be an illusion.

In *Daniel* and in the dialogue "With a Monist," Buber, anticipating his "primary words," distinguished between two types of reality: the realizing and the orientating. But *realizing* still retained too much of the sense of "to make real" and signified an immense exertion and straining of the creative faculty. What Buber at that time attempted, in the language of *I and Thou,* was an integration of both primary words by means of a creative act. In *I and Thou,* however, the unifying man *receives* his I as a result of meeting. It all depends on the "complete acceptance of the present"; not only must the partner be accepted but the fact that the moment is *not* eternity must also be accepted, the "discontinuity" of the I-Thou relation.

Buber came closest to these insights in his dialogue "With the Monist," in which he pointed out that there was something in things of the nature of a gift, a secret form that reveals itself only to the one who loves and who embraces them with his whole being. Reality arises through the "contact between the ineffable cycle of things and the experiencing powers of my senses . . . which are corporeal spirit." [32] With this "effective" presentness of things, with the knowledge of the cosmic love-unity inherent in things and in beings which is to be realized "between" them, Buber came close to what in *I and Thou* signifies "mutuality."

But only in the certainty of the "eternal Thou," the revelation of God as absolute Person, was the meaningful center in whose light "realization" became possible, an incomprehensible resting point around which revolve all isolated ecstatic raptures and attachments: "God may be seen seminally within all things; but He must be realized between them. . . . In every human being there is present the beginning of universal being, but it can unfold only in his relatedness to universal being, in the pure immediacy of his giving and taking, which surrounds him like a sphere of light, merging him with the oneness of the world." [33]

Just as the youthful microcosm belief is both preserved and transcended, so does the preface to *Daniel* present in a remarkable way the continuity between the prewar work and *I and Thou*. It consists of two paragraphs, of which the second (except for the first sentence) was added after the work appeared, but which is nevertheless highly appropriate. The first paragraph describes how Buber once pressed the point of his walking stick against the trunk of an oak tree: "Then I felt in twofold fashion my contact with being: here where I held the stick and there where the stick touched the bark. Appearing to be only where I was, I found myself nevertheless there too where I found the tree." The last sentence, later incorporated in the new paragraph, reads: "At that time dialogue appeared to me."

Buber now interpreted the essence of dialogue, and in doing so he placed his own excess of inwardness and superlingual contact in a human situation that is familiar and accessible to every man, whereby the revelatory touch of God and the speechless mutuality in the life with nature became reality. We actually experience how the empty space of *between* is filled with the oscillations of being to being: "For like that stick so is the speech of man wherever it is genuine speech, and that means: truly directed address. Here, where I am, where ganglia and the organs of speech help me to form and send forth the word, here I 'mean' him to whom I send it forth, I 'intend' him, this one unmistakable person. But also there where he is something was delegated by me, something not at all like a substance, like that being-with-me, but pure vibration and impalpable which tarries there with him, the one who was meant by me and takes part in receiving my word. I encompass him to whom I address myself."

This testimony is important because *Daniel* is a transitional work in which the "I" still occupies too central a position and the "Thou" has not yet been fully attained. In the material he subsequently added, Buber still retained this transitional character: in his description of the dialogue the partner remains passive and does not "comprehend"; he is still being "realized" and is not yet "munificent Thou." The impression gained from Buber's description is that his own experiences did not take place in the realm of the unreal, but that he possessed more delicate organs with which to penetrate and express the hitherto speechless reality of *between* and find for it "a local habitation and a name." And he could do so precisely because of the "transmitting soul element," by sending forth something "which is not at all like a substance . . . but pure vibration and impalpable."

And thus in the late epilogue to *I and Thou* where the question of mutuality in relation to speechless and invisible forms is treated once more, Buber spoke in the confident tone of one who has had reality experiences that have not been vouchsafed to others, and of one who knew that others can and will follow him, just as someone in Goethe's day might have known of radio and telephone. What he proclaimed is the complete answer of the "primal memory," [34] the possibility of communication from being to being which is assured because it is God who reveals himself in and between his creatures. That revelation as pure being is ultimately a messianic category becomes clear when Buber in his address "Herut" looked into the future and saw a time when no image of God will be adequate or needed, because life itself in the miracle of its fellowship has become a symbol, and "God is truly present when one man clasps the hand of another." [35] This messianic being of pure, fulfilled relation is however inherent in the elemental relational force in the life of primitive people. Redemption applies to *entire* creation: it was not only Paul who heard the sighs of the dumb creature. God's spirit pervades the whole of creation; he appears like a light in every wholeness when it is taken as a whole, the form he intended. Not only does the "Thou" that shines for a brief moment in the glance of an animal "answer" man but also the "living wholeness and unity" of the tree, "the simple mutuality of being," discloses itself to us when we create it by saying Thou—not by selfishly realizing it but by finding our proper place within creation. And this reciprocity of Being reaches "from stones to stars."

The *between* in the back and forth movement of vibration, filled by a stream of being to being which is only the breath of things and beings, bathed in God's refulgent light—thus does the epilogue to *I and Thou* describe the life of mutuality which man is able to lead with the forms of nature and spirit. To grasp the active life form in a visible, immovable natural phenomenon and to experience the spirit which "wafts about us and breathes into us" with our senses constituted two complementary revelations: the "mystery of the real" is the sacramental penetration of spirit and sensibility.

Is this then mysticism after all? No and yes! No, when compared to all that mysticism has meant in the past, as is clearly shown in the introduction to *Ekstatische Konfessionen*; no, also, when the reader is inclined to brush aside as "mystical" those spiritual experiences that are strange to him and beyond his reach. Yes, if thereby is meant "the mystery of the real," apprehended in the secret of "ontic participation" whose element is relational force. Yes, if thereby is meant, as Buber himself expressed it, "religion as presentness." At any rate, Buber shared with most of the mystics his opposition to a concept-bound orthodoxy.

His own early mysticism was pantheism in which God is One and All. God as well as man are comprehended under the category of substance; mystical union was to result in fusion and in a transformation of essence. Thenceforth, however, it was a matter of the mutuality of an Opposite in which the category of relation comes more to the forefront, and the nature of God's essence is not inquired into. At one time Buber believed that it might be possible to unite the pantheistic life feeling of his generation with the old myth of the realization of God— but this myth was derived from a time in which the theological-philosophical conceptual world and real life were united by allegorical interpretation, which both combined and separated them and which always kept in view the otherness of man with respect to God. Buber's own life feeling, however, is symbolic-sacramental and sensitive to the direct penetration of spirit and sense. Like Hölderlin he sought a natural sacramental unification with the universe. But even Hölderlin failed in his attempt to reconcile the divine forces in nature, which blessed him and "smote" him, and to bring them into harmony with the one God as absolute Being. Lightning contacts are not sufficient to create a coherent structure of spiritual reality.

Both the boldness and the perils of Buber's thinking became evident again and again in the intensity with which he converted abstract conceptual contexts into sensible events. This made for severe tensions and crises that became a matter of life and death but which in the end led to a more deeply conceived reality of the spirit. Thus, in his younger years the inner compulsion to conceive the world in time and space as finite or infinite brought him to the edge of despair. A second crisis is intimated at the end of the second part of *I and Thou*. Here we see what happens when philosophy entertains two mutually contradictory thought possibilities, conceiving the world idealistically, on the one hand, as the idea of the "I," and materialistically, on the other hand, taking man as the product of an evolutionary process. We thus have a rupture in the relationship between God, man, and the world in that the thinking subject places itself at the center of being. Buber was not affected by this extreme individualism which dominated his age with its opposition of idealism and materialism, but he was profoundly influenced, on the contrary, by the universal myth of the "realization" of God which, in place of an ontological system, dominated his religious thinking. There was also a danger of imposing a ghostlike conceptual structure on life itself. As long as Buber did not conceive God as "Person" and "eternal Thou" but as "the Absolute," "the world-spirit" that dwelled in unattainable transcendence, his realizing man was too much in the center of world events. Life, which in theory proceeded from God and returned to God, could in practice revolve imperceptibly around "realizing" man, around the "I of the world," as he is called in *Daniel*. God and world are then realized *in* the "I." A realizing pan-sacramentalism thus remains subjectively bound to the I, severing man from God and the world, instead of binding him to both. It is not "the one stream from I to Thou, always more unending, the one boundless stream of real life"—relation as "ontic participation."

The juxtaposition of two quotations in the third part of *I and Thou* shows that Buber in this work achieved the reconciliation of two conceptions of life. He described the revelatory presentness of the spirit first in the language of the Bible: "But they who wait for the Lord shall renew their strength" (Isa. 40:31), and then in Nietzsche's dictum: "One takes and does not ask who gives" (I.152). Buber, like Nietzsche, had experienced the lightning flash of relation leaping from the elemental dynamic of being which, when isolated and without a redeeming attachment to spirit, is a shattering force. The meeting with the "eternal Thou," however, is a life moment which reveals the rest-

ing point and the spiritual center around which all relational force revolves. It will help us understand the old and the new points of view
better if we compare Daniel's experience with the fir cone in the first
dialogue with the meaning of the ash trunk in the preface of the work.
Here as there "the mystery of the real" constitutes the basic idea. But
whereas in the former the Opposite reveals itself as a struggle of mythical forces transplanted to the inner sphere of man, it appears in the
preface as the gentler mystery of "ontic participation" in the more
spiritual sphere of the embracing touch.

It is precisely the thematic similarity of both processes which
shows how Buber's path from *Daniel* to *I and Thou* took the same
course as it did in the *Addresses on Judaism*, and is characterized in the
preface as "clarification" and not "conversion." The struggle of the
soul and the spirit for the reality of "the religious" is always the same in
all of life's spheres but "the theophany changes," as it is expressed in
"The Holy Way"; the nature of revelation had undergone a change
during the years of the war.

What assurance have we that Buber escaped from the coils of the
subjective? We know this because Buber finally came to realize that
the unending relation and mutuality in being are for man no longer exhausted in a moment of bliss but that man is now burdened with an
equally universal responsibility, the "unending ethos of the moment,"
the "love responsibility" in its involvement in world events, which ultimately means man's co-responsibility in establishing the kingdom of
God on earth: "The world is not divine sport; it is a divine destiny!" [36]
The "spark" in the innermost recesses is godlike in its essence—but
man is involved in one great spiritual reality of which he is but a part
and no longer the central point.

Only now has the "mystery of the real" truly become the "religion as presentness." The concepts *creation, revelation, redemption* can
now be translated into the language of contemporary man for whom
they acquire a reality that permeates all of life, a reality around which
all being revolves. From this trinity, which is always a promise and a
summons, there emerges ultimate unity, a unity that is seminally inherent in the "mystery of the real": the kingdom of God. The whole substance of Buber's message to his contemporaries, and the course which

he inflexibly pursued in all his writings, has to do with its realization.

In his article "I and Thou in the Philosophy of Martin Buber," the French philosopher and poet Gabriel Marcel objected to the imprecision of the term "in the beginning." [37] In his "Answer" that appeared in the same volume, Buber replied that in using this expression, "In the beginning is relation," [38] he had in mind the early stage of the I-Thou relation among primitive people, the "vital original words" which precede the "primary words." The attentive reader will not fail to detect that the imprecise term used here has a profounder meaning, a meaning that is both obvious and concealed and, although only intended as adventitious, is indispensable in revealing a deeper dimension of *I and Thou,* namely, a reference to the words "in the beginning" in the first chapter of Genesis and in the prologue of the Gospel of John. This reference is meant to indicate not only the "vital original words" which precede the "primary words" temporally but also the divine word of creation spoken beyond time. God spoke as he created the world, addressing man, and this was the real beginning of relation. The allusion is obvious to those readers who detect it; the others must remain content with the reference to the prehistoric period. The conjoining of these two primary realities, the religious and the historical, reveals the full span of human existence.

The world became real through God's word; and the world becomes real for man through the word and comes into being with the word: "Speak that I might see thee," as Hamann said.[39] The substance of the world is relation, and speech consummates the relation. As early as 1930 Hans Kohn pointed out the linguistic-philosophical basis of *I and Thou,* and he cited verses from Buber which summed up his philosophy of language and religion: "We are the sounds that the primal mouth speaks,/ And yet we are only isolated words and not words in context./ When shall we be words that find their place/ In a sentence, to do justice to primordial speech." [40] In this same connection reference is made to a passage in an unpublished preface to *I and Thou* which states: "What is here called speech is the primary act of the spirit, which is consummated in human beings with the help of sounds and signs." Kohn emphasized the magical power of words and names in

Jewish religious history from time immemorial. The giving of names was also a dialogic act and, as seen from man's point of view, proceeded from the divine words: "I have called thee by name." All human speech takes place, imperfectly to be sure, within God's speech, in which the Word is identical with creation. In an unpublished lecture on Lao-tzu, Buber spoke of an "inwardness of the name," emanating from things that strive to attain form in man and through him reach the sphere of the spirit: "Name is meeting, as is all reality. The reality in which we live is the reality of the relation between the things of the world and me, man. Reality is an in-between and the name is an in-between." [41] Here we see clearly the mutuality of all beings and things, a mutuality which eludes rational comprehension and which constitutes the basis of the three spheres of relation in *I and Thou.*

In the epilogue to the *Writings on the Dialogic Principle* (1953) Buber pointed out the connection between *I and Thou* and the tendency in the philosophy of language prevalent at the time, a connection not in the sense of dependence but rather of a significant coincidence of insights arrived at independently. The two most important contemporary parallels are Ferdinand Ebner's *Das Wort und die geistigen Realitäten* [The word and spiritual realities] (1921) and Franz Rosenzweig's *The Star of Redemption [Stern der Erlösung]* (completed 1919, published 1921 in German; English trans. by W. H. Hallo, 1971)—the one written in the spirit of Hamann and Kierkegaard, the other a product of a new existential "meeting" with the Bible and Jewish tradition.

In this epilogue Buber said of himself: "The possibility and reality of a dialogic relation between man and God, that is, of a free partnership of man in a dialogue between heaven and earth, whose speech in address and answer is itself an event, the event from above to below and the event from below to above, was a question that had already challenged me in my youth." [42] The problem was brought closer to him by Hasidism as the question concerning the nature of man's vocation. In the introduction to the *Legend of the Baal-Shem* (1908) we find: "The legend is the myth of the calling." In the preface (written in 1919) to *Der grosse Maggid und seine Nachfolge* (1922), the meeting between God and man is already recognized as the basis of Hasidism, so that when Buber's critics accuse him of reading his dialogic existentialism into the Hasidic writings, the reverse is true: his conception of Hasidism contributed to the clarification of the problems treated in *I and Thou.*

In one of his essays Buber characterized Franz Rosenzweig's "philosophizing theology" as "having rediscovered the fundamental identity of revelation and language." [43] The original thinker to whom we owe this alliance between the philosophy of religion and the philosophy of language was Hamann. To him, man was primarily a creature that possessed speech and hence, unlike Kant, he did not inquire into the nature of reason but into the nature of language. Language is at the same time sense and spirit, wherein the total reality of man as body-soul finds direct expression. God created man in his own image and gave him language. Every word is a sacred sign, a hieroglyph, in which the miracle of creation is reenacted: "Without the Word there is no reason—no world. Here is the source of creation and of government." [44] Hamann understood the world to be the word of God addressed to man who is so constituted by nature that he can perceive truth and the essence of things only in the image of the sensuous given. Every natural being is a word of God through which He speaks to man. The real meeting between God and man, however, takes place in the world of history: nature and history are for Hamann "the two great Commentaries of the divine Word, which is the only key capable of disclosing their meaning to us." [45] Human acts in history are the answer to the divine Word of creation. History as God's actions and as man's answer found its culmination in Jesus Christ. Hence, according to Hamann, God's word can be understood only by him who has heard it spoken by Jesus Christ. God's self-revelation in the Bible is, in the same sense as in history, God's meeting with man, the word of God and the word of man as one. God wished to speak in the language of men. "God reaches down into the history of mankind and of man by means of language. Language is the middle ground between God and man. . . . It always comes as God's language in human speech. It *is* not, it happens. And in it and with it the history of God happens with man. . . ." [46]

History for Buber is also the arena where God and man meet. Everything that is said in *I and Thou* about "spirit" as man's answer to the Thou that addresses him out of the mystery revolves around this thought, as well as everything that is said about an event of "meeting" on which every great culture has been founded, but which later no longer takes place and is forgotten. The full significance of Buber's assertion that "spirit is the word" can be understood only in connection with his philosophy of language and its relation to Hamann: "And just as talk in a language may well first take the form of words in the brain of man, and then sound in his throat, and yet both are merely refractions of the true event, for in actuality speech does not abide in man, but man takes his stand in speech and talks from there; so with every word and every spirit" (p. 39). Man moves and has his being in God's speech and he is looked upon as God's partner in the world's work. Man's relation to God is chiefly characterized, according to Schleiermacher, by a feeling of dependence; but Buber considered this a partial definition that stresses one aspect only: "You need God, in order to be —and God needs you, for the very meaning of your life" (p. 82). Man's response is his responsibility for the fate of the world; he is God's coworker since the goal of creation is redemption.

Hamann's conception of biblical revelation as being both the Word of God and the word of man was taken seriously by Buber, and it acquired a new meaning in his life and work. God's revelation is "modified" by man; there is no purely divine revelation, and the more that the divine image of revelation is reflected in a religion, the more humanized does it become.

"Word" in *I and Thou* signifies the union between God and man; it is the language of relation—proceeding from God and from man. Thus it says of the three spheres in which the world of relation arises: "All are gates leading into the *presence of the Word*" (p. 102); or: "In turning the *Word* is born on earth" (p. 116); "Disintegration of the *Word* has taken place"; "The essence of the Word is in revelation, its effectiveness in the life of form (God's image), and its validity in the power of those who have passed away" (p. 119). In this comprehensive sense of "speech" between God and man "Logos" became for Buber a primary symbol which accompanies his "in the beginning is relation." In a letter to Henri Borel in 1917 Buber wrote: "Word creation, the production of the word, is for me one of the mysterious processes of the spiritual life; yes, I confess, that in my view there is no essential difference between what I here call the "production" of the word and that which has been called the emergence of the Logos." [47] Even in the essay "The Teaching of Tao," the Logos of the prologue of the Gospel of John is called "the symbol of primal existence taken significantly from the world of speech" (p. 36). It is the primary symbol of unity as well as of life that creates unity; it is the teaching of the great founders of religion that is at the same time both word and life. Just as Hamann compared God's word with "the light that contains all colors within itself," [48] so did Buber speak of "the teaching" in which all opposites of the wholeness are elevated into the One "as the seven colors of the spectrum fuse into white light" (p. 34). At that time, however, Logos, as well as Tao, had for Buber a meaning that is close to that of Heraclitus; it is "the unknowable Logos that yet works in all," the "harmony of opposites," the eternal order that makes the human world our "common" world (p. 58).

Through his word, which is at the same time an answer and a turning to God, man finds his place in the "double movement" of the world, and in this context Buber saw the primary words: "Estrangement from the primary Source, in virtue of which the universe is sustained in the process of becoming, and a turning toward the primary Source, in virtue of which the universe is released in being" (p. 101). This formulation also expresses a concomitant thought that was significant in Buber's thinking, namely, that besides primordial creation and millennial redemption there is eternal creation and redemption.

Are we still in the realm of myth and the cosmological production of myths? "A neglected, obscure primal reality" was to be made visible.[49] Is Buber concerned as well with discovering the primordial myth of mankind and reviving it for his time? Is *I and Thou* a myth and does it explain the conjunction of spirit and expression found between religion, philosophy, and poetry? Again the answer to this problem, which has been so perplexing to critics, is both No and Yes.

If we define the intellectual attitude of philosophizing as a rupture of the individual with the whole, which is the definition given by E.

Levinas,[50] then *I and Thou* does not belong to philosophical literature. Buber remains a "life-experiencing thinker" and seeks to avoid that very rupture between philosophy and life which is the essential element in Levinas's definition. He takes his stand where spirit remains life, the place where it arises and comes into being. *I and Thou*, using the resources of philosophy, seeks to express more than philosophical knowledge. Buber traced the presuppositions of all philosophizing to their "original reality" where they impinge upon sacramental experience and mythical expression. His philosophizing does not shun the overtones and undertones that characterize the mysterious nature of reality. He supplemented rational knowledge with a language symbolism that had found its expression in the very title *I and Thou*.

The symbolic character of this philosophy of language extends dialogic life far beyond the spoken word; it includes a communicating silence, dialogue as pure inwardness of the Other, as that wordless contact of being with being, which was of special significance in Buber's conception: "Only silence before the Thou—silence of all tongues, silent patience in the undivided word that precedes the formed and vocal response—leaves the Thou free, and permits man to take his stand with it in the reserve where the spirit is not manifest, *but is*" (p. 39). We can thus speak of the "strict sacrament of dialogue" with respect to the "eternal Thou"; among people where unreservedness rules we find the dialogic word "sacramental." [51]

Since "word," as Buber's basic symbol, is a living, spirit-sensuous unity, all being is seen by him as life form and felt to be in constant, imperceptible motion which is at once the breath of the spirit and the elemental radiation of being, an unending stream of mutuality with which the I-Thou relation, as a peculiar elemental consciousness without content, harmonizes. In Buber's work, reality around the light orb of rational knowledge remains a mystery; the sensible world is everywhere transparent and extends beyond itself. God is not experienced as concept in a rational definition of being, but as symbol and absolute Person in the "eternal Thou." Those who are not disposed to recognize the prerational and suprarational as part of a philosophical work would designate *I and Thou* as myth, for where myth reigns truth is experienced in the symbol, in the indivisible and undivided unity of spirit and life. In *I and Thou*, however, we are dealing with a myth which does not exclude but which comprehends rationality.

Mysticism, myth, and teaching were the spiritual forces which determined Buber's path up to the time of *Daniel*. The "impossible message" of mysticism, its voice in which "the word burns" and which seeks to express the inexpressible, led Buber to the language of myth where "word" is both life and teaching and where teaching means "Way," the one thing that is needful. In *Daniel* Buber attempted to understand the basic facts of life mythically against the background of his own time, to create a life teaching of the free religious relation to God. But it is precisely when we compare *I and Thou* with *Daniel* and the other forms of myth that appeared in the first two decades of the century that we realize its uniqueness. It is not the private ivory tower of a poet or thinker, attesting to nothing more than personal life feeling, but the "word" that is within the reach of all: the "primordial reality" of the primary words is common to all men. The *Dialogues on Realization* somehow always terminate in monologues. *I and Thou* is addressed directly to the reader who is often addressed as a "Thou" or included by the author in a "we."

When we speak of myth in connection with *I and Thou*, we must bear in mind that this myth is neither self-created nor the renewal of the century old theological myth of the realization of God. Buber took his stand in the mythical language of the Bible, in its dialogue between God and man. The spirit of the Bible is the life air that animates his work. As a result of experiencing the "eternal Thou," the personal God, all being is tacitly made to accord with the biblical categories of creation, revelation, and redemption. Because there is creation, there is "nothing but being-mutuality," a common participation, and what Buber called the "grace of things," obviously in contrast to Vergil's "tears of things." [52] By means of a universal speech symbolism, the identity between language and revelation is established in *I and Thou*.[53] Creation and revelation, as mutual communion of things and as a dialogue of being to being, bear within themselves the seeds of redemption. By leaving all earthly spheres of the Thou open toward God, man participates in redemption by his responsibility and his sanctification of

the world. Thereby, in addition to mysticism and myth, a third factor
in Buber's development, the "teaching," is both preserved and transformed.

There is still a final dimension in Buber's speech symbolism that
needs to be clarified: the "word" of the teaching, the word which is
Way and attitude. In Buber's early period, "teaching" was frankly
oriented to the prophets and to the founders of religion. God once
"spoke," and the prophet spoke as his mouthpiece. In the age of the
"eclipse of God" there are no prophets and no voice that proclaims a
message. The beings and things of the world are the message because
they are the speech of God, and through them the "supra-lingual transmission of the mystery" must take place: the hidden message corresponds to the God who has concealed himself, the *deus absconditus*. A
definite hour in world history is destined to lead us along the arduous,
thorny ways of the "task." Within the framework of this task the revelation of *I and Thou* unfolds in different areas of the I-It world as philosophic anthropology, religious history, sociology, and ethics. The criteria of the teaching are no longer the great men among the messengers
of God, but the "servant" who completes his work in the deepest silence of being, whose activity is to a certain extent a nonactivity, and
who represents the ever-recurring figure of Israel.[54]

CONTINUATION OF THE DIALOGIC PRINCIPLE

Dialogue

That Buber published *Die Schriften über das dialogische Prinzip* in
1953 does not mean that he elaborated his *I and Thou* into a kind of
system. His thoughts on dialogic life continued to develop in accordance with a comprehensive design of the nature of the two primary
words, a design that was self-contained but also pointed in all directions
beyond itself. Insights that had only been hinted at in *I and Thou* demanded completion and clarification. In addition there were objections
and misunderstandings on the part of readers and critics which called
for refutation and corrections. This gave rise to further writings on the

subject of I and Thou: *Dialogue* (first printing 1930, published in book form 1932), the three "Talks on Education" (written in 1925, 1935, and 1939, collected in book form 1953); "The Question of the Single One," (1936); and "Elements of the Interhuman" (1953). That nothing had been changed in the basic view of *I and Thou* as a result of the elaboration of this theme in subsequent works can be seen from the epilogue to the new edition of the book issued in 1958 which retains unchanged the principle that had been so often attacked concerning our relations to inanimate and invisible forms, only treating it now with greater discernment and mature reflection.

To set forth the presuppositions of human philosophizing in *I and Thou* and then to continue to philosophize on that basis were two different things. Buber now found himself in a situation similar to his teacher Dilthey, who was convinced that until his time "the whole, uncurtailed and unimpaired realm of experience had never been made the basis of philosophizing, and hence reality in its entirety never comprehended." [55] Just as Dilthey's primary concern, ever since his preface to *Einleitung in die Geisteswissenschaften*, [Introduction to the social sciences] had been to be a philosopher not as a "knowing subject" but with his whole unique person, so did Buber direct his basic philosophical principles to regain a dimension of reality that had been lost. In this attempt he was mainly concerned not with historical but with creaturely uniqueness, placing man not in the stream of history but in the depths of creation. Creation also "happens," to be sure, and changes from moment to moment; but its historical aspect coincides only in part with that which world history records and preserves: "And thus the whole history of the world, the secret real world-history, is a dialogue between God and his creature." [56]

Just as Dilthey had to create a special method of "understanding" in order to be able to capture the peculiar spiritual vitality of historical phenomena, so did Buber attempt to extend the province of philosophical anthropology through an "understanding" that extended far beyond Dilthey's intention and found its proper language in the dialogic principle. The extension of reality from which both men proceeded makes it equally impossible for them to develop a systematic philosophy. They could only illuminate partial areas of being out of the fullness of their basic insight, so that the teaching of man—which each envisaged in a different way—developed naturally and unsystematically and not as a coherent theory.

Of all the writings on the dialogic principle, *Dialogue* is the closest to *I and Thou* and demonstrates in a convincing manner how far Buber was removed from any desire to systematize his basic theme. His main concern was to show that the "ontic participation" on which the dialogic principle rests is not a defective or problematic mysticism, but a reality that leads to the depths of being, a reality whose mysterious nature is emphasized in the dream "Urerinnerrung" ["Original Remembrance"] at the beginning of the work, but which requires no special predisposition or training and can be tested in daily life. We read in the concluding argument with the imaginary opponent: "Dialogue is not an affair of spiritual luxury; it is a matter of creation, of the creature . . ." (p. 35). Only spontaneity and fortitude are needed to get the whole of reality into focus and to learn to trust it implicitly. To this end Buber sought to imbue his readers with courage. After describing the nature and function of the primary words in *I and Thou*, he attempted, by means of a series of separate questions and by referring to fragmentary though exemplary life situations, to contribute to the ontic basis of the I-Thou relation.

It is not basic *concepts* but rather basic *attitudes* which Buber took for examples; the I-Thou relation is for him above all a way into life and not a philosophical principle. As in *Daniel* he was now not so much interested in elaborating a life philosophy as in finding a life teaching that would serve as an antidote to the crisis of the age. Although Buber had always inquired into the unchanging basic conditions of human existence, from the very outset he deliberately directed his word to the needs of his own age. This interest is apparent in *Daniel* where he sought to resist the predominant "orientating" thinking of his day and the mechanized, unreal life of our large urban centers. The second part of *I and Thou* was also written with conscious awareness of the impending crisis and the urgency of conversion. Buber has often been accused of not doing justice in his philosophy to the It-world. In his "Answer" he admitted this but justified it by saying that even a philosopher must depart from the world-hour in which he was born: "In another hour it would perhaps have been granted to me to sound the praises of It; today not: because without a turning of man to his Thou no turn in his destiny can come." [57]

Buber saw the real danger for our time in the ominous disappearance of our personal life. Man becomes a "person" through real meeting, through entering into an I-Thou relation. But in *I and Thou* Buber stated that without a sane personal life there can be no genuine community. In an essay written in 1942, at a time when his worst fears had come true, Buber again spoke out with all clearness: "A people in the real sense of the term exists only when there is throughout, below as above, among those led as among the leaders, the element of the person, the sphere of the person, the freedom and responsibility of the person. The substance of a people and the latent substance of the person are one; where the one is suppressed, the other will be suppressed. The totalitarian mass marks not only the end of personal life, it is also the end of the life of a people." [58]

Even before 1930 Buber had recognized in the "modern zeal for collectivity," in the anonymous masses marching step in step, a danger equally as great as the extreme individualism of the educated classes who without any real consciousness of responsibility for the people as a whole regarded man only as a thinking and experiencing subject. Even the youth movement, which was animated by the noblest motives to strive for community life, could not summon up the "elemental force of being a Person" that was needed to achieve its goal. The cause that was espoused was turned into a problem; one "experienced" one's "I" instead of pledging one's self without reservation to the ideal.[59]

The lecture "Wie kann Gemeinschaft werden" [How can community arise?] [60] in 1930 is addressed to the German Jewish youth and is based on the proposition that modern man is left today with only the remains of community, since all his striving has been increasingly directed to rationalizing life instead of humanizing it. Our task is to break through this entrenched rationalization, not in a mood of heroic desperation or impelled by a spirit of unattainable perfection but in the midst of active life in which one happens to find oneself. The problem is, as Buber stated in his dialogue: how to break through into "the tiny strictness and grace of every day," so that I do not look upon my daily work as a senseless treadmill but see in it "unassuming and glorious, the effective creaturely reality given to me in trust and responsibility." [61] This does not mean that we should insinuate meaning into things, but that we should help meaning come into being "between" things. To establish a mutual and unified relation to the world is man's natural prerogative: "No factory and no office is so abandoned by creation that a creative glance could not fly up from one working place to another, from desk to desk, a sober and brotherly glance which guarantees the reality of the creation which is happening: quantum satis. And nothing is so valuable a service to the dialogue between God and man as such an unsentimental and unreserved exchange of glances between two people in an alien place." [62] Ultimately it is a question of putting in place of the "I," which knows only objects and goals, the I of relation, which Buber in his old age also called "the I of love." [63]

The problem of "speech" that was dealt with in *I and Thou* reappears in *Dialogue*. Life as such is in every lived moment a dialogue of man with God who speaks to man through world events. What the individual experiences is incommunicable but unmistakably a feeling that he is being spoken to in "signs," as one of the symbol concepts is called whereby Buber rendered the speech of unification. Such signs happen continually, and they contain nothing that leads beyond the natural order of things: "Nothing is added as a result of being spoken to." And thus man, protected by the armor of *ratio*, fails to hear the silent language of events, as if it were not directed to him: "The waves of ether roar on always, but for most of the time we have turned off our receivers." [64] To him who is attentive, however, every concrete hour with its world content and fate content is "speech"—a speech that knows no alphabet, for it is identical with constantly changing creation: the speech addressed to man is in the form of questions put to him by "ongoing creation" which he cannot evade. Nor is our answer "speech" in the usual sense; we answer by our actions and by our failure to act, by the way in which we enter or do not enter a given situation with our being. Since the whole of creation addresses us in each situation, we cannot completely master any one situation, "but we subdue it in the substance of the lived life" [65] in that we are responsible for it as far as it lies within our power to do so.

Dialogue also takes its starting point from the basic difference between I-Thou and the I-It world which confront one another as "world concreteness," which is addressed to me and which challenges me every moment as the "world-continuum of time and space." The one is the world as creation whose essence is the dialogue of unification, the other is the world as knowledge, the "titanic work of the human spirit"—titanic also in that its excess endangers the work of the creator. "World-concreteness," on the other hand, is not recognized as such; it is "amazingly unique" in its presentness, "inseparable, incomparable, irreducible." [66] But lived responsibility can deal with it, and fidelity to each moment's demand produces a life that is more than the sum of its moments.

Dialogue added nothing that is basically new to *I and Thou*. Buber was trying to think through what it means in concrete life to stand in the I-Thou relation. A kind of thinking in which human relations are paramount, and with which the theme of *I and Thou* is once more illustrated, gives this work its peculiar character. In a section "Vom Denken" [On thinking] [67] Buber points out the danger of indulging in monologues, even for a thinking man, and urges us to think *between* I and Thou. In *Dialogue* he directed his thoughts to the "otherness" of the reader, and took pains to reach those who did not share his basic assumptions and to take into consideration their possible objections.

In those areas in which the I-Thou meeting could take place Buber restricted himself to the relations between man and man and to the dialogue with God, and omitted the problematical question of "meeting" with the speechless forms of nature, although he did not fail to indicate its basic possibility. But as in *I and Thou*, his chief consideration was to point out that the dialogue with God and with the world belong together: "Above and below are bound to one another. The word of him who wishes to speak with men without speaking to God is not fulfilled; but the word of him who wishes to speak with God without speaking with men goes astray." [68]

At the beginning of this work Buber was primarily concerned with presenting the elements of the I-Thou relation and illustrating them by examples from lived life—"In the house of speech there are many mansions." [69] He started from the premise that "speech" is more than the spoken word, and that without sound or gesture it can still remain speech; on the other hand, even long and animated discussions can fail to produce the slightest understanding. "Speech" is a process which the spoken word helps to consummate. It is a natural mode of human expression in relation to creation, a form of "ontic participation" that can express itself effectively in a "communicating silence," and can also be absent in speech which is not truly addressed to the other. Buber insisted that we are not dealing with "mysticism" but, on the contrary, with something that has become concrete and has assumed bodily form, whereas in a vocal exchange of opinions reality all too easily vanishes.

To illustrate this, Buber tells us of a religious discussion he had with a former pastor, Florens Christian Rang, in which complete mutual unreserve, without sacrificing personal convictions, ended with the kiss of brotherhood: "The discussion of the situation between Jews and Christians had been transformed into a bond between the Christian and the Jew. In this transformation dialogic was fulfilled. Opinions were gone; in a bodily way the factual took place." [70]

Dialogic speech is directed to the being of others; it is an attitude of "unreserve." By turning to the world without reservedness, an "inner awareness" takes place. Buber made a distinction between this form of apprehending reality and other forms of perception: e.g., observation which conceives the Opposite as an object in which we record as many features as possible, or the attitude of the observer which he called the "artistic" attitude. This "inner awareness," on the other hand, is an attitude which binds the Opposite to one's own life; it starts from the premise that all reality as such can "tell me something"—as, for example, a complete stranger who in a receptive mood sits next to me on a bench. In this it all depends on my "accepting" the fact of meeting, even if I fail to appreciate its significance for me at the moment: "It may be that I have to answer to this very man before me; it may also be that saying it has a long and manifold transmission before it and that I am to answer some other person at some other time and place, in who knows what kind of speech, and that it is now only a matter of taking this answering upon myself. But in each instance a

word demanding an answer has happened to me." [71] "Word" is also
taken in a deep sense that goes beyond all speech, the sense in which it
is often used in *I and Thou*: as a ray of relation directed to me, through
which Being addresses me directly. In the sense of a "communion"
from one sphere of being to another, "where unreserve has ruled, even
wordlessly, between people, the word of dialogue has happened sacramentally." [72]

The basic dialogic movement of unreserved turning to the Other
is contrasted by Buber with the attitude he called "re-flexion" *(Rückbiegung)* and which he characterized as an attitude that regards the
Other only as a thinking and experiencing object, and permits the
other to exist only as "part of myself," without recognizing the otherness of the Other or comprehending it with love.[73]

This "loving comprehension" of the Other, which is still a connotation of the Hebrew word "to know," finds its highest expression in
the love between man and woman, when that love truly represents the
human fulfillment of Eros as a cosmic force. The experience of the
lover is then bipolar, a silent dialogue which comprehends what both
the lover and the loved one have in common: "Only the being whose
otherness, accepted by my being, lives and faces me in the whole compression of existence, brings the radiance of eternity to me. Only when
two say to one another with all that they are: 'It is Thou!' is the indwelling of the Present Being between them." [74] To unite "the indwelling of the Present Being," the shekinah, with the world means for
each man to be a coworker, wherever he may happen to be, in helping
to fulfill the meaning of the world.

At the same time this also serves to illustrate what Buber meant
when he said that the spoken human Thou is always accompanied by
the "eternal Thou," that the I-Thou world is a transparent world that
looks out to God. Even our relation to God need not involve esoteric
experience, such as mysticism and gnosis; it is rather a question of dialogue in a concreteness that is attainable by all people. In the religious
relation man can also behave as a knowing and experiencing subject
and desire to draw God into his "I." He can overestimate ecstatic experience that leads us out of our humdrum daily life and excludes the
world from a relation to God and make this experience his criterion.

The episode "A Conversion" on the other hand, acknowledges the union between man and man, and a religion which is "simply all that is lived in its possibility of dialogue." [75] Being takes refuge in mysticism; in dialogue it is converted into responsibility, into the "strict sacrament of dialogue" in the midst of the life of the world, which in its elemental core is not denied but hallowed.

"Simply all that is lived in its possibility of dialogue!" shows how Buber found the essence of religion in the "world concreteness" of every moment in its summons and responsibility and "strict sacrament of dialogue"—which he considered in the section "Morality and Religion" as a possible unity, representing as an ideal condition the complete integration of the ethical into the religious. A clarification of the term "world concreteness" in connection with Buber's unusual use of the concepts "sacrament" and "sacramental" is necessary at this point for a proper understanding of his personal spiritual development.

"World concreteness," which differs from the "world continuum of time and space" in that it is a sign and a summons addressed to me, goes back to Buber's characterization of mythical experience. To recognize a sensuous-real event as a sign of a supracausal connection, to experience it in its total irrationality absolutely and as a divine event—these were the criteria of mythical world experience as outlined in the address "Myth in Judaism." [76] Corresponding to "world concreteness," an event also has an absolute and irrational effect and is experienced as a sign—and thus the question arises why Buber described man's responsive reaction sometimes as "myth" and sometimes as "sacramental word." What change has taken place?

Between these two views lies the experience of the one personal God and His holiness. Myth in its strict sense is the expression of the union between man and God and of their essential equality; it still knows nothing of the confrontation of I and Thou.[77] Dialogue is possible only with a personal God. "Sacramental dialogue" anticipates what Buber some years later in relation to Hasidism called "sacramental existence." [78] In a section about the Hasidic message, originally given as a lecture in 1934, there is an explanation of sacrament: "That the godlike and the human unite with one another, without mutual dissolution, is the chief meaning of sacrament." [79] Sacrament was for Buber the consecration of unification which affects the entire person; it is part of the very nature of sacrament that the Absolute, meaning, should be given bodily form.

Sacramental existence means that lived life as such is the path to salvation and needs no special instrumentality of grace. A theoretical basis for this is provided by the Jewish doctrine, lovingly elaborated in Hasidism, that God is both transcendent and "indwelling" in the world. "Through the world-indwelling of God, the world, speaking in terms of general religion, becomes a sacrament," as was stated in the foreword to "Chassidische Bücher" [Hasidic books] of 1927.[80] This should be understood in the sense that to man things and beings "are available in their sacramental possibility," so that he could consecrate them to God or, speaking Hasidically, redeem the divine sparks in them. The world concreteness of every lived moment consists in the possibility of becoming sacramental, of bearing redemptive events. Sacramental existence means the active acceptance of God's work in all things; man communicates with God through his service in the work of creation. In this sense Buber could speak of the "indwelling of the Present Being" between men who have become Thou to one another.

At the time of his mythical world interpretation Buber's attitude can be described as naive pan-sacramentalism. Sacramental dialogue seeks to comprehend the whole of life, but its meaning is responsibility in diversity and complexity which are immeasurable: "We respond to the moment, but at the same time we respond on its behalf. A newly created concrete reality has been laid in our arms; we answer for it. A dog has looked at you and you answer for its glance; a child has clutched your hand and you answer for its touch; a host of men moves about you, you answer for their need." [81] Buber was at all times an enthusiast of the Unconditioned: "responsibility" is demanded in *Dialogue* just as passionately as "realizing" is in *Daniel*—in both cases there is the danger of carrying human possibilities too far. "Responsibility" is in Buber's sense "realization" of the possible godliness of the world, and hence contains a creative element; but this realization does not mean a formative activity but rather service and dedication. "You shall not hold yourself back" was written by Buber as early as 1919 in an article "What Is to Be Done?" *(Was ist zu tun?)*.[82] The unreserved giving of one's entire person is the element that distinguishes Buber's conception of responsibility from the meaning of the word in its purely ethical significance to denote the suppression of opposing impulses.

"In the unconditionality of his deed man experiences communion with God" is already stated in the address on "Jewish Religiosity." [83] Wherever the unconditioned deed reveals "a hidden divine Countenance, there is the core of Judaism." [84] Buber's "responsibility" goes beyond the postulate of the categorical imperative and points to the biblical command: "Be holy for I your God am holy." The realization that man is made in the image of God, which is the meaning of this commandment, precludes ethics as a special sphere of being: "One serves God not with the spirit but with the entire reality of being without reservation. There is not one realm of spirit and another realm of nature, but only one becoming realm of God; and God is not spirit, but that which we call spirit and that which we call nature equally stem from God who is above both in equal unconditionality, and whose kingdom attains its fullness in the complete unity of spirit and nature." [85]

"Elements of the Interhuman"

It may be said that between the singular and plural of beings, Buber's speech symbolism discovered the dual as man's genuine being-form: "The basic fact of human existence is man with men," we find at the end of the essay "What Is Man?" (*Das Problem des Menschen,* Hebrew edition, 1943; German special edition, 1948).[86] The "Prospectus" of this socio-historical introduction to a philosophical anthropology introduces the "sphere of the in-between" to which Buber in 1953 devoted a short study called "Elements of the Interhuman." Buber called this "between" a "primordial category of human reality," which is created together with man's existence but which is conceptually not yet comprehended.

In all nature man alone knows the other as an independent Opposite, whereas an animal's participation in the world is an activity determined by and involving its body. One man can participate with another without violating his otherness; he is able to "communicate" with him in a common sphere that transcends the individual spheres of the two partners. Through this contact from life to life there arises a "creative middle" (Gabriel Marcel), an excess (Maurice Friedman), a reality that is not a continuity but arises from the meeting and then disappears, and is more than the individual soul but still not yet the world: "Beyond the subjective, on this side of the objective, on the narrow ridge where I and Thou meet, is the realm of the in-between." It is a field of energy, as it were, which actualizes man's personal aspects: to the extent that man says "Thou," he becomes I. The "interhuman" is the sphere that must be strengthened if modern man's fast disappearing personal life is still to be saved so that genuine community, beyond individualism and collectivism, might be restored.

Accordingly, "man with man" must constitute the basis for a science of man that includes anthropology and sociology. In "Elements of the Interhuman" Buber undertook to clarify the suppositions for such a philosophical anthropology by means of a separate study of the sphere of the in-between, setting forth in five sections its underlying principles and limits. In *Dialogue* as well he had contributed only fragments toward an ontology of the dialogical life, and since this as reality is not a continuity but lightning flashes that dart back and forth, it does not lend itself to systematic treatment but can only be illumined from different points of view.

If we follow Buber's presentation of the dialogical from *I and Thou* to "Elements of the Interhuman," we understand what Buber meant when he said at the beginning of his "Answer" [87] that it was his task to find a generally understood conceptual language for a non-conceptual unique experience. The change that occurred in his language between these two writings is a clear indication of his efforts to find a suitable language and a philosophic method—not because he was loath to abandon the rules of the game but because of his characteristic urge to communicate. *Dialogue* was still looked upon as "a thing of creation, of the creature"; this work is, to be sure, far removed from a religious tract, but the basic religious experience and the knowledge of mutual ontic participation within creation are still conspicuous. In "Elements of the Interhuman" Buber took pains to keep this basic experience in the background; he did not speak of it but out of it, and confined himself to the limited sphere of the problem he was discussing.

The first section deals with a basic distinction: "the social and the interhuman." In the introduction to the first volume of the series *Die Gesellschaft*,[88] Buber used the concept "interhuman" *(zwischenmenschlich)* which he had coined in 1905–1906 in the sense of "social," thus following common usage by relegating relations between individuals to the sphere of the social.

"We may speak of social phenomena wherever the life of a number of men, lived with one another, bound up together, brings in its train shared experiences and reactions." [89] Collective being-together and personal being-for-one-another are two radically different and incompatible concepts. Since the former liberates man from anxiety and loneliness while the latter sets high standards for him to follow, it is understandable that preference should be given to closely knit group life. Buber had experienced the sustaining power of the group when on one occasion he joined the marchers of some movement and felt that merely keeping step with them integrated him into the ranks of the procession so that he lost all personal contact with the marchers beside him.

The sphere of the interhuman reaches further than that of sympathy. Its peculiar effectiveness, the "secret of contact," can also apply to two strangers or even enemies. The decisive factor is not the feelings of the two partners, but that they should not become an object for one another. In contradiction to the social, Buber once more emphasized that the interhuman is not concerned with lasting relations but with actual meeting which deeply affects the two people.

A special set of problems arises with respect to the interhuman because people are not always what they appear to be. Some people live from the center of their being while others seek to create a definite image of themselves and behave accordingly. Where appearances and falsehood prevail, the very existence of the interhuman is threatened, for its truth rests on the assumption that people will present themselves as they are. The behavior of an "image-man" is often dictated not by a conscious will to deceive but by shame and cowardice, by the fear to appear as he really is. As in all ethical questions, Buber was also convinced of the possibility of repentance and conversion, and he considered the view that regards human character to be unalterable as false: "Man as man can be redeemed." [90]

At the same time Buber took a stand against the fatalism in modern literature as represented, for example, by Sartre. Man's need to turn directly to man has not been entirely lost, and can be restored, despite the mood of our age, for it belongs to man's very existence. Nothing more is needed than a willingness to accept the one I am dealing with as a person, even when I am compelled to oppose his convictions. This means that I must experience him in his wholeness, that I must "become aware" of him, as Buber said, that is, comprehend the dynamic center which gives to each of his utterances and actions its peculiar character. I must respect the mystery of his person and refrain from reducing his personal uniqueness to recurrent and comprehensible structures. This requires an aptitude that is generally designated as intuition but for which Buber prefered the concept "imagining the real," which he had already introduced in 1951 in "Distance and Relation," describing it as the capacity "to hold before one's soul a reality arising at this moment but not able to be directly experienced." [91] As "personal making present," imagining the real means that when I find myself in a common situation with another person, I experience his participation in a vital way, not as something detached but as *his* life process.

This concept of intuition brings us to the subject of Bergson's influence on Buber which is generally taken for granted since Buber's prewar writings reveal a certain affinity with the basic thoughts of the French philosopher. However, Hans Kohn pointed out in his book as early as 1930 that Buber did not know Bergson's works when he wrote *Daniel*,[92] and that at no time had they ever had any appreciable influence on him.[93] In his introduction to the Hebrew edition of Bergson's works, the conclusion of which appeared as an independent essay in German under the title "Zu Bergsons Begriff der Intuition" [Bergson's concept of intuition],[94] Buber pointed out a number of basic differences in their thinking. Bergson starts from the experiencing I, Buber from the vital contact with the otherness of the Thou. To Bergson intuition is sympathy which insinuates itself into an object until the duality of the viewer and the thing viewed vanishes, at the same time claiming for intuition absolute knowledge; whereas for Buber the peculiar being of the two partners in the meeting remains intact, and this is in no sense a question of knowledge but of "a substance experienced in giving and taking."

It is precisely in "Elements of the Interhuman" that Buber emphasized that an "image" I have of my partner can inhibit the development of the interhuman—either because my partner wants to appear different from what he really is or because my own perception of him is too schematic and fails to comprehend him in his wholeness and uniqueness. Another inhibition is mentioned in the section "Imposition and Unfolding," in which two fundamental ways of influencing others are described. One of these ways is direct and importunate, having no regard for the person of the other and its individual qualities, being concerned only with the imposition of a definite opinion. For this method of influencing others, propaganda can serve as a model.

In contradistinction to this type of influence, unfolding or disclosure represents the proper effective method of the educator. He too desires to have others adopt what he has recognized as right: "Because it is right, it must also be alive in the microcosm of the other, as one possibility among others. It is only necessary to evoke the potentiality of the other person; moreover, this evocation is not brought about essentially by teaching, but by meeting, by existential communication between someone who is in actual being and someone who is in a process of becoming." [95] The educator will always proceed from the view that every pupil entrusted to him is a person and hence the bearer of a definite mission in the fulfillment of his being, in the development of which the educator must help. It is of utmost importance that, together with the self-realization of the individual, the creation meaning of his existence should also be realized; the mutual help extended in this way is the highest effect of the interhuman.

In the concluding section Buber summarized the criteria of genuine dialogue. Here another element must be added to those already mentioned, namely, that he who takes part in the dialogue must "give of himself" and not withhold what he has to say. Genuine dialogue is an ontological sphere; the common life of the word must be respected by all the participants: "At such times, at each such time, the word arises in a substantial way between men who have been seized in their depths and opened out by the dynamic of an elemental togetherness." [96] Genuine dialogue cannot be arranged beforehand; it takes its own course: "the course of the spirit, and some discover what they have to say only when they catch the call of the spirit." [97] With this explanation of "word" and "spirit," Buber returned at the end of the work to the secret sphere of the dialogic life.

DIALOGIC LIFE WITHOUT FULL MUTUALITY

Addresses on Education

In his preface to *Addresses on Education*, Buber stated that the addresses belong to three clearly differentiated stages of his pedagogical activities and owe their origin to totally different situations. The address "On Education" was given in 1925 at the Third International Education Conference in Heidelberg; the subject of discussion was "The Development of Creative Powers in the Child." The second address "Education and World View" took place at the Jewish Lehrhaus for Adult Education in Frankfurt in 1935 in connection with Buber's untiring efforts to help German Jews achieve a new orientation after the catastrophe of 1933 had taken the ground from under their feet and to lead them back to the spiritual values of Judaism. The address on "The Education of Character" was delivered in Hebrew in 1939 at the National Conference of Jewish Teachers in Tel Aviv.

Common to all three periods is Buber's participation in the problems of adult education. The decades after the beginning of the century, especially the twenties, were an age of far-reaching educational reforms in Germany. Buber's passionate interest in adult education was demonstrated in his participation in the work of the Hohenrodter Bund. This enabled him after 1933, as the director of the Central Office for Adult Jewish Education, to devote himself to the training of teachers who were needed for Jewish children who had been excluded from the German schools to help them cope with their new problems and, at the same time, give them instruction in Judaism. After he had settled in Palestine Buber's pedagogical work was placed in the service of the practical demands of Palestinian Zionism. In 1949, after the establishment of the state, he founded the University for Teachers of the People and became its director in 1953. His main concern in this educational work within his own country was the training of teachers who would be able to awaken in the Jews who had emigrated to Israel from all parts of the world an interest in Judaism and a civic sense of common goals.

Despite the different character of these world events, the spirit of the three addresses is of an impressive and convincing unity. The pedagogical problems are treated with great insight and are not compromised by the political upheavals of that period. For Buber the catastrophe was not unexpected; an awareness of the crisis in European culture is evident in his prewar writings and was intensified by the enthusiasm with which his newly discovered dialogic principle filled him.

The unified spirit that pervades the addresses is apparent from two sentences taken from the first and third address respectively:

"The relation in education is one of pure dialogue."

"Education worthy of the name is essentially the education of character." [98]

The education of character, which has nothing to do with the transmission of knowledge and the training of individual functions in the pupil but with the person as a whole, presupposes a personal relation between teacher and pupil. The basis of pedagogical influence is for Buber the pedagogical meeting, the I-Thou relation between teacher and pupil. The primary situation of the teacher, who cannot select his own pupils, gives rise to a basic contradiction at the very outset which militates against the indispensable requisites for meeting, namely, "the Thou meets me out of grace; it is not found by seeking," as we read in *I and Thou*. [99]

Hence, in the epilogue to *I and Thou* of 1958 Buber spoke of those meetings which under the laws of our common social life do not admit of full mutuality such as the pedagogical relation and the relation between a legitimate therapist and his patient. Full mutuality cannot

exist in a relation in which a deliberate attempt of one party to influence the other constitutes an essential part of the relation itself:
"Healing, like educating, is only possible to one who lives over against
the other, and yet is detached." [100] Another example Buber gave is that
of the influence of the pastor where full mutuality would infringe on
"the sacred authenticity of his mission." All other things that happen to
man out of grace and which permit him to influence the being of others
with his life have become a matter of law and routine. Does not this
paradox deprive the I-Thou relation of its basis and thereby destroy its
essence? One must realize the deep significance of the I-Thou primary
word in order to understand the high regard that Buber had for the
profession of teaching.

It is not an accident that Buber should point out, before he spoke
of the pedagogical relation in the Epilogue to *I and Thou*, that full and
lasting mutuality "does not inhere in people living together," and that,
like all things human, it is subject to limitations that stem from man's
inadequacy. The human Thou inevitably becomes an It; the "inborn
Thou" is realized in the case of each individual and can complete itself
in none: every human Thou is a mediator to the "eternal Thou,"
which alone can never become an It.

This mediation to God holds good for the profession of the educator, doctor, or pastor in an eminently high sense. The teacher is a representative of God not only through the word of trust spoken to him.
From the very nature of his office, which those entrusted to him may
not choose, from the "Thou" of his primary address which comprehends them all, a mediating position is conferred upon him from above
to below; in his love for them all he stands in God's stead: "He enters
the school-room for the first time; he sees them crouching at the desks,
indiscriminately flung together, the misshapen and the well-propor-
tioned, animal faces, and noble faces in indiscriminate confusion, like
the presence of the created universe; the glance of the educator accepts
and receives them all . . . for in the manifold variety of the children
the variety of creation is placed before him." [101] In the third address,
Buber added another important element to this initial situation. Again
we read: "These boys—I have not sought them out; I have been put

here and have to accept them as they are—but not as they now are in this moment, no, as they *really* are, as they can become."

This projection of the pedagogical into the religious sphere was not a matter of secondary importance to Buber. It did not appear to him as an unattainable ideal but as the great figure of the zaddik in the Hasidic communities, who was teacher, doctor, and pastor in one, combining in his person all three professions mentioned by Buber in his epilogue to *I and Thou* that in our time are practiced separately.

From the very beginning of his Hasidic studies Buber looked upon the zaddik as the perfect man, for he was the perfect helper. In his early days he called these "righteous men" an "institution of mediators" which arose from the distress of the people.[102] The love of the "righteous man" manifested itself in three spheres. The largest sphere included the sick and needy who came to him from afar with their troubles, expecting to be healed and saved. The second sphere was the community which freely became attached to him as the spiritual leader. The third and narrowest sphere consisted of the students with whom he often lived in a common household community. They all experienced the radiation of his charismatic being; they were healed and instructed by "supra-lingual transmission of the mystery," by the "non-arbitrariness of his being as he is." The effect of this teaching and learning arose because "in the atmosphere of the Masters, in the non-arbitrary activity of their being, the ineffable How hovered in the air and descended as testimony." [103] The high pedagogical value of Hasidic community life, as it emerged in Buber's transmission, has recently been examined in a dissertation by one of Heidegger's students who is extremely critical of the dialogic principle.[104] The zaddik, however, was not a completely independent figure in his own right but reflected a still greater tradition of the past, namely, the prophets of the prehistoric biblical days who were workers of miracles and popular leaders and whose teaching was life and word in one.

In *Addresses on Education* Buber did not refer to Hasidism, and in his address "On Education" he called the master of former times the model teacher. For in those days when journeymen and apprentices lived together with the master, the unintentional effects of teaching proceeded from the wholeness of being. The students not only learned "handwork or brainwork" but also, without being aware of it, "the mystery of personal life: they received the spirit."

The convictions and presuppositions which Buber brought to the Pedagogical Conference in 1925 serve to explain his statement at the opening of his address "On Education"; he found the subject under discussion, The Development of Creative Powers in the Child, highly questionable, except for the last two words, the child—not just millions of individual children but the child as an indisputable reality. A newborn child means the grace of being able to make a new start: "In every hour the human race begins." [105]

Buber thus introduced his hearers to the meaning of creation: the creation that is constantly taking place, the unique creation. He then pointed out how the word *creative* had been misused and how its meaning has deteriorated in recent centuries: "Creation originally means only the divine summons to the life hidden in non-being." [105a] The autonomous and underivative instinct in a child to see something come into being that did not exist before is called by Buber the *Urhebertrieb*, "the originator instinct." This is an instinct that can never degenerate into lust or greed because it is directed not to possessions but to activity. The child demands its share in the becoming of things.

But is it the task of the teacher to develop this instinct alone? Man as "originator" is solitary; education leads him into the community, addressing itself not only to the "originator instinct" but above all to another equally original drive, the instinct for unification.

The infant's striving for relation, which appears like a primordial recollection of the prenatal union with his mother, like a "wordless prefiguration of the Thou-saying," was one of the basic elements of Buber's dialogic principle: here, as in the life of primitive people, he found a concrete example of "the a priori of relation," the "inborn Thou." The development of the child's soul is above all bound up with this instinct for unification.

The educator is to give direction to the child's striving for relation, his almost boundless capacity for comprehending the world. He creates a selection of the actual world, and to do this he must be for the child an elemental reality; he must rely not on compulsion but on a genuine union which is addressed to the child in a personal manner and which awakens a response in the "tiny spark" of the child's soul.

The task of education then is not the release and unfolding of creative powers, nor is it that other tendency of the "new" education whose adherents generally contrast Eros with the "will to power" of former generations. Neither is it the will to power, according to Buber, but the power of tradition which former educators set up over against the natural existence of their pupils. With the general weakening of traditions, teachers find that they must rely on themselves and their own resources. But Eros cannot be the basic principle of education. Eros is choice and is not compatible with the peculiar objectivity of the teaching profession which resists "mingling with the private spheres of the person."

Buber illustrated the sober, ascetic character of certain professions by introducing the concept of "inclusion." [106] It is not a new term in his writings; he had used it in *Daniel* to describe the consummation of a polarity, the realization of the counter-pole in one's own inner self.[107] Now, however, it means an elemental bipolar experience in the actual confrontation of two people: the common situation experienced from the standpoint of the other, not with imagination but with the entire person. "Inclusion" is not empathy: one's own reality is not excluded in favor of the other but is extended by it. Only when mutuality includes the presence of the other does Eros become love.

A relation of two people which is more or less characterized by the element of "inclusion" was called by Buber "dialogic," without being necessarily dependent on the spoken word. A small child knows when he is being "addressed" by his mother without understanding her words. "Trust, trust in the world because this human being exists" is the innermost core of the dialogic relation in education. Because this human being exists, therefore he must really be there in a constant potential presentness; he must truly accept the child as one of the bearers of his communion with the world, one of the focal points of his responsibility for the world.

No other relation is based on "inclusion" as much as the pedagogical, but this must necessarily be a one-sided inclusion. To illustrate this

Buber cited three main types of the dialogic relation. The first refers to the other individual as a spiritual person and recognizes his responsible attitude to being and truth, even when this is opposed to his own. The second basic relation, the pedagogical, is directed to the entire person. Here the educator must "include" the pupil and must experience the educational process from his point of view; the pupil's viewpoint, however, must not include that of the teacher, for this would disrupt the pedagogical relation or lead to the third basic type, friendship. Education means selection of the effective world by a single person. But there are no rigid maxims as to how and to what end one should be educated; there are only cultural periods in which society sets up a universally valid educational ideal.

But in a time when all traditional values have broken down, what remains to be built up, and to what end must we educate the youth? Nothing, but the image of God!

Buber, who at the beginning of his address alluded only briefly to the existence of creation and the misuse of the concept "creator," set forth his own faith experience and thus erected a bridge that led to his Hasidic ideal of man. He reminds us that man is made in the image of God and that the educator, like all of us, stands in the *imitatio Dei*: "Man, the creature who forms and transforms the creation, cannot create. But he, each man, can expose himself and others to the creative Spirit. And he can call upon the Creator to save and perfect His image." [108]

These grave words spoken in 1925 led to the second address, "Education and World View," given in the darkest hour of Jewish history. In the essay "Imitatio Dei," which in point of time is close to "On Education," Buber wrote: "The secret of God which stood over Job's tent [Job 29:4] . . . can only be fathomed by suffering, not by questioning, and man is equally forbidden to question and to imitate these secret ways of God." [108a] To imitate God can only mean to walk in His ways of mercy and justice (Deut. 13:5). For Buber the Jew differs from the heathen in that he "recognizes" God in all of His manifestations—even when God afflicts him and His hand is heavy upon him. The concluding words of "Imitatio Dei" are thus deeply moving in their anticipation of the impending calamity: "Only when the secret no longer stands over our tent but breaks it do we learn to know God's ways with us . . . and we learn to imitate him." [108b]

Buber's very first warning to the German Jews in 1933 bore witness to his indestructible faith. He saw the historical catastrophe as an ordeal of Judaism in which its innermost being was questioned by God: "If we would turn to him, abandon the false freedom with all its deceptive assurances, turn to God's freedom which is a binding to God, then this reeling through the dark mountain pass will reveal itself as a way, our way to the light." [109]

Buber was one of the first to recognize that, after all external assurances had failed, the Jews needed a new, personal, existential hierarchy of values, and that they must rediscover the sources and goals of their Jewish destiny. This is the road he pointed to in all his addresses to his people in the time of crisis.

German Jewry at that time—and "Education and World View" confirms it—was by no means in agreement, but was split into a number of groups with different world views, religious and non-religious. To many, *education* appeared to be a luxury they could ill afford in the light of the pressing practical problems of that day. Buber recognized, however, that those who strive toward a goal must not neglect their point of departure lest they lose sight of the goal. The point of departure, needless to say, should not be chosen at random, but should represent an original stand, a primordial reality.

Education, as Buber saw it, is not concerned with a world view but with world and reality. It is a matter of confronting all the various groups having different world views with the whole of the peoplehood, so that each could learn to find its place there and thus grow into a genuine community. The participating groups should have a common view of the constructive forces of the people and be imbued with the ideal of common service: "Community is the overcoming of *otherness* in lived unity." [110] The various groups within a people are not united by feverish activity directed toward different ends but by the common unfolding of the common reality.

A further consideration to be borne in mind is that only when a world view ceases to be pure thought and is tested in life do we know whether it has "air roots" or "earth roots"; and this will decide its reality content, verification, and reliability. In all world views there is a "dialectic of the inner line," an inner front between truth and falsehood, between the real and the fictive conviction. Educational work helps to implant a world view in the soil of one's own world; it trains our "world view conscience" with which the individual is existentially responsible for a world view: "In the uniform marching line of the group today there is no distinguishing any more between one person's step which is the expression of his direction-moved existence and another person's step which is nothing else than an eloquent gesture. And yet this distinction, which cuts straight across each group, is more important than that between groups. For only those who realize with their life-substance will establish new viable reality. Success may depend on the impetus of the troop, but upon the genuineness of the individuals depends what this success will announce in the depths of the future: genuine victory or its counterfeit." [110a]

Buber did not include this address to the German Jews in his collection of Jewish writings. What it contains concerning education and world view is of general human interest. To those who were able to read between the lines, it must have sounded like the summons of a divine decree. To the German reader of today it appears as a *mene tekel* that proved true ten years later.

Buber also demanded of his Jewish brethren that they turn from their ways, for they too must stand the test and prove themselves. This confirmation is the theme of "The Education of Character."

To train character means to impress upon it the connection between the essential unity of an individual and the consequences of his actions. In this respect life itself is already educational. He who is called to the profession of teaching stands in the midst of his "impressing infinity": with his conscious selection of the world that he brings to the pupil, with his responsibility, and with the set limits within which character training can succeed.

These limits are already drawn because ethics cannot be taught. Character does not signify knowledge but confirmation; and thus it can well be that the most unabashed liar in the class could write the best essay on the destructive power of the lie without drawing the necessary consequences from it for himself. Another difficulty is that the most self-reliant students could be the ones least likely to accept arbitrary standards as to what is good and what is evil on mere authority. Character training is possible only through the pupil's confidence in the teacher and in the truth of his human existence. The pupils must accept the teacher as person and know that they are confirmed by him. Buber's insistence that pedagogical meeting and pedagogical intention should be considered the basis of educational influence goes back to the address he gave in 1925.

The chief difficulty for character training in our time lies in the breakdown of tradition and of traditional values of the last centuries. The concept of ethical character based on established maxims is today obsolete for character training: "We cannot conceal from ourselves that we stand today on the ruins of the edifice whose towers were raised by Kant." [111] The gap today between older people and youth represents not only the conflict between two generations but also the conflict between an old world that for thousands of years has "believed that there is a truth superior to man and an age that does not believe in it any longer—will not or cannot believe it any longer." [112]

In "Education and World View" Buber demanded Jewish educational work as a constructive inner-forming power as opposed to the dismal uniform step of marching columns. He appealed to the "common memory" that had been preserved for centuries, to the long history of Jewish spiritual fortitude. The Zionist community in Palestine was to realize social and national justice: a "people" as a model society living in peace and justice, a chosen people in the biblical sense of election, was the goal of spiritual Zionism to which Buber for decades had been summoning the youth. But when he came to Palestine in 1938, he found the country in turmoil, and the relations between Jews and Arabs extremely tense. Under the pressure of historical events the youth in the country had succumbed to rabid nationalism, rejected religious calling, and in a desire to be like all the other nations, were prepared like them to suspend the Ten Commandments if the existence of the people was at stake. Much of this can be read between the lines of "The Education of Character"—an impressive testimony to Buber's incorruptible sense of justice and love of truth.

In this situation it was hopeless to attempt to demonstrate with arguments that unconditional norms still existed. Radical changes do not come from conceptual thought but from being: collectivity and the group have today taken the place of absolute values and constitute the highest court of appeal against whose decrees there is no redress. A serious illness has infected the human race, but "it is idle to call out to a mankind that has grown blind to eternity: 'Look! the eternal values.' " [112a]

The many grave difficulties that attended character training in Buber's time were now clearly seen, but it was under such difficulties that his pedagogical genius was fully revealed. Despite the fact that he was deeply rooted in the tradition of his forefathers, he could "accept" the young generation wholeheartedly and "comprehend" it. His success in this respect can be attributed to the fact that he did not believe that "moral character" based on maxims of unconditional validity was an ultimate value. That he personally experienced the sickness and need of his time on the religious plane aggravated the seriousness of the situation. Not only has ethical autonomy been abandoned in our day but the holy has also been violated—the meaning of creation itself. But other hopeful paths are beginning to appear in the religious sphere: a turning *(tshuva)*, the grace of a new beginning. A young generation that has sold out to collectivity has also renounced its human prerogative to be a "person." But since man was created to be a "person" and to bear personal responsibility, there will always be moments in which he will feel something missing in his relation to himself. In the midst of this inner struggle and restless longing the educator must stand by the young person and strengthen him. Buber's point of departure was his trust in creation, in "its being permeated throughout by vital dialogue," in the common participation of its creatures and their need of one another. If direct contact is restored between man and man, the eternal Thou will by that same token also be the object of personal address, and we shall have entered the sphere of reconciliation.

The capacity was given to Buber, as to few people of the older generation, to "accept" the young generation and to confirm it in its refusal to have fixed values imposed upon it. It is in such a situation that the educational ideal can be realized, the ideal that Buber regarded as the highest, even though it appeared so seldom: a person of great character, one who in every situation acts with his entire substance, who realizes that every situation is a unique portion of life that has never been before and will never return, and demands the entire person: "It demands presence, responsibility; it demands you." [113] He who in every instance is responsible for "world-concreteness," that is, meets the demands of the situation out of a sincere readiness to assume responsibility for his entire life; such a person's being, impelled by the unifying force of this urge for responsibility, will be prepared for unity of action. A great character does not stand outside the norm—but the norm is for him not maxims but forms of personal address. [114]

An ethical destiny in this sense entails the sanctification of life, as was seen by Buber in Hasidism, the sanctification of daily life which he hoped would be practiced by the Jewish settlers in Palestine as pioneers of a religious as well as a social renewal of man. Thus, Ernst Simon stated "that Buber sees and loves the halutz [pioneer settler] as the real successor of the *hasid,* whose actualization he is in our day in the sense of his religious-socialistic solution: 'The true community is the Sinai of the future.' " [115] Here as well the forms of the sanctification of life are not to be prescribed but are determined by the situations in which man is placed.

"Situations, too, have something to say in the matter" [116] is a dictum with which Buber began a reflection that continues to deepen his thoughts concerning the "dialectic of the inner-line" present in all world views. [117] In the world view theory everything is clear and simple; real historical and biographical situations, however, contain a contradiction within them: "You stand before a political decision or, more exactly, before your part in a political decision, and for the man whom I mean a political decision is also a moral one. You are impelled by the commandment of justice and, your heart moved by it, you look into the almost chaotic depths of a situation, there where the contradiction stares back at you." [118] In the soul struggle that now ensues, it can happen that a great feeling of serenity and certainty comes upon a man involuntarily; nevertheless, his decision remains a daring step.

Buber, then, did not insist on the demand "all or nothing," but only asked that no more of one's own truth be realized than the insight into the situation and its contradictions permits. Ernst Simon has justly called the teaching of the "demarcation line" that is daily drawn anew, besides the concept of "inclusion," Buber's most original contribution to pedagogical theory. [119]

"Genuine education of character is genuine education for community" [120] means that the aim is to educate youth to personal responsibility for world and life, a responsibility of which it has been relieved by collectivity at the price of unity and wholeness of being. That there could be true community only between persons had already been stressed by Buber in the first address and in *Dialogue.* Only true community will lead us beyond the fatal alternatives of individualism or collectivism.

Character education helps above all else "to place man before God's Face." In a collection *Philosophical Interrogations,* recently published in the United States, Buber was asked: How could modern youth be given a sense of the holy and recover its lost wholeness of being? He answered that no teaching could bring this about, that only the personal involvement of the educator could help: his simple personal life in which his daily acts are sanctified and in which those entrusted to him, who knowingly or unknowingly lead unsanctified lives, could take part: "But what is meant here by holy? Now, quite simply this, that the one who lives in contact with this man feels against his will, against his *Weltanschauung*: that is genuine to the roots; that is not a shoot from an alien stem; its roots reach into that sphere from whose inaccessibility I suffer in the overlucid hours of midnight. And at first unwillingly, then also willingly, the man thus affected in contact is himself drawn into connection with that sphere." [121]

It becomes plain how closely related are the tasks of the educator, doctor, and pastor. Buber placed the educator and the pupil in a direct relation to one another, a situation which had hardly ever been achieved before—without pedagogical methods and without assurances, but with trust in the powers that carry man aloft over every abyss of human history: "the fluttering wing of the spirit and the creative word."

The Dialogical Relation in Psychotherapy

In his public discussion with Carl Rogers, who was at that time (April 1957) a professor of psychology at the University of Chicago, Buber was asked how he had acquired so much knowledge about people and interhuman relations without being a psychotherapist himself. Buber replied that in his youth he had studied clinical psychiatry for three semesters and had also taken part in some psychological laboratory experiments under Wundt in Leipzig.

Buber's interest in psychiatry and psychotherapy thus reaches far back. From early youth he had been interested in that narrow line that separates spiritual health from sickness.[122] Public remarks by Buber on matters relating to psychotherapy appeared in the fifties. He did not carry out his early plan to write a criticism of Freud's psychoanalysis.[123] His first statements on this subject are in his preface to Hans Trüb's posthumous work "Healing through Meeting" (1952).[124] Buber began with the idea that in no profession is the contradiction between spirit and life so glaring and no activity so paradoxical as in that of the psychotherapist who, confronted by the "naked abyss" of man, seeks to master it by relying on traditional scientific theory and method and the mechanics of the *ars medica*.

But there will always be psychotherapists—Hans Trüb was one—who will be terrified by these paradoxes and will undergo personal crises when they realize that something altogether different than this reliance on safe professional methods is expected of them, namely, that they forego all attempts to objectify the case before them and enter into the elemental situation of one who appeals for help and one who is appealed to, both of whom come together in a personal meeting that takes place in the "abyss of being-human."

If this term "abyss of being-human," as the common ground between doctor and patient, is to have any meaning, it must presuppose a different relation to sickness than is found in psychoanalysis where guilt in general is taken only as guilt feeling and neurotic illness. Buber, however, saw in guilt a fundamental life process of a superpersonal ontic character. Guilt is not in man, but man stands in guilt—just as man, as we find in *I and Thou*, "lives in his love." This means that the repression of the knowledge of guilt must be treated as more than a psychological problem. Guilt demands penance; the soul must be cleansed. Not every guilt can be expiated where it has been incurred—but life must continue to be lived as expiatory. The psychotherapist is mainly concerned in making his patient's life painless by silencing his guilt consciousness: "I call this successful cure changing hearts. The artificial heart functioning with maximum efficiency no longer pains; only a heart of flesh and blood can pain. . . ."

The psychotherapist who has gone through the crises of his profession will of course have to return to the methodology of his science; but in such a case he will risk taking the path of personal involvement and unreserved confrontation.

In the spring of 1957 Buber gave three public lectures in Washington which were designed to be a contribution of philosophical anthropology to psychiatry. This gave rise to his "Guilt and Guilt Feelings" in which he resumed the thoughts set forth in his preface to "Healing through Meeting." In connection with his lectures Buber also took part in a seminar on the problems of the unconscious given for the benefit of the instructors and assistants of the School of Psychiatry. The above mentioned discussion with Carl Rogers fell within the framework of this American lecture tour.

In "Guilt and Guilt Feelings" Buber began with the statement that psychotherapy of the old school was concerned only with conscious and "unconscious" feelings of guilt, while the problem of guilt itself was left to the theologians. There is surely some justification for such a restriction of the practical field of operations demanded by scientific methodology, the sphere in which the doctor is competent. However, this restriction to psychic guilt—which excludes problems of actual experiences of guilt in the patient's biography—appears in a different light when we consider the psychotherapeutic theory of the fathers of psychoanalysis, Freud and Jung, and their attitude to the question, What is guilt? It turns out that in both of these systems guilt is not granted an ontic character. Freud was a late child of the Enlightenment and a naturalist, and as such he opposed all religious teachings of the existence of an Absolute. This basic attitude compelled him to regard guilt only as violation of a taboo and social authority. But for Jung, whose theory Buber characterized as psychological solipsism and panpsychism, God has no being outside the soul of man. The highest authority for Jung was the "self" that is to be realized and integrates within itself the opposites of good and evil. He also took guilt in the ontological sense to be at most a transgression against the process of individuation, but not as a fact in the relation between the human person and the world he faces.

But actually there are not only purely neurotic feelings of guilt but also illnesses of the soul which arise as a result of something that has gone amiss in the interhuman and social sphere. It is not enough to trace this guilt feeling to a repressed instinctive core in the unconscious and make it conscious. Guilt feelings of this kind go back to fully remembered life processes which torment man and make him ill, although he does not expect to be punished by any authority; these feelings spring from an ever-renewed terror of not being able to undo what has been done, from the dread of being identical with one's self even though one has become another. Buber here spoke of "authentic guilt-feeling" based on man's person and on the fact that he can become guilty and knows it. Such guilt that is incurred by man as person and in a personal situation was called by Buber "existential guilt" and it occurred "when someone injures an order of the human world whose foundations he knows and recognizes as those of his own existence and of all common existence." [125] One can in this sense also, by failing to do something or by participating in a social guilt, become burdened with an existential guilt. A grave existential guilt may be a boundary case and an exception, but every authentic guilt feeling is bound up with the existence of the person and with his participation in the order of being, with his relation to other people for which he bears the responsibility.

An existential guilt cannot be reached with such categories of psychoanalysis as "repression" and "becoming conscious." The doctor must also confront the ontic character of guilt and dare to depart from the safe foundations of his science, knowing that every step he takes involves a risk. The task he now faces, "the regeneration of an atrophied personal center," could only be accomplished "by one who grasps the buried latent unity of the suffering soul with the great glance of the doctor; and this can only be attained in the person-to-person attitude of a partner, not by the consideration and examination of an object." [126] He can, of course, be successful within the limits of his methods in diverting an authentic guilt feeling and reducing it to silence. But this ignores the possibility of repentance through a newly won relation to the world. For this painless life the patient pays a price, that is, he foregoes the opportunity of becoming the being to which his highest aspirations have destined him.

It is instructive to compare the task of the psychotherapist with the often incomprehensible healings performed by the *zaddikim* of the Hasidic communities and attested to by the believers. In this connection Buber remarked that nothing can affect the process of healing so directly as a "comprehensively moving, psycho-synthetic proclamation of a whole unified soul that advances the process of crystallization; it does not 'suggest' but creates in the fellow soul that appeals to it a central unifying core; and the more genuine and perfect this soul is, the greater its care that the appealing soul does not remain dependent upon it: the helper creates the steadfast center not by introducing his own image in the soul that is to be regenerated but by enabling it to look through him into being as through a glass and then having him discover being in himself and making it the core of the living unity." [127] Buber was well aware that the doctor is not a pastor and that he could easily lose himself in dilettantism should he attempt to enter into the personal life of the patient. He could only help the patient help himself and find his own way. But the doctor must recognize the existence of real and personal guilt and, if he would be a conscientious psychiatrist, he must have the courage to confront the patient with his guilt.

But to be equal to this task the doctor must be aware of the spheres in which expiation of guilt can take place. The first sphere is the law which is concerned with the demands that society makes on one who has incurred guilt. Here expiation takes the form of confession, penalty, and indemnification. In this sphere the doctor is not competent, except when it is a question of the patient's anxiety and his fear of censure and punishment. The doctor is also denied access to the highest sphere, that of faith, where confession of sin, repentance, and penance take place between man and God or His representative acknowledged by the guilty man. Only the sphere of conscience concerns the doctor. Man is the only living being who has been given the capacity to see himself from the outside, the capacity to confirm or to reject himself. His conscience is a constant source of anguish and torment, driving those who feel guilt into a state of neurosis, the effects of which are the concern of the psychotherapist.

Only the "great or high conscience"—which, together with existential guilt, is answerable for the relation to its own being—can reach the "ground and abyss" by elevating itself from the entanglements and torments of the soul to a threefold action: to self-illumination, in which man becomes inwardly aware of the full extent of the guilt in relation to his own being; to perseverance, that is, the humble acknowledgment of guilt as belonging to his own being, even when he has in the meantime become another man; and to expiation of the violated order-of-being by means of a new relation to the world around him: "for the wounds of the order-of-being can be healed in infinitely many other places than those at which they were inflicted." [128] To this view of conscience the doctor can lead the patient—but the proper road to be taken by the patient must be walked by him alone.

In "Guilt and Guilt Feelings" the element of one-sided inclusion in the relation of the psychotherapist to the patient is not expressly stated. In the epilogue to *I and Thou* it is emphasized in connection with the situation of the educator: "In order that he [the doctor] may coherently further the liberation and actualization of that unity in a new accord of the person with the world, the psychotherapist, like the educator, must stand again and again not merely at his own pole in the bipolar relation but also with the strength of present realisation at the other pole, and experience the effect of his own action. But again the specific 'healing' relation would come to an end the moment the patient thought of, and succeeded in, practising 'inclusion' and experiencing the event from the doctor's pole as well." [128a]

The question as to whether or not the relation between doctor and patient is based on full mutuality was one of the main questions raised in the public discussion between Buber and Rogers.[129] To Rogers the mutuality of the I-Thou relation is given in those moments in which the relation to the patient is fully effective and unrestricted, when both partners have entered completely into the relation and have undergone a change as a result of this experience.

In the discussion Rogers started from the experience of the doctor who "accepts" the patient as he is, as a whole, as a unique creature of indubitable worth whom he might not only help but whom he also seeks to understand fully in his situation. Over against this reflection from within, Buber started from the respective situations of the two people involved, which are different but irreversible: the patient cannot understand the situation of the doctor and is not in a position to help him. Whether the therapist wishes it or not, his part in the common relation is "detached presence"; he is, as Buber stated in the epilogue to *I and Thou*, "the one who lives over against the other, and yet is detached." [129a] The two partners in the common situation do not stand on the same plane.

In the course of the discussion Rogers always returned to his basic concept of the "acceptance" of the patient by the doctor as the person he is at present in all his feelings and utterances, and saw in this acceptance the factor that has the strongest effect on the patient and contributes most to his healing. In this he proceeded from the premise that it is the task of the doctor to probe to the deepest layer of the patient's being, where he will surely find that in him which is positive and constructive.

Here as well Buber's thinking is more realistic. He was convinced that deep down in man there is the tension of a polarity, the ground *and* the abyss, the positive and the negative—chaos and lack of direction—so that the real task is to give man direction, to strengthen him in his struggle with himself. Over against the concept of acceptance Buber placed that of "confirmation." Confirmation adds to acceptance an element of direction. What is confirmed is the hidden possibility in man, the person he was created. To accept a human being as he now is in his present state is but the beginning. Love that accepts has a premonition of the goal for which this human being was created and of his highest possibilities. Confirmation directs itself to that which a man really is according to his nature and not to the image of the man I now see before me. And it is this confirmation which is met on the other side by a more than personal trust, by an existential trust: "Trust in the world because this human being exists" [129b]—this is not only the innermost core of all education but also the certainty needed by the patient in his struggle against the destructive forces within him.

"In the strongest illness that appears in the life of a person, the highest potentiality of this person may be manifesting itself in a negative form. The therapist can directly influence the development of those potentialities. Healing does not mean bringing up the old but shaping the new: it is not confirming the negative but counterbalancing with the positive." [130]

To arrive at a clearer conception of Buber's understanding of the effect that the therapist has on the patient, we must briefly examine his criticism of Freud's interpretation of dreams and the theory of the unconscious as revealed in the notes of the seminar course.

In his treatment of the unconscious, Freud had fallen into an error, according to Buber, by starting from the assumption that the unconscious must be either physical or psychological. In contradistinction to his predecessors he attached the unconscious to the soul, and in this he was followed by Jung and the psychoanalytical schools. But the positing of these alternate points of departure is unwarranted: the unconscious is a condition in which the two phenomenal modes, the physical-psychical, are still indistinguishable and from which both proceed. The unconscious is our being itself in its still undivided wholeness. It does not manifest itself as such, but by observing states of consciousness we can infer that it has effects that can be investigated by the psychologist. Of the unconscious itself we can say nothing, for it is never given to us: "The radical mistake that Freud made was to think that he could posit a region of the mind as unconscious and at the same time deal with it as if its 'contents' were simply conscious material which was repressed and which could be brought back, without any essential change, into the conscious" (Friedman).

The distinction we make between inner and outer is connected with the fact that the unconscious unity of our being manifests itself only in inner and outer perceptions. Man can experience his unity to a certain extent through his actions, but it is never given to him as an object of cognition. He who deals with the unconscious only within the individual person will regard the basis of human reality as psychic and not as interhuman, and he will tend to psychologize the relations between people.

"The positing by most psychological schools of a non-phenomenological yet psychical reality means the assumption of a quasi-mystical basis of reality. . . . The assumption of an unconscious psyche that exists as something exists in space is either a metaphor or an entirely metaphysical thesis about the nature of being for which we have no basis at all in experience" (Friedman). Buber called Freud a "simplificator," as was Marx in another sphere, whereby he characterized one who deals with a new aspect of reality as if he were solving a life riddle—in Freud's case a great tragic attempt.

From Buber's point of view, Freud's dream interpretation had far-reaching consequences. What we call dream, or the content of dream, is never the real dream itself but always a construction of our formative memory: it is not the reality of the dream but a new reality which is created by our attitude to the reality x, the dream. Our daily life takes place in a common world which is summoned up by a kind of ordering faculty in our consciousness. The dreamer, however, has no part in the common world from which there is no access to the dream world and to that which gives to dreams sequence and coherence.

Dreams are only *one* of the forms of the unconscious. In judging Freud's interpretation of dreams and theory of repression we must bear in mind that: "The unconscious is not something psychical that can be preserved in the underground but just a piece of human body and soul-existence: it cannot at all be raised again as it was. We do not have a deep freeze which retains psychical fragments that may be delivered up intact to the conscious. The unconscious has its own existence which can again be dissociated into physical and psychic phenomena, but this dissociation means a radical change of substance" (Friedman).

In this new transition from the unconscious to the conscious, the participation of the therapist plays a far greater part than has hitherto been assumed. The concept of transference, of the personal binding of the patient to the doctor, appears in a new light. There is a great difference between a doctor who only helps to make conscious something that was already lying unconscious at the bottom of the soul, making his work comparable to that of a midwife, as it were, and a doctor who helps create the new form in which this transition to consciousness takes place: the new element that now makes its appearance is the product of the relation of the patient to the therapist.

It is interesting to note that in this view the responsibility of the doctor is considerably greater. We must now distinguish more clearly than formerly between two types of therapists: those who follow a definite method strictly and hence know more or less the desired result beforehand and those who do not. With the former the doctor runs the danger of imposing himself on the patient more than he himself suspects. A therapist's real ability, however, is shown in his knowing how to listen and, as far as possible, how to keep from relying on any given method.

Existential healing takes place more often through meeting than through insight and analysis. Buber was convinced that for complete healing, down to the very depths of a patient's being, the person of the doctor is more important than method. If we look upon the unconscious as the undivided unity of body and soul, we begin to see its significance for the future development of interhuman relations. It becomes the bearer and guardian of a direct and undivided contact in which body and soul become indistinguishable—and this contact can be established with the mere clasp of the hand. In the patient's full trust the unconscious is directly active, and it will render decisive support to the objectifying mechanism of the analysis.

Even the incomplete indications contained in the notes reveal that Buber had a strong faith in the future development of psychotherapy. It will in time have to turn its gaze from the inner sphere of the soul to the interhuman and cosmic spheres. Buber pointed out that the instinctive sexual life of early childhood has perhaps been exaggerated and that more attention will have to be paid to the "social and cosmic puberty" of late childhood. He predicted that the methods and terminology of psychotherapy will change, just as in our day the terminology of physics has changed, an apt comparison corroborated by the views of Werner Heisenberg, who says with reference to the natural sciences: "the current divisions of the world into subject and object, inner world and outer world, body and soul are no longer applicable . . . Natural science no longer stands before nature as a spectator but recognizes itself as part of this interplay between man and nature. The scientific method of selection, explanation, and systematization is becoming aware of the limits imposed by such a procedure in that it changes and reforms its object, so that the method can no longer remove itself from the object." [131] Psychotherapy is now making rigorous demands on man himself, and they can be met only if the psychotherapist is conscious, like the physicist in our day, of the paradoxes of his task; if he realizes that he is in the same boat with the patient, and that it is not only the scientific method that fills the sails of the boat but also a humble trust in the sustaining power of creation. Buber, whose teaching of "ontic participation" involves the elemental radiation and oscillations of being to being and the hitherto neglected micro-life of unification, was also a pioneer in this sphere.

"THE QUESTION TO THE SINGLE ONE"

Sören Kierkegaard could also have characterized himself, like Buber, "atypical," as one who found no place in the philosophy and theology of his day. In his case he had to contend with both those disciplines—although two generations later philosophical existentialism and dialectic theology were to claim him as their spiritual father. His similarity to Buber is also evident in his poetical gifts and his deep psychological interests. They both found the language of reflective prose inadequate to describe the fullness of the non-conceptual they sought to express, and yet neither regarded poetry as an end in itself but only as an adjunct enlisted in the service of their faith experience.

Kierkegaard classified the atypical aspect of his personality under the category of the "single one," to define which Buber in 1936 devoted the essay "The Question to the Single One," which likewise belongs to the writings that deal with the dialogic principle. Buber had become familiar with Kierkegaard when he, as a student,[132] first read "Fear and Trembling." The work made a lasting impression on Buber and compelled him to reflect on the problem of the relation of the ethical to the religious, a problem that engaged his mind throughout his life and which he treated at length in one of his last works, *The Eclipse of God.*

Buber's close relation to Kierkegaard can also be seen in the similarity of their linguistic usage—an important consideration when we realize what language meant for Buber. In reading "Fear and Trembling" Buber experienced the unprotected hour of decision,[133] which again and again represents the real confirmation of standing-in-existence. Buber's highly personal use of the term *communicate* is also found in Kierkegaard, whose assertion that "the only way that God communicates with man is the ethical" is quoted by Buber.[134] The phrase "the one thing that is needful"—which was for Buber the essence of what "teaching" meant to the great founders of religion—is the title of a talk Kierkegaard gave in 1848 and is found elsewhere in his writings.[135]

The interest in language which united both men points to a common source, the Bible. As a result of his study of Kierkegaard, Buber was one of the first to adopt an attitude of greater understanding for Christianity, which is finding greater acceptance today through the efforts of the church and synagogue to enter into dialogue with one another. Both thinkers are brothers in Abraham, and both are bound by a common response to Abraham's faith. And yet Kierkegaard in his early stage took the fateful path of occidental Christianity by way of Greek philosophy and found in the Socratic doctrine of ignorance a kind of divine service since it "expressed in Greek the Jewish idea that the fear of God is the beginning of wisdom." [136] Kierkegaard's conviction that there is but one mode of time in relation to the unconditioned, the present,[137] was shared by Buber: Kierkegaard's "contemporaneousness" with Christ corresponded to Buber's "stepping before the Countenance." Contemporaneousness with Christ takes us beyond the "scandal"; it demands the paradoxical passion of faith. Christ is the paradox that is never comprehended and subsumed by history. He can never be "known"; he is only "there" for the believer.[138] To be contemporary with Christ means above all to take the "scandal" seriously. But present-day Christianity no longer knows the "scandal"; it has "relaxed the paradox" and "has done away with Christianity without really being aware of it." [139]

God and man are incommensurable magnitudes, and hence paradox is the form which expresses their relation to one another. Paradox is the form which expresses the absolute within the finite; it creates the "scandal" which summons us to make a decision, to the "passion of faith" which is a self-overcoming of man, whereas the "passion of the understanding" runs aground at the "boundary" and founders at the edge of the "unknown." [140] For Kierkegaard, as for Pascal, man is a paradox unto himself and gets to know his true nature only from the Lord.[141] Also for Buber it is only the language of paradox that can do justice to the meeting with God in its "incomparable, non-subsuming uniqueness";[142] the soul can comprehend the entire relation only as *coincidentia oppositorum*. God is "the wholly Other"; but he is also "the wholly Self"; he is the *mysterium tremendum*, but he is also "the mystery of the obvious which is closer to me than my own I." The principle of contradiction loses its validity in the lived relation: freedom and necessity are lived together as one.[143]

Buber's study of Kierkegaard in his early youth must have strongly influenced his conception of Christianity. His own early defense of "religiosity" over against religion as well as his limited understanding for religious forms and institutions owed much to Kierkegaard's struggle against the church of his day. Just as Kierkegaard, "the great arch-critic of Christianity in the nineteenth century," [144] confronted Christian life with Christ's teaching, so did Buber in *Addresses on Judaism* examine the faith reality of the Jewish life of his time. He recognized that Kierkegaard's "leap" out of despair into faith was a legitimate consequence of Luther's theology, and that it was in its uncompromising unworldliness a boundary phenomenon. However, the meanings that "decision" and "direction" had for him were close to that of the Danish thinker, although considerably influenced by the Bible and Hasidism.

Kierkegaard, like Buber, was a religious thinker who refused to be regarded as a prophet. Up to 1849 he looked upon himself as a poet, but he gradually came to the conclusion that the times needed martyrs and not geniuses;[145] consequently in the last years of his life he considered himself to be one of those who in every age are destined to be sacrificed "in order to advance the idea." [146] The desire to confirm his faith was at the basis of his struggle against the Danish church. Faith for him was genuine only when it was rooted in the life of the believer and "becomes substance and form of the life he lives," [147] or, to quote from a note in his journal of 1851: "Spirit is: the power a man's knowledge has upon his life." [148] Thought cannot certify or accredit itself; it must be confirmed by life. This was expressed in one of Buber's formulations of 1937: "Human truth emerges when a man seeks to realize his relation to truth with his whole life; and the imparting of the truth becomes possible when he endorses it with his own person and stakes his Self upon it." [149] That attitude is valid which is lived in the wholeness of the person, whether the Absolute to which one turns is called God or not. The philosophical existentialists who followed Kierkegaard were for the most part not religious thinkers.

"Metaphysics here takes possession of the actuality of the living man with a strength and consistency hitherto unknown in the history of thought. Its ability to do this springs from the fact that man is considered not as an isolated being but in the problematic nature of his bond with the absolute. It is not the I, absolute in itself, of German idealism that is the object of this philosophical thought . . . but the real human person, considered in the ontic connection which binds it to the absolute." [150] Although he did not reject the theological basis of belief, Kierkegaard became the pioneer of a philosophical anthropology.

In this connection Buber has repeatedly been described as an "existentialist," although he rejected this appellation, as he did all "isms" that were applied to him. In the essay "The Question to the Single One," as in *I and Thou* and *Dialogue*, he developed his own point of view from a historical perspective. This step into the sphere of history was significant for his further development. But here he attempted to see one component of his own being in a brotherly "Thou," in its present closeness and historical "otherness." He was constantly aware that Kierkegaard's "single one," in its isolation from God, concerned only one aspect of his own spiritual existence, the soul's becoming one, of which he speaks in *I and Thou*, the ingathering of strength in the being's core.[151] To it must correspond, like the diastole to the systole, the soul's radiation into relation, into the undiminished life relation that is not confined to God alone. For this other aspect of his being as well, there was a historical authority who had symbolic significance for him, namely, Ludwig Feuerbach. In "The Question to the Single One," where Buber developed his theme historically, without reference to himself, Feuerbach is hardly mentioned. But in the essay, "The History of the Dialogic Principle" (1954), he appears as the spiritual counterpart to Kierkegaard and, as the representative of a "pseudo-mystical atheism" in contradistinction to the Dane's "monadic theistic piety," makes his own discovery of the "Thou" questionable.[152] Here we have two opposite figures from an objective historical point of view and, above all, as significant influences in Buber's development: "Of the intellectual forefathers I had already known Feuerbach and Kierkegaard while I was still a student. Yes and No to them had become a part of my existence . . ."[153] In "What Is Man?"[154] Buber confessed that in his youth he had been inspired by Feuerbach, referring to his discovery of the "Thou," which Karl Heim has called "the Copernican turning-point" of modern thought. Buber's assertion that the fundamental fact of human existence is man with man[155] reminds us of Feuerbach's observation in *Principles of the Philosophy of the Future* (1843): "The single individual by himself has not the essence of the human being within him, neither as a moral nor as a thinking being. The essence of man is contained only in the community, in the unity of man with man—a unity, however, that is based only on the reality of the distinction of I and Thou" (par. 59).

Feuerbach was the first to demand a philosophic anthropology whose subject matter was not to be abstract spirit, but "the real and whole being of man" (par. 50). He saw the new philosophy as a complete reduction of theology to anthropology, not to human reason alone but to the entire man as a being of flesh and blood (par. 52). This philosophizing, however, must take into account the fact that man's being is never found in isolation but only in society. Its starting point must be the "secret of the necessity of the Thou for the I," and it must recognize the unity of man with man as its highest principle: "Man by himself is man (in the ordinary sense); man with man, the unity of I and Thou, is God" (par. 60).

In "What Is Man?" and in "The History of the Dialogic Principle," Buber clearly showed that Feuerbach's sensualistic materialism produced a conception of man devoid of all problems. A philosophical anthropology cannot deal with man without relation to the Other, in a tension of being to non-being, and without making man problematical. Furthermore, by dispensing with the theological concept of God with his formulation, "the unity of I and Thou is God," Feuerbach transgressed the limits of anthropology proper in favor of a pseudo-mystical God substitute.

In his early essay on the philosophy of Jacob Boehme (1901)[156] Buber had taken this thought of Feuerbach more seriously, because he was still absorbed in vague mystical experiences of his own. He related this thought to Boehme and to his myth of a God who realizes himself in the world, and he placed it beside the teaching of Francis of Assisi and the Vedanta. At that time the world was for Buber a divine self-revelation, God's becoming in which man is a coworker: he saw "the longing movement of things to one another" as the way "to the new God whom we create, to a new unity of forces." Feuerbach's unity of I and Thou, in which all beings unite to God, was understood by him as the primordial cell of the harmony of all individual forces in the Boehmean sense: in connection with an ontic double movement from above to below and below to above, and corresponding to Boehme's image of the organ in which "every voice, yea, every pipe gives its tone and yet there is but one kind of air, the same air that is in all the voices that resounds in every voice . . . ," Buber was careful not to follow Feuerbach in basing the new unity on the distinction between man and man, for he was concerned even at that early date with the basic need in man for mutuality that came from God and returned to him. At that time it was mainly a matter of finding a mythical image for what he later understood as "ontic participation," the mutual openness and cooperation of beings and things in the world.[157] He was concerned with the problem of being as "primordial community," and of spirit that inheres in all life in sparks.[158] For the full sensible concreteness of all this, he found corroboration in Feuerbach, the fact, namely, that the I attains consciousness of itself only through the Thou. Buber always looked upon Eros as a cosmic force, and he never disavowed his belief in the image of man as microcosm (which presupposes the macrocosm) that had been impressed on his youthful mind by Boehme—and we still meet it frequently in "Elements of the Interhuman." [159] Just as the individual was for him a microcosm, so was the "unity of I and Thou," as it were, the microcosm of "being-housed" in the universe, and in this Feuerbach was for some time his spiritual authority. It may very well be regarded as a fruitful misunderstanding that in this connection he overlooked the materialism and sensualism of his predecessor, but we must make allowances for a young man who culled isolated sentences out of context in the works of an admired philosopher in order to clarify his own vague relation to being.

This peculiar double influence of Kierkegaard and Feuerbach on Buber's prewar development is reflected in the first dialogue in *Daniel*: in the tension with which at the beginning Daniel's soul is directed "to above," in the loneliness of the spaceless universe, and in the concluding symbolic image of his unity with the woman, which seems an apt illustration of Feuerbach's I and Thou as conceived by Buber. This also sheds light on Buber's atypical, world-rejoicing "existentialism" which is anticipated in *Daniel*. But still another utterance during the last years of his life shows that this peculiar early influence of Kierkegaard and Feuerbach continued to the very end, albeit in another form. When he was asked about his relation to philosophical existentialism, Buber answered in *Philosophical Interrogations*: "I have never included myself in such, but feel myself standing perhaps between an existential thinking in Kierkegaard's sense and something entirely different, something which is still out of sight." [160] To this concept of the "wholly Other," which was provided by Kierkegaard, we must add Feuerbach's influence during Buber's early years in order to understand his point of view more fully.

On looking back we see that Feuerbach was a transitional phenomenon and that he was succeeded within the space of a few years by more radical contemporaries: Karl Marx and Max Stirner, who in different ways surpassed him in their anti-Hegelian criticism of materialism.

Stirner regarded Feuerbach's reduction of Christianity to anthropology as a half-hearted measure. To him "man" no longer was a possible point of departure, but only a "single one" who was at the same time the "unique one" with all his uniquely acquired possessions. Also the distinction between the essential and the non-essential in man, all that is transcendental and goes beyond itself in search of a universal idea, was for Stirner an illusion: Feuerbach was relegated by him to "the remains of idealism." We must get rid of not only the theological distinction between the divine and the human but also the anthropological distinction between what man essentially should be and what in fact he is.[161] The unique one is concentrated on his own ego; his task is not to realize universal essence but only to satisfy himself, to be what he *can* be, no more and no less.[162] The idea of humanity is reduced to the individual ego which acquires for itself what it needs.

This unique one, who raises himself to the sole I, to the bearer of his world, knows of no essential relation outside the one to himself; the Other and his responsibilities to him are no concern of his. He feels ethically free, for he does not recognize anything outside himself. On the basis of this rejection of responsibility and the relation of a suprapersonal truth, Buber took Stirner seriously and in "The Question to the Single One" treated him as Kierkegaard's proper historical antagonist. Stirner's "unique one," who is real to himself alone, severs all existential connection with the Other; the beings outside himself are only "nourishment" for his own uniqueness.[163] He simply does not know what "of elemental reality happens between life and life; he does not know the mysteries of address and answer, claim and disclaim, word and answer. He has not experienced this because it can only be experienced when one is not closed to the otherness, to the ontic primal otherness of the other." [164] The role that Stirner played in modern spiritual history is as much a "curious interlude" as that of the Sophists in antiquity.

Buber examined the peculiar similarity and the basic difference between the concepts "the single one" and "the unique one." As far as the destruction of the Hegelian intellectual edifice is concerned and the disintegration of truth, Kierkegaard and Stirner are in agreement. But there is a great difference whether one says with Stirner: "I am the unique one" or with Kierkegaard: "Man must become the single one." Both lift man out of society and confront him with Nothing. With Kierkegaard this happens in the conviction that only the leap into Nothingness can place man before God's Face. With Stirner, however, the impulse is an individualistic anarchism, a creative pleasure in destruction, as noted by Löwith in an observation that is valid far beyond the individual case of Stirner: "The Germans are the first and foremost exponents of the historical vocation of radicalism; they alone are radical, and they alone justly so. There are no others so relentless and ruthless; not only do they bring about the collapse of the existing world so that they may themselves stand fast, they also bring about the collapse of themselves. When Germans demolish, a god must fall, a world pass away. To the Germans destruction is creation, the pulverization of the temporal is disintegration of eternity." [165] Kierkegaard's "single one," who leaves the whole world behind, reminds one of Abraham's boundary situation of faith. Here, too, truth is not something that one can "have"; it is the "real-relation of the whole human person to the unpossessed, unpossessable truth." [166] The daring to take part in that which is: this is "existential" truth, personally conditioned but absolutely binding.

Kierkegaard was convinced that man must free himself from worldly ties if he is to have contact with God; that he must make a choice whether he wants to speak with God or with the world: for him the sacrifice of the world is an act of obedience. In the section "The Single One and His Thou," Buber introduced the question whether the exclusive relation to God must, according to Kierkegaard, necessarily exclude all other relations. In this connection he pointed out that Kierkegaard, the Christian who strives for "contemporaneousness" with Jesus, did not speak in the sense of his master who took the "double commandment" as one, the love of God and the love of our fellowmen. God, who created man and revealed himself to him and who will redeem him, leaves room, in our love for him, for the love of all creatures: "We are created along with one another and directed to a life with one another; creatures are placed in my way so that I, their fellow creature, by means of them and with them, find the way to God." [167] There is but one task that concerns man: to see things "in God," to include all relations in one relation to God, uncurtailed. Just as God comprehends his entire creation, so must man comprehend the limited portion of the world assigned to him. He confirms having been made in God's image and realizes it when he says "Thou" to the beings in his sphere. God cannot be reached by renouncing all worldly rivals. He is not the cosmos, but "far less is he Being *minus* cosmos. He is not to be found by subtracting and not to be loved by diminishing." [168] Buber saw Kierkegaard as a man of exceptional gifts whose intense vision was blurred by an inveterate melancholy: "We have much to learn from him, but not the final lesson." [169]

Kierkegaard's renunciation of marriage, as Buber observed in "The Single One and the Body Politic," was for him "the zero of a spiritual graph" with respect to which every other point received its value. Buber explained his behavior as a symbolic act, as a counterpart to Luther's symbolical marriage whereby a recluse with an overzealous religious fervor was led back to a life with God in the world. For his own day and age Kierkegaard held the reverse process to be necessary: at a time when the masses are dominant, men must again become individuals. In addition to his disinclination for marriage, Kierkegaard feared to be drawn into "the body politic," for he was repelled by the "deformed shape" it had assumed in his day, which seemed to him to be a falsification and denial of creation.

Marriage, which permits us to experience the life substance of another human being, is the strongest and most exemplary bond that leads to the "manifold-otherness" of the body politic. Marriage teaches one to affirm the right and legitimacy of the other, since I affirm this one human being just as he is. He who enters into marriage steps into the most decisive relation to otherness. He has learned "that I cannot legitimately share in the Present Being without sharing in the being of others; that I cannot answer God's lifelong address to me without answering at the same time for the other; that I cannot be answerable for myself without being at the same time answerable for the other as one who is entrusted to me." [170]

The body politic, that "reservoir of otherness," has in our day become the anonymous, unfamiliar crowd whose creaturely affirmation is well-nigh impossible. Its otherness appears to be unfathomable and beyond our reach—except for those "historical hours of enthusiasm" in which the individual transfigures the crowd and submerges himself in the movement of the body politic. In daily life for the most part we "go along with" the others, unwillingly and half-heartedly, without having genuine personal opinions or making personal decisions. He who would truly live with the body politic would have to do so as the single one and attempt to "unmass" the masses, and find in its otherness individual forms that could become his "Thou." The single one need not remove himself from the masses; he must endeavor to convert them into "single ones." "And if he does not achieve much, he has time, he has God's own time. For the man who loves God and his companion in one—though he remains in all the frailty of humanity—receives God as his companion." [171]

Kierkegaard's category of the "single one" was thus changed by Buber into the "single one in responsibility." The biographical hour and the historical hour in which I have been placed cannot be separated and kept apart: the responsibility is *one*—and it is always God to whom I must answer in the language of the situation with which he addresses me. "World-concreteness," as it is called in *Dialogue*, also includes participation in the affairs of the community: political decisions must also be made from the personal ground to which God's word and address are directed.

But these genuine decisions in the political sphere are being threatened more and more by collective decisions. The community is split into groups, each of which is convinced of its right to relieve its followers from making political decisions. A genuine faith relation to God, however, must include everything within itself. Religion cannot content itself with being one more department of life among others or tolerate other spheres besides its own in which it has no power to make decisions. What God demands of me each hour, I learn only in that hour; his "word" comes to me in a unique, unanticipated situation, "a word that is to be found in no dictionary, a word that has now become word." [172] And I answer it with the decision of my conscience which, it is true, can only give me an "uncertain certainty" as to the right way; but these struggles of the soul that take place in the depths of our personal life are necessary in the struggle "between the world's movement away from God and its movement toward God." [173]

There are two things which Buber saw as having become questionable in our day: the person and the truth. The first has become questionable because of the inroads of collectivization in the life of modern man; the second, because it has been made political. It is precisely the "single one in responsibility," the one who is responsible for his truth, who is most vulnerable to this danger. The process of collectivization began as a reaction to an overpowering individualism, as a struggle against "the idealistic concept of the sovereign, world-embracing, world-sustaining, world-creating I." [174] As a result the creaturely nature of the human person was now stressed, his involvement in a manifold We and in communities of different kinds.

This being bound to a community, however, must be a genuine binding that does not infringe upon or violate personal existence; nor must it lead to a blind obedience to the collectivity. The struggle for personal truth must be carried on in the group as well. The collectivity must not become the sole reality; it cannot relieve the individual of the responsibility of making decisions: "The collectivity cannot enter instead of the person into the dialogue of the ages which the Godhead conducts with mankind." [175] Nor must there be a separation between the spheres of private and public life: the entire undiminished reality of the person must take part in its "existential" relation to truth; the will to truth must be unconditioned and it must include the whole of thought and the whole of life.

Kierkegaard proclaimed the simple teaching that the truth is present for the individual only when he produces and preserves it actively. Here human truth is bound to personal responsibility. This personal discovery of truth through confirmation excludes the collectivity whose language is: "True is what is Ours," which is but a summation of Stirner's: "True is what is Mine"—and it is in this, aside from the content of his philosophy, that we find the real demoralizing influence of Stirner on his contemporaries.

Humanity is in danger when truth is no longer believed in as something independent, as the bearer of all that the individual cannot acquire by himself but with which he must enter into a lifelong "real relation": "But in order that man may not be lost, there is need of persons who are not collectivized, and of a truth which is not politicized." True community cannot exist without the individual's responsibility to truth; it can only be achieved to the extent "to which the Single Ones become real, out of whose responsible life the body politic is renewed." [176]

In extending Kierkegaard's category of the "single one" by adding to it the concept of world responsibility on the part of every individual, Buber wished to indicate that the ethical and the religious were in the final analysis inseparable. We cannot have ethics existing as a separate sphere over against the wholeness of being any more than we can have an autarkic religion that is divorced from the ethical. The ethical cannot be a "stage," in Kierkegaard's sense, from which one can "leap" into the wholly different sphere of the religious: "but it dwells in the religious, in faith and in service." [177]

We are confronted here with two basic conceptions of holiness. Kierkegaard's insistence that man should abandon the world and concede the victory to his implacable antagonist, an august God, can appeal to a thousand year old tradition of unworldliness in both the Orient and Occident. To Buber holiness meant integrating the ethical into the religious, and was based ultimately on the biblical "double commandment" which enjoins the love of God and the love of man. The ethical thus becomes an area of concern for both man and God: "The true ethical deed is done with God in view." [178] He who does not love the world loves God only as the Lord of his own solitary soul, but loves not the God of the Universe who in his love has mercy on his creation. Existence for Buber meant "sacramental existence";[179] man bears the responsibility that things and situations "in their sacramental possibility have been placed in his reach" by God, and that the world should become the kingdom of God.

Responsibility in this sense means love, as stated in "The Question to the Single One": "But the ethical in its plain truth means to help God by loving his creation in his creatures, by loving it toward him." [180] In this same essay Buber could only vaguely indicate his meaning by the use of philosophical language; with this language he could only express the juxtaposition of God and the world, but not the profound thought that in the ultimate depths there is no longer any duality.

This mystery Buber was able to capture in a poetical vision which constitutes the climax of his novel *For the Sake of Heaven*. The main character, the "holy Jew," shows that Buber knew the bliss and the need of "loving God alone," which has been experienced by every great religious figure. The "holy Jew" is first of all a "single one" in Kierkegaard's sense, and like him he shuns woman, the messenger of the elements, and loves God's freedom that he finds in self-communion and other worldliness. One night shortly before his death he is granted an apocalyptic vision:[181] the appearance of the shekinah, the indwelling of God, in sublime grandeur and yet bearing the features of a woman, the woman that the "holy Jew" had shunned. From her mouth come the words: "Do you wish to help?" The mutual involvement of the two figures, their similarity and their otherness, and the undiminished "God above all" over against the world below, could only be depicted poetically. The figure of the "holy Jew" thus reveals much of Buber that is not to be found in his other writings.

Struggle for Israel:
Buber's Zionism

NOW THAT the state of Israel is a reality and an increasing number of tourists can see that the Jews are a nation, it is becoming more and more difficult to describe the beginnings of the Zionist movement and to appreciate the utopian idealism of those early days.

The hatred and hostility of non-Jews contributed to the establishment of the new state. Before national independence was achieved millions of Jewish martyrs suffered simply because they were Jews; even today the enmity of the Arab nations and the threat they present to the new state have brought an increasing number of Jews from all over the world to Israel.

Before the beginning of the present century anti-Semitism gave rise to the great "utopian vision of the Jewish State" (Robert Weltsch) in the soul of the Viennese journalist, Theodor Herzl. In Paris, where Jewish emancipation originated, the founder of political Zionism came to the conclusion that the Jews were a people and that their only hope was national independence. The Dreyfus case and its virulent anti-Semitism demonstrated to him the hopelessness of individual assimilation as long as the world refused to grant the Jewish people emancipation and continued to vent its hatred against the individual Jew—an insight which the German Jews for the most part acquired only after the catastrophe of 1933.

Herzl had gone as far along the road of assimilation as it was possible in those days. As a student he was a member of a national society, and at one time even conceived a plan to have all the Jewish children of Vienna baptized indiscriminately in one common public act[1]—a thought no less fantastic than that of a Jewish state, which also showed its author's indifference to religion as plainly as his willingness later to have the national homeland of the Jews in Uganda instead of in Palestine. His basic conception was the establishment of a Jewish state and not the idea of Zion. As a true liberal he had not the slightest notion of Israel's religious mystery. The establishment of a Jewish state was to put an end to the suffering of the Jewish people, and the exigencies of the historical moment would have to determine the geographical details. But Herzl's liberal attitude did not ignore human dignity and freedom; it displayed, moreover, a political talent that was conspicuously absent in the people's religious leaders.

Herzl's idea of a Jewish state arose spontaneously, although he had forerunners among the Jews of the East and the West. Richard Lichtheim in his *Geschichte des deutschen Zionismus* [History of German Zionism] names a number of highly placed Christian personalities in the West who were interested in the idea of creating a Jewish state in Palestine;[2] to these must be added the names of Jewish philanthropists, scholars, and theologians of the nineteenth century who had a similar interest. Chaim Weizmann refers to groups of East European Jewish students in Germany in the eighties and nineties of the last century and the Kadimah society in Vienna who were devoted to this same ideal.[3]

In Germany the Rhinelander Moses Hess had experienced a similar conversion thirty years before Herzl. In his book *Rome and Jerusalem* (1862) he turned from Marxian revolutionary materialism to a form of national socialism and to the idea of a renaissance of the Jewish people in Palestine. He was thoroughly imbued with Jewish tradition and Western thought, and his independent solution of the Jewish problem anticipated all the essential points of later Zionism.[4]

In 1881–1882, after the assassination of Alexander II, pogroms broke out anew in Russia, and this in turn gave rise to *Choveve Zion* (Friends of Zion) which for the most part attracted young Jewish intellectuals. The first *aliyah* to come to Palestine arrived in small groups and under the greatest difficulty, for the Jews were forbidden by the Russian government to leave the country and by the Turkish government to enter Palestine. In 1882 Leo Pinsker published *Auto-Emanci-*

pation, in which he supported the idea of national Jewish autonomy through the acquisition of territory and, like Herzl, without first insisting on Palestine. Pinsker was a physician in his native city of Odessa and, as an enlightened liberal who, like Herzl, sympathized with the plight of Eastern Jewry, he understood their passionate longing for Zion and their insistence on Palestine as the national homeland.

Achad Ha'am (Asher Ginzberg) came from a Hasidic family in the province of Kiev. As a representative of a national spiritual renaissance and "renewal of heart," he became for Buber the most influential advocate of the Zionist movement. Imbued with the spirit of the Haskala and deeply influenced by the school of Mill and Spencer, he undertook to unite the two basic forms of the Zionist idea, the religious-mythic and the emancipatory.[5] His understanding of the full significance of the Zion idea is closer to Hess than to Herzl and Pinsker. In his Memorial Address of 1927 Buber emphasized the fact that Achad Ha'am had faithfully translated the language of the religious past into that of a national Jewish culture without sacrificing the enduring values to the exigencies of the present. His conception embraced the whole of Zion and not one partial aspect; in thinking of a cultural center that was to grow out of the Jewish settlement in Palestine, he did not fail to consider the Diaspora as a vital element of the new Jewish spirit.[6]

Achad Ha'am and Pinsker were supported by the distressed masses of East European Jews, whereas Hess and his comrades in Germany stood alone without a following. In the sixties and early seventies the most hopeful prospects for the solution of the Jewish problem were to be found among those who believed in complete emancipation and assimilation. Full civil equality for Jews, which had first been put forward in 1848, became state law in Austria in 1867, in the North German Union in 1869, and in the entire country in 1872.

The adoption of German manners and culture by Jews had at that time made great progress. The great majority of German Jews wished to be distinguished from their fellow citizens by religion alone. While the Jews adopted German culture and made it their own, Jewish life and studies were unfortunately not part of the curriculum of German education. In this connection H. G. Adler[7] cites Leopold Zunz, the founder of the science of Judaism: "The disparagement of Jewish authors, even those who have been baptized, will continue in Germany until Jewish history and literature will be taught in all the universities by Jews who are full professors." While almost total ignorance of Jewish religion and history prevailed in those German circles which were well-disposed or indifferent to Jews, the enemies of the Jews knew how to disguise their hostile feelings and justify their caricature of Judaism with objective scientific terminology. All that was known of Judaism in German intellectual circles were scraps of modern literature, mostly the creation of second-class writers and journalists of the Jewish press, which reflected the inner turmoil that resulted from the Emancipation more than the original world of Jewish thought.

While the Jews often had a deeper understanding of the great figures of German life and literature than the Germans themselves, the latter had an inadequate and distorted knowledge of Judaism. In those instances where Jews and Germans were friends, the Jewishness of the Jew was for the most part carefully ignored and did not affect the social relationship, very often for the simple reason that the Jew himself would have found it embarrassing to be reminded of it. At any rate, the German was rarely confronted with a clear-cut, unprejudiced picture of the real world of Jewish thought. Even under the best of circumstances the relations between the two tended to take place in an intellectual no-man's-land and never reached the roots of the other personality. This ignorance of things Jewish on the part of the Germans explains why they were later ill-prepared to defend their Jewish friends as Jews and to present a true picture of the Jew based on objective facts against the odious clichés of the Nazis.

Equality in civil rights acquired by the Jews at the beginning of the seventies gave their enemies no rest. In 1873 Wilhelm Marr's *Der Sieg des Judenthums über das Germanenthum* [The victory of Judaism over Germanism] appeared, in which for the first time hatred for the Jews was called anti-Semitism and the basis laid for the biological-materialistic historical conception of National Socialism. Two years before then the lampoon *Der Talmudjude* [The Talmud Jew] was circulated in Austria, an abusive work which merely intensified the existing prejudices against the Pharisees. The financial crash caused by reckless speculation after the Franco-German War (1870–1871) gave anti-

Semites an opportunity to direct the anger of the injured middle class against the Jews. The hard-hearted, avaricious Jew, who was blamed for the scandal, perpetuated the image of the Jewish usurer of the Middle Ages. The influx of impoverished and abject East European Jews at the beginning of the eighties only intensified the hostility against the Jews.

The Berlin court preacher, Stöcker, founded his Christian Social Workers Party in 1878, about the time that Bismarck began to adopt a national conservative policy. In 1881 the hostility against the Jews took a more obvious form in the Antisemiten-Petition[8] bearing 267,000 signatures, which was sent to Bismarck demanding that equal rights for Jews be curtailed. That the myth of Jewish ritual murder of Christian children was still believed in Germany was demonstrated by the trials that took place in Xanten-Cleve in 1891–92 and in Konitz near Bomberg in 1900. In Russia accusations of ritual murder ceased only after the trial at Kiev in 1913.[9] These accusations then gave way to the malicious legend of the Protocols of the Elders of Zion, according to which the world was ruled by a secret organization of three hundred Jews—a forgery concocted in Russia in 1905 and still effective as Nazi propaganda.[10]

All these ominous signs are, of course, clearer to us today than they were at that time. In the course of their long history the German Jews had learned to be patient and for the most part did not take these signs seriously. They believed that anti-Semitism was a curable disease and that it would be overcome by the ultimate victory of reason, aided by the spirit of liberalism which united them with a large segment of the non-Jewish population. Their undisputed talent and industry had given them a prominent place in the intellectual and artistic life of the country despite intense secret opposition and, through intermarriage with influential families, they were able to attain highly respectable positions in the economic and financial spheres. The influx of poor Jews from the East, who had fled from the Russian pogroms after the accession of Alexander III, made them appreciate all the more their own affluence and security. A considerable number of German Jews became converts to Christianity. Despite equality in civic rights, the baptismal font was the only entrance to high official posts in government service and to an academic career. It was not uncommon for German professors at the universities to advise bright Jewish students and young scholars to embrace Christianity in order to aid their careers, even if only for the sake of appearances, just as one might purchase a new suit of clothes to go to court. The vast majority of Jews, however, remained faithful to the religion of their fathers, although many of them were indifferent to its observance. In a real sense they were not Jews, but they remained attached to one another as the members of one big family. They desired nothing more than to be regarded as Germans of Mosaic persuasion, which they proclaimed by founding the Centralverein deutscher Staatsbürger jüdischen Glaubens [Central Society of German Citizens of Jewish Faith] in 1893. It is therefore not surprising to learn that the Jewish community of Munich protested against Herzl's original plan to convene the First Zionist Congress in that city and that after the Congress had met in Basel the governing body of the Rabbinical Assembly in Germany issued a proclamation declaring that religion and love of country imposed upon Jews the duty to refrain from taking part in Zionist activities or attending the proceedings of the Congress.[11]

It was the liberal and cosmopolitan Germany of the classical period that was most congenial to Jews and where they felt most at home—a sentiment expressed in 1890 in lofty terms by Heymann Steinthal, the philosopher and founder of folk psychology: "No, there is no contradiction between being a Jew and being a German and being a man, but these three are so intermingled that we can be one of them only by being the other two . . . Besides the prophets, we are also inspired by Lessing and Herder, Kant, Fichte and Schiller, Goethe and the Humboldt brothers, who could have arisen outside of the German people as little as the prophets outside of Israel." [12] And even among Herzl's followers there was the so-called Revisionist movement, whose members supported the creation of a national culture in Palestine but at the same time insisted on remaining good Germans. Thus, Franz Oppenheimer declared in 1914: "I unite within myself the German and the Jewish national feeling. I and my friends stand firmly on the ground of the Basel Program, and our good German world-sentiment does not prevent us from being good Zionists." [13] This sentiment was expressed by Gustav Landauer in even simpler and more heartfelt language: "My Germanism and Judaism do not harm one another, but rather do each other much good" [14]—words that were spoken in 1913, six years before he lost his life at the hands of his German compatriots.

The Jewish problem in all its stark reality confronted Theodor Herzl in Paris where the unjust conviction of the Jewish officer, Dreyfus, clarified once for all his thoughts concerning the relation between Jews and the people among whom they lived. His solution was to cut the Gordian knot rather than to answer the question concerning the nature of the Jewish community and its destiny. Political Zionism did not arise from inner necessity but from a reaction to anti-Semitism. Even in Herzl's *Der Judenstaat* [The Jewish state] we read: "Perhaps we could disappear everywhere among the surrounding nations without leaving a trace if we were left alone for only two generations. But they will not leave us alone. After short periods of tolerance, hostility is again and again aroused against us." [15] Herzl's Zionism presupposes civil equality and the subsequent disillusionment of attempts to assimilate; it is "post-assimilatory Zionism," as it was called in the following decades, the phrase being one that was originally used by Kurt Blumenfeld, the propagandist and ideologist of the Zionist Organization.[16] This "post-assimilatory" situation, however, existed only for western Jews; it was as inapplicable to eastern Jews as the one-sided reduction of Judaism to the concept of a nation that does not take into consideration its religious component. Herzl's "nation" was too much orientated to European nationalism and its minority problems, so that it is not surprising that Zionism should have been called a gift of Europe to the Jews.[17] In Judaism itself, however, religious consciousness cannot be divorced from national consciousness. Religion was not given to an individual but to an entire people; the religious community and the racial community are mutually pledged to one another. Until the Enlightenment the Jews lived under the peculiar conditions of ghetto life as a separate national minority, apart from the general cultural development of Europe. In the rigid medieval framework of traditional intellectual forms and fixed social stratification the Jews found their peoplehood only in their religion; the individual Jew felt secure only within the wholeness of the community.

The French Revolution envisaged the emancipation of the individual Jew and tacitly assumed that the group would dissolve within the
Christian environment. The Enlightenment adopted the optimistic
view that all men were equal and that national differences could be
transcended. The liberalism of the nineteenth century, which was a
continuation of the Enlightenment, was a secular and individualistic
cultural movement; every man, as a member of his linguistic and cultural community, was expected to advance the progress of mankind.
Emancipated from a fixed order that had endured for centuries, and
prevented by the precepts of his religious law from engaging in the
professions, the Jew was now wholly on his own as an individual and as
such was expected to preserve the substance of his Jewish faith. Since
he was unequal to this task, it is understandable that after attaining
equal rights he should seek to remove himself more and more from his
origins in his desire for greater security. But now the Jewish question
arose in another form. Having attained all civil rights, living in prosper-
ity and security, the Jews were obliged to acknowledge that the preju-
dice against them had not ceased and that they were still looked upon
as an undesirable foreign element.

In East European Jewry, on the other hand, we find not only
great insecurity and material distress but also a sense of community and
the consciousness of a vital, unbroken Jewish tradition. This was experienced even by Herzl when he first met the seventy delegates of East
European Jewry at the Zionist Congress of 1897, a meeting which
made a deep impression upon him and which he describes in his impul-
sive and naive manner: "They still feel an inner attachment, which is
no longer true of western Jews. They have a pronounced national Jewish consciousness, without any national narrow-mindedness and intol-
erance. They do not find the idea of assimilation painful, for they feel
unpretentious and imperturbable in their inner selves. They do not ad-
just to other nations, but endeavor to learn what is best in them. In this
way they manage to remain honest and original. And yet they are
ghetto Jews! The only ghetto Jews in our time! When we look at them
we understand whence our forefathers took the strength to survive
even the bitterest times." [18] The leading East European Zionists missed
in Herzl that warm Jewish feeling of national community and destiny;

and this was felt even by those who, like Achad Ha'am and Chaim Weizmann, were completely at home in the culture of European Enlightenment. They found his idea too abstract and too little rooted in the emotional life of the Jewish people which, in the final analysis, was their ultimate source of power; and they found his *Judenstaat*, with its emphasis on power politics and diplomatic strategy, its organizational problems and extensive propaganda, unfamiliar and even forbidding. From the very beginning Herzl's "political" Zionism and the East European "practical" Zionism constituted two opposing camps—the one by attempting to realize the national idea on the vast stage of world history, the other by creating the new type of chalutz who was prepared to translate his idea into reality by becoming the vanguard of Jewish colonization in Palestine and to suffer hardship and danger in following the luminous goal that summoned him to a brighter future.

The opposition between the Western and Eastern manifestations of Zionism came into open conflict when Herzl, after the Kishinev pogrom in 1903, was prepared to surrender Palestine as the Jewish homeland and to accept in its stead Uganda in East Africa. The East European Jews, whom Herzl's proposal was intended to benefit, were the very ones who resolutely refused to endorse this project. The unexpected conflict, which threatened to split in two the young Zionist party, and which contributed to Herzl's early death, was only a superficial manifestation of the deep cleavage between western and eastern European Jewry that began with the Enlightenment. A different conception of national rebirth was the apparent issue that threatened to split the Zionist Organization to the detriment of the general welfare; yet, the Zionist ideal and national renewal remained the common goals which both groups inflexibly pursued and around which they could ultimately rally. To point the way that was to be taken to this end was the task appropriate for Buber, "the East-West Jew," as Ernst Simon called him.[19]

Years later Buber recalled two occasions when he participated in the great Jewish movement of the century: once in a short article called "Three Stations" (1929) and again in the comprehensive volume *Der*

Jude und sein Judentum [The Jew and his Judaism], a collection of his shorter writings on the subject of Israel and its renewal.

The "three stations" to which Buber referred in 1929 were designated by three concepts: culture, religious renewal, reality. "When we began our service for Israel our slogan was: culture." [20] This term was understood by Buber as the visible expression of the Zionist idea, the incarnation of the spirit of national rebirth. Zion meant to him, as it did to Achad Ha'am, a national homeland, above all a spiritual center to which all the forces of the Diaspora could turn. But the acquisition of culture, like the development of personality, cannot be made a goal that one consciously strives for. The new values and creative works cannot spring from the mind of the individual but must arise from the collective life of the entire people. "The primordial depths of life must be stirred; this is what we mean by religious renewal."

But least of all must "religion" be pursued for the sake of the people; and even he who seeks it for its own sake falls too easily into aestheticism and unreality, just as the conscious striving for creative achievement can lead to pseudo-intellectuality. Religion also can give man a distorted view of God's Face. The right path has been taken only by him who understands religion to be the whole of reality, God's holiness in the life of the individual and in the life of the people, the world as the arena of God's kingdom to come. Reality in this sense means the "lived daily life" or, as it is called in *Dialogue*, religion, which is "simply all that is lived in its possibility of dialogue," that is, of responsibility that one assumes.[21]

The tremendous task that inheres in such an attitude to religion helps us to understand why Buber in his second review, as he looked back on his activity in behalf of the Zion idea, spoke of his "struggle for Israel." Under this title he had published in 1933 shorter essays and talks on Judaism, which had been preceded by the two volumes of *Die jüdische Bewegung* [The Jewish movement] in 1916 and 1920. In the preface to *Der Jude und sein Judentum*, Buber spoke of this "struggle" in a threefold sense: "First, an external struggle against those forces of the age which challenge the unrestricted right of the Jewish community to exist, whether in the Diaspora or in its ancient home. Secondly, an inner struggle against those forces in Judaism itself which were opposed to the erection of a center of Jewish life in 'Zion.' Thirdly, an innermost critical struggle, first within the Zionist movement in the Diaspora and then, with increasing political and economic realism, in the course of building the new Israel in Palestine."

Buber's "struggle" in the sense described here began not only when the state of "reality" was reached, of which he spoke in 1929; on the contrary, his fighting spirit was evident in his early and still immature participation in the Zionist movement. He had joined Herzl as early as 1898 when the Zionist organization was still in its infancy, consisting mostly of small groups of young people. While he was still a student in Leipzig, he founded a local Zionist group in the winter of 1898–1899 and took part in the Third Zionist Congress in Basel as a delegate. His independent views of Zionism are clearly seen in the discussions he conducted there as a consultant of the Agitation Committee. "Zionism is not a matter of party interest; it is a world-view, to develop which is the task of the inner 'Agitation' which will encourage the growth of all the different ideas without forfeiting their subtle distinctions. Those who will be won over by the external 'Agitation' are to be Zionists not in the sense that one is a conservative or a liberal but as one is a human being or an artist." [22]

In the winter of 1900–1901 Buber had already organized in the Zionist Society of Berlin a department of Jewish art and science that was to concern itself with the cultural forces in Jewish life. At that time Buber regarded his age as an "epoch of cultural germination," [23] and Zionism as part of a great movement of "the self-awareness of peoples' souls."

The first station of service to Israel, cultural Zionism, looked to Achad Ha'am as its guide and teacher, but beyond this it was strongly influenced by Nietzsche.[24] Buber's vague revolutionary fervor, his heroic pathos over against an alienated tradition, his passionate interest in the development of art and myth, clearly reflect Nietzsche's influence. His overestimation of the role that art was to play in the new movement was, as Ernst Simon has indicated, not without justification: "Jewish deficiency in the fullness of life," which can be explained historically, was especially evident in the realm of art; Buber struggled against one-sided Jewish intellectualism.[25] "Auto-emancipation," however, as self-redemption through creative, artistic activity, envisaged by Buber in his early essays on Zionism, overestimated art as the "great educator" for life and true Judaism.

Achad Ha'am and Nietzsche could not so easily be combined and reconciled; another East-West synthesis proved more promising. Buber, as a student of Dilthey, began at an early date to look upon the national rebirth of Judaism historically and to think of it in conjunction with his teacher's conception of the European Renaissance. In "Renaissance und Bewegung" [Renaissance and movement] (1903), the only essay of that early period which Buber included in his collected works, he investigated the origins of the cleavage that took place between East European and western Judaism, and he saw the Jewish "new era" from both points of view—from the standpoint of western intellectual freedom, which was too dearly bought at the price of assimilation, and as the slowly won synthesis of the Enlightenment and Hasidism as it was interpreted by East European Jewry. "The Jewish Renaissance is, like its earlier renowned namesake, more than a mending of torn threads. Nor does it mean a return—and this must again be emphasized—but rather a rebirth of the whole man, a rebirth that has been going on from the days of the Haskalah and of Hasidism down to our own day and which will continue. A new type of Jew is gradually emerging." [26] Here in Buber's cultural Zionism we already find indications of a "Hebrew humanism"; like Dilthey, he appreciated the significance of the rising national culture for the renewal of mankind.

In 1901 Buber moved from Berlin to Vienna to become the director of the central Zionist publication *Die Welt*. A few months later a conflict arose between him and Herzl during the Fifth Zionist Congress. In the course of a talk on Jewish art Buber, as spokesman of a group to which Chaim Weizmann also belonged, asked for the means to found a Jewish publishing house. The refusal to grant this request resulted in his separation from Herzl and the termination of his activity as editor of *Die Welt*. Shortly thereafter he founded Der Jüdische Verlag in Berlin, and one of its first publications was a collection called *Jüdische Künstler* with an introduction by Buber, who also contributed an article on Lesser Ury.[27]

In the autumn of 1903 a prospectus appeared in which Buber and Weizmann announced the publication of a monthly *Der Jude*, conceived in the manner of a modern European journal, which was not to be a party organ but an independent magazine devoted to a free and dignified discussion of Jewish matters. The economic, social, political, and cultural conditions of Jewish life, with reference to their peculiar effects and mutual influences, were to be discussed candidly from different points of view. But it was not until 1916, in the midst of World War I and under changing conditions, that Buber could realize this plan.[28] In the intervening twelve years Buber had also changed: the founding of the magazine had now become the expression of that form of activity which he had, in 1929, designated as the third station, as "reality." During these years his chief interest had been "religious renewal," which he now saw as a deeper and more comprehensive phenomenon of what he had formerly understood as "cultural Zionism." In his work *My Way to Hasidism* (1918) he spoke of having professed Judaism without having really known it. In 1904 he retired from all party activities and began his studies in Hasidism as an "eye-to-eye recognition of the people in its creative original documents." [29] After long and diligent study he attained the personal "reality" of a great Jewish teacher, and in that role he appeared for the first time in his *Addresses on Judaism.*

The early intellectual beginnings of German Zionism, its literary life, its idealism and romanticism, have been described in Hans Kohn's book on Buber, which is particularly valuable for its elaboration of the movement's historical and intellectual connections. Kohn describes the cultural group of the young movement and Buber's central position within it as one who has himself experienced the awakening strength of this great teacher. The author's absorbing interest in cultural activities so peculiar to the books of the twenties helps us to recapture the atmosphere of those early days. The memoirs and historical accounts published after the establishment of the state look back on the decades of struggle concerning the social and political structure of Israel and evaluate Herzl's Zionism and that of his co-workers much more soberly. If we read Weizmann's autobiography *Trial and Error*, R. Lichtheim's

Geschichte des deutschen Zionismus [History of German Zionism], or Kurt Blumenfeld's *Erlebte Judenfrage* [The Jewish question personally experienced], we are surprised to find that in these personal and historical accounts of Zionism Buber has practically no part. The statesman, the historian, and the propagandist find no place for his atypical character either as a teacher who sought to establish the intellectual foundation of the movement or as the admonitory conscience of the movement.

The extreme attitude was that of Weizmann who around the end of the century stood side by side with Buber in cultural opposition to Herzl—for even then he was interested in the Jewish University in Jerusalem. Weizmann's portrayal of Buber as aesthete in 1903 was superficial even for that early date and would have to be supplemented at least by Buber's years in Jerusalem. But the future first president of the state of Israel also describes Herzl with the same critical detachment and reservation,[30] stating that he found not a single new idea in Herzl's *Judenstaat* and accusing its author of being ignorant of the work of his predecessors. Even the concept Zionism does not come from Herzl but from Nathan Birnbaum. Weizmann was a well-known chemist and diplomat; he was disconcerted above all by Herzl's journalistic dilettantism, and the *Chovev Zion* [Friend of Zion] in him was repelled by Herzl's uprooted liberalism and his condescending, philanthropic attitude to East European Jewry. But he admired Herzl's personality with its intense, persuasive force, which was very attractive to East European Jews—the imponderable element that distinguishes the leader from the statesman. It was around the figure of Herzl that the myth of the Zionist movement crystallized, attested to by the Mt. Herzl memorial in Jerusalem: an heroic life in an unheroic age, his motto being, "If you but will it, it is no legend."[31] In 1907 Weizmann described his own Zionism as "synthetic," which he understood to be diplomatic-political activity combined with the demands of colonization. That Buber's Zionism was approaching more and more a synthesis escaped him.

Buber's disagreement with Herzl covered a period of four decades.[32] It was first evident in literary form in the two memorial addresses delivered in 1904, and it terminated with the fourth section of *Israel and Palestine* (Hebrew edition 1944, German 1950, English

1952) which deals with the Zionist idea. In the same year (1944) another article appeared, "Herzl vor der Palästina-Karte," which takes us back to 1901 and describes one of those "exemplary" moments the memory of which accompanied Buber all his life. From the intervening years we have a memorial address on Herzl's fiftieth birthday called "Er und wir" [He and we] (1910) and a contribution to an anthology for the twenty-fifth anniversary of Herzl's death called "Sache und Person" [Cause and person] (1929).

In his objective criticism of Herzl we find Buber close to the East European bloc. He points out that the Jewish question had never become for Herzl a question of Judaism, and in support of this contention he cites from *Der Judenstaat*: "We are a people—the enemy has made us such without our will." [33] Herzl did not see Judaism from the inside, in its continuity and heroic new beginning; he was completely engrossed in the phenomenon of Jewish suffering. But his understanding of the nature of anti-Semitism and its effects was more realistic than that of most of his German contemporaries. In his very first essay, "Theodor Herzl," Buber spoke of *Der Judenstaat* not as a creative intellectual achievement but merely as a program of action on which the Zionist organization could be based. He had already criticized Herzl's one-sided diplomatic efforts in his essay "Gegenwartsarbeit" [The work of the present] written in 1901,[34] and demanded that such efforts be supplemented by popular education and a deeper understanding of the people as a whole. In an essay in 1903 called "Zionistische Politik" [Zionist politics],[35] Buber raised the question as to whether the Zionist Organization had not been created prematurely. Herzl's negotiations with the world powers had been hampered because there was as yet no significant Jewish colonization in Palestine to which he could point. Similar considerations led to the founding in 1901 of the Democratic Party, to which Buber and Weizmann belonged, which called for the creation of a well-organized, productive settlement as the basis for all negotiations. Buber himself, however, was mainly concerned with the task of educating the people in preparation for the future settlement of Palestine: propaganda, political negotiations, and colonization must be based on cultural work.

In the memorial essay "Herzl and History" [36] an objective criticism of Herzl is made from a historical point of view. Buber confronts the author of *Der Judenstaat* with his literary predecessors who had envisaged the Zionist goal just as clearly, but who had presented the idea of Zion with a deeper understanding of Judaism. It is interesting to note that the distinction made here between Herzl, on the one hand, and Moses Hess, Leo Pinsker, and Achad Ha'am, on the other, reveals almost all the essential features to be found in the later presentation in *Israel and Palestine*. Herzl's predecessors are described as "East-West Jews" who labored to achieve the great synthesis of the national rebirth of a people; Herzl, however, was an out-and-out Western Jew who had become the leader of a movement that had its roots in the East. Again Buber starts from the idea of a Jewish renaissance, as outlined by him the previous year in *Renaissance and Movement*: "A movement is not historically justified by helping people but by enriching mankind with new values." [37] It was, nevertheless, a source of pride to know that Herzl was the first Jew since the Exile to engage in Jewish politics on a large scale. But there was still a long way to go before real progress could be made in the "regeneration of hearts" and in the education of the people.

Buber's objective criticism of Herzl, however, was only a part of his long-standing quarrel with him. What strikes us is his constant search throughout all his essays to find something deeper behind the man, something peculiarly dialogic. His very first essay seeks not so much to evaluate Herzl's intellectual achievements as to depict his personality or, rather, to indicate the disparity between his personality and the task to which he was called. Buber went deeply into this matter where others were content with superficial observations. The practical inadequacy of the literary man who had become the leader of a great movement presented Buber with a deep, spiritual problem—the problem of the poet whose fatal gifts produce nothing salutary or enduring and who, overwhelmed by the vanity of his labors, turned his fantasy to the work of fashioning a new life for himself and for others—a poet who does not create heroes but who himself becomes a hero. Buber was interested in the peculiar affinity between the hero and the poet and, ultimately, in the deeper mystery of the hero as well as the prophet, a problem which engaged him in those years, namely, the origin of myth. He described Herzl as a man of elegant gestures with an innate aesthetic dignity that never deserted him, and a flair for the dramatic gesture of the hero on the stage, oblivious of the obstacles in his path in the attainment of his goal, characteristic of the poet in dealing with the problems of practical life. In this case the "hero," critically considered, was in reality a dictator "with far-reaching decisions and far-reaching errors, with generous power and despotic repression of opinions but, above all, with admirable energy dedicated to action." [38] The material first employed by Herzl was words, and then it was men. He had an enviable talent for winning over people and controlling them: "Folk-fantasy wove a tender legend around him, removed his actions to the twilight of mystery, adorned his brow with a messianic halo." [39] Even the disillusion that attended his Uganda project could not deprive him of this glory.

In the second essay "Theodor Herzl and History" this personal portrayal was continued with bolder strokes and greater detail. Again Buber began and ended with the contradictions in Herzl's personality: "He was both harsh and gentle, unrestrained and well-poised, chivalrous and vindictive, a man of moods and a man of action, a dreamer and a practical statesman. The riddle of his personality is unsolved." [40] At the end of the essay Buber ventured a personal insight: "Theodor Herzl may or may not have been an outstanding poet in words and in artistic form. He certainly was a great poet in the unconscious of his own life. Living, building, erring, working good and evil for his people, he erected, without being aware of it, a statue in the sight of the people, which the people called by his name—a statue beyond fault or blame, bearing the pure features of genius." This peculiar interplay of poetry and life belongs to the intellectual atmosphere at the turn of the century and shows us Herzl as one who was deeply rooted in his age. A strong aesthetic element also dominated Buber's ethics and was especially characteristic of his early period. Even in his early meeting with Herzl in 1903 Buber was surprised to find that this "hero" was in reality a poet; but now he realized that the tragedy of his life was that, blinded with a consuming passion like the hero of a tragedy, he was unable to distinguish between his own person and the cause to which he devoted his life. Buber remembered this experience for many years and in 1929 recorded it in *Sache und Person* [Cause and person].

Even in *Israel and Palestine* Buber spoke of this peculiar mixture of life and poetry in Herzl's personality. He recalled how Herzl was most diligent in writing his novel *Altneuland* [Old-new land], the literary utopia of the Jewish state, during those periods when his exertions to further his cause seemed most hopeless, and in this connection he cites the following entry in Herzl's diary: "The hopes of success in the practical sphere have faded; my life is no novel now, so the novel is my life." To this Buber observed: "What he really needs is that his life should be 'a novel'; writing novels is only a substitute for that." [41]

In the essay "Theodor Herzl and We" (1910), the dispute takes place on another level and Buber's appreciation of Herzl's greatness reaches a high point. Objective criticism is not abandoned and is in part repeated but, as Ernst Simon puts it, the dimension of truth that was lacking in his cause "he possessed as person." [42] Herzl's image had undergone a change because Buber's own criteria of judgment had been clarified, so that he now no longer inquired into the truth and error of Herzl's conception of Zionism nor into the opposition of life versus poetry, but sought to assess his talent for direct action and subsume it under a new category, for which he coined the concept of "the elemental active" which he set up in contrast to the "we" of the problem-man.

"Theodor Herzl and We" falls in the period of *Addresses on Judaism*. After 1909 Buber was occupied with this total conception of Judaism and the destiny of the Jews in connection with which he ventured to suggest a spiritual synthesis between East and West in the manner of Hess and Achad Ha'am, and was also able to find a suitable occupation as teacher in the Bar Kochba Circle. At the same time he clearly saw the inner disunity of the exiled Jew, his tragic oscillation between two extremes, as the basic spiritual condition of life in the Diaspora: "To be a Jew is an inconceivably deep tragedy," which he had earlier discussed in *The Creators, the People and the Movement*. More and more the qualities of unity, decision, unconditionality became for Buber the highest values, and he learned to look upon Herzl as a man of action in a new light—a change that was in no small measure due to Nietzsche's ambiguous and vague concept of "creation." This had been his ideal of national rebirth in the early years of the century; in the meantime he had clarified it for his own ends. The disillusion that followed his discovery that Herzl was not a genuine intellectual creator was gradually succeeded by the supplementary insight that the literary activity of the man of letters, the heroism of the pen, is far from being "creation" in the sense of the world's work and its moving events. This was not expressed directly in "Er und wir," but it emerged in a later article "Herzl vor der Palästina-Karte," with which Buber concluded his recollections of the political leader of his youth.

By 1901 Herzl saw the reality that was later to absorb all the energies of the state of Israel: the opening up of the desert; a great reservoir at the Jordan river which was to support the entire economy of Israel; Haifa as a great world harbor. Buber recognized only much later that Palestine was for Herzl something concretely given, a land with definite geographical limits, a task for the man of action, whereas to him it represented the Promised Land and, even more, a land of the soul and of the miracle of redemption.

Buber's image of Herzl may be dismissed as poetical and of little importance to the historian who undertakes the task of recording all the activities of the Zionist movement and the names of those who participated in it. No one will deny the usefulness of works of reference. But one who wishes to gain a deeper understanding of Buber's protracted quarrel with Herzl over a period of four decades and retain an unforgettable image of an indomitable leader will be grateful for this human portrait. Although Buber's description deals with the vague imponderables of human character, it is by no means inaccurate; on the contrary, it abounds in authentic details and, because of its insights, raises questions that are of significance beyond the historical personality under discussion, such as: the extent to which the "hero" of former times is today's dictator; the justification of that indestructible method of historical writing which we call myth. Buber's portrayal of Herzl is typical of his general attitude toward historical personalities. Misgivings which may arise in this connection will reappear when we come to his presentation of Hasidism.

Many of us today on looking back to the *Addresses on Judaism* will be inclined to regard them as too aesthetic. It is difficult for later historians to recapture the lost enthusiasm of a vanished age. Buber had a deeper understanding of the problem of Jews, seen in its larger historical context as the problem of Judaism, than any of his contemporaries. The realization of the dream of national rebirth—like all realizations—took a different turn from what had been anticipated by Buber and his young friends of the Bar Kochba Society. But since the hopes for a real renewal of Judaism still lie in the future, it may be that some future generation will be inspired by this ineluctable inspiration "from within": "Youth is the eternal opportunity given to mankind that is always presented to it anew and always missed. Again and again a youthful generation comes upon the stage of history with an arduous longing for the unconditioned, with an unreserved dedication to the ideal. . . ." [43] It is always youth above all to whom Buber would speak and on whom he pinned his hopes.

For Buber's relation to Zionism, as well as his intellectual development in general, World War I represented a definite turning point. The basic intellectual principles of *Addresses on Judaism* pointed to a path that had to be taken and which Buber called "the holy way." His personal breakthrough to "reality" merged with the stream which in those years carried the Zionist movement toward its goal. All the "realities" of the movement at that time stood out in sharper outline and were more clearly defined. The situation in the Diaspora was seen more realistically because of the Jewish soldiers who fought on the various fronts and because of the internal struggle with the national assimilationists, who patriotically defended their respective host countries. The meeting between East European and western Jews became a reality when German troops pressed forward into Poland and Lithuania. The strongest impetus to the Zionist cause was given by the Balfour Declaration in which the English government promised the Jews a national homeland in Palestine. As a result, the political leadership of the Zionist Organization, which after Herzl's death had transferred its central office to Germany, went without a struggle to Chaim Weizmann who had been living in England since 1904 and had succeeded during the war in joining the fate of Zionism with that of the great colonial power of Europe. Nevertheless, that German Zionism retained its importance, at least in the intellectual sphere, is to a large extent due to Buber's personality. In the spring of 1916 he realized his old plan of publishing a representative Jewish magazine, *Der Jude*, in which all practical and intellectual problems of Judaism were freely discussed. In the introduction to the first volume, Buber declared that the problem was not that of the individual but that of the Jew as the bearer of the peoplehood. The struggle now waged was not for freedom of worship but for freedom to live and work on behalf of a repressed community: "We want to realize the Jew, whose lofty image we bear in our memory and in our hopes."

PRACTICAL ZIONISM

Palestinian Politics

For German Jewry of that day and its essentially political orientated Zionism, the appearance of *Der Jude* meant an "extension of the horizon" (Ernst Simon). For Buber it meant the task of dealing with problems at closer range: the need to take an active stand and to defend it. The periodical now became the organ of his struggle for Israel, and the very first issue announced the forthcoming "theological-political debate" between Buber and Hermann Cohen concerning the nature of Jewish religion and nationality.[44] Buber, who was described by Robert Weltsch as "a polemicist of grand style," [45] defended his views against one of the most formidable representatives of assimilated liberal Judaism in Germany with such sober eloquence and sustained vigor that he won the admiration of even such a convinced non-Zionist as Franz Rosenzweig.[46] In an essay "Zionism and Religion" Cohen had taken issue with Zionism's "equivalence" of religion and nationality, wherein he saw a great danger. He himself acknowledged his attachment to the Jewish religion and to Jewish nationality which he described as "a fact of nature," as the "anthropological means for the propagation of religion"; but he challenged the claim of Zionism that the Jews were a nation. A nation arises as the creation of the state and is determined by it; it can include several nationalities, just as the German nationality includes, among other minorities, the Jewish.

Buber, on the other hand, saw nationality as a historical community and an ethical task, as "reality of spirit and ethos in history," having its roots in nature, as all things human, but fulfilling itself only in the spiritual sphere, in the struggle for the idea of humanity. Only a strong Jewish peoplehood can be the bearer of the Jewish religion, of a creative religiosity that bears witness to God not only in a passive way. Buber contested Cohen's assertion that the fulfillment of Judaism is bound up with the dispersion of the Jews among the nations, that the humiliation and homelessness of the Jewish people are indispensable for the advent of messianic humanity.

The second half of the debate makes it clear that the real point at issue has to do with the conception of the state, that is, the relation between the state and religion or, more broadly conceived, the relation between the state and the spirit and what that signifies for the idea of humanity. For Cohen the nation and the state community are not only identical; the state is for him "the realization of morality on earth," the idea of the state is "the quintessence of ethics," and, as Buber added, Cohen finds it necessary to have religion supervised by ethics. Buber, however, held with the prophets, who defended God's cause over against the state and its sovereigns. He regarded the *Volk* as the creative power in the history of mankind and the state as only an ordering principle: and so it will remain "until in the messianic form of the human world creation and order, *Volk* and State will be fused into a new unity, into the community of salvation."

In this connection Buber asserted in opposition to Cohen that in his conception of the ultimate goal of Zionism it was not the state but the Jewish settlement in Palestine which was to realize the inner forces of Judaism independent of other nations and all external politics: not a "state" but "only this hard crust of earth, the promised pledge of the *final* and *sanctified* enduring abode, the hard clod in which alone the seed of the new unity could sprout. And not out of 'the need for power,' but solely out of the need for self-realization, which is the need to increase God's power on earth."

Reservations concerning the state, the Jewish settlement as the basis of national renewal, and Palestine as its possibility and guarantee —here we already have the essential factors which subsequently were

to determine Buber's Zionism. To disengage Zionism from the traditional methods of European nationalism and attach it to the social and
human aspects of national existence—this was the goal envisaged by
Buber in his Struggle for Israel within the movement itself, a struggle
which he conducted with great vigor in the pages of *Der Jude*. He had
opposed Herzl's policy of diplomatic negotiations, and he continued to
oppose it now when it was being conducted as "political" Zionism by
his old friend in the "democratic party," Chaim Weizmann, who more
and more was gaining the upper hand in the international play of
power politics.

It was Weizmann's personal influence and diplomatic skill that
were responsible for the Balfour Declaration, addressed to Lord Roth-
schild, whereby the Jewish people were promised the support of the
British government for the erection of a national homeland in Palestine. Zionism thereupon became "a political factor," a phrase used by
Buber (as the title of an essay) to describe the situation in 1917, that is,
even before the promulgation of the Declaration. He still believed that
"the hour for secular re-formation has been given to the world of
men" [47] by the war—the course of the Russian Revolution could not at
that time be foreseen, and the Congress Movement of the American
Jews was arousing new hopes.[48] On the other hand, it appeared to
Buber questionable that the Zionist movement, which had not been
permitted to take sides in the war, should be used as a pawn in the
power play of the great nations; with this in mind he called for greater
vigilance and a deeper sense of responsibility.

In January 1918, Palestine was occupied by English troops, by the
same power that had promised the Jewish people its national homeland.
This turn of events gave Buber cause for renewed reflection, and he
expressed his ideas in an article in *Der Jude* called "Die Eroberung Palästinas" [The conquest of Palestine]. Palestine could be occupied by
any power whatsoever by the use of force—but it could be "conquered" only through service, work, and sacrifice. Only the dedication
of the Jewish people will extract from the Land its hidden resources:
the "ancient bond" between Land and People is a metaphysical bond
and belongs to the realm of mystery; it has been given only to the Jews
to "redeem" the Land.

The next essay on the political situation, "Vor der Entscheidung" [Before the decision], is dated March 1919. The great powers in Paris, which were considering European and Near Eastern territorial questions, had recognized the Jewish people as a nation, and it was expected that the Jewish settlement in Palestine would gradually develop into an autonomous community in the free atmosphere of the British Empire. The initial pride and joy that Buber felt at this prospect were mixed with apprehension. It was already becoming clear that the general new order being created in Paris was not advancing the cause of justice and truth among nations but was only concerned with safeguarding the spoils of victory. The devastating war that had been fought for the noblest ideals seemed to give rise to deeper entanglements rather than sober afterthoughts. What was called the League of Nations was in reality a league of political systems intent on retaining their wartime gains. It is true that the existing civilized powers recognized the Jewish people as a nation, but the Jews themselves could not in good conscience acknowledge this power structure. This is not to be interpreted as a readiness to give up Palestine, but simply as an inner resolve not to engage in politics that, under the mask of humanity, was intent only on the extension of power. For Palestine to become involved in the prevailing system of injustice and wrongdoing would make of it a "Zionised galuth dependency" and, as "an agent of economic and political imperialism," render it incapable of fulfilling its great mediating role between East and West. Only if Judaism acknowledged its essential peoplehood and its attachment to the Land, fully conscious that the Jews are a Semitic race and Palestine a Near Eastern country, would it be able to remain true to its mission.

At the Conference of San Remo in April 1920, Great Britain was entrusted with the Mandate of Palestine, which was confirmed by the Council of the League of Nations in 1922 and put into effect in 1923 after Transjordan had been separated from Palestine. In the summer of 1920 British military rule was replaced by a civil administration under a High Commissioner. In September 1921, the first postwar Zionist Congress met in Karlsbad, and for the first time after many years Buber took an active part as the representative of the Socialist Workers Party in Palestine, Hapoel Hatsair, which he had joined some years before when he was convinced that this movement, under the leadership of A. D. Gordon, represented the conceptions of life in Palestine that were closest to his own ideal of the renewal of the people.

At the Karlsbad Congress Buber delivered two addresses: one that dealt with the fundamental principles of "nationalism" in general and of Jewish nationalism in particular, and one in support of the adoption of a resolution to create a basis for mutual understanding between Jews and Arabs in Palestine. Buber was one of the first to recognize the importance of the Arab question for Zionism. During the English occupation and administration of the country, the number of Jewish immigrants had risen considerably, resulting in increased Arab hostility which led to bloody acts of violence. From the outset Buber supported the idea of cooperation with the Arabs, which in an article written in 1922 he had called "Landespolitik" [Palestinian politics]:[49] building the country together out of a common love of the land; the economic exploitation of the country would be undertaken for the mutual benefit of both peoples and would finally lead to a bi-national state, which Achad Ha'am had urged in 1920 [50] and which had been envisaged by the Brith Shalom, founded in 1925 to promote Jewish-Arab understanding. Buber was deeply perturbed by acts of injustice against the Arabs, by the violation of their rights, and by the failure of the Zionists to win their confidence; indeed, the Jews in Palestine tended to regard themselves as the culturally superior master race. In the spring of 1920 it was quite clear to Buber[51] that the favorable hour for reaching an understanding had been missed. After the expulsion of the Turks the English occupying power should have taken seriously the support promised in the Balfour Declaration and made it clear to the Arabs in Palestine that Jewish immigration would benefit them economically and culturally.

The resolution that Buber had in mind in Karlsbad was to be the beginning of a sincere pan-Palestinian policy based on the conviction that with an intensive and planned cultivation of the soil the country could support both peoples. Buber insisted that Jewish immigration into the country was the natural and sacred right of a people who had no other way to survive and renew itself. This very people, however, who for two thousand years had been an oppressed minority in all countries of the earth, emphatically rejected imperialistic methods of which it had itself been a victim. The object of its colonization was not the capitalistic exploitation of the land, but the cultivation of a common soil by free men: "In this social character of our national ideal lies the mighty pledge of our assurance that between us and the working Arab people a deep and lasting solidarity of true interests will emerge which will perforce overcome all the oppositions created by the confusions of the moment." [52] In an open letter on the occasion of J. L. Magnes's seventieth birthday in 1947, Buber recounted his experiences in connection with his proposal.[53] The resolution in its final form was interpreted as not strictly binding, and it was finally adopted for reasons of political expediency. To see how the sincere words of the original draft had been hardened into an ideology by his own party and its ethical principles turned into political propaganda was more than Buber could bear and, disillusioned, he retired for a long time from active politics.

This bitter experience found expression in "Kongressnotizen zur Zionistischen Politik" [Congress notes to Zionist politics] which Buber published a month later in *Der Jude*. He began with a historical summary of the Zionist program from its early beginnings and then asked about the extent to which the present leadership of the movement has remained faithful to its own formulation of "synthetic Zionism." The problem that was involved here was how to combine the program of the East European Choveve Zion—colonization and popular education —with Theodor Herzl's diplomatic policy. The "democratic party," which had adopted this goal twenty years before, took the view that politics is always the expression of real power relations and, as long as planned colonization failed to create a basis for any claim to Palestine, the purpose of negotiations was only to provide colonizing work for the settlers. Hence, it was imperative that the declaration of a claim and the organization of the settlement should be presented together and treated as inseparable.

With the outbreak of World War I and Palestine's involvement in the conflict the implementation of the "synthetic" program became impossible. This again called for a preponderance of diplomatic negotiations, and in the course of the war the neutral attitude that had been adopted by Zionism had to be abandoned. The Balfour Declaration appointed England the official protecting power of Zionist aspirations. To the indigenous people of that area this seemed to make Jewish immigration the cat's-paw of European imperialism. Although England won the sympathy of world Jewry, it still retained its full freedom of action. The assurance of a national homeland remained just a declaration without authentic interpretation or a well-defined plan of implementation. A general principle was enunciated, but no practical scheme of execution was mentioned. It was later disclosed that England had made promises simultaneously to both Jews and Arabs which would be mutually contradictory to fulfill. In practice the English administration adopted the principle of "divide et impera," which had been proved successful as a political tactic. Buber, however, was fair-minded enough to appreciate the deeper causes that made such a policy necessary in the Orient: England had passed the apex of its power and was now cautiously proceeding to loosen and decentralize the solid structure of its colonial empire; in so doing it was compelled to take the nationalism of the Arab world into consideration.

Diplomatic promises were as yet not realities. Zionist leadership was contented with the declaration of its goal and overlooked the proper moment for stipulating the number of immigrants to be allowed into the country and their specific working conditions. In its diplomatic negotiations it had neglected the systematic preparation for colonization on a large scale, and the favorable moment for setting up a well-organized settlement with a fair prospect of success was missed for lack of a convincing conception of the real nature of the work to be done.

Buber realized that the slogans of political Zionism—the creation of a Jewish majority, sovereignty, the "Jewish state"—were under the circumstances battle slogans and not principles of peace, and that the only principles that held forth any hope for peace were community of interests with the Arabs and an end to unjust acts that were not absolutely necessary for survival, a concept for which Buber in 1921 had coined the term *demarcation line,* that is, the line that must constantly be drawn with a sense of responsibility, within which one was permitted to defend his right for survival. To Buber the limited goal of the Jewish state represented a great danger. He saw the necessity for gradual colonization over a period of several generations through the constant recruiting of a working elite of the people; only thus could a completely new life form arise in Palestine that would be basically different from existence in the *galuth,* and a society be built up gradually[54] in which Jews would be represented in all walks of life, from the basic production and consumption of goods to the cultural professions. This would solve the sociological problem of Jewish life among the nations, namely, the inability of the rootless intellectual classes to renew themselves from a native soil. Only under changed conditions of life could new social communal forms be tested and developed.

Buber realized that to maintain itself the Jewish community in Palestine would have to create new human values. As a latecomer to European nationalism a small Jewish state could not long endure. He was deeply disturbed because the movement understood Zionism to be nothing more than "normalization" [55] that would make it "like all the other nations," and had a goal no different from that of the many small states artificially created in 1919. This form of Zionism, however, is merely a kind of "national assimilation," and one which is more dangerous than any other because through it the very essence of Judaism is vitiated.

Buber thus considered it imperative at the Karlsbad Congress, where political questions were being discussed with great heat, to deliver a basic address on "nationalism," [56] and to draw the "demarcation line" between its lawful and unlawful forms. His aim was to impress upon the representatives of the Zionist movement the need for the Jewish community in Palestine to present to the world a new form of nationalism that was different in every way from the power hungry, aggressive nationalism of modern Europe. It must resist the temptation to rush into statehood, but must constitute itself as a people, that is, as "a new organic order built on the natural forms of the life of the people," an order whose structure is nationally determined and constructed out of the elements of the people's tradition.

Modern European nationalism, which arose in the wake of the French Revolution, is state nationalism directed from a centralized organization whose aim is to gain and retain power, and in it the group egoism of the individual has found its modern form. Buber, unlike Jakob Burckhardt, was not convinced that power in itself is evil. Evil is the inordinate desire for more power *(pleonexia)*, which Buber called power hysteria, a form of greed which he regarded as an illness of modern man. Buber distinguished between people, nation, and nationalism. A people arises as a community with a common destiny, and endures more or less as a unity based on blood; it becomes a nation when it grows conscious of its peculiar strength, organization, and task. Nationalism, however, denotes an exaggerated function of this national consciousness and is thus symptomatic of an illness in the life of the people.

A certain amount of nationalism is necessary to enable a nation to fulfill its mission within mankind. A false nationalism, however, has power as its goal and holds up the nation as an end in itself; it is nothing more than the idolatry of a people. To draw the line between legitimate and illegitimate nationalism thus becomes the indispensable task for the leaders of a national movement and of utmost importance for its future. The only criterion that can be used to draw this line, however, is the recognition of a supernational responsibility on the part of the nation.

When an unlawful nationalism gains the upper hand not only within a single people but also throughout an entire epoch, the very substance of peoplehood is threatened and the life of mankind endangered. This seemed to represent to Buber the nature of the world crisis of his day, a crisis that coincided with the awakening of the Orient from its slumber of centuries. If Judaism is to fulfill its mission as the intermediary between the East and the West, it should refrain from becoming the emissary of a hypertrophic European nationalism in Palestine. The principle of the centralized state prevalent in Europe proved unsuitable for the new social order and for the changing relations between nations—and this completed the train of thought that had begun the debate between Buber and Cohen. If Zionism withstands the temptation of an unlawful nationalism and if it reshapes its public life in conjunction with the elemental forces of the community now stirring among all peoples, so that work communities will be combined with larger communal units imbued with a strong sense of social justice, it will be able to grant the Asiatic peoples the opportunity to achieve their own emancipation and lead ultimately to the genuine soli-

darity of a common social life. Judaism must complete its national consolidation in the service of a supernational mission, for this is the only
enduring assurance that the young "Volksland" in Palestine will become "a spiritual power capable of creating new forms of national life,
exemplary relations among the nations and a genuine bond that will
unite the Orient with the Occident and, on the basis of this preparatory work, proceed to ally itself with the future elements of all peoples." [57]

Buber's thoughts concerning a gradual national consolidation in
Palestine by means of a Jewish settlement that understood how to
awaken a consciousness of solidarity among the Arabs would have
needed a peaceful development of generations if it were to have any
prospect of success. But in the twenties the differences became more
acute and tension increased, and there developed on both sides an aggressive nationalism after the European pattern which Buber had
feared and which appeared among the Arabs sooner than could have
been anticipated at the time of the Balfour Declaration. The real leader
of this new movement was the religious head of the Palestinian Arabs,
Mohammed Emin el Huseini, the Mufti of Jerusalem, who in 1926 had
been appointed by the Mandate government as Grand Mufti and the
chairman of the Supreme Islamic Council. Bloody battles between
Jews and Arabs broke out in 1929. In 1937 an official commission
headed by Lord Peel recommended a partition of the country into a
Jewish and an Arab state, a plan which the Arabs, who regarded themselves as the rightful owners of the country, bitterly opposed.

The outbreak of World War II proved unfavorable to the Jews in
Palestine. Because of its proximity to the Suez Canal and the oil supply
lines from Iraq, the country was an important English base in the Near
East. This obliged England to consider Arab sensibilities, and thus the
White Book of 1939 drastically restricted Jewish immigration and the
sale of land in Palestine, despite the catastrophic condition of the Jews
in Germany. A Jewish legion took part in the struggle against Hitler;
but there was little hope that the Labor government would rescind the
provisions of the White Book after the end of the war. Acts of terror
by the Arabs were now answered more and more by retaliatory meas-
ures of the Jewish self-defense and underground forces. Again in 1946

an Anglo-American Commission came to investigate the situation on the spot. The group that was friendly to the Arabs, the Ichud (Union), led by Buber and by Dr. J. L. Magnes, President of the Hebrew University, appeared before this Commission and recommended the creation of a bi-national State.[58] The Security Council of the United Nations, which had been asked to serve as arbiter, recommended the partition of the country with economic cooperation between Jews and Arabs, and the neutralization of Jerusalem. The British government thereupon announced the termination of the Mandate and the withdrawal of its troops, to take effect in May 1948. On the fourteenth of that month the state of Israel was proclaimed. The civil war with the neighboring Arab states began and, after the intervention of the United Nations, ended with an armistice and with more or less accidental boundaries which remained until the Six Day War in 1967.

Buber did not conceal the fact that he deplored this fateful development: "Everything proceeded with fearful logical succession and at the same time with fearful meaninglessness." [59] But in an article that appeared in the United States in 1958, he left no doubt that he stood foursquare behind the new state: "I have nothing in common with those Jews who feel impelled to contest the factive form of Jewish independence. It is now incumbent upon us to fulfill the command to serve the spirit in this State, and from this State as a basis." This does not preclude the will for reconciliation with the Arab people. We must continue to labor to open up paths that will lead to an understanding with the Arabs and to compensate them for any wrongs done against them: "Under such difficult conditions it is still the command of the spirit, and today more than ever, to pave the way for the cooperation of the nations." [60]

Revolutionary Colonization

In his address "The Holy Way" (1918), Buber described the Zionist settlement whereby Palestine was to become a "new land with a social structure" as "revolutionary colonization," a concept which implicitly contradicted the principle of revolution. Since the time of the French Revolution people had believed that the human desire for a new social order and for social justice could be realized by means of political upheavals; after the Communist Manifesto the radical socialists in all countries proclaimed world revolution as the goal of their party programs.

Buber had been a socialist since his student days. In 1899 he became acquainted with the circle of the New Community in Berlin where he met Gustav Landauer whose friendship he enjoyed until the latter's death in 1919. After Buber returned from Italy, they lived as close neighbors in Hermsdorf near Berlin (1906–1907). They shared in common a love for Meister Eckhart and Hölderlin, an abiding interest in the philosophy of language and in the various social and cultural movements of that day. But they also had a peculiar gift for discovering great spirits of the past with whom they formed a highly personal relationship. Landauer, who on one occasion stated that his view of life could best be described by the word *anarchism*,[61] was at bottom a mystic—in the sense in which it was used at that time as complementary to skepticism. Like Buber, he saw man as a microcosm,[62] in a mysterious and ineffable cosmic relationship. On June 21, 1900, he wrote to Hedwig Lachmann: "The deeper we descend into the depths of our individual life the more will we become part of this real community with the powers of race, of humanity, of animality and, finally, when we withdraw into our most secret depths and into the ineffable stillness away from conceptual thought and sensible images, part of the infinite world. For this world lives in us since it is our source and origin, that is, it is constantly active within us, else we cease to be what we are. What is most individual in us is what is most common." [63] His mysticism, like Buber's cosmic unification, could go far back into the past to summon up long-forgotten communal powers as well as into the future for the realization of which he staked his life. The relentless critic of the intellect and its generalized concepts was also an ardent believer in an emergent humanity and, as such, was more fit for the role of a martyr than that of a leader of a political movement.

In one of his works[64] Ernst Simon recalls that Franz Rosenzweig once called Landauer "a great half" *(einen grossen Halben)*. Harsh as such a judgment may sound for one who died a martyr for his convictions, it is nevertheless true that Landauer was a problematical figure in his attitudes and achievements. Early in his career he experienced the woes of the spiritual man who seeks to enlighten his people. Hans Kohn quotes from an early essay, "Durch Absonderung zur Gemeinschaft" [Through separation to community], the testimony of an intellectual anarchist who longs for community but who remains imprisoned in his own ego and there finds the world: "We are too far advanced that our voice could still be understood by the masses." [65] His later articles and appeals are also interspersed with literary allusions and quotations, and are too lofty for mass consumption. In his essay "Der Krieg" [The war], written in 1911, he asks the question: "Are we socialists today not far too much thinkers and poets?" [66] And on October 18, 1912, he writes: "I believe I am somewhat unusual and fit no category, and this is because I am neither an agitator nor a poet, but a synthesis of both that has no name . . ." [67] The alternative agitator poet is inadequate, and the double epithet so characteristic of that day, poet thinker, must be added. Landauer's thoughts on mysticism are aesthetic and literary; his writings are of unequal value, and his essays often give the impression of having been composed under the pressure of time and financial distress. On the other hand, his excellent lectures on Shakespeare, posthumously published by Buber, gave a generation of young people a deeper understanding and appreciation of Shakespeare: here his admirable love of freedom and candor, which are revealed to us so convincingly in his letters, his ideal of humanity and his talent for seeking the answer to the world's riddle in man and in his relation to himself, found their most appropriate subject matter.[68]

Revolution was, for Landauer as for Buber, not only a political and social process but also a spiritual phenomenon in its most inclusive sense, a "permanent revolution," and of far greater significance than was understood by the author of this phrase. The meaning of revolution is regeneration, and every revolution brings with it a temporary regeneration. Until World War I every revolutionary impulse, including the socialist, always ended in a victory for capitalism and imperialism. The real enemy of social forces was for Landauer the state: "Inwardly we do not take part in the compulsory State because we wish to create the true federation of man, the society that springs from the spirit and hence from freedom." [69] Only he truly desires peace who rejects the state. Wars break out because there are states, and will continue to do so as long as states exist. What is today called peace is not a genuine peace but an armed truce. These and similar thoughts are to be found in the essays which Landauer published in the journal *Der Sozialist*, which he directed from 1909 to 1915. He was a revolutionary, but he belonged to no particular political group; he was an opponent of all rigid party programs and tactics.

Landauer's socialism, in contradistinction to that of Marx, does not start from the historical process and its epochs, but from the individual human being and the possible transformation of his life. Revolution meant to him not changes in political institutions but a change of heart in the individual and a new beginning for the spirit of man: "In the fire, the enthusiasm and the brotherly feeling of such aggressive movements there rises, again and again, the image and consciousness of positive solidarity brought about by harmonizing forces, by love which is strength. Without such transient regeneration we should be unable to live on, and we would wither away." [70]

In his *Aufruf zum Sozialismus* [Appeal for socialism] (1911), Landauer again stated that the future of revolution stands and falls with the individual human being. Only a total awareness of new necessities in the midst of daily life can be the basis of a genuine and lasting revolution. Buber wrote in his preface to *Lebensgang in Briefen* [Life in letters], which he published: "He understood socialism as something with which one can and should begin at the place where one happens to be, and there alone; and his own existence was for him a place of realization."

Years later Buber, in *Paths in Utopia*, honored Landauer's memory with his sympathetic insight into the broken glimpses and partial illuminations of his friend's fragmentary conceptions and aspirations.[71] Buber placed Landauer in the succession of those men whom Marx described as "bourgeois-socialists" and "socialist utopians," and who are to this day dismissed by scientific Marxism as visionaries and romantics. The image of a future "just order" is shared by both utopians and Marxists, but whereas the latter believe that the new order will necessarily arise from the conditions of production, the former appeal to the will of the individual and his ability to make decisions. If we take socialism as secular messianism, then the utopians may be regarded as being in the succession of the prophets who preached conversion and repentance, and the Marxists in the role of the old apocalyptical figures who awaited with assurance the catastrophic end of the historical process.

The utopians whom Landauer found most congenial were Proudhon and Kropotkin. Kropotkin's socialist village and his federation principle for settlements and voluntary associations appealed to Landauer, who also translated his book, *Mutual Aid, a Factor of Evolution* (1902) into German. With Proudhon he shared the conviction that a social and not a political revolution will bring about peaceful construction and create a new social reality—although it cannot dispense with political revolution to achieve its ends. But the revolution can be prepared in prerevolutionary society through individuals banded together into groups and then into associations, and through their reciprocal influences.

Landauer was distinguished from his predecessors, according to Buber, by his new insight into the nature of the state and its relation to the community. He saw the state as one of the ways in which men are related to one another; but this relation that is represented by the present order of the state can be overcome by the adoption of a different relationship, one that is more like that of a growing organism, which Landauer called *Volk*. This new relationship can flourish outside of the state and parallel to it, for it is at bottom the revival of an everpresent but forgotten reality. Socialism is thus possible at all times, and is independent of the existing state.

Landauer thus saw the state as "status," a condition which must be reduced to an indispensable minimum by a voluntary association that promises greater justice. As individuals and families combine to form communities and these in turn larger associations, the state as a centralized compulsory community will disintegrate from within. In all this restructuring of society, it is a matter of evoking creative forces that have long been dormant and of resurrecting old communal forms suppressed by the state. To revitalize these forms and make them significant in men's lives, it is necessary, in Landauer's view, to start from a concrete situation, from the here and now; but, above all, it is essential that the individual experience a rude awakening and a change of heart before direct contact between men can be restored.

Landauer's socialism combines the revolutionary with the conservative spirit. He believed that the rebirth of a people arises from the spirit of the community. Hence, he called for the creation of the socialist settlement because in the village communities the common spirit and communal life of the past are still alive in the memory of the people. Here, in all tranquillity, the preparatory work can be done that will later be completed by the political revolution. Continuing Kropotkin's ideas, Landauer saw the basic form of the new society as a combination of community, agriculture, handwork, and village productions, so that the workers do not work for an employer but for one another. Buber pointed out that for Landauer socialism was never something finished and absolute but signified the "growth of the human community within the human race to the extent and in the form of that which is desired and which, at definite times and under given conditions, can be accomplished." Revolution was to him something which of necessity belonged to the social order to keep it from growing too rigid and inflexible. Thus, he placed himself at the disposal of the socialist revolution that had broken out in Bavaria in 1919; but, as a member of the Revolutionary Committee which at that time was conducting the affairs of the state, he found little understanding for his ideal of a truly human social order. He was already a martyr to his convictions, even before the counter-revolution demanded his life.

Buber's social philosophy was greatly influenced by Landauer, especially in his thoughts about the work of Jewish settlement in Palestine. The views of the two friends developed from animated discussions and an intimate exchange of ideas, so that it became difficult to determine to whom to attribute the original idea. Both were convinced that the renewal of society must begin with the "cellular structure" of community life and proceed from communities and settlements, for here was to be found the living core of humanity. This was the view that was represented in German sociology by Ferdinand Tönnies who, in his *Gemeinschaft und Gesellschaft* [Community and society] (1887), divided social life into these two basic forms. His bold definitions and the vague language of his fundamental principles lent an air of novelty to his writings and exerted a strong influence on the young people of his day. In his view *community* is an organic form of living together, based on voluntary cooperation and free consent; on the other hand, *society* represents an artificial structure directed to a definite end, having no inner cohesion and containing tensions that could be controlled only by a highly centralized, coercive authority. In this negative image of society Tönnies was influenced by Marx. But whereas for Marx community is a future ideal into which society is converted when it becomes absolute as a result of the dialectical historical process, community for Tönnies looks back into the distant past where the dormant natural and organic forces are to be found which must be brought to the surface and developed into new communal structures. Community, in Tönnies's view, has its roots in the vegetative and organic life, in the blood community, in marriage and family, whose natural growth gives rise to the settlement and the village community. Although it is no longer possible to return to the primitive forms of kinship and tribal community life, we can still recapture the spirit of natural association and brotherly feeling in our common life and work and fashion it into new communal forms. Whereas for Tönnies community is predominantly a natural, organic phenomenon, Hermann Schmalenbach's *Bund* [Union] introduces us to a community of the spirit and of voluntary association.

Buber's idea of community, as set forth in the second volume of *Worte an die Zeit* (1919), is closer to Schmalenbach's *Bund*, which stresses the personal and selective character of the community, than it is to Tönnies. Buber's community is a community of kindred souls organized around a religious center,[72] a voluntary association of people for the purpose of preparing an abode for the kingdom of God. Buber's "My Way to Hasidism" appeared in 1918. The Hasidic group had realized the image of human community as envisaged by Buber: "genuine fellowship and genuine leadership; something ancient, primordial. . . ." Here in this community, which proceeded with earnest joy to sanctify the undivided world of their daily lives, "the ancient Jewish relation to God, world and man" had remained alive. "Never before in Europe had a community—not an order of recluses, not a select brotherhood, but a 'Volksgemeinde' in all its intellectual and social distinctions and with all its diversity—set its life with such singleness of purpose on that which is inwardly perceived. Here we find no separation between faith and works, between truth and confirmation or, as it is now called, between morality and politics; here all is One Kingdom, One Spirit, One Reality." [73]

Buber's idea of community is distinguished from that of Landauer's in that it is firmly rooted in the religious life. Both recognized that the free, unmediated contact between man and man is today the only way a community can again find God; through a new beginning made in common and through a common labor of reconstruction our wordless life will one day be transformed into the authentic binding Word. Landauer would have agreed with Buber's words in "The Holy Way": "The true community is the Sinai of the future." [74] In his view communism and religion belonged together, and in the "community of love" which shared all things in common he saw the realization of religion. [75]

In rejecting the domination of state centralism, the two friends were in agreement. Buber also saw the state as "status," as he wrote in a letter to Florens Christian Rang: "You know what I see in the State: the 'status,' the recurrent expression of the non-realization of God's kingdom made manifest—for men, between men, in every man. Only when we accept it unreservedly with all its uncompromising facts can it lead us toward God." [76]

Landauer, unlike Buber, was never a Zionist: "On the way to the evolving man of the future he forgot the Jew of today or could not see him." [77] A nation for Landauer was defined by the function it was destined to fulfill in the construction of the true human community: "To be a nation means to have a sphere of duty; and where that is there is my fatherland." [78] He could not see that the task of the Jews to labor for the coming of the messianic kingdom was to be fulfilled in the land of their fathers. That he had so little understanding for the problematical position of the Jews in the life and culture of Germany constituted his greatness, but it also represented a distinct danger. He thought of himself as a Jew and a German, and he experienced "this singular and intimate juxtaposition as something precious." Ernst Simon has pointed out that Landauer's concept of *nation* is surprisingly ambiguous[79]— sometimes being used as if *humanity* were its complementary concept

—and thus it often appears as a sterile philosophical concept with no parochial attachments. The tension within him between the thinker and the practical revolutionary remained unresolved. Like Herzl, he would have liked to descend into the arena as an "elemental activist" and attain heroism by abandoning the pen. His failure to bridge the gap between his literary talent and his "faithful dedication to the works of the earth" sapped his strength and in the end made him unsuitable for the role of a revolutionary.

In Buber also there was a great tension between his practical Zionism and his inner need to comprehend intellectually all aspects of Judaism. His unconditionality and his uncompromising attitude in the pursuit of the highest ideals made him as disturbing a figure at Zionist congresses as Landauer was among the anarchists.

Cohen's liberalism and Landauer's utopian socialism had this in common: in the pursuit of social messianism they bypassed Judaism or deliberately neglected it. In 1930 Buber also acknowledged: "I believe in an evolving humanity";[80] but he did not shut his eyes to the existence of individual nations and to the still more disturbing fact that all men are not of *one* faith, from which he concluded that it is precisely within this diversity of peoples and religions that God speaks to us and presents man with his task. Buber was Landauer's literary executor, and by publishing his works preserved the memory of his friend for posterity. But he felt his responsibility to extend beyond this; it is as if the conversations of the two friends concerning the realization of the true human community had never ceased. Buber took up and defended Landauer's noblest thoughts where alone they had the prospect of being realized, that is, in the Jewish settlement in Palestine. The fate of the German revolution of 1918 strengthened the conviction in Buber that the Jewish people had a mission to create a divinely ordained community, and to reconcile spirit and politics. In Palestine alone there were possibilities for a genuine new beginning. The communal life that will arise here could become the "new-land of social significance"—not through revolutionary upheavals but as a "colonizing revolution," representing "a constructive element" at the beginning of mankind's regeneration. The Jewish settlement was not burdened with existing institutions and traditional constitutional forms, but for its own purposes and to meet its own needs it created forms that were not taken "out of an intellectual vacuum and introduced into reality: in our folk-memory, transmitted to our inner history, we bear the lofty command for a genuinely communal but still unrealized society." [81]

In those years Buber acquired a clearer image of the halutz, the pioneer settler, whose "religion" is to dedicate his life to the work of the community, and he came to see him as the legitimate successor of Hasidic piety. Although this new type of man was exemplified by A. D. Gordon, Landauer was the one who died a martyr for a human ideal which he pursued with a singleness of purpose and intense vision, and which lived on in Buber insofar as he bore witness to this ideal. The mystery of the transmission of the spirit that bound all three was called by Buber "being-tradition." Gordon lived the life of cosmic unification that reaches from the earth to the stars,[82] of which Landauer had spoken in his letter to Hedwig Lachmann, and whose truth Buber attested through his word, thus binding together these two thinkers.

If the regeneration of the individual is to become a human process, it must take place within the larger sphere of a renewal of the people. Without the genuine unification of the people as a whole, the rebirth of the individual will not succeed and in our present-day mechanized society will dry up like drops of water in the desert. Every elemental national movement, as described by Buber in "Regeneration eines Volkstums" [Regeneration of a People] (1943),[83] produces, at least for a brief period, a new human type which represents in visible form the historical hour in which a deep change is taking place in the life of the people. Zionism thus produced the halutz, who not only opened up the country of Palestine with the work of his two hands but who is at the same time the pioneer of a new life form; not only is his achievement important but also his exemplary way of life. In this figure the Zionist movement demonstrated its authenticity and its historical justification.

The phenomenon of regeneration has, as Buber showed, a psychological and biological aspect and, in conjunction with a change in one's mental attitude, effects a change of the entire being. In the case of the halutz this means a dedication to work for the common good of the people and a new feeling of solidarity: "The common unification with the center, that is, with the welfare of the settlement and its future and with something larger that is represented in it, unites the comrades with one another. . . ." [84] At first the conditions everywhere are miserable; behind the work there is a constant struggle for existence, which leads to mutual aid and responsibility. But we also find everywhere a common desire for a life of human dignity: "a common dream, a common summons, a common awakening to new necessities." [85] Every group feels itself to be part of the entire people as it moves forward; the soil it cultivates is almost always the common property of the people which the group only holds in fee. Whatever is done is considered as an experiment; all is in flux and open to various possibilities, the most significant of which is that the collectivity can combine into greater communal units according to the same principles by which the smallest cells are formed.

The larger historical communal formations, a "people" and a "community of believers," have become congealed into the rigid structures "state" and "religion." State people and church religion today are no longer genuine destiny communities and life associations for the sake of a living center of faith; they now contain only the remnants of community. Buber shared Landauer's view that beside these forms and outside of them there can be another relationship between people which is found, for example, in the underground movement of the Russian revolutionaries. Buber called this third way "community as process," [86] to be found wherever a group experiences a critical, fateful situation in common and meets it with unified resolution. The Jewish settlers in Palestine constitute such a communal association, dedicated to the concrete and realistic work of social transformation—not through utopian romanticism or through institutions and organizations, but through "direct contact between men," which at the same time means identification with the soil and with work. One can dismiss these beginnings of a new comradely life as an insignificant experiment from the standpoint of numbers; but what is here taking place is something that points to the creation of a new community of the future, a peculiar force beyond all political power conflicts and historical claims: "the right of colonization is that of power capable of coping with the settlement situation." [87]

We can understand the halutz only when we see him as the ideal union of the national and the social; the synthesis of people, land, and work that is taking place in Palestine is a social one. The chief requisites needed for a socialist reconstruction of Palestine—common ownership of the land, independent work, and the right of the settlers to determine the norms of their community life—could be achieved during the Mandate period only within small groups and associations. Nevertheless, Buber would not have us underestimate these early beginnings: the people in the *kvutsa*, the voluntary socialist collective later called *kibbutz*, are a *"living* experiment." [88] A new combination of production and consumption associations arose here not for ideological reasons but out of necessity, and this brought with it a humanization of labor: one does not work as a living machine but as a whole man with undivided will and in sincere cooperation with one's comrades. In all this the most important element is decentralization and community autonomy which through federation can gradually displace state centralism.

As early as 1928, in his address "Why Must the Development of Palestine Be Socialistic?" [89] Buber set up a third crystallization point over against the two political power centers, Moscow and Rome: "I believe in Jerusalem." In Russian communism the idea of a universal community ended in state centralism that was more totalitarian than its predecessor; and fascism became a national power state without any idea of humanity. When *Paths in Utopia* appeared, fascism was already in its decline, but the Moscow-Jerusalem alternative continued to occupy Buber's thoughts. In the section called "Another Experiment" he once more summarized his experiences and ideas relating to the Jewish community village. The Russian development, which had established a net of compulsory associations in place of the old village settlements, made the voluntary collective in Israel even more significant for the reconstruction of society: now as before it was to be regarded as the primary cell for a new socialistic society, which was to be based on the union of production and consumption, whereby production refers not only to agriculture but to its combination with handwork and industry. From the collective in its strict sense other forms were derived in the meantime, forms which permitted a certain amount of private property and closer family life; the socialistic principle was thereby not violated and, at the same time, the vitality of the idea and its capacity for growth were preserved. Everything was still in a fluid condition; the initial difficulties of opening up the land were overcome in the old settlement, but new problems arose.

Buber set forth the most important of these problems on which the future of the communal villages depended. First, the problem of inner cohesion: whether the feeling of comradeship that had sprung up of necessity in a period of distress could be maintained. Further, the problem of the new generation: whether the young people of the next generation will remain faithful to the life style of their fathers or whether they will flee to the cities. Another problem concerns the question of federation: the original communal village felt itself to be the primary cell of a new society; the settlements were to unite into larger associations in which the principle of common ownership would be preserved. But this became increasingly difficult with the emergence of semi-individual types of settlements side by side with the original kibbutz. In addition, politicization followed with the penetration of party programs and the imposition of fixed political points of view. The real test of the new communal form, however, lay in its radiating strength, in its power to influence the whole of society, especially in effecting a decentralization of urban society. The social pioneers of the first waves of immigration were inspired in their settlement work by the idea of a new order of society.

We cannot speak of their work as a success for in the long run it was impossible to maintain the natural selective principle which attracted only those who were willing to undergo privation and hardship out of idealism and love of country. A development that should have taken place gradually was accomplished in a decade, in the thirties. Hosts of refugees descended upon the country, too many to be absorbed by the older settlements, not because of Zionist convictions but out of desperation, for they could go nowhere else—violently interrupting the gradual line of tranquil development. On the other hand, this mass immigration of persecuted people was the real cause for the creation of the Jewish State. Perhaps something of greater significance, something unique, might have arisen had events taken a different turn; nevertheless, Buber spoke in *Paths in Utopia* of an "exemplary non-failure" of the work of settlement: the paths that lead into the future were still open.

National Humanism

In the years before World War I Buber sought to comprehend the spiritual condition of Judaism in all its varied aspects. The essays and articles he wrote on questions of Judaism and Zionism after 1917 sought to concretize specific problems. The underlying principle here was that politics also belongs to spirit and that this includes not only political activities in the narrower sense—Buber's experiences at the Zionist Congress of 1921 convinced him that this was not the path he was destined to take—but is to be understood rather as an attitude to specific problems in the larger sphere of national affairs. As early as 1903 Buber regarded Zionist politics[90] as culture politics, but even then he was not content to understand it as dealing exclusively with spiritual matters but rather with the deep changes that occur in the life of the people and with the creation of new forms of living together. In an article written in 1917,[91] he rejected "cultural work" as a misleading concept, for the end in view is not primarily culture but life: "We wish to transform Jewish life, and that means: we wish to make the life of Jews a Jewish life . . . we wish to build a Jewish community life."

The concept that must replace cultural work is education. The education of the people is indispensable if the national goal, which is the building of Palestine, is to be more than a passing collective passion, and if its dynamism is to be preserved.[92] Popular education is not to be confused with propaganda. With reference to Zionism its task is to produce two types of men: the pioneer for Palestine and the helper in the Diaspora, both of whom are to establish a tradition of work and carry forward the Zionist movement from generation to generation.

For an education of this kind, instruction alone is not sufficient; it must be based on a life lived in common. In the twenties Buber was anxious to see his theories of education and adult instruction[93] for Zionist work, to which he had devoted long years of earnest thought, put into practice and bear fruit. Education in Palestine must be adapted to the requirements of the country, just as Grundtvig's voluntary residential folk schools had been adapted to German conditions. In this way "the institutional nodal points in the concatenation of the generations" could be created to guarantee the preservation of ideas and of the human type to transmit them. The popular schools that Buber had in mind must not have as their goal the popularizing of university education, but rather the training of a special type of man for a definite task. General education and Jewish education are not to run parallel, but must be joined together as national and social education, combining training for Judaism and for the community. This educational goal, which applies principally to the settlement in Palestine and to the Diaspora, is designed to awaken forces that make for unification and to develop an attitude that could at all times become a firm support.

Buber was thus able to appeal to the people in the great crisis of 1933: "Let it not be asked for which country we wish to educate. For Palestine, for those whose country it should be. For some other land, for those whose country it must be. For Germany, for those whose country it could be. It is *one* image, *one* goal, *one* education." [94] But whereas in the previous decade Buber had treated concrete questions of education, being concerned with the involuntary, elemental, and incommensurable aspects of education and community building, he was, in the crisis he now faced, concerned with elaborating the normative, universally valid character of the goal of Jewish education. At a time when those who dealt with this question could only propose practical ways and means, Buber was interested in creating a common spiritual stand and in indicating the historical framework of the present distress. This above all showed him to be the great Jewish teacher who sought to introduce spirit and a sense of reality in assessing a given situation and to restore the lost equilibrium.

In those efforts as well, he was able to recall ideas that had influenced his youth and needed only to be deepened and clarified. Just as the concept "cultural work" had to be realized through education, so also must the idea of national "rebirth" be given concrete content. To a

small group of people who were interested in founding a Jewish country boarding school in Germany in 1913, Buber suggested that its entire curriculum be put under the inclusive concept of "Hebrew humanism." [95] In this same spirit Konrad Burdach continued Dilthey's
basic thoughts concerning the renaissance of the fifteenth century, conceiving Western humanism to be "a re-formation of our entire inner
life," and having for its goal the "return to the primal ground."

The purpose of the essay "Biblical Humanism" (1933) was to
help the Jew find his way back to this primal ground of his being: "The
Hebrew man is he who allows himself to be addressed by the Voice
that speaks to him from the Bible in its Hebrew tongue." [96] Humanism, according to Buber, combines two mysteries: the mystery of
speech and the mystery of the human person. As for the relation of the
Jewish people to the Hebrew language, Buber had already expressed
his thoughts in a lecture that he had delivered in 1909.[97] Language is
the consciousness form of a people, guaranteeing the cohesion and integrity of its internal relations and its relations with others, and we can
therefore describe it as the unifying form in the life of a people. It is
thus symptomatic of a grave illness in a people when a language loses
its vital continuity and no longer serves as a bond to unite the members
of a group. Only in Palestine will Jewish children speak their first
words in the language of their people. Here the Zionist movement can
truly become a "Renaissance" by recapturing the spirit of the people's
great classical period through its language. He who makes the Hebrew
language his own also "makes the creative function of the folk-spirit his
own," and is thenceforth a Jew in the deepest sense. But neither the
national homeland nor its language can create by themselves a "renewal," and thus at the XVI Zionist Congress in 1929 Buber demanded a "Hebrew humanism in its most real sense" as the determining factor for education in Palestine.[98] This Hebrew humanism must
proceed from the view that Zionism is more than a Jewish nationalism,
and that it signifies not only national self-determination but also a
supernational mission in whose service national consolidation is undertaken: "Zion is something greater than a piece of land in the Near East,
something greater than a Jewish community in this land; Zion is recol-

lection, admonition, promise; Zion is the new sanctuary in the image of the old; from Zion the teaching shall again go forth as of yore. It is the foundation stone of the messianic edifice of mankind." [99]

This supernational mission of Judaism has been indicated in the Bible from time immemorial. The primordial powers which the biblical word transmits to the Jew have a normative character. It was to a community that the biblical word was once addressed. Community in its primary biblical sense can again arise only when every individual who hears the word will let it penetrate to the core of his being. To hear the word means not only to understand its content but to realize that it is also being spoken to the individual.

In the Greek language the word has been severed from its spoken character and lives on in its written form; it stands before me. The word of the Bible is Voice: appeal, exclamation, consolation; it always has the dialogic character of living reality. Its essence is mutuality, and it demands an answer. Word and deed constitute a unity from the very beginning; God's speech is creative. The biblical word *is* not, it happens; it creates the relation and is fulfilled in its confirmation. It does not permit one to escape into the realm of the logos and the perfect form; it demands obedience and response: "This fearful world is the world of God. It challenges you. Prove yourself in it as God's creature." [100] Biblical humanism means the rebirth of the normative primordial energies of Israel.

In 1933 Buber had indicated the "primal ground" to which the Jew is to return; in the essay "Hebrew Humanism" of 1941,[101] he elaborated the concept of humanism, not from the linguistic point of view but from the standpoint of the basic word *humanitas, Menschlichkeit*, "Hebrew humanity." By means of language a people can summon up out of its past a classical image of man, and it does so to help posterity preserve its own *Menschlichkeit* and to keep it from sinking into inhumanity and barbarism.

The humanistic attitude is always both receptive and critical. It requires selectivity, a distinction between the time-conditioned and the supra-temporal. The return to the "primal ground" requires, furthermore, that the normative values found there be preserved in the material content of a changed world. But it is a question of realizing that what the Bible says to us today is no different from what it said to us in ancient days, namely, that there is truth and falsehood, justice and injustice, and that man's welfare depends on his not neglecting any realm in which this distinction is not valid; private and public life must be pervaded by the same spirit. If an injustice is unavoidable, then conscience must draw the "demarcation line" within whose limits it assumes responsibility. Hebrew humanism demands a national humanistic attitude in public life which is distinct from the national egoism of other nations. Israel is both a nation and a religious community, and it can preserve its innermost life only if it is willing to be God's people. In our age an ominous division has set in between the nation and the people of faith. The nation flourishes, religion withers; but in the long run neither can prosper without the other.

The address "The Spirit of Israel and the World Today" (1939), which Buber included with three other addresses of 1951 in a second series of *Addresses on Judaism*,[102] begins by taking note of this fatal division. All the addresses are informed by the idea of Hebrew humanism which Buber illumined from different points of view. The subtitle *Addresses on Judaism* is no doubt intended to remind us of the addresses that were given three decades before. Robert Weltsch points out that the questions which now engage Buber are *mutatis mutandis*, the same as before; the new addresses, however, were written in Jerusalem and directed to the Anglo-Saxon world where the Jewish Diaspora for the most part was now to be found.[103] The questions raised in the first address in 1909—"Why do we call ourselves Jews? Is there a living Jewish religion?"—are still relevant three decades later. The new "worldword," which Buber had hoped would be spoken by Judaism in Palestine, the religious-social synthesis with which it was to anticipate the coming development of mankind, had not yet been realized. In his earlier days Buber addressed young intellectuals who had been uprooted from their peoplehood and to whom he wished to convey an idea of the greatness of Judaism and a deeply rooted feeling of national pride; but in 1939 he had to deal with an exaggerated national consciousness, and his initial questions were: "What have you in mind when you speak of the spirit of Israel? Your own spirit? Or that which we have betrayed and continue to betray day in and day out?" And again the question is asked at the end of the second address: "Are we still Jews? Is Judaism still a living religion?"

The Jews are on the verge of becoming like other peoples: to fall prey to the collective egotism of an overweening nationalism, to make of the nation, which is but an extension of the ego, an idol and replace its traditional religion with a state myth. This kind of assimilation is the most dangerous that the Jewish people have ever had to experience. The real spirit of Israel, however, is the spirit of realization—again a concept that reminds us of the former addresses—the realization of the simple truth that the world was created by God for a purpose, with a view to some future day when mankind will live in peace and harmony. Israel as a people was entrusted with the task of laboring toward this end and becoming for the peoples of the earth a model of peaceful existence, social justice, and brotherly love. Throughout the centuries Israel preserved this mission in its teaching; but it has never fulfilled it and has not been an example to the nations in realizing God's truth. It now often acts as if the mere return to its original home will usher in the messianic period, but it "knows no longer of a king or of a royal will." Important social experiments have undeniably been made and different types of community settlements have been created and these could be of great significance for the future of mankind. But they have not had any appreciable effect on the total picture of Palestine. Israel is in danger, as are the Western nations, of making religion a private affair of the individual soul and letting the material world go its own unredeemed way.

The second address, "Judaism and Culture," resumes the comparison of Judaism with the great world cultures, a theme to which Buber had devoted considerable time in former years. He began with the basic notion that every genuine culture in its early period is a living system in which all areas of life develop around a supreme principle which is both religious and normative—religious because it signifies a concrete binding of man to the Absolute, and normative because it always refers to a transcendent Being that not only reigns throughout the entire cosmos as a regulating force but also determines man's ethical conduct and community life: "Everywhere the basic features of a true human society are prefigured in Heaven." [104] But everywhere man resists this binding, and out of his struggle with spirit arises a great culture.

Among the cultures of the ancient world Israel occupies a special place. In all areas of its private and public life this relation to a transcendent principle was conspicuous in its incomparable immediacy and concreteness: God had made a covenant with the people and charged them with the task of realizing justice and thus aiding Him in the creation of the coming Kingdom.

Every culture at a certain stage of its development strives to become autonomous and to free itself from an absolute binding principle: it confines its aspirations to the cultic sphere; its norms become convention. This development took place especially in the West so that, despite the extraordinary achievements in all the various spheres, it lost unity of spirit. In the Orient the spiritual deterioration was not as radical. But in Israel men of spirit arose to challenge the emancipation of culture, namely, the prophets who opposed having the divine commandment relegated to the purely sacral sphere, and they defended its claims over against the kings who abused their power. This failure on the part of the kings gave birth to the promise of the Messiah, the figure of the fulfilling king. Judaism has preserved a confident, realistic belief in the possibility of realizing the divine mission on earth: nations and cultures can repent, just as individual sinners, and find forgiveness. This conviction that the messianic promise will be fulfilled in human life and in human history the Jews took with them into exile and preserved it through the centuries. But now, when they reentered the history of nations, a deep division set in between people and religion. National freedom and independence had been achieved, but "Israel has been separated from its principle." Basic religious ideas were being secularized and applied to purely political processes. Judaism thus found itself in the midst of the general social crisis in Europe when all the ancient foundations were crumbling and all the traditional values disintegrating. The times were ripe for conversion, and the address ends with the question: "How shall we become the ones that we are?"

The third address, "The Secret Question," begins with the basic view that the deepest questions of our day are ultimately of a religious nature, an unconfessed cry for help arising out of doubt and despair. It is not directed to dogmas, nor can these provide an answer, but to the unmediated life-and-faith reality of the religions. In this sense people also turn to Judaism for guidance and help, although it is something of a novelty for the world to expect any answers from Judaism: "For many centuries Judaism was unknown and disregarded beyond its surface appearance"—attention was paid only to Jews, and not to Judaism. A change came about with the terrible persecution of Jews and the establishment of the state of Israel, two astonishing phenomena of death and life. It is of course still true that Jews themselves know nothing or very little of their religion, e.g., Bergson and Simone Weil, whose indictment of Judaism Buber answered by pointing out the social and religious humanity of Judaism on which the Jewish relation to God, world, and man is based. In Judaism the love of God and the love of man are twin commandments, and one who establishes peace is God's collaborator in the work of creation. Buber's teaching contests the autarchy of the soul; the inner truth must become a life reality: "A drop of messianic fulfillment must be mixed with every hour, else it is godless despite all piety." Not justice but the sanctification of all earthly things is the real Jewish concern. Judaism can answer the secret question of humanity if it would turn to its ancient origins for renewal and be lived sincerely by Jews themselves.

What distinguishes the Bible from the holy books of other peoples is the dialogue between God and man that runs through it, and for this reason Buber called the last of his four addresses "The Dialogue between Heaven and Earth." Again and again God addresses man in the Bible and informs him of His will, and man answers Him in direct speech or with his wordless soul. Even when we hear the voice of man alone, as in the Psalms, God's presence is revealed: "The basic teaching that runs through the Bible is this: that our life is a conversation between Above and Below."

But is this still valid for our lives today? This is contested by believers as well as unbelievers. The worshiper today also stands before God, but he no longer dares hope for an answer; and the unbelievers see the entire dialogic of the Holy Scriptures as a collection of myths no longer relevant to our day and age. Over against this, Buber contended that the Bible has given imperishable graphic expression to an ever-recurrent event: "In the unending, eternally changing signs of events and situations, obvious to one whose eyes are open to them, transcendence speaks to our hearts in the critical hours of our personal life." The language in which we can answer it is the language of our actions; our answer is the attitude of responsibility that we adopt over against the world.

But in the Bible it is not only the individual who is addressed but also, as in no other sacred book, the community; the entire people, as well as the individual, is called upon to sanctify itself in its common life and become a "holy people." God created not only the individual but also the peoples of the world, and he wishes to make use of them for the completion of his creation. His commandment is directed equally to individuals and to peoples.

A judgment is thus passed on our modern life which, so to speak, carries on double entry moral bookkeeping: that which is culpable in the life of an individual is in public life considered unavoidable. Man's life thus falls into two spheres, a private and a public sphere: to a private individual lying is considered disgraceful, but in a politician it is acceptable. But if the first basic principle of the Bible is that man is spoken to by God, then its second basic principle is that human life is meant to be lived as a unified whole. In every hour man's whole being is confronted with the decision to be for or against God; and the sinner who repents is granted the grace of conversion.

In the Bible, however, God speaks both to the individual and to the community at certain hours in their respective histories. All being and all becoming is God's speech, an unending procession of signs: nature also is a self-communing of the creative God and always expresses its might and glory in the same way. In history, however, where man collaborates with God, the great periods in which God's rule is perceptible alternate with those which appear God empty, as it were, and in which no sign of his Presence can be detected. The Lord of history is a revealing and a concealing God. In this connection we must bear in mind that the Bible knows two kinds of periods in which the contact between heaven and earth seems to be interrupted: one, when man becomes sinful and unworthy of himself, and the other, which emanates from God himself, an incomprehensible and uncanny concealment of the *deus absconditus,* which makes life unbearable to one who knows the living God. Such periods are not unfamiliar to the men of the Bible. Buber referred to Job who remonstrates with God and refuses to yield until he can again approach Him and hear the words spoken to him. And if the man of today should ask how a life with God is still possible in the time of an *Auschwitz,* then he can only be helped in this hour of concealment by a steadfast and humble struggle for his Presence: "In such a situation we wait for his Voice, whether it comes out of the storm or out of a stillness that follows it. Though his appearance in the future may be like no other in the past, we will recognize our fierce and gracious Lord again."

In remonstrating with the people and accusing them of religious betrayal, admonishing and consoling, Buber stood in the succession of the prophets, who are no longer to be found among us today in the old sense. The teacher who points the way has taken their place; he has no message to bring, but his word is spoken in a definite historical situation and in a definite hour and demands decision. He seeks to regain the vitality and relevance of the Jewish religion, and admonishes the people to return to the ways of God. And he is also in the succession of the prophets in that his voice is not heard and his word not heeded.

Israel and Palestine

In the official theology of the state of Israel, which is represented by the Chief Rabbinate, the return of the Jewish people to the land of its fathers and to national independence has been called "the beginning of the redemption," [105] without giving the phrase any concrete content. In reality there is an uneasy, tolerant relationship between the new state, which is a modern democracy, and the representatives of the traditional religion who adhere to the letter of the law and to the old forms. In public life the state has granted them a number of concessions relating to the dietary laws and to the keeping of the Sabbath, and has left to the rabbinical courts the jurisdiction of a person's legal status. But the Israelis are for the most part not "practising" Jews who adhere to religious observances, and feel many of these restrictions to be a superimposition. Never before has there been so wide a cleavage between nation and religion as we now find in the state of Israel. What Buber had previously deplored did not change in the land of the fathers: "Israel has been separated from its principle."

Since the end of World War I Buber considered the Zion idea, as it had survived among Eastern Jewry, and Herzl's national idea as one. In 1918 he had told Jewish youth: "Zion is the new sanctuary in the image of the old; from Zion shall once more go forth the Law. It is the foundation stone of the messianic edifice of humanity." [106] This also contains a reference to the promise of redemption, not as something that is ascertainable but as "the immense task of the Jewish folk-soul." And the Law that is to go forth from Zion is not a verbal proclamation, but a new life form in which the national, social, and religious elements will be fused into a divinely ordained community: "It was from the tillers of the soil that the last great, peculiarly Jewish religious movement in Erets Israel grew, the Essenes—a rural people which sought a pure common life and found God. Tillers of the soil, rural folk are those on whom I set my hope. It is they, and also we—such is my belief—who will seek a pure life and will find God. Then will Zion become, as was promised, a house of God for all peoples." [107]

In his long dialogue with Karl Ludwig Schmidt in 1933,[108] Buber presented to the Christian world the view that Israel is neither a nation nor a religion but something unique and singular that cannot be conceptually subsumed under any category of world history; this is indicated because the patriarch was given a name by God and not by his father and mother. Israel became a people at the very hour in which it received its decisive faith experience; it received its religion not as individuals but as a community, and its God became at the same time its king to whom it swore fealty "in world-time and eternity": "The Lord will reign for ever and ever" (Exod. 15:18). God made a covenant with the people, so that they might become "the first fruits of his harvest" (Jer. 2:3). But even then Israel wanted to be like all the other nations—and Jerusalem was destroyed because the people had betrayed their mission to build the just state.

Israel has again been given the opportunity to establish its community as a model of God's kingdom, to realize the just social order among men, and again it longs to be like other nations and is prepared to separate politics from religion, public from private life, the profane from the holy. For this reason Buber, after his many addresses on Judaism, again gave a special series of lectures, which appeared as a book in Hebrew (1944), in German (1950), and in English (1952) with the title *Israel and Palestine*.

In this book Buber undertook to explain the essence of Judaism from the initial standpoint of the experience in Palestine so that all those who listened might in some manner comprehend it: the inseparability of land and people, and the mystery of their interdependence. In the first of his former addresses on Judaism, his starting point had been the bond of common blood, which at the same time represents the elemental soul of the individual; now, however, he spoke of the concrete unity of people and land and its ultimate metaphysical basis: "Thus from the very beginning the unique union between this people and this land was characterized by what was to be, by the intention that was to be realized. It was a consummation that could not be achieved by the people or the land on its own but only by the faithful co-operation of the two together." [109] The mystery of this union of people and land, which every Jew in Palestine felt consciously or unconsciously, was called Election, and its meaning lies hidden in the word *holiness*. The land guarantees the incarnation of the new spirit that is to be. The national movement of Zionism is only the inheritor of "an ancient and at the same time religious and popular spiritual reality." And this reality was the holy matrimony of an elected people with a chosen land consecrated in the name Zion. This holiness by election cannot be dismissed as an obsolete religious function. If Israel renounces its mystery, it forfeits the kernel of its reality; if it should content itself with less than what it is intended to fulfill, then it will also fail to achieve the lesser goal. [110]

In a time of feverish nationalistic unrest and passion, Buber undertook to bring home to the people this unwelcome teaching: that people and land were chosen for mankind, for the sake of a mission. It is above all biblical testimony that he recalled, beginning with the superscription and prefatory verse in connection with the annual offering of the first fruits of the harvest (Deut. 26), where the worshiper thanks God for the gift of the land, and generation after generation speaks as one

who has himself come to the land and received it from God. The taking of the land, just as the covenant, concerns all generations, an ever-
renewed gift of God. Buber then referred to the biblical relation of
man and earth, of *adam* and *adama:* from earth man was created and to
earth he returns in death. The earth also suffers from the sins of the
people; the curse pronounced against man also afflicts the land. And
just as man rests on the seventh day to honor God, so shall the earth
celebrate every seventh year by lying fallow. There is a cosmic-ethical
relation between man and the earth: the attitude of man to God's command directly affects the land for good or ill. Buber interprets God's
promise to Abraham, "Unto thy seed will I give this land" (Gen.
12:7), as a unique event in the history of religion: "The Promise means
that within history an absolute relationship between a people and a land
has been taken into the covenant between God and the people." [111]
Also the prophecy of redemption unites people and land. Mt. Zion is
seen by Isaiah as the seat of God's throne, and in the reinterpretation of
Deutero-Isaiah the redeemed Zion becomes the eschatological center of
the redeemed world: "In this doctrine the biblical view of the unique
significance of the connection between this people and this land
reaches its climax." [112]

In the next section Buber treated "the interpretive and transfigu-
rative teaching of the talmudic-midrashic epoch of the meaning of living in the land of Israel." The third part of the book, "The Voice of
the Exile," takes us from the Middle Ages to the journey of the Hasidic
zaddik Rabbi Nachman to Palestine, which had already been included
among the *Stories of Rabbi Nachman.* At the beginning of this section
Buber recounted the story in Judah Halevi's "Kuzari" concerning the
conversion of the tribe of the Khazars to Judaism about the year 800.
At the end of the story the Rabbi, who had instructed the Khazar king
in the faith and explained to him the election of people and land, leaves
the royal court and departs for Palestine. The mystery of the connection between people and land is completed in the Cabbala: "Just as 'the
Assembly of Israel,' the power that unites the people of Israel, is
blended with the Shekhina, so also 'Zion' is taken up into the emana-
tions of the divine substance itself, without however thereby losing its
earthly reality." [113] In the section "The Beginning of the National

Idea," Buber tells us about the "lofty Rabbi Liva" of Prague who at the end of the sixteenth century had already formulated the basic rights of nations, among them the principle that every people has a right to a natural dwelling place and ought not to be subject to any other people. A transition is thereby created leading to the last part of the book which presents the Zionist idea.[114]

Of special significance are the two figures treated in the concluding part of the book, Rav Kook and A. D. Gordon, for they provide us not only with an outlook into the future but also with a backward glance to biblical beginnings. Rav Kook gave visible form to the holiness of people and land within the Zionist movement, and incorporated in his person as no other contemporary figure "the holy substance of Israel." But this element of holiness was in him organically combined with the demand for national independence and return to nature. It was not holiness in the sense of the exile, but a new kind of holiness that radiated from the land itself: a becoming whole again and a becoming one again through contact with nature. To Rav Kook, as well as to Buber, holiness was not a separate sphere of being that excluded natural life, but signified rather "the realm open to all spheres" in which the profane can fulfill and perfect itself. A holiness of spirit that turns its back on nature arose among the people only after they had been separated from the land; in the exile Israel lost the holiness of nature. But messianic perfection requires not only a spiritual soul but also a vital soul. On returning to the land the people may at first attach themselves to nature too ardently and with exaggerated activity, but the land will have the power to reunite the natural and the holy and create "the unified soul"; through election an inner power inheres in the land from eternity, and in it the soul is taught to reach out and "grasp the principle of the unified world."

A. D. Gordon, the last of the leading Zionist figures, is represented as "one who realizes the idea of Zion"—"realization" is almost always used by Buber as a concept of religious relation. Gordon was impelled to return to nature, which was at the same time a return to the source of holiness, by an insatiable longing to become part of the life of the cosmos; the land was to him a mother, and to be its son his human prerogative. But he knew that this was a prerogative that had to be earned by dedicated labor. He recognized intuitively that a new spirit of cosmic relation to nature will bring about the revival of the people. He experienced, as did no other personality of the modern Jewish people's movement, the unique connection between this people and their land by recognizing "that the nature of Truth, of Holiness, of Beauty, of Power, the nature of all spheres is open to the soul . . . in another way," [115] and that in the light of this land things are revealed which elsewhere remain concealed. Gordon knew that a new essential relation must be achieved if we are to restore our connection with the Eternal—even though the soul can find no name for it. The "holiness" of becoming-whole-again proclaimed by Rav Kook is realized through A. D. Gordon's cosmic unification, and his idea of possessing the land in a spirit of sanctification goes back to biblical origins.

What is the significance of *Israel and Palestine* in Buber's life work, and how is it to be judged against the background of the history and culture of the time? There is no doubt that Buber spoke out of a deep sense of personal involvement which put him in the company of Rav Kook and A. D. Gordon. A reflection with which he concluded his recollections of Achad Ha'am is in this context tantamount to a confession. Achad Ha'am's reference to "the power of historical feeling" that binds people and land led Buber to observe that "historical feelings" can, like all feelings, be deceptive, and that it is necessary to discover the reality behind them. Are we dealing here with a simple historical reality that is transitory like all historical phenomena, or with the token and expression of a suprahistorical relationship? "Is the 'election' of this people and this land for one another and for a third something that embraces them both and is greater than both of them? Is the Election of which the Scriptures tell, which the Haggada interprets, of which the voices of the exile sing and which they discuss, an illusion, or is it a true picture of the Eternal drawn with the strokes of history? It is difficult for those who live today, in a time in which Eternity is eclipsed, to cherish the belief in such a true picture. But this is precisely what is needed. Faith alone will obtain the proof that it is true." [116]

It is thus not a question of a scientifically demonstrable proposition but of a "being-truth," as Buber called it elsewhere, a truth that is revealed to faith and which a man cannot "have," but which he must confirm with his whole existence. It is in this sense that Buber spoke of Gordon's participation in the life of the land: "Gordon's knowledge is a faith and his faith is a life." Also for being-truths there is a historical continuity which Buber called a "being-tradition." It is characteristic of this tradition that the word which proclaims it is inseparably connected with the memory of the one who spoke it, for his word is only one of the functions of his life, the one which expresses his life.

When Buber in *Israel and Palestine* described the history of an idea in bold strokes, he no doubt thought of himself as a "speaker" in Gordon's sense, that is, "the mouthpiece of a reality in process." In many places in his address a messianic note is struck, a note of hope for the beginning of the redemption, the intimation of a "new creation." The being-truth of the past becomes a message, and proclaims what is to be; it casts a light on that which is. Buber took his stand in the midst of the becoming reality by means of a function which he had long considered to be one of his most important tasks: popular education. He was opposed to the rising tide of nationalism, and he spoke to the people about Israel's mission for humanity, about the true human community which they are to realize.

By thus taking a stand in the midst of evolving reality, by participating in the common task of the people, *Israel and Palestine* is distinct from Buber's biblical scientific works which in the thirties coincided with the immense task of translating the Bible, namely, *The Kingdom of God, The Anointed One, The Faith of the Prophets*.

What did the return to the homeland mean to Buber? Several times he cited the talmudical saying of Rabbi Seira that the air of Palestine makes one wise. As for himself he confessed that the country had given him the strength for a new beginning.[117] It gave him renewed vigor to continue his work in Hasidism, and inspired him after an interval of several decades to complete his literary works *For the Sake of Heaven* [*Gog und Magog*] and *Elijah*. A new beginning in 1938 meant in practical terms the transition from the German to the Hebrew language and from teaching *Religionswissenschaft* in Frankfurt-am-Main to a professorship in social philosophy at the Hebrew University in Jerusalem.

The strength for a new beginning in Buber's case was found in the exhilarating new life in the Promised Land. After those harrowing years in Germany, where he had been isolated in the midst of a people that had grown strange to him, he began to find himself again in the new society, in an atmosphere in which time and space were mythically transformed and replete with hidden power. God's election was first announced in this land, and it was here that eternity had been since time immemorial. Holiness was its life air, and this was felt by Buber's sensitive nature as a touch of transcendence. Out of this holiness grew the "inner power" of the land to create "one soul" of which Rav Kook had spoken, the oneness and the wholeness of being that Buber had already demanded in his early addresses. Everything here was sign and revelation, bringing him close to the myth-creating soul of his people: before him stretched the world of the Bible in visible form and in all its sensuous concreteness.

According to the testimony of the Bible, the life of the Jew in and with the land was a relation established by God and, as such, was "sacramental existence"; it denoted the constant presence of revelation. The "original relationship" between people and land, that which Buber had called "ontic participation," was made manifest through suprahistorical decree and held up as a model of the meaning of creation: the interrelationship and mutual dependence of beings and things in God's world. This was to be the general condition of creation in a messianic future; but the seeds of future perfection, through the grace of creation, were planted in this one people and land to serve as a paragon: the seeds of a holiness that is communicated from being to being.

What the Bible has to say about this being-for-one-another was remarkably similar to Buber's inner experiences as recounted in his *Urerinnerung*[118] and confirmed the basic principles of his philosophical anthropology. The myth of the people and the myth of his own soul coincided, both finding their historical expression in *Israel and Palestine*; and the testimony of millennia served to guarantee that it was not an illusion.

Israel and Palestine appeared at a definite historical hour, the hour of the emergent state. It was not meant to provide "informative knowledge" but a "panoply for being." [119] The development of the state, however, took a different turn from what Buber had hoped, and with the passing years he saw only too clearly that "being-tradition" could not easily be translated into a discursive, cognitive context. As a testimony of the being-tradition, *Israel and Palestine* took the form of address and admonition, which was to lead to confirmation. As a presentation of the history of an idea, the book comes dangerously close to a historico-theological disquisition.

Buber's vigilant self-criticism quietly evaluated the consequences of this situation, and in the final edition of his works he included only parts of *Israel and Palestine*. The introduction of the book, the essay on Rabbi Liva, and the fourth part, "The Zionist Idea," are to be found in the volume *Der Jude und sein Judentum*; "Biblisches Zeugnis," which was included in volume 2 of his *Collected Works*, and "Ein Zaddik kommt ins Land" were assigned to the volume on Hasidism. The book as a whole belonged to a historical period in which the past and the present for the author had become unification, meaning, and mission: he thus conceived his mission to reside in a historical message. He was well aware that one cannot recognize the objective meaning of historical events and had already expressed himself to this effect in 1933: "The meaning of history is not an idea which I can formulate independently of my personal life; it is only with my personal life that I am able to grasp it, for it is a dialogic meaning." [120]

The Message of Hasidism

IN PALESTINE the "sacramental existence" of the Jew, which is only present by reason of Election, became evident to Buber as the inseparable unity of land and people. His purpose in *Israel and Palestine* was to call attention to an ancient "religious and at the same time popular spiritual reality" at a critical hour in the life of the people when a new national form was in the making. History was now inclined to adopt the language of the message that was to proclaim the advent of the future.

Not far removed from the time and spirit of this book is another of Buber's works in which the force of the past is expressly designated as "message," applying this term which he ordinarily reserved for the prophets to a historical phenomenon: *The Origin and Meaning of Hasidism* (Hebrew edition 1944; German 1952; English 1960). The book was not written all at once, but developed, as Buber states in the preface, "in the course of many years as the slowly growing product of a long work of scholarship and interpretation of the great literature of the Hasidic teaching and legend." The earliest part is the fourth chapter called "Spirit and Body of the Hasidic Movement," which had formed the principal part of the introduction to one of Buber's earliest writings on Hasidism, *Der grosse Maggid und seine Nachfolge* (1921); the third chapter, "Spinoza, Sabbatai Zvi and the Baal-Shem," was the introduction to the *Chassidische Bücher* (1927); and the fifth chapter, "Symbolic and Sacramental Existence," was the subject of a lecture given by Buber in 1934 to the Eranos Society in Ascona. The other parts of the book were written in Jerusalem from 1940 to 1943. The strength of a new beginning that Buber felt in his ancestral homeland is reflected in the unity and coherency of this work, which expresses "the message to the human world that Hasidism did not want to be but that it was and is. . . . It is because of its truth and because of the great need of the hour that I carry it into the world against its will." [1]

Hasidism was for Buber what the composition of Faust had been for Goethe, who in his old age used to call it his "chief occupation." Buber's interest in Hasidism cannot be assigned to any definite period of his life. The study of its vast literature began two decades before his work on the Bible and continued to an advanced age. His presentation of the subject reflected the different stages of his development, and each new literary form revealed new aspects of his rich personality. This versatility of style, however, is not to be interpreted as signifying any basic changes in his conception that, in its essential features, remained the same over the decades, for his mind was not concerned with doctrine and theory but with the reality of a religious community whose chief concern was the sanctification of its existence. That this living reality cannot be reduced to concepts or adequately communicated by scientific knowledge explains why, at the beginning and at the end of his long study of Hasidism, Buber attempted poetical compositions. His earliest expositions began with free renderings of tales and legends, and his final insights are found in the comprehensive chronicle *For the Sake of Heaven*, which presents in artistic form the activities and contrasting personalities of two opposing Hasidic schools, which no conceptual analysis could adequately describe and to which only "the cruel antitheticalness of existence" could do justice.

Buber never identified himself with Hasidism, nor was it his purpose to find his personal teaching reflected in it since, as he repeatedly stated, he had no teaching. In the foreword to *For the Sake of Heaven* (which is the epilogue to the original German edition, *Gog and Magog*),[2] Buber explained at length his relation to Hasidism and the misunderstandings to which it could give rise. As a modern thinker he could not accept uncritically a historical phenomenon like Hasidism which belongs to the past: "My heart is at one with those among Israel who today, equally distant from blind traditionalism and blind contradictoriness, are in the vanguard in the struggle to renew the forms of both faith and life." He felt that the present had claims upon him and that Judaism of today must build on the foundations laid by the pious Hasidim of the past. His personal life is related to theirs "in a living unity"; he grew up amid scenes where they had flourished, and their ways of life had been impressed upon him in his childhood "as image and feeling."

The number of scholars who know Hasidism from its original sources is small even today. In the nineteenth century Hasidism was an obscure sect whose superstitious piety attracted little interest. It was the Zionist movement that first called attention to East European Jewry where a genuine sense of Jewish peoplehood was still preserved. At first poets like Perez and Berdyczevski, moved by a romantic impulse, became deeply interested in Hasidic legends. Buber's early fascination with this subject, which soon led to intensive study, arose from a similar interest: the desire to study Jewish *Volkstum* from its creative ancient records.[3] In the decades that followed he made this East European Jewish literature available to European readers in a series of collections of Hasidic legends, anecdotes, and gnomic wisdom, and later added it to the classics of world literature with his publication of *The Tales of the Hasidim* and *For the Sake of Heaven*.[4] In this manner a basic stock of Hasidic texts was presented to the European reading public, together with interpretations in the form of instructive introductions and essays. This body of interpretation after several decades grew into a theoretical exposition which Buber called *Die chassidische Botschaft* [The origin and meaning of Hasidism]. Nevertheless, it was not the theory of the movement but the pious lives of its adherents that affected him from the very beginning as a personal "message" to which he must bear witness and which led him to a serious study of Hasidism, extending over a period of several decades. In "My Way to Hasidism" (1918), he recalled that after he first became acquainted with the Baal-Shem's "legacy," he knew that his vocation was to reveal this Hasidic piety to the world. He was first inclined to regard this task as a literary one. In his later years he spoke of the widespread tendency of those early days "to display the contents of foreign religions to readers who wavered between desire for information and sheer curiosity."[5] But as early as 1924, in the preface to *Das verborgene Licht* [The hidden light], he viewed the matter differently: "Since then I realized that the teaching is there that one may learn it and the way that one may walk on it. The deeper I realized this, so much the more this work, against which my life measured and ventured itself, became for me question, suffering and also even consolation." The title of the book pointed in the same direction. A passage in the Talmud recounts that after man's sinful fall the primeval light, whereby man could see the world from one end to the other, was concealed by God in the Torah, whence it is extracted by the righteous by lifelong study. This "hidden light," which in Buber's legend *Revelation* rests over the head of the Baal-Shem, is "free of all earthly aspects and only in secret revealed to the beholder." [6]

Buber was not concerned with a conceptual elaboration of Hasidism but with the "way" of its adherents and with their teaching insofar as it was lived life. Hence, after his first collections—*The Tales of Rabbi Nachman* and *The Legend of the Baal-Shem* (of which a revised second edition had already appeared in 1916)—he confined himself primarily to those sources of Hasidic literature in which legend appears as "legendary anecdote," which Buber understood to be an anecdote that relates a single incident in condensed form,[7] that is, a short legend in which the teaching emerges as the main point and which is addressed directly to the reader. The wisdom and piety of a great religious folk movement were in this manner designed to be wholly untheoretical and to be transmitted from life to life, thus helping to restore that direct contact both between men and in man's relation to God, so sadly missing in our time.

Out of an original stock of about ten thousand such short legends that he had collected, Buber chose some five hundred which were included in two books: *Der grosse Maggid und seine Nachfolge* (1922), isolated parts of which appeared in *Tales of the Hasidim* (1961), and *Das verborgene Licht* (1924). In the former, the anecdotes are arranged according to the personalities to whom they are attributed; in the latter, according to the subject matter which is arranged not to reflect a world view but rather to illustrate the Hasidic way of life. In *Die chassidische Bücher*, Buber again combined *The Tales of Rabbi Nachman* (1907), *The Legend of the Baal-Shem* (augmented by addenda), *Der grosse*

Maggid, and *Das verborgene Licht*; "My Way to Hasidism" also found its way into this collection; and in a lengthy preface the author attempted to clarify the historical and religious significance of Hasidism. This collection was preceded by the sayings of the Baal-Shem which Buber had gathered under the title *The Baal-Shem-Tov's Instruction in Intercourse with God* (1927). The collection of Hasidic writings from the first half of Buber's life was followed twenty years later by three works, the product of "the strength of the new beginning": *Gog und Magog* (Hebrew, 1943; German, 1949; English: *For the Sake of Heaven*, 1946); *Die chassidische Botschaft* (Hebrew, 1944; German, 1952; English: *The Origin and Meaning of Hasidism*, 1960); and *Tales of the Hasidim* (1949), which Buber felt belonged together as a "life-and-work unity," neither one by itself being sufficiently complete to give justice to his total view. Side by side with "The Baal-Shem-Tov's Instruction in Intercourse with God" we may place his booklet, "The Way of Man according to Hasidic Teaching" (1948) (now chapter 4 of *Hasidism and Modern Man*), which Gershom Scholem characterized as "not only a jewel of literature but also an unusual document of religious anthropology in Hasidic language." [8]

Buber's works on Hasidism, which by and large remained undisputed for decades, have for some time now met with serious criticism, and it is precisely its cardinal aspect, the "message," that has given rise to the gravest misgivings. In *The Philosophy of Martin Buber* (*The Library of Living Philosophers*, vol. 12), Rivkah Schatz-Uffenheimer, one of Scholem's students, takes issue with Buber's presentation of Hasidism; this was followed by an equally severe criticism by Scholem in an article in the *Neue Zürcher Zeitung*—not a light matter considering that it came from the foremost scholar in the field of Jewish mysticism in all its aspects, especially the Cabbala. Scholem contests the authenticity of Buber's interpretation of the Hasidic "message"; by reading his own religious existentialism into the Hasidic texts, Buber distorted the essence of Hasidism. His very selection of Hasidic writings is prompted by subjective considerations, and his restriction of its extensive literature to legends and folk books is unwarranted. Such an arbitrary restriction is calculated to produce the erroneous impression that Hasidism was a lay mysticism that had developed into an unexpressed, but nevertheless sharp, opposition to the Cabbala and this, according to Scholem, is out of the question, since Hasidism never severed its connection with the Lurianic Cabbala which was a gnostic teaching. Hasidism is not to be regarded as a self-contained life form, as a "category of life"; on the contrary, life here can be understood only from the standpoint of the teaching. Scholem concludes with the words: "If we would really understand the phenomenon of Hasidism, in its greatness as in its decline (which are in many ways closely related), we shall have to begin again from the beginning." [9]

Hasidism's "message," according to Buber, resides above all in its relation to concrete reality. Scholem, however, insists that the practical activities of the Hasidim that flowed from this relation were dependent on contemporary mystical theory. How did Hasidism understand the myth of the divine sparks which since time immemorial lie hidden in things waiting to be restored to God through man? In Buber's interpretation the sparks are redeemed by sanctification and "sacramental existence," by every deed performed in holiness and with man's whole inner being turned to God. The essential message of Hasidism can be summed up in a single sentence: God can be seen in every thing and reached by every pure deed. Buber's critics, on the other hand, insist that the myth of the sparks, which Hasidism took over from the Cabbala, is to be interpreted gnostically, that is, things must be reduced to their nothingness before God through meditation, and are not to be fulfilled in their concreteness, if the sparks are to be raised up to God. It is not a matter of holiness but rather of dematerialization and of reducing the world to nothingness: the concrete is here only "a vehicle for the abstract and hence to the ultimate source of all being." [10]

In the concluding section of *Library of Living Philosophers*, vol. 12, which is devoted to answering questions and objections raised by the various contributors to the volume, Buber replied to Schatz-Uffenheimer's criticism.[11] He candidly confessed that his presentation of Hasidism was based on "the principle of selection," which lies in the nature of the task he set himself. His selection, however, was not based on any subjective preference. The essential truth of Hasidism and its importance for the history of the human spirit are not its elaboration of the cabbalistic tradition but "the bursting forth of a mighty originality of the life of faith alongside which only a very little in the history of religions could be placed." Regarded from the standpoint of its theories, Hasidism is in fact "pure epigone"; it owes its greatness to its devotion to the divine and the hallowing of the lived life through this devotion.

Buber agreed with Scholem that "cleaving to God" must be acknowledged as Hasidism's central concern. But it attained this through a twofold development: first, through "spiritualization," whereby the reality of the lived life is elevated to the nothingness of pure spirit; and second, in a more popular direction through the "hallowing of life," whereby transformation takes place without eliminating concreteness, not a nullification or reduction to nothingness but a "bridge-building" toward the Absolute. Both possibilities emerged in the movement from the very beginning. This inner dialectic of Hasidism is clearly evident in *For the Sake of Heaven*, where the "metaphysics" of the Seer of Lublin and his magical practices are contrasted with the simple human "existence" of the holy Yehudi of Pshysha who, without surrendering the basic cabbalistic teaching, proclaims *teshuva*, repentance, and a life directed to God.

In his reply to Scholem's strictures[12] Buber again declared that his task was not that of a historian who is obliged to present a historical phenomenon as completely as possible but to help a faithless generation regain its faith in God and its direct contact with Him. This cannot be achieved by adopting or reinterpreting some conceptual system of the past but only by pointing to a form of life in the past that could serve man as a guide and inspire him with new enthusiasm. Only by returning to the sphere of personal and communal existence can this vital spark be communicated. In the lives of the great founders of religion we see how teaching and life are inseparable. In the history of mysticism two types have always existed: the masters of mystical speculation, with whom Buber was not concerned, and those religious currents which concentrate on the "sphere of the realizing mode" and on the lived truth. They are fascinated by the "mystery of the indescribable situation" and attempt to capture it in the form of legend. This tendency of mysticism Buber saw best represented outside of Hasidism among the Islamic Sufis and in Zen Buddhism, whose legends first circulated orally and were put in writing only at a relatively late period—

which does not militate against their authenticity for, according to Buber, experience has shown early religious oral tradition to be surprisingly reliable.

Scholem's intensive studies have enabled non-Jews to find a place for Jewish mysticism in the historical development of Western religious thought,[13] for he is primarily interested in spiritual phenomena that can be studied scientifically and placed in a historical context. Buber's exposition of Hasidism thus appeared to him to have been forcibly detached from the history of mysticism and treated as a separate phenomenon. Buber's statement at the end of *Origin and Meaning of Hasidism* that "Hasidism explodes the familiar view of mysticism" is challenged by the historian Scholem who convincingly argues that the religious substance of a mystical movement is bound to its theory and can be recognized as such only through this theory. Buber's unmediated relation to God, which defies all formulation, appears to him as "religious anarchy," [14] with which Hasidism has nothing to do.

It is clear that in the end the historian's arguments which are precisely formulated are more persuasive than those of Buber which are attested only by the course of human conduct embedded in man's nature and can dispense with the external corroboration afforded by the intellectual disciplines, even that of theology, for he is not concerned with theological categories but with the stream of lived religious life. Scholem dismisses Buber's reply in a brief note[15] as being too general and maintains his charge of subjectivity and religious anarchy. To Buber, however, the confrontation of man and God was the basic fact of our existence, and nothing could be less subjective. His "anarchy" may be said to be the teaching that one "is" and not "has." This teaching establishes a common meeting ground in the sphere of lived religion between teacher and student, and invests it with the spontaneity of the "indescribable situation," the "supra-verbal transmission of the mystery" that cannot be defined but only pointed to. The language of Buber's answer is calm, but it lacks the vital rhythm and assurance of the polemicist. He knows that it is not a question of detecting and exposing fallacies but of defending an intense vision at the heart of his work. Here also, in the conflict of two opposing points of view in interpreting the ultimate experiences of mankind, we come upon "the cruel anti-theticalness of existence."

What basic impulse may be detected behind Buber's attitude that may be said to govern his relation to history and tradition? In his Answer in volume 12 of *The Library of Living Philosophers*, he pointed out[16] that the selective principle he adopted with regard to Hasidism was the same as the one that informs his view of Judaism in general, which from the very beginning insisted on the "immovable central existence of values."

In an address given at the Lehrhaus in Frankfurt-am-Main in 1934 called "Teaching and Deed" [17], Buber distinguished two kinds of propagation in the life of nations: the biological and, using Rudolf Pannwitz's phrase, "the propagation of values." Just as organic life is transmitted from parents to children, so is the spirit in each generation transmitted from one entire person to another. In Judaism this "propagation of values" penetrated the natural life of the nation in a special sense. Both in the Diaspora, where the natural survival of the people was threatened, and in the early days of its history, Israel considered spiritual propagation to be as vital as its bodily propagation. Israel became a people by receiving the Torah, and thenceforth the transmission of life and the transmission of values were indissolubly bound to one another. "Spirit begets and gives birth; spirit is begotten and born; spirit becomes body." [17a] If this image is taken seriously, it follows that in the propagation of values we are dealing not with the transmission of something that remains unchanged but with new creations; new forms emerge in the process of transmission. Just as a child represents a new beginning, so does a generation truly receive a teaching only in the sense that it renews it: "In the living tradition it is not possible to draw a line between preserving and producing." [17b]

But the real mystery of this living tradition which Buber calls "being-tradition" is that what has changed is again brought forth as something that remains the same: "The total living Jewish human being is the transmitting agent; total living Jewish humanity is transmitted." [17c] In Judaism teaching is inseparably bound up with doing and should not be considered as simply a collection of knowable material; it demands life as fulfillment, that unity of life and deed "through which alone we can recognize and avow the all-embracing unity of God." [17d] Nor is the deed alone enough; the deed without teaching might bring success but it destroys the substance, the permanent element. The spirit that is lived, which is a Way, permits the unchanging features of Jewish humanity to emerge during the process of transformation. Nothing that ever existed is broad enough to represent the teaching of Judaism; generations must continue to meet generations in which all teaching assumes the form of a human link, awakening and activating the common bond with God: "The spark that leaps from him who teaches to him who learns rekindles a spark of that fire which lifted the mountain of revelation to the very heart of heaven" (Deut. 4:11).

Buber had already treated the history of his people as "being-tradition" in his early addresses on Judaism. At that time, however, he did not inquire into religion but into the "religious reality" of Judaism. Here again his starting point is "biological propagation," and in his first address on Judaism he finds the common basic experience in present-day Jewish life, which goes back to the creative depths of history, to be the blood-community. He interprets Jewish history not as a series of objective events but as a chain of basic attitudes.[18] The Jews are a recollection community in which every generation is physically aware of the experiences of its ancestors. The religious feasts that are repeated year after year and the power of the Zion idea that was rekindled in our time testify to this passion for the "propagation of values." Genuine Judaism, the essential attitude of the believing Jew, was in Buber's view not to be found in the official religion of the rabbis but rather in the perennial folk religion which has survived underground from ancient days until our own time, being the bearer of myth and the unmediated living faith of the people. This folk religion appeared in three great movements: in the Essenes, in early Christianity, and in Hasidism. In all three movements the unchanged substance of the religion was preserved even while the Jewish spirit was being transformed, the paramount concern being the continued vitality of the spirit and the unity of teaching and doing.

Buber's conception of Judaism was from the very beginning based on "the theologumena of a folk-religion," [19] whose deepest expression he found in the community structure of Hasidism. Here he encountered the being-tradition which he, as an "epigone" or as one who was born later, felt has a claim upon him: "I bear in me the blood and spirit of those who created it, and out of my blood and spirit it has become new," he wrote in the preface to the *Legend of the Baal-Shem* (p. 10). Since he approached the past of Judaism from the standpoint of Zionist aims, Buber's mind is always directed to the people as a whole, and the renewal of faith is always considered in conjunction with the regeneration of the people, spirit and body being inseparable. As early as 1903 he declared that the two seemingly contradictory movements, the Haskalah and Hasidism, both contributed to the rebirth of Judaism in our time.[20] His own task, as the historian Hans Kohn saw it in 1930, was to create a synthesis between these two spiritual forces. At no time did Buber regard Hasidism as a segment of history that could be considered apart from his own development. In his introduction to the *Legend of the Baal-Shem* we note that he was primarily concerned not with the principles of Hasidism but with the forces which determined its lived piety and which he saw as a double movement of "cleaving to God" and of service to the world. While ecstacy and intention permit man to appear as cosmic mediator capable of leading the world back to divine unity, the soul is reduced to "nothing" through service and humility, so that it may bind things to their upper root. In this double movement that is inherent in Hasidism, Buber detected the tension which he later discussed in *For the Sake of Heaven* in the form of the conflict between two opposing schools of Hasidism.

Buber's interest had never been the history of religion but always the history of faith—a distinction he sought to clarify, when he was still under the influence of Simmel in his early days, by opposing religion to religiosity. In the history of faith he went back to the great founders of religion whose "teaching" was the unity of life and word, and he discovered religiosity among people whose myths had not yet become conceptually petrified but which were preserved as symbols that could always be revived to new life throughout the centuries. Hasidism with its teaching that the divine is hidden in things and with its belief that man can help to reunite God's majesty with his exiled shekinah was for Buber the distinctive, popular Jewish myth of the One which develops into the manifold only to be again restored to unity.

In Judaism religious myth cannot be separated from the history of the people, and God as the creative force of nature remains bound to Yahwe and to the deeds He performed for the people. His encounter with Hasidism saved Buber from the secret burdens and private broodings of a vague mysticism that was in the air at that time: "My narration stands on the earth of Jewish myth, and the heaven of Jewish myth is over it"—he observed in the introduction to the *Legend of the Baal-Shem*. Here Buber succeeded in formulating the encounter between God and man which anticipates his later "dialogic principle": "The legend is the myth of the I and Thou, of the caller and of the called, of the finite which enters into the infinite and of the infinite which has need of the finite" (p. 13). On the other hand, as a result of the pantheistic influences of the so-called "life-philosophies," nothing remained mere thought in Buber's intellectual world, but all spirit became life. "Ontic participation," the vital contact of being with being, is not possible without this "corporeal" aspect of all being as well as of all history: that is, without "being-tradition."

This helps us to understand why Buber called the first two parts of his introduction to the *Origin and Meaning of Hasidism* "Spirit" and "Body";[20a] and in the concluding section he saw the development of Hasidism as being determined by these two aspects of the movement. The foreword to the book gives the impression that even at that time Buber anticipated difficulty in explaining what he regarded to be the characteristic aspect of this movement. This characteristic aspect is neither a monastic nor a reformatory piety, but the preservation of the tradition with its general articles of belief and with its precepts, only renewing their vitality and radiating power without changing their substance: "Its own contribution cannot be codified; it is not the material of a lasting knowledge or obligation, only light for the seeing eye, strength for the working hand . . . .[21] More clearly than any other movement, Hasidism proclaims "the infinite ethos of the moment." [22] The permanent is here bound to the transitory, to the individual life, and to transmission from person to person—to all that which was included by Buber under the aspect "body." Hasidism, as Buber saw it, is being-tradition.

Being-tradition is not identical with the totality of historical tradition. It transmits knowledge which creates values and at the same time deepens man's roots in being. Just as the immediacy of the I-Thou relation must be added to the world of I-It which can be described and communicated objectively, that is, the I of unification must be added to the world around us and to the Absolute, so also are we in need of "meeting" for the understanding of historical life, in need of the leaping spark from the past. It is precisely the "cosmically unhoused" man of our time who is most in need of "ontic participation" to enable him to participate with his whole person in the life of the present and the past. Only genuine unification can give rise to a new revelation: "The true community is the Sinai of the future." [23]

When Scholem speaks of the proper understanding of the "real phenomenon of Hasidism," which Buber failed to give us and which still remains to be achieved, he is referring to the scientific treatment of the entire historical movement as a whole, whereas for Buber reality in its truest sense is given only where there is a "meeting" which in some way affects man. Scholem sees the prospect of a science of Judaism in our time in a growing comprehension of the living peoplehood without theological, apologetical, or political considerations; Buber is concerned with the inculcation of teaching and of values to be achieved anew in every generation. In this connection it is of interest to recall that as early as 1924, in a letter to the Executive Committee of the Zionist Organization,[24] Buber urged the establishment of institutions for Palestine capable of transmitting being-tradition: adult education, rural student homes, and especially popular education in its broadest sense were more important to him than the establishment of a university. In the development of a Palestinian system of education there should be no attempt to emulate European models which grew out of different conditions; what is important is not the erection of cultural showpieces but the needs of the settlers. The new science of Judaism should not slavishly adopt the criteria and categories of Western research, but should consider how the ancient Jewish method of learning, the inner Jewish methodology, developed over a period of two thousand years and how it can be used with advantage for modern scientific work. In opposition to the external aspect of European science which excludes value judgments, and recalling his grandfather Salomon Buber, he urged the adoption of the view from within and the "earnestness of the spiritual reality," whereby he understood the determining elements of the value-renewing "being-tradition." In this sense through *Israel and Palestine* he intended to call the attention of the Jews of the settlement to the two dimensions of "ontic participation": the present with its deep sense of identification with the land, and the past with the historical figures who bore witness to the idea of Zion.

THE ZADDIK

That Hasidism had always meant "being-tradition" to Buber and never "history" is attested in all his writings and requires no further external corroboration. The question still remains, however, whether the new point of view that he had achieved with *I and Thou* affected his attitude to the Hasidic texts to the degree assumed in Scholem's criticism; in short, whether Buber later read his own existentialism into these texts which in his youth he regarded as "the flower of Jewish mysticism." When Scholem, in referring to the earlier legends, states that Buber "tinctured them with mystical hues," he acknowledges by this very wording that Buber's free renderings are not to be evaluated in the same sense as the existential statements of his later works, but are to be viewed primarily as poetical compositions designed to create an atmosphere of holiness and of mysterious cosmic unification.

Since Buber recorded the great faith experience of his life as happening between 1912 and 1919, his work *Der grosse Maggid und seine Nachfolge* (1921), published at the same time that *I and Thou* was being composed, occupies a central position among the works on Hasidism. In the introduction, which for the most part was later included in *Origin and Meaning of Hasidism*, Buber attempted for the first time to classify this religious movement from a historical and typological point of view.

Hasidism took over and united two traditions, and extracted from them new light and new strength: a tradition of religious law and the teaching of the Cabbala. Without adding anything essentially different, it adapted them both to the realities of its own life and community. It accomplished this by placing at the center of its religious life the Cabbalistic concept of God's fate in the world and man's ability to influence the fate of the universe through his actions. For man this meant responsibility in an unconditioned, transcendent sense—responsibility for God's fate in the world. God contracted himself to become world; in his "indwelling" of the shekinah he takes part in the world because he wanted to allow relation to emerge: "because he wanted to allow to arise from his primally one Being, in which thinking and thought are one, the otherness that strives for unity." [25] Man's power and mystery culminate in the supreme task of reuniting God with his world-indwelling majesty. His task is to redeem the sparks of light which in primordial time were imprisoned in matter, when the divine light fell flaming from the upper to the lower spheres, and to lead them from their earthly prison back to their source. Buber felt that, compared to the Cabbala, Hasidism strives—and in this he agreed with Scholem—for the "deschematization of the mystery" through the intensity with which it elevates man's cosmic-metacosmic power and responsibility to the central place in his life and community. The world was created so that man can choose God; its "shells," that is, its material being, exist so that he could penetrate to their kernel. Buber cited a saying of the Baal-Shem to the effect that "in all corporeality is a holy life and that man can lead everything back to this its root and hallow it." [26] This happens when man directs all his works to God. Hasidism is the teaching of the sanctification of daily life, "the Cabbala that has become ethos."

In *Der grosse Maggid* Hasidism is interpreted on the basis of concepts and ideas found in the Cabbala: God's self-contraction to become world, *tsimtsum*,[27] the teaching of the sparks that are to be redeemed by man, the act of *yichud*, of reuniting the disjoined spheres and restoring the union of God with his shekinah, a process which can be influenced by man. *Yichud* has nothing to do with psychology; the "consecration" of things to God is not a subjective process: "*Yichud* means the ever-new joining of the spheres striving to be apart, the ever-new marriage of the 'majesty' with the 'Kingdom'—through man; the divine element living in man moves from him to God's service, to God's intention, to God's work. God, in whose name and command of creation the *yichud* takes place, is his goal and end, himself turning not in himself but to God, not isolated, but swallowed in the world process, no circle but the swinging back of the divine strength that was sent forth." [28] *Yichud* signifies "the working out of the objective in a subjectivity"; it is "the dynamic form of the divine unity itself" [29]—the divine unity of creation.

Since the world process as a whole is involved, as well as God's presence and realization in it, nothing is excluded from sanctification. All of daily life is appropriated and related to the kingdom of God, and "eschatalogical messianism" must be resisted by the greatest possible measure of "messianism that takes place at all times." *Yichud* is "cosmic consecration." [30] Within this world process that returns to God every deed has an "inner consecration," [31] which is not subjective even when it is connected with magical processes in the cabbalistic tradition. The binding of man to God as part of the cosmic binding is above all magic as the "swinging back of the divine strength that was sent forth." [31a]

The basic concepts of Hasidism are examined in the introduction to *Der grosse Maggid* under the heading of "Spirit." The second section called "Body" discusses primarily what must be added to Hasidism, as Buber saw it, so that it may be regarded not as a historical phenomenon but as a "being-tradition," namely, the figure of the *zaddik* and his close relationship with the circle of his students and with the people. The seventeen portraits of the heads of Hasidic schools assembled by Buber in his book find the material of their teaching in the living circles around them, particularly in the relation between teacher and student and in "the force, the fruitfulness and the tragedy of this relation." [32] The problem that is dealt with here is the conceptually incommensurable concretization of the spiritual which Buber can compare only with the process of reproduction and incarnation, that is, the ineffable "how" whereby the masters succeed in the "supraverbal transmission of the mystery" and which unites the Hasidim into a community. In all this the texts are never discarded; talmudic learning and cabbalistic teaching continue to be studied and retain their influence.

During the period in which he wrote *Der grosse Maggid*—that is, during the most important years in Buber's religious development—there can be no question of a break or of a decisive change in his conception of Hasidism. The conceptual interpretation in the introduction starts from the basic concepts and symbols of the Cabbala and stands, as it had in the *Legend of the Baal-Shem*, "on the earth of Jewish myth, and the heaven of Jewish myth is over it." [32a] A truer understanding, however, may be gathered from what Buber said in 1923 in the preface to the complete edition of *Addresses on Judaism*, namely, that the basic principles of his subject were "clarified" in the course of the ten years it took to write the book. That the question we are dealing with here is not that of a break with his earlier views is confirmed by his attitude to Hasidism.

The new element that entered Buber's life, the "turning," does not pertain to the realm of thought but to the "realizing mode." Through a direct experience of God, the critical areas within the vast conceptual structure of religion and myths surveyed by Buber appear in a new light. Such an experience not only rendered a break in Buber's conception of Hasidism unnecessary; it provided a basis that helped him understand "the bursting of a mighty originality of the life of faith" that appeared in this movement, without anything essential being changed conceptually or in its relation to tradition. Since Hasidism continued to cultivate the Lurianic Cabbala which it had adopted, there was no need for Buber to surrender the symbols of the great myth of humanity written in the language of the Cabbala because of his subsequent God experience. And yet everything changed as a result of the new vital polarity between a "personal God" and "individual man." The teaching became in a new sense a concern of life and of transmission.

Even after the faith experience of the period of World War I, *yichud,* "union," did not refer to God and the soul. The union of God with his shekinah continued to be the primary concern: "Man effects the unity of God, that is, through him takes place the unity of becoming, the divine unity of creation . . . in which the original unity overarches the enduring differences and finds its cosmic counterpart: the unity without multiplicity which dwells in the unification of the multiplicity." [33] Similarly, the idea of God's self-contraction in the original act of creation remained for Buber a fundamental thought of the Cabbala. The question concerning the relation of the transcendental primordial ground of all being to the personal God, which had occupied him before from the theoretical point of view, now became a burning issue as a result of his God experience. Again it was a Hasidic thinker, the Great Maggid, who came to conclusions which surpassed those of Meister Eckhart in boldness, and who helped him to comprehend God as "absolute Person." "God and Soul," a chapter in *Origin and Meaning of Hasidism*, traces in detail the steps which made such a union of biblical belief and mystical speculation in Hasidism possible.

Corresponding to the dialectic between the divine primordial ground and the personal God we find in Hasidism the twofold possibility of power and service that inheres in the figure of the zaddik, the inner dialectic between man as "cosmic mediator" and as "perfect helper"—the two ways characterized by Buber in his dispute with Scholem as "spiritualizing" and "sanctifying." The zaddik for Buber is above all the figure of the "realizing man," the one "through whose existence the Absolute resting in its truth can acquire the character of reality." [34] The Baal-Shem's "zeal" that is capable of creating worlds is also found in Daniel's dialogues on realization—"realizing" being just another word for the task of drawing forth into the light "the sparks," the godlike in things. At that time Buber was convinced that it was possible to recognize "the signs of the primordial being," the "secret form" in all things, by an "inclusion" that meant both devotion to the task at hand and a new creation.

In the case of the *zaddik* we are dealing with "clarification," that is, with a decision between two possibilities. The "turning" here is also in the "realization mode," along the road that leads from creative knowing to sanctifying service. Here as well there was no need for a break with earlier views, but only a changed emphasis from the power of the zaddik to his service: the decision for personal emulation and a readiness to imitate the figure of the zaddik not only in theory but in fulfilling as many of his tasks as was possible in another age.

The zaddik as a historical phenomenon and in his relation to the age-old movements in Judaism has been treated with impressive scholarship by Scholem in *The Mystical Form of the Godhead*. Buber's interest was from the very outset more personal and less informed by the desire for knowledge. As a boy in Sadagora he had felt an inexplicable aura of holiness surrounding the zaddik who in his relation to man and in his ability to overcome "world-concreteness" revealed the Way that was to be taken by the Jews, the way of sanctifying piety that led at once to both the past and the future.

Buber wrote of his gradual initiation into the being-tradition of the zaddik in his essay "My Way to Hasidism," [35] in which he also described how his contemplation of the life and activities of the pious Hasidim deepened his knowledge of the movement. He had come in contact with a Hasidic community in Sadagora in his boyhood at a time when the movement had degenerated and when the zaddikim had become superstitious wonder-rabbis who preyed on the credulity of the people; and yet he felt something of their inborn dignity and steadfast faith that could not be wholly eradicated. It was mostly with material wishes that the people turned to them; but something of a divinely ordained relationship between a fortunate and an unfortunate soul impressed him: "Here was, debased yet uninjured, the living double kernel of humanity: genuine *community* and genuine *leadership*. Ancient past, farthest future were here, lost, longed for, returned." [35a]

This growing familiarity with the tradition of the zaddik from within is illustrated by an anecdote that Buber recounted in "My Way to Hasidism," an anecdote that also reflects the religious life of the Hasidim of that period, distorted to a point of non-recognition and yet retaining its deepest meaning intact. After a lecture that Buber had given in Czernowitz in 1910, he was approached by the brother of a former steward of his father's estate who begged him for answers to some highly personal matters about which Buber could not possibly have known anything, firmly convinced that Buber could help him. Even this trivial incident reminded Buber of the figure of the zaddik as "the helper in spirit, the teacher of world-meaning, the conveyer of the divine sparks." [35b] At that time he had gathered from all the myths of the world the idea of the God-realizing, the "perfect" man—and that revealed to him what is today, as always, the task of such a man, namely, to be a teacher and helper. All of Buber's thoughts on education and therapy were henceforth determined by the image of the zaddik. It was above all the experience of the Hasidic community and its zaddik that determined his ideas of the Palestinian community village. Although Buber portrayed the zaddik in the human image of the "perfect helper," he remained within the bounds of Jewish tradition when he also described him as the "conveyer of the divine sparks." This is corroborated in an essay written in 1956 in which he spoke of how he had often been urged to emancipate Hasidic life-teaching from its "denominational limitations" and to proclaim it as an unfettered teaching for all mankind. This, however, would have seemed to him an arbitrary procedure, and he refrained from taking this universal path: "In order to speak to the world what I have heard, I am not bound to step into the street. I may remain standing in the door of my ancestral house; here too the word that is uttered does not go astray." [36] Buber thus saw every religion as a house whose doors and windows lead out into the world—but whose walls may not be pulled down.

A zaddik is neither priest nor monk; he merely applies himself with greater soul energy to the task which confronts every man. This was brought home to Buber by a personal incident that affected his whole life,[37] when on one occasion a visitor in deep despair sought his advice about the meaning of life and soon thereafter met an untimely death. This shattering experience finally placed Buber within the tradition of the zaddik, for it compelled him to recognize the unending sphere of responsibility presented to us with every moment of life: "Each man with all his being and doing determines the fate of the world in a measure unknowable to him and all others; for the causality which we can perceive is indeed only a tiny segment of the inconceivable, manifold, invisible working of all upon all." [38] There is a causality of deeds which we can only surmise. The zaddik in his relation to the "infinite ethos of the moment" is aware of the measure of responsibility that accrues to him hourly. If it is now urged that Buber read his "existentialism" into the Hasidic movement, his own words are closer to the truth when he states that Hasidism "was in a mysterious manner involved in the task that claimed me." [39] This is confirmed by Robert Weltsch: "The origin of Buber's turning to dialogic thinking lies at least partly in his immersion in the immediacy of Hasidic speech." [40]

The image of the zaddik, the man as "perfect helper" who is ready to aid all who need his advice and guidance, became the criterion for Buber's so-called "existentialism." The idea of responsibility, not in the moral but in the metaphysical sense, such as the zaddik bears for God's fate on earth, he developed further in the dialogic relation of I and Thou into the relation of man to "world-concreteness" as elaborated in *Dialogue*.

All esoteric knowledge, all ecstatic cleaving to God are now relegated to the background to give way to the daily involvement of man's entire being demanded by the zaddik, to his being present for the sake of others. Buber had been remiss in this respect to one who was in need and in deep despair, so that it is not surprising that in the preface to *The Baal-Shem-Tov's Instruction in Intercourse with God* he should call the essence of Hasidic mysticism "presentness." As early as 1906 he had called this piety "the Cabbala that has become ethos"; but it occurred to him only much later what it meant "when a gnosis becomes ethos: it is the true religious revolution that is only possible as work of *devotio*." [41] Again and again it is this same return to religious practice that Buber had in mind: in the case of the zaddik from mystical power and glory to the perfect helper, and in his own case from realization that remained conceptual and literary to the presentness of the entire person for the sake of others.

An additional factor must be kept in mind. From the very beginning Buber's interpretation of Hasidism placed particular emphasis on the popularity of the movement among the people. Besides the intimate circle of students and the restricted community there were the common people seeking help and guidance, in which the zaddik's quality of "presentness" had to be proven, for it was his duty to impart instruction and comfort to the people as a whole as well as to his students and the community. That there is no hierarchy in Hasidism and no wall that separates the initiated from the people was regarded by Buber to be of immense benefit to the movement, foreshadowing its subsequent fate: "On the combination of both elements, leading the students and leading the people, the teaching element of the Diaspora together with the judging element of the ancient community rested the power and growth of the Hasidic movement. Its decline is in a great measure de-

termined by the conflict between both." [42] Only when mysticism becomes a people's movement can it achieve the vital renewal of the religious substance which Buber regarded as essential, a view which is also
confirmed by the mysticism of the Christian Middle Ages. Buber saw
Hasidism as a reaction to the failure of Sabbatai Zvi's messianic movement. Polish Jewry, deeply shaken and bewildered, demanded leadership and spiritual authority, and Hasidism was able to meet its needs
because of its un-hierarchical structure and because of the many personalities it provided who came forward at the same time to show the
people the way to God.

The task of being a teacher of the people beyond the narrow circle of students and readers was another Hasidic principle that impressed Buber. In 1933 he became aware of German Jewry's need for
responsible leadership in the field of adult education, and he was equal
to the challenge that it presented. At that time he was deeply rooted in
the being-tradition of Hasidism and, as once the zaddikim in their day,
he now became a "light for the seeing eye, strength for the working
hand" for groups of bewildered German Jews who, expelled from their
former communities, were now seeking guidance. This guidance Buber provided by teaching them the imperishable values of Judaism. But
beyond that it was his personality which testified to the vitality of these
values in the sense in which it was once said of the zaddikim that they
not only interpreted the Torah but were themselves Torah, not only
the bearers and apostles of the teaching but also "effective reality," that
is, they themselves were the teaching—as we find stressed again and
again in Buber's writings on Hasidism.

In a lecture given at the Frankfurt Lehrhaus in November 1933,
Buber presented the entire phenomenon of the Jewish being-tradition
in conjunction with a historically articulated development of folk education: the *"instructive"* phase, based on the Torah in its literal meaning of instruction, was placed at the beginning and this was followed
by the folk education of the prophets *"admonishing"* and preaching
natural brotherliness; the third form of folk education arose in the
Exile, the *"traditional,"* which can be called the "recollecting" form,
for Judaism also existed in the Dispersion as a recollection community.
The Jewish folk education that was now needed may be called "regen-

erative," for it presupposes a reevaluation of its values and essential contents.[43] It bears the same meaning as "renewal" in *Der grosse Maggid*, where it is referred to as the peculiar life principle of the zaddik.

THE BEING–TRADITION OF SANCTIFICATION

At the catastrophic turning point of 1933 both lines of development met: being-tradition as "propagation of values" and the chain of "realizing" men whose image Buber tended more and more to incorporate in his description of the zaddik. Buber's address on "Symbolic and Sacramental Existence," which was delivered in Ascona in 1934 (and later included in *Origin and Meaning of Hasidism*), constitutes his contribution to the interpretation of Hasidism in the thirties. In it he compares the zaddik, as a phenomenon in the history of faith, with the Old Testament prophet from the standpoint of rank and significance.

Two years before the Ascona address, Buber's first large scientific work on the Bible, *The Kingdom of God*, appeared. Since the middle of the twenties he devoted himself, in addition to his work on Hasidism, to an intensive study of the Bible, which was first undertaken in preparation for a new translation of the scriptures but soon assumed a more comprehensive scope. Thus, in his essay "Biblical Leadership," [43a] he distinguishes five basic types of biblical leaders in accordance with the different situations in which they appeared.

From the standpoint of the Bible the history of Israel is a dialogue of God with his people, in which the efforts of the human partner are again and again frustrated and end in failure. This is exactly contrary to the judgment of world history which glorifies the expansion and elevation of man's mind and its singular achievements. Failure, on the other hand, is indispensable to the success of the prophetic mission: the failure of man's venturesome schemes and short-lived audacities. The suffering servant in the book of Isaiah speaks for these prophets of God when he declares: "He made my mouth like a sharp sword, in the shadow of his hand he hid me: he made me a polished arrow, and in his quiver he hid me away" (Isa. 49:2). Among the "servants" who did not remain hidden in the quiver, Buber counted the messianic pretenders from Jesus of Nazareth to Sabbatai Zvi. Since history is conceived as events that take place between God and mankind, it was possible for Buber in the first chapter of "Chassidische Botschaft"—which was composed as early as 1927 to be the introduction to the *Chassidische Bücher*—to establish a relationship between the Baal-Shem and the religious-historical significance of Spinoza and present it as an "answer" to Spinoza's attempt to undermine the belief in a personal God. In the essay "In the Midst of History" ["Geschehende Geschichte" (1933)], Buber regarded the events that take place between man and God as the real, essential movement of world history. In *Addresses on Judaism* he had declared that religious reality precedes the morphology of its age: "theophany begets history." [44] Seen in this light, the history of power appears superficial and its leaders have failed in the dialogue with God. The history of salvation also knows victory and defeat. The crowning event in the life of its heroes is martyrdom; their sufferings are intensely personal and seldom bring them glory. There is also the fleeting, vanishing martyrdom, testimony that no one accepts, as Buber characterized the catastrophe that overtook German Jewry in his open letter to Mahatma Gandhi.[44a]

In the Ascona address Buber distinguished between the "symbolic" existence of the prophets and the "sacramental" existence of Hasidism, whereby he understood two different ways in which the union of the absolute, the eternal, with the concrete and transitory can become known. The biblical prophet was chosen in his mother's womb that he may serve as a mouth to utter with his whole person, being, and life the sound of "the hovering silence" (1 Kings 19:12) that passes through him, and to make it understandable to the people—the sound in which the woe and misery of the human heart is concentrated and seeks expression. The prophetic word, spoken in a situation that is always ambiguous and unresolved in man's dealings with God, is not enough; it needs in addition to be supplemented by significant deeds that serve as signs. In the dialogue between biblical man and God, a sign means the embodiment of an idea by means of symbolical action and symbolical existence. When, for example, the prophet Hosea marries a woman of unchaste habits of whom it is implied that she will not be faithful to him, and then changes the holy names of the children of this remarkable union to their opposites (2:1), his whole existence becomes symbol and sign of Yahwe's experience with unfaithful Israel.

Sacrament differs from symbol, which is the appearance of meaning in bodily form, in that it is the consummation of a reciprocal binding between the divine and the human without a fusion of the two. To achieve this it is essential that man should perform the act with his whole being. Primitive man was a naïve pan-sacramentalist: the divine could appear to him in every thing and in every function—the danger of this attitude being a tendency to rely on magic, the desire to gain power over the sacred effective force inherent in things.

The historical religions make a distinction between the holy and the profane, the consecration of unification being confined to definite things and actions. The danger is that the full involvement of man's whole being is no longer guaranteed and that the sacrament can degenerate to mere gesture. The sin offering of the Old Testament is thus meaningful only when man takes part with his innermost being in the death of the sacrificial animal which dies for him vicariously. Where the full force of this demand is absent or ignored, the fate of the religion in question will depend on whether a reformation will really be able to renew man's presence in the sacramental unification.

Among all the reformatory religious movements, Hasidism, as seen by Buber, occupies a special position because it had developed a new pan-sacramentalism, and it succeeded in doing this not by reverting to a more primitive level of religious life, but "through the fulfilling presentness of the whole, wholly devoted man, through sacramental existence." [45] This renewal is not to be interpreted as the revolt of feeling and sentiment against religious rationalism, but rather as a change in man's conception of God's image which strengthened man's sense of devotion and will for realization. Through its central teaching of the indwelling of God in the world and man's task to redeem the divine sparks hidden in beings and things, Hasidism remains closely bound to the Cabbala. But it has no direct interest in the image of the divine inner circle of the upper world projected by the Cabbala, the "map of the primal mysteries in which the origins of the contradictions also have their place." Buber described Hasidism as "agnostic" in its own restricted sphere, by which he meant that it is not concerned "with objective knowledge that can be formulated and schematized, but with vital 'knowledge,' with the Biblical 'knowing' in the reciprocity of the essential relation to God." [46] Hasidism is opposed to "the schematization of the mystery." The world of man is a world of contradictions, and it is man's duty to accept this unpleasant fact with fortitude; to flee from it to loftier spheres is to forsake his mission.

"Through the world-indwelling of God the world becomes, speaking in general terms, sacrament," as Buber had written in the preface to *Origin and Meaning of Hasidism*.[47] To this he added in 1934 that there had always been a strong tendency in Judaism for the sacramental life and that since biblical times there have always been "masters of an unmistakably sacramental form of existence" in whose whole life attitude and actions "the consecration of the covenant was present and operative": the Hasidic zaddik is only "an especially clear, theoretically delineated stamp of the same archetype, originating in the Biblical world and pointing into a future one." [48] Hasidism succeeded in transferring an esoteric mysticism to the sphere of man's personal life within the community, to the sphere of lived and shared experience. This change meant a definite return to the personal character of biblical piety and to Israel's common acknowledgment of the One holy God and King, for whom the earth is to be prepared as a dwelling place of perfection. The essence of Hasidic piety is the effective fulfillment in life of an ancient commandment: "Be ye holy, for I am holy."

Buber saw in Hasidism not so much a reformation as a regeneration of Jewish faith through the formation of community cells that arise around the central figure of a holy religious leader and that, through their striving for the establishment of God's kingdom and for the unity of spirit and world, renew the life of biblical piety: "The original intention of the religious community, the realization of 'holiness' in the whole breadth and fullness of the common life, shall now be fulfilled; with it, fulfillment is begun." [49] This tradition of sanctifying and sanctification which has its source in the Bible and which acknowledges the unity of the all-comprehending God through the unity of teaching and life, imparting to the divine Spirit ever-new forms of human unification, is for Buber the true being-tradition of Judaism in which he placed Hasidism and his own life.

The essay "Imitatio Dei" (1926) provides the basis for this idea, and is of the utmost importance for the understanding of Buber's conception of sanctifying and sanctification. Here the commandment enjoining us to imitate the invisible, imageless God of Israel, which is a corollary of man's having been created in the image of God, is characterized as "the central paradox of Judaism." [50] We are destined to be like God through our own human efforts to complete the image in which we were created and which we bear within us: "We perfect our souls towards God; this means that each of us who does this makes perfect *his* likeness to God, his *yehida,* his soul, his 'only one,' his uniqueness as God's image." [51] That our imitation of God means that we are to walk in his ways is attested in the superscription at the beginning of the essay, a saying of Aristides of Athens concerning the Jews, "They imitate God's mercy," and here "the perfect helper" appears as the God-ordained image of man.

In this essay the commandment to be holy because God is holy is traced back to the primary root of God's likeness in man. The essay is important because it takes seriously the creation of man and the world by God, and the ways in which we are to become holy as set forth in the Bible. He who accepts the creation of the world by God in its full reality is bound to affirm the uniqueness and singularity of every creature that fulfills the meaning of its creation by striving to perfect itself towards God. The reduction of the world to "nothingness," as practised by the gnostics—apart from the fact that it can take place only in man's thinking—must from this point of view appear to be the wrong way.

As Buber examined the biblical view of the problem of the "God-realizing man," he discovered two fundamental ways in which man seeks to fulfill the divine image within him: *devotio* and gnosis.[52] The former refers to man's adoration and sanctification of God with his whole being, while the latter for Buber plays the part of the forbidden apple of the Tree of Knowledge. The gnostic finds God in the depths of his own Self. Unperturbed by life's riddles which he believes are insoluble, he undertakes "to present the mysteries of transcendental being as items of knowledge." In this sphere of "pneumatic sovereignty" the relation of Hasidism to concrete reality is as Scholem presents it; it deals with those representatives of the movement whose tendency Buber described as "spiritualization." Here the divine sparks are removed from things by an act of abstraction which destroys the "concrete" element of reality. To bind the divine life in things to their "upper root" means to find different ways of "using the concrete as a vehicle to the abstract and thereby to the ultimate source of all being." [53] Only by leading things back to their nothingness can they be restored to their true position before God. By means of a contemplative act, another dimension is reached in which the concrete as such has disappeared: "For it is not the *concrete* reality of things that appears as the ideal result of the mystic's action, but something of the *messianic* reality in which all things are restored to their proper place in the structure of creation, and have as a result of this restoration become deeply transformed and transfigured." [54] In addition, Hasidism has always tolerated more primitive practices in which "the holy sparks no longer appear as metaphysical elements of the divine Being, but as subjective feelings of joy and affirmation which are projected into man's relation to his environment." [55]

This, however, is not to be understood as Buber's idea of the tradition of "sanctification" as the perfection of the meaning of creation any more than his use of the term "consecration" is to be understood as subjective, aesthetic feeling. With regard to the meaning of "the quality of zeal," which Scholem called "a significant and impressive formulation of the basic principle of religious anarchism," [56] Buber stated in unmistakable terms in an explanatory note to *The Baal-Shem-Tov's Instruction*: "What is meant is the divine attribute of 'readiness,' the power to effect that is accorded to man who is created in the image of God." [57] Here the direct relation to the biblical notion of *imitatio dei* is obvious.

Since Buber's point of departure is the Here and Now of man and not of things, he wanted in the preface to *The Baal-Shem-Tov's Instruction* to translate Hasidism by the German word *Gegenwärtigkeit*, "presentness." "Sacramental existence" he characterized as "the fulfilling presentness of the whole, wholly dedicated man." [58] In Buber's own philosophical language this presentness of man signifies that "the I of relation," which he also called "the I of love," is turned toward things. The essential element in this act of turning-toward-things, however, is the actual effect that proceeds from it and which constitutes for Buber in *I and Thou* the real criterion of Meeting. The zaddik is commissioned as "cosmic mediator," and called upon "to awaken a holy reality in things through holy contact with them." [59] The sanctifying unification with beings and things makes them transparent toward God—just as every earthly relation in *I and Thou* becomes transparent toward God. Buber was therefore consistent in translating *hasiduth*, "Hasidic piety," with "to love the world in God." [60] What is experienced in *I and Thou* as the grace of Meeting is demanded as Service in the *devotio* of sanctification.[61]

Things are "transformed and transfigured" not only in mystical contemplation; something of "messianic reality" also flares up in them in the act of sanctification. In his answer to Rivkah Schatz-Uffenheimer's criticism, Buber spoke of sanctification as "a change without removing concreteness." [62] Through holy contact a holy reality can be awakened in things and thus contribute to the redemption of the sparks, which is the perfection of the world toward God. Buber insisted that we are here concerned not with an intellectual process within man but with his daily life, the contact of being with being; and in this connection he introduced the concept of "erecting bridges" as over against "reduction to nothingness."

The perfection of things with a view to their messianic form takes place through "holy contact," through the consecration of unification. In the legend "Revelation" (1907), the Baal-Shem is presented as one who with his "over-arching presence" bridges the abyss between things; "the helper" is the man who is able to unite all that is separated in being, so that there is no longer an abyss "but a light space of seeing and touching, and all that was therein." [63] Beings and things then "recognize" one another, and their cosmic unification points to a divinely ordained perfection of the world. Here in poetic presentness something of messianic reality is intended—only later "the realizing mode" is different.

The sanctifying relation to concrete reality, as Buber explained it, also involves a "reduction to nothingness." This does not concern things and beings outside of us which must be confirmed and perfected in their concreteness, but refers to the arbitrary will of the one commissioned to be the helper and cosmic mediator. By a "fulfilling presentness" is meant a "turning" and a rebirth that has gone through "nothingness." Buber asserts in the *Legend of the Baal-Shem*: "If man desires that a new creation come out of him, then he must come with all his potentiality to a state of the nothing, and then God brings forth in him a new creation. . . ." [64] The perfect helper is now the humble man who "rests in himself as in the Nothing," and "help" is not regarded as a virtue but as an "artery of existence." [65] In *Der grosse Maggid* too, the zaddik appears as the one "in whom metaphysical responsibility is consciously turned into organic existence," [66] that is, one who has attained that degree of integration of the ethical and the religious which for Buber signified "holiness." From the very outset the "fulfilling presentness" of the zaddik is for him the life of sanctifying unification which is only possible in the dedication of the *devotio*; he who addresses himself wholly to God can attain it. The juxtaposition of *devotio* and gnosis still seemed possible to him in his early days, and only later did he realize that mystical contemplation in itself remains isolated and that here all abstraction remains a triumph of the one who finds the divine in himself. Holiness, however, demands unification. To participate actively in the work of perfecting the world means to render honor to God; it is *devotio*, service, bringing to light the seeds of God's kingdom that are hidden in things.

The apostle Paul had also admonished the Ephesians to imitate God: "Be ye therefore followers of God" (5:1). In his essay "Imitatio Dei" Buber referred to this passage in order to make a distinction between the Christian and the Jewish understanding of this concept, between those who can recall the life history of the founder of their religion and those who are urged to imitate the imageless God of Israel. For the Christian there is a direct connection between the command "Follow me!" of the Son of God as the way to "perfection" and the commandment to be holy because God is holy, so that in the contemplation of holy life within the Church he will have many occasions to confirm Buber's Jewish being-tradition of holiness.

In this connection one must bear in mind the revitalization of the gospels through those who became the founders of the various Christian orders and who were mainly concerned not with doctrinal reforms but with the regeneration of Christian life as a result of the unconditionality of their *imitatio Christi,* with that same unity of truth and confirmation which Buber regarded as the essential nature of the Hasidic communities. The Christian orders are also living cellular structures whose propagating spirit constantly keeps renewing the total organism of the Church from within. Just as the being-tradition of Judaism, which is ever-changing and yet essentially the same, is for Buber inconceivable without the divinely preordained trinity creation-revelation-redemption, so is the powerful influence exerted over the centuries by the Christian exhortation, "If you would be perfect, follow me," inconceivable, were it nothing more than the work of man. Buber spoke of the incarnation of the spirit of holiness through human unification, of sparks leaping through generations and centuries. Hans Urs von Balthasar also sees in the survival of the great religious orders the mystery of a "substantive holiness" which was preserved and transmitted with the life substance of their founders: "The elemental impulse which issued from them, comparable to a natural catastrophe, whereby they became the fathers of entire legions of children throughout the centuries, all of whom mysteriously bear the unmistakable stamp of the personal God-inspired spirit of the founder, this impulse lies too wholly in the overflowing grace of their supernatural mission to be explained by any earthly power of personal suggestion." [67]

Devotio is Buber's translation of the trusting faith of the Old Testament *emuna,* which in Christianity mysteriously developed into the trinity faith, hope, and love. In the religious orders *devotio* is realized in the three vows of poverty, chastity, and obedience. It can never be anticipated when and where the spirit of sanctifying devotion will assume a new historical embodiment. Nor is this union of "spiritualization" and "sanctification," which Buber imputed to Hasidism, foreign to the Church. Side by side with the strongholds of scholasticism, and without conflicting with their aspirations and achievements, we find the community of St. Francis which desires nothing more than "life in accordance with the teaching of the gospel of Jesus Christ." In St. Francis, who takes seriously the instruction: "Sell all you have and give it to the poor," even if this should mean begging for one's daily bread, the "incarnation" of the innermost contact with Jesus Christ attains the visible manifestation of the stigma. Of all the founders of orders, he was the one who most vigorously opposed the strict traditional rules. Holy life is joy in God and joy in His creation, and needs no external precepts and rigid forms: "This life means holiness, unification with God arising out of loving imitation of Christ in heroic poverty and humility. Preaching is secondary; study, work, writing, nursing the sick, etc.— all this is secondary and tertiary. He who bears this life in him, however, shall be free: he can seize initiatives that present themselves, embark on suitable undertakings, create new forms of the apostolate, cultivate science or lead the life of a hermit removed from the world, insofar as this does not militate against his own soul and the Vita." [68] Could we not also speak of the rigid class structure of the medieval world as "religious anarchy," as argued by Scholem in opposition to Buber? This seemingly grave accusation, however, does not appear so damaging on second thought. The ordeals of obedience imposed on so many saints by their superiors at the beginning of their careers demonstrate that the unconditionality of their genuine desire to realize holiness could come into conflict with the ordinances of traditional teaching and ecclesiastical hierarchy and easily be misunderstood.

The indomitable spirit that prompts one to take upon himself the *imitatio Christi* or the Kingdom of God is common to the Christian and Jewish being-tradition of holiness. "To sanctify" meant for Buber to fulfill God's commandment from within, to live each moment in such a way that a spark of messianic perfection could flare up from it, to be faithful to the "messianism that takes place at all times" which, in Buber's view, must precede the eschatological one. That the totality of all of these hallowed moments constituted man's proper "way" was already envisaged by Buber in his earliest utterances on Hasidism in 1903: "All that is done with pure heart is God's service. The goal of the law is that man himself should become a law." [69] To replace the external prescriptions of ritual law with a "law of life" is still Judaism's uncompleted task in which Hasidism seemed to Buber to have made a beginning. He pointed out that in Hasidism *devotio* absorbed and overcame gnosis. In the Church it is again and again the spirit of *imitatio Christi* that preserved its vitality. Buber's observation, which was criticized by Scholem, namely: "Where the mystic vortex circled, now stretches the way of man," [69a] reflects a recurrent development in both religions whereby faith is repeatedly brought back from the isolation of "spiritualization" to the community of "sanctification." In "Revelation" we find that the Baal-Shem was the one who paved the "Way" for the Rabbi who was threatened by the entanglements and confusion of the "vortex"—this being another example of how Buber remained faithful to the images and symbols of the religious life he experienced in his youth.

Buber stressed the fact that the Jewish being-tradition reveals unchanging features, especially its constant striving to open up new areas of reality for the Kingdom of God. The Christian orders also have retained their basic conception of the *imitatio Christi,* although as social institutions and in their "realization mode" they are subject to change. The founding of new orders has given rise to the development of new communal forms corresponding to the exigencies of the Church's world situation. The path leads from the earliest Oriental hermits to the modern Third Orders, whose members keep their vows in the midst of the world, or to the Small Brothers of Jesus who in all lands share the life and work of the poorest of the poor, which in no way impairs their ecclesiastical position within the Church. This is comparable to what Buber reported of Rabbi Zusya, who was very popular among the people: "He does not sequester himself; he is only detached. His loneliness in the face of the eternal Thou is not the loneliness of a recluse but of one who is composed and true to the world, a loneliness which includes intrinsic oneness with all human beings. He leads his life among his fellows, detached and yet attached, regarding their faults as his own, rejoicing in them, and in all creatures in the freedom of God." [70] Buber, who has so often found a common ground in different world views, now found confirmation in the Christian brother-religion. Both religions contain paths of "spiritualization" and of "sanctification," although differently expressed, and in both religions the being-tradition of holiness is transmitted as a leaping spark which provides not only "informative knowledge" but a "panoply for being."

But even when we see the Hasidic community as a vital form of Jewish tradition of holiness, we cannot fail to recognize that the relation of lived truth to cognitive truth must be different from what it is in Buber's view. A religion stands not only in a being-tradition of holiness but also in a theological and philosophical tradition, and bound to a historical situation. Buber was conscious of the inner identity of Hasidic truth and the truth he lived, and since the one thing they have in common is "the one thing that is needful," he was impelled to proclaim it as a "message." But his "ontic participation" in Hasidism was basically beyond all conceptual formulation because the two partners, although having a common language of life, lack a common language of concepts. Buber was consequently obliged to translate Hasidism's "message" into modern concepts so that it could be introduced into contemporary life with the result that it was not recognized as Hasidic teaching. The being-tradition of sanctification, which directed Buber to Hasidism, makes it difficult to describe his attitude as "existentialism"; yet his critics cannot be blamed for insisting on retaining the historical image of Hasidism.

Buber continued to think through his conception of Hasidism, which he called the "de-schematization of the mystery," and ended by thinking of it as a "de-dogmatization and de-formalization of religion," which accounts for the emphasis he placed on the unmediated dialogue between God and man in the world and the resultant significance that accrues to "the infinite ethos of the moment." This gave rise, according to Rivkah Schatz-Uffenheimer, to a "disproportion in his rendering of the Hasidic world-image." [71] Scholem states that Hasidism remained at all times bound to Jewish tradition and to the commandments of the Torah. By lawfully setting forth the rules of what was to be done, limits were placed to the sanctification of all being, and the distinction maintained between good and evil, pure and impure. In considering a historical movement of the past there is always the danger that the extreme limits of what had been achieved will be overestimated, for it is looked upon by those who come later as a normal condition: "In the living tradition it is not possible to draw a line between preserving and producing," as Buber stated in his address "Teaching and Deed." [72]

From our consideration of Buber's early mystical studies we have seen that he had as little relation to the theological conceptions underlying mysticism as he had to the rigid forms and institutions of any particular religion. This is obvious in his conceptual treatment of the Hasidic message. Buber underestimated the effect on the religious life of a community as a result of the believer's participation in the stable order of institutional religion with all its dogmas and rituals. The behavior of a Christian or Jewish mystic will as a rule be influenced more profoundly by theological conceptions than Buber was willing to believe. Not only the beliefs and experiences of the mystic but also his thoughts revolve around God and delve into his mysteries. God is for the Occidental mystic not only the personal God of the Bible but also the source of the world of ideas from which all being originates. The understanding of the sensible world remains related to cognitive realities. Until quite late in modern times the mystic was an allegorist, who regarded sensible form as another way of expressing a concept, as the image of an abstract thought. Since the peculiar truths of salvation are not intuitive, they cannot be adequately rendered by sensible reality. Thus, the relation of the allegorical thinker to reality is derived from afar, from a region where conceptual thought cannot penetrate. He can turn to the concrete Here and Now without being riveted to it, for he is always aware of the transcendental meaning expressed therein. From the standpoint of the history of mystical thought Scholem's presentation of the relation of Hasidism to concrete reality is convincing. That the Hasidim should have been aware of their "sacramental existence" in the manner described by Buber, even when this term is used to characterize their innermost life, is difficult to imagine. Their sanctification of daily life had its deep roots in the traditional forms of religion and in the "cultic-sacramental," its root and anchor. Sentences such as "The primal danger of man is religion" [73] or "Everything tends to become sacrament," "The moment is God's garment," [74] lead us too far away from the historical situation of the Hasidim not to be challenged by the historian.

The Hasidim may have lived to a large extent a renewed "pan-sacramentalism," but they certainly could not have been conscious of it as such, for this presupposes a consciousness with respect to God which appeared only with the transition of religious thinking to secularism, when the unmediated contact between the absolute and the concrete, a contact not transmitted by thought, regained the significance that Buber attributed to it. In German and Jewish mysticism, symbols are not sharply separated from allegory; we find a subtly linked connection between theological-philosophical thinking, symbolic experience, hypostasizing imagination, and allegory, in which the naked concept is given sensuous dress. The symbol is for Buber a self-contained personal revelation which "descends from on high" and which proclaims itself in things and in situations as unmediated intuition. The modern distinction between symbol and allegory that we take for granted was first elaborated by Goethe,[75] who speaks of the "symbolical or sacramental meaning";[75a] this is the source of Buber's unusual use of the word "sacrament."

What we find in *Origin and Meaning of Hasidism* concerning primitive and sanctifying pan-sacramentalism is largely autobiographical. In his youth Buber had a genuine affinity for mythical thinking in which every event can become a sign and miracle. As the lightning contacts with the divinely experienced cosmic life give way to the *devotio* of the God of the Bible, God's language summoning man to a sanctifying responsibility tends more and more to replace that of mythical signs. But in the paradox of God as Absolute Person, something has remained of the "momentary God" of Buber's youthful ecstasies— for to him only unmediated dialogue was of consequence.

As early as 1918 Buber discovered Judaism's proper way, which he called "the holy way." This is not a way of thought but a way of life "in the face of God," an "unmediated relation to existence" wherein God is an elemental Being in whose light all creatures breathe in common and disclose themselves to one another. In the "Herut" address of 1918, Buber regarded such a life, a life in which all beings and things are the manifestation of God and every happening a sign and revelation, as the basis of the Jewish myth. The Jewish myth "by its very nature" had for him a historical continuity which exists side by side with the continuity of thought; and this myth is always present in the history of Judaism and can appear at any time wherever a group has developed into a community.

This emergence of such an unmediated faith existing beside and beneath the conceptuality of contemporary history Buber found in Hasidism. In the short legends and pointed answers of the teachers, an elemental and popular language was found, a pithy, expressive language which reminds us of Jewish wit. This style of writing is not an end in itself, but serves to integrate the natural into the religious, to hallow beings and things in a single context of God unification. In an address at the Frankfurt Lehrhaus[76] in 1934 Buber recognized that "the power of the spirit" in Judaism was derived from this intense dedication to hallow the world. These instances of God unification from ancient times down to our own day Buber sought to comprehend by the modern concept "sacramental existence." The extensive accumulation of short legends which he published attests to the prevalence of the sanctification of daily life in the Hasidic communities—and it alone could provide a message for our time.

Buber was aware that he lived in an age in which Judaism was struggling to achieve "a new form of faith and life." "In this struggle Hasidism persists at a perilous hour when the fading light has departed and darkness has descended, waiting with soul in readiness until the dawn breaks and a path becomes visible where none suspected it." [77] The non-Jewish world is also affected by "the eclipse of God" in our time when the "holy" is no longer lived but has become a historical concept. Our age no longer finds God in religion; only in the world, "in the holy contact with all being," can man hope to meet Him again. But the contact with beings and things, "the marrow of our existence," is today unsound and ailing.[78]

It might be instructive to compare these reflections with those of Dietrich Bonhoeffer, the Protestant pastor who was executed by the Nazis: "We are entering a world that is devoid of religion. People as they now are simply cannot be religious any longer. What is the significance of this for Christianity? Are there Christians without religion? In such a world without religion what is the meaning of a Church, a congregation, a sermon, a liturgy, a Christian life? How do we speak of God—without religion? How do we speak of God in secular terms?" [79] Buber was convinced that the "hope for this hour" could only be the renewal of direct contact with the human Thou: "If our mouths succeed in genuinely saying 'thou,' then, after long silence and stammering, we shall have addressed our eternal Thou anew." [80] Only the realization of a genuine community can give rise to a new revelation. In this time of distress Hasidism brings to us the message that Buber found in it: "You yourself must begin. Existence will remain meaningless for you if you yourself do not penetrate into it with active love and if you do not in this way discover its meaning for yourself. Everything is waiting to be hallowed by you; it is waiting to be disclosed in its meaning and to be realized in it by you. For the sake of this your beginning, God created the world. He has drawn it out of himself so that you may bring it closer to Him. Meet the world with the fulness of your being and you shall meet Him. That He himself accepts from your hands what you have to give to the world, is His mercy. If you wish to believe, love!" [81]

For the Sake of Heaven, Tales of the Hasidim

The Hasidic message that Buber had in mind could be transmitted only imperfectly in conceptual language. *Origin and Meaning of Hasidism* met with the objections of historical criticism, and was one of his least read books; thirteen years after it appeared in German, it still had not reached a second edition. The cause of its neglect is not difficult to discover. The essays of which it is composed cover a period of three decades and, although it is a work of admirable industry and amplitude, it betrays its rudimentary limitations and lacks the deeper harmonies that come from organic coherence and the natural cohesion of its parts.

While Buber was finishing this book,[82] he made another significant attempt to present a total view of Hasidic life in *For the Sake of Heaven* [*Gog und Magog*], which significantly has the subtitle *A Chronicle*, for it lays claim to greater historical fidelity than the free imaginative writing of a historical novel. The book deals with the two opposing Hasidic schools at the time of the Napoleonic Wars: "Hence it is not a legendary symbol but a simple fact that in this conflict both sides were annihilated." [83] Within a single year the heads of the two conflicting schools died in a mysterious manner, a sign that the spiritual sphere in which they were involved consumed their mortal being.

The outbreak of a war always ushered in a period of religious ferment for East European Jewry, accompanied by pogroms and unpredictable persecution. The longing for redemption, which in the seventeenth century drove the masses to follow the banner of the false messiah, Sabbatai Zvi, now seized upon the figure of the world conqueror, Napoleon, with whose appearance "the pangs of the Messiah" and the final catastrophe seemed close at hand. To the pious Jews of Eastern Europe he seemed to be the "God of the land of Magog," who was prophesied by Ezekiel and whose appearance precedes the redemption by the Messiah. Although those who were learned in the law had always warned the people not to "force the end," yet the Cabbala, whose mystical speculations the Hasidim had adopted, knew of exceptional ways to bring the prayers of the believers before the throne of the Highest. Thus, "the Seer of Lublin," the head of the most respected Hasidic school, undertook, in common with the zaddikim of other congregations, to exert pressure on the higher Powers by means of theurgic performances as envisaged by the Cabbala.

These activities were opposed by the school of Pshysha, led by the "holy Yehudi" who rejected the magical practices of his former teacher and, in imitation of the biblical prophets and God's servants, insisted on the return to God as the only way to attain salvation. But the struggle, into which Yehudi was drawn against his will, consumed his strength and, after intense prayer and sanctification, he was finally drawn in a mysterious way into the magic circle of the "Seer." A year after his death the Rabbi of Lublin, whose plans had been frustrated, was taken ill and also died.

In the careers of these two men, Buber developed what he understood to be the "dialectic inner line" of Hasidism. The reader cannot help but regard it as symbolic that the heads of the opposing schools bore the same name, Yaakob Yitzhak—the same spiritual phenomenon of the zaddik appears in them in a double form. The two basic types, "spiritualization" and "sanctification," are portrayed with rare purity, and yet they are not irreconcilably opposed but find their proper place in the complex world of East European Jewish piety. Carl Kerényi places *For the Sake of Heaven* among the classics of the world's religious literature because in communion with the divine it penetrates to the depths of religious experience.[84] Even Buber's critic, Rivkah Schatz-Uffenheimer, speaks highly of this work: "Here we stand solidly on the ground of the Hasidic world: the court of Lublin here is flesh and blood; every conversation in this book, *For the Sake of Heaven*, is a chapter of life in the spiritual world of Hasidism, a chapter sifted of all banality and sentimentality, all of it polished by the masterful use of adumbration." [85]

Buber's study of Hasidism, which extended over decades, bore fruit in this poetical presentation. It succeeds in comprehending the phenomenon of holiness in everyday life, without ignoring its "original situation" and the constant opposition between lonely service and community life. All that Buber had thought about concerning holiness and community, the kindling and the leap of the spark in personal confrontation, emerges in epic form more clearly here than in the theoretical formulation of *Origin and Meaning of Hasidism*. The poetic treatment shows Buber to be more realistic than the theoretical exposition in his earlier work would lead us to believe—which is also true of many other areas in which Buber had to come to grips with concrete situations. The chronicle leaves room for the contradictory aspects of Hasidism, whereas *Origin and Meaning of Hasidism* tends to interpretations which strike the reader as one-sided: what appears to be mutually exclusive in the world of thought is in the everyday life of the Hasidim experienced as an undivided whole. The author's realism is evident in his impartiality to the schools with magical and anti-magical tendencies, which he compares with the tradition of Saul and the tradition of David. Their struggle is not conducted in bad faith, but reflects "the cruel antitheticalness of existence" itself; Buber was conscious of "standing on the ground of tragedy."

The Rabbi of Lublin is thus presented as "the acknowledged leader of the generation," intellectually and physically a strong, outstanding personality. He is the only zaddik to whom legend has accorded the epithet "The Seer" to denote the power of clairvoyance which he employed in his treatment of suppliants who sought to be cured. This gift denotes not only genuine intuition that penetrates to the limits of time and space but it also makes its possessor dependent on supernatural "signs" which he trusts more than the clear knowledge of the heart. That he is shortsighted is symbolic, and the first chapter of the chronicle depicts him as "blind" in contrast to the messenger from the world of demons who walks among his students. The Seer is the embodiment of the zaddik as cosmic mediator, whose social and metaphysical position derives from his charismatic personality, because, more than anyone else, he "works in the higher worlds" and labors in the work of redemption.[86] But together with these authentic qualities of holiness and intuitive vision, the Seer combines a strong elemental will touched with melancholy and a consciousness of power that brooks no rival: "He stood in the world of his spiritual impulses." [87]

The Seer's most distinguished student, the "holy Yehudi," was soon felt to be an intruder in that intimate circle, one who rose up against the mystery that surrounds the Master: "against the sacred majesty of the high man who stands in the middle of the world, against his covenant with the higher powers, against his influence on the blendings of the spheres of heaven, against his combat with demonic forces" (p. 214). Buber's description of the Seer agrees with that of the zaddik drawn by Schatz-Uffenheimer. Between teacher and student there existed from the very beginning a "relation woven of nearness and distance." [88] The "Yehudi" began as an ecstatic visionary who was driven by the temptation of the world to seek God's freedom; he flees from the world and longs for death since he could find perfection nowhere on earth. The Seer teaches him that one can accept the world and be part of it without losing one's direction toward God. The beautiful symbol of the Yehudi overcoming his insomnia in Lublin indicates that he found his way back to his own nature whose essence is "the giving of one's self."

But the Seer lacks the "clarity of love under whose auspices the life-substances of the students are formed, each one forming them out of their elements." [89] The Yehudi does not find in him the fulfillment of the teacher-student relation, the trust of soul to soul, and he feels compelled to rebel against the teacher who "imposes himself." A dispute concerning the problem of good and evil brings things to an open rupture. The Seer wanted to bring about a temporary victory of Napoleon as "Gog" of the Bible by means of mysterious practices, without considering the harm that would thus be done to the souls of countless individuals. In this, according to the Yehudi, he transgressed the limits assigned to man: "But the good . . . I do not mean God's good . . . I mean the good that exists on earth, mortal good—if it seeks to make use of evil unnoticeably and without noticing it itself, it is dissolved in the evil and exists no longer" (p. 58). God's thoughts are not those of man: the sphere assigned to man is the life between soul and soul, and he cannot help the coming of redemption "if life does not redeem life" (p. 256).

Behind this dispute there is also the problem of the alternatives gnosis-*devotio,* the twofold direction of the human likeness of God and the lament of the Yehudi: "The Rabbi is terrible" is significantly based on the Seer's outcry against God: "He is terrible, terrible, terrible"— which is constructed on the analogy of the thrice-holy God. In contrast to the Seer, the Yehudi represents the work of sanctification, of the healing and hallowing contact with human souls, so that on one occasion he could say: "God is our prototype," to which Buber added: "Therewith the congregation of Pshysha was founded" (p. 185). On the other hand, the Rabbi once sent a shirt to the Yehudi that he might wear it; the latter, however, took it as a symbol of secret, magical power and was unable to wear it because his whole being was opposed to magic (p. 65).

Every congregation for the Yehudi is the beginning of a great human congregation of the future; on one occasion he asked whether the Holy Books must not suffice to bring this about if they speak as a living voice to living hearts. But God is not only concerned with *what* men do but also with *how* they do it—and this is not to be found in books: "A congregation does not arise out of a man's will, but out of his being what he is" (p. 157). The return to God depends on *teshuvah,* our return to the good, and this true mystery man can reveal only through his own life and death (p. 246). What does it mean to be a leader? The community as the original source of holiness, the mystery of togetherness (p. 125), is based on the one called upon to be a zaddik: whoever has any dealings with him receives that "togetherness" in his heart. Of a mere assemblage of people he makes a congregation by his mere existence: God is with us wherever we are, "but the dawn of his Kingdom can arrive only among us . . ." (p. 232).

This does not preclude the fact that the service of the zaddik is a lonely one. He performs this service with a feeling of both detachment and obligation, faithful to the world yet serene and imperturbable. Just as the Rabbi of Lublin recognizes what is distant in time and space more clearly than what is close to him, so does the Yehudi's influence extend to the holy community of the Hasidim and not to the natural circle of the family. He also has "the far-away eyes" (p. 160) with respect to his immediate surroundings; and his relation to his two wives shows that the freedom of him who chooses God is not an unmixed blessing. He acknowledges this: "He who falls into the hands of the living God is unfit to be either husband or father until God dismisses him" (p. 86).

The Yehudi with all his involvement in the world was still given to ecstasy; the longing to reach out beyond this imperfect world never left him. The consciousness of living in an age in which God's Face is hid only intensified his desire "to cleave to God." All his prayer is directed to the end of unifying God with his world indwelling Glory and preparing "the great turning" which God expects of man. This is also true of the moving sermon he delivered to his congregation after the nocturnal vision of his approaching end: God's majesty took on the twofold form of a servant out of love—he sent his shekinah into exile in the world and had it share its fate and degradation; and he placed the redemption of the world, the coming of the Kingdom, into the hands of man who has been given the task of reuniting God with his shekinah, and he will not be reunited with it until we bring it to him as a gift: "For this reason all calculations concerning the end of time are false and all attempts calculated to bring nearer the coming of the Messiah must fail. In truth, all such things deflect us from the one thing needful, which is this, to reunite Him and the shekinah by virtue of our return to good . . . Redemption is at the door. It depends only and alone upon our return to good, our *teshuvah*" (p. 230). Like one of the concealed servants of God, the Yehudi suffers from the unredeemed condition of the world.

This "messianism without eschatology" [90] seems to be contradicted by his death through which he joined the company of those "who force the end"; he undertakes an act of unification which can only be consummated with impunity in the land of Israel. Buber saw his death as an act of obedience. In an external sense this is true because he could thereby carry out an instruction of the Seer of Lublin; in reality, however, he can only close the gaping wound in the body of Hasidic piety with the sacrifice of his life, the wound that had been opened by the conflict with his teacher. Only by his death can the Yehudi regain the "unification" of his own life, and as he lay dying, he achieved this by clasping together his raised hands, a symbol we find in *Daniel* as the sign for a mysterious renewal of being. Seen from the perspective of redemptive world history, where the decisive question is not one of power but of salvation, his death appears as crowning martyrdom: "God marches to His victory by the path of our defeats" (p. 103).

The Yehudi represents not only Buber's conception of Hasidism but also a large part of his own nature, particularly that predisposition in his own affections that attracted him to the world of Hasidism. In *For the Sake of Heaven* we encounter for the first time the symbol of "the eclipse of God," which was later used as the title of a book in which he discussed the religious and philosophical situation of our time (p. 116). Beneath the immemorial linden tree and under a crescent moon and starry sky the two characters speak about the hidden God, and the natural mood of modern man accompanies their religious discussion like muted music in the background. The words of the Yehudi that the language of being is *one,* no matter how many languages there are in the world, reflects one of Buber's convictions: "All aboriginal speech is to be understood at that point where word and gesture are still inextricably blended" (p. 218). The Yehudi, like Buber, sees nature as that aspect of creation that discloses events and happenings; "miracle" is an aspect of revelation and refers to our receptivity to eternal revelation; an event becomes a miracle not through its opposition to nature, but through its significance for the receiver (p. 112). The tension between God's freedom, on the one hand, and service to man, on the other, the idea that "God does not compel me," was deeply felt by Buber for whom every earthly Thou was transparent toward God and whose direct contact with men led to direct contact with God.

In connection with this question of freedom we have the conversation of the Yehudi with his departing friend Yeshaya (pp. 98 f.), which Ernst Simon has interpreted so convincingly.[91] The question is whether prayer is the spontaneous expression of the individual soul on the road to self-discovery or whether it should be conducted within the traditional framework of congregational life: "We do not pray according to the inspiration of the individual heart. We join an ordering of the word of prayer which generations of our fathers organically built. We subordinate ourselves to and within this ordering not as this *I* or this *you*, but as part of that congregation in the act of prayer with which you and I are integrated. What your single heart bids you tell your Creator you can utter in the solitariness of your waking at dawn or in your lonely walks. But the order of prayer has its place and its appointed times, which you should respect" (pp. 101 f.). The Yehudi, however, stoutly maintains that the word without spirit does not exist: "The word, that it may be a living word, needs *us*." The word needs worshipers who wait until they can enter fully into the prayer and who in their solitariness "prepare the rebirth of the congregation"—without the fiery spirit of the ardent worshiper the living word of the congregation is "not there" (p. 102).

Ernst Simon interpreted this conversation as a reflection of the controversy between Buber and Franz Rosenzweig concerning the validity of the law and the personal observance of the commandments. He failed to add that in later years he defended Rosenzweig's view in opposition to Buber that the law is not promulgated by man. Yeshaya's objection, "That is not the way to be trodden. . . . What you believe is not communicable, cannot be handed on," can be maintained with equal justification as the answer of the Yehudi: "You shall not withhold yourself"—an exhortation which Buber emphasized in his essay written in 1919, "What Is to Be Done?"[92] At the conclusion we read: "They parted with their friendship unimpaired, but their mood was one of unconquerable melancholy" (p. 103).

This poetical work culminates in the vision of the shekinah through which the world mystery is revealed to the Yehudi as well as his approaching death. The impenetrable darkness of the night without moon or stars, the blast of the heavenly *shofar,* the primeval light from which the womanly form arises, the apocalyptic winged beings with the double command, "Thou shalt prophesy," "Thou shalt die"—in all this the end of time and the here and now have coalesced into one indistinguishable present. The earthly woman from whom the Yehudi once fled speaks with heavenly majesty: "When ye are hostile to each other, ye hunt me down. When ye plot evil against each other, ye torment me. When you plunder each other, ye deny me. Each of you exiles his comrade and so together ye exile me. . . . One cannot love me and abandon the created being. I am in truth with you. Dream not that my forehead radiates heavenly beams. The glory has remained above. My face is that of the created being" (p. 229). The primeval light that has become the "hidden light" through the sins of man[93] has in the moment of vision disclosed its mystery.

The way that is shown to the Yehudi is the way of the *imitatio dei* which leads through the mystery of the suffering servant of God: the words and commandments of the Bible are the common ground of meeting for Buber and Hasidism. In *For the Sake of Heaven,* the "modern" features of Buber's piety appear in the authentic portrayal of Hasidism—the structure of its group life, its atmosphere of learning and of brotherliness, its will to holiness. That which is common to all times, which remains the same, and which thought cannot make visible are present in the confrontation of man to man. The ways to God are all different and yet they all lead to the same goal when man's fervor is directed with undiminished power to God's destiny in the world. The joy in concrete reality bears the primordial sorrow of the created being and is given only to him who desires nothing but divine joy—"nothing but joy in itself." [94] What Buber found in the legendary anecdotes of Hasidism was "the reality of the experience of fervent souls," which do not give an account of themselves but of what stirred them;[95] and he who came later adopted them "with Hasidic fervor." [96] The reality of relation is given where the will to sanctification is the unmediated, fervent speech of the heart.

Judaism as being-tradition, "the permanent and enduring amid the changing," was never more beautifully presented by Buber than in *For the Sake of Heaven*. "Spirit begets and gives birth, spirit is begotten and born; spirit becomes body." [97] All that Buber had thought about the "propagation of values" and their transmission from generation to generation through ever-renewed community cells came to light in this book, in the enduring will of the Jewish people for study and sanctification, and in the destiny of individual Jewish personalities whose recurrent features are mysteriously renewed from age to age. On this plane the holy Yehudi meets his descendant of the age of "the eclipse of God"; the way from the ecstatic visionary to the great Jewish teacher and God's servant was the same.

In the introduction to *Tales of the Hasidim* this way is traced back to the beginnings of Hasidism in the comprehensive figure of the Great Maggid, the first real teacher of Hasidism. Only then does it become clear to us why Buber turned to the work of the Great Maggid when, after being awakened to "the fervent life" by the Baal-Shem, his understanding of "sanctification" moved from the sphere of ecstasy to that of instructive responsibility: "But we cannot grasp all this in its full significance until we remember that obviously the Maggid had always been a man given to ecstasy, only that this ecstasy, under the influence of the Baal-Shem, was diverted from ascetic solitude to the active life of teaching disciples. From that moment on, his ecstasy assumed the shape of teaching . . . and to accomplish this service he regarded himself, his thinking as well as his teaching, only as a vessel for divine truth. To use his own words, he 'changed the something back into the nothing.' Seen from this point of view, we can understand the effect he had on his disciples, described by the youngest among them, who later became the 'Seer of Lublin,' after his very first visit to the Maggid: 'When I came before the master, before the Maggid, I saw him on his bed: something was lying there which was nothing but simple will, the will of the Most High.' That was why his disciples learned even more and greater things from his sheer being than from his words." [98]

Buber was fond of saying: "When I am well disposed to a person I tell him stories"—and since, by his own testimony, he was "inescapably destined to love the world," [99] he kept telling it Hasidic stories. After his theoretical exposition of the "message" of Hasidism in *Origin and Meaning of Hasidism* and his poetical presentation in *For the Sake of Heaven*, which was prompted by "the telluric crisis" in his own time, we have the comprehensive and definitive collection of *The Tales of the Hasidim*. The hope of witnessing "the great conversion" of the people which Buber still cherished at the beginning of the forties, when *Israel and Palestine, For the Sake of Heaven*, and *Origin and Meaning of Hasidism* were being written, was not fulfilled with the establishment of the state of Israel. The collection of the *Tales* is designed to give the reader a general picture of the development of Hasidism without messianic overtones. The failure of this great religious movement and its decline from the time of God's departing light until the darkness of our own time received greater emphasis than the message to the emerging nationhood of the new state. The holy Yehudi's summons to return, *teshuva*, went unheeded by those who came later; but his words, "This also will be corrupted," continued to live in Buber's mind in his concern for the popular Zionist movement. One of his introductory stories about the life of the Hasidim ends with a description of Rabbi Mendel of Vorki whose peculiar piety manifested itself in silence, not a "soundless prayer" but a "soundless scream": "The soundless scream is the reaction to a great sorrow. It is in general the Jew's reaction to his own great sorrow; it 'befits us.' By reading between the lines we discover that it is particularly his, Mendel of Vorki's reaction to the hour in which 'the present too is corrupted.' The time for words is past. It has become late." [100]

The historical survey of the development of Hasidism in the lengthy introduction to the *Tales* still emphasizes being-tradition, the "spirit" and "body" of a great folk movement. Buber's attitude to history had not changed essentially. The account adheres as closely as possible to the vital current of tradition. His portrayal of Hasidism is confined to the characterization of a number of personalities, to the great figures of the founders of the movement, their descendants and disciples. After the theoretical and poetical survey of Hasidism, simple biography still has the last word: the tragedy of life is apparent not only in the human beings living side by side with one another but also in the destinies of the leading personalities in the history of the movement.

Here again Buber emphasized at the very outset that he has utilized legends as a source for his presentation and that their reliability is to be judged by other standards than those of a historical account, for they document the life of a "holy community" from within. Ardent souls speak with fervor about the ambient influences that vivified their spirits, about the spontaneous movement of the awakening soul toward God, about the spell exercised by the original force of the zaddik who was for them a helper for body and soul, a healer in the physical and spiritual spheres, and whose mere presence was "God's teaching." In the early days of the movement the relation of the community to its leading figure, the zaddik, was a pre-pedagogical relation, an awakening and unfolding of forces within three overlapping spheres of life: those who came from near and far to seek help, the congregation, and the intimate circle of disciples. The figure of the zaddik was not that of an effective teacher but that of the Master who kindles the light of "sanctification" and who in turn is illumined by the flame of "the fervent."

He was followed by a generation of great teachers in whom the basic pedagogical relation was kindled in holy zeal and who created the conceptual basis for the charismatic efficacy of the zaddik. Over a period of several generations all varieties of religious community leaders were developed: the preacher, the judge, the ascetic, the ecstatic visionary, God's fool in the sense meant by St. Francis, the man of prayer. With this increasing variety of different types the movement gradually became infected with rivalry, the lust for power, superstition, simony, and abuse of privilege, so that the zaddikim fell into disrepute and finally degenerated into dynasties of wonder rabbis, who were still familiar to Buber in his childhood.

In the introduction Buber confined himself to the biographical portrayals of the heads of the Hasidic schools; in the *Tales*, however, he returned to the succinct form of the legendary anecdote and the terse answers of the teachers. His object was to reconstruct the events as they appeared in folk books, mostly in crude form, as accurately and simply as possible and to clarify their obscure meanings. The legendary anecdote is a condensed story with definite form, whose "teaching" is represented, consciously or unconsciously, in actions which have the effect of symbols and which mostly culminate in a saying which contributes to the interpretation.[101] Buber called them anecdotes because they relate a self-contained incident, and he designated them as legendary because they represent the attempt of "enthusiastic witnesses" to relate an experience that transcends conceptual reality: "It was the reality of the exemplary lives reported as exemplary, of a great series of leaders of the Hasidic communities. They were not reported in connected biography, but in a tremendous series of instances, limited events in which something was at times spoken, not seldom, however, only done, only lived. Yet even the dumb happenings spoke—it told the exemplary. And, indeed, it did not tell it didactically; no 'moral' was attached to the event, but it spoke, even as a life-event speaks, and if a saying was included, its effect too was like that of a life-event." [102]

A comparison of the poetical legends of the early days with the brief, almost meager legendary anecdotes transmitted to us in the *Tales* of the Baal-Shem reveals the self-discipline in Buber's intellectual development: the restless chafing of the imprisoned spirit against its limitations and the constant striving of the soul toward the deeper harmonies of the Whole, toward "the perfect relation" of the beginning, which in the end is always a conscientious self-limitation to the factual and the necessary. Buber had perhaps never seen the unity of the dissimilar elements in the Hasidism of the old folk books so clearly as in the free renderings of the early *Legend of the Baal-Shem*—a holiness which was at the same time magical force, the power and impotence of evil, cosmic unification, and the abyss between things, the world loneliness of the Baal-Shem and his common life with his students. In *The Baal-Shem-Tov's Instruction* this magical note of wholeness and the union between God, man, and the world has not altogether vanished, and the perfect service of man and his fervor in cleaving to God is still the key to the secret of creation: "This is the mystery of the oneness of God, that at whatever place I, a tiny bit, lay hold of it, I lay hold of the whole. And since the teaching and all the commandments are radiations of His being, so he who fulfills *one* command in love to its very ground, and in this command lays hold of a tiny bit of the oneness of

God, holds the whole in his hand as though he had fulfilled all." [103] For "the proved ones," the world is "lived cosmic multiplicity" whose innermost realization does not impair the rigor of the "responsive service" which God expects of man: "Man should unite all things of the world with all his thinking, speaking, doing, toward God in truth and simplicity. For no thing of the world is set outside the unity of God. But he who does a thing otherwise than toward God separates himself from Him." [104]

Here we find the same basic principles of "a realistic and activistic mysticism" [105] which also appear in the *Tales*. Here as there the Baal-Shem points to a new way that does not involve asceticism and renunciation of the world: the love of God, the love of Israel, the love of the Torah.[106] Although the anecdotes of the *Tales* were composed with some regard for the "inner biography" of the individual characters, a complete exposition of doctrine and of biographical details was clearly not intended. The fragmentary character of the work is conspicuous, but this makes it even more "exemplary." The exemplary without the didactic, without the moral being explicitly stated—this new way of transmitting religious teaching permits the events of life to speak for themselves. Whoever takes this path must keep in mind a saying of the Baal-Shem: "Alas, the world is full of enormous lights and mysteries, and man shuts them from himself with one small hand!" [107] The clear teaching should not become for the student "a small hand" that blocks out the lights and mysteries of the religious life. The attitude of the "sanctifying" association with men demands here as well the reduction of oneself to nothing, a liberation freely undertaken by the student which at the same time preserves his implicit faith in the imponderabilia of the awakening and the return to God.

In his preface Buber stressed that an essential part of the innermost life of the Hasidic community was to have their leaders tell stories. To tell a story is considered an event in itself and possesses the consecration of a holy act because it is based on inner experience, so that "the holy essence" testified to in the story lives on: "The miracle that is told acquires new force; power that once was active is propagated in the living word and continues to be active even after generations." [107a] The historian will point out, as Scholem has, that the legends propagated in this manner are at bottom a commentary to that which is actually lived and that a religion, such as Catholicism, cannot be comprehended on the basis of even the most beautiful sayings of its saints.[108] This is no doubt true; but the Way of *imitatio Christi* and *imitatio dei*, the being-tradition of sanctifying life which is handed down from generation to generation, is surely comprehended in this manner. And with every one of the Hasidic legends man can recover the grace of the beginning.

7
The Bible

Confession of the Writer

Once with a light keel
I shipped out to the land of legends
Through the storm of deeds and play,
With my gaze fixed on the goal
And in my blood the beguiling poison—
Then one descended to me
Who seized me by the hair
And spoke: Now render the Scriptures!

From that hour on the galley
Keeps my brain and hands on course,
The rudder writes characters,
My life disdains its honor
And the soul forgets that it sang.
All storms must stand and bow
When cruelly compelling in the silence
The speech of the spirit resounds.

Hammer your deeds in the rock, world!
The Word is wrought in the flood.[1]

THIS CRYPTIC poem with its enigmatic allusions is a reflection of
Buber's intellectual development. The voyage under full sail, which is
followed by the exhausting toil on the galley, refers to the facile literary
composition of the young man which must eventually give way to prolonged application and stern discipline in the service of the true word.
This change takes place against the will of the writer in obedience to a

summons which reminds us of the biblical scene (1 Kings 19) in which Elijah hears the still small voice of the spirit after the storm has ceased. The command, "Now render the Scriptures!" indicates to the writer the manner in which he is to fulfill his calling: the Word is not a diaphanous dance of the soul; its body, formed from the dust of sensation, must also be made manifest, else it walks unseen and unheard among men. The last two lines of the poem refer to Buber's double view of history:[2] first, the stark, inflexible visibility of success, and second, the suffering obedience of God's servant bound to a streaming element of fleeting boundaries and uncertain destination, the "Word" in the very heart of world events.

This, however, does not exhaust the poem's depth. The capitalization of a single letter—"Now render *The* Scriptures" (Nun stelle *Die* Schrift)—in the command gives the poem a new dimension. In his youth Buber had a vision of acquiring the power and authority of the poet, and now it was made plain to him that he was to dedicate his poetical talent to God's Word and not to his own "honor." The meaning of the final verse is thereby extended. The figure of the writer and the contrasting succession of flood, Word, and rock remain unchanged. Through "The Scriptures" the writer is led to the original sources where the Word that is wrested from the flood is the living Word of revelation. Looking back to the years 1916 to 1920, critical years in his intellectual development, Buber recalled[3] how significant Goethe's line in the *Westöstlicher Divan* had become for him, leading him to the "original depths" of the human race: "How important the word was there,/ Because it was the spoken word." [4] Goethe had contrasted this "spoken" word of the Orient with the figures of the Greek artists formed in clay: "Water drawn by bards whose fame/ Pure is, may be rounded" [5]—a reference to the oriental belief in the power of the pure to roll water into a crystal ball. The Orient is here regarded as man's original home. In *Addresses on Judaism* the Orient is also regarded as the cradle of the world's great religions and the unconditionality of the teaching which is word and life in one. The contrast Orient-Greece is again found in "Biblical Humanism" (1933) in which Buber took language as his point of departure.[6] The Greek word is divorced from its spoken expression and molded into pure form. The Word *is* here—the logos of the Greeks is eternal.

The biblical word, on the other hand, *happens;* it does not exist outside of its vocal utterance. It is the word in its original state, still wet with intuition. It is not changed into a structured form or pattern but remains an address, an exclamation, the human voice, preserving the character of living reality, of the stream of events, of the "flood." The Word does not find its ultimate perfection in form but in the confirmation of the moment. All being in the world is derived from the spoken nature of the original divine Word: through God's speaking the world was created. Ever since God first spoke to man all human speech is addressed to God in open or secret dialogue. Biblical man is not a figure enclosed within himself but an "open person," a human being in relation.

All these connotations of a linguistic-philosophical nature are to be found in this poem of 1945, and had indeed determined the choice of the title *I and Thou* as early as 1922. They represent the basic principles with which Buber approached his work of translating the Bible.

The project of translating the Bible into German may be said to have begun in the spring of 1925 with the "providential suggestion" (G. Scholem)[6a] of the young Lambert Schneider who wished to print a translation of the Old Testament as the first work of his newly founded publishing house, on condition that it be undertaken by Buber. This idea had occupied Buber's mind for many years, and he took this request from a Christian as a "sign" and consented to undertake the task. The initial plan to adhere to a revision of Luther's Bible, which had been recommended by Buber's associate, Franz Rosenzweig, proved to be ill-considered and was abandoned.

On the title page of the first volume *Im Anfang* [In the beginning], which appeared in 1926, we find: "Die Schrift/ zu verdeutschen unternommen/ von/ Martin Buber/ gemeinsam mit/ Franz Rosenzweig" [The Scruptures/ Rendered into German/ by/ Martin Buber/ together with/ Franz Rosenzweig]. At the time of Rosenzweig's death at the end of 1929, nine volumes had been published (up to and including the book of Kings), and the translation had reached the fifty-third chapter of the book of Isaiah. Six more volumes appeared subsequently, three with Lambert Schneider and three with Schocken Press. When the latter publishing house was liquidated at the end of 1938, the work was finished up to and including the Book of Proverbs. The edition now found in bookshops is a revised translation of the Bible which Buber began in 1950 when the Jakob Hegner Press requested him to revise and complete the work. The Bible was now issued in four volumes: *Die fünf Bücher der Weisung* [Pentateuch] (1954), *Die Bücher der Geschichte* [The historical books] (1955), *Bücher der Kündung* [Prophets] (1958); early in 1961 the translation was completed, and the fourth volume *Die Schriftwerke* [Hagiographa] appeared in 1962.

It was a fortunate coincidence that had brought these two ideally mated translators together and made their monumental work possible. The Bible formed the basis of their philosophy of language, as developed by Buber in *I and Thou* and by Rosenzweig, who was eight years younger, in *Star of Redemption* which was completed at the beginning of 1919. The "germ-cell" [7] of this universal symbolism in which the two triangles (God, man, world; creation, revelation, redemption) are combined into a six-pointed "star" is not only relational thinking—the three "substances," God, man, world, of which the book treats, can be comprehended only in relation to creation, revelation, redemption—but is primarily speech thinking. Language is for Rosenzweig the peculiarity of faith; it is not the work of man and is not based on rationality; it appears at the very beginning of human existence and points to a goal of perfected human communication in the future.[8]

Thinking, unlike speaking, does not take place in time. The spoken word, in contradistinction to the word that is thought, presupposes a partner. Only through his fellowman, through the spoken "Thou," does man become conscious of his "I": Rosenzweig's speech-thinking is also dialogic. He rediscovered "the fundamental identity of Revelation and Speech." [9] He shows in his book that until the beginning of the nineteenth century the I and Thou in speech between man and man was generally considered to be also the I and Thou between God and man; in language the difference between immanence and transcendence vanished.[10] Rosenzwieg's basis is a theological one, but this theology needs to be supplemented by philosophy. Its starting point is Revelation, although it knows no dogmas but only objects of thought. Buber called the "Star of Redemption" a "piece of good fortune" in the relations between philosophy and theology,[11] and Rosenzweig explains the relation of the two spheres as follows: "The theological problems want to be translated into the human sphere, and the human problems want to be driven forward into the theological." [12]

Translation is "applied thinking-in-language," a mutual revelation of languages. In accordance with the theological origin of language, Rosenzweig starts from a principle of unity, inherent in all languages, which permits us to see their diversity and differences as part of one Whole. "There is but One language," he declares in the epilogue to his German translation of the poetry of Yehuda Halevi, "Sechszig Hymnen und Gedichte des Jehuda Halevi" [Sixty hymns and poems of Jehuda Halevi] (1922–1923). The peculiarities of one language are to be found in every other language, at least in a rudimentary and germinal state: "On this essential unity of all language and on the imperative of universal human communication that flows from it is based the possibility of such a task as that of translation, its Can, May and Should." [13] The free rendering of a text has in our day become the criterion of translating, whereby we attempt to impose our language on that of the text—to irrigate foreign pastures, as it were, with the stream of our native tongue. This, however, misconceives the proper task of translation which is to enrich our own tongue with foreign treasures, as Luther enriched the speech of his day with biblical German.

It is always a momentous hour in the history of a people when it appropriates the Bible and makes it its own, Rosenzweig writes in his study *Die Schrift und Luther* [The Bible and Luther]. For the monumental German translation of the Bible this is especially true, for through it German became a literary language, and for the Protestants it became what institutions were to the Catholic Church, the bearer of its visibleness.[14] Rosenzweig insisted that a new German translation of the Bible was needed because of the new attitude to faith brought about by scientific biblical criticism. The "holiness" of the Bible is no longer taken for granted; it must communicate its truths to us in a new way.

The man of today does not approach the Bible with the strong assurance of traditional faith, but rather with an indeterminate readiness for belief *and* unbelief at the same time. The Bible must find a new persuasive language if it is to convince modern man of its holiness, and for this it is necessary that the Hebrew original should appear in a new translation.

Buber affirmed [15] that the versions of the Bible extant today have transformed it into a palimpsest. The original meaning of the word has been "overlaid by a veneer of conceptuality, of partly theological and partly literary origin" which has distorted its true sound to a point of non-recognition. This is true not only of the German translations but also of the original Hebrew. The modern reader of the Bible no longer hears the pure spirit that became Voice in it, but "a compromise of the intellectual notions of two millennia." The Hebrew Bible is read today as if it were a translation, a poor translation in blurred, conceptual language. The various translations have until now failed to render the full meaning embedded in the original Hebrew vocabulary, sentence structure, and rhythmic articulation. Even the great translators of the Bible were primarily concerned with giving Christian worshipers a reliable version by rendering the original "content" into another language. But this "content" cannot be divorced from its "linguistic bodily form." Although the Word of God is valid for all ages and all places, we must not fail to consider the original soil in which it grew: "Complete revelation is always human body and human voice, and always means this body and this voice in the mystery of its uniqueness." [16]

The Bible, in contradistinction to all other holy books, contains the history of a people; the events that occur are nothing more than "the revealed mystery of the folk-history itself." [17] Buber and Rosenzweig read the Bible as an organic unit; this was clear to them from the coherent language of the message that pervades it, particularly in the prophetic books. But other parts of the Bible are also inspired by a message. "Apparently purposeless series of names in the early genealogies, because of the manner of their selection and arrangement, turn out to be precursors of the message. We read stories, such as that of Gideon's son Abimelech, which seem to belong entirely to secular history until we detect the hidden intent to strengthen the message, in this case that of 'naive theocracy.' In the midst of the most tedious legalistic prescriptions, some touching pathos is suddenly communicated to us. We read Psalms that seem to us nothing more than the anguished cry to God of one in distress, only to discover on listening more closely that it is not a common call for help but the lament of one who stands under Revelation. We read Wisdom literature and through its skepticism shine forth luminous bits of the message. No matter what the previous nature of any part of the Bible was, once it became part of the Bible it became message: in every member of its body the Bible is Message." [18] This message is at the same time both revelation and command, all spheres of nature and history are pervaded with the task of sanctifying life. The message is not conveyed in the sense that a "moral" is attached to the biblical stories, but it is part of the composition without depriving the story of its epic unity, and it contains "its own earmark and point." Rosenzweig expresses it in his essay "Das Formgeheimnis der biblischen Erzählungen" [The secret of form in the biblical narratives], when he speaks of a "subterranean didactic" that prevails in this sphere.[19]

To learn the language of this message one must go back to the "fundamental oral nature" of the Bible, to the sphere of "sacred spokenness" in which it was recited and listened to. To attain this spoken effect in German, Buber articulated the text according to "breathing-units" or "colons," in lines arranged to accord with the expressed meaning which supersedes articulation by punctuation. An example of two complete sentences being spoken in one breath would be Cain's breathless:

Ich weiss nicht. Bin ich meines Bruders Hüter? (Gen. 4.9)

(I know not; am I my brother's keeper?)

On the other hand, "breathing-units" can also reflect the measured epic solemnity of an account:

Am Tag, da ER, Gott, Erde und Himmel machte,
noch war aller Busch des Feldes nicht auf der Erde,
noch war alles Kraut des Feldes nicht aufgeschossen,
denn nicht hatte regnen lassen ER, Gott, über die Erde,

und Mensch, Adam, war keiner, den Acker, Adama zu bedienen:
aus der Erde stieg da ein Dunst und netzte all das Antlitz des
  Ackers
und ER, Gott, bildete den Menschen, Staub vom Acker,
er blies in seine Nasenlöcher Hauch des Lebens,
und er Mensch wurde zum lebendigen Wesen. (Gen. 2:4–7)

(In the day that the Lord God made the earth and the heavens;
and every plant of the field before it was in the earth, and every
herb of the field before it grew: for the Lord God had not caused
it to rain upon the earth, and there was not a man to till the
ground. But there went up a mist from the earth, and watered the
whole face of the ground. And the Lord God formed man of the
dust of the ground, and breathed into his nostrils the breath of life;
and man became a living soul.)

Buber also pointed out that in a discourse containing commands and
prescriptions the rhythmic articulation is often interrupted when an instruction is meant to indicate the divine purport of the preceding prescriptions. Thus, after detailed instructions concerning a sacrifice we
find in Num. 15:14–16:

Und wenn bei euch ein Gastsasse gastet
Oder wer in eurer Mitte sei, für eure Geschlechter,
und beteitet Feuerspende, Ruch des Geruhens IHM,
wie ihrs bereitet, so soll ers bereiten.
Versammlung!
Einerlei Satzung sei für euch und für den Gastsassen, der gastet,
Weltzeit-Satzung für eure Geschlechter:
gleich ihr, gleich sei der Gastsasse vor IHM,
einerlei Weisung und einerlei Recht
sei für euch und für den Gastsassen, der bei euch gastet.

(And if a stranger sojourn with you or whosoever may be among
you, throughout your generations, and will offer an offering made
by fire, of a sweet savour unto the Lord: as ye do, so he shall do.
As for the congregation, there shall be one statute both for you,
and for the stranger that sojourneth with you, a statute for ever
throughout your generations; as ye are, so shall the stranger be for
the Lord. One law and one ordinance shall be for you, and for the
stranger that sojourneth with you.)

Here, as Buber explained, the statute proclaiming equal rights to the stranger living in the land is emphasized by the exclamation *Versammlung!* "Congregation," which appears in no other place.[20] Luther renders the passage as follows:

> 14. und ob ein Fremdling bei euch wohnet oder unter euch bei euren Nachkommen ist, und will dem Herrn ein Opfer zum süssen Geruch tun, der soll tun, wie ihr tut.
> 15. Der ganzen Gemeinde sei *eine* Satzung, euch sowohl als den Fremdlingen; eine ewige Satzung soll das sein euren Nachkommen, dass vor dem Herrn der Fremdling sei wie ihr.
> 16. *Ein* Gesetz, *ein* Recht soll euch und dem Fremdling sein, der bei euch wohnet.

Another principle of composition that must be kept in mind, and one that was much more effective in recitation than in the written text, is the recurrence of basic words within the same section or in a later passage. The repetition of the same or similar sounds, the recurrence of words or phrases with the same or similar roots within a section or a book or a series of books, have "a quiet but overwhelming impact on the reader who is willing to listen." [21] The meaningful repetition of a word or root creates an atmosphere which Buber designated as "latent theology." The problem in translating is to direct the attention of the German reader to the repetition of a word or root by using similar words and not synonyms. Buber made it a rule to render a Hebrew root by a single German root and to find a related root wherever possible, although this may entail the use of quaint or unfamiliar expressions. This stylistic principle was consciously employed by Luther in those passages which he regarded as theologically significant, for example, the verse in Psalms (68:18): Du bist in die Höhe gefahren und hast das Gefängnis gefangen, "Thou hast ascended on high, thou hast led captivity captive," that is, you have not only freed the prisoners who are at present held captive therein, but also made it impossible for the prison to "capture" others, that is, Jesus achieved redemption.

This "subterranean didactic" is clearly evident in the story of Jacob, whose guilt over against his brother is designated by his father as *Trug*, "guile" (Gen. 27:35). Later, however, it is he who must ask

Laban: "Warum hast du mich betrogen?" "Wherefore then hast thou beguiled me?" (Gen. 29:25). His sin had to do with the firstborn, and his punishment consisted in his receiving the firstborn as wife. Similarly, in the expiation of his guilt the central words are *bless–blessing*. Jacob wrestles with the unknown angel until the latter "blesses" him; and his atonement offering to his brother is designated as "blessing," a word that would ordinarily not be used in this context. Jacob names the place of his nocturnal struggle Peniel (God's Face, *Gottes-Antlitz*), for:

> Ich habe Gott gesehn
> Antlitz zu Antlitz,
> und meine Seele ist errettet. (Gen. 32:30)

(I have seen God face to face, and my life is preserved.)

And after his reconciliation he says to his brother:

> Denn ich habe nun doch einmal dein Antlitz angesehn, wie man
> Gottheitsantlitz ansieht, und du warst mir gnädig,
> so nimm denn meine Segensgabe, die dir gebracht wurde! (33:10)

(For therefore I have seen thy face, as though I had seen the face of God, and thou wast pleased with me. Take, I pray thee, my blessing that is brought to thee.)

The connection between reconciliation in the divine sphere and in the human sphere is thus made prominent by the choice of words.[22]

The manner of rendering JHWH distinguishes Buber's translation from all others. This problem is discussed by Franz Rosenzweig in his essay "Der Ewige" [The eternal],[23] a title that represents Moses Mendelssohn's solution and that was thereafter adopted by most of the German translators. Another solution would have been to adopt the old substitute pronunciation for JHWH—*adonai, Herr,* "Lord"—but Christianity had already claimed this title for Jesus, and so it was abandoned. The rendering Yahwe, adopted by the Christian scholars of the Old Testament, was regarded by both translators as "the degradation of God's name to that of an idol," which dispelled the peculiar mystery of Revelation. Here was one of the points where a new language had to be found to express the holiness of the Bible, so that the modern reader could sense something of the awe and the fear of God that was felt in ancient times.

Mendelssohn correctly recognized that the rendering of the Name must be bound to the revelation of the Name. His translation is based on his interpretation of Exod. 3:14, which is as follows: God spoke to Moshe: I am the Being that is eternal. He spoke to him thus, Thou shalt speak to the children of Israel: "The Eternal Being who calls himself I am eternal has sent me to you." [24] The Buber-Rosenzweig translation of this verse is:

> Gott sprach zu Mosche:
> Ich werde dasein, als der ich dasein werde.
> Und sprach:
> So sollst du zu den Söhnen Jissraels sprechen:
> ICH BIN DA schickt mich zu euch.

(And God said unto Moses: I AM THAT I AM; and he said: Thus shalt thou say unto the children of Israel: I AM hath sent me unto you.)

The question does not concern God's "eternity" but rather God's "presentness, His being-present for you and with you, now and in the future." He who is Present at all times is also "The Eternal." The "ICH BIN DA" of the last verse, where the Name becomes transparent, gave Rosenzweig the idea of rendering it in the three forms of the personal pronoun written in capital letters: God speaks as ICH, is addressed as DU, and referred to as ER. Despite his departure from Mendelssohn's solution, Rosenzweig is of the opinion that his recognition of the need to bind the Name to the moment of Revelation was of crucial significance: "Nothing less than the unity of the Bible depends on making this connection visible, its unity as the coherent expression and emanation of the revelation of the one God." [25] It is characteristic of Jewish belief in general to regard the Godhead as One and Eternal and at the same time as the ever-present God of Abraham who is closer to us than breathing.

In conclusion we present an example where specific effects are attained by the deliberate use of the various stylistic devices referred to—rhythmic stress, the repetition of words, accentuation by means of a series of parallel sentences, and, finally, by the use of God's name:

> Darum
> will ich so dir tun, Jissrael!
> Deswegen,
> dass ich dir dieses tun will,
> bereite dich,
> deinem Gott gegenüberzustehn,
> Jissrael!
> —Ja denn, wohlan,
> der die Berge bildet,
> der den Geistbraus schafft,
> der dem Menschen ansagt,
> was sein Sinnen ist,
> macht nun aus Morgenrot Trübnis
> und tritt einher auf den Kuppen der Erde,
> sein Name:
> ER IST DA, der Umscharte Gott. (Amos 4:12f)

(Therefore thus will I do unto thee, O Israel; Because I will do this unto thee, Prepare to meet thy God, O Israel. For lo, He that formeth the mountains, and createth the wind, And declareth unto man what is his thought, That maketh the morning darkness, And treadeth upon the high places of the earth; the Lord, the God of hosts, is His name.)

The completion of the translation in February 1961 was celebrated in Buber's home when G. Scholem reviewed Buber's contribution to biblical studies over a period of more than three decades,[26] throughout which Buber was the severest critic of his own work, "as artist, master of language and *homo religiosus*." His painstaking accuracy and fidelity to the text often clarify obscure passages. But he never attempted to conceal or to pass over difficulties, and thus compels the reader to earnest reflection. He had a keen eye for the peculiarities of the Hebrew language—its oriental imagery, hidden allusions, and architectonic structure—and he tried to bring the reader closer to this alien idiom without supplying chevilles and transitional words. His whole purpose was to lead the reader to the spoken word, and this is especially evident in his revised version where the language is more fluent without forfeiting its accuracy and where, as Scholem puts it, "urbanity supersedes the traces of fanaticism to be found in the first edition." Others, however, have found strong indications of expressionism in the translation.[27] The language that Buber intended was one of "sanctifying spokenness" lifted out of daily life, a characteristic that led Scholem to ascribe to the translation a "utopian element." The language of Buber's Bible translation is not that of his age, for it drew on "present continuance and potential possession." [28] He revived the disappearing treasures of an ancient tongue and its hidden possibilities. To say that this work will have a lasting effect seems to Scholem questionable because of the unforeseen historical developments: German Jewry, for whom the translation was primarily intended, no longer exists; and the German spoken language has changed considerably since the twenties.

It is clear that Buber was primarily interested in leading German Jews back to the original Hebrew text by way of his translation. But he also knew that with the Bible we are dealing with an "original truth" common to both Judaism and Christianity, and that its disclosure was of great significance for the future of mankind. In his answer to Scholem he referred to a letter by Franz Rosenzweig in which he foresaw a time approaching when men would turn away from the Old Testament, not the period of Hitlerism but an era of "Neo-Marcionism"; nevertheless he retained the firm belief that the translation would make its influence felt, if not in his own time then in a later age.[29]

Buber ardently hoped that a cheap popular edition of the translation might be published during his lifetime. He was fully aware of the sincere efforts made recently by both Catholics and Protestants to form a new image of Judaism and to arrive at a juster appreciation of the Jewish element in Christian belief. This genuine desire for a better understanding of Judaism has created a new reading public for the translation that could not be counted on in the twenties. German theologians in greater numbers will today feel obliged to consult his interpretations. Nor must we underestimate the influence of the *Frei-*

burger Rundbriefe addressed to all Catholic teachers of religion or the activities of the working groups of "Jews and Christians" in the Protestant synods. A popular edition of the translation would be welcomed today by many German readers who would profit immensely from Buber's interpretation and from his struggles to keep alive the spirit of Hebrew in a foreign tongue. In the twenties Buber's translation created great interest and was widely discussed, for it was a period of literary experimentation. But aesthetic considerations were of secondary importance compared to the need for adopting new attitudes such as we now see among theologians and laymen in the Christian church.

"Do we mean a book? We mean the Voice," we read in Buber's essay "The Man of Today and the Jewish Bible." [30] The rediscovery of the spoken word refers not only to our reading of the Bible but above all to our ability to listen. Today a return to the Bible that fails to consider the prevailing mood of skepticism is no longer possible, but we can still hope for the biblical "re-turning" to the Voice that pervades the Bible as message and revelation. The readiness to listen can become meeting, a being-touched by the wholly Other which imparts to us knowledge whose origin we cannot explain. There may be moments when revelation becomes "presentness" and shows us, today as always, the way that leads from Creation to Redemption, to the realization that "God every day renews the work of the Beginning but also daily anticipates the work of the end" [31]—that the man of today could also experience merciful rebirth and deliverance. For this is indeed his plight, that he knows no beginning and that history without meaning "sweeps him on into a posthistorical cosmic age." [31a]

Buber would lead his reader along the road where he meets the "Voice" and thenceforth recognizes his life and the life of the world as a sign language to which he must respond with the daily acts of his life. For one who was born after the Age of Enlightenment, this presupposes a "turning" or change of heart, such as Hamann experienced when he discovered that all the miracles of the Bible take place in our soul: "Make this desolate earth a fruitful land," he wrote after his conversion in London,[32] "a garden of your hand, through the spirit of your mouth, through your Word." In estimating Buber's influence it should be noted that the deep-rooted affinity between religion and language that he had developed became more elaborate as a result of his confrontation with Jacob Boehme and especially with Hamann,[33] that is, with a Christian tradition primarily derived from Luther. In his discourse on the Psalms in 1513 and 1514, Luther had already looked upon creation as God's "language" and placed it together with Revelation in the medium of human speech.[34] In contrast to the works of creation the form of God's speech is veiled, expressing itself in the Old Testament through the mouth of the prophets, then in the incarnation of the Son, and subsequently by means of a pneumatically determined exegesis of the biblical Word through the medium of the sermon.

For Luther language was also a divinely instituted phenomenon wherein human speech and divine spirit combine into a unity that cannot be sundered. The bearer and mediator of the Universal is not reason but the Word through which the spirit is grasped. Luther was still bound to the tradition of the four principles of hermeneutics according to which the Bible is interpreted—historical, tropological, allegorical, and anagogical—but he sometimes deviated from them to go back to the natural sense of a word and from it press forward to its proper spiritual sense which can be grasped only by him who opens himself up completely to the divine Word.

In the twenties Buber's translation was felt to be somewhat strange and its contrast to Luther's Bible more evident than it is today. The ardor of the prophet's spoken word follows in the tradition of Luther. Indeed, a close examination of the two translations reveals a number of related features that can be traced to a common basic conception of the nature of language, namely, that all men live and move in the speech and in the address of the one divine Spirit whose reproductive execution is consummated in the act of speaking, that the revelation of the Holy Scriptures resides in the Word of God and the word of man as one. In the Christian tradition the Word that has become flesh is an indispensable element in its philosophy of language which, of course, we do not expect to find in Buber's reflections on language. His mind was nevertheless directed to the living Word which is for him both teaching and life in one, the ideal mediator between sense and spirit, the bright focal point where heaven and earth meet. This inner affinity between the two monumental translations of the Bible must today appear providential in the light of the closer understanding between Jews and Christians.

BIBLICAL HUMANISM

Buber's writings on Old Testament themes were the products of his activity as a translator. His original plan was to write a theological commentary under the title *Der biblische Glaube* [Biblical faith], which would treat the problems of the Jewish Bible in the exact order of succession in which they appear in the text. But he was soon compelled to recognize that this project surpassed his strength and that he would have to confine himself to formulating those questions he deemed most important. He therefore contemplated a work in three volumes: *Das Kommende. Untersuchungen zur Entstehungsgeschichte des messianischen Glaubens* [The coming one. Investigations with reference to the genetic history of the messianic faith], of which the first volume *Königtum Gottes* [Kingship of God] appeared in 1932. The purpose of the work is to demonstrate that the idea of a folk kingdom of God in Israel's early history was a historical recollection. The discussion starts with the book of Judges and refers to historical texts from the Pentateuch and Joshua. The second volume, *Der Gesalbte* [The anointed], which is based on the books of Samuel, seeks to explain "how the conception of a human governor of God intersects and transforms that primitive-theocratic tendency—both common to the ancient Orient and both, nevertheless, occurring here in a configuration of a peculiarly new nature." [35] The kingship of man is conceived religiously and hallowed in the sacrament of the anointment. The third volume was to treat the eschatologization of both conceptions. The messianic belief, according to its central theme, was directed to the fulfillment of the relation between God and world in a consummated kingly rule of God. This belief, which was at first historical hope, then became eschatologized through a growing historical disillusion, and seized upon the future as the unconditioned turning point of history. Another theme in this volume was the relation between folk kingship and world kingship of Yahwe; finally, the third and last theme would deal with the changes in form of the messianic person up to the Deutero-Isaiah mystery.

The second volume was about half finished and printed at the end of 1938 when Schocken Press, which was publishing the work, was dissolved by the Gestapo. Buber discontinued the work, and *Der Gesalbte* was later included as a fragment in the volume of his writings on the Bible.[36] He was compelled to suspend his work at that time because of his appointment in the spring of 1938 as professor of social philosophy at the Hebrew University in Jerusalem. He had, moreover, been requested at the same time to write the religious history of Israel for the Dutch series *The Religions of the World*. His contribution, which he called *Der Glaube Israels* [The faith of Israel], was confined to the prophetic faith from its earliest period up to the end of the Babylonian exile. It appeared in book form in Hebrew in 1942, in German in 1950, and in English in 1949 under the title *The Prophetic Faith*. The monograph *Moses* (Hebrew, 1945; German, 1952; English, 1946) was prompted by a remark of Eduard Meyer, the well-known historian, who had declared that Moses was not a historical personality and that no one has ever been able to present him as a concrete historical figure or to produce anything that he had actually accomplished or that might be regarded as his historical achievement. In approaching this task Buber founded his views on what he regarded as "the obvious basis of unprejudiced critical investigation, dependent neither on the religious tradition nor on the theories of scholarly turns of thought." [37] Briefer studies on Old Testament themes that should be mentioned are: "Abraham the Seer" [37a] (Hebrew, 1939; German, in *Sehertum*, 1955), "Prophecy, Apocalyptic, and the Historical Hour" [37b] (German, in *Sehertum*, 1954), and "Images of Good and Evil" (1952). A religio-historical critique of Buber's writings lies beyond the scope of this work; we shall, however, set forth some of his basic conceptions which can be understood only in connection with his total work.

Buber's works do not pertain to the Old Testament but to the Jewish Bible as seen from within, a view that differs considerably from that of the Christian biblical scholars, for whom ancient Israel and Judaism of the post-Christian Diaspora constitute two completely distinct realities. Israel is for them a vanished world to be studied in conjunction with ancient oriental cultures; it is significant from the theological point of view because it gave rise to the Church of Christ, to the "new Israel." The scientific study of the Old Testament is a child of Western humanism: "The Greek-Germanic view of the Christian Occident misunderstood the Jewish roots of the Old Testament, so that Old Testament theology—even where it was consciously 'theologically' oriented—was driven to adopt a conceptual system which violated the Old Testament." [38] Even when such outstanding contemporary Jewish thinkers as Buber, Rosenzweig, and Leo Baeck had presented their interpretations to the Christian world, there was no fruitful dialogue concerning the problems that the two religions had in common: "An entire dimension of Old Testament theology remained neglected." [38a] In his "Gespräch mit Martin Buber" [Conversation with Martin Buber],[39] the author of the above quotation, Hans Joachim Kraus, demonstrates how the confrontation with the inner view of the Old Testament deepens the Christian standpoint. Similarly, the Catholic theologian, Hans Urs von Balthasar, declares that Buber's voice reminded the Christians at the appropriate moment of the deep existential participation of the Jew in the substance of Revelation: "Not merely isolated individuals, but the anonymous mass of praying and suffering Israelites have, in their hearts, created those words which remain the word of God to the Christians, the 'People's Prayer' of the New Covenant, daily singing their psalms. In prayer the Christian soul feels what the Jewish soul has felt." [40]

In his Bible studies Buber was not concerned with the history of religion but with the history of faith. Religious teachings, symbols, and practices as such are not his subject, but, instead, the place that theological, symbolical, and institutional elements occupy in the total life of Israel, in its social, political, and spiritual existence.[41] As in *Addresses on Judaism*, he was again primarily concerned with the lived reality of religion, with what he called the "body" of a religious movement,[41a] understanding the history of faith as the extension and more precise formulation of the being-tradition.

Buber came to the Bible by way of Zionism, from which he learned that a regeneration of the people is possible only by returning to the sources of Judaism. This conception of the renewal of the human content of Judaism took Buber back to the glorious period of Jewish history as recorded in the Bible, a heroic period that is still vital for Jews of today and which reaches them in an uninterrupted stream through the community of blood and the propagation of values. Judaism may at times have been vitiated and debased by assimilation, but it has never been deprived of access to the Bible and to the normative primal forces of the Jewish spirit. The hard core of Judaism had never yielded to Christianity and surrendered its claim to be "the true ecclesia, the ever-faithful community of divine immediacy." [42] The return to biblical sources was intended to renew the bond between the people and the community of faith. In the seclusion of the ghetto this union of the national and religious community had been taken for granted, and the consciousness of being the chosen people was kept alive despite adversity and persecution. Around the turn of the century the Jews of the West had not only lost their national cohesion but also to a large extent the faith of their fathers which had become feeble and timid, and it was imperative that the individual Jew should restore the unity of both and reassert their influence in his personal life.

That this situation applied not only to Zionists is evident in the case of Franz Rosenzweig, who at one time had contemplated conversion to Christianity and had rejected Zionist nationalism as *Judenvolks-Theologie,* and yet was deeply convinced that the Jews constituted a people, the "eternal people," as he later called them in his "Star of Redemption." In a lecture in 1919 [43] he explained how the Jews through their Election were lifted out of time, so that their history knows no epochs as other nations, but extends from exile to exile. It began with Abraham who was sent forth to seek a land that was promised him but which was to remain God's possession even after he had taken it. During the flight from Egypt peoplehood was achieved through the covenant at Sinai. The Jewish state ended in exile. Even the destruction of the Temple did not represent a radical discontinuity as is generally assumed. Rosenzweig points to the unifying role of the Talmud which had become a bridge from which one could look back to the past and forward to the future. Even before the destruction of the Temple, we find foreign domination and a flourishing Diaspora, the synagogue and the Greek Bible. Spoken Aramaic had become the vernacular, distinct from the holy language of divine service; custom and law were set apart as holy and were no longer subject to the laws of growth and development. The Jews were never a people as other nations.

In an age characterized by the decline of traditional religious values, Buber and Rosenzweig have as individuals preserved the substance of Jewish faith and found for it a new personal language. Their existential appropriation of the Bible came from the realization that in it God, despite his transcendence, deigns to speak to man and impart to him a message that runs through all the books of Holy Scriptures. This dialogical situation is not confined to the relation between God and individual man. The whole history of the world, "the hidden, real world history" [44] was for Buber a dialogue betwen God and His creature: "God in all concreteness as speaker, the creation as speech: God's call into nothing and the answer of things through their coming into existence, the speech of creation enduring in the life of all creation, the life of each creature as dialogue, the world as word—to proclaim this Israel existed. It taught, it showed that the real God is the God who can be addressed because he is the God who addresses." [45] Creation, Revelation, Redemption—the great "triad of world time" [46]—are not confined to the earliest beginnings of mankind and to its end; the life of every person stands under its sign. Faith is not knowledge but the union with God that does not touch the mystery of being. Truth is the confirmation of one's being-true in the participation of the being of the world.

In the center of this personal conception of the Bible we find Revelation, which in its purest form is the divulgation of the divine Presence; there are indications in Buber's work that he experienced this as *mysterium tremendum* and *mysterium fascinosum*.[47] Every divine Revelation, however, is in his view speech-less and needs to be "translated" into human speech by the one who has received it. This view of Revelation determines our attitude to Jewish law and its observance, and in this matter the two friends were in complete disagreement. Rosenzweig felt bound to observe the ceremonial laws revealed by God, for once we submit to the yoke of His government we are in duty bound to do His will and cannot disencumber ourselves of His laws. Buber, however, draws a sharp distinction between Revelation and Law: "I do not believe that Revelation is ever Legislation; and in the fact that out of it legislation is always derived I see the fact of human contradiction, the fact of man." And in another place he writes: "Since I regard man alone and not God as Legislator, the Law for me is not universal but personal, namely, only that part of it which I must acknowledge as being spoken to myself." [48] The defenders of the Law challenge him on this point with the biblical verse: "Hear, O Israel, the statutes and judgments which I speak in your ears this day, that ye may learn them, and keep, and do them. The Lord our God made a covenant with us in Horeb. The Lord made not this covenant with our fathers, but with us, even us, who are all of us here alive this day" (Deut. 5:2–3). But Buber defended his position with the unconditionality of a man of religious convictions who in ecstasy and despair has heard the Voice. *Herut,* "freedom," alluding to an ancient interpretation, was in 1918 the theme of his last address on Judaism: "God's writing on the tablets constitutes freedom . . . God's original tablets are broken. The religious forces of eternal renewal persistently strive to restore the blurred outlines of divine freedom on the second tablets, the tablets of teaching and the law." [49]

Buber recognized also that we are being spoken to in the Decalogue: "The soul of the Decalogue, however, is to be found in the word 'Thou'. . . . Thanks to its 'thou,' the Decalogue means the preservation of the Divine Voice." [50] He acknowledged that the command, "Ye shall be holy, for I your God am holy" (Lev. 19:2), is addressed to him; but he would replace the prescriptions of the Law, which are meant to safeguard the sanctification of life from without, with the fulfillment of the Law from within through "sacramental existence," through a "pan-sacramentalism" to which Hasidism points the way. Sinai is not for him the mount of the Law but the mount of Revelation where God's royal proclamation was addressed to Israel. He is prepared to take upon himself "the kingship of God" and acknowledge His dominion over the undivided reality of lived life. This constituted for him the essence of the covenant entered into and sealed at Sinai. The work of *imitatio dei* through the sanctification of creation and of the human community is for him the real obligation that has bound the Jew throughout the centuries and is still valid today: "It is the community through whose ever purer perfection man is to consummate the *imitatio dei:* community as the work of unification . . . All sanctification means the union between essence and being, between being and being; the highest degree of world sanctification, however, is the unification of the human community in God's sight. This is the proper answer of creation to the Creator, and the only appropriate body of the spirit." [51] Speech is the organ that binds man to God, as it is the token of his having been created in the image of God. It is through this same medium of language that we address God and man. Buber's dialogical principle is also part of the *imitatio dei* and is a secular proclamation of the double biblical command to love God and to love man. The perfect human community is a "messianic category." To turn wholly to God—this is the contribution that every man can make to redemption, that "messianism that takes place at all times" which Buber placed beside the eschatological—and for which he has often been criticized.

Buber's personal understanding of the Bible is in its form and substance between a theological and philosophical conception, between historical knowledge and living presentness. It expresses the religious thinking of his Hebrew humanism which is oriented to biblical man and his relation to God. His scientific writings on Old Testament themes were the product of direct personal involvement. With all their learning they are so intimately connected with his character and personal philosophy that it is impossible to attribute them to any particular school of biblical interpretation. He was acquainted with the findings of contemporary research, but he approached the Bible as part of the living reality of the human spirit that could not be fully appropriated by the methods of impartial science: "Also my book here is not intended to express faith, but a knowledge about it; it asserts admittedly that one can possess a knowledge about faith legitimately only when the eye remains directed on the cosmic margin, never given as object, where faith is given a habitation." [52] He was earnestly concerned with traditional and textual problems, but his primary task was to help the reader appropriate the Bible existentially by bringing him closer to its "genuine spokenness." In his "Herut" address of 1918 he had insisted that the Bible be read with "knowledge as a service" and that it be made the subject of reverent and unbiased knowledge, at the same time setting forth the principles which later governed his own work of translation and research: "Whatever his [the scholar's] knowledge of old as well as new exegesis, he will search beyond it for the original meaning of each passage. No matter how familiar he is with modern biblical criticism's distinction between sources, he will penetrate beyond this criticism to more profound distinctions and connections. Though unafraid of bringing to light the mythical element, no matter how initially alien it may be to him, he will not advance a mythical interpretation where there exists an adequate historical one. He will read the Bible with an appreciation of its poetic form, but also with an intuitive grasp of the suprapoetic element which transcends all form." [53]

If Buber's work with all its erudition has found no acknowledgment in the standard religious-historical works of contemporary Christian and Jewish scholars such as Martin Noth or E. L. Ehrlich,[54] it is for the same reason that we have found in his dispute with G. Scholem concerning Hasidism.[55] The auxiliary method of "scientific intution"[56] which he recommended to scientific investigators presents religious historians with serious difficulties. His introduction of supra-scientific elements to fill in the gaps that remain after a conscientious examination of the material and his concrete language—likewise attesting to his comprehension of the subject from within—violate the method and style of today's highly technical biblical criticism. Just as his presentation of Hasidism broke through the prevailing concept of mysticism, so did his view of the early stage of the Israelite belief in God, the "kingship of God," present a unique phenomenon that cannot be subsumed under any category of religious history. In both instances it is clear that although Buber employed methods from the sphere of comparative religion, they are not properly religious-historical: "Against the background of the west and south Semitic early typology (showing through in the *malk*-concept) of a divine leader, of the way, and of existence, for clan, tribe and confederation, we are confronted here by a religio-historical uniqueness in the strictest sense: the ever and again realized but always intended relation of dialogical exclusiveness between the One who leads and those who are led." [57]

The dialogic sanctification of concrete life which Buber stressed in Hasidism is here traced to its origins. "The Bible has, in the form of a glorified remembrance, given vivid decisive expression to an ever-recurrent happening," [58] so that in the critical hours of our personal life, transcendence speaks to us out of events and incidents in the language of signs. The objection that Buber read his I-Thou primary word into the past is plain. But we must bear in mind that at a time when Jews no longer experienced the traditional God, the invisible yet ever-present God of their fathers, it was he who recognized the ancient dialogic character of Judaism as it appears in the "Thou" of the Decalogue, in the cry of the Psalms, and in the language of Job. Similarly, the Zionist movement, which had developed in the wake of secular nationalism, made Jews aware—even such non-Zionists as Franz Rosenzweig—of the indissoluble union of religion and peoplehood, the paradoxical unity of blood and election. The renewal of the Zion idea and of the Hebrew language in our century indicates that the mysterious revival of the true essence of Judaism is possible at all times and attests to the subterranean "bodily" continuity of the living tradition, which was Buber's primary concern. The return of a people to the land of their fathers that had been inhabited by another people for centuries, the revival of a "dead" language, the War of Independence of 1948 which was conducted in the spirit of the Maccabean Revolt two centuries before Christ—all contradict political and historical experience, and yet these are the indisputable facts of our time. The preservation of the people in the Babylonian exile and the rebuilding of the Temple in Jerusalem also belong to these unique historical events and were possible, according to Buber, only because of the restorative character of the theocratic idea in Persian times which permitted it to go back to an ancient tradition for support: "the shore of antiquity with which it connects is not a fiction sprung from the post-exilic hankering for foundation, but the remembered reality of early time, without perceiving which, one cannot perceive Israel." [59] Buber was chiefly interested in awakening an appreciation for this recurrent paradox which is particularly evident in the history of Judaism.

Buber felt that from the very beginning the faith of Judaism was distinguished from that of other peoples not by its greater spirituality but by the immediacy and concreteness of relation, by God's governance of all history. Fortified by this dialogic relation to God, the Jewish faith has survived centuries of persecution and the greatest catastrophes, faithful to its peculiar "collective memory" and its "passion of transmission." In his scientific investigations as well, Buber started from the continuity of the lived being-tradition in Judaism, recognizing the peculiar dynamic of Jewish existence in its will to realize an invisible presentness in its association with the Absolute which runs through its history from the "primitive theocracy" of the period of the Judges to the idea of the kingdom of God and to the social utopias of our own day.

In the Bible the connection between traditions can often be restored only by "scientific intuition" directed to the concreteness of a situation, insofar as this expresses a real relation to actuality. What Buber called the "uniqueness of the fact" means an actual, unique faith-relation that is expressed in concrete situations; for the early period of Israel's history, this method permits us to investigate its historical possibility only, not the factual course of events. If, however, we investigate the meaning and significance of the recurrent concept "uniqueness," we come upon, as H. J. Kraus has pointed out,[60] "an indissoluble union of the intuitive literary aspect with the election belief of Israel. Israel's election is the mystery of the 'uniqueness of the fact' which is the criterion for all traditions." This is the rock bottom on which Buber took his stand as a religious thinker.

Buber's Old Testament writings, however, can not be described as theological in the proper sense of the word. The same reason that once turned him away from mysticism also prevented him from being a theologian, namely, the conviction that finite man can make no adequate statement concerning God. Just as the ecstatic confessions could not comprehend the *unio mystica*, so also was the I-Thou relation between God and man fully effective only in the direct confrontation of speechless address and answer. A revelation that is expressed is a humanization of experience. But the possibility of actual confrontation is the primal *humanum* from which Buber started and which is expressed in the Bible for all time and beyond all demythologizing: God speaks to us "out of the burning bush of the present." [61] Biblical man stands in relation to God, and this relation is reciprocal.

The dialogical confrontation of God and man is the "narrow ridge" where Buber's philosophy and biblical studies meet and where his own experience merges with the traditional faith of the fathers. In *Dialogue* he expressed the thought that the God of I and Thou is "the God of a moment, a moment-God," but that the sum of all the signs through which we are addressed means more: "In such a way, out of the givers of the signs, the speakers of the words in lived life, out of the moment Gods there arises for us with a single identity the Lord of the voice, the One." [62]

It is no different with the biblical stories whose images express man's deep emotional experiences in the presence of God, presenting us in their totality with the dialogic confrontation of man and God in various concrete situations. With Israel's election and in the course of its historical vicissitudes, this fundamental human phenomenon became more prominent. Just as Buber once broke away from mystical teachings and turned to the great religious myths in which teaching appeared as a way through lived life, so he now understood the Bible primarily as the way of man in the sight of God. He regarded the election of Israel not as a "theological conception" but as a unique historical fact of how a people in the hour of their national unification also became a faith-community and the bearer of a revelation: "God wishes man whom he has created to become man in the truest sense of the word, and wishes this to happen not only in sporadic instances, as it happens among other nations, but in the life of an entire people, thus providing an order of life for a future mankind, for all the peoples combined into one people. Israel was chosen to become a true people, and that means God's people." [63] It would be difficult for the reader not to see a "theological conception" in such a statement in which the course of history is outlined as far as it is accessible to human cognition. The peculiar mixture of theology and thoughtful understanding, which is characteristic for Buber's conception of the Bible, is fully apparent. Since his basic form of man is man in relation to God, he did not strictly distinguish between philosophical humanism and theology which, in his exposition of biblical "faith-history," tend to pass into one another. Faith and science are not as rigidly separated as we often find among Christian scholars of the Old Testament, which is an additional obstacle in the path of mutual understanding.

Buber's lonely stand on the "narrow ridge" at the outposts of human knowledge, the mute crepuscular spot where the mind relinquishes the irritable pursuit of facts, is too perilous for many Christian theologians who cannot share his exhilarating experience. They are often vexed by his inhospitable juxtaposition of theology and secular philosophy, and chide him for converting God's historical deeds against His people into comprehensible universal truth,[64] or express the fear that in his philosophical writings "the principle of the dialogic could become a metaphysical idea that would attach itself to the free life and activity of God." [65] A consistent theological standpoint that ventures statements about God based on revelation would meet with greater acceptance among theologians than the attempt to introduce as part of our intellectual history his own faith experience with its deep conviction that man's life lived in the sight of God is the most primary human experience. Buber expressed this view in unmistakable words: "The theological element has indeed influenced a large part of my scholarship and reporting. It is the foundation of my thinking, but not as a derivative of anything traditional, as important as that also may be to me. It has, therefore, not been to 'theology,' but rather to the experience of faith that I owe the independence of my thought. I am not merely bound to philosophical language, I am bound to the philosophical method, indeed to a dialectic that has become unavoidable with the beginning of philosophical thinking. But I also know nothing of a 'double truth.' My philosophy serves, yes, it serves, but it does not serve a series of revealed propositions. It serves an experienced, a perceived attitude that it has been established to make communicable." [66]

For the Christian, the Old and New Testaments supplement one another as promise and fulfillment. God, who spoke to the fathers through the prophets, speaks at the end through his Son; the creative Word at the beginning of Genesis points to the "Word" in the prologue to the Gospel of John. Christian theologians recognized in the books of the Old Testament history set in motion by God's Word, the creative Word that continues to bring new promise and fulfillment until the coming of the Son of man. But they see these acts of God for His people, acts that come from the unfathomable depths of time, as "de-historicized" by Buber's philosophy (Hammerstein) and transformed into a timeless dialogic confrontation, and this they censure as an evasion of the ultimate historical consequences that flow from the Old Testament. Buber, however, regarded the confrontation of man and God as the basic phenomenon of biblical man that, to be sure, is subject to the vicissitudes of history but whose essential core remains the same throughout all changes.

Buber's humanism is Hebrew humanism which has a precise pedagogical ideal and a definite conception of man, to attain which present-day Judaism must be brought back to the humanity of the Bible. Buber was also aware that a return to the origins of Judaism was fraught with incalculable consequences for the future of mankind. His humanism, like every genuine humanism, is imbued with a strong faith in man's undamaged integrity and in his capacity to share God's wisdom, a venturesome claim that runs counter to the Christian conception of fallen man. To take upon oneself the yoke of the kingdom of God does not preclude this faith in man. Judaism knows no original sin, but only the certainty that God will keep faith with the handful of dust He chose to be his co-worker in the work of salvation and in the progressive deification of man.

This inner theological-humanistic view of Judaism constitutes one of the basic differences between Buber's understanding of the Bible and that of the Christian scholars of the Old Testament. Another characteristic difference stems from his long study of myth in the decade preceding World War I when he became acquainted with the early forms of historical transmission in primitive societies by means of song and legend. The third criterion that he often mentioned refers to the recurrent stylistic methods he discovered in his work of translation during which his experiences with the text as such led him to appreciate more highly than most scholars the art of composition in the Bible.

In the historical accounts of the Bible Buber discovered ideas that had been alive and active in folk history for many generations, ideas of such "original force" as that of messianic belief which had existed from time immemorial: "Out of the transmitted experience of divine *melekh-ship*, out of organic memory there develops for the cultic, and for the eschatological as well, the corporeality which hinders them from becoming apparatus and schema, and on the strength of which they exert influence down to our own day. If they had not attained this they, like the innumerable instances of the merely-religious in the history of ideas, would long ago have been buried in museums and libraries." [67] Buber acknowledged that in his investigations he took pains to understand the attitude of scientists and their reluctance to consider traditions whose origin and development are attested by no extant documentation and of which we know only the final literary product. He emphasized, however, as early as 1936, that the amazing methods of source criticism must be reexamined because they deal only with the results of a long process of tradition formation and never arrive at an examination of its developing stages. It is recognized today "that a judgment concerning age or youth of a literary stratum by no means involves one concerning age or youth of the corresponding stratum of religious development, because it still remains to be investigated, for example, whether an early genuine tradition has reached us in a late form or transformation; it is recognized that without the co-operation of an investigation of tradition—to be sure, still in the process of becoming—or rather investigation of the compilations of tradition and the forms of bias which determine them, the criticism of sources must miscalculate and lead astray." [68]

Overpowering historical events gave rise among primitive people to a passion for creating sagas. Ancient man met the great events which transformed the life of his community "with a fundamental stirring of all the elements in his being." [69] The saga is the original record that tells of the encounter of a people with events so awe-inspiring that it sees in them the work of a heavenly power, and fills man with a "primeval state of amazement" which sets all the creative forces of the soul to work: "The historical wonder is no mere interpretation; it is something actually seen." [69a] What is involved is actually a religious *viewing* of history: "The wonder is beheld by a wonder-expecting person and imagined by the wonder-gripped person in narrative language. It is not fantasy that is active here, but memory; but precisely that believing memory of individuals and generations of early times which, driven by extraordinary occurrence, builds for it in a manner free of arbitrariness the extraordinary context—a poetizing memory, certainly, but one which poetizes believingly." [70] Saga which is still close to events contains genuine historical substance. An "objective state of affairs" cannot of course be derived from it; secular history cannot be dissevered from the historical wonder. But the experience which has been transmitted to us as wonder, like the case of Israel, can itself be history, for we must bear in mind that the forces that formed the saga are in essence identical with those which reigned supreme in history: the power of a faith. [71]

What we know of Israel's ancient history cannot be divorced from this kind of transmission, and to attempt to derive a "profane history" from it is, in Buber's view, hopeless. The peculiar nature of Jewish myth had interested Buber as early as 1907 when he referred to it in his introduction to the *Legend of the Baal-Shem*. The Hasidic legend was for him the last form in which Jewish myth appeared. Even at that early date he took pains to distinguish the legend as the "myth of the I and Thou, of the caller and the called" from the "pure myth in which there is no distinction of being." In *Moses* he explains more clearly what is meant by this: "The central figures of the people are not, as in so many hero-tales, merged in or amalgamated with persons belonging to mere mythology; the data regarding their lives have not been interwoven with stories of the gods. Here all the glorification is dedicated solely to the God who brings about the events. The human being acting under God's orders is portrayed in all his untransfigured humanity." [72] The God of the "pure myth" begets the hero. The charisma of the ancient oriental kings is also based on the myth of the begetting or adoption by God. The God of the Bible "calls" those chosen by him.

Jewish myth, accordingly, bears a special relation to history. In "Myth in Judaism," Buber pointed out that "the Jew of antiquity cannot tell a story other than mythically; an event is to him worth telling when it is grasped in its divine significance: all story-telling books of the Bible have but one subject matter: the account of Yahwe's encounters with His people." [73] In contrast to the common concept in the history of religion, Jewish myth is nothing more than "the report by ardent enthusiasts of that which has befallen them"; in prehistorical reports it might be preferable to describe them as a "mythization of history" rather than a "historization of myth." [74]

In *Philosophical Interrogations* (1964) Buber was asked by Hugo Bergmann what he meant by "the ontic status of the mythical image," taking as his example the biblical story of Bileam's speaking ass and the cloud that guided the Israelites in the wilderness. Bergman offers four possible interpretations of the myth and asks Buber if he could identify himself with any one of them: 1. the naively pious attitude; 2. the transformation of myths into psychic realities, as found in Jung; 3. the rational explanation; 4. the view that the mythical world is a reality *sui generis,* experienced by some special sense organs which contemporary man no longer possesses or does not as yet possess.[75] Buber was unable to identify himself with any of these interpretations, for he believed that the story is based on some basic reality that can only be expressed in a mythical image. Thus, in the case of Bileam the trusted animal that refused to go further would indicate that nature refused to take part in his resistance against God: "The mythical image is no allegory; what is involved here is not something abstract that has been carried over into the sphere of sensory perception; it is bodily experience that has engendered the image"—an experience of bodily contact with the animal which sounded in his ears and which he perceived as "speech." In the second example of the shining cloud that precedes the Israelites and in which the tribes recognize their divine leader, Buber saw the cloud neither as a reality *sui generis* nor as an experience of a purely psychic reality. The belief in the divine leader and natural phenomenon must coincide, so that the Israelites can see what they see—and this coincidence remains an insoluble mystery.

The most instructive example is Buber's description of the coincidence of natural phenomenon and revelation when Moses ascends Sinai with Aaron and the seventy elders (Exod. 24:10): "And they saw the God of Israel; and there was under his feet as it were a paved work of a sapphire stone, and as it were the body of heaven in its clearness." Buber explained this as follows: "They have presumably wandered through clinging, hanging mist before dawn; and at the very moment they reach their goal, the swaying darkness tears asunder (as I myself happened to witness once) and dissolves except for one cloud already transparent with the hue of the still unrisen sun. The sapphire proximity of the heavens overwhelms the aged shepherds of the Delta who have never before tasted, who have never before been given the slightest idea of what is shown in the play of early light over the summit of the mountains. And this precisely is perceived by the representatives of the liberated tribes as that which lies under the feet of their enthroned *Melek*. And in seeing that which radiates from Him, they see Him. He has led them by His great might through the sea and through the wilderness. He has brought them "upon eagles' wings" to the mountain of His revelation. Here He has entered into the Blood Covenant, the King's Covenant, with them. He has invited them to eat here before Him; and now that they have reached unto Him, He allows them to see Him in the glory of His light, becoming manifest yet remaining invisible. [The retina of their eyes captures nothing more than ours are able to, but they see the Revealer]." [76]

In this description we detect again the characteristics of a believing humanism with which Buber approached the Bible. The naive rational understanding with which the historical wonder is explained is likely to astonish a man of the present century, despite the poetic beauty of the presentation. But genuine humanism, faith in man, also needs a touch of enlightened optimism such as we find in the German classical period, an innocent approach which reverently stops at the limits of that which cannot be reached by man's finite mind. In *For the Sake of Heaven* the holy Yehudi had already expressed the conviction that there was nothing unnatural about a miracle: "I am unwilling to believe that God confuses our poor understanding with artifices which contradict the course of nature. It seems to me rather that when we say 'nature,' we mean the aspect of creation of all that takes place; when we say 'miracle' we mean the aspect of revelation. On the one hand, we mean what is called God's creative hand; on the other hand, we mean His pointing finger. The happening, though seen under the two aspects, is the same . . . 'Miracle' means our receptivity to the eternal revelation. And as for 'nature,' since it is God's, who would presume to draw its boundaries!" [77] In this attitude to miracles and revelation we hear echoes of Lessing and Goethe.

Buber's believing humanism also rests on the universal harmony of creation-revelation-redemption to which all world events are attuned, a harmony which does not permit nature and revelation to contradict one another and which ordains ultimate congruity between nature and spirit in man: "We can only receive revelation, if when and so long as we are a whole." [78] In this wholeness reason must not be absent; it should rule within its domain, but it must also find its proper place in the wholeness of our substance. This is the spirit that also pervades Buber's description of the Revelation on Sinai.

To counterbalance the preponderance of *ratio* in our time Buber emphasized physical participation in receiving revelation as it appears in the myths of antiquity. He is naturally inclined to comprehend the spiritual from the standpoint of its incarnation: "Revelation is continual, and everything is fit to become a sign of revelation. What is disclosed to us in the revelation is not God's essence as it is independent of our existence, but his relationship to us and our relationship to him." [79] The meaning of man's encounter with God is sought by Buber not in conceptualized assertions but in lived situations, recollected as faith history, the traces of that melting fusion of human substance by divine fire, which is what revelation means to him: the way of Israel, which is the real teaching of the Bible, consists of reports of real situations.

Buber was also a humanist in his relation to language and to the philosophy of language. Language in its sensible spiritual double nature is the real mark of our humanity and unique creation; it is the receptacle of divine Revelation: "Humanism moves from the mystery of language to the mystery of the human person. The reality of language must become operative in a man's spirit. The truth of language must prove itself in a person's existence. That was the intent of humanistic education, so long as it was alive." [80] The creative powers of antiquity have been preserved and transmitted by means of language. The native vigor of Hebrew humanity has come down to us in the biblical word which can still move us to spiritual restoration. A strong element in Buber's humanism is his feeling for the mystery of the spoken word. His biblical studies began in the service of the biblical word as translation. All that he had written in *Die Schrift und ihre Verdeutschung* attests to the importance of this basically humanistic approach. Starting from the "body of the word" he acquired insights into the inner aspects of biblical language and style, whose nature and significance had not been sufficiently appreciated. His German translation of the Song of Deborah and its interpretation attest to this interest and have been widely acknowledged. But it is precisely in this respect that Hans Joachim Kraus, despite his admiration for Buber's intuitive gifts, detects an untheological element which he finds questionable: "The vibrating power of a sentence as experienced by the exegete determines its faith-historical relevance." [81] Kraus expresses this dangerous aesthetic element in the concept "congeniality," but perhaps it was more like the joy felt by German classicism in the folk songs of all nations—to which we must refer in comparison—a sense for the untainted word in its virgin womb, "engendered in the spirit" and not "made." [82]

The section in *Moses* which treats of the "natural" wonder on Sinai is not the only place in which Buber's Hebrew humanism is evident. In none of his other writings do we feel so vividly the biblical conception of man. Something of the "splendor of poetry" (Max Brod) seems to suffuse the work or perhaps it is the charismatic spell of the Bible induced by an austere discipline of long years of study. Buber demanded of Hebrew humanism "a seer's selection" which aspires to the classical Jewish conception of biblical man in his purest state.[83]

The figure of Moses has in recent years become the most controversial in the Old Testament and the subject of the most contradictory views. Until the beginning of the last century he was acknowledged and revered as the founder of the Israelite religion, and as such has suffered the fate of most such figures, namely, the traditions about him were subjected to historical philological criticism, and the historical reality of his very existence questioned. As a result of these scientific analyses various aspects of his personality and activity were stressed at different times and placed in the foreground—prophet, priest, legislator, magician, popular leader, etc.

"The most impressive book on the figure of Moses we owe to Martin Buber," writes Rudolf Smend in his *Das Mosebild von Heinrich Ewald bis Martin Noth* [The image of Moses from Heinrich Ewald to Martin Noth].[84] The section *(Verstehende Gesamtschau)* in which Buber's work is treated is introduced by some reflections of Karl Jaspers concerning the methodical possibilities for understanding "leading figures" (Socrates, Buddha, Confucius, Jesus). In all these instances of great men we meet with the same difficulty, namely, that the texts from which we derive our knowledge of them came into being only after their death and that they themselves tend to disappear behind a cloud of myth and legend. Modern methods of research have been successful in separating and sifting the various layers of overlapping traditions, but the secret of the greatness of these personalities eludes the researchers, for the known historical facts turn out to be negligible and inconsequential and altogether disproportionate to the world historical importance of the figure in question.

The reality of these great men can only be understood from the history of their activity and from the influence they exerted on their contemporaries and on posterity. The images they inspired are historical reality, having been formed by those who were directly affected—a factor not to be underestimated by modern historical criticism if it is to arrive at a total conception of the phenomenon under consideration.[85] That Buber's presentation of the subject should meet the requirements demanded by Jaspers, which are the product of a philosophic humanistic existentialism, is not surprising.

The strictly historical view, on the other hand, as represented today by Noth's *History of Israel*, despairs of arriving at a complete conception of Moses. Noth is also of the opinion that a history of Israel must remain a venturesome project since "the traditions at our disposal cast only sidelights on the totality of events and this can be comprehended only within the framework of a definite point of view." [86] The exposition of a historical event carries conviction only when it does justice to all the extant reports in an objective manner.

Israel as a historical reality, accordingly, exists for Noth only after the union of the twelve tribes into a sacred confederacy on Palestinian soil, as reported at the Assembly of Shechem (Josh. 24). This is the proper point to begin the exposition of the history of Israel, for all the accounts concerning the prehistorical period are only available to us in that great composite collection of traditions, the Pentateuch, which presupposes the historical reality *Israel*, and reports the prehistorical period in the form in which it had been retained by those tribes that were already settled on the soil of Palestine as the basis of their faith.[87]

In this welter of traditions certain individual themes are conspicuous: the promise of the land to the Patriarchs, the Exodus from Egypt, the wondrous rescue at the Red Sea, the Covenant at Sinai. In these last three sagas Moses emerges in the Pentateuch as the leading personality. Noth considers it beyond all doubt that Moses was originally not connected with all these traditions, although he cannot state with certainty which single tradition he was part of at the beginning. The historical role of Moses cannot be conclusively determined.

Smend justly points out that Buber was thoroughly familiar with all the scholarly research about Moses of the last two centuries. His work, nevertheless, stands as an "erratic block" among the historical critical presentations of our time,[88] for he endeavors to present the incommensurable, the "individuality" of Moses which cannot be subsumed under any category of religious science. There is no office to which Moses can be assigned or by which he is conditioned; he can only be defined by a unique historical situation: "What constitutes his idea and his task: the realization of the unity of religious and social life in the community of Israel, the substantiation of a ruling by God that shall not be culturally restricted but shall comprehend the entire existence of the nation, the theo-political principle; all this has penetrated to the deeps of his personality, it has raised his person above the compartmental system of typology, it has mingled the elements of his soul into the most rare unity." [89] The category of the "uniqueness of the fact" applies to Moses, although it is a category to be used only in special circumstances and with the utmost caution. Figures like Moses are not fabricated.[90] Similar thoughts have recently been expressed by Walter Eichrodt in his *Religionsgeschichte Israels* [Religious history of Israel] and by E. L. Ehrlich; both point out that "the older traditions of the Old Testament agree in their description of the unique religious and political significance of Moses, and there is no reason to regard as unhistorical the more important incidents of his life story as contained in the Old Testament." [91]

We also find that Buber, whose portrait of Moses retains the large outlines of the historical account in the Pentateuch, made a distinction between saga that is produced "near the historical occurrences" and saga that is "further away from the historical event," and in each case endeavored to come as close as possible to the "historical core" of a tradition. With intuitive humanistic insight he detects the tradition in its entirety—as an uninterrupted change of form within the great stream of continuity: "The Moses who had his being long ago is properly expanded by the one who has come into being in the course of long ages. . . . We must hold both in view without confusing them; we must comprehend the brightness of the foreground and gaze into the dark depth of history." [92] The continuity between the various layers of tradition develops because the same forces of faith which reigned supreme in the history of the people also formed the sagas. This faith was not subsequently imposed on the narratives transmitted from the early period of Israelite history. No matter how fact and legend may have been mixed, "the indwelling story of faith which inheres in them is authentic in all its main lines." [93]

In Buber's opinion Israel as a people first appeared in history with the Exodus from Egypt. He adhered to the historical reality of the Covenant at Sinai, and saw in the Diet of Shechem only its renewal. The God with whom Israel concluded the King's Covenant is the God of the fathers. In the narrative of the Patriarchs in the book of Genesis the later religio-political relation of the people to God is germinally foreshadowed in a family. The faith of Israel must be understood from the standpoint of a double God experience, from the experience of the community—"God leads us"—and from the experience of individuals who feel that God addresses them and speaks to the people through them. The Exodus account has always remained in the center of Israelite religious life because it presents in unsurpassable concreteness the historical warrant of this leadership. Even to Abraham, God showed himself as the God who "singles out and summons forth" and shows the way: Abraham is the first *nabi*, "announcer"; his life is "lived prophecy." The road that Israel had traveled from the Exodus to the Exile was also the development of its original "monotheism" in the sense that ever new realms of being were appropriated for the one God. The God who is experienced as the Partner of the I-Thou relation is again recognized. [94]

The sacral legal basis of this confrontation of man and God is the Decalogue, which Buber called Yahwe's royal proclamation. Its meaning will not be properly understood if it is looked upon as a kind of catechism, for it is not concerned with articles of faith or principles of moral conduct, but with legislation in the strict historical sense, with basic laws of communal life under God's rule.

From Buber's discussion we clearly see how the confrontation of man and God has its roots in the Decalogue. The "soul of the Decalogue" is to be found in its "Thou," and thanks to this "Thou" the Decalogue means the preservation of the Divine Voice. It is never the isolated individual who is addressed, however, but man in relation to God or to the community.

The first part of the Decalogue contains five prohibitions, all beginning with Thou shalt not, which refer to man's relation to God. The third part also contains five prohibitions designed to safeguard the basis of the community and which Buber summed up in one sentence: "Do not spoil the communal life of Israel at a point upon which you are placed." [95] These sections deal with the common life of the members of a community as it is lived in *space,* whereas in the middle section, which enjoins the sanctification of the Sabbath and the honoring of one's parents, the element of *time* enters into the constitutional basis of the people. Here the commandment to observe the Sabbath concerns the relation to God, and honoring one's parents concerns the life of the community: "Both of them together ensure the continuity of national time; the never-to-be-broken consecution of consecration, the never-to-be-broken consecution of tradition." [95a] Buber's primary *humanum,* man as "open" person in confrontation with God and his fellow man, is rooted in the innermost section of the Bible.

From this standpoint Buber was able to survey Jewish being-tradition as a whole, past and future. When he pointed out, at the end of the preface to his book, that our age more than any other is in need of Moses, he again had in mind "the realization of the union of religious and social life in the community of Israel," which was once the task of Moses and has again in 1944 become necessary in Palestine. But this third "message" that Buber addressed to the renascent people, going back to the lessons of ancient history for guidance, fell on deaf ears, and so did his *Israel and Palestine* and *Origin and Meaning of Hasidism.*

Buber was well aware that the journey back through history from the Covenant between God and people at Sinai to the period of the Patriarchs, which again recognized JHWE in the "God of the fathers," touches "the most important question in the history of Israel's faith." [96] But he is convinced that a content of tradition can be wrested from the problematical material that "will enable us to reconstruct hypothetically some traits of its origin." [97] In "Abraham the Seer" he followed the biblical account of Abraham and at the same time examined the details of composition, style, imagery, and vocabulary to lend support to the views he derived from his activity as translator: "the story-telling theology" of the Bible with which he tried to acquaint the reader in *Die Schrift und ihre Verdeutschung.* The book of Genesis especially demands "complete concentration" if one is not to miss the complicated relations it contains.

Traces of the three great elements of faith which Buber detected in the Song of Deborah, in Joshua's address at Shechem, and in the beginning of the Decalogue—"God's accompanying leadership, the people's 'loving' devotion, and the zealous demand for decision" [98]—he again discovered in the saga of the Patriarchs: the God who singled out Abraham and sent him forth is a God who leads and whose demands and tests require decision, and Abraham pledges himself to God in full trust and in complete dedication. Buber was of the opinion that the book of Genesis was compiled by the literary prophets in the final period of Solomon's reign; but that the whole work should have acquired such a homogeneous character points to a long tradition, to a common spiritual atmosphere of story telling which Buber calls "the proto-biblical, that is, the biblical atmosphere that existed before the Bible." [99] All who contributed something to the history of beginnings—the beginning of the world, the human race, Israel—were ultimately concerned with one thing: "to show the people how their God prepared the goal and road for them, even before they were yet a people." [100]

That the early experiences of tribal life, the wandering, and a multitude of people being led, go back to an old tradition is obvious. How can we account for the fact, however, that in Abraham's being singled out and taken from his natural surroundings we detect the later experience of the prophets, for Abraham appears as seer and *nabi* and his existence signifies "lived prophecy"? Here as well Buber believed there is a core of genuine prehistorical experience: "Regardless of when the *concept* of the prophet arose, the *existence* of prophets is as old as Israel itself. This sort of thing does not appear suddenly in the midst of a community's history, but is in its original, spontaneous form as old as that history itself. And without the archaic experience of being singled out, being taken out—that is, without the certainty of a man of primitive times that what he is doing springs not of his own will but from the will of God—the faith of Israel would not exist." [101] Buber's exposition sheds light on his Hebrew humanism.

Buber took great pains to determine the place that Abraham occupies in the context of the biblical historical narratives and in the structure of the history of beginnings—beginning of the world, beginning of the human race, beginning of Israel. The cosmogony is related for the sake of the ethnogony, for the sake of the origin of a people. The meaning of this people's history is to be traced back to the meaning of the world's origin. [102]

The book of Genesis begins with two accounts of creation which complement one another: in the one, man stands at the outskirts of nature; in the other, he is at the center of the world. The sin against God led to the expulsion from Paradise; the sin of men against one another, which begins with fratricide, ends with the Deluge. From the remnant preserved from the Deluge the second generation of men is established on earth and again, as at first, receives God's blessing, the blessing of fecundity and growth, but it is now made contingent on the commandment not to commit acts of violence. The first generation of men failed because of division and strife, the second by sinning against God. The Tower of Babel does not lead to destruction but to dispersion: mankind is divided into different tongues.

The third beginning is marked by Abraham's appearance. He is chosen to be the father of a people in whose history command and promise are implicit from the very outset, obliging them to seek the right way that they may be the beginning of a future family of nations united as one common humanity. Abraham's personal vocation anticipates the election of Israel. How his life means "lived prophecy" that points to the past and the future, how the seven revelations experienced by him represent an elaborate account of ordeal and blessing, are convincingly explained by Buber on the basis of numerous stylistic considerations. Abraham, whom God made "the nomad of faith," enters history with the blessing of promise. The Bible associates him with three things: the origin of the people, the task of Israel in establishing one humanity from all nations, and the birth of prophecy: "Three traditions seem to be merged in the story of Abraham: the tradition, preserved among the people, of a family of ancestors; the tradition, preserved by the Torah, about a divine revelation at the beginning concerning the road for the future; and the tradition, preserved by the prophets, about the historic origin of the prophetic gift." [103]

Command and promise to Abraham anticipated the task that God gave to Israel to become a blessing for mankind. The Election meant responsibility. A people was to become God's people and the true community of mankind, an example to the other nations of living together in justice and love. This can only come about when all nations bind themselves together in the divine center of a single humanity.[104] On the other hand, only a community can help man to realize fully his potentialities as a creature made in God's image.

World history as the dialogue of God with man can only mean the fulfillment of the meaning of creation as the "answer" of entire humanity. Again and again man fails to live up to his task. The leading figures of the Bible embody projections or blueprints of man's answer, feeble and halting efforts of responsibility that arise from the situation in which they make their appearance. Their leadership is at the same time a submission to God's leadership, the assumption of an assigned task. The Patriarchs, the fathers of the people and of the faith, are followed into the Promised Land by the real leaders, and these in turn are followed by the Judges who endeavor to establish the kingdom of God but who fail in the end because of outer and inner tensions. Israel's "primitive theocracy" of the early period was bound to the existence of "charismatic" leaders, those vested with power on whom rested the *ruach,* the breath (spirit) of God as a gift of grace which was no guarantee of continued power but which demanded constant confirmation since it could at any time be withdrawn. To the King's Covenant of God and man, to the leader and those content to be led, belonged the person of the "mediator"—the revelations and commands of Yahwe needed the "translating" activity of mortal man; "the species of man that bears the word from above downwards and from below upwards is called *nabi* announcer." [105] It is relatively unimportant to determine when the concept was coined and came into use: "At all events no age in the history of early Israelitish faith can be understood historically, without considering as active therein this species of man with his mission and function, his declaration and mediation." [105a] In the early period the multitude is led by God, represented by one who is called by Him and empowered by grace—but the mystery of his personal vocation is not transferable. The *nabi* represents the divine Lord and King, commands in His name and enunciates His message. This "ministry of the word" binds him to the later prophets; their appearance, however, corresponds to an altered situation between God and people.

In the time of the Judges there was neither a magical relation to God nor inherited succession as in the neighboring ancient oriental cultures. The struggle for existence against the Philistines demanded the continuity of the charismatic representation of God, that is, the dynasty. The period of the Judges passes into that of the Kingdom which is sanctified by sacramental anointing: the folk order becomes the state. The continuity of succession presupposes a continuity of representative responsibility. Through the anointment of the king comes the transformation of a man into the bearer of a mission: "The history of the kings is the history of the failure of him who has been anointed to realize the promise of his anointing." [106] The belief in a messiah, the hope placed in the anointed one, who with his person realizes the purpose and intention of anointment, is closely related to this failure of the kings. The belief in a messiah is the belief in a leader who fulfills a mission, one who in dialogue with God finds the answer that corresponds to the creation-meaning of mankind.

The situation brought about by the unsuccessful rule of kings led to the appearance of the prophets. They came from the circle of the *ne-biim,* of the charismatic "announcers" who had maintained themselves from the time of the post-Mosaic and post-Joshuanic convulsions. They had their origin in the religious movement which at the time of Joshua opposed the merely cultic centralization of tribes in an Amphictyonic Covenant designed to safeguard the unity of the people, and they advocated militant devotion to YHVH and to the Covenant of Sinai—a sentiment expressed with great passion in the Song of Deborah.[107] This early Israelitish *nabi*-dom arose, according to Buber, from a group of those who were endowed with charismatic power, an "association of speakers" whose members prophesied under the inspiration of an irresistible spirit.[108] The distinctive characteristic of this peculiar group was its belief that "something descends from the divine sphere upon man." [109] *Nabi* was originally not the designation of a class or profession but of a condition that from time to time seizes those who are exposed to *ruach.*[110]

It is in connection with these circles and as a precursor of the prophets who struggled against the kingship and the sacrificial cult of the priests that Buber considered the great narrator to whom we owe the composition of the book of Genesis from the creation of man to the sacrifice of Isaac and who gave Israel's historical faith its most important document. With his "storytelling theology," he first set before the people the unfulfilled command "to become a blessing." The faith of Abraham is presented by the narrator as an admonition to the royal court which had endeavored to pervert the people's relation to God by making it purely mythical and cultic.[111]

The prophets now become God's messengers and the mediators between heaven and earth, exercising little power and moving further and further away from the community—from kingship, priesthood, and people. Their association with the Divine is governed by God's word which descends upon them like a flash of lightning. The priestly rites and ceremonies proceed from man to the sphere of the Divine where they are either accepted or rejected; the Word always descends anew from above and breaks through the order of the human world.[112] The prophet becomes the mouth of God, receiving his words intuitively in revelatory symbols; he is called to the ministry body and soul.

Thus, some twenty years before the destruction of Jerusalem, Jeremiah is sent to the potter's house where he realizes that Israel is as clay in the hands of the divine Potter who breaks and re-forms imperfect vessels.

But the prophet is not a mere soothsayer; he remains God's messenger to human souls capable of *teshuva*, "repentance." His word goes forth in a memorable, decision-open hour—even when he proclaims disaster. Man is not deprived of his freedom of choice, even in his most wretched and abandoned state. To prophesy means to confront the community to whom the word is addressed, directly or indirectly, with a choice and decision.[113] Human decision is an indispensable element in the workings of God's grace. One who has "turned" cooperates in the work of redemption. God still keeps waiting for Israel's fulfilling answer.

From prophecy as the highest form of dialogic meeting with God two roads may be taken. One is the apocalyptic, which is the province of the future and to which only those things are "disclosed" which can no longer be averted—and this is regarded by Buber as a late form of prophecy shot through with Persian concepts which lead from Judaism and to Christianity and Hellenism. The other road points to the figure of the *ebed*, the suffering servant of the Lord in Deutero-Isaiah: "Out of the depth of the community's suffering there arises the conception of God as the God of sufferers." [114]

After the national catastrophe the significance of suffering began to occupy a central place in Israel's relation to God. Job's question is at the same time the question concerning the meaning of historical destiny. The personal *I* and suffering Israel are inseparable.[115] Why does a righteous God permit the just to suffer? Man, the individual as well as the faithful remnant of Israel, begins to feel the chill wind of the modern spirit as he contemplates a "hidden God" whom he could no longer address—and this becomes Job's complaint. The book offers no solution to the vexing questions it raises, and Job's complaint is not even considered. The answer is merely God's Presence, which Job experiences anew in the light of his suffering. The decisive element here is not God's revelation in itself, but the particular revelation given "as an answer to the individual sufferer concerning the question of his sufferings, the self-limitation of God to a person, answering a person." [116]

The servant in the second part of the book of Isaiah is both person and more than person. Buber points out that Deutero-Isaiah saw himself as one of the figurations of the *ebed* and, indeed, as the one to whom was disclosed the mystery of the servant's concealment and his emergence in the future.[117] The servant is the prophet whom God called in his mother's womb and in whose soul he implanted a marvelous potency. And yet the task for which he is destined, that of restoring and rebuilding the saving remnant of a truant Israel, is denied him. The image in which this is proclaimed is frequently cited by Buber: "And He hath made my mouth like a sharp sword, In the shadow of His hand hath he hid me; And He hath made me a polished shaft, In His quiver hath He concealed me" (Isa. 49:2). The servant feels he is an arrow in God's quiver.[118] God chose him to be a light unto the nations. Great suffering is laid upon him and he willingly endures it, for it is a suffering for God's sake to bear the sins of the multitude. The magnificent conclusion with its vision of lasting peace, the reign of a divine order among the nations of the world whose center will be Jerusalem, the figure of the suffering servant—all point beyond the individual to the future path of Israel's history.

But the mystery of suffering in the fifty-third chapter of Isaiah is supra-personal: "Whoever accomplishes in Israel the active suffering of Israel (i.e., takes it upon himself for God's sake and out of love), he is the servant, and he is Israel, in whom YHVH 'glorifies Himself.' The mystery of history is the mystery of a representation which is at bottom identity. The arrow, which is still concealed in the quiver, is people and man as one." [119] The servant is the figure of Israel in the Dispersion.

We obtain an understanding of the historical depth of Judaism's "being-tradition" only from the Bible; from biblical humanity Hebrew humanism receives its measure and norm. Buber's presentation is neither theology nor religious history but the history of faith. He did not wish to impart the faith itself but "knowledge about it." The biblical texts, however, are not pages from the past which he regarded as something apart from his own person. The biblical figures, whose attitude to faith he investigated with modern scientific methods, attest to a deeply human religious experience *(Ur-humanum)* in man's encounter with God which had been his own basic religious experience.

In dealing with the Bible, as in his treatment of Hasidism, Buber's method was selective. His underestimation of the apocalyptic reflects his disregard of the historical effects of biblical faith; but even more significant is his lack of understanding for the visions of the prophet Ezekiel which have had such a strong influence on the development of Jewish mysticism. He holds fast to one great theme, the biblical dialogue between God and man, this being for him the primary phenomenon of human existence and the outermost limit of what finite man can say about God.

Humanism is defined by the distinguished German philologist, Konrad Burdach, whom Buber quotes, as "the desire of humanity to return to its origins." [120] Buber's Hebrew humanism was directed to that conception of man which realizes his creation-meaning. Just as his *I and Thou* was not concerned with the development of a new philosophy but with investigating the presuppositions of all philosophizing, so was he concerned later with the basic principles of theology in general. In both cases his desire is "to uncover a buried ancient treasure," a long neglected, submerged, primordial reality—as he expressed it in "The Holy Way." [120a] The ideal of European humanism had become in the reality of the twentieth century the caricature of the alienated intellectual. Hebrew humanism sees man "in relation," as an "open person" over against God and fellowman; and in addition to this the people are summoned to become the "open" community to humanity. The national ego of the European nations is to be overcome by a national humanism; and Israel, faithful to its election as God's people, would also become the true people of mankind.

Mankind is today in danger of succumbing to nihilism. All of mankind's traditional bonds are being dissolved and its basic values questioned. Can the roots of our humanity still be saved? This is the question that Buber attempted to answer in "Judaism and Civilization" (1951): "Let us recognize ourselves: we are the keepers of the roots. How can we become what we are?" [121]

In the early *Addresses on Judaism* Buber envisaged the way to the true human community to be that of realizing God in history. The "holy way" always meant to him the sanctifying way—Hebrew humanism signifies "the power of the spirit" to hallow natural life and consecrate it to God [122]—but true community with God and being, which to him meant holiness at all times, was now seen by him to consist in the realization of man, and with this a clearer recognition of the limits of man's having been made in God's image. In an early poem "The Word to Elijah" the prophet appeared to him as "the son of man," and the transmission of the creation word "Let it become!" was bound up with his having been created in God's image. In the mystery play *Elijah*, which was completed rather late and which Buber included in his biblical writings, Israel's election signifies a heavy burden which man again and again vainly seeks to cast off, an inner need to serve and a willingness to serve out of love, and a boundless suffering endured for God's sake. The features of the "suffering servant of the Lord" are anticipated in the figure of an early prophet.

Something of this development is also reflected in Buber's spiritual attitude. His presentation of Israel's history of faith in *Kingship of God* and *The Prophetic Faith* makes it abundantly clear that the figure of the prophet belongs to a distinct, clearly defined period and that other uses of this term are unwarranted. In his youth, however, Buber had imbibed the "seductive venom" of the false prophet Nietzsche whose ecstacies of "inspiration" confirmed the significance he attached to his own calling. In that age "prophecy" denoted one of the forms in which human genius expresses itself, somewhat akin to that of the poet. It was also in the high sense of a prophetic literary task that Buber at first understood his calling. In the figure of the Hasidic zaddik, as well as in his own guilty feelings of having failed, he recognized that holiness must not only be represented in poetical form but must also be lived as responsible and sanctifying service. From that time on the spirit of the zaddik as teacher, helper, and leader served to light up the path before him and to guide his steps. In the upheavals of World War I he had a revelation which scattered the mists of self-glorifying creativity and clarified his innate knowledge concerning man's relation to God.

The words "Then one descended to me," in *Confession of the Writer*, are almost the same words that Buber used to describe the basic experience of the biblical *nebiim*. The study and translation of the

Bible, to which he now devoted his energies, not only disclosed to him the whole panorama of Jewish "being-tradition" but also deepened his understanding of his own calling. All this came to him from the religious life of prehistoric times in which he recognized traits related to his own being, and from which he learned the true meaning of "inspiration." The zaddik and his Hasidim, the Great Maggid who turned from ecstatic visions to teaching—these were the successors of the biblical "enthusiasts" who reported their overpowering experience under the spell of inspiration, as did the narrators of early biblical history.[123] All their "objective enthusiasm" Buber called in Jacob Grimm's phrase "primordial amazement," which sets in motion all the formative powers of the soul and creates reality, a reality which, to be sure, is legendary, but gives us information of its effects on body and soul and sets in motion an original kind of historical continuity.

In his mind's eye Buber saw "the bands of prophets" (1 Sam. 10:5) who, unlike himself, were given to ecstasy without being mystics. They were not thinkers and masters of the word, but "its listener and executor, its worshipper and proclaimer." [124] These *nebiim* were nameless, and yet throughout the centuries they were the core from which arose great men, leaders and prophets. "The ministry of the word" [125] was common to them all, those who were called and those who were chosen, something that "descends from the divine sphere upon man." [126] Nameless also remain the great ones among them, like the narrator of the book of Genesis whose history of beginnings is retold by Buber in "Abraham the Seer." He may be said to have followed in the footsteps of this narrator when he, in *Israel and Palestine*, *Moses*, and *Origin and Meaning of Hasidism*, transmitted to a regenerate Israel the knowledge of the past as "sensitive selection," [127] when he speaks of history as recounted by the editors of the Bible as "storytelling theology." The "archaic experience of being-singled-out" [128] unites the *nebiim* of all times. Buber was separated from his mother and parental home at the tender age of three, an experience which he described in the first of his *Autobiographical Fragments* as the most instructive of his life in determining the road he was to take.

Singled out and sent forth to wander like Abraham were also the first Zionist settlers in Palestine; they too were enthusiasts to whom

God spoke "out of the burning bush of the present." [129] It is, then, not surprising that Buber should have hoped that this community would give rise to a new theophany, the "Sinai of the future." [130] The German word with which Buber wished to translate the mysticism of the Hasidim was *Gegenwärtigkeit*, "presentness." [131] The full presentness of the present, "the full grasping of the present," [132] was for him the distinctive mark of the prophets. This is his broad-minded realism that seemed utopian to the political leaders of Zionism and for which he was again and again reproached in his controversies with them. "Humanism moves from the mystery of language to the mystery of the human person." [133] Knowledge and confirmation are united in him as one.

The varied forms of finding-oneself-again and participating in the submerged life of history did not constitute for Buber an aesthetic experience, but a genuine "ontic participation" that was inseparable from his being. It is expressed with deep feeling and doubtlessly unfeigned sincerity in the discussion between "synagogue and church" that he had early in 1933 with Karl Ludwig Schmidt. In the course of the discussion Buber described how he would from time to time visit the Jewish cemetery in Worms and from that lonely spot look across to the cathedral: "There below not the slightest vestige of form, only stone and ashes beneath the stones . . . One feels the corporeality of the men who once were. One possesses them. I possess them. Not indeed as bodily form in the space of this planet, but as bodily form of my own recollection reaching down to the depths of history, as far back as Sinai. I stood there, bound to the ashes and through them to the patriarchal forefathers. This is the recollection of the experience with God which is given to all Jews. I cannot be talked out of it by the perfection of Christian divine-space; nothing can induce me to exchange it for Israel's divine-time. I stood there and experienced everything in my own person. Death itself came to meet me: all the ashes, all the disintegration, all the voiceless woe is mine. But the Covenant has not been abrogated. I lie on the ground, cast off like these stones—but I have received no word of its abrogation." [134]

Such self-recognition reaches far beyond the experience of a single individual. It conjures up the biblical figure that accompanied Israel in the Dispersion, the servant of the Lord: "When the nations look at him, they look at the truth of Israel, the truth chosen from the very beginning." [135] It has not been vouchsafed to the "servant" to lead his own people back to their God; his destiny is to be a light unto the nations.

THE DIALOGUE WITH CHRISTIANITY

"What have you and we in common?" Buber asked the Christians in 1930 at one of the study sessions held by the German mission societies in Stuttgart. "If we take the question literally, a book and an expectation. To you the book is a forecourt; to us it is the sanctuary. But in this place we can dwell together, and together listen to the voice that speaks here. That means that we can work together to evoke the buried speech of that voice; together we can redeem the imprisoned living word." [136] The last sentence presupposes a solidarity between Judaism and Christianity which was to be found in wider circles only after 1945 as a result of the persecution both had suffered during the period of National Socialism; in all this, however, Buber did not forget the vital differences between the two religions. The Christian expectation awaits a return, the Jewish expectation an unanticipated redemption. The two worlds of faith are fatefully separated from one another "premessianically." The Church has looked upon Jews to the present day as obdurate and impenitent, rejected by God for not recognizing Jesus as the Messiah and deprived of all consolation in this world and the next. Animated by a strong assurance in the merits of its cause, the Church turned the Old Testament into a quarry to prove its extraordinary claims of being the new and true Israel. For the Christian world events had been determined by a caesura; for the Jews they flow from creation toward completion. The Christian assertion that redemption has been consummated seems to the Jew unwarranted, even preposterous, since he more than anyone else has experienced the unredeemed character of the world: "He feels this lack of redemption against his skin, he tastes it on his tongue, the burden of the unredeemed world lies on him. Because of this almost physical knowledge of his, he *cannot* concede that the redemption has taken place; he knows that it has not." [137]

This does not mean that the individual Jewish soul does not feel again and again salvation taking place, for "the Jew experiences as person what every openhearted being does in an hour when he is most utterly forsaken, a breath from above, the nearness, the touch, the mysterious intimacy of light and darkness." [138] But Buber was careful not to separate a redeemed soul from an unredeemed world: "There is not one realm of the spirit and another of nature; there is only the growing realm of God." [139]

The differences between the two religions cannot be bridged by an easy tolerance nor removed by any human power. Their unity must not be anticipated. Christians and Jews must hold fast to their respective beliefs, which to Buber meant their "own real relation to truth," without timidity or remorse. They are not merely to tolerate one another's errors but are to attempt something much more difficult, because their own real relation to truth seems to contradict the believer's attachment to God, that is, to respect the other's faith-reality and acknowledge it as a mystery, even when it runs counter to one's own convictions.

"What is permitted, however, at this hour of history, and what is indeed imperative, is dialogue—a greeting extended from both sides, and an honest attempt to discuss our common concerns as God's creatures." [140] In 1926 Buber, together with Joseph Wittig and Viktor von Weizsäcker, founded the journal *Die Kreatur*. The suggestion that a literary organ be published together by a Jew, a Catholic, and a Protestant came from Buber's friend, Florens Christian Rang, who was not able to realize it himself. The title that was first considered, *Grüsse aus den Exilen* [Greetings from the exiles] was designed to emphasize the inevitable separation of religions until the coming of the one Kingdom of God. It was then decided, however, to take a name that would emphasize more strongly that which the different faiths had in common: the certainty of having been created, "the yea to the unification of the creaturely world, to the world as creature." People from different walks of life were to speak of the world in such a way as to make manifest their creatureliness. The journal was not to deal with theology, but rather with "cosmology, in spiritual humility." Beyond the differences that separate them theologically, a unifying humanity was sought, a common interest of the lived relation of God.

A common origin and goal, and a common waiting! In the religious dialogue with Karl Ludwig Schmidt it was still possible for Buber to stress an aspect of faith held in common by Jew and Christian, a power of common possession beyond the irreconcilable contradictions: the spirit which Jews call *ruach ha-kodesh,* "the spirit of holiness," and Christians *pneuma hagion,* "holy ghost." [141] By virtue of this power it is possible to respect the mystery of the other religion which cannot be known from without: "How it is possible that these mysteries exist beside one another, that is God's mystery." [142] The spirit that God implanted in men turns them to Him and to human freedom in their relations with one another.

Buber's view of the two religions is again that of an "open" humanity directed to God. They have in common creation and redemption as origin and goal, but they are separated by a different conception of revelation. "Every religion has its origin in a revelation. No religion is absolute truth, none is a piece of heaven that has come down to earth. Each religion is a human truth . . . The religions must become submissive to God and his will, each must recognize that it is only one of the shapes in which human elaboration of the divine message is presented, that it has no monopoly on God." [143]

In this utterance we again discern Buber's believing humanism with its peculiar affinity for the spirit of the Enlightenment, which should however not be overestimated. The distinction made by Lessing in his ring parable between true, false, and lost revelation did not exist for him. As a believing thinker he took seriously every revelation that comes from God, and urged men to stake the whole reality of their lives upon it. His own conception, however, was confined to the divine revelation that came from the burning bush on Sinai which, in Buber's interpretation, is not "I am that I am" but "I shall be there as the I shall be there," that is, God cannot be pinned down to any one of His revelations, for He is above any of His utterances. Hence, the Jew attributes to "none of his revelations finality, to none the character of incarnation." [144] Besides the strong conviction of the unredemptive character of the world, the two religions are separated by the belief of "the non-incarnation of God who reveals himself to the flesh and is present in a mutual relationship." [145] The God to whom Jews are pledged does not unite with human substance on earth. He has chosen man to be His partner in the work of redemption, and no prehistoric Fall or original sin can relieve him of this task or induce him to forfeit this prerogative, "for the intention of God is mightier than the sin of man." [146] Man was created in God's image which was stamped on him; it can grow feeble but cannot be obliterated: *teshuva* and a new beginning are at all times open to the sinner. God created man to be His partner in the world dialogue, addressing him by giving him life and expecting from his actions response and responsibility. Buber demanded of us an attitude that is close to revelation in which there can arise for man at any place and at any time revelation as "the pure shape of meeting" with God.[147] This presupposes that man's whole life reality must be turned to God and that religion has not become for him just another sphere of the spirit, a mere segment of his total existence. There is always a tendency for religion with its rigid forms and institutions to relieve man of the immediacy of living before God, a danger which Buber expressed in rather strong words, namely, that "there is nothing that is so apt to obscure the face of God as a religion." [148]

It is an integral part of the character of Israel and its election that its history of faith should have preserved this immediacy to God as found in early biblical humanity. In Judaism dogma was elaborated relatively late and plays a far less significant role than in the Christian Church; in his dispute with Christianity Buber also underestimated the importance of the law as a fixed religious form for the preservation of Judaism. In his view the essence of Judaism is not law and teaching but rather "Abraham's soul," [149] which is the pre-Sinaitic soul of Judaism, whose substance is that it is pledged to God whom it clings to through all trials and temptations. The specifically Jewish element in man seemed to Buber to be the recognition of God in all his manifestations, even the "God who conceals himself" and who leaves his creatures utterly abandoned. He knows that even when he is distant from God he is not forsaken: "In the prophetic books God is depicted to a sinful people as One to whom it cannot bind itself in power but only in darkness and suffering." [150] In dispersion and in persecution Israel knows itself to be the "servant of the Lord" who takes suffering upon himself for God's sake.

In his dialogue with Karl Ludwig Schmidt, Buber pointed to the historical uniqueness of Israel, which is neither people nor religion but a combination of both that cannot be subsumed under any category of national life and sociology. The Bible states clearly what Israel's election means: God had destined it to be "the first fruits of his increase" (Jer. 2:3), and its survival in history and the mystery of its continued preservation testify to its continued task. The Christian nations, to be sure, have granted emancipation to a great number of Jewish individuals, but have not recognized Israel's divine mission. Even in the early days of 1933, shortly before the Nazis seized power, Buber still hoped that a genuine acceptance of Israel might take place by those Christians who believed in the Bible "in a difficult but blessed common struggle." [151]

The martyrdom of the Jewish people which was at that time inconceivable, and which the Christians of Germany and the world did not prevent, began only a few weeks after these words had been spoken, interrupting for a number of years the dialogue with Christianity. After 1945, the sense of guilt and the consciousness of being isolated in a world that was turning away from Christianity caused the Church to look upon the mystery of Israel's suffering in the Pauline sense as "an addition to the mystery of the suffering which the Church contemplates in the Cross." [152] Hans Urs von Balthasar has stated that in an age that has witnessed a rebirth of heathenism both the synagogue and the church stand in the pillory: "The Jews have suffered and keep on suffering, as if this were their privilege and not that of the Christians. Does this escape the notice of Christians? By what right do they withhold from the sufferer the distinctive Christian gesture of understanding love? The dialectic between Jews and Christians is inescapable and will remain thus to the end of the world, for it cannot be revoked or rescinded, being an offense and a scandal and a thorn of envy for both, as the Holy Ghost assures us through Paul." [153] Both churches, Catholic and Protestant, have in the last two decades been disposed to discuss controversial questions that the religions have in common in the hope of being able to uproot confirmed prejudices. In this sense a new basis was created for the relationship of the Catholic Church to Judaism by the second Vatican Council of 1965.

Buber, in *Two Types of Faith* (1950), once more expressed the hope that a dialogue of faith between Judaism and Christianity will at some future date prove to be fruitful. Both religions find themselves at present in a crisis. The Christian, who in sanctifying his own soul does not forget the sanctification of the world, and the Jew, who today is no longer born into the community of faith as a matter of course but finds himself facing a division between the people of God and a secularized nation—both could have "something as yet unsaid to say to each other and help to give to one another—hardly to be conceived at the present time." [154]

Buber was also regarded by world Jewry as the Jewish teacher through whom the message of the Old Testament was presented to the Christians with a new urgency. He was the spokesman for Judaism who gave Jewish answers to Christian questions, "the kind of answer Christians must hear if they are to understand themselves." [155] Buber has been highly respected among Jews for his biblical studies and translations. His disparagement of apocalyptic revelation in favor of prophecy was controversial and aroused much criticism. It is universally acknowledged that, through his interpretation of the prophets and his openminded attitude to the figure of Jesus, the greatest possible understanding has been reached between Jews and Christians. His efforts in this direction were often regarded as extreme, and in some quarters his attitude, although not openly expressed, was characterized as Christian in a deeper sense.[156] He was reproached for having given the figure of the "holy Yehudi" in *For the Sake of Heaven* a Christian bias, consciously or unconsciously, and he took this criticism seriously enough to refute it.[156a]

"From my youth onwards I have found Jesus my great brother. That Christianity has regarded and does regard him as God and Saviour has always appeared to me a fact of the highest importance which, for his sake and my own, I must endeavor to understand . . . My own fraternally open relationship to him has grown even stronger and clearer, and today I see him more strongly and clearly than ever before.

I am more than ever certain that a great place belongs to him in Israel's history of faith and that this place cannot be described by any of the usual categories." [157] These words are found in the preface to *Two Types of Faith*, a work in which Buber is concerned more than in any other with the relation between Judaism and Christianity and which proceeds not from the standpoint of the respective essence and content of the two religions but from the difference in their attitude to faith. He is thus able to find a place for the figure of Jesus as it emerges from the synoptic Gospels in the history of Israel's faith and to consider Christianity, with its belief in the divinity of Jesus, as a new type of faith beginning with the apostle Paul and the Gospel according to John. This introduces into the relationship between Judaism and Christianity a new perspective which we find in Buber's early writings, such as *Addresses on Judaism* in which he presented the beginnings of Christianity as a religious folk movement like that of the Essenes and later Hasidism, each of which manifested the unconditionality of Jewish faith in its characteristic relation to reality.

At that time he was of the opinion that *Urchristentum* should really be called *Urjudentum* because it proclaimed the essential teaching of the prophets: the unconditionality of the deed. In "The Renewal of Judaism" we find an observation which Buber in later years never repeated, but which he never retracted: "Whatever in Christianity is creative is not Christianity but Judaism; and this we need not approach; we need only to recognize it within ourselves and to take possession of it, for we carry it within us, never to be lost. But whatever in Christianity is not Judaism is uncreative, a mixture of a thousand rites and dogmas; with this—and we say it both as Jews and human beings—we do not want to establish a rapprochement." [158] At that time Jesus appeared to Buber, together with Buddha and Lao-tzu, as one of the great religious masters of the Orient, whose teaching is not knowledge but a Way: "the one thing that is needful." He is one of the "central, fulfilling people" who go along different paths the *one* way of God in history[159]—the way of realizing God and uniting the world with him. In this sense he interpreted in 1914 the resurrected Christ of the Isenheim Altar: "This is the man, the man of all times and of all places, the man of the here and now, who perfects himself into the *I* of the world." [160]

Man in his ultimate relation to God throughout the ages was even then Buber's real theme, and it is in this context that Jesus appeared to him as his "great brother."

In *I and Thou* Jesus is referred to as the one who in the history of mankind uttered the primal word I-Thou in its purest form. As Socrates spoke of the "I of endless dialogue" from man to man and Goethe of the "I of pure intercourse with nature," so Jesus spoke the "I of unconditional relation" to the eternal Thou, "in which the man calls his *Thou* Father in such a way that he himself is simply Son, and nothing else but Son." [161] Hence, Buber in this same work called the Gospel of John "the Gospel of pure relation": "Here is a truer verse than the familiar mystical verse: 'I am Thou and Thou art I.' The Father and the Son, like in being—we may even say God and Man, like in being—are the indissolubly real pair, the two bearers of the primal relation, which from God to man is termed mission and command, from man to God looking and hearing, and between both is termed knowledge and love. In this relation the Son, through the Father dwells and works in him, bows down before the 'greater' and prays to him." [162] That this relation to God, apart from Buber's interpretation of Jesus, is simply designated as the "primal reality" of dialogue will perhaps be deeply disconcerting not only to Christians but also to Jews who could not help remarking that the relation to God of a man of prophetic type is taken here as a model of the confrontation of God and man, a charismatic father-son relationship which appears possible through election which operates in human nature at all times—just as creation, revelation, and redemption were for Buber processes that endure for all time. The words of Meister Eckhart, "The noble man is that only-begotten Son of God whom the Father eternally begets" (condemned by the Pope in 1329), were always understood by Buber in connection with the verse in Psalm 2:7: "Thou art My son, This day have I begotten thee." [163] He also interpreted the baptism of Jesus as adoptionism in this sense according to Mark 1:11: "Thou art my beloved Son, in whom I am well pleased." In *Addresses on Judaism* Buber spoke of "Jesus' truly Jewish proclamation that every man could become a son of God by living unconditionally." [164] In his later years Buber based the charismatic relation to God not on the "unconditionality of the deed" but on the hidden depths of suffering of the "servant" who out of love to God remains concealed "in His quiver."

Buber's historical portrayal of Jesus in *Origin and Meaning of Hasidism* was conceived from the standpoint of this late perspective. Here he held it to be an error to regard Jewish messianism as exhausted by the belief in a unique eschatological event involving but one human being. From generation to generation "God's servants" bear the woes of the world and transfigure its failings and imperfections. Their part in the messianic mystery lies in a concealment that reaches down to the innermost core of existence. This "messianism of continuity" explains Judaism's attitude to Jesus as the messiah: "Whatever the appearance of Jesus means for the Gentile world (and its significance for the Gentile world remains for me the true seriousness of Western history), seen from the standpoint of Judaism he is the first in the series of men who, stepping out of the hiddenness of the servant of the Lord, the real 'Messianic mystery,' acknowledged their Messiahship in their souls and in their words. That this first one in the series was incomparably the purest, the most legitimate, the most endowed with real Messianic power . . . alters nothing in the fact of this firstness; indeed it undoubtedly belongs just to it, to the fearfully penetrating reality that has characterized the whole automessianic series." [165] This line of messianic pretenders runs through Bar Kochba to Sabbatai Zvi and Jakob Frank. The significance of the "servant of the Lord" in Deutero-Isaiah was suggested to Buber by Albert Schweitzer. Buber's assertion that Jesus of Nazareth stood "in the shadow of Deutero-Isaiah's servant of the Lord" [165a] and from the Jewish point of view occupies, as it were, a rank inferior to the "holy Yehudi" of Pshysha, who remained hidden in the quiver, is a hard saying for Christians and as difficult to understand as Buber's failure to see that the "messianism" of Jesus Christ and that of Sabbatai Zvi took place on such different levels that a juxtaposition of the two would seem impossible.

The inner view of *Two Types of Faith* shows the image of Jesus as determined by Buber's conception of prophecy and revelation. Buber still endeavored to understand Jesus completely from the standpoint of Judaism: in the great line of prophets and servants of the Lord, of those who place their full trust in God and engage Him in dialogue. The sermon of Jesus begins, like that of his predecessor John, with the demand for a "turning" and the tidings that the kingdom of God was nigh. The ethics of the Sermon on the Mount, because of its eschatological expectation of God's dominion, was taken by Buber as going far beyond the limits set by the Pharisees. An entire people, in an effort that surpassed all human strength, was determined to take the kingdom of God "by storm," and to have Jesus himself come forth from concealment among the servants as the proclaimed Savior. His most radical demands, like that of loving one's enemies, although "originating from the enthusiasm of eschatological actuality," derive their light from the world of Judaism.[166] Because of the failure of the people and of the Pharisees, Jesus is able to experience the mystery of the suffering of the "servants" and to relate it to the idea of the heavenly "son of man" who came down on earth to become a light unto the nations, an idea that was still alive among the people of that day: "Here, in a continuation of Deutero-Isaiah's conception, the ascending man is interwoven with the descending into an earthly-heavenly dual life. Jesus finds this in the popular conception; and so he appears to conceive his own present and future in a personal crisis, the office of suffering for the preparation and that of glory for the fulfillment." [167]

Buber's reverent interpretation of the New Testament takes us far back into the religious life of Judaism at the beginning of the common era. Every Christian of good will is grateful for being shown the Jewish roots of Jesus' teachings. The Jewish exegete is frequently more conservative than the Christian biblical scholar whom he cites in the footnotes. Biographical questions are tactfully confined to those indispensable in determining the "type of faith"; just as the Old Testament adheres to the witnesses of faith and not to secular history, so did the evangelists record the "message" and not biographical details. The real mystery of Christ is, of course, comprehended only by the Christian who stands in his faith—and this is freely acknowledged by Buber: "There is a something in Israel's history of faith which is only to be understood from Israel, just as there is something in the Christian history of faith which is only to be understood from Christianity." [168] Yet, now and then Buber had some profound insights into the nature of Christianity which come close to explaining its mystery as, for example, when he spoke of the significance of the *imitatio Christi* for the disciples and their striving to preserve it beyond his death, calling it "the fiery center" in the history of Christianity.[169] Just as the early Israelites felt themselves to be "led" by JHWH in a literal sense, so did Jesus repeatedly summon individuals to join him, and "when the challenge touched the man's very heart, 'he went after him' and shared his life." [169a] This command to "follow after me" has been heard again and again throughout the centuries by the elect and has kept Christianity alive. Buber had a profound, although not ultimate, comprehension of what took place among the disciples in the week following Easter, especially the instance of "doubting" Thomas who, through his exclamation "My Lord and my God!" (when he saw Jesus' wounds), became "among all the disciples of Jesus . . . the first Christian in the sense of the Christian dogma." [170] Karl Thieme had already pointed out in his review of *Two Types of Faith* that this did not mean the collapse of a world, as Buber thought, but the concrete fulfillment of that "folk-idea," mentioned by Buber, of one who had descended from heaven and then risen to heaven.[171]

With the demand that the one who had been resurrected be recognized as Christ, the Jewish *emuna*, the unconditional relation of trust in God which characterizes the Jew becomes belief as *pistis* as found in the apostle Paul and in the gospel of John, namely, the belief that we are saved only by the crucified Son of God and that Jesus Christ is the Way on which alone we come to the Father. This confession of faith constitutes the Christian Church. It is a faith that is held and perfected by the individual believer, as Buber pointed out, but does not affect him as a member of society or as part of the entire people. The difference between the two types of faith was summed up by Buber as follows: "If we consider the Synoptic and Johannine dialogues with the disciples as two stages along one road, we immediately see what was gained and lost in the course of it. The gain was the most sublime of all theologies; it was procured at the expense of the plain, concrete and situation-bound dialogicism of the original man of the Bible, who found eternity not in the super-temporal spirit, but in the depth of the actual moment. The Jesus of the genuine tradition still belongs to that, but the Jesus of theology does so no longer." [172] The opposition between the two religions is even greater when considered from the standpoint of the later dogma of the Trinity: "God suffers as the Son in order to save the world, which He as the Father created and prepared as one which needs salvation. The prophetic idea of man who suffers for God's sake has here given way to that of God who suffers for the sake of man." [173]

Paul was seen by Buber as a representative of Hellenistic Diaspora-Judaism, a marginal form of the genuine Jewish faith, and his manner of thinking as a syncretism of the Pharisaic, apocalyptic, and Hellenistic spirit. The figure of Jesus had unexpectedly been recovered for Judaism by the bold interpretation in *Two Types of Faith*, in which Paul emerges as the antithetical figure who broke with the faith of his fathers. Buber shared Schweitzer's view that Jesus must be understood from an eschatological standpoint as awaiting the end of time, but he could not agree with his attempt to find the roots of Paul's ideas in the Jewish world of thought. He saw Paul as taking the first step on the road that led to Marcion; the biblical text with which he was most familiar was no longer the original Hebrew but the Greek Septuagint. As a translator of the Bible Buber was well aware of the difficulties of establishing the real meaning of many biblical words, and he always insisted that the Greek version of important biblical concepts failed to give the full import of Jewish tradition. The translation in the Septuagint of *Torah* as *law* changes the basic meaning of the Hebrew word which, according to Buber, should be translated as "direction, instruction, information" [174]—to which Shalom ben Chorin, in *Antwort des Jona*, adds "reproof" (forewarning penalties) and "proof" (of God's deeds).[175] Buber went on to explain the meaning of this concept: "The Torah of God is understood as God's instruction in His way, and therefore not as a separate *objectivum*. It includes laws, and laws are indeed its most vigorous objectivizations, but the Torah itself is essentially not law. A vestige of the actual speaking always adheres to the commanding word, the directing voice is always present or at least its sound is heard fading away. To render Torah by 'law' is to take away from its idea this inner dynamic and vital character. Without the change of meaning in the Greek objective sense, the Pauline dualism of law and faith, life from works and life from grace, would miss its most important conceptual presupposition." [176] Buber admitted that in the course of the post-exilic centuries Torah was to a large extent identified with law and the observance of its precepts—but this never applied to more than one segment of the population.

In *The Teaching of the Tao* (1910) Buber had described Paul as "a violent man of action" through whom the teaching of Jesus, "the one thing that is needful," was turned into dialectic.[177] The attempt to relate the Pauline conception of the impossibility of fulfilling the divinely ordained law with Hegel's dialectic of history, according to which "the god of the philosophers, 'Reason,' forces by its 'ruse' the historical process unwittingly to urge on its perfection," [178] reveals the weakness of Buber's comparative religion method which makes no pretension to being a history of religion. Its strength lies in permitting Buber to see a religious phenomenon from the inside and to participate in it. Even when, at the end of *Two Types of Faith*, he seeks to classify the periods of Christian history in accordance with the degree of Paulinism they exhibit, the resulting determination is very vague; his interest, moreover, is obviously directed only to the Evangelical church. Of the four theologians to whom he acknowledges his indebtedness in the preface of the book—Rudolf Bultmann, Albert Schweitzer, Rudolf Otto, and Leonhard Ragaz—not one is a Catholic. The Catholic church has a greater appreciation for the union of faith and works, and does not regard the Epistle to James as a "right strawy epistle" (Luther). When Buber in the same section (xvi), referring to our present age, spoke of "Paulinism without Christ," whereby he understood "a way of seeing and being indwelling in life itself"—which can mean an "eclipse of God," an unbridgeable dualism between the redeemed soul and the unredeemed world, or else the deliverance to demonic powers, depending on the nature of one's faith—then the conceptual basis is too vaguely defined and the view from within too divergent from the view from without to permit fruitful discussion.

Karl Thieme pointed out in his review of *Two Types of Faith* that Buber in his discussion of the Epistle to the Romans spoke of "the wrath of the Pauline God" who no longer has any of the qualities of the Father, but did not sufficiently appreciate the passage (Rom. 9–11) which is of decisive importance for the relation of God to the Old Testament. Here the *heilsgeschichtliche* interpretation of the obduracy and impenitence of Israel reveals the Apostle's love for his people whose "zeal for God" he acknowledges. Israel's painful self-deception with respect to Jesus Christ has not robbed it of its election nor caused God to abrogate his ancient Covenant: "I say then, Hath God cast away his people? God forbid" (Rom. 11:1). The gifts and calling of God are without repentance (11:29). The holiness of the Covenant and its continuing validity are evident from the symbol of the "noble olive tree" Israel; some of its branches are broken off and in its place the wild olive branches of heathen Christianity are grafted which will then "partake of the root and fatness of the olive tree" (11:17). The Apostle admonishes the converted heathens not to become arrogant: "Boast not against the branches. But if thou boast, thou bearest not the root, but the root thee" (11:18). When God's plan of salvation will be fulfilled with the heathen, all of Israel will be saved: "Touching the election, they are beloved for the fathers' sakes" (11:28).[179] Paul concluded by rejoicing over the inconceivable greatness of God. This central piece of the Epistle to the Romans, with its admonition to the Christians not to become arrogant because of their apparent preference, has been fully appreciated only in recent times and is today the biblical basis for all those who accept the divinely ordained, mysterious coexistence of Israel and the Christians.

Buber belonged to that school of biblical scholarship which places great emphasis on the gnostic element in Paul's thinking. The American scholar, Malcolm L. Diamond,[180] finds in Buber's interpretation of Paul something akin to Persian dualism. The body has another law from that of the spirit, and this accounts for the moral incompetence of human nature in the presence of an acknowledged ideal; so that it is not surprising to find that the verse in the Apostle's epistles most frequently cited by Buber is: "For the good that I would I do not: but the evil which I would not, that I do" (Rom. 7:19). Buber's conception of Paul's character is described by Diamond as "extremely onesided": "Not only is there a 'law in his body' that opposed the 'law of his reason,' there was a Hebraism in his thinking that struggled with his Hellenistic dualism. The Hebraic side is the one Buber neglects." Paul was also closer to Jesus than it would appear from Buber's interpretation, a fact pointed out long before Diamond by Albert Schweitzer in *The Mysticism of Paul the Apostle in the Light of Jewish Religious History* (London, 1931).

Schweitzer's conception was followed by Hans Joachim Schoeps' in his comprehensive and significant work, *Paul, the Theology of the Apostle.* The author characterized his work as a kind of "homecoming of the heretic," and has accordingly continued in his treatment of Paul what Buber had begun with the figure of Jesus. His book presents us "with a profusion of traditional Jewish material which makes it possible to understand the Apostle not only as having an affinity with (as Schoeps believes), but as being wholly 'the Yehudi in concealment' himself . . . whose praise is not from men but from God, as he wished it to be (Rom. 2:29—with an allusion to Gen. 29:35)." [181]

Schoeps also proceeds from the belief that in the Septuagint we have a pronounced ethicization of Judaism which strongly emphasizes justification by works. Paul, like Jesus, was opposed to a "religion of performance" that tends to lose sight of the fact that it is not the observance of the law that makes men righteous but God. The argumentation and exegetical method of the Pauline Epistles are rabbinic. Paul had studied with Gamaliel in Jerusalem and had retained the rabbinic custom of citing biblical verses, singly and in combination, to support his arguments. The apocalyptic element in his thinking provided him with the idea of the Son of Man and the aeon speculations which first appeared in the book of Daniel. Schweitzer also regarded Paul as an aeon theologian: for the Apostle is of the belief, also found throughout rabbinic writings, that with the coming of the Messiah the Torah will lose its validity. Schoeps speaks of a messianic interval which will terminate with the return of Christ and the resurrection of the dead. The aeon *pneuma*, however, is ushered in with the resurrection of Jesus.

In his detailed study of Paul's messianic belief Schoeps insists that the historian of religion is obliged to take the Damascus incident as seriously as the Covenant at Sinai, for it bears evidence of a true theophany and its language is similar to the theophanies found in the Septuagint. Unless the Damascus incident is taken to have a real content, no understanding of Paul is possible. In discussing Jewish messianic ideas Schoeps came to the conclusion that the belief that "Jesus

Christ is the Son of God," is the only "basic un-Jewish principle" in the Apostle's thinking, and that all other un-Jewish ideas are derived from this fundamental principle. Moreover, his doctrine of salvation can be traced to Jewish elements which he combined in a novel manner.

Schoeps expresses the view that Judaism has not yet sufficiently realized that since the time of Christ other nations have been able to share the belief of the fathers through Christianity. He agrees with Franz Rosenzweig that the ancient Covenant is valid for Jews for all time, but that this does not preclude God's having entered into another Covenant. In his letter to Rudolf Ehrenberg, in which he retracts his decision to become a Christian, Rosenzweig even takes the view that for the peoples of the world Jesus Christ is the only way to the Father: "What Christ and his Church mean in the world, in this we are agreed: no one comes to the Father except through him. No one *comes* to the Father except the one who no longer needs to come to the Father because he *is* already with him. And this is the case with the people Israel." [182] Israel will remain the priestly people until the day when the Father will be "all in all" (1 Cor. 15:28). As for the Jews and Christians who in common await the end of God's ways, Schoeps declares that "it might well be that He who comes at the end of time, He who has been alike the expectation of the synagogue and the church, will bear one and the same countenance." [183] In the meantime it would help improve the Christian-Jewish dialogue if the Christians would understand the law not only as it is viewed in the Epistle to the Romans but also as it appears in Psalms 19 and 119—which reveal all the meanings of the Torah as the "Way" to God—and realize what the concept "rejoicing in the law" means in Judaism. The law is the mediator of the Old Testament, as Jesus Christ is for the Church, and has therefore not only ethical but also sacramental significance. The Psalter is filled with expressions of "the Law's beauty, sweetness, or preciousness"; it is clean and everlasting and its order is for the Jews "the mirror of divine order." [184] "It is not monotheism," writes Franz Rosenzweig,[185] "but the Torah that makes the Jew." On the other hand, the Jews must make an effort to understand Paul's "law of Christ" (Gal. 6:2; 1 Cor. 9:21); in the eyes of the Apostle the ultimate meaning of the Torah had been fulfilled by Christ and had become the "personal divine-human pointing of the way" (Thieme).

Ernst Simon in "Martin Buber and the Faith of Israel" (Hebrew ed., 1958), cited in Diamond's book,[186] has chided Buber for his inconsistency in condemning Paul for abrogating the law when he himself fails to observe it. This is but another element, seen from a Christian point of view, that makes Buber's relation to Paul more complicated than he was probably aware of.

Buber's interpretation of Paul is shown by Diamond to have been influenced by Kierkegaard, whose views of the Apostle were colored by his own brooding, melancholy nature and for whom salvation could be achieved only by a "leap" of faith and a transformation of existence through faith. Kierkegaard was for Buber the pioneer of a philosophical anthropology. Although he severely criticized Kierkegaard's category of the Single One, he was at the same time deeply influenced by it.[187] Religious thinkers who, like himself, had experienced a deep religious conversion, a kind of revelation which compelled them to rethink man's position in the world and to seek a new basis for it, engaged Buber's mind to a very large extent. Besides Paul and Kierkegaard, there was also the figure of Pascal who influenced him and, above all, Hamann, whose philosophy of language and symbols of existence he made his own.[188]

In this respect Buber did the least justice to Paul. Just as the early disciples of Jesus regarded the Pharisees as their chief adversaries, for precisely where much is held in common, there opposition is most intense and contradictions most glaring,[189] so is Buber spiritually closer to Paul than one would surmise from the nature of his polemic. He criticized Paul's dualism, although in his earlier years he had regarded the disposition to dualism as a basic Jewish trait. "The breath of unconditionality,"[190] which he took to be the uniquely Jewish element in the prophetic message, was also characteristic of Paul. The Apostle was also disposed to ecstasies and visions, and he was faithful to his divine revelation to the point of martyrdom. The theophany at Damascus was accompanied by dazzling light and an overpowering voice, as we find with all the prophets, but it was Christ as God's speech—and here was the parting of the ways. The revelation, as always in Judaism, effected in Paul a complete transformation and renewal of life. Buber had described the Greek concept *metanoia,* by which the Septuagint translates the Hebrew *teshuva,* as a reduction of the "turning" of the whole person to nothing more than a mere "change of mind"—this being one of the points where, as Franz Rosenweig said, "world history is found in the dictionary." [191] But Paul's conversion was so absolute that the "Christ lives in me" became for him new life and new creation. He was the only non-believer to whom the Resurrected One appeared, and it was from the standpoint of this special charismatic calling that he carried out his mission despite the opposition of the disciples of Jesus. His Damascus experience had transformed the substance of traditional faith from within into the sacramental existence of the Christian, following the same direction as Buber's interiorization of Judaism: the idea of the Church as "the mystic body of Christ" and participation in the death and resurrection of the Lord go back to him. He places "being under the law" over against "being in Christ," in which every believer takes part through the sacraments, that is, through ontic participation. Paul was concerned, like Buber, to make Christian *humanum* visible out of his revelation and to find a conceptual basis for the "new Israel," so that Albert Schweitzer could call the Apostle "the patron saint of thought in Christendom." [192] But his faith did not remain contemplative; his life was consumed in the realization of the true Christian community and concern for its hallowing way of life. Just as Buber characterized the Jewish soul as "the soul of Abraham," so did Paul recognize in Abraham the father of all believers. He saw that the promise that had been given to Abraham was to be a blessing for all mankind and was to be fulfilled by preaching Christ to the nations. In Buber's attitude to faith there is a constant spilling over of Judaism into the universally human, a desire to fathom its original condition and elemental power: a transformation that rises above the merely national bond of faith.

Buber did not include *Two Types of Faith* among his biblical writings but in the volume of his philosophical works. He did not wish to appear to speak as a theologian, for his main concern was to discover the basic human relations to God in the same sense in which he wished gnosis to be understood as not only a merely historical but a universally human category also.[193] His initial assumption was that only the diversity of faiths can fully reveal the changing content of faith. His purpose in *Two Types of Faith* was not to draw historical limits but to set forth two principles, one of which "found its representative reality" among Jews, the other among Christians—whereby the religio-historical notion emerges "that Jesus and central Pharisaism belong essentially to one another, just as early Christianity and Hellenistic Judaism do." [194]

The book was written during the siege of Jerusalem in the War of Liberation waged by the new state of Israel against the Arabs. Under such circumstances it is understandable that he should become keenly conscious of the "unredeemed character of the world," of which he reproachfully reminded Christianity; and the Christians on their part will understand how in this "chaos of destruction" Jesus was close to him as a great son of Israel who could be subsumed under no category of his history of faith. Nevertheless, no believing Christian will recognize his faith in what Buber had to say about it. Buber's interpretation of the Jewish Bible is based on its coherent character which consists essentially in the spoken word and in its message; the New Testament also has a coherent character, and is in the same sense revelation and proclamation.

Two Types of Faith has been the subject of criticism by Christians since it first appeared. The two Catholic reactions which deserve special mention are those of Hans Urs von Balthasar in *Martin Buber and Christianity* (London, 1961; original German: *Einsame Zwiesprache*, 1958), and the valuable contributions of Karl Thieme in *Freiburger Rundbriefen*; on the Protestant side we have the excursus devoted to Buber in the third volume of Emil Brunner's *Dogmatik*.[195] Buber's relation to Christianity has also been treated by Balthasar and Brunner in the volume of critical essays devoted to Buber's life and works. The critics are at one in acknowledging their indebtedness to Buber; at the same time their internal sectarian differences recede in the face of a common rejection of assertions that a Christian cannot accept. Balthasar describes the significance of Buber's concentration on the theocratic, prophetic, and sacramental principle in the history of Israel from the standpoint of Christianity as a consistent method of a reduction of

Judaism that runs counter to the historical current.[196] Apocalypse is treated only as a continuation of prophecy that is essentially alien to the people. Buber's interpretation tends to ignore the historical line of development from prophecy to the conviction that the kingdom of God cannot be established by man's unaided strength and plainly leads to the idea of the "Son of Man." As Karl Thieme pointed out, it is not a question of different "types of faith," but of different "times of faith" and a shift of emphasis.

Brunner, who regards *Two Types of Faith* as "a major attack on Christianity," sees it as being written by a Jew who set forth his reasons for not being able to accept Christianity.[197] Behind the early Christian's "I believe that," however, was a deep emotional involvement in the overpowering message and promise of salvation spoken by the Apostle: "You have words of life": the proclamation of the love of God in the fulfilling love of Christ. Beside the trusting faith of the Old Testament must be placed the triune faith, hope, and love, which belong together in the New Testament, or the conjunction of faith and hope found in Paul, or faith and love in John.[198] Josef Pieper in *Ueber den Glauben* [On belief] [199] points out that the fact of believing someone and believing something always belong together, and he cites passages from Aquinas and Luther to corroborate this view. Christian faith seeks, above all, communion with God, which Cardinal Newman sums up in the words: "We believe because we love." [200]

The Christian of today finds himself in a "super-nation of the Church," [201] just as the Jew finds himself in a national faith; the Christian also waits and hopes as a "we" and not as a lonely, unredeemed soul.[202] In its effort to combat erroneous teachings, early Christianity was constantly compelled to set forth its dogmas and to express its mysteries in concepts. Bishop Hilary, as Thieme informs us, had complained of this necessity in the fourth century, and Thomas Aquinas declared that the *explicatio fidei*, the conceptual elaboration of a faith-content, is justified only in order to combat erroneous beliefs.[203] Christian dogmas are for the non-Christian just as incomprehensible as the law is for the non-Jew; there are prejudices on both sides that need to be removed. Karl Rahner, in the most illuminating essay for the understanding of dogma in recent times, "Was ist eine dogmatische Aus-

sage?" [What is a dogmatic statement?] [204] states that a dogmatic statement can only be an analogous one, corresponding to the infinite
diversity of divine and human reality, and that our concepts remain
bound to human nature and to the terminology of the historical epoch.
The dogmatic statement is spoken *ex fide ad fidem:* it proceeds from the
light of faith, and the *habitus fidei* must penetrate and comprehend the
habitus scientiae. A dogma is a statement that penetrates the mystery:
an infinite object is designated by finite concepts. Rahner gives as an
example the word *person,* which in the ecclesiastical doctrine of the
trinity is something quite different from what it is usually considered.

It is a sign of genuine mystery, rooted in revelation and faith experience, that through it new spheres of life are constantly being disclosed. From the time of St. Augustine down to our own day Christian
thinkers have discovered trinitarian structures in the world and in man:
God's trinitarian character is reflected in creation. Romano Guardini's
attempt to develop a Christian anthropology in *Welt und Person*
[World and person] [205] is noteworthy in that he also proceeds from the
revelation of the Old Testament, according to which the things of the
world are God's "language," and finds it consummated in the logos
doctrine of the Gospel of John. God is Person in that he speaks; man
also is person in that he enters into dialogue. His I-being consists essentially in the fact that God is his Thou. In the epilogue to *Schriften über
das dialogische Prinzip* Buber indicated that the meaning of the I-Thou
relation had been discovered simultaneously in several quarters, but
failed to mention Guardini in this connection; nor do we find Buber's
name mentioned in the works of Guardini. Man's personality is related
by Guardini to the triune God.[206] The essence of the Christian message resides for him in the "mysterious and exuberant manner in which
God is Person." That there is only *one* God is found in the Old Testament: "The new revelation is the way in which this God says *I'*"—the
convergence of the unity of God-being with the Opposite of existence.
This relationship is interpreted in the New Testament in two ways:
Christ as the "Son" of God and as the "Word" of God—begetting and
speaking are the two ways in which life is revealed. Something of a primary symbolism is thus suggested, but the mystery is not explained.

The human person and its I-Thou relation are for the Christian the attenuated and explicated image of the divine trinity.

Still another thought of Guardini is essential for the dialogue with Judaism. In *Two Types of Faith* Buber spoke of his feeling that the Christian's immediacy to God is obstructed by Christ who as the Son of God, leader, and Savior takes the place of God.[207] Guardini asserts that the real and ultimate Thou is the Father; but Christ is the one who alone speaks the true "Thou" to the Father. In the deepest sense we do not say "Thou" to Christ, but we partake in his Thou-saying in that we follow him—for he is the Way.

God is represented in his relation to man, according to Buber, in the paradox of the "absolute Person." The trinity is the mystery of the absolute I-Thou relation. The third divine person is the primal image, as it were, for the ontic "between" which Buber sought to apprehend in the realm of human existence as a special sphere within the I-Thou relation, the sphere "between man and man." Here we have a mysterious correspondence. The simultaneous return of both religions to the biblical image of man, which has drawn the religions closer together in our day, remains inexplicable. At a time when every Jew is called upon to defend his faith, Buber's Hebrew humanism summons the priestly people to recall the charisma of a personal God-immediacy. From the primal symbol of the trinity, Guardini deduces that to be a person does not mean an isolated individualism but an "open" personality toward community. The transparency of every earthly Thou toward God is a conviction shared by both thinkers.

Balthasar's book seeks an earnest dialogue between Israel and the Church, between the two parts of God's people who have become estranged, but are divinely ordained, as Franz Rosenzweig recognized, to exist side by side. Decisive for our day is not the theoretical "dialogue" but its realization, the personal participation of life to life, and the courage to venture a confrontation in a spirit described by Buber in his discussion with a Christian in 1914: [208] "I no longer know how from that I came to speak of Jesus and to say that we Jews knew him from within, in the impulses and stirrings of his Jewish being, in a way that remains inaccessible to the peoples submissive to him. 'In a way that remains inaccessible to you'—so I directly addressed the former clergy-man.[209] He stood up, I too stood, we looked into the heart of one another's eyes. 'It is gone,' he said, and before everyone we gave one another the kiss of brotherhood. The discussion of the situation between Jews and Christians had been transformed into a bond between the Christian and the Jew. In this transformation dialogue was fulfilled."

FROM 1933 to 1938 Buber was the undisputed spiritual leader of German Jewry. It was not until the spring of 1938, after the prohibition that forbade him to teach or lecture had been extended to include private Jewish gatherings, that he left for Palestine to join the faculty of the Hebrew University in Jerusalem. Now, as a responsible teacher in his own land, would his earlier *Addresses on Judaism* retain their influence, and would he be able to help the new generation of young Zionists find their way?

The situation was far different from what it had been in 1910. It was no longer a question of appealing to the national sentiments of the students, for the political tension in the country was becoming acute, and patriotic feeling ran high. Buber was faced with the unpopular task of reaffirming the ideals of humanity and justice and of reminding the people of Israel's religious mission and historical responsibility. Furthermore, he was not officially authorized to teach religious subjects, as he had been in Frankfurt, but instead social philosophy: "This was a consequence of the Orthodox opposition to Buber's being entrusted with anything that had to do with religion." [1] His long years of research in the field of biblical studies thus found no outlet in his new academic post and, despite his distaste for all rigid systems, he was constrained to develop his philosophical thoughts methodically. In 1938 he began to expand his theme of dialogic existence in the direction of a philosophical anthropology.

Buber's first steps to this end led him to history; but the historical problems formulated by him involved highly personal views of actual

events. His first series of lectures on "The Problem of Man" from
Kant to present-day philosophical thought, corresponded to the situation of the German Jew who "has passed through every heaven and
hell of the Occident" [2] and now, returning home after having taken
farewell of Europe, is prepared to give an account of its spiritual values.

This is the viewpoint already expressed in his inaugural lecture in
Jerusalem, "The Demand of the Spirit and Historical Reality," in
which he contrasts Plato with Isaiah, the spirit of the West with that of
the Bible. This lecture not only served as an introduction to social philosophy, defining its aims and possibilities, but also provided a masterful
description of the condition of the Jews in Palestine viewed in the light
of the past.

The pioneer thinkers of sociology were philosophers who in the
turbulent aftermath of the French Revolution recognized the crisis of
the modern spirit, and sought to establish the spiritual foundations of a
new social structure, convinced that the human spirit could avert the
imminent dissolution of our society by a discriminating and systematic
analysis of social concepts. Sociology thus made its appearance at a time
when the human spirit was confronted by a crisis in its social life of
such magnitude that it could no longer be ignored by the critical
thinker. This required an independent, judicious attitude on the part of
the sociologist, which in turn demanded a new relation to reality, "a
new dialogic relation that purifies him." [3] This seems to be contradicted by modern sociology which is no longer concerned with the individual but with social structures and institutions. Buber insisted that
innovations can only be effective when people undergo at the same
time a change in their living together. To this end sociological education is necessary. Although sociology is now established as an independent science, free of subjective evaluations, Buber demanded a philosophy which includes evaluation that is undertaken with a conscious
awareness of a higher responsibility, following in the spirit of Ferdinand Tönnies whose "social philosophy" as theoretical sociology comprehends society as a whole, investigates its ruling categories and their
relations to other spheres of life, and raises the question concerning the
meaning of social life itself. The student of sociology must learn to

think independently on the basis of his social obligations and experiences, as far as his finite understanding permits him to possess the truth.

But even if one is able to attain this inner freedom, how can one maintain an independent attitude in the face of external obstacles? Has the spirit the power to assert its claims and realize them as historical reality? Buber answered this question by citing two contrasting historical situations. The first refers to Plato who in his Seventh Letter tells us of his repeated attempts to cooperate in Syracuse in the establishment of a state founded on philosophical principles—an undertaking which finally came to nought because of the death of his disciple, Prince Dion, master of Syracuse. Plato was convinced that a just state can be created only by a philosopher who is brought up to be king or by a king who has been trained as a philosopher. He believed in the office of the spirit to exercise power and to regenerate corrupt power. In accomplishing this task he looked upon himself as the heir and deputy of Socrates. But he was not entrusted with political leadership in Greece; nor was his disciple, the philosopher-king Dion, able to carry out his ideas successfully in Syracuse. Spirit here believes itself to be in possession of the truth, but fails when it encounters reality. What is the reason for this? It is the spiritual father of Utopia whose image Buber deliberately held up to his countrymen as they searched for new social forms along "paths in Utopia."

Buber then described an altogether different kind of failure, that of the prophet Isaiah, whose relation to spirit is wholly distinct from that of Plato, for in the Bible spirit is something that descends on man from above and spurs him on. Power is also seen by Isaiah to belong to man as little as spirit. The king is only the representative of God, the real King, and is held to account by God's messenger before whom he is powerless and inevitably condemned to fail. Isaiah does not propound an idea; he only has a message to deliver. He knows he is unclean before God, as his king is, but he also knows that it is required of every individual to do justice. He urges the people to remain faithful to its divine king and not to rely on alliances but to acknowledge God's dominion over all areas of social and political life. For this very reason Isaiah's failure is different from Plato's, for his demand struck root in Israel and gave it "this new chance to translate the spirit into reality of which we have a presentiment. We may yet experience an era of history which refutes 'history.' The prophet fails in the hour of history, but not in so far as the future of his people is concerned." [4]

The social thinker of today is not a prophet but a philosopher. He has no message and can only express his knowledge. He does not desire to build a universally valid, just society, like Plato, but to criticize its shortcomings and injustices, as Isaiah did, regardless of failure or success. Buber concluded with a word of hope for Jerusalem's historical hour and for the opportunity "to advise and prepare," even without a message.

Buber thus saw his position in Palestine confined to the narrow, precarious ridge between the attitude of the philosopher and that of the prophet, faced with the task of making visible and accessible in the form of knowledge "the one thing that is needful," but which today can no longer be transmitted as message. The divergent conceptions of the Greek and Hebrew view of man, as set forth in the inaugural lecture, reveal the serious nature of this task. It reminds us of how Buber before World War I wrote a book in the form of a Platonic dialogue which bore the name of the prophet Daniel because it takes us through the world-age of the spirit and ends with a highly personal view of God's kingdom. It was Buber's life problem to find a middle term to bridge the gap between philosopher and prophet.

The solution attempted in "What Is Man?" follows the lines of sociophilosophical criticism: "This work, the first part of which is essentially the historical treatment of a problem and the second expository, proposes to arrange historically the subject matter of the dialogical principle set forth in other works and to contrast it critically with some contemporary theories. At the same time it would serve as an introduction to a work not yet published" (preface).

The question What is man?—which is the theme of the book—was formulated but not answered by Kant. That this basic question was left open has made it possible for present-day philosophical anthropology to go back to Kant; every answer to the problem only made us aware of the distance that separates us from Kant. The philosophy of the Enlightenment saw man as a being determined by reason, and did not yet contemplate those problems which for us are bound up with Kant's question, that is, "man's special place in the cosmos, his connexion with destiny, his relation to the world of things, his understanding of his fellow-men, his existence as a being that knows it must die, his attitude in all the ordinary and extraordinary encounters with the mystery with which his life is shot through." [5]

In the historical part of the book Buber dealt with the question which concerns the conditions that made the anthropological problem so critical in the history of the Occident. This is because a philosophical anthropology is bound to comprehend man in his relation to non-human existence and to treat him as problematical. To illustrate this, Buber made a distinction in the history of the human spirit between epochs of habitation, in which man lives in the world as in a house,[6] and epochs of homelessness in which man feels like a stranger in the world. The first world-house of the Occident in which man found a firm place was built by Aristotle, but this provided no answer to the anthropological question as to the nature of man. The first to raise the anthropological question, more than seven centuries after Aristotle, was Augustine who turned for his solution to God, because he found something in man that could not be understood from the standpoint of this world. Christian faith in the Middle Ages built the new cosmic house which filled space from heaven to hell and time from the creation of the world to the end of days, a house in which man felt secure because of Christ's redeeming sacrifice. Toward the end of the Middle Ages the question concerning man arose again, but as a conceptual and not as a vital question. Only with the emergence of the new Copernican world-image does man become aware of his insecurity in the infinity of space and, at the same time, of his spiritual indestructibility. Pascal was the first who combined in himself a knowledge of these two extremes.

The anthropological question thus arises from man's insecurity and loneliness in the world. The problem was enormously deepened by Kant's insight that time and space are not attributes of the external world but forms of human perception. After Kant, another great thinker undertook to restore man's lost security: Hegel built "the world-house of history." Time was now to be man's new abode, for there was no more room in Copernican space to build another house. The new edifice was to be time in the form of history: "Hegel's system is the third great attempt at security within western thought; following Aristotle's cosmological attempt and Aquinas's theological attempt it is the logological attempt." [6a] Here world reason goes its own way through history, revealing itself to man in its dialectical development in which thesis is relieved by antithesis and antithesis by synthesis. Man is ensconced in a well-constructed house and in a reliable order of history—and the anthropological question seems to be solved.

The Hegelian house, however, proves to be uninhabitable for the real man of flesh and blood. Time, in which the self-realization of the spirit takes place, is in Hegel's system thought-time and does not coincide with time as it is actually experienced by man: "An intellectual image of the universe, which incorporates 'the goal of universal history,' has no power in this part of it to give assurance." [7] Such assurance can only be given by faith, as we find, for example, in Iranian messianism with its belief in the final victory of light over darkness or in the Israelite belief in a messianic kingdom. Hegel's system is a secularized messianism, but one which is powerless to imbue man with a feeling of unconditioned trust in the future based on faith.

Following Hegel, and in opposition to him, Marx succeeded in making such trust possible, at least for some time. His doctrine of history is likewise secularized messianism; it is, however, no longer a complete world-picture but what may be called a "sociological reduction" to society. The world of man is society, and a new society is to become man's house of the future. But Marx also depended too much on the lawfulness of the dialectic process and underestimated man's power of decision; the security he provided for the future was only apparent and failed to stand the test of time.

Feuerbach's "anthropological reduction" may be placed at the side of the sociological reduction of the Hegelian world-image. It starts with man, but man is not made the problem. Hegel's universal world-reason was to Feuerbach but another concept for God, and God in turn was only man transposed to heaven. The new philosophy was to deal exclusively with man, and made no claim to be anything more than anthropology. But it did not lead to the depths of human existence nor beyond the threshold of Kant's fourth question: What is man? In one point alone Feuerbach discovered something new: he took man not as an individual by himself, but as I and Thou, as man with man, as community.

The first one to concentrate on the problem of man and place him in the center of his philosophical speculation was Nietzsche. Man is for him "the animal that is not yet established," not a definite final species but a transitional form, something that is becoming, an embryonic superman. Nietzsche was a "mystic of the Enlightenment," and he had fantastic notions of man's role in the universe. He saw man as related to the animal world and from this he derived his formulation of the problem, but he did not see man's "primal distance" from nature which is peculiar only to the human species.

In the second half of the book Buber explained how the anthropological problem became acute only in our time because of two factors. The first, which is chiefly sociological in nature, refers to the disintegration of the old organic forms in the life of man with man—the family, small work groups, the village community. The social forms that replaced them—clubs, trade unions, political parties—could not restore man's lost security, and only deepened his solitude. The second factor which made the anthropological problem critical is that modern man was outstripped by his works. His soul was too faint to master the world he created. The machines which were to serve him enslaved him and impoverished his life. The economy has become a huge, unwieldy apparatus, and politics a demonic power that threatens man with annihilation. It is with these far-reaching sociological and psychological changes that a philosophical anthropology in our time has to deal.

Before considering the two most important representatives of this philosophical anthropology, Buber first turned to Kierkegaard, from whom wholly different philosophical and theological movements today derive their "existentialist" attitude. Kierkegaard's rejection of Hegel's philosophy and the absolute *I* of German idealism, which believes it can create a world by thinking it, was radical and final. More than any other thinker he demonstrated that thought "cannot authorize itself but is authorized only out of the existence of the thinking man." [8] As a result of this new perspective of the relation between truth and existence Kierkegaard's influence extended far beyond his time. He discovered this relation because his interest was mainly in faith, not in thought. The question he asked concerned the congruence between thought religion and lived religion. Faith is genuine only when it is rooted in and confirmed by the existence of the believer. Kierkegaard's view of man was theological anthropology, but it contributed greatly in advancing the philosophical question of our time.

The two contemporary representatives of the anthropological problem with whom Buber took issue are Max Scheler and Martin Heidegger. Scheler did not complete his philosophy of anthropology, but his description of the intellectual-historical situation from which it proceeded is penetrating and realistic, namely: man in our time has become problematic as never before in that "he no longer knows what he essentially is, but at the same time also *knows* that he does not know. Only by being willing to make a complete *tabula rasa* of all traditions about this question, and by learning to look in extreme methodical aloofness and astonishment on the being called man, can we reach tenable insights again." [9] The discussion of traditional theories about man was to lead to the impartiality and independent reflection demanded today—anthropology was to become a history of human self-consciousness.

Scheler was a fascinating personality of unusual intellectual force and broad vision, but he was more effective in the give and take of conversation than in the systematic elaboration of ideas. It was precisely this intellectual vigor that enabled him to think through the problem of man from various metaphysical points of view. He was at first a student of Eucken, and then became one of Husserl's disciples. During this theistic-phenomenological period he developed a material axiology and a metaphysics of person in which the basic principles of Catholicism were elaborated. In the twenties he became interested in the relation between the sociological conditions of culture and the formation of values. He then turned away from Catholicism and drew closer to a teaching which was based on the dualism of spirit and impulse, namely, the metaphysics of Schopenhauer.

It is to this point that Buber's criticism was directed. Scheler's affinity to Spinoza, which seems to stem from his world-ground and its two attributes, spirit and impulse, is deceptive. Spinoza's attributes are based on an eternal unity that transcends world and being; for Scheler the essence of the Absolute consists in the duality of spirit and impulse. Being is thus confined to time and to the world process which occurs in time. In place of Spinoza's attributes Scheler puts Schopenhauer's two basic principles, will and idea. The world-ground must "lift the brakes" of impulse and release it. Spirit, which Scheler also calls *deitas*, in itself has no power, and it can only influence the world process by guiding life's impulses and sublimating them, so that spirit and impulse break through and rise to a higher form of life. In this process that goes on in man, Scheler saw the self-realization of the divine, for man is the only available place for deification, for the becoming of God. The idea of a "realization" of God through man had also occupied Buber in the days before World War I, but he was always aware that "only a primal certainty of divine being enables us to sense the awesome meaning of divine becoming, that is, the self-imparting of God to His creation and His participation in the destiny of its freedom." [10]

In Scheler's teaching of the impotence of the spirit, Buber recognized the peculiar malady of our time and the consequent deterioration of society. It is not an accident that the thesis of the sublimation of the impulses employs Freudian categories. According to Buber, spirit is in its original reality "event," being "something that is not expected but suddenly happens." [11] Buber cited the "event" of speech in the child and the way simple people arrive at insights by participating in the being of the world. In both cases spirit and impulse coordinate; spirit arises from its concord with impulse. Spirit stands in a primal relation to being.

Buber found in Scheler, as he did in Hegel, Marx, and Nietzsche, an ontological overestimation of the significance of time as historical time, a characteristic German phenomenon. In Hegel and Marx it is expressed in a "secularized messianism," in Nietzsche in the significance given by this "mystic of the Enlightenment" to becoming in time for the transition of man to superman. Through Scheler's "becoming God," however, the Absolute is placed completely in time and made dependent on it; he "lets being itself be resolved in time." [12] By absolutizing time man's relation to the supratemporal is severed.

This question of the relation of being and time is of special interest to Heidegger, and he made it the subject of his chief philosophical work, that is, the question of how time belongs to the meaning of being. Buber also placed Heidegger in the line that leads from Hegel to our present-day historization of being and absolutizing of historical time: "For Hegel world history is the absolute process in which spirit attains to consciousness of itself; so for Heidegger historical existence is the illumination of being itself; in neither is there room for a suprahistorical reality that sees history and judges it." [13]

When Buber described Heidegger and Scheler at the end of the essay (in the section called "Prospect") as representatives of an "individualistic anthropology," he reduced two unequal magnitudes to the same common denominator. Unlike Scheler, who had a broad and far-ranging view of philosophical problems, Heidegger was a philosopher in a strict and exclusive sense, so that he cannot be adequately comprehended from the standpoint of a philosophical anthropology—which can be seen from the basic question of his *Introduction to Metaphysics*: "Why is there being at all, and not rather nothing?" The subject matter of philosophical anthropology is for Buber "concrete human life," [14] and he criticized Heidegger for dealing only with a partial segment of life and not with the whole, with a "metaphysical homunculus," as it were. Heidegger, like Buber, began with Dilthey's attitude and his efforts to find a basis for philosophy and for a new understanding of history. But Dilthey, according to Heidegger, had also left the basic concept "life," with which he wished to imbue philosophical understanding, in "ontological indifference." His conception of history remained imprisoned in Greek metaphysical thought which is oriented in seeing, an ideational thinking which regards the existent as a permanent being present in time and space. Such a conception, however, fails to do justice to temporality in which factive life takes place and is unable to think time in its peculiar essence. It could think of that which is *(das Seiende)* in its being *(Sein)*, but not inquire into being itself.[15] Heidegger makes the meaning of being a problem and, in conjunction with his question concerning the "being of that which is existent" *(Sein des*

Seienden), he comprehends man as *Dasein,* that is, as that entity *(Seiende)* which has a "self-understood status" (existence) and an understanding of being. The question concerning the nature of being thus remains closely connected with the question concerning man. In an "existential analytic of *Dasein,*" the ground of *Dasein* is to be thought within the relational triangle *Dasein*-time-being. The first part of *Being and Time* is divided into three sections: 1) Preparatory Fundamental Analysis of *Dasein*; 2) *Dasein* and Temporality; 3) Time and Being. But the work terminates abruptly at the end of the second section: "Since temporality is conceived as the meaning of the being of *Dasein*, the decisive step still remains to be taken: to derive from this temporality the temporality of every understanding of being, the time-bound nature of the meaning of being prior to thought." [16] The "chemical purity" of the *Dasein* concept, with which Buber reproached Heidegger, was methodically demanded as a consequence of raising the question.

Heidegger interpreted the "basic state of *Dasein*" as "Being-in-the-world," whereby the world is not conceived as an entity over against which man sees himself. Being-in-the-world means a "structural totality" out of which neither man nor the world can be lifted. When Buber found the dialogical character of life absent from Heidegger's "concern, solicitude, Being-with," he was not doing justice to Heidegger's formulation of the problem: "The I and the Thou belong in the sphere of the authenticity of *Dasein*; they refer to existence and not to the inauthentic Being-in-the-world whose preliminary interpretation we are here considering." [17] Also L. Binswanger placed "love" over against Heidegger's "concern," which he considers to be a one-sided interpretation of human existence; he later admits, however, that he misunderstood Heidegger's "a priori exposing to view the concern-structure of existence" as "anthropological teaching." [18] To both Buber and Heidegger man is in his totality and in every expression of life distinct from animals; for Buber this was because of man's capacity for "primary distance and relation," for Heidegger it was because man possesses a "being-understanding." The significance of I and Thou, the "we" that arises from the I and Thou, is beyond Heidegger. He was constantly striving to gain firm ground from which to approach such questions, but it eluded him. In his later years he increasingly emphasized the "being-on-the-way" of his philosophy. In the preface to his *Lectures and Essays* he spoke of himself as an author who under the best of circumstances can only "show the way," that is, indicate to others a way of thought. In *On the Road to Language (Unterwegs zur Sprache)* Heidegger recorded a conversation he had with a Japanese in which he assumed the role of "interrogator," [19] which alone would contradict Buber's opinion that Heidegger's "self" is a "closed system." [20] For it was not a scientific conversation conducted in the "avid pursuit of explanations" or with the desire to gain information, but a genuine conversation which leaves what is really meant vague and even "hospitably hidden in obscurity." In such a conversation, according to Heidegger, "the vagueness not only does not divert the participants from the content, but grows more radiant and vigorous as it proceeds"—and thus the dialogic character seems to be fully preserved.

A philosophical anthropology which has its center of gravity in social philosophy is certain to miss the mark when it criticizes Heidegger. Philosophical anthropology was for Heidegger the end of the road that began with Descartes's conception of man as *subjectum*. Since Nietzsche's time Western metaphysics has dissolved into anthropology—a development which, according to Heidegger, cannot be overcome without first creating a new ontological basis.[21]

Since Buber started from Kant's question What is man?, he judged Heidegger chiefly on the basis of the latter's book on Kant,[22] a transitional work with which in the last analysis Heidegger failed as he did with *Being and Time*. When Buber delivered his lecture "The Problem of Man" in 1938, the work of Heidegger's that would have been most appropriate for him to consider in his criticism had not yet been published, namely, *Letter on Humanism*, addressed to the Frenchman Jean Beaufret. This work appeared in 1947 together with *Plato's Doctrine of Truth*, in which Heidegger removed a number of misunderstandings that *Being and Time* had occasioned in the minds of its readers.

In the meantime Heidegger had proceeded from the problem of "being and time" to that of "being and language." As long as he associated himself with existing philosophical currents of thought and attempted to deepen their presuppositions he failed. Now he left the path that had taken him back to the beginnings of Occidental thought, "into the nameless"—as he called it in his conversation with the Japanese. Language was to lead him back to the premetaphysical thinking of the Greeks, to the time when language was not yet an instrument for subduing being, nor thinking the "technique of explaining from highest causes." Here Heidegger sought to discover the original nature of truth as "exposing something to view," the Greek *aletheia.* In this light language appears as the "house" of being: "In its abode man dwells; thinkers and poets are the guardians of this abode." [23] Until now each humanism was indebted to the Being-conception of the late Greek philosophical schools which took it for granted that man's nature was something permanent and fixed. In a new humanism man must again become "the shepherd of Being" and guard the truth of Being "so that in the light of Being *(Sein),* being *(das Seiende)* may appear as the being that it is." [24] Man's nature must be thought further back to its beginnings in order to bring it back to "the vicinity of Being." Only in a "new proximity to Being" can man's destiny of "homelessness" be overcome; only here will it be decided whether "the holy" will again appear, which is the indispensable condition for the return of the godly and of God. Heidegger's humanism is not concerned with man as such but with the dimension "in which man's nature, determined by being itself, is at home." [25] Heidegger stresses the fact that the sentence "Man's nature rests on the Being-in-the-world" contains no decision as to "whether man in the theological-metaphysical sense is only a being of this world or of the world beyond." The existential determination of man in itself decides nothing as yet concerning "the existence of God" or his "non-existence," and this because of the observance of the limits set to human thought. In our time the man who "has strayed into subjectivity" can only descend into the "poverty of ex-istence of the *homo humanus.*" Heidegger maintains that the kind of thinking which proclaims God as the highest value debases God's nature by making it the object of man's evaluation.[26] Fundamental ontology, on the other hand, goes back to the essential ground from which the thinking of the truth of Being originates. The "beginnings" of thought that Heidegger had in mind he elucidated by two sayings of Heraclitus: "Man, in so far as he is man, lives in the vicinity of God"; and his words to his visitors when they expressed their disillusion at seeing him warming himself at the oven, "Here also the gods are present." [27]

Buber has more in common with Heidegger than one would assume from his sharp criticism in "The Problem of Man." Both thinkers had come under Dilthey's influence, and the nature of history had become for them a problem. Buber also inquired into the historical as the direct consummation of life and as "actual living events"; he was concerned with the "body" of a historical movement and the sparks that leap from person to person, with the "being-tradition" of the generations. Buber distinguished between epochs of habitation and epochs of homelessness in the history of the human spirit; Heidegger sought to disclose to his age the "house of Being" as that of language. Both thinkers have in common a deep and intimate relation to the poetry of Hölderlin, an understanding for the significance of myth in the development of humanity and for the "beginning" philosophy of Heraclitus. Above all, we must not omit the affinity of the two thinkers for the poetical word and its use in philosophical writing, including their zeal for extracting the secret wisdom of words by way of etymology, whose application is apparent in Buber's translation of the Bible and in Heidegger's philosophical language.

Kierkegaard's influence on both thinkers is evident in their attempt to keep the religious sphere free of intermixtures. Buber would have nothing to do with the "God of the philosophers," and he called theology a questionable type of philosophy.[28] Similarly, the "God of onto-theology" is not the "divine God" for Heidegger; he holds that only after the experience "God is dead" and after a long detour through "being-illumination" can the divine be restored. He lacks the sense for the religious mystery of Israel: "The beginning is for Heidegger not a truth-event as it is revealed in Jewish biblical faith; the Jewish biblical element is rejected by him without the slightest appreciation of its originality." [29] Buber correctly asserted that Heidegger had misunderstood the prophets of Israel and added that he had never encountered such a far-reaching misunderstanding of the prophets of Israel coming from such a high philosophical plane.[30] Christian thinkers, like Pascal and Kierkegaard, whose philosophical statements are based on a personal experience of faith, are reproached by Heidegger for retaining metaphysical conceptuality and thus combining two irreconcilable conceptions of history.[31] Heidegger himself started from theology; and from early Christianity he learned, as Pöggeler informs us, the essence of the historical: the time of the new Being of early Christian faith lasted until the second coming of Christ. Paul not only lived in time; he lived time itself: he experienced the present from the standpoint of the unknown future. The main concern of the early Christian experience of life was precisely a "non-objectifying consummation" which is "historical." In early Christianity Heidegger recognized "that the God of philosophy is not at all the living God of faith, and metaphysical theology not the last answer to the question of thinking." [32] The relation between language and Being emerged for Heidegger, as he expressed it in his late conversation with the Japanese visitor, from the relation of the biblical Word to theologic-speculative thought: "Without this theological background I would never have found the road of thought. Background always remains foreground" [33]—that is, it cannot be denied in any present.

"The Problem of Man" demonstrates Buber's ideas of dialogic existence as they progress to a philosophical anthropology. After setting forth the historical presuppositions of the question concerning man and analyzing the most important contemporary theories, Buber stated his own position with respect to the problem simply as thesis and "prospect." [34] At that time he was evidently still considering writing an independent study of the subject, What is man?

In the section called "Prospect," individualism is taken to be a great danger that threatens mankind in the twentieth century, and equally dangerous is the counter-movement of collectivism. Both world views prevent man from realizing his life relations with his whole being; both are the result of "cosmic and social homelessness, dread of the universe and dread of life." [34a] Collectivism promises man the security he craves; but in reality it is only a sop for his loneliness and not a remedy. A true relation can exist only from person to person, and only as a result of breaking through to the Other.

Life and thought today face the same problematical situation. Not only in reality but also in theory we believe that a choice must be made between an individualistic anthropology and a collectivistic sociology, and thus miss the opportunity of a third choice, which alone is the proper one: "The fundamental fact of human existence is man with man." [34b] Only from person to person do things take place that can be found nowhere else in nature, things which make man truly man—and these are localized neither within the individual nor in the world around him, but in the sphere where two human beings communicate with one another apart from their respective spheres. This sphere, to which Buber later devoted a separate work,[35] he called "between man and man" *(das Zwischenmenschliche)*. He described it as a "primal category" of human reality, but he was aware that it cannot as yet be conceptually comprehended. It deals with a dimension accessible to two people in meeting, and hence knows no continuity, for it is always constituted anew. In a spontaneous conversation, in a non-routine hour of instruction, or in a genuine embrace—wherever the barriers of individual being are broken through—a situation arises where "one life opens to another, not steadily but, so to speak, attaining its extreme reality only from point to point, yet also able to acquire a form in the continuity of life; the other becomes present not merely in the imagination or feeling but in the depths of one's substance, so that one experiences the mystery of the other being in the mystery of one's own. The two participate in one another's lives in the very fact, not psychically, but ontically." [36]

In *I and Thou* Buber spoke of "primary words," in the foreword to "What Is Man?" of the "dialogical principle," and in the section "Prospect" he explained the sphere of the "between," which is given with the I-Thou relation as an ontological dimension, and called it the "primal category" of human reality. Buber, in elaborating the experiences of the dialogic life as the basis of a philosophical anthropology, used the language of Western metaphysics. To find a place in the "human inheritance of thought" for the reality that had been disclosed to him as a religious experience, he was constrained "to express what is by its nature incomprehensible in concepts that could be used and communicated (although at times with difficulty)." [37] From Heidegger's point of view Buber, like Pascal and Kierkegaard, was a thinker destined to fail in that he appropriated a philosophical conceptual language which is unable to express his experiences. But, even apart from this, Buber's philosophical language remains a problem that cannot be ignored in a study of his intellectual development.

HEBREW HUMANISM AND THE LANGUAGE OF PHILOSOPHY

Man's homelessness in the universe, which was the starting-point of Buber's anthropological investigations, had been experienced by him at the age of fourteen as a phenomenon of "cosmic puberty," when the compulsion to imagine the world in time and space as finite or infinite produced in him a grave psychological disturbance. The inner necessity to translate abstract concepts into concrete, sensible images was not in his case a passing symptom of growing pains. Concepts had for him a dynamic quality, whether life-enhancing or inimical; symbolical concepts, especially, were felt by him to be endowed with a sensible-supersensible relational force. He thus appropriated Boehme's concept of the microcosm as well as the Hasidic teaching of the divine sparks in all things and beings. The leading ideas of his own *Talks of Realization* were both concepts and life-processes in one.

That the late, disintegrating, tragic-heroic form of Nietzsche's humanism became a dangerous influence in Buber's thinking was as characteristic for his dynamic intellectual life as was the fact that the German poet of Greek life was for him not Goethe but Hölderlin who knew the life of the gods and the "mystery of the zephyrs of the spirit." [38] Even the late Goethe address of 1949 [39] shows how Buber infused a different kind of humanity into the life air of German classicism by stressing the great poet's nearness to God, an intimate relationship that was free of all theological dogma. In the *Sorrows of Werther* the hero appears as the "son" of the eternal Father and utters Christ's words, "Why hast Thou forsaken me?" The "noble man" of Goethe's poem *Das Göttliche* [The divine]—"Edel sei der Mensch, hilfreich und gut"—Buber related to Meister Eckhart's saying of the *homo nobilis:* "The noble man is that begotten son whom the Father eternally begets," and this in turn indicated to him the adoptionism of the Bible.

The language of *I and Thou* reflects Buber's character and spiritual quality more perfectly than any other of his works, since it was at the same time a panegyric and a religious tract, a philosophical treatise and a modern myth in one. The Bible does not appear in the book, but the spirit of the biblical confrontation of man and God and its juxtaposition of the love of God and the love of man have become the language of a worldwide humanity and a life teaching that is accessible to all: the Thou which is directly addressed is a human and eternal Thou within the same life movement. The uniqueness of this work, which was composed in a spirit of "irresistible enthusiasm" and which ranges from mysticism to the speech usages of primitive peoples, thus anticipating an anthropological basis of a highly personal experience of faith, was apparent from the very outset. The work *Dialogue,* which was written many years later, is calmer in tone, but it is characterized by the same dreamy indifference to philosophical conceptual language. In it the author is concerned with illustrating dialogic life by giving examples of concrete situations in which it appears in the daily life of individuals and society. His own religious experience is freely acknowledged, illuminating every page with a warm and intimate light. The presentation of *Dialogue* makes no claim to completeness, but it adheres as closely as possible to lived life.

The language in which Buber in the twenties expressed the experience of the "eternal Thou" as a world view is unsystematic and unphilosophical from a technical point of view, but highly appropriate for his conception of the Bible. Hebrew humanism is the source from which he draws the abundant material he here presents to the reader. The "ontic" character of the I-Thou relation, which he emphasized from the very beginning, became for him a certainty through his meeting with the "eternal Thou." Such an experience is so overpowering that one never emerges from it the same as he was before. The revelation of the Voice that Buber heard is the same as that attested to in the Bible, the great document of the dialogue between heaven and earth. The revelation that comes to us at the destined hour teaches us anew to understand beginning and end, creation and redemption. From the presence of revelation we learn that there is a world-preserving creation that is unceasing, and that redemption goes on hour after hour.

When Buber in *I and Thou* spoke of "a world-life of association," of "the one boundless flood of actual life," he seems to have captured the dynamic aspect of the biblical account of creation: "*Ruach elohim,* the hovering, roaring manifestation is neither natural nor spiritual, but both at once; it is the creative breeze which arises from both nature and spirit . . . God is to be relegated neither to the natural nor to the spiritual sphere. He is neither nature nor spirit, but both have their origin in him." [40] There is only *one* undivided action that comes from God which flows down to earthly being.

In the twenties the double nature of the human "primary words" —I-Thou and I-It—appeared to Buber as the expression of a metacosmic "double movement": "Estrangement from the primal Source, in virtue of which the universe is sustained in the process of becoming, and of turning toward the primal Source, in virtue of which the universe is released in being." [41] These two basic movements, one toward individual being and one toward unification in which man is involved, constitute one single reality.

From the outline of the lecture, "On the Psychologizing of the World" *[Von der verseelung der Welt]*, given in 1923, around the time that *I and Thou* was published, we learn more about how Buber conceived the life of the world in philosophical language. He started from the one reality in which man and world confront one another: "The arch of relation arises, as it were, on these two clearly individual pillars." [42] When Buber designated I and world as two separate entities and observed that in place of world we could put "being," it is evident that he was not interested in using the philosophical language of any particular school. The confrontation of I and world is in his opinion endangered by two conceptions that arise from philosophical systems: by "psychologism," which draws the world into the soul and treats it in its most ordinary form as "idea," and by the contrary movement of "cosmologism" which regards the soul as a product of the world. This theory, however, does not comprehend "what is essential in the soul (the I)" even as the being-character of the world is *not* comprehended in the idea. The designations "psychologism" and "cosmologism" also reveal a wholly personal philosophical language.

These two contrary aspects must, according to Buber, be replaced by a third element that, however, is today "not even comprehensible in the form of an image" and that can be indicated only with the utmost caution. The more comprehensive reality into which the concepts of the psychic and cosmic are absorbed may be designated as "pneumatic reality": "This reality understood as existing being, as existing being into which all that is psychic and that is cosmic and all that is opposite and all that is inclusive of the two is embedded, this *ontologism* we can, with all foresight and self-limitation, set up for a moment as the third to the two—psychologism and cosmologism—a third which unites them." [42a]

That this ontologism is to be understood in conjunction with the metacosmic double movement discussed in *I and Thou* can be gathered from the fact that Buber understood soul and spirit not from the standpoint of the isolated individual (not "I-bound") but from the standpoint of the relation between I and world-bound or non-world-bound being: "Characteristic of both (soul and spirit) is the dynamic, that is, that they stand in a continually developing double movement, in the unfolding or realization of the relationship and in the I's withdrawing-into-itself or being-withdrawn from the relationship (the spirit is different in this from the soul; the spirit points to something from which it stems, points to something new which arises ever again, what exists from of old in a nonindividuated, unconditioned manner.)" [42b]

In all this we must keep in mind that as soon as the soul is comprehended as I-bound, it is comprehended as an abstraction and no longer in its full existence. Similarly, the spirit must not forget that it exists not *in* man but *between* men and that which is neither man nor world. Spirit and soul are both relation surfaces. Soul is to be understood from the standpoint of the relation between man and world, spirit from that of the relation between man and that which is not world, between man and being which does not appear world-bound and which is not absorbed in world-bound phenomena.

Spirit tends "to bend back on itself" again and again—"bending back" is for Buber an important concept in other places as well [43]—and in this Buber detected man's real backsliding which leads to "the spirit's illusion about the soul," of which he speaks in *I and Thou*. [44] In this connection Buber explained the two metacosmic movements in the history of man's relation to God, but he did not speak of "psychologism" or "cosmologism" but of "subjectivism" and "objectivism": "Subjectivism empties God of soul, objectivism makes Him into an object—the latter is a false fixing down, the former a false setting free, both are diversions from the way of reality, both are attempts to replace reality." [45] Buber saw the two metacosmic movements as not always running the same course, but rather as the "way" in which "the Kingdom" is to be realized in our midst. From this view the concept "pneumatic reality" is seen in its full significance. In another place Buber stated that only the perfect human society will be "the appropriate body of the spirit." [46]

The lines of thought that connect *I and Thou* with the lecture "On the Psychologizing of the World" indicate that Buber went back to the Bible as his starting point and that he was translating the dynamic of its confrontation of man and God into a philosophical language: "reflexion or bending back" is the secularized equivalent of first man's fall as recounted in the Bible. "Ontologism" means creation in its participation with God on the way to redemption toward the full "pneumatic reality" of God's kingdom, of "the appropriate body of the spirit." God created the first human couple—I and Thou are for Buber "the microcosm of being-housed." Equally characteristic is Buber's interpretation in *I and Thou* of the concepts Cosmos, Eros, and Logos from the standpoint of his experience of the "eternal Thou." Cosmos is given for man only "when the universe becomes his home, with its holy hearth whereon he offers sacrifice . . . There is Eros for man only when beings become for him pictures of the eternal, and community is revealed along with them . . . And there is Logos for man only when he addresses the mystery with work and service for the spirit." [47] That the proper "house for mankind," the "house of true life," was for Buber the messianic Kingdom is evident in his early *Addresses on Judaism*.[48]

The real difference in the two modes of thought, the Greek and the Jewish, is that the Bible is concerned with the person, the uniquely concrete individual man and his relationships, whereas the thinking that has come down to us from the Greeks conceives "man" as a generalized abstraction, that is, as self-subsistent. In the Bible reality is created by God and is pervaded by his Presence; in philosophy reality is the essence of things *(res)* that I behold. In an address that Buber gave in 1928 at a session of the Hohenrodter Bund called "Philosophical and Religious World View," [48a] he illustrated this contrast with the two meanings of the verb *to know,* which in our language denotes "to regard a thing as an object," whereas its biblical meaning refers to the relationship of being to being. The one kind of knowing is peculiar to philosophy, the other to the religious world view.

Philosophical thinking is able to achieve conceptual continuity whereby man acquires a special position in nature, but it is unable to establish a community, since its basic presuppositions compel it to ignore the concrete situation as a result of which human thinking, which in man is only a partial function, becomes totalized. Buber continued with a further thought which supplemented the lecture he gave in Zurich in 1923 ("On the Psychologizing of the World") in which spirit was understood as "a plane of relationship" between men and "nonworldly being" and which "points to something from which it stems." [49] In a later address Buber referred to this idea: "Being, insofar as it metes itself out to the human thought contents, is *also* in the thinking of men, and the knowing spirit is a spark of the *pneuma,* even though a detached spark—spirit in the attitude of self-contemplation." [50] If then it will be demonstrated in what follows that scientific and philosophical thinking not only disrupts the totality of the concrete person but also separates man from God, it is clear that in the foregoing sentence "being" stands for God and that Buber was here naively "translating" into philosophical language.

In this same address [50a] Buber spoke of the great difficulty that attends every religious statement, namely, that in the realm of the religious the law of contradiction does not apply: "The religious situation is simply the abode of the *lived complexio oppositorum.*" Belief, according to Buber, is "lived life in dialogue," and the religious statement testifies to this dialogue: "The religious man knows only the mystery to whose nature the inscrutability belongs and to which only standing firm and involvement open access." Here it becomes clear why Buber's path to philosophical anthropology led through Kierkegaard's religious existentialism. Existential thinking means to stake one's life on what one thinks.

In 1933, because of the inhumanity of his Christian contemporaries, Buber again became aware, as in the early days of *Addresses on Judaism,* of the universal world-open humanity of the Bible as Israel's national heritage in contradistinction to European culture. The divergence of spirit and reality, which even then he clearly perceived in the West, had now reached an ominous stage in Germany: "The reality of language must become operative in a man's spirit. The truth of language must prove itself in the person's existence. That was the intent of humanistic education, so long as it was alive." [51] The formative influences of the Bible were to create a Hebrew man who not only speaks the language of the Bible but also answers its challenging call with his life.

The principal significance of this essay is that Buber here was highly conscious of the sharp contrast of the two spiritual worlds of Israel and Greece as reflected in the life of their respective languages. The word of the Bible is the spoken word which preserves the dialogic character of the reality of life; the word of the Greeks is the form resting in itself without the immediacy of being spoken: "The Greek logos *is;* it possesses eternal being (Heraclitus). Although the prologue of the hellenizing Gospel of John begins, like the Hebrew Bible, with 'In the beginning,' it immediately continues with the totally un-Hebraic *'was* the Word.' In the beginning of the Bible's account of creation there *is* no word; it comes to be, it is spoken. In this account there is no 'word' that is not spoken; the only being of a word resides in its being spoken. But then all being of things that are comes from having been spoken, from the being spoken of the primary word: 'He himself spoke and it was.' " [51a]

The word as event and spokenness, not as logos and form but as the organ of dialogic life, also has a corresponding pedagogical aspect. Western humanism releases man's creative powers; biblical humanism has to do with the "open person" directed to the community and as such is not concerned with noble form but with relation conceived as immediacy to God and as justice, love, and faithfulness within the present community. Its meaning is not to be found in structure and form but in confirmation from moment to moment.

Buber's world view is based on the primary fact of biblical "dialogue." "The vital dialogic, demanding the staking of the self, which is the heart of the world," [52] is a dialogue of action that proceeds from God to man, for every hour with its world content and fate content is word and sign addressed to us. Corresponding to this dialogue from above to below we have the elemental being-spoken-to through the existence of the human Thou. Both constitute one event, the vital core of that great being-complex which Buber envisaged as "ontologism." Man transcends his *I* through the "embrace" of the Thou; this communicating with the "other," however, is but the answer to the primal movement with which God "embraces" His creation: "The Single One corresponds to God when he in his human way embraces the bit of the world offered to him as God embraces his creation in his divine way." [53] The ontic "otherness of the other" is experienced with respect to God as "being approached, grasped, addressed," and is again recognized in the human Thou.[54] Man's answer is the same in both places: responsibility. Buber's "ontologism" is symbolized by the one great symbol "dialogue," the central point around which all is ordered and which replaces a systematic philosophical terminology of static concepts incapable of rendering the dynamic events between God and world. Dialogue is relation and event, and remains "open" teaching in accordance with the biblical *humanum* of the "open person." It is designated as "sacrament," and presupposes the basic principles of faith in the Bible; "it is a matter of creation, of the creature, and he is that, the man of whom I speak." [55] Dialogue is word, answer, and responsibility; and this corresponds, in a manner that cannot be fathomed conceptually, to the trinity: creation, revelation, redemption.

"The Question to the Single One" is still pervaded by this speech symbolism. Most important is "that as the situation is presented to me I expose myself to it as to the word's manifestation." [56] I am responsible for it by my answer "from the depths, where a breath of what has been breathed in still hovers." [57] The dispute with Kierkegaard concerning the relation of man to God need not be translated into philosophical language. Only several times is God spoken of as Present Being: "the relation of faith to the one Present Being" or "the real relation to the Present Being." Even in "Dialogue" the *shekinah* was rendered in one passage as "the indwelling of the Present Being." [58] Buber spoke of the "claim of the fearful and kind God, the Lord of history and our Lord," but also of the God who is "the infinite *I* that makes every *It* into his *Thou*." [59] This work deals with the sphere of existence, with the truth as it is lived and not as already possessed; man as "person" in contradistinction to the "individual" is shown to be the bearer of dialogue.[60] From Kierkegaard's theological anthropology Buber learned the limits of his own position. "The Question to the Single One" is a transitional work on the way to the language of a philosophical anthropology.

In "What Is Man?" Kierkegaard saw the stages and conditions of life as "links in an existential process, in an ontic connexion with the absolute"—to which Buber added, "as elements of an existence 'before God.' " [61] He insisted that the object of philosophical thought should be "the real human person, but considered in the ontic connexion which binds it to the Absolute." [61a] God is thus translated into a concept of philosophy. Elsewhere in "What Is Man?" we find "the Absolute" put in the place of "God";[62] in one passage there is the phrase "the Absolute or God." Buber also spoke of "supra-temporal being" or of the "ground of being," and then again of the "mystery of being . . . which the philosopher calls the Absolute and the believer calls God." [63] The question remains whether such a juxtaposition is not problematical: "the Absolute" is by no means the only possible philosophical translation for God or the mystery of being. The concept seems rigid and isolated, whereas for Buber the biblical principles of faith and his own experience of God succeeded, by means of a few great symbols, in struggling through to a "pneumatic reality" whose dynamism is apparent when, in his criticism of Scheler, he spoke of "the spirit as happening" and as "primal community with the whole being." [64]

Only from the standpoint of Buber's religious presuppositions can we fully understand the concept of "ontic participation" [65] as the participation of creation in the life of God and the product of its creaturely interdependency. In the larger context of creation the soul is "that tender surface of personal life which longs for contact with other life";[66]

and a dialogic relation, although hardly perceptible, makes for an ontic "between," a sphere of being common to two people, which "has its being between them, and transcends both." [67] This dimension, which is accessible only to the two participants and in which they communicate with one another, shows no continuity; it assumes form and then disappears. In "Prospect," it is called a "primal category of human reality." [68] "Primal category" is again a concept derived from another spiritual world, one which is as little suited to capture this tender and elusive element of a "pneumatic reality" as is the designation "dialogical principle" for the mysterious sphere of dialogical life which Buber in his advanced age described as "the grace that appears ever anew in earthly material." [69] The "between" happens and withdraws, being unpredictable and indeterminable, so that Buber spoke of "the mystery of contact." [70] In the subject-object-conceptuality of modern philosophy, the sphere of the *Zwischenmenschliche* cannot be subsumed as an ontic sphere. It is essentially an element of the evolving kingdom of God and not an ontological principle of a philosophical anthropology, and is thus rejected by the philosophers again and again and dismissed as mere experience or as "intersubjective." [71]

"Being" was for Buber event and relation within a "pneumatic reality." The "ontologism" he has in mind is an unending dynamic structure of communicating acts which arise from the relation of creation. The *Zwischenmenschliche* is not; it occurs as a process of that mysterious interweaving in which creation, revelation, and redemption take place continuously. Buber's world image had always retained something of the dynamic of a religious myth that could not be rendered in the language of modern philosophy. A coherent presentation of the theme What is man? was not possible starting with such presuppositions, and Buber had to be content with elaborating the basic principles of his dynamic "ontologism" as contributions to a philosophical anthropology.

Contributions to a Philosophical Anthropology

"Distance and Relation"

Das Problem des Menschen concluded with the "prospect" that the fundamental fact of our existence is "man with man," and designated the ontic sphere of "between" as a primal category of human reality. Buber's basic contribution to philosophical anthropology is not to be found in his "Elements of the Interhuman," however, but in his essay "Distance and Relation" which, though small in size, is generally acknowledged as among his most important philosophical works.

At the beginning of the essay Buber raised the question concerning the principle of human life whose task it is "to consider, in all its paradox and actuality, the category of being characterized by the name of man," [72] thereby accepting the challenge of Nietzsche's thesis that man is an animal that has not yet been defined. Neitzsche understood man as a being who had been driven to the dizzy edge of nature and, as a consequence of this violent separation from his animal past, has been painfully dislocated and seriously damaged. He saw man only in relation to nature and no longer as a being in his own right who, to be sure, came from nature but who also stepped beyond it in a way that cannot be comprehended by means of natural concepts alone. A creature that knows about Being and about its own being is not to be understood in terms of the animal world. If Nietzsche saw man as a still unfinished form, it is because he had in mind the superman he is to become; when Buber, however, spoke of a "creature of transition," he meant man on the way to the perfect community and to the realization of his creation-meaning. In all this, however, he was aware that man's nature must first be investigated in order to determine whether man is distinct from the animal world by virtue of a special mode of being.

In this manner Buber reached the conclusion that the category of man is based on a twofold movement, that is, on two primal movements, of which the one is the presupposition of the other. Man is man by virtue of his sense of distance and relation.

"Primal distance" answers the question: how is man possible? It "establishes the human situation": man is the only living creature that has "world" in the sense of an independent opposing entity. Only man has a coherent spatial and temporal world of sense. An animal gathers sense-data for its vital needs and necessities in the particular surroundings in which it happens to find itself, its selection being governed by its vital functions. Only man knows the world as a whole, as an entity that can be imagined or thought. Man's relation to time is also different from that of animals: man sees the future before him; the animal instinctively provides for it with predetermined bodily activities.

Only he who is capable of sensing distance can enter into relation. Buber placed the other primal movement of human life in two spheres: in relation to things and in relation to other people. The animal also associates with people and learns to use things for its purposes; but these things are never assigned a definite place in a world. Only man is able to see things as detached from himself at a distance, and put them where they could readily be found again, arranged according to function. Every technique is built on this elementary basis: "Technique only fulfills what has been given by the primary choice and assignment, by a primary nomos."

The beginnings of art attest even more convincingly to man's desire for a personal relationship to things. Whether the first signs and ornamental figures scratched on utensils signify magic or play, "we have to turn to the principle of human life in its twofold character in order to establish what has happened. Picture signs give rise to independent forms of art work which cannot be adequately explained as objects of nature or as products of man's inner spirit. Art is "the work and witness of the relation between the *substantia humana* and the *substantia rerum;* it is the realm of 'the between' which has become form."

In connection with one's fellowmen, relation is above all the capacity for the individual supplementation and recognition of function which facilitate forms of union involving action and adjustment. An animal also knows community and hostility, but only man can enter into relation with his equals. Man alone has the need to be confirmed in what he is and can be, and also to confirm his fellowmen. The organ that makes this possible is language. An animal uses calls and signals; speech is peculiar to man alone, based on the recognition of the independent otherness of the other with whom he enters into relation. In the transition from the holophrase (the sentence condensed into a word) to the independent, isolated word, language bears witness to the principle of human life. Man can remove himself from objects and see them from a distance. He now makes his signals, like his utensils, independent; he converts them into words.

Every genuine conversation is more than an exchange of opinions concerning an object. It is a relation in which the elemental otherness of the other is not only taken into consideration but is also affirmed. Human life is realized in genuine meeting in which people confirm one another in their elemental being. The high point of this entering-into-relation was found by Buber in a process he called "making present," which rests on man's capacity to grasp with his soul a reality that exists at this moment but which cannot be experienced by the senses. This capacity is based on intuition—Buber called it *Real-phantasie*—and through it one can feel another's pain even as one's own; the pain I inflict on another is felt by me, and only then does the other become a "self" for me. This process is not to be understood psychologically but in a strictly ontological sense, and may be designated as a "becoming a self with me." The process is completed only when the other knows that he is being made present by me in his self and when this knowledge contributes to his self-becoming, for the self does not grow out of the relation of man to himself but out of mutual affirmation and confirmation. An animal is what it is; for man it is essential that he be confirmed by others and have a presence in the being of others: "Sent forth from the natural domain of species into the hazard of the solitary category, surrounded by the air of chaos which came into being with him, secretly and bashfully he watches for a Yes which allows him to be and which can come to him only from one human person to another. It is from one man to another that the heavenly bread of self-being is passed."

The remarkable thing about this small work is that it speaks the language of philosophical anthropology without forfeiting any of the dynamic force of Buber's experience of faith and the world. The principle of human life rests on two primal movements. The one is transcendental and prior to consciousness, and constitutes the basis for our idea of an independent world. Through this first movement space is created for the second movement whereby human life is realized: "It is only at this point that the real history of the spirit begins." Here we see how spirit becomes "event," whereby man attains his "finished form" and independent being-category—not as subject that thinks the world but as person meeting other persons. This meeting takes place in being and is consummated by the whole person. "By this double movement, man is situated at the center of being, and philosophy is identifiable with anthropology. But he is not at the center in so far as he is a thinking subject, but with respect to his whole being, since only a total commitment can be the realization of his fundamental situation." [73] Man at the center of creation: this is also the biblical conception whereby man is destined to be God's co-worker. The twofold principle of human life can be understood as part of the twofold movement of the cosmos that Buber assumed. Man's capacity for "distancing" makes him an independent being, capable of constant recreation and of fashioning the world anew. "Being made present" through the embrace of the other is the beginning of the counter-movement in the process of unification. In the "between," spirit emerges as the beginning of redemption.

In the "Elements of the Interhuman" the mutual help toward self-becoming is called "unfolding." Buber pointed out that the innate self-realization which can be comprehended in the Aristotelian image of entelechy is an entelechy of the work of creation: the self as such is not ultimately the essential thing; the important thing is that "the meaning of human existence given in creation again and again fulfills itself as self." [74]

Logos

The two talks published in 1962 under the title *Logos*—"The Word That Is Spoken" (1960) and "What Is Common to All" (1956)—were included by Buber in the first volume of his collected works as *Contributions to a Philosophical Anthropology*. The "contribution" illumines the principle of human life by explaining the primary phenomenon of human reality which is both spirit and life in one. Spirit as "event" is the element in which Buber's Hebrew humanism and a philosophy of man could meet.

The very title "The Word That Is Spoken" reminds us of the essay "Biblical Humanism" which elaborated the distinction between the Greek word that becomes form and the spoken word of the Bible. Buber made it clear in his talk that God "had placed man in speech" by speaking to him, and man's answer is for him, now as in 1933, the confirmation of the truth of the word. One of the basic assumptions in *I and Thou* was that the speech usage of primitive people demonstrated that the I-Thou relation was prior to the primary ground-word I-It. Even later Buber's contribution to a "philosophical science of man" was based primarily on the results of research in the early stages of language. The scientific insight "that the mystery of the coming-to-be of language and of the coming-to-be of man are one" [75] confirmed for him the biblical view which is expressed in the language of myth—although this connection is not always obvious in Buber's presentation. In developing the theme of language in this talk, Buber went back to his essay "Distance and Relation," and showed how language is "the great characteristic of men's lives with one another," [76] attesting to the principle of human life. The development of language also involved a new function of distance. The speech of primitive man "sets the word outside itself in being, and the word continues, it has continuance. And this continuance wins its life ever anew in true relation, in the spokenness of the word." [77]

It belongs to the nature of the spoken word "that it does not want to remain with the speaker." [78] It reaches out to the hearer and is meant to be heard. It has its dimension "in the oscillating sphere between two persons," [79] the sphere in which the different meanings of a word are experienced and at the same time overcome through understanding. A lyrical poem, for example, is not a monologue, for it is directed to a person (although unknown) who is capable of understanding it. A poem cannot be translated into concepts, for its truth resides in its unique form. Thus, the truth of the spoken word is one with the speaker's unique being, and is confirmed in three ways: in relation to the reality that was once perceived and is now expressed, in relation to the person addressed, and in relation to the expression of the speaker's own existence.

The first and second talk supplement one another in the twofold sense of the Logos: word and meaning, both of which establish community and are hence in Buber's view definitive for "man's being-category."

In "Distance and Relation" Buber stated that man alone of all the creatures has "world." The world of sense as the spatial-temporal whole which confronts man presupposes an act of "distancing" that is prior to consciousness. In "What Is Common to All" Buber was concerned with the deeper meaning of the fact that men have a common world. He started with a saying of Heraclitus: "One must follow that which is common"—one of the basic insights by which the Ionic sage enriched Western thought. To the Greeks the one common world form meant primarily something that was seen. It is in this sense that Plutarch, through whom the fragment has been preserved, explains that the common cosmos ceases when man closes his eyes in sleep.

The nature of being, according to Heraclitus, is to be found in the "pairs of opposites," in the tension between polarities; and yet there is but *one* cosmos which is common to the human race as the Logos, the meaning that dwells in the word: "Meaning can be in the word because it is in being. Thus it stirs deep in the soul which becomes aware of the meaning; it grows in it and develops out of it to a voice which speaks to fellow souls and is heard by them." [80] The meaning comprehended by people when they speak with one another is part of the common work of the cosmos in which all participate: "They associate with one another in the world, helping one another through the power of the logos to grasp the world as a world order, without which ordering grasp it is not and cannot be a world." [81] This can be done by men only when they are truly awake and shake off the dreamlike illusions that they call insight—when they exist in common.

Heraclitus's interpretation of the meaning of being as the things all men have in common which we should all pursue is not to be taken as something that is self-understood in the history of the spirit, as a glance at the teaching of the Chinese Tao and of the ancient Upanishads shows. Also Tao, the Way, is the ordering of the many opposites which are regarded as the phenomenal expression of two complementary primary essences, *yang* and *yin*. But in its sphere neither logos, cosmos, nor the things we have in common has undisputed sway: the realm of dreams and the special province of him who turns away from day and community have the same claim to be "world," and are even considered to be more real than the waking state.

The teaching of the Upanishads goes even further in this direction. Here dreams are regarded not only as a prelude to deep sleep but also as the liberation of the spirit for the performance of its sovereign transformations. But it is only when this preliminary stage is overcome in deep slumber amid the pageant of melting shapes and shadowy images that the personal self unites with the self of the world, both being in truth a single Self. That they are taken to be two in the waking world is an illusion, and in sleep one is free of this deceptive duality. Existence with people in the waking world is illusory; unity is found only in the loneliness of deep sleep.

In the West of our day this insight of Heracleitus which urges us to follow the common way is endangered by two world views which proclaim another teaching. The one is collectivism which distorts the meaning of community, the other individualism which seeks the meaning of existence in relation to one's own being, identifying the self of the I with the Self as such. Here also one believes one can gain real life by leaving the life of the community.

In this connection Buber spoke of a peculiar type of individualism which seeks the complete isolation of the individual and "flight out of selfhood and environment," as it is described in Aldous Huxley's *The Doors of Perception*," [82] a title derived from William Blake's observation: "If the doors of perception were cleansed, everything will appear to man as it is, infinite." Huxley started with the assumption that the urge for self-transcendence, for overstepping the bounds of I-conscious selfhood is extremely ancient. The use of drugs for ritual purposes has been known for centuries. Among such drugs Huxley regards mescalin, which is extracted by the Indians from peyotl cactus, as desirable and salutary, affording the one who partakes of it "chemical holidays from the petty I and repugnant surroundings" [83] and transporting him, at least for a short time, to "artificial paradises." On his return through "the Door in the Wall" he will "never be the same as the man who went out. He will be wiser but less cocksure, happier but less self-satisfied, humbler in acknowledging his ignorance yet better equipped to understand the relationship of words to things, of systematic reasoning to the unfathomable Mystery which it tries, forever vainly, to comprehend." [84] A characteristic effect of mescalin, as described by the author, is that under its influence one becomes indifferent to time and space. The expected visions fail to come; one feels empty within, but experiences things in the environment with a heightened intensity of color and an overpowering presence of the individual object—at first with the eyes of an artist, but then as a "sacramental vision of reality"—for "all is illumined by an inner light and becomes infinite in its significance." [85] The primal ground of being opens, and there is no longer an inner and outer. The resemblance between the teachings of Asia Minor and the mysticism of the Far East is striking, and is stressed by Huxley.

But Buber justly pointed out that an arbitrarily conducted experiment in which the person under observation is constantly aware of his actions and never loses control of himself cannot be compared with the experiences of the creative artist or mystic who is lifted out of the common life, overwhelmed and irresistibly drawn to his vocation. The teachings of eastern Asia also claim all existence. This is particularly true of Heraclitus. Every soul bears the logos within it; however, it never attains its fullness *in* us but between us. It requires speech which becomes true between people and which is common to all: "To man as man belongs the ever renewed event of the entrance of meaning into the living word. Heracleitus demands of the human person that he preserve this occurrence in life in such a way that it can legitimately take part in the reality of the common logos." [86] Those who truly speak to one another also think with one another. Through common service to the logos this also becomes the manifest, formative total order in the cosmos.

The logos, meaningful speech, is the element in which the genuine "we" has its life—not a collectivity or some observable group, but an essential relation between persons which is actualized and then disappears. Man has his experiences as an *I*: "but it is as We, ever again as We, that he has constructed and developed a world out of his experiences." [87] The flight from the common cosmos into a special sphere in both the East and the West is "a flight from authentic spokenness of speech in whose realm a response is demanded, and response is responsibility." [88]

We can learn much from Heracleitus, but not the ultimate truth. He knows of no transcendence. What it means to live before God as a "We," this mankind learned from the prophets of Israel, who lived close to the time of the Greek philosopher and who served, like him, as a bridge between the real Orient and Europe.

"Man and His Image Work"

Buber's thoughts concerning man as creative artist, which he set forth in 1955 in "Man and His Image Work," constitute a basic contribution to philosophical anthropology. In this essay he was prompted by considerations that go far beyond the concern and special province of the artist. We have found indications of this interest in "What Is Man?" which investigates the historical conditions under which the question concerning man became critical, namely, in those periods "when the original contract between the universe and man is dissolved." [89] This is the condition of our own time as a result of the revolutionary findings of physics which makes the world appear strange and inimical to man: "This universe can still be thought, but it can no longer be imaged; the man who thinks it no longer really lives in it." [90] Ernst Simon reports a conversation which shows Buber at the age of seventy-eight occupied with the same problem, and he connects it with the autobiographical fragment "Philosophers": "Buber used the meeting as an opportunity to clarify the disturbing problems which arose in the wake of Niels Bohr's 'complementary theory,' according to which light could be understood either as the motion of corpuscles or of waves, depending on the standpoint of the experimenter, but never as both at the same time. He now struggled, just as he had sixty years before, to find an answer to the question as to what happens to the unambiguous relation of truth to reality in the face of two such irreconcilable statements." [91] Buber also pointed out in "Man and His Image Work" that according to Niels Bohr even the verbs "to be" and "to know" have lost their simple meaning. Man wants to live in a world he can really imagine, but the new world image does not permit him to make for himself an *image* of the world, and he sees himself confronted with the contradiction that the world he names and uses and the world of science are "fearfully dual." [92] It is clear that what was at stake for Buber was the possibility of a genuine "ontic participation," a cooperative task in the sphere of creation.

Buber was helped here by a saying of Dürer's which he had heard while a student in Vienna from the art historian Conrad Fiedler: "For art truly is hidden in nature; he who can tear it out, has it." The essence of artistic production was seen by Fiedler—in the light, of course, of neo-Kantian idealism—as originating in man's distinctive nature, thus anticipating the anthropological question. It is comprehensible that Buber, after more than half a century, should return to this interpretation. Fiedler correctly took artistic activity to be a natural, further development of the event of perception, but he tied it to the doctrine of the world-producing subject and to the cognitive faculty, whereas for Buber cognition and art complement one another "like the electric poles between which the spark jumps." [93]

Buber then raised the question as to whether Dürer's words are still valid for our day and age. We are related to the world of sense that comes to us through perception and movement. Science teaches us to distinguish between the things of the sensible world and the It-self on which it is based, which Buber designated by a small x since it is not imagable. Kant designated it as the thing-in-itself, and said that we know nothing of it except that it is—to which Buber added: "and that the existent meets us." [94]

Standing in front of an ancient linden tree Buber asked himself the meaning of such a meeting. Whatever the science of botany may say of the fragrant, verdant tree that enters my sensible world, the fact of communication with this linden tree x remains. An animal lives with its surroundings as with its organs, but outside of its vital needs it knows little of them. Through the primary act of "distancing" nature first becomes real nature, a whole which makes its appearance piece by piece. All the qualities conditioned by sense come into the world through perception: "Let us proceed confidently from x, from its unfathomable darkness: its being has intercourse with my being when it dispatches to my senses the representatives to which scientific language has lent the name of stimuli, and out of our intercourse arise the clearly outlined forms that people my sense world in color and sound. It itself, the sense world, arises out of the intercourse of being with being." [95] The multiplicity of stimuli that emanate from the unknown x becomes a unity through my perception; the wholly insensible connection in x that meets me has found an intuitive, formed correspondence. Man answers the unknown x with his vision: "Vision is the figurating (in the sense of making the figure fully manifest) faithfulness to the unknown and does its work in co-operation with it. It is faithfulness not to the appearance, but to being—to the inaccessible with which we associate." [96]

Our sensible world belongs in a twofold sense to the sphere of the "between": first, as a result of meeting between man and the unknown x of nature and, second, because it contains *in posse* what the artist completes—the figure. The "world-filter" of our senses yields that which the species *homo sapiens* needs in order to exist. Here also something that is embedded in nature is extracted. Dürer was still of the opinion that the world of sense was an independent entity that confronted the artist; but this world arises as such only as a result of the confrontation, of its meeting with the species. Through the formative power of the artist the finished figure is wrested from nature. The artistic confrontation is the meeting between the being of the artist and the being of x. The fine arts draw from the spheres of time and space; meeting here takes place through a single sense, through the eye or the ear. There is only one art that is not determined by one of the senses, namely, poetry which draws its material from language and is dependent upon it alone.

How can we explain this ability to surpass the universally accessible "figure" in the process of artistic creation? The nature of art, according to Buber, can only be disclosed when one considers the four potencies "with which man transcends the natural and establishes the human as a unique realm of being." [97] An animal also plays, and in this reaches out beyond the satisfaction of its needs. But man alone has an additional peculiarity which Buber described as the "longing for perfected relation or for perfection in the relation." [98] This refers to the four areas of life—knowledge, love, art, and faith. Man alone wants "to get to the bottom" of things with his knowledge, and attain the perfection of the cognitive relation. An animal is also attached to its family—but the love of person for person is the radiation of perfected relation. In this manner the artist also desires to experience in his vision and in his work the perfect relation to the substrata of sensible things and to incorporate it in his work.

"Vision" is not confined to artists alone; it also applies to man as person, and to the extent that he is person. This capacity for vision explains how the linden tree could become a Thou for Buber. Mutual speech and answer are not the essential criterion of the I-Thou relation, but rather "the intuition on the part of man of the full ontological dimension of the other." [99] Perfect relation is for Buber the unfolding of the I-Thou relation. He pointed out that the four potencies aid man against the "alienation" of the world. Here again Buber had in mind the shock he experienced as a result of the revolutionary conclusions of modern natural science.

In the same year that the conversation recorded by Ernst Simon took place (1956), the Bavarian Academy of Fine Arts held a series of lectures on "The Arts in a Technical Age." The main lecture—"The Nature Image of Present-Day Physics"—was delivered by the distinguished scientist, Werner Heisenberg, who pointed out that we cannot recognize atoms and their movements *an sich,* that is, apart from the presuppositions of our experimentation. The object of research is no longer nature *an sich,* but nature as it is revealed to human experimentation: in the last analysis man comes face to face with himself. Heisenberg declared that natural science constitutes only part of the great confrontation between man and nature. Fundamental dislocations have taken place simultaneously in many important areas of our lives, so that the customary divisions of subject and object, inner and outer world, body and soul no longer apply. [100]

Emil Preetorius in his lecture attempted to draw the consequences of this situation for the fine arts which, in his view, can no longer rely on nature, since the earlier "mysteriously fruitful relation between nature in us and nature around us has been irreparably disturbed." Objective nature is completely exhausted for the fine arts, so that art today is "object-less art." The new world image arises from the confrontation of the artist with himself, with a creative *must* within him. Here also man confronts only himself. An incomprehensible change of form is taking place throughout all reality; an epoch has come to an end.[101]

In connection with some observations concerning Leopold Krakauer's drawings of the year 1959, Buber took issue with the view put forward by Preetorius who in his opinion had failed to make a distinction between *Gegenstand*, "passive object" and *Gegenüber*, "face-to-face being." Only in the latter can we have dialogue that leads to a work of art; it can never take place within a person by himself. The "how" of the work of art can never be divorced from the "what" that is given by perception. It is not the perception of an object that furnishes us with a *what* "but the being accosted by face-to-face being that enables the human person to behold superobjectively." [101a] Buber pointed out that the change now going on in the world is not independent of man's will and cooperation, and he was convinced that a coming generation of artists will attempt to find a new kind of meeting with nature. He saw the promise of such a breakthrough in the work of Leopold Krakauer whose artistic destiny was his meeting with the landscape of Jerusalem, to which he had turned with such an intense devotion that he was able to comprehend it from within, as it were, "in the dynamic of its solitude that corresponded to and answered his own." [102]

For man as artist, meeting emerges as a primary fact. In his "Answer" Buber frankly acknowledged that he "never succeeded in grasping a metaphysical totality and accordingly in building a metaphysical system." [103] His contributions to philosophical anthropology are fragments of his dynamic ontologism—"fragments" in the significant sense in which Buber had also described his own life in *Autobiographical Fragments*, namely, "meeting." In meeting being becomes event; the "between" happens. It is both life process and meaning as one.

ECLIPSE OF GOD: STUDIES IN THE RELATION BETWEEN RELIGION AND PHILOSOPHY

"Eclipse of the light of heaven, eclipse of God—such indeed is the character of the historic hour through which the world is passing. But it is not a process which can be adequately accounted for by instancing the changes that have taken place in man's spirit. An eclipse of the sun is something that occurs between the sun and our eyes, not in the sun itself." [104] Here by means of a single image that is comprehensible to all people Buber characterized the religious situation of our time as an event between God and man. In the early *Addresses on Judaism* God was seen as an elemental presentness, as the "sun of the soul" in the light of whose rays the realizing "between" takes place: "Just as the sun's substance has its being among the stars yet beams its light into the earthly realm, so it is granted to human creatures to behold in their midst the radiance of the ineffable glory. It glows dimly in all human beings, every one of them; but it does not shine in its full brightness within them—only between them. In every human being there is present the beginning of universal being; but it can unfold only in its relatedness to universal being, in the pure immediacy of his giving and taking, which surrounds him like a sphere of light, merging him with the oneness of the world." [105] The binding element of the divine rays opens the "prison of the person," so that immediacy is established between beings and, "in the Between, in the apparently empty space," community takes place. The sphere of the "between" was anticipated as early as 1918, not as "category" but as image reflecting all beings grounded in God.

The symbol *sun* is addressed to all people, but it applies to Israel in a special manner, reminding us of the petition in the Psalm that God let His countenance shine and of Isaiah's words (45:15) of the God that has concealed Himself, which has often been realized in Israel's historical experience. In his late address, "The Dialogue between Heaven and Earth," Buber distinguished between those periods in the Bible in which the disrupted relation between man and God was clearly the fault of the former and could have been averted through repentance, and those periods in which God is the first to turn aside as if He were no longer interested in life on earth. But it is Israel's prerogative to recognize its God in all His appearances and to preserve its trust in the hidden Countenance. In *For the Sake of Heaven* the "holy Yehudi" speaks of the "eclipse of God," and it seems to him as if the earth is no longer illumined by his Countenance and must grow cold. But he knows it is the great awesome event, the total return and repentance, that God is waiting for, the breaking up of the deep, primordial sources that can be brought about only by the greatest sorrow and affliction.[106] The history of faith has taught the Jews that in the world hours of the hidden God only waiting and praying can avail, an invincible trust that God's light, though dim, has not been extinguished.

That it was Buber's chief concern in *Eclipse of God* to distinguish between the idea of the God of philosophy and the personal God of the Bible is evident from a "Report of Two Talks" which Buber placed at the beginning of his book: "Both times it was a dispute about God, about the concept and the name of God, but each time of a very different nature." [107] The essential thing was that the first conversation, which seemingly came to an end, actually remained unconcluded, but the second, which was seemingly unfruitful, found a completion seldom arrived at in conversations.

The occasion of the first conversation was a series of lectures given by Buber in Jena after World War I on "Religion as Reality." In a discussion with workers that took place after the lecture a convinced materialist said to him that he had no need of the hypothesis "God" in order to be at home in the universe. Buber recognized immediately that the man's certainty could only be shaken by a philosophical argument which would appeal to his scientific world view. He therefore cited Kant in support of his own view to the effect that the world of phenomena arises from the meeting of an incomprehensible subject with an unknown object. The man had to admit the postulate of a Being outside of the world that had become problematical, and the conversation seemed to have come to an end. But it then became clear to Buber that he had not shown the man the way that he must take. He had brought him to a point where he acknowledged a philosophical idea of God, but not to the God whom Pascal called the God of Abraham, Isaac, and Jacob, to the God we call upon in prayer: "I could not enter into the factory where the man worked, become his comrade, live with him, win his trust through real life-relationship, and help him to walk with me the way of the creature who *accepts* the creation. I could only return his gaze." [107a]

In the second conversation the philosopher, Paul Natorp, criticized Buber for his naive use of the word "God" in one of his works, a word which is in truth the most misused, defiled, and desecrated of all human words, and it seemed to him blasphemous that the Highest, that which is above all concepts, should be called "God" hereafter. Buber assured him that by taking the purest, most sparkling concept from the inner treasure chamber of the philosophers he could only capture an unbinding product of thought and not the presence of Him whom the generations of men have honored and degraded, the one living God to whom men pray in distress: "We cannot cleanse the word 'God' and we cannot make it whole; but, defiled and mutilated as it is, we can raise it from the ground and set it over an hour of great care." [108] The conversation reached an end not by exhausting a theme but by the brotherly Thou exchanged by the two partners of the conversation, and Buber added: "For where two or three are truly together, they are together in the name of God." [108a] Not all believers of a faith will regard such a conversation as having come to a successful conclusion, but for Buber it was a genuine religious conversation, a dialogue from open person to open person in which the essential concern was the living God and not an Idea.

Buber was well aware that it is part of the dynamic of dialogical life that every man should speak his own language and that the participants in a conversation never use words and concepts in precisely the same sense. When people speak of God, however, it should first be made clear whether they mean an idea or a reality of faith: "In that moment when the name of God is mentioned, most human circles break asunder as persons without knowing it. In that moment the commonness of thinking—the fact of thinking together—is disrupted. The difference between the world with God and without Him is so enormous that discussion of God must divide except in a group united by a real common faith." [109] In a dialogue about God it is essential that the participants be unreservedly accountable to one another and sincerely "in conversation." Here the answer of him who is asked about God is in the highest degree "responsibility"—the responsibility to keep the dialogue alive "between" the participants and to attend not only to one's own truth but to consider also the understanding of the other and make a sincere effort to grasp it, so that the conversation will "mean" and "include" one's partner, as was stated in the foreword to *Daniel*.

To acknowledge the God of the Bible, however, is no guarantee of a dialogical relation to God in the sense intended by Buber. In *Autobiographical Fragments* two further conversations are reported in which both partners, a Christian and an observant Jew, cite the text of the Bible to support their conviction. The first conversation took place in May 1914. The Christian visitor, Reverend Hechler, had been a tutor of princes and was highly esteemed in many European courts. Through a genuine eschatological faith in the living Christ, he supported the Zionist cause from the very beginning, because the return of the Jews to Palestine was the necessary condition for the return of Christ. He showed Buber a graphic representation of the prophecy of Daniel and pointed to the exact spot, as on a map, where we now find ourselves. He prophesied that "world war" would break out that very year. On departing, Buber was asked whether he believed in God, and he answered the aged man who feared the impending chaos in the affirmative. It was only on the way home, however, that it became clear to him in what sense his affirmative answer was understood: "The God who gives Daniel such foreknowledge of this hour of human history, this hour before the 'world war,' that its fixed place in the march of the ages can be foredetermined, is not my God and not God. The God to whom Daniel prays in his suffering is my God and the God of all." [110] The prediction of an impending world war proved to be correct and yet the man who proclaimed it, like all those to whom the future "discloses" itself, was not a true prophet. He was not able to distinguish between divine revelation and personal insight, between his interpretation of Daniel and current political information.

As a result of the many years spent in translating, Buber was well aware of biblical passages in which the human word seems to contradict the divine Voice. One such passage, which was the subject of his conversation with the observant Jew, is the account of Saul and Agag in the Book of Samuel which relates how Saul disobeyed God's command and spared the life of the conquered prince of the Amalekites, whereupon Samuel delivered a message to him in the name of God to the effect that his dynasty will be taken from him, after which he slew the enemy king with his own hand. Buber's conviction that this could not have been God's message and that Samuel had misunderstood God because of some human error at first startled the observant Jew and filled him with indignation, but after some reflection he agreed. His reaction conforms to the Jew's trust in God as described by Buber in *Two Types of Faith.* "There is in the end nothing astonishing in the fact that an observant Jew of this nature, when he has to choose between God and the Bible, chooses God." [110a]

As far as answering his partner in his own language and according to his own understanding and thus attaining a limited but common insight, the conversation as dialogue had come to an end. But the problem of man's understanding and misunderstanding of a revelation accompanied Buber throughout his life. What is essentially involved is the fact that "in the work of throats and pens out of which the text of the Old Testament has arisen, misunderstanding has again and again attached itself to understanding, the manufactured has been mixed with the received. We have no objective criterion for the distinction; we have only faith—when we have it. Nothing can make me believe in a God who punishes Saul because he has not murdered his enemy. And yet even today I still cannot read the passage that tells this otherwise than with fear and trembling. But not it alone. Always when I have to translate or to interpret a biblical text, I do so with fear and trembling, in an inescapable tension between the word of God and the words of man." [111]

Buber described his own religious position over against God as that of the insecure "narrow ridge," meaning that he was not content to "rest on the broad upland of a system that includes a series of sure statements about the absolute, but on a narrow rocky ridge between the gulfs where there is no sureness of expressible knowledge but the certainty of meeting what remains, undisclosed." [112] The four conversations, by juxtaposing complete freedom of spirit and the unconditioned binding of faith in God, clearly illustrate Buber's position. All the essays in the volume *Eclipse of God* serve to define more exactly this "narrow ridge" between religion and philosophy.

A living religion that comprehends and pervades all reality can give man no certainty over against God; it can only help him to live with the mystery. Even in *I and Thou*[113] Buber was disturbed because religions are gradually losing the original force of the I-Thou relation. Man is tempted to make God his spiritual possession, to see in Him an object of ritual worship and cognitive knowledge, and consequently to find himself in a position of false security over against God. For this reason Buber was able to say of religion that it is apt to obscure the face of God.[114] That religion always succeeds in becoming an end in itself is because "it is far more comfortable to have to do with religion than to have to do with God who sends one out of home and fatherland into restless wandering." [115] Theology, with its demonstrable assertions, can become a rather questionable type of philosophy.[116]

The more the original I-Thou relation to God gives way to an I-It relation, the more does religion approach philosophy, whose hybrid development—characterized by Nietzsche's phrase "God is dead"—determines the situation of our time. "In our age the I-It relation, gigantically swollen, has usurped, practically uncontested, the mastery and the rule. The I of this relation, an I that possesses all, makes all, succeeds with all, this I that is unable to say Thou, unable to meet a being essentially, is the lord of the hour. This selfhood that has become omnipotent, with all the It around it, can naturally acknowledge neither God nor any genuine absolute which manifests itself to man as of non-human origin. It steps in between and shuts off from us the light of heaven." [117] Religion must be life "in the sight of God"—"the complete, the over-arching existence of real man that unites all incompleteness in the real world of God"; it must be a Way that leads from the concrete lived hour as something unique and unforseeable. All philosophizing begins with abstracting from the concrete situation, lifting oneself into the sphere of strict conceptuality. By thus giving up our attachment to concretion, "world" is created as thought continuum through which objective understanding becomes possible. Man makes his way through history spurred on by his desire for knowledge and his duty to attain it.[118] All essential knowledge in its origin is contact with an existing being and in its completion is possession of an enduring concept.[119] There is such a thing as a religious understanding between people who recognize in each other a readiness to stake life on a principle; and there is such a thing as the communication of a religious con-

tent in the form of paradox which preserves the unique and incomparable character of experience. Religious experience is objectively
communicable only within philosophy and its methods—whereby we
must understand thought truth not as a "cognitive possession of being"
but as a "cognitive real-relation to being." Buber admitted that to make
his basic experiences generally accessible and not to make his explanations unduly difficult, he had to adopt psychological and philosophical
terminology; in this connection he spoke of the "encroachment of bor-
rowed terms." [120]

The position on the "narrow ridge" means religious thinking but
not thinking that is bound to a religion. In the religious reality in which
Buber lived the human person is a total entity which includes thought
but does not permit it to become absolute. Every conception that
claims complete knowledge is here rejected.[121]

In connection with a refutation of one of Heidegger's statements,
Buber made a very instructive observation with respect to his "dialogical principle," namely, "That is a testimony to that which I call the dialogical principle, to the dialogical relation between a divine and a
human spontaneity." [122] The mysterious "spontaneity" which cannot
be subsumed in any conceptual language is meant to express the real
immediacy and mutuality of the contact of being with being in the
midst of life. We have already encountered this thought: "Always,
again and again, men are accosted by One who of Himself disconcerts
and enraptures them, and, although overcome, the worshipper prays of
himself to Him." [123] The chief aim of *Studies in the Relation between
Religion and Philosophy* is to convince the reader of the concreteness of
this becoming obligated. The purpose of the criticism that is made of
historical or contemporary phenomena in this connection is to stimu-
late appreciation for the genuineness of an experience of God and to set
forth the criteria for recognizing dialogical immediacy in the religious
relation.

The *Eclipse of God* is too often considered exclusively as a polemic
against contemporary philosophy in the manner of Nietzsche, as a criticism directed by a religious existentialist against the non-religious existentialism of his day. This criticism had been made in "What Is
Man?"; *Eclipse of God* was written considerably later and reflects the

wisdom of an older man and his "pervasive concern not with theories but with the living Thou." [124] It summarizes the whole complex of the primary words I-Thou and I-It in the light of the accumulated experience of a long life and transports it to a historical plane. *Eclipse of God* is a deeply human work which illumines, with the aid of examples taken from past and present-day history, the various aspects of man's religious situation, just as *Dialogue* had pointed to concrete possibilities for a dialogic life in the daily experiences of an individual. In all this the question revolves around two basic types of human living: "For man the existent is either face-to-face being or passive object. The essence of man arises from this twofold relation to the existent—meeting and contemplation." [125]

That the personal aspects of the godly are not necessarily involved in this is demonstrated by Buber's example of Buddha who, to be sure, did not oppose too earnestly the intimate relation between the gods of popular belief and man, but who also knew the genuinely divine—an "Unborn, Unoriginated, Uncreated"—about which he made no assertion but to which he was related with his whole being. This is also religious reality, although it is not bound to a divine service. Buber considered it entirely possible to live toward an unknown God and thereby really mean God; on the other hand, by limiting God to immanence and drawing Him completely into the sphere of man, the "godliness of the godly" is reduced to nought. Buber illustrated this by comparing two passages from Greek tragedy in which Zeus is mentioned. The chorus in Aeschylus' *Agamemnon* still experiences God as its face-to-face opposite, whereas in *The Trojan Women* of Euripides the supplication of Queen Hecuba to Zeus is no longer true prayer, and a real religious relation is absent. This simple juxtaposition of two quotations thus casts an interesting light on Greek religious history. Only where reality as a whole is sustained by deeds and suffering and answered without reservation does it disclose its meaning. The answer of the Israelites on receiving the law on Sinai, "We shall fulfill it and obey it," expresses with incomparable aptness that this meaning will be found only where man is willing to stake his entire person on its realization.

Nor is criticism as such the essential ingredient in the dispute with contemporary philosophy and psychology, but rather a human concern for man's fate in times of crises, such as Buber had experienced in his early days. His keen and judicious criticism comes from the fact that he had experienced the crisis of Western culture as the crisis of his own life. What had happened in this situation was that the thinking and experiencing subject had unexpectedly found itself lodged at the center of being and had made itself the "I of the world" and the bearer of "world-tension," as was the case in *Daniel.* The relation to God is disrupted when man draws the godly into his own self. In retrospect Buber characterized this phenomenon as "soul-madness of the spirit" or "subjectivism" which plunged him into a "shuddering confusion of a reduplicated ego," into a "confrontation with himself" which he vainly sought to interpret as a religious relation: "If a man does not represent the *a priori* of relation in his living with the world, if he does not work out and realize the inborn *Thou* on what meets it, then it strikes inwards. It develops on the unnatural, impossible object or the I, that is, it develops where there is no place at all for it to develop. Thus confrontation of what is over against him takes place within himself." [126] In this way a God-realizing man can be lead astray by an intoxicating self-dramatization and find himself on the way to self-deification.

The two contemporary intellectual representatives of present-day thought dealt with by Buber in *Eclipse of God* are Martin Heidegger and C. G. Jung. The dispute with Heidegger, which began in "What Is Man?" was now concentrated on the problem of religion in our time. It thereby acquired a deeper dimension, so that Heidegger is no longer seen from the standpoint of philosophical anthropology but rather as a thinker searching for an ontological basis for contemporary philosophical thinking. Buber made a sincere effort to understand his philosophical opponent. In "What Is Man?" he had attempted to understand Heidegger's central problem, that of being, by way of Hölderlin: Heidegger, influenced by Hölderlin, the great poet of this mystery, has undoubtedly had a profound experience of the mystery of being which is dimly apparent through all that is; but he has not experienced it as the one which steps before us and challenges us to yield the last thing, so hard fought for, the being at rest in one's self, to breach the barriers of the self and to come out from ourselves to meet with essential otherness." [127] Can we speak of Heidegger "as being at rest in one's self?"

There are not many philosophers of Heidegger's stature whose teaching has undergone such incessant transformation. Buber, who as late as 1958 described the I-Thou relation as "grace appearing ever anew in earthly matter," compared to Heidegger spoke like a dogmatist of the dialogical principle. In *Eclipse of God* he quoted from Heidegger's *Letter on Humanism:* "*Being*—that is not God and it is not a ground of the world. Being is more than all that exists and is nonetheless nearer than any existing being, be it . . . an angel or God. Being is the nearest thing." To this Buber added: "If by the last sentence, however, something other is meant than that I myself am, and not indeed as the subject of a *cogito,* but as my total person, then the concept of being loses for me the character of genuine conceivability that obviously it eminently possesses for Heidegger." [128] Even such a determined opponent of Heidegger as Paul Hühnerfeld saw that in the continuation of "Being and Time" a conception was involved for whose realization "the quality of a prophet, or at least that of a genuine mystic, was necessary." [129] Buber's apparent inability to understand Heidegger reminds us of his similar failure to understand the Apostle Paul—which is not accidental, for in both cases he felt he was dealing with a renegade of the spirit. Buber also believed in the forgiveness of sins against the Holy Ghost through repentance and return to God. But is it not the possibility for such a return that bursts the self grace, yes, grace *itself?* Heidegger not only believed in Nietzsche's proclamation that God is dead but he also felt conscious of having participated in this event. Because of his Catholic upbringing he was familiar with confession and the forgiveness of sin; but since he could not believe in its saving grace, it remained for him only to persevere in combating error in the knowledge that the past continues both to exert its influence and to be the source of the future.

In "What Is Man?" Buber stated that every individual by virtue of his nature and condition has a threefold living relation: a relation to the world and to things, a relation to people, and a relation to God or the Absolute.[130] In the course of his reflections he pointed out that the first two living relations are found in Heidegger only in a reduced form and that the third is missing altogether. Heidegger could justly be charged with the absence of a God experience, but surely not with the absence of a restless searching which grew increasingly calmer.[131] In his lecture, "What Is Common to All," Buber indicated that the artist and the mystic are lifted out of the community to enable them to fulfill their task; and in "Man and His Image Work" the human need "to attain the perfection of the cognitive relation" is one of the four potencies that pertain to the essence of man. Is not the philosopher often enough a tragic figure that has been "lifted out" of the community and whose piety remains a restless questioning? Must it necessarily be characterized as extravagant romanticism when Heidegger feels compelled to go back to the "beginnings" of philosophy in the pre-Socratic period? We must not forget that Heidegger came from a rural environment and that he had spent a good part of his life in a lonely ski hut in the mountains. The words of Heracleitus as he warmed himself at the oven, "Here also the gods are present," may also be applied to Heidegger. Just as Buber went back to the Patriarchs, Heidegger turned to the forces of the earth; he also went back to the root of a word and to its etymological significance: "Like an archaeologist Heidegger investigates the word that he has dug up down to its root; he plants the root of the word into the earth again." [132] The result is often enough a disconcerting artificial language, but in his treatment of the language of poetry there flashes forth in the dark night of godlessness something of "the grace of things," a luminous premonition of godliness.

From a statement made by Buber [133] in a seminar on the subject of "The Unconscious" held in 1957 at the School of Psychiatry in Washington, it appears that since the middle twenties he had been in contact with a number of psychotherapists who were interested in the effect on their work of his "dialogical principle." One of the leading representatives of German psychosomatics, Viktor von Weizsäcker, had with Buber been the editor of the journal *Die Kreatur*, which was first issued in 1926. Another prominent psychiatrist who appreciated the significance of the I-Thou meeting and found it to be highly useful in healing treatment was Ludwig Binswanger.[134] From the school of C. G. Jung came Hans Trüb who learned from Buber to reinterpret the task of the psychiatrist. The psychoanalyst was accustomed to consider the guilt feelings of the patient as an illness. Buber taught him, however, that there is also ontic guilt that has to be repented and of which the soul has to be cleansed, so that the therapist under certain conditions must have the courage to confront the patient with his guilt.[135]

Still another disciple of Jung, Arie Sborowitz, was attracted by Buber's work and personality, and in his writing *Beziehung und Bestimmung* [Relation and vocation] [136] he sought to clarify the basic principles of both Jung and Buber and to reconcile their teachings. Sborowitz justly points out that for Buber being and event are experienced under the "category of creation." The I-Thou relation is at the same time an act of freedom and grace which releases the subjective reaction of humility and awe. In the earthly Thou the divine Thou is recognized, and this confers on our fellowman an incomparable worth as a concrete face-to-face being.

The most important discovery in Jung's science was the "collective Unconscious." The unconscious to Freud included only the contents of one's personal life. Jung gave to this cardinal concept of psychoanalysis as a medium for comprehending the human soul a significance far beyond its medical aspect. Beneath the personal unconscious he found a still deeper sphere common to all mankind, a sphere of collective images and alleged possibilities of psychological events—the great symbols of mankind's spiritual experience or, as Jung called them, archetypes. Jung devoted his researches to the mysterious effect of these archetypes, which he considered just as important for the life of the soul as the contents of conscious life and of the personal unconscious. He found them in ancient symbols, in the psychological life of primitive people, in the folk tales and myths of all cultures. The archetypes are "centers of unwholesome as well as salutary influence"; they beget dangerous addictions which could lead to grave illnesses.

These "powers of the unconscious being" are no intellectual and manipulative concepts; they are "numinous *typi*, or unconscious contents, processes and dynamisms. These *typi* are, if it can so be stated, immanent-transcendent." [137] By virtue of their autonomy they constitute a counter position to the subjective ego and represent a portion of the objective psyche. For Jung this involves a genuine psychological confrontation, a psychic factor which he designated "Thou." Its efficacy is attested by man's inhumanity to man. The dialectical relation to the autonomous contents of the unconscious constitutes an essential element of therapy. The God image is for Jung an autonomous psychological content whose presence is attested by the history of nations and by psychological experience. Jung, in his dispute with Buber, went back to the assertion that everything that is said of God is a human statement, that is, psychical. It cannot be the task of an experiential science to ascertain "the extent to which such psychological content is influenced and determined by a metaphysical Godhead." Jung spoke ironically of "metaphysicians . . . who for some reason or other believe they have an intimate knowledge of unknowable things in the world beyond."

The criticism that Buber directed in *Eclipse of God* against Heidegger and Jung rests on the assumption that modern thought in its ontological or psychological form is not authorized to judge to what extent religion is to be granted the character of human life reality. Buber recognized the service rendered by Jung in illuminating religious phenomena, and he respected the results of psychological research as of any science which observes its limits. He was well aware that there is no room for faith in the realm of science, and as early as 1928 he asserted that the history of religion has nothing to do with the acts of God, but deals with religion as a human expression of life. But he refused to admit that science has the right to declare objectively demonstrable that which is beyond its competence.

This, as Buber saw it, is the position of Jung who went beyond the interpretation of religious phenomena and proclaimed a "religion of pure psychical immanence." Religion is for him "a vital link (a living relation) with psychic processes independent of consciousness and beyond it, in the dark hinterland of the psyche." This is not the only passage cited by Buber to show that in Jung's view God does not exist absolutely and apart from man. The ironic tone in which Jung expressed himself in his reply to Buber and other representatives of historical religions clearly reflects his attitude: "I do not doubt Buber's conviction that he stands in living relation to a divine Thou, but I remain of the opinion that this relation stems from an autonomous psychic content which would be defined in one way by him and in another by the Pope. Consequently, I do not hazard the least judgement about whether, or to what extent the problem has to do with a metaphysical God, who has revealed Himself to the devout Jew as He was before the incarnation, to the Church Fathers as the subsequent Trinity, to Protestants as the one and only Savior, and to the present-day Pope (at that time Pope Pius XII) as accompanied by a *co-redemptrix.*" [137a]

In answering this ostentatious indifference to God's influence in the world Buber adopted a severe tone: "We should at last extricate ourselves from this ingenious ambiguity!" [137b] He once more formulated the controversial question with great precision and again asserted that Jung knew no transcendental God, being of the opinion that the effects which the believer ascribes to a trans-psychical Being come from a deep layer within man himself. Such an assertion, however, is beyond the competence of psychology: "Neither psychology nor any other science is competent to investigate the truth of the belief in God. It is the right of their representatives to keep aloof; it is not within their disciplines their right to make judgements about the belief in God as about something which they know." [137c]

A transcendent God is not explicitly denied by Jung; He is merely excluded and replaced by the "self," a totality which was developed in connection with an ancient Indian teaching and which is realized through the integration of the unconscious contents in consciousness. Buber characterized this all-embracing totality as a gnostic solution. His reference to one of Jung's early works, which represents a kind of acknowledgment of a gnostic God, is dismissed by his opponent as a youthful error. Actually, Buber did not have historical gnosis in mind in searching for an intellectual classification for Jung, but rather gnosis as a "universally human category," which in our time has again acquired special significance. It is an intellectual tendency which approaches the ultimate mysteries without an attitude of faith, arrogating to itself a knowledge that has not been vouchsafed to man. In a later essay, "Christ, Hasidism, Gnosis," [138] the basic peculiarity of gnosis was characterized by Buber as "a knowing relationship to the divine, knowing by means of an apparently never wavering certainty of possessing in oneself sufficient divinity." In our time this is expressed by having the mysteries embedded in an "unassailable psyche." Again and again we find in the gnostic attitude the tendency to understand one's self as *the* Self—and in this Buber saw the real antithesis to the reality of faith.

Buber agreed with Jung that all statements made by man, including those about God, can only be "human." This was expressed by Jung as follows: "It goes against my grain to think that the metaphysical God himself is speaking through every one who quotes from the Bible or ventilates his own religious opinion." [139] Buber insisted that his own faith in revelation is not to be identified with any "orthodoxy" and does not mean "that finished statements about God were handed down from heaven to earth. Rather it means that the human substance is melted down by the spiritual fire which visits it, and there now breaks forth from it a word, a statement, which is human in its meaning and form, human conception and human speech, and yet witnesses to Him who stimulated it and to His will. We are revealed to ourselves—and cannot express it otherwise than as something revealed." [140] Buber's conviction that a man's relation to God can be deduced from his speech is impressively confirmed by this contrast: "The difference between the world with God and without God is so enormous that discussion of God must divide except in a group united by a real common faith." [141] No bridges can span this difference; but perhaps a distinction could be made between Jung's skeptical self-assurance and Heidegger's need to question.

The crisis of our time was viewed by Buber as the struggle between gnosis that wants to know and *devotio* that wants to serve and sanctify. Gnosis is a powerful force in the history of the human spirit. Of the power of *devotio* little can be seen on the surface of history; its highest trial of strength is martyrdom.[142] Gnosis is essentially concerned with self-redemption. But where man's salvation no longer appears to be dependent on a divine Opposite, conscience, as the court which distinguishes right from wrong, becomes vacillating: "False absolutes rule over the soul, which is no longer able to put them to flight through the image of the true. Everywhere, over the whole surface of the human world—in the East and in the West, from the left and from the right, they pierce unhindered through the level of the ethical and demand of you 'the sacrifice'. . . . In the realm of Moloch honest men lie and compassionate men torture. And they really and truly believe that brother-murder will prepare the way for brotherhood!" [143]

This danger of the "suspension of the ethical" in our age of the "eclipse of God" prompted Buber to insert in his book a section on "Religion and Ethics" which describes the natural and the disrupted relation between the two spheres. The ancient dispute between ethics and religion had already been dealt with by Buber in the section "Love of God and Love of Neighbor" in *Hasidism and Modern Man* (Hebrew edition, 1944). Should the good be done because it is good or because it is commanded by a higher Power? Or, seen from the standpoint of religion, should one do "good" at all or do that which is God's will? To Buber both questions, expressed in this form, proceed from a false conception.

If one does not believe in a God who commands and makes demands, he can and should do what is good simply because it is good; and his acts are not less meritorious just because they are not prompted by religious motives. Such a man can lead an exemplary life that represents a Whole, but he is not dealing with the totality of being and he cannot draw from his soul absoluteness for his scale of values. This, according to Buber, is something that can be understood only by a religious man, for here we have reached the limit of conceptual understanding.

In the section "Religion and Ethics" in *Eclipse of God* Buber went on to show that in the great ancient oriental cultures and in ancient Greece the moral order was identical with the cosmic order. Gods and men were subject to the same principle which in China was called Tao, in India Rita, in Iran Urta (usually pronounced Asha), and in Greece Dike. This principle, whereby the heavenly powers devised the pattern of right behavior for man to follow, was questioned in Greece by the Sophists for whom man was the measure of all things, and it was Plato who opposed this disintegrating, relativizing process with his doctrine of Ideas.

The second great attempt to bind the separation of good and evil to the Absolute came from Israel. Here the determining factor was not the cosmic order but the will of the one God and Creator who taught man to distinguish between good and evil, even as He himself had distinguished between light and darkness. He is the God who took man with Him into the world which now became the place of man's salvation, a salvation to be achieved through *imitatio dei,* that is, in accordance with the commandment: Be ye holy, for I your God am holy. The difference here between "the ethical and the religious is suspended in the breathing-space of the divine . . . The absolute norm is given to show the way that leads before the face of the Absolute." [144] In the teaching of the great Asiatic cultures, only the normative side of the one Truth is directed to man; in the teaching of Israel, ethos is "an inherent function of religion."

In a genuine face-to-face relation with God a living religion even today will produce a living ethos whose distinctive mark is "that the critical flame shoot up ever again out of the depths, first illuminating, then burning and purifying." [145] It is always religion, however, which bestows and the ethical which receives; and this in Buber's view by no means signifies moral heteronomy, that is, externally imposed laws as over against the self-imposed laws of moral autonomy. A genuine religious relation safeguards man's independence; freedom of decision belongs to the mystery of his creation.

In *Hasidism and Modern Man*[146] Buber set forth what this means for the man of today who no longer recognizes guiding lines for the conduct of his life in accordance with God's will in the tradition that has come down to him. In hours of personal illumination he will conduct himself with an inner assurance and confident sense of rectitude; but he will also know hours of unalleviated sorrow in which he feels completely abandoned, when God's word no longer speaks to him and when he can no longer rely on his conscience. He hears God's questions and demands in the events of the hour, but this does not provide him with the precepts of right conduct; for these must be wrested from conscience and then ventured in "fear and trembling." The fear of God is for Buber as for biblical man the basis of religious reality; it is the dark gateway that leads to an open site where one can live with the mystery and persevere in the face of the doubts and terrors of daily life. He who begins with the love of God without having previously experienced the fear of God loves an idol that is easy to love. Only he who goes through the gate of fear knows "that he endures in the face of God the reality of lived life, dreadful and incomprehensible though it be. He loves it in the love of God, whom he has learned to love." [147]

Buber's writings on the subject of religion and ethics include another small work which was published at about the same time as *Eclipse of God*, namely, *Images of Good and Evil* (1952). To illustrate the contrast between good and evil Buber attempted to make the problem of evil more comprehensible by examining myths by means of images which mankind in its infancy made for itself. In this connection he cited two myth cycles: the biblical account of first man's fall and its consequences and the Iranian myths, especially the saga of King Yima and his lie of being; this king had been given the task of governing the world in the spirit of the god Ahura Mazda, but he rebelled against him by putting himself at the central point of being. The motif of the two myths is the same, namely, the desire to be like God—and yet they express two different types or levels of evil.

After an interval of many years Buber, in his search for a more profound knowledge of man, turned again to his early interest in myth, this time with reference to Jung's myth researches and in conscious opposition to his findings. His point of departure is his serious attitude to evil, the knowledge of its "existent actuality." [148] The question for Buber is not merely the transgression of a social tabu. His view is directly opposed to that of modern psychology which "is concerned to penetrate 'behind' that which is remembered, to 'reduce' it to the real elements assumed to have been 'repressed.'" [149] Buber, on the contrary, considered it to be our business "to call to mind an occurrence as reliably, concretely, and completely remembered as possible, which is entirely unreduced and undissected." [150] The images of the collective Unconscious which, according to Jung, confront the ego do not constitute for Buber a real face-to-face confrontation. It is true that the individual "has to do with the totality of being," but this involves the real correspondence of the "order" within man and in being, of the factual face-to-face meeting of man and the Absolute. In myth this reality that is common to world and soul becomes poetry; it manifests "truth" which, as Plato had already noted, could not be adequately transmitted in a conceptual manner. Myth is pure process; it has to do, like the soul, with the evil that actually *happens,* with good and evil as they exist in human reality and not with ethical abstractions. Buber characterized his way of looking at myth as "anthropological definition of good and evil." [151] In dealing with the problem of evil he found a way, as in his other contributions to philosophical anthropology, of transmitting the principles and the dynamic of his Hebrew humanism without falling into the abstract terminology of a conceptual ethic.

The problem of the correspondence of the inner and outer, with which Buber was concerned here, also appeared as one of the cardinal themes in *"For the Sake of Heaven."* [152] The words of its chief character, the "holy Yehudi," are quoted by Buber in the preface to *Images of Good and Evil*: " 'Rabbi,' he said in an almost failing voice, 'what is the nature of this Gog? He can exist in the outer world only because he exists in us?' He pointed to his own breast. 'The darkness out of which he was hewn needed to be taken from nowhere else than our own slothful and malicious hearts. It is our betrayal of God that has made Gog grow so great.' " The Rabbi, who wishes to use evil as a means to the good, puts himself in the place of God who embraces both opposites, and thus goes beyond the limits of man who stands *in* them and who has to choose between them.

The "anthropological definition" recognizes evil as something that happens within us. The images show that this involves three stages: the fall of first man is on a different plane from that of Cain's murder and the perpetual lying and demonism of Yima. The eating of the apple of the Tree of Knowledge as recounted in the Bible Buber interpreted to be "spun out of play and dream"; it is an act that must be attributed more to man's failure to decide for God than to conscious malice. Cain is attacked by a demon and succumbs to him; Yima's conscious and determined decision against God and for evil falsifies the truth of being.

To what extent does human reality today correspond to the images of these ancient myths? [153] Evil can also become simply "event" in us; it can attack us by reason of the false orientation of our being toward God; we can fall into a demonic state which, as with Cain, can come forth in a monstrous deed. Just as the narrator of Genesis must have experienced Adam and Cain in the depths of his own heart, so every young person today finds the chaos of disorientation within himself. The evolving human person "is bowled over by possibility as an infinitude." [153a] Numberless possibilities rush in on reality; the chaos of possible acts overwhelms the imagination which plays with them: an irresistible consuming passion and a circling lack of direction are the signature of our age. A restless desire to attempt all things and an innate grace of "direction" confront one another as "chaos and the spirit that hovers above it." To transform chaos into cosmos the whole man must direct himself to God; the "evil impulse" must be enlisted in the love of God and pressed into the service of being.

Buber's assertion that the "images of good and evil" correspond to definite anthropologically comprehensible processes in the life of the human person is based on the assumption that man is a being in whom the category of possibility is embodied, so to speak, and whose reality is constantly subject to a variety of possibilities. He lacks the instinctive certainty of an animal; he is "an audacity of life." In "Distance and Relation" Buber also spoke of man as the only being who desires confirmation of his existence and who becomes a "self" through the confirming Thou of his fellowman. In both instances we detect a latent opposition to Jung's findings.

In *Images of Good and Evil* we are given a further criterion for defining the nature of man: "Every man, yes, every man has an implanted but sadly neglected premonition of the nature that is meant to be his and his alone—whether it be from the standpoint of creation or of 'individuation.'" There is in man himself a court of appeal which confirms his way as true or false; this explains why man, on looking back, is aware of his lack of direction, and he feels a sense of guilt in failing to choose the proper way.

But the lack of direction and the opposition to God acquire a new perspective because of man's desire for confirmation. The decision to turn away from God is a decision that is not confirmed by one's inner nature—"evil cannot be done with the entire soul"—so that one who makes such a decision is compelled to alter the order of the world and seek its confirmation. In this way evil is radicalized and acquires "substantive character."

The secret knowledge of man, of what he is and should be, Buber called an "anthropological criterion"; it can assume as many forms as there are individuals and still never be relativized. This anthropological criterion attests Buber's Hebrew humanism, his conception of man which he placed in the category of creation. His concern was not with man as such, but with man as he lives over against God and with the being-mystery of his person. The uniqueness of human personality is only a projection, and it needs man's cooperation for its consummation. To this end his soul has been imbued with the knowledge that he was created in order to fulfill a being-intention that is personal but which at the same time contributes to the realization of world order and the goal of creation. The good that man does, so conceived, cannot be subsumed in any ethical coordinating system. All ethos has its origin in a revelation that shows us the proper way to cooperate in the work of creation. We can thus better understand the deeper meaning of Buber's mysterious words addressed to Jung: "We are revealed to ourselves—and cannot express it otherwise than as something revealed." My "self" is realized by taking the direction toward the point of being "at which, executing for my part the design which I am, I encounter the divine mystery of my created uniqueness, the mystery waiting for me." [154]

NOTES

A work is referred to by its English title whenever a translation is readily available; the German title follows in parentheses. After the first mention the English title only will be used. When the work has not been translated into English, the German title is used, but when first mentioned is followed by the English translation in brackets with only the first word capitalized.

Chapter 1

1. Stefan Zweig, *The World of Yesterday* (London, 1943), pp. 21 f.
2. Friedrich Heer, *Land im Strom der Zeit. Oesterreich gestern, heute, morgen* (Vienna, 1958), pp. 236 f.
3. Cf. Hans Kohn, Karl Kraus, Arthur Schnitzler, Otto Weininger, *Aus dem jüdischen Wien der Jahrhundertwende* (Tübingen, 1962), pp. 3 f.
4. Zweig, p. 28.
5. Cf. Kohn et al., p. 63.
6. Olga Schnitzler, *Spiegelbild der Freundschaft* (Salzburg, 1962), pp. 67, 129.
7. Richard Beer-Hofmann, *Gesammelte Werke* (Stuttgart: S. Fischer Verlag, 1963), p. 5.
8. Kohn et al., p. 19.
9. Schnitzler, pp. 54 f.
10. Heer, p. 301.
11. Ibid., pp. 294 f.
12. Zweig, p. 16.
13. "Autobiographische Fragmente" [Autobiographical fragments] (Stuttgart, 1960), written as a contribution for the volume *Martin Buber* in the series *Philosophen des 20. Jahrhunderts* (Stuttgart, 1963), pp. 1–34. Appeared in English as vol. 12 of *The Library of Living Philosophers*, ed. P. A. Schilpp and M. Friedman, with title *The Philosophy of Martin Buber* (LaSalle, Ill., 1967). Hereafter cited as M.B. with page number.
14. Cf. Buber, *Hasidism and Modern Man* (New York, 1958), bk. 1, p. 26.
15. Buber, "Erinnerung," in *Martin Buber zum 80. Geburtstag, Schriften des Zentralrats der Juden in Deutschland*, no. 2 (Düsseldorf, 1958), p. 33.
16. M.B., p. 5.
17. Ibid., p. 6.
18. Beer-Hofmann, p. 654.
19. M.B., p. 4.
20. Ibid., p. 10.
21. Ibid., p. 6.
22. Buber, *Between Man and Man* (Boston, 1947), pp. 136 f.
23. M.B., pp. 11 f.

24. *Between Man and Man*, pp. 136 f.

25. Simon, *Deutsches Judentum. Aufstieg und Krise*, ed. Robert Weltsch (Stuttgart, 1963), pp. 27 ff.

26. Ibid., p. 28.

27. "My Way to Hasidism," in *Hasidism and Modern Man*, bk. 2, p. 57.

28. M.B., p. 12.

29. Lou Andreas-Salomé, *Friedrich Nietzsche in seinen Werken, Unveränderter Neudruck der Ausgabe von 1894* (Dresden, n.d.), p. 54.

30. Buber, *Nietzsche und die Lebenswerte, Die Kunst im Leben*, no. 2 (Berlin, 1900), p. 13.

31. Otto Friedrich Bollnow, *Die Lebensphilosophie* (Heidelberg, 1958), pp. 4 f.

32. Karl Jaspers, *Nietzsche* (Berlin and Leipzig, 1936), p. 130.

33. Thomas Mann, "Nietzsches Philosophie," in *Neue Studien* (Frankfurt, 1948), pp. 126 f.

34. Friedrich Nietzsche, *Complete Works*, trans. Oscar Levy, "Thoughts Out of Season II" (London, 1910), 5: 34.

35. Ibid., p. 55.

36. Cf. Hans Kohn, *Martin Buber. Sein Werk und seine Zeit*. 2d ed. enl. (Cologne, 1961), p. 29.

37. Cf. Ernst Bertram, *Nietzsche* (Berlin, 1921), pp. 64 ff.

38. Buber, *Die jüdische Bewegung I, Gesammelte Aufsätze und Ansprachen 1900–1914* (Berlin, 1920), pp. 68–77; quotation, p. 73.

39. Nietzsche, *Works*, "Thus Spake Zarathustra," 11:356, 357; cf. Jaspers, p. 145.

40. Bollnow, p. 15.

41. Cf. Jaspers, p. 145.

42. "What Is Man?" in *Between Man and Man*, p. 185.

43. Kohn, *Martin Buber*, p. 295.

44. Nietzsche, *Works*, "Ecce Homo," 17:101.

45. Nietzsche, *Works*, "The Will to Power," 2:417–18; cf. Jaspers, p. 305.

46. Jaspers, p. 321.

47. Bollnow, *Das Wesen der Stimmungen*, 3d ed. (Frankfurt, 1956), p. 234.

48. "Erinnerung," p. 34.

49. Buber, *For the Sake of Heaven* (Philadelphia, 1947), p. xii.

50. Heer, esp. chap.: "Judentum und österreichische Genius."

50a. First appeared in Buber's *Begegnung*; English translation is from M.B., pp. 14 f.

51. Georg Misch, *Dilthey versus Nietzsche, Die Sammlung* (Göttingen, 1952), 7:388.

52. Wilhelm Dilthey, *Gesammelte Werke* 7:250; 8:226; 4:528 f.; hereafter cited with volume and page number in the text.

53. Bollnow, *Dilthey*, 2d ed. (Stuttgart, 1955), pp. 218 f.

54. Cf. ibid., p. 64, and the section "Das Leben und die Welt," pp. 43 ff.

55. Cf. ibid., pp. 19 f.

56. Cf. Gerhard Masur, "Wilhelm Dilthey und die europäische Geistesgeschichte," *Deutsche Vierteljahrsschrift* 12, no. 4 (1934):493.

57. Hugo von Hofmannsthal, *Gesammelte Werke* (Berlin, 1934), 3:156.

58. Dilthey, 8:220–26.

59. *Buch des Dankes an Georg Simmel*, ed. Kurt Gassen and Michael Landmann (Berlin, 1958), p. 223.

60. Ibid., Paul Fechter, p. 160.
61. Simmel, *Brücke und Tür* (Stuttgart, 1957).
62. Margarete Susman, *Die geistige Gestalt Georg Simmels* (Tübingen, 1959), p. 14.
63. *Buch des Dankes*, Otto Heuschelle, p. 183.
64. Ibid., p. 221.
65. Susman, p. 12.
66. *Brücke und Tür*, p. 68.
67. Cf. "Elements of the Interhuman," in *The Knowledge of Man* (London, 1965), chap. 3, pp. 71 f.
68. Cf. Kohn, *Martin Buber*, pp. 310 ff. and 89 f.
69. *Buch des Dankes*, p. 9.
70. Cf. Hellmuth Bohner, *Untersuchungen zur Entwicklung der Philosophie Georg Simmels* (Offenburg i.B., 1930), p. 24.
71. Susman, p. 17.
72. Ibid., pp. 4, 24.
73. Simmel, "Die Religion," in *Die Gesellschaft*, 2d ed. (Frankfurt, 1912), 2:95.
74. Cf. Bohner, pp. 52, 59.
75. *Buch des Dankes*, Leo Mathias, p. 192.
76. Cf. "Verhandlungen des ersten deutschen Soziologentages," in *Schriften der Deutschen Gesellschaft für Soziologie*, ser. 1 (Tübingen, 1911), 1:204–7, 213 f.
77. Simmel, *Lebensanschauung. Vier metaphysische Kapitel* (Munich and Leipzig, 1918), p. 225.
78. (Leipzig, 1920), pp. 243 f.

Chapter 2

1. Simmel, *Hauptprobleme der Philosophie, Sammlung Göschen*, 7th ed. (1950), 500:13.
2. Cf. Franz Rosenzweig, "Aus Bubers Dissertation," in *Aus unbekannten Schriften*, Festgabe für Martin Buber zum 50. Geburtstag (Berlin, 1928), pp. 240–44. Prof. Buber kindly permitted me to use the manuscript of the dissertation.
3. Dilthey, *Die grosse Phantasiedichtung* (Göttingen, 1954), p. 68.
4. Jaspers, *Nikolaus Cusanus* (Munich, 1964).
5. Ibid., p. 212.
6. Ibid., p. 122.
7. Ibid., p. 263.
8. Ibid., p. 229.
9. Ernst Hoffmann, "Nikolaus von Kues," *Die grossen Deutschen I* (Berlin, 1935), p. 259.
10. Boehme, *Works* (London, 1764–1781), chap. 6: "The Threefold Life of Man."
11. Ernst Benz, *Die christliche Kabbala* (Zurich, 1958), pp. 27, 57 f., note; Gershom Scholem, *Major Trends in Mysticism* (New York, 1946), p. 233.
12. *Wiener Rundschau* 15 (June 1901).
13. Cited in Ernst Benz, *Der volkommene Mensch nach Jakob Böhme* (Stuttgart, 1937), p. 5.
14. Buber, *Die Schriften über das dialogische Prinzip* (Heidelberg, 1954), pp. 287 ff.
15. From the poem, "Manche freilich."
16. *I and Thou*, 2d ed. (New York, 1958), postscript, pp. 123 f.

17. "Original Remembrance," in *Between Man and Man*, pp. 1 ff.

18. *I and Thou*, p. 18.

19. Cf. Romano Guardini, *Hölderlin. Weltbild und Frömmigkeit* (Leipzig, 1939), p. 410.

20. *Daniel, Dialogues on Realization* (New York, 1965), chap 5: "On Unity. Dialogue by the Sea," p. 135.

21. "Dialogue, A Conversion," in *Between Man and Man*, p. 13.

22. Cf. chap. 1, n. 44.

23. Cf. Grete Schaeder, "Hugo von Hofmannsthals Weg zur Tragödie," *Deutsche Vierteljahresschrift* 2, no. 3 (1949):308, where the sources of the quotations are given.

24. Cf. Walther Brecht, "Hugo von Hofmannsthals 'Ad me ipsum' und seine Bedeutung," *Jahrbuch des Freien Hochstifts* (1930), pp. 322, 324.

25. Dilthey, *Die grosse Phantasiedichtung*, p. 3.

26. Kohn, *Martin Buber*, pp. 296, 310.

27. Kadima Kalender für das Jahr 5667. (Berlin: Verlag der Jüdischen Rundschau, 1906); also Buber, *A Believing Humanism* (New York, 1967), p. 35.

28. *Die jüdische Bewegung I*, p. 68.

29. "Education," in *Between Man and Man*, p. 85.

30. Buber, *Hinweise, Gesammelte Essays* (Zurich, 1953), pp. 231 f.

31. "My Way to Hasidism," p. 58.

32. "The Altar," in *Pointing the Way* (New York, 1957), p. 18.

33. *Between Man and Man*, pp. 184 f.

34. *Der grosse Maggid* (Frankfurt, 1922), p. 37; cf. *Origin and Meaning of Hasidism*, p. 130; also Goethe, "Concept of Humanity," in *Pointing the Way*, p. 78.

35. Cf. "Meister Eckhart der Prediger." Festschrift zum Eckhart-Gedenkjahr, ed. Udo M. Nix and Raphael Ochslein (Freiburg: Herder, 1960).

36. "Renaissance und Bewegung," in *Der Jude und sein Judentum* (Cologne: Joseph Melzer Verlag, 1963), p. 273.

37. "My Way to Hasidism," pp. 57 f.

38. *The Tales of Rabbi Nachman* (New York, 1958), p. 44.

39. *Tales of the Hasidim, Early Masters* (New York, 1947), p. 156; *Die jüdische Bewegung I*, p. 126; Ernst Simon, *Martin Buber und das deutsche Judentum*, pp. 36 f.

40. "Drei Stationen," in *Der Jude und sein Judentum*, p. 751.

41. *Der grosse Maggid*, p. 31; *Hasidism and Modern Man*, p. 33.

42. *The Tales of Rabbi Nachman*, p. 12.

43. *The Legend of the Baal-Shem* (London, 1956), p. 49.

44. Wilhelm Michel, "Martin Bubers Gang in die Wirklichkeit," in *Das Leiden am Ich* (Bremen, 1930), pp. 267–93.

45. *The Legend of the Baal-Shem*, p. 10.

46. Ibid., p. 27; *The Tales of Rabbi Nachman*, p. 12.

47. *The Legend of the Baal-Shem*, p. 32.

48. The preface to the *Legend of the Baal-Shem* (p. 13) has a reference to the "son of man" as prophet and saint.

49. Buber, *Ekstatische Konfessionen* (Jena: Eugen Dietrichs, 1909), p. xxv.

50. *Tales of the Hasidim, Early Masters*, p. 11.

51. *The Legend of the Baal-Shem*, pp. 72 f.

52. Cited by Hans Kohn, *Martin Buber*, p. 305.

53. Ludwig Strauss, "Georg Munk," *Der Kunstwart* 42, no. 1: 225 ff.

54. Paula Buber, *Geister und Menschen* (Munich, 1961), pp. 182 f.

55. "Demon in the Dream," in *Pointing the Way*, p. 11.

56. (Frankfurt, 1911; new ed., Zurich, 1948).

56a. Cf. *A Believing Humanism*, p. 51.

57. Cf. Kohn, *Martin Buber*, pp. 87 f.

58. "Das Epos des Zauberers," in *Hinweise*, p. 100.

59. *The Legend of the Baal-Shem*, p. x.

60. *A Believing Humanism*, p. 31.

61. *Ekstatische Konfessionen*, p. xvi.

62. Chap. 1, n. 73.

63. Chap. 2, n. 25.

64. Nietzsche, *Works*, vol. 1: *The Birth of Tragedy*, p. 174.

65. Landauer, "Die Revolution," in *Die Gesellschaft* 13 (Frankfurt, 1907):24.

66. Liebert, in *Kantstudien* 27 (Berlin, 1922): 399–455.

67. "Myth in Judaism," in *On Judaism*, ed. Nahum N. Glazer (New York, 1967), pp. 95 ff.

68. *I and Thou*, p. 27.

69. "Rainer Maria Rilke, Lou Andreas Salomé," *Briefwechsel*, ed. Ernst Pfeiffer (Zurich, 1952), p. 353. Cf. Grete Schaeder, "Rainer Maria Rilke und Lou Andreas Salomé," *Die Sammlung* (Sept. 1953), pp. 436 f.

70. Rilke, *Ausgewählte Werke*, "Erlebnis" (Leipzig, 1942), p. 256.

71. Ibid., p. 259.

72. Lou Andreas- Salomé, *Mein Dank an Freud* (Vienna, 1931), p. 83.

73. Cf. H. E. Holthusen, *Der späte Rilke* (Zurich, 1949), p. 8.

74. Ernst Bertram, p. 6. In Buber's preface, legend is taken to be a late form of myth.

75. Ibid., p. 7.

76. Cf. Wera Lewin, *Die Bedeutung des Stefan George-Kreises für die deutsch-jüdische Geistesgeschichte*, yearbook VIII, Publications of the Leo Baeck Institute (London, 1963), pp. 184 ff.; for Buber and the George Circle, esp. p. 210 to the end.

77. Cf. chap. 2, n. 15.

78. "The Spirit of the Orient and Judaism," in *On Judaism*, p. 57. The following quotations are taken from this address.

79. "Renewal of Judaism," in *On Judaism*, p. 44.

80. "The Teaching of Tao," in *On Judaism*, p. 37.

81. Cf. "Production and Existence," in *Pointing the Way*.

82. "The Teaching of Tao," p. 50.

83. "The Spirit of the Orient and Judaism," p. 68.

84. "Renewal of Judaism," p. 44.

85. "The Teaching of Tao," p. 52.

86. Ibid., p. 58.

87. Cf. chap. 2, n. 60.

88. "The Teaching of Tao," p. 35.

89. "Myth in Judaism," p. 106.

90. "The Altar," in *Pointing the Way*, p. 18.

91. "With a Monist," in *Pointing the Way*, p. 28.

92. Ibid., p. 29.

93. Ibid., p. 30.

94. Hugo Bergmann, "Martin Buber and Mysticism," in M.B., p. 300.

95. "The Teaching of Tao," p. 43.

Chapter 3

1. Buber, *Ereignisse und Begegnungen* (Leipzig: Insel Verlag, 1917), pp. 3–9.

2. Martin Buber, *Daniel*, p. 56; in this chapter, page numbers in parentheses will follow quotations in text.

3. "The Teaching of Tao," p. 54.

4. Ibid.

5. Cf. Kohn, *Martin Buber*, p. 123.

6. "The Spirit of the Orient and Judaism," p. 60.

7. Cf. chap. 1, n. 19.

8. Cf. Kohn, *Martin Buber*, p. 123.

9. Cf. earlier discussion in chap. 2.

10. "With a Monist," p. 29.

11. Ibid., p. 28.

12. Ibid., p. 29.

13. *Daniel*, p. 44.

14. *Die jüdische Bewegung I*, pp. 7–16; Cf. Kohn, p. 50; also, "The Holy Way," in *On Judaism*, p. 143.

15. "The Holy Way," p. 140.

16. "Renewal of Judaism," p. 54.

17. Ibid.

18. "The Holy Way," p. 110.

19. *Daniel*, p. 95.

20. "Warum gelernt werden soll," in *Der Jude und sein Judentum*, p. 745.

21. "Herut: On Youth and Religion," in *On Judaism*, p. 164.

22. Cf. Robert Weltsch's introduction to *Der Jude und sein Judentum*, p. xxiii.

23. In *The Credo Series* (New York, 1964), cf. esp. "The Zionism."

24. Ibid., p. 144.

25. P. xxii.

26. Rosenzweig, *Kleinere Schriften* (Berlin: Schocken, 1935), pp. 106 ff.

27. Bergmann, pp. 297 ff.

27a. "Judaism and the Jews," in *On Judaism*, pp. 11–22.

28. Kohn, *Martin Buber*, pp. 94 ff.

29. Kohn et al., pp. 64 f.

30. Landauer, *Sein Lebensgang in Briefen*, ed. Martin Buber, 2 vols. (Frankfurt, 1929), 1:60.

31. Landauer, *Skepsis und Mystik* (Berlin, 1903), pp. 37 f.

32. For the quotations from this address, cf. "Judaism and Mankind," in *On Judaism*, pp. 22–34.

33. "Renewal of Judaism," in *On Judaism*, pp. 34–56.

34. Pp. 56–79; pp. 95–108.

35. Cf. chap. 2, n. 67.

36. "Judaism and Mankind," p. 39.

37. "Jewish Religiosity," in *On Judaism*, pp. 79–95.

38. "The Holy Way," pp. 108–49.

38a. "Herut: On Youth and Religion," in *On Judaism*, pp. 149–74.

39. "Jewish Religiosity," p. 83.

40. Bergmann, pp. 297.

41. Cf. chap. 2, n. 14.

42. Cf. chap. 1, n. 42.

43. "Spirit and Body of the Hasidic Movement," in *Origin and Meaning of Hasidism*, p. 133.

44. P. 150.

45. Ibid.

46. Cf. *Die jüdische Bewegung*, pp. 205 ff.

47. M.B., p. 689.

48. "Dialogue," in *Between Man and Man*, pp. 14 f.

49. Preface to *Addresses* (1923), in *On Judaism*, p. 6.

50. "God and Soul," in *Origin and Meaning of Hasidism*, pp. 193, 196.

51. Cf. Hans Kohn, *Martin Buber*, p. 392; now in *A Believing Humanism* (New York, 1967), p. 18.

Chapter 4

1. *I and Thou*, p. 98.

2. "To the Contemporary," in *Pointing the Way*, pp. 59 ff.

3. Cf. chap. 2, n. 50.

4. "Dialogue (A Conversion)," in *Between Man and Man*, p. 13; cf. chap. 2, n. 20.

5. Georg Simmel, *Die Religion*, 2d ed. (Frankfurt, 1912), p. 16; cf Kohn, *Martin Buber*, p. 214.

6. Cf. Margarete Susman, *Die geistige Gestalt Georg Simmels*, p. 39.

7. M.B., p. 689.

8. M.B., pp. 49, 235.

9. Simon Maringer, "Martin Bubers Metaphysik der Dialogik im Zusammenhang neuerer philosophischer und theologischer Strömungen" (Ph.D. diss., Zurich, 1936), pp. 22 f.; Hermann L. Goldschmidt, Hermann Cohen, and Martin Buber, *Collection Migdal* (Geneva, 1946), p. 75.

10. M.B., p. 703.

11. M.B., p. 742.

12. Landauer, *Der werdende Mensch*, ed. Martin Buber (Potsdam, 1921), p. 244.

13. M.B., p. 693.

14. M.B., p. 222.

15. Buber, *Dialogisches Leben* (Zurich, 1947), preface, pp. 7–13.

16. *I and Thou*, trans. R. G. Smith, 2d ed. (Edinburgh, 1958), p. 3; hereafter in this chapter quotations from *I and Thou* are cited in the text by page number in parentheses.

17. "The Holy Way," p. 110.

18. Cf. chap. 2, n. 61.

19. M.B., p. 701.

20. *I and Thou*, pp. 6, 33 f.

21. Ibid., pp. 123 ff.

22. M.B., p. 273.

23. M.B., p. 714.

24. "The Two Foci of the Jewish Soul," in *Israel and the World* (New York, 1948), p. 31.

25. "Spirit and Body of the Hasidic Movement," in *Origin and Meaning of Hasidism*, p. 144.

26. M.B., p. 716.

27. "The Two Foci of the Jewish Soul," p. 35.

28. "The Holy Way," p. 146.

29. "Spirit and Body of the Hasidic Movement," p. 116.

30. Cf. earlier discussion in chap. 2.

31. Cf. chap. 2, n. 19.

32. "With a Monist," p. 28.

33. Cf. chap. 3, no. 38.

34. Cf. chap. 2, n. 17.

35. "Herut," p. 151.

36. *I and Thou*, p. 82.

37. M.B., p. 45.

38. *I and Thou*, p. 18.

39. J. G. Hamann, *Schriften* (Leipzig: Insel, 1921), "Aesthetica in nuce," p. 263.

40. Kohn, *Martin Buber*, p. 240.

41. Ibid., p. 242.

42. *Geschichte des dialogischen Prinzips*, p. 297.

43. "Franz Rosenzweig," in *Der Jude und sein Judentum*, p. 820.

44. Hamann, p. 368.

45. Ibid., p. 179.

46. Martin Seils, *Wirklichkeit und Wort bei Johann Georg Hamann* (Stuttgart, 1961), pp. 20 f.

47. Cf. chap. 2, n. 60.

48. Hamann, p. 130.

49. Cf. chap. 4, n. 12.

50. Cf. Gabriel Marcel, in M.B.

51. *Between Man and Man*, pp. 4 f., 17 f.

52. Ibid., p. 194; Vergil *Aeneid* 1.462.

53. Cf. chap. 4, n. 40.

54. Cf. Buber, *Einleitung zu "Die chassidischen Bucher"* (Hellerau, 1928); and Hans Kohn, p. 271.

55. Dilthey, *Gesammelte Werke* 7:171; cf. chap. 1, n. 55.

56. "The Faith of Judaism," in *Israel and the World*, p. 16.

57. M.B., p. 704.

58. "People and Leader," in *Pointing the Way*, p. 154.

59. *Between Man and Man*, p. 32.

60. "Wie kann Gemeinschaft werden," in *Der Jude und sein Judentum*, pp. 358 f.

61. *Between Man and Man*, p. 36.

62. Ibid., p. 211.

63. "The Silent Question," in *At the Turning, Three Addresses on Judaism* (New York, 1951), p. 41.

64. *Between Man and Man*, p. 11.

65. Ibid., p. 17.

66. Ibid., p. 10.

67. Ibid., pp. 25 f.

68. Ibid., p. 15.

69. Ibid., p. 10.

70. Ibid., p. 6.

71. Ibid., p. 10.

72. Ibid., p. 4.

73. Ibid., p. 23.

74. Ibid., p. 30.

75. Ibid., p. 14.

76. In *On Judaism*, p. 104.

77. Cf. the introduction to *The Legend of the Baal-Shem* and the preface to *Der grosse Maggid*.

78. *Origin and Meaning of Hasidism*, p. 165.

79. Ibid.

80. "Spinoza, Sabbatai Zvi and the Baal-Shem," in *Origin and Meaning of Hasidism*, pp. 95 f.

81. *Between Man and Man*, p. 17.

82. "What Is to Be Done," in *Pointing the Way*, p. 109.

83. "Jewish Religiosity," in *On Judaism*, p. 86.

84. Ibid., p. 89.

85. "The Two Foci of the Jewish Soul," p. 34.

86. For the following, cf. the concluding chapter "Prospect" of "What Is Man?," in *Between Man and Man*, pp. 199 f.

87. M.B., p. 689.

88. Cf. chap. 1, n. 67.

89. Buber, *Knowledge of Man. Selected Essays* (New York, 1965), p. 72.

90. Ibid., p. 78.

91. Ibid., p. 70.

92. *Daniel*, pp. 21 and 116.

93. Personal communication from Buber.

94. *Pointing the Way*, p. 81.

95. "Elements of the Interhuman (Imposition and Unfolding)," in *Knowledge of Man*, p. 82.

96. *Geschichte des dialogischen Prinzips*.

97. Ibid.

98. Cf. the two essays on education in *Between Man and Man*: "Education," p. 98; "Education and Character," p. 104.

99. *I and Thou*, p. 11.

100. Ibid., p. 133.

101. "Education," pp. 94.

102. *The Tales of Rabbi Nachman* (Indiana Univ. Press, 1956), p. 17.

103. *Der grosse Maggid*, pp. 56 f.

104. Johannes Ernst Seiffert, "Das Erzieherische in Martin Bubers chassidischen Anekdoten" (Ph.D. diss., Freiberg i.B.; Japan: Takatsuki, 1963).

105. "Education," p. 83.

105a. Ibid., p. 84.

106. Ibid., pp. 97 f.; cf. chap. 4, n. 73.

107. *Daniel*, p. 117.

108. *Between Man and Man*, p. 103.

108a. "Imitatio Dei," in *Israel and the World*, p. 76.

108b. Ibid.

109. "Das Erste 1933," in *Der Jude und sein Judentum*, p. 581.

110. "Education and World View," in *Pointing the Way*, p. 102.

110a. Ibid., p. 103.

111. *Between Man and Man*, p. 110.

112. Ibid., p. 110

112a. Ibid.

113. Ibid., p. 114.

114. Cf. chap. 4, n. 6.

115. Simon, "Martin Buber, the Educator," in M.B., p. 548; this essay is an important contribution to Buber as educator.

116. "Aus einer philosophischen Rechenschaft," in *Werke* 1:1119 f.

117. Cf. chap. 4, n. 110a.

118. Cf. *Werke* 1:1120.

119. M.B., pp. 572 f.

120. *Between Man and Man*, p. 116.

121. *Philosophical Interrogations*, ed. Sidney and Beatrice Rome (New York: Holt, Rinehart and Winston, 1964), pp. 61 f.

122. Cf. chap. 2, n. 20.

123. Personal communication from Buber.

124. Buber, "Healing through Meeting," in *A Believing Humanism*, pp. 138 f.; also in *Pointing the Way*, pp. 93–97.

125. "Guilt and Guilt Feelings," in *Knowledge of Man*, p. 127.

126. *I and Thou*, p. 133.

127. *Der grosse Maggid*, pp. 51 f.

128. *I and Thou*, p. 133.

128a. Ibid.

129. The conversation was recorded on tape. Professor Buber kindly placed at my disposal a copy of the conversation in MS. form, as well as the notes and summary of the Seminar on the Unconscious. Both MSS. are critically interpreted in the introduction by Maurice Friedman to Buber, *The Knowledge of Man*. The appendix also has the conversation with Rogers. Cf. also *A Believing Humanism*, p. 153.

129a. *Between Man and Man*, p. 198.

129b. Ibid.

130. From the summary of the Seminar on the Unconscious by Maurice Friedman in section VIII of his introduction.

131. Werner Heisenberg, "Das Naturbild der heutigen Physik," in *Die Kunste im technischen Zeitalter*, annual register, vol. 3: *Gestalt und Gedanke* (Munich, 1954), pp. 62, 67.

132. "Zur Geschichte des dialogischen Prinzips," *Werke* I:298; also "Suspension of the Ethical," in *Eclipse of God* (London, 1953), chap. 7.

133. "Love of God and Love of Neighbor," in *Hasidism and Modern Man*, pp. 227 f.; M.B., pp. 33, 704.

134. "The Question to the Single One," in *Between Man and Man*, p. 57.

135. For example, *Philosophische Brocken* (Düsseldorf, Cologne: E. Diederichs, 1952), p. 31.

136. For Kierkegaard and Socrates, cf. H. Knittermeyer, "Die Philosophie der Existenz," Sammlung *Die Universität* 29:110.

137. *Einübung im Christentum* (Düsseldorf, Cologne: E. Diederichs, 1951), p. 63.

138. Ibid., pp. 23 ff.

139. Ibid., pp. 33 f.

140. *Philosophische Brocken*, pp. 42 ff.

141. Cf. H. Knittermeyer, p. 57.

142. M.B., p. 701.

143. *I and Thou*, pp. 81, 80, 96.

144. *Eclipse of God*, chap. 7, p. 113.

145. Kierkegaard, *Die Tagebücher*, ed. Th. Haecker, 3d ed. (Munich, 1949), p. 259.

146. Ibid. (1853 edition), p. 535.

147. *Between Man and Man*, p. 162.

148. Kierkegaard, *Die Tagebücher*, p. 463.

149. "The Prejudices of Youth," in *Israel and the World*, p. 46.

150. *Between Man and Man*, p. 163.

151. *I and Thou*, pp. 86, 89.

152. *Geschichte des dialogischen Prinzips*, p. 295.

153. Ibid., p. 298.

154. In *Between Man and Man*, pp. 146 f.

155. Ibid., p. 203.

156. Cf. chap. 2, n. 12.

157. *Between Man and Man*, p. 170.

158. Ibid., pp. 195 f.

159. "Elements of the Interhuman," pp. 82, 79, 83.

160. *Philosophical Interrogations*, p. 23.

161. Cf. Karl Löwith, *From Hegel to Nietzsche, the Revolution in Nineteenth-Century Thought* (London: Constable, 1965), p. 357.

162. Ibid., p. 317.

163. "Question to the Single One," p. 44.

164. Ibid.

165. Löwith, p. 355; Max Stirner, *Kleinere Schriften* (Berlin, 1914), p. 19.

166. "Question to the Single One," p. 46.

167. Ibid., p. 52.

168. Ibid., p. 58.

169. Ibid., p. 55.

170. Ibid., p. 61.

171. Ibid., p. 65.

172. Ibid., p. 68.

173. Ibid., p. 70.

174. Ibid., p. 80.

175. Ibid.

176. Ibid., p. 82.

177. Ibid., p. 56.

178. "Love of God and Love of Neighbor," in *Hasidism and Modern Man*, p. 24.

179. Cf. chap. 4, n. 80.

180. "Question to the Single One," p. 57.

181. *For the Sake of Heaven*, pp. 228 f.

Chapter 5

1. Ernst Simon, "Siegmund Freud," in *Juden, Christen, Deutsche* (Stuttgart, 1954), p. 333.

2. Lichtheim, *Geschichte des deutschen Zionismus* (Jerusalem, 1954), pp. 31 ff.

3. Chaim Weizmann, *Trial and Error, the Autobiography of Chaim Weizmann* (London: East and West Library, 1950), p. 61.

4. Lichtheim, pp. 44 ff.; Buber, *Israel and Palestine*, pp. 140 f.

5. Lichtheim, pp. 21 ff.; Buber, *Israel and Palestine*, pp. 181 f.

6. "On Achad-Ha'am 1927," in *Der Jude und sein Judentum*, pp. 755–62 ff.

7. H. G. Adler, *Die Juden in Deutschland* (Munich, 1960), p. 91.

8. Cf. Adler, pp. 103 f.

9. Simon, *Deutsches Judentum. Aufstieg und Krise*, pp. 127, 143; Adler, p. 123.

10. Cf. Adler, pp. 141 f.

11. Lichtheim, pp. 133 f.

12. Adler, pp. 114 f.

13. Ibid., p. 126.

14. Landauer, *Vom Judentum. Ein Sammelbuch* (Leipzig, 1913), p. 254.

15. Cf. Adler, p. 158.

16. Cf. Blumenfeld, *Erlebte Judenfrage* (Stuttgart, 1962), p. 43.

17. Lichtheim, p. 13.

18. Weizmann, p. 86.

19. Simon, "Martin Buber und das deutsche Judentum," *Deutsches Judentum*, p. 39.

20. "Drei Stationen 1929," in *Der Jude und sein Judentum*, pp. 751 f.

21. "Dialogue," in *Between Man and Man*, p. 14.

22. Cf. Kohn, *Martin Buber*, pp. 24, 27, 292.

23. "Jüdische Renaissance," in *Die jüdische Bewegung I*, p. 7.

24. Cf. chap. 1, n. 34, 35.

25. Simon, "Martin Buber," p. 40.

26. "Renaissance und Bewegung," in *Der Jude und sein Judentum*, pp. 274 f.

27. Cf. Kohn, pp. 41 f.

28. Cf. Weizmann's statement on p. 92 of his *Trial and Error*, "It was in Geneva that we founded the first Zionist publishing house Der Jüdische Verlag, which grouped around itself a number of men, some of them already well known, others with their mark still to make, [who] collaborated with us." This statement is obviously due to a faulty memory and applies only to Der Jüdische Verlag.

29. *Hasidism and Modern Man*, p. 58.

30. Cf. Simon, p. 55.

31. Cf. R. Weltsch, "Theodor Herzl and We," pp. 155 ff. The Young Jew Series, no. 2 (1929).

32. Cf. Simon, pp. 54 ff.

33. Buber, "Theodor Herzl (1904)" in *Der Jude und sein Judentum*, p. 778.

34. *Die jüdische Bewegung I*, pp. 17–22.

35. Ibid., pp. 108–20.

36. Cf. The Young Jew Series, no. 2, pp. 5 ff.

37. Ibid., p. 11.

38. "Theodor Herzl," p. 780.

39. Ibid., p. 782.

40. The Young Jew Series, no. 2, p. 16.

41. *Israel and Palestine*, pp. 135 ff.

42. Simon, p. 57.

43. "Zion und die Jugend (May 1918)," in *Der Jude und sein Judentum*, p. 700.

44. Cf. Simon, pp. 63 ff.

45. Introduction to *Der Jude und sein Judentum*, p. xxxii.

46. "Völker, Staaten und Zion," in *Der Jude und sein Judentum*, pp. 280 ff.

47. "Ein politischer Faktor (Aug. 1917)," in *Der Jude und sein Judentum*, pp. 501 f.

48. Cf. R. Salman, "Ein Bekenntnis," pp. 414 f., and Leo Herrmann, "Aktivierung," pp. 217–23, in *Der Jude 2* (1917–18).

49. "Frage und Antwort," in *Der Jude und sein Judentum*, p. 348.

50. Cf. Robert Weltsch, epilogue to Kohn, *Martin Buber*, p. 434.

51. "In später Stunde, 1920," in *Der Jude und sein Judentum*, pp. 515 f.

52. Lecture, XII Zionist Congress, Karlsbad, 1921, in *Der Jude und sein Judentum*, p. 475.

53. Cf. Robert Weltsch, pp. 436 f.

54. "Selbstbesinnung," in *Der Jude und sein Judentum*, pp. 496 f.

55. "Zweierlei Zionismus," in *Der Jude und sein Judentum*, pp. 349 f.

56. "Nationalismus," XII Zionist Congress, Karlsbad, 1921, in *Der Jude und sein Judentum*, pp. 309 ff.

57. Lecture, XVI Zionist Congress, Basel, 1929, in *Der Jude und sein Judentum*, p. 523.

58. For this development, cf. Robert Weltsch, epilogue.

59. "Der Weg Israels," in *Der Jude und sein Judentum*, p. 541.

60. Ibid., p. 542.

61. Cf. Kohn, *Martin Buber*, p. 350.

62. Landauer, "Die Revolution," in *Die Gesellschaft*, ed. Martin Buber, vol. 13 (Frankfurt, 1907): 21.

63. Landauer, *Sein Lebensgang in Briefen*, ed. Martin Buber (Frankfurt, 1929), 1:60.

64. Simon, "Priester, Opfer und Arzt," in *In zwei Welten* (Tel Aviv, 1962), p. 414.

65. Kohn, pp. 31 ff.

66. Landauer, *Rechenschaft* (Berlin, 1919), p. 17.

67. Landauer, *Lebensgang*, 1:424.

68. Landauer, *Shakespeare. Dargestellt in Vorträgen*. 2 vols. (Frankfurt, 1920); cf. foreword by the editor.

69. Landauer, *Rechenschaft*, p. 22.

70. Landauer, "Die Revolution," pp. 108 ff.; cf. Kohn, pp. 199 ff.

71. In the following, cf. *Paths in Utopia* (London, 1949), chap. 26.

72. Kohn, pp. 195 ff.; cf. also pp. 188 ff.

73. "My Way to Hasidism," pp. 50, 52 f.

74. "The Holy Way," in *On Judaism*, p. 139.

75. Landauer, *Der werdende Mensch. Aufsätze über Leben und Schriftum*, ed. Martin Buber (Potsdam, 1921), p. 61.

76. Florens Christian Rang, *Deutsche Bauhütte* (Sannerz and Leipzig, 1924), p. 184.

77. Ernst Simon, "Der werdende Mensch und der werdende Jude," in *Der Jude* 6:466.

78. Landauer, "Sind das Ketzergedanken?" in *Vom Judentum*, p. 254.

79. *Der Jude* 6:464.

80. Buber, "Wie kann Gemeinschaft werden," in *Der Jude und sein Judentum*, p. 371.

81. "The Holy Way," p. 142.

82. Cf. "Der Acker und die Sterne," in *Der Jude und sein Judentum*, p. 773.

83. "Regeneration eines Volkstums, in *Der Jude und sein Judentum*, pp. 249 ff.

84. Ibid., p. 257.

85. Ibid., p. 262.

86. "Wie kann Gemeinschaft werden," p. 369.

87. "Jüdisches Nationalheim und national Politik in Palästina," in *Der Jude und sein Judentum*, p. 332.

88. "Warum muss der Aufbau Palästinas ein sozialistischer sein?" in *Der Jude und sein Judentum*, p. 379.

89. Ibid., p. 376.

90. *Die jüdische Bewegung I*, "Zionistische Politik," pp. 109–23.

91. "Kulturarbeit," in *Der Jude und sein Judentum*, pp. 671 f.

92. Cf. "Volkserziehung als unsere Aufgabe," in *Der Jude und sein Judentum*, pp. 674 f.

93. Cf. section, "Reden über Erziehung," pp. 152 ff.

94. "Unser Bildungsziel," in *Der Jude und sein Judentum*, p. 601.

95. "Biblical Humanism," in *On the Bible*, pp. 211 f.

96. Ibid., pp. 1088 f.

97. "Die hebräische Sprache," in *Der Jude und sein Judentum*, pp. 723 ff.

98. Lecture, XVI Zionist Congress, Basel, 1929, in *Der Jude und sein Judentum*, pp. 525 f.

99. "Zion und die Jugend," in *Der Jude und sein Judentum*, p. 705.

100. "Biblical Humanism," in *On the Bible*, p. 216.

101. "Hebrew Humanism," in *Israel and the World*, pp. 240 f.

102. *At the Turning*. Three addresses on Judaism (New York, 1952).

103. Robert Weltsch, Introduction to *Der Jude und sein Judentum*, pp. xiii f.

104. "Judaism and Culture," in *At the Turning*.

105. Cf. Schalom ben Chorin, *Die Antwort des Jona* (Hamburg, 1956), p. 52.

106. Cf. "Zion und die Jugend," p. 705.

107. Ibid., p. 707.

108. "Kirche, Staat, Volk, Judentum," in *Der Jude und sein Judentum*, pp. 558 ff.

109. *Israel and Palestine*, p. xi; "Zion und die nationalen Ideen," in *Der Jude und sein Judentum*, p. 327.

110. *Israel and Palestine*, p. xiii; "Zion und die nationalen Ideen," pp. 328 f.

111. "Zion und die nationalen Ideen," p. 34; *Werke* II, p. 1011.

112. "Zion und die nationalen Ideen," p. 55; omitted in *Werke* II.

113. *Israel and Palestine*, p. 18.

114. For this, cf. section, "The Beginnings—Buber and Herzl."

115. *Israel and Palestine*, p. 158.

116. Ibid., p. 143.

117. *Tales of the Hasidim, Early Masters*, p. xii.

118. Cf. chap. 2, n. 17.

119. "Adult Education," in *Torah*, Magazine of Nat. Fed. of Jewish Men's Clubs of United Synagogue of America, June 1952.

120. "In the Midst of History," in *Israel and the World*, p. 82.

Chapter 6

1. *Origin and Meaning of Hasidism*, foreword, p. 22.

2. *For the Sake of Heaven*, foreword.

3. G. Scholem, *Martin Bubers Deutung des Chassidismus, Judaica* (Frankfurt, 1963), p. 166; Buber, "My Way to Hasidism," pp. 47 ff.

4. Karl Kerenyi, "Martin Buber as Classical Author," in M.B., p. 635.

5. *Hasidism and Modern Man*, p. 22.

6. *Legend of the Baal-shem*, p. 72.

7. Cf. *Der grosse Maggid und seine Nachfolge*, preface.

8. Scholem, *Judaica*, p. 171.

9. Ibid., p. 201.

10. Ibid., p. 195.

11. M.B., pp. 731 ff.

12. Ibid.

13. Scholem, esp., *Major Trends in Jewish Mysticism*, 3d ed. (New York, Schocken, 1961).

14. Scholem, *Judaica*, p. 197.

15. Scholem, pp. 203 ff.

16. M.B., p. 731.

17. In *Israel and the World*, pp. 137 f.

17a. Ibid., p. 138.

17b. Ibid., p. 139.

17c. Ibid.

17d. Ibid., p. 140.

18. "Warum gelernt werden soll," in *Der Jude und sein Judentum*, pp. 745 ff.

19. "The Faith of Judaism," in *Israel and the World*, pp. 13 f.

20. Ibid., p. 275.

20a. The section called "Schicksal" in the German is added to chapter 4 of the English translation without any title. [Trans.]

21. *Origin and Meaning of Hasidism*, p. 116.

22. Ibid., p. 117.

23. "The Holy Way," p. 139.

24. "Renaissance und Bewegung," p. 275.

25. *Origin and Meaning of Hasidism*, p. 119.

26. Ibid., p. 125.

27. "Spirit and Body of the Hasidic Movement," in *Origin and Meaning of Hasidism*, p. 120.

28. Ibid., p. 134.

29. Ibid., p. 139.

30. Ibid., p. 134.

31. Ibid.

31a. Ibid.

32. *Der grosse Maggid*, preface.

32a. *Legend of the Baal-Shem*, pp. 10 f.

33. *Origin and Meaning of Hasidism*, p. 133.

34. Cf. chap. 1, n. 42.

35. "My Way to Hasidism"; *For the Sake of Heaven*, foreword.

35a. "My Way to Hasidism," p. 52.

35b. Ibid.

36. *Hasidism and Modern Man*, p. 42.

37. Cf. chap. 4, n. 4.

38. *Hasidism and Modern Man*, pp. 67 f.

39. Ibid., p. 24.

40. Kohn, p. 467.

41. "Christ, Hasidism, Gnosis," in *Origin and Meaning of Hasidism*, p. 252.

42. *Der grosse Maggid und seine Nachfolge*, p. 67.

43. "Aufgaben Jüdischer Volkserziehung," in *Der Jude und sein Judentum*, p. 602.

43a. In *Israel and the World*.

44. Preface to *Early Addresses*, in *Der Jude und sein Judentum*, p. 5.

44a. Cf. "A Letter to Gandhi," in *Pointing the Way*.

45. *Origin and Meaning of Hasidism*, p. 170.

46. Ibid., p. 178.

47. Ibid., pp. 97 f.

48. Ibid., p. 173.

49. "Love of God and Love of Neighbor," in *Hasidism and Modern Man*, p. 232.

50. *Israel and the World*, p. 71.

51. Ibid., p. 73.

52. Cf. "Christ, Hasidism, Gnosis," pp. 242 ff.

53. Scholem, *Judaica*, p. 195.

54. Ibid., pp. 194 f.

55. Ibid., p. 196.

56. Ibid., p. 199.

57. *Hasidism and Modern Man*, p. 214.

58. Cf. chap. 6, n. 45.

59. *Hasidism and Modern Man*, p. 33.

60. Ibid., p. 179.

61. This is also true of the teaching profession; cf. chap. 4, n. 99.

62. M.B., p. 631.

63. *Legend of the Baal-Shem*, p. 70.

64. Ibid., p. 40.

65. Ibid., p. 48.

66. *Der grosse Maggid*, pp. 37 f. Cf. *Origin and Meaning of Hasidism*, p. 131; the original German (in Buber, *Werke* 3:815), as well as the published English translation has "transcendental responsibility" instead of "metaphysical responsibility."

67. "Die grossen Ordensregeln," in *Menschen der Kirche in Zeugnis und Urkunde*, ed. Hans Urs von Balthasar, 8:7.

68. Ibid., p. 230.

69. "Renaissance und Bewegung," p. 273.

69a. *Origin and Meaning of Hasidism*, p. 253.

70. *Der grosse Maggid*, p. 75; *Tales of the Hasidim, Early Masters*, pp. 26 f.

71. M.B., p. 416.

72. *Israel and the World*, p. 139.

73. *Origin and Meaning of Hasidism*, p. 94.

74. Ibid., p. 181.

75. Cf. "Das Symbol als Mittler," in Schaeder, *Gott und Welt. Drei Kapitel Goethescher Weltanschauung* (Hameln, 1947).

75a. Goethe, *Autobiography, Poetry and Truth from My Life*, trans. R. O. Moon (London, 1932), bk. 7.

76. "The Power of the Spirit," in *Israel and the World*, pp. 173 f.

77. *For the Sake of Heaven*, p. xiii.

78. *Hasidism and Modern Man*, p. 40.

79. Bonhoeffer, *Bestandaufnahme*, ed. H. W. Richter (Munich, 1962), p. 191.

80. "Hope for This Hour," in *Pointing the Way*, p. 229; also *World Review* (Dec. 1952).

81. "The Silent Question," in *On Judaism*, pp. 202 f.

82. Cf. chap. 6, n. 8.

83. *For the Sake of Heaven*, p. ix.

84. M.B., p. 635.

85. Ibid., p. 434.

86. Ibid., p. 417; hereafter quotations from *For the Sake of Heaven* are cited in the text by page number in parentheses.

87. *Der grosse Maggid*, p. 92.

88. Ibid.

89. Ibid.

90. M.B., p. 430.

91. Simon, *Martin Buber und das deutsche Judentum*, pp. 75 ff.

92. In *Pointing the Way*, p. 109.

93. Cf. chap. 6, n. 6.

94. *Tales of the Hasidim*, p. 4.

95. Ibid., p. 1.

96. *For the Sake of Heaven*, foreword.

97. "Teaching and Deed," in *Israel and the World*, p. 138.

98. *Tales of the Hasidim*, pp. 16 f.

99. *Origin and Meaning of Hasidism*, p. 99.

100. *Tales of the Hasidim*, p. 46.

101. Ibid., p. vi.

102. *Hasidism and Modern Man*, pp. 25 f.

103. Ibid., p. 190.

104. Ibid., p. 199.

105. Ibid., p. 180.

106. *Tales of the Hasidim*, p. 52.

107. Ibid., p. 74.

107a. Ibid., p. v.

108. Cf. Scholem, *Judaica*, pp. 177, 179 f.

Chapter 7

1. *A Believing Humanism*, p. 33; also, Oliver Roy, *The Wanderer and the Way* (London, 1968), p. 6.

2. Cf. chap. 6, n. 44.

3. In Sonderdruck, *An einem denkwürdigen Tag* (Tel Aviv); cf. "Schlussbemerkungen," p. 18. This special pamphlet is the record of the proceedings at the celebration held in Buber's home on the completion of the translation.

4. Wie das Wort so wichtig dort war/ Weil es ein gesprochen Wort war. Cf. Goethe, *Westöstlicher Divan*, foreword.

5. Goethe, "Lied und Gebilde," in *The Poems of Goethe*, trans. E. A. Bowring (New York, 1881), p. 395.

6. "Schlussbemerkungen," p. 18; in German this appears, slightly altered, in Buber's collected works, vol. 2, 1175 f., where it is called "Zum Abschluss."

6a. Sonderdruck.

7. Cf. Rosenzweig, "Urzelle des *Stern der Erlösung*," in his *Die Schirft*, ed. Karl Thieme (Bibliotheca Judaica, 1954), pp. 177 ff. Cf. the following also: Epilogue by Willehad Eckert and K. Thieme, *Die Schrift-Uebersetzung von Martin Buber und Franz Rosenzweig, Freiburger Rundbriefe*, 14:35 ff.

8. Cf. Else Freund, *Die Existenzphilosophie Franz Rosenzweigs* (Hamburg, 1959), pp. 140 ff.

9. Cf. "Franz Rosenzweig," in *Pointing the Way*, p. 88.

10. Rosenzweig, *The Star of Redemption*, trans. W. H. Hallo (New York, 1971), part 2: Song of Songs.

11. Buber, "Franz Rosenzweig," p. 89.

12. *Das neue Denken, Die Schrift*, pp. 201 f.

13. Ibid., p. 84.

14. *Die Schrift*, pp. 51 ff.

15. "Zu einer neuen Verdeutschung der *Schrift*," Beilage (appendix) to *Die fünf Bücher der Weisung* (Olten, 1954), p. 5; hereafter referred to as Beilage.

16. Ibid., p. 6.

17. Ibid., p. 3.

18. Ibid., pp. 10 f.

19. *Die Schrift*, pp. 13 f.

20. Beilage, p. 19.

21. Ibid., p. 13.

22. Ibid., p. 18.

23. *Die Schrift*, pp. 34 f.

24. Quoted in *Die Schrift*, p. 37.

25. *Die Schrift*, p. 44.

26. Scholem, *Judaica*, pp. 207 ff.; also Sonderdruck.

27. Cf. Thieme, *Die Schrift-Uebersetzung von Martin Buber und Franz Rosenzweig*, p. 34.

28. In *Knowledge of Man*, p. 110.

29. Sonderdruck.

30. In *On the Bible*.

31. Ibid., p. 8.

31a. Ibid., p. 7.

32. Hamann, *Schriften*, p. 136.

33. Cf. chap. 4, n. 39.

34. Cf. Peter Meinhold, *Luthers Sprachphilosophie* (Berlin, 1958), pp. 11 ff.

35. *Kingship of God* (London, 1967), preface to 1st ed., pp. 15 f.

36. Buber, *Werke*, 2:725 ff.

37. *Moses. The Revelation and the Covenant* (New York, 1958); cf. preface.

37a. In *On the Bible*.

37b. Ibid.

38. Hans Joachim Kraus, *Geschichte der historisch-kritischen Erforschung des Alten Testaments* (Neukirchen, 1956), pp. 386 f.

38a. Ibid.

39. Kraus, "Gespräch mit Martin Buber", in *Evangelische Theologie* 12 (1952–53): 59 ff.

40. M.B., p. 345.

41. *Moses*, preface, p. 9.

41a. *Der grosse Maggid*, intro.

42. "Jewish Religiosity," in *On Judaism*, p. 90.

43. "Geist und Epochen der jüdischen Geschichte," *Die Schrift*, pp. 129–42.

44. "The Faith of Judaism," in *Israel and the World*, p. 16.

45. "Spinoza, Sabbatai Zvi and the Baal-Shem," in *Origin and Meaning of Hasidism*, pp. 91 f.

46. "The Faith of Judaism," p. 25.

47. *Between Man and Man* (Boston, 1955), p. 13; cf. chap. 4, n. 25.

48. Cf. Martin Buber, "Offenbarung und Gesetz, Aus Briefen an Franz Rosenzweig," in *Almanach des Schocken-Verlags auf das Jahr 5697* (Berlin, 1936–37), pp. 147–54.

49. "Herut. On Youth and Religion," in *On Judaism*, p. 169.

50. *Moses*, p. 130.

51. "Das Judentum und die neue Weltfrage," in *Der Jude und sein Judentum*, p. 237.

52. *Kingship of God*, preface to 1st ed., p. 20.

53. "Herut. On Youth and Religion," p. 173.

54. Martin Noth, *The History of Israel* (London, 1960); Ernst Ludwig Ehrlich, *A Concise History of Israel* (London, 1962).

55. Cf. chap. 6, n. 9.

56. *The Prophetic Faith* (New York, 1949), p. 6.

57. *Kingship of God*, preface to 3d ed., p. 56.

58. "Dialogue between Heaven and Earth," in *On Judaism*, p. 215.

59. *Kingship of God*, preface to 2d ed., p. 45.

60. Kraus, p. 66.

61. "The Holy Way," in *On Judaism*, p. 137; also, somewhat changed, in Buber, *Werke* 2:235.

62. *Between Man and Man*, p. 15.

63. "Hebrew Humanism," in *Israel and the World*, p. 251.

64. Buber, *Das Messiasproblem bei Martin Buber* (Stuttgart, 1958), p. 46.

65. Kraus, "Gespräch mit Martin Buber," p. 64.

66. "Replies to My Critics," in M.B., p. 690.

67. *Kingship of God*, preface to 2d ed., p. 39; preface to 3d ed., pp. 57, 58.

68. Ibid., p. 81; preface to 2d ed., p. 43.

69. *Moses,* p. 14.

69a. Ibid.

70. *Kingship of God,* p. 63.

71. *Moses,* pp. 16, 19.

72. Ibid., p. 17.

73. "Myth in Judaism," in *On Judaism,* p. 105.

74. *Moses,* p. 17.

75. *Philosophical Interrogations,* pp. 105 ff.

76. *Moses,* pp. 117 ff.; the last sentence of the German quotation is omitted in the published English translation.

77. *For the Sake of Heaven,* p. 112.

78. *A Believing Humanism,* p. 113.

79. Ibid.

80. "Biblical Humanism," in *On the Bible,* p. 213.

81. Kraus, p. 62.

82. *A Believing Humanism,* p. 31.

83. "Biblical Humanism," p. 212.

84. Smend, *Das Mosebild* (Tübingen, 1959), p. 66.

85. Ibid., pp. 62 f.

86. Noth, p. 48.

87. Ibid., chap. 2.

88. Smend, p. 66.

89. *Moses,* p. 186.

90. *The Prophetic Faith,* p. 6.

91. Walter Eichrodt, *Historia mundi* 2:381 ff.; Ehrlich, p. 12.

92. *Moses,* pp. 18 f.

93. Ibid.

94. Cf. *Kingship of God,* pp. 118, 22 f., 108 ff.

95. *Moses,* p. 134.

95a. Ibid., p. 132.

96. *The Prophetic Faith,* p. 23.

97. Ibid., p. 30.

98. Ibid., p. 31.

99. "Abraham the Seer," in *On the Bible,* p. 24.

100. Ibid., p. 24.

101. Ibid., p. 30.

102. Ibid., p. 25.

103. Ibid., p. 43.

104. "The Election of Israel," in *On the Bible,* pp. 87 ff.

105. "Holy Event," in *The Prophetic Faith,* p. 57.

105a. Ibid.

106. "Biblical Leadership," in *On the Bible,* p. 147.

107. *The Prophetic Faith,* p. 63.

108. *Kingship of God,* p. 154.

109. *The Prophetic Faith,* p. 64.

110. Ibid.

111. Ibid., p. 89.

112. Ibid., p. 164.

113. Ibid., p. 2.

114. Ibid., p. 3.

115. Ibid., p. 189.

116. Ibid., p. 195 f.

117. Ibid., p. 230.

118. Ibid., p. 225.

119. Ibid., p. 234.

120. "Biblical Humanism," p. 112.

120a. "The Holy Way," p. 143.

121. "Judaism and Civilization," in *On Judaism*, p. 201.

122. "The Power of the Spirit," in *Israel and the World*, pp. 173 f.

123. *Tales of the Hasidim*, intro.; *Moses*, p. 13.

124. "Biblical Humanism," p. 216.

125. *The Prophetic Faith*, p. 18.

126. Ibid., p. 64.

127. "Biblical Humanism," p. 212.

128. "Abraham the Seer," p. 30.

129. "The Holy Way," p. 137.

130. Ibid., p. 139.

131. "Baal-Shem Tov's Instruction," in *Hasidism and Modern Man*, p. 181.

132. *The Prophetic Faith*, p. 175.

133. "Biblical Humanism," p. 213.

134. "Kirche, Staat, Volk, Judentum: Zwiegespräch mit Karl Ludwig Schmidt, Jan. 14, 1933," in *Der Jude und sein Judentum*, pp. 569 ff.

135. *The Prophetic Faith*, p. 234.

136. "The Two Foci of the Jewish Soul," in *Israel and the World*, p. 39.

137. Ibid., p. 35.

138. Ibid.

139. Ibid., p. 34.

140. *Die Kreatur* 1 (Berlin 1926–27), preface by Martin Buber.

141. "Kirche, Staat, Volk, Judentum," p. 569.

142. Ibid., p. 563.

143. *A Believing Humanism*, pp. 115 f.

144. "Kirche, Staat, Volk, Judentum," pp. 562. f.

145. "The Two Foci of the Jewish Soul," p. 38.

146. Ibid., p. 32.

147. *A Believing Humanism*, p. 135.

148. Ibid., p. 115.

149. "The Two Foci of the Jewish Soul," p. 28.

150. "Kirche, Staat, Volk, Judentum," p. 565.

151. Ibid., p. 568.

152. H. U. von Balthasar, *Martin Buber and Christianity, A Dialogue between Israel and the Church* (London, 1960), p. 12.

153. Balthasar, *Was halten Sie vom Christentum?* List-Bücher no. 105 (Munich, 1957), p. 83.

154. *Two Types of Faith* (London, 1951), p. 174.

155. James Muilenburg, in M.B., p. 382.

156. Cf. Malcolm L. Diamond, *Martin Buber, Jewish Existentialist* (New York, 1960), p. 174.

156a. *For the Sake of Heaven,* preface.

157. *Two Types of Faith,* pp. 12 f.

158. "Renewal of Judaism," in *On Judaism,* p. 47.

159. "The Spirit of the Orient and Judaism," in *On Judaism,* p. 62.

160. "The Altar," in *Pointing the Way,* p. 18.

161. *I and Thou,* pp. 66 f.

162. Ibid., p. 85.

163. Cf. "Spirit and Body of the Hasidic Movement," in *Origin and Meaning of Hasidism,* pp. 129 f., and Hans Joachim Kraus, *Begegnung mit dem Judentum* (Hamburg, 1963), pp. 64 f.

164. "Jewish Religiosity," in *On Judaism,* p. 83.

165. "Spinoza, Sabbatai Zvi, and the Baal-Shem," pp. 109 f.

165a. *For the Sake of Heaven,* preface.

166. *Two Types of Faith,* p. 76.

167. Ibid., pp. 112 f.

168. Ibid., p. 13.

169. Ibid., p. 96.

169a. Ibid., p. 69.

170. Ibid., p. 128.

171. Cf. *Freiburger Rundbrief,* no. 10–11 (1950–51), pp. 18 ff.

172. *Two Types of Faith,* p. 34.

173. Ibid., pp. 149 f.

174. Ibid., p. 57.

175. Chorin, *Antwort,* p. 75.

176. *Two Types of Faith,* p. 57.

177. "The Teaching of the Tao," in *Pointing the Way,* p. 57.

178. *Two Types of Faith,* p. 90.

179. Cf. Karl Thieme, "Das Mysterium Israels," *Freiburger Rundbriefe,* nos. 5–6, 7 (1949–50), pp. 19 ff., 9 ff.

180. Diamond, pp. 181–93.

181. Karl Thieme, *Freiburger Rundbrief* no. 12 (1959–60), p. 43.

182. Franz Rosenzweig, *Briefe* (Berlin: Schocken, 1935), p. 73.

183. H. L. Schoeps, *Paul, the Theology of the Apostle* (Philadelphia, 1961), p. 258.

184. "Sweeter than Honey," in C. S. Lewis, *Reflections on the Psalms* (London, 1958), pp. 64 f.

185. Rosenzweig, *Briefe,* p. 212.

186. Diamond, pp. 166 f.

187. Cf. chap. 4, n. 176.

188. Cf. chap. 4, n. 46.

189. Cf. Buber's essay "Pharisäertum," in *Der Jude und sein Judentum,* pp. 221 ff.; also, the work of the Christian scholar, R. Travers Herford, *Pharisaism, Its Aim and Its Method* (New York, 1912).

190. "Jewish Religiosity," p. 89.

191. *Two Types of Faith*, p. 26; Rosenzweig, *Briefe*, p. 78.

192. Quoted by Schoeps, p. 298.

193. *Eclipse of God. Studies in the Relation between Religion and Philosophy* (New York, 1957), p. 136.

194. *Two Types of Faith*, foreword, p. 11.

195. Brunner, *Dogmatik* (Cologne-Olten, 1958; Zurich, 1960), pp. 186 ff.

196. Balthasar, in M.B., pp. 347 f.

197. Brunner, in M.B., p. 313.

198. Cf. Brunner, *Dogmatik*, pp. 190 ff.

199. Pieper, *Ueber den Glauben* (Kösel Verlag, 1962).

200. Ibid., p. 46.

201. *Two Types of Faith*, pp. 10 f.

202. Karl Thieme, *Biblische Religion heute* (Heidelberg, 1960), p. 68.

203. Ibid., p. 116, no. 1, 2.

204. In *Zeitschrift Catholica* 15, no. 3 (1961).

205. Guardini, *Welt und Persen* (1939; 3d ed., Würzburg, 1950).

206. Ibid., pp. 123 ff.

207. *Two Types of Faith*, p. 132.

208. *Between Man and Man*, "Dialogue," pp. 5 f.

209. Florens Christian Rang in a personal communication from Buber.

Chapter 8

1. Robert Weltsch, in Hans Kohn, *Martin Buber*, p. 450.

2. "The Spirit of the Orient and Judaism," in *On Judaism*, p. 77.

3. "The Demand of the Spirit and Historical Reality," in *Pointing the Way*, pp. 177 f.

4. Ibid., p. 190.

5. "What Is Man?" in *Between Man and Man*, p. 120.

6. Cf. *I and Thou*, pp. 101 f., 118 f.

6a. *Between Man and Man*, p. 139.

7. Ibid., p. 141.

8. Ibid., p. 161.

9. Ibid., p. 182; also, Max Scheler, *Philosophische Weltanschauung*, p. 62; cf. H. J. Schoeps, *Was ist der Mensch?* (Göttingen, 1960), pp. 202 ff.

10. *On Judaism*, preface to 1923 ed., p. 9.

11. "What Is Man?" p. 193.

12. Ibid., p. 184.

13. "The Validity and Limitation of the Political Principle," in *Pointing the Way*, p. 215.

14. Cf. "What Is Man?" pp. 163 ff.

15. Cf. Otto Pöggeler, *Der Denkweg Martin Heideggers* (Pfullingen, 1963), pp. 30 ff.

16. Ibid., p. 64.

17. H. Knittermeyer, *Die Philosophie der Existenz von der Renaissance bis zur Gegenwart* (Vienna-Stuttgart, 1952), p. 228.

18. Cf. Pöggeler, p. 302.

19. Heidegger, *Unterwegs zur Sprache* (Pfullingen, 1959), pp. 83 ff.

20. "What Is Man?" p. 171.

21. Heidegger, *Holzwege* (Frankfurt, 1950), pp. 91 f.

22. Heidegger, *Kant und das Problem der Metaphysik* (1929; 2d ed., Frankfurt, 1951).

23. Heidegger, *Platons Lehre von der Wahrheit. Mit einem Brief über den Humanismus* (Bern, 1947), pp. 60, 58, 53.

24. Ibid., p. 75.

25. Ibid., pp. 85 f., 94 f.

26. Ibid., pp. 101, 103, 99.

27. Ibid., pp. 109, 106 ff.

28. *Eclipse of God*, p. 43.

29. Cf. Pöggeler, p. 195.

30. *Eclipse of God*, p. 73.

31. Cf. Pöggeler, pp. 191 f.

32. Ibid., pp. 46, 36 ff.

33. Heidegger, *Unterwegs zur Sprache*, p. 96.

34. For the following, cf. the concluding chapter "Prospect," in "What Is Man?"

34a. Ibid., p. 200.

34b. Ibid., p. 203.

35. Cf. chap. 4, n. 87.

36. "What Is Man?" p. 170.

37. M.B., p. 689.

38. Cf. Buber, *Werke* 2:864; this passage does not appear in the abbreviated English translation of "The Man of Today and the Jewish Bible," in *Biblical Humanism*, ed. N. Glazer (London, 1968).

39. "Goethe's Concept of Humanity (1949)," in *Pointing the Way*, p. 77.

40. Cf. Buber, *Werke* 2:862.

41. *I and Thou*, p. 101.

42. For the following, cf. *A Believing Humanism*, p. 145.

42a. Ibid., p. 146.

42b. Ibid., p. 147.

43. Cf. chap. 4, n. 74.

44. *I and Thou*, p. 93.

45. Ibid., pp. 118 f.

46. "Das Judentum und die neue Weltfrage," in *Der Jude und sein Judentum*, p. 237.

47. *I and Thou*, p. 102.

48. "The Renewal of Judaism," in *On Judaism*, p. 50.

48a. *A Believing Humanism*, p. 130.

49. Ibid., cf. p. 147.

50. Ibid., p. 131.

50a. Ibid., pp. 132 f.

51. Ibid., p. 213.

51a. "Biblical Humanism," in *On the Bible*, p. 215.

52. "Dialogue," in *Between Man and Man*, p. 32.

53. "The Question to the Single One," in *Between Man and Man*, p. 56; cf. chap. 6, 20.

54. "The Question to the Single One," p. 50; also pp. 44 f.

55. "Dialogue," p. 35.

56. "The Question to the Single One," pp. 69, 80.

57. Ibid., p. 66.

58. Ibid., pp. 67, 47, 30.

59. Ibid., pp. 66, 56.

60. Ibid., p. 41.

61. "What Is Man?" pp. 162, 163.

61a. Ibid., p. 163.

62. Ibid., pp. 183, 185, 184.

63. Ibid., p. 177.

64. Ibid., p. 196; also p. 193.

65. Ibid., p. 170.

66. Ibid., p. 201.

67. Ibid., p. 204.

68. Ibid., p. 203.

69. M.B., p. 743.

70. "Elements of the Interhuman," in *Knowledge of Man*, p. 74, where "mystery of contact" is translated as "fact of content."

71. Cf. Seiffert, pp. 130 f.

72. For the following, cf. "Distance and Relation," in *Knowledge of Man*, p. 59, 65–71.

73. M.B., p. 140.

74. "Elements of the Interhuman," p. 85.

75. "The Word That Is Spoken," in *Knowledge of Man*, p. 117.

76. "Distance and Relation," p. 68.

77. "The Word That Is Spoken," p. 118.

78. Ibid., p. 112.

79. Ibid.

80. "What Is Common to All," in *Knowledge of Man*, p. 98.

81. Ibid., pp. 90 f.

82. Aldous Huxley, *The Doors of Perception* (London, 1954).

83. Ibid., p. 52.

84. Ibid., p. 65.

85. Ibid., p. 17.

86. "What Is Common to All," p. 104.

87. Ibid., p. 107.

88. Ibid., p. 108.

89. "What Is Man?" p. 132.

90. Ibid., p. 133.

91. Simon, *Martin Buber und das deutsche Judentum*, p. 30.

92. "Man and His Image Work," in *Knowledge of Man*, p. 155.

93. Ibid., p. 152.

94. Ibid., p. 157.

95. Ibid., p. 158.

96. Ibid., p. 159.

97. Ibid., p. 163.

98. Ibid.

99. M.B., p. 237.

100. Cf. Heisenberg, *Die Künst im technischen Zeitalter*, pp. 43–69.

101. Ibid., pp. 109–29.

101a. *A Believing Humanism,* p. 106.

102. Ibid.

103. M.B., p. 704.

104. *Eclipse of God,* p. 23.

105. *The Holy Way,* pp. 109 f.

106. *For the Sake of Heaven,* p. 116.

107. *Eclipse of God,* p. 3.

107a. Ibid., p. 6.

108. Ibid., p. 8.

108a. Ibid., p. 9.

109. *A Believing Humanism,* p. 171.

110. M.B., pp. 24, 25.

110a. Ibid., p. 32.

111. Ibid., p. 33.

112. "What Is Man?" p. 184.

113. *I and Thou,* pp. 112 f.

114. *A Believing Humanism,* pp. 115 f.

115. M.B., p. 742.

116. *Eclipse of God,* p. 43.

117. Ibid., p. 129.

118. Ibid., p. 42.

119. M.B., p. 692.

120. Ibid., p. 701.

121. Ibid., p. 742.

122. *Eclipse of God,* p. 76.

123. Ibid., p. 75.

124. M.B., p. 685.

125. *Eclipse of God,* p. 44.

126. *I and Thou,* pp. 69 f.

127. "What Is Man?" p. 179.

128. *Eclipse of God,* p. 74.

129. Hühnerfeld, *In Sachen Heidegger* (Hamburg, 1959), p. 109.

130. "What Is Man?" p. 177.

131. Also Jean Wahl, in M.B., p. 499.

132. Max Picard, *Wort und Wortgeräusch* (Hamburg, 1953), p. 31.

133. *A Believing Humanism,* pp. 153 f.

134. Cf. Binswanger, *Grundformen und Erkenntnis menschlichen Daseins* (Zurich, 1942).

135. Cf. chap. 4, n. 125, and Buber's introduction to Trüb's posthumous work "Healing out of Meeting," now in *A Believing Humanism,* p. 138; cf. also Friedman, *The Life of Dialogue,* pp. 184 f.

136. *Wissenschaftliche Buchgesellschaft* (Darmstadt, 1955).

137. Cf. Jung, "Reply to Buber," in *Spring* (New York, 1957), p. 6; also Buber's reply, "Religion and Modern Thinking," in *Eclipse of God,* pp. 77 f.

137a. Jung, p. 6.

137b. *Eclipse of God,* p. 136.

137c. Ibid.

138. "Origin and Meaning of Hasidism," p. 243.

139. *Spring*, p. 8.

140. *Eclipse of God*, p. 135.

141. *A Believing Humanism*, p. 171.

142. *Origin and Meaning of Hasidism*, p. 245.

143. *Eclipse of God*, pp. 119 f.

144. Ibid., pp. 104 f.

145. Ibid., p. 95.

146. "Love of God and Love of Neighbor," p. 225.

147. *Eclipse of God*, p. 37.

148. Buber, *Images of Good and Evil* (New York, 1953), p. 122.

149. Ibid., p. 123.

150. Ibid.

151. Ibid., p. 131.

152. Cf. chap. 4, n. 89.

153. *Images of Good and Evil*, pp. 115 f.

153a. Ibid., p. 125.

154. Ibid., p. 142.

INDEX

Grete Schaeder received her degree from the University of Vienna in 1926 and is a private scholar and free-lance writer. She is editor-in-chief of the publication of Martin Buber's correspondence in three volumes with the title *Martin Buber: Correspondence of Seven Decades*. The first volume from 1897–1918 was published in 1972.

Noah J. Jacobs, the translator, has degrees in linguistics, theology, and philosophy. He has published books and articles in German and English and has made various translations from the Hebrew and German.

The manuscript was edited by Marguerite C. Wallace. The book was designed by Joanne Kinney. The typeface for the text is CRT Janson originally cut by Nicholas Kis about 1690; and the display face is American Uncial issued in 1953 based on the design by Victor Hammer in 1923.

The text is printed on Neshoba paper and the book is bound in Columbia Mills' Llamique cloth over binders boards. Manufactured in the United States of America.